Monarchies, States Generals and Parliaments

This book charts the history of the States General – the parliament – of the Netherlands and its relations with two phases of monarchical rule in the fifteenth and sixteenth centuries, and places the States General for the first time at the centre of the country's political history.

Unlike the English Parliament, the States General was a composite body representing the local Estates of the separate provinces which were anxious to keep their autonomy. The history of the States General was determined by this structure, and by its relations with the monarchy: dukes of Burgundy in the fifteenth century, and Spanish Habsburgs in the sixteenth. Theirs was a composite monarchy of which the Netherlands were an important but rarely central part. Ideally, everyone was meant to cooperate. In practice, there was already a major crisis by the 1480s, and an even more serious crisis from the 1560s led to decades of civil war in which the two sides quarrelled violently about religion, sovereignty and local privileges. By 1600 the Netherlands had split. In the north, the United Provinces became a parliamentary regime, governed as a republic by the States General. In the south, the Spanish Netherlands remained part of the Habsburg composite monarchy.

H. G. KOENIGSBERGER is Professor of History Emeritus, University of London, and Fellow of King's College London.

CAMBRIDGE STUDIES IN EARLY MODERN HISTORY

Edited by Professor Sir John Elliott, University of Oxford
Professor Olwen Hufton, University of Oxford
Professor H. G. Koenigsberger, University of London
Professor H. M. Scott, University of St Andrews

The idea of an 'early modern' period of European history from the fifteenth to the late eighteenth century is now widely accepted among historians. The purpose of Cambridge Studies in Early Modern History is to publish monographs and studies which illuminate the character of the period as a whole, and in particular focus attention on a dominant theme within it, the interplay of continuity and change as they are presented by the continuity of medieval ideas, political and social organisation, and by the impact of new ideas, new methods, and new demands on the traditional structure.

For a list of titles published in the series, please see end of the book

Monarchies, States Generals and Parliaments
The Netherlands in the Fifteenth and Sixteenth Centuries

H. G. KOENIGSBERGER

CAMBRIDGE
UNIVERSITY PRESS

CAMBRIDGE UNIVERSITY PRESS
Cambridge, New York, Melbourne, Madrid, Cape Town, Singapore, São Paulo

Cambridge University Press
The Edinburgh Building, Cambridge CB2 8RU, UK

Published in the United States of America by Cambridge University Press, New York

www.cambridge.org
Information on this title: www.cambridge.org/9780521803304

© H. G. Koenigsberger 2001

This publication is in copyright. Subject to statutory exception
and to the provisions of relevant collective licensing agreements,
no reproduction of any part may take place without the written
permission of Cambridge University Press.

First published 2001
This digitally printed version 2007

A catalogue record for this publication is available from the British Library

Library of Congress Cataloguing in Publication data

Koenigsberger, H. G. (Helmut Georg)
Monarchies, States Generals and Parliaments: The Netherlands in the Fifteenth and
Sixteenth Centuries / H. G. Koenigsberger.
p. cm. – (Cambridge Studies in Early Modern History)
Includes bibliographical references and index.
ISBN 0 521 80330 6
1. Netherlands. Staten-Generaal – History. 2. Netherlands – Politics and government –
1477–1556. 3. Monarchy – Netherlands. 4. Netherlands – Politics and government –
1556–1648. 5. Netherlands – Foreign relations – 1556–1648. I. Title. II. Series.
DJ146 .K64 2001
949.2′02–dc21 2001025656

ISBN 978-0-521-80330-4 hardback
ISBN 978-0-521-04437-0 paperback

To the European Parliament

King Richard: . . . lions make leopards tame

Thomas Mowbray,
duke of Norfolk: Yea. but not change his spots

Richard II, 1, 1, 5–6

Machiavelli was barred from Parnassus
'because he was found at night with a flock of sheep whom he taught to use false dogs' teeth . . . so that in future they could not be kept in obedience by the whistle and the staff'.

Traiano Boccalini, *Ragguagli di Parnasso*, LXXXIX

Contents

	Illustrations	page x
	Acknowledgements	xii
	Abbreviations	xiii
	Glossary	xiv
	Maps	xvi
1	Prologue	1
2	The beginnings of the States General	16
3	The first crisis (1477–1494)	42
4	The Netherlands becomes part of a composite monarchy (1506–1531): Philip the Handsome (1494–1506)	73
5	*Dominium politicum et regale* in a composite monarchy: the regencies of Margaret of Austria (1507–1530)	93
6	*Dominium politicum et regale* in a composite monarchy: the regency of Mary of Hungary, I (1531–1550)	123
7	The Netherlands at the centre of the Habsburg composite monarchy: the regency of Mary of Hungary, II (1550–1555)	151
8	The Netherlands at the centre of the Habsburg composite monarchy: the governor-generalship of Emmanuel Philibert of Savoy (1555–1559)	172
9	Rule from Madrid: the regency of Margaret of Parma (1559–1567)	193
10	The governor-generalships of the duke of Alba (1567–1573) and of Don Luis de Requesens (1573–1576)	220
11	The beginnings of parliamentary government: Holland and Zeeland (1572–1576)	241
12	Rule by the States General: myths and realities (1576–1581)	262
13	Parliamentary government and *dominium regale* (1580–1600)	301
14	Epilogue	325
	Bibliography	344
	Index	356

Illustrations

PLATES

1 Rogier van der Weyden (attrib.), *Philip the Good*. Groeningemuseum, Bruges © IRPA/KIK Brussels — page 17
2 Rogier van der Weyden (attrib.), *Charles the Bold*. Staatliche Museen zu Berlin, Preussischer Kulturbesitz, Gemäldegalerie (Photo: Jörg P. Anders) — 31
3 'The tree of class struggle' – nobility, clergy and commons fight to reach the top. MS 9079 f. 10v (H. Bovet, *L'arbre des batailles*, c. 1461). © Bibliothèque Royale de Belgique, Brussels — 45
4 'Not all is strife' – urban May celebrations. MS II 158 f. 5v (*Book of Hours of Notre Dame*). © Bibliothèque Royale de Belgique, Brussels — 47
5 Coin commemorating the marriage of Maximilian of Austria and Mary of Burgundy. © Bibliothèque Royale de Belgique, Brussels — 51
6 Albrecht Dürer, *Harbour Front at Antwerp*, 1520. Graphische Sammlung Albertina, Vienna — 74
7 Bernard-Barend van Orley, *Margaret of Austria*. Musées royaux des beaux-arts de Belgique © IRPA/KIK, Brussels — 94
8 Hans Bolsterer, medallion of Charles V with the pillars of Hercules on the reverse, 1548. Kunsthistorischesmuseum, Vienna — 101
9 Leone Leoni, *Mary of Hungary* (bronze). Kunsthistorischesmuseum, Vienna — 124
10 Frans Hogenberg, engraving showing a scene of the transfer of sovereignty to Philip II. MS 196 C 30, f. 11, Koninklijke Bibliotheek, The Hague — 168
11 Petrus van der Borcht, engraving of the Antwerp stock exchange from L. Guicciardini, *Descrittione di tutti Paesi Bassi*, Antwerp, 1581 — 178
12 Titian, *Philip II*, 1554. Private collection, Switzerland — 181

Illustrations

13	Bartholomeus de Momper, engraving of the court of Brussels, 1558–60. Print cabinet S. II. 11445, Koninklijke Bibliotheek Albert I/Bibliothèque Royale Albert Ier, Brussels	189
14	Antonio Moro, *The duke of Alba*. Musées royaux des beaux-arts de Belgique © IRPA/KIK, Brussels	215
15	Satirical engraving of 'Alba's throne', 1569. Atlas Van Stolk, Rotterdam	224
16	Adriaen Thomas Key, William I, prince of Orange. © Rijksmuseum, Amsterdam	243
17	Engraving of the Polish Sejm, with Sigismund II Augustus presiding, from A. Guagninus, *Sarmatiae Europae Descriptio*, 1581. British Library, London	328
18	Elizabeth I in Parliament, from Sir Simonds d'Ewes, *Journals of the Parliaments of Queen Elizabeth*, 1672. British Library, London	329
19	Engraving of the French Estates General, 1614. Bibliothèque Nationale, Paris	330
20	Engraving of the Regensburg Reichstag, 1653. Photo courtesy of the late Professor Dr. Volker Press	331
21	The seal of the Estates of Holland, in use from 1572, with the lion of sovereignty as its emblem. Rijksarchief, The Hague	334

MAPS

1	The Burgundian Netherlands	xvi
2	Europe and the Mediterranean	xvii
3	The Habsburg Netherlands, mid-sixteenth century	xviii
4	The division of the Netherlands at the beginning of the seventeenth century (from Geoffrey Parker, *The Dutch Revolt* (Harmondsworth, 1977), © Geoffrey Parker)	xix

Acknowledgements

This book was made possible by a one-year fellowship at the Historisches Kolleg in Munich, 1984–5. My thanks also to the John Simon Guggenheim Memorial foundation for a six-month fellowship in 1971; for help, at various times, with travel expenses to the University of Manchester and to the American Council of Learned Societies. There are many individual historians with whom I have discussed aspects of my work. The following read the whole or parts of this book and made valuable suggestions: Prof. Wim Blockmans, Prof. Sir John Elliott, Dr Dorothy Koenigsberger, Prof. Maria-José Rodríguez-Salgado, Dr Mark Steele, Dr Guy E. Wells.

Abbreviations

AAGB	*Afdeling Agrarische Geschiedenis. Bijdragen. Landbouwhogeschool, Wageningen*
ACM	Archives Communales de Mons
AESC	*Annales: Economies – Sociétés – Civilisations*
AGRB	Archives Générales du Royaume à Bruxelles
AGN	*Algemene Geschiedenis der Nederlanden*, ed. J. A. van Houtte *et al.*, vols. III, IV, V (Utrecht, 1952)
AÖG	*Archiv für österreichische Geschichte*
ARSLBA	*Académie Royale des Sciences des Lettres et des Beaux-Arts de la Belgique. Mémoires. Classe des Lettres*
APAE	*Anciens Pays et Assemblées d'Etats (Standen en Landen)*
BARSBL	*Bulletin de l'Académie Royale des Sciences et Belles Lettres de Bruxelles*
BBR	Brussels, Bibliothèque Royale
BCRH	*Bulletin de la Commission Royale d'Histoire*
BGN	*Bijdragen voor de Geschiedenis der Nederlanden*
BMGN	*Bijdragen en Mededelingen betreffende de Geschiedenis der Nederlanden*
BMHG	*Bijdragen en Mededelingen van het Historische Genootschap*
BN	*Biographie Nationale*
BVGO	*Bijdragen voor Vaderlandsche Geschiedenis en Oudheidkunde*
ESR	*European Studies Review*
GAE	Ghent. Archives de l'Etat
HR	*Historical Research. The Bulletin of the Institute of Historical Research*
HSR	*Holland Staten Resoutiën* (The Hague, 1772–)
HZ	*Historische Zeitschrift*
MIÖG	*Mitteilungen des Instituts für Österreichische Geschichtsforschung*
NAGN	*Nieuwe Algemene Geschiedenis der Nederlanden*, 15 vols. (Haarlem, 1980)
PER	*Parliaments, Estates and Representation*
RBPH	*Revue Belge de Philosophie et d'Histoire*
RSH	*Resolutiën van de Staten van Holland* (an alternative name for *HSR*)
TG	*Tijdschrift voor Geschiedenis*
TRHS	*Transactions of the Royal Historical Society*

Glossary

aides = *beden* = parliamentary grants of money by means of some special tax
alcabala = sales tax in Spain
bandes d'ordonnance = provincial cavalry militia commanded by the provincial governor
chambre des comptes = *Rekenkammer* = treasury of a province
congie = *verloofgeld* = export tax on grain
contado (Italian) = area or province surrounding a city and subject to it
dominium regale and *dominium politicum et regale* = both terms coined by the fifteenth-century English Chief Justice, Sir John Fortescue. The first term meant untrammelled princely power, especially over taxation and legislation, although the prince was expected to respect existing laws. France was regarded as a typical *dominium regale* regime. The second term, sometimes designated as mixed monarchy or *Ständestaat*, required the prince to obtain consent for new taxes from a representative assembly and, in many cases, for new legislation. On the continent the word 'political' was often used to designate limited princely authority.
encabezamiento = in Spain composition of the *alcabala* into a global sum
Eternal Edict = Perpetual Edict = slightly modified form of the Pacification of Ghent, signed by Don John of Austria in 1577.
Franc de Bruges = het Vrije van Brugge = area of small towns and castelries between Bruges and the sea which the Burgundian dukes made into a 'Member' (*leden*) of Flanders with separate representation in the Estates of Flanders
gracien = discount on the *aides*, allowed to individual towns
gueux = literally beggars; in fact those who opposed the Spaniards by force of arms. Cf. also Sea Beggars
joyeuse entrée = *blijde inkomst* = succession oath taken by the dukes of Brabant: a charter of rights
leden = member or consitituent body of a city council or constituent part of a province
legibus solutus of a prince = not bound by laws, i.e. able to legislate and tax by his own authority
pensionary = secretary of a city government or of the whole province of Holland
placards = publicly displayed posters of laws against heresy

Glossary

quota, quotisation = fixed share of a tax of the various members of the Estates
renouvellement de la loi = annual appointment of city magistrates
rentes = *renten* = *juros* (in Spain) = annuities funded by the government or the Estates
ruggespraak = reference back by the delegates to the States General to their principals
schepen = town councillor(s)
schutters = armed citizen guard
tercio = regiment of Spanish infantry
vervangen = the crown paying the contribution of a member of the Estates who had refused to pay its part of a tax granted by the rest of the Estates
vroedschap = ruling oligarchy of a town

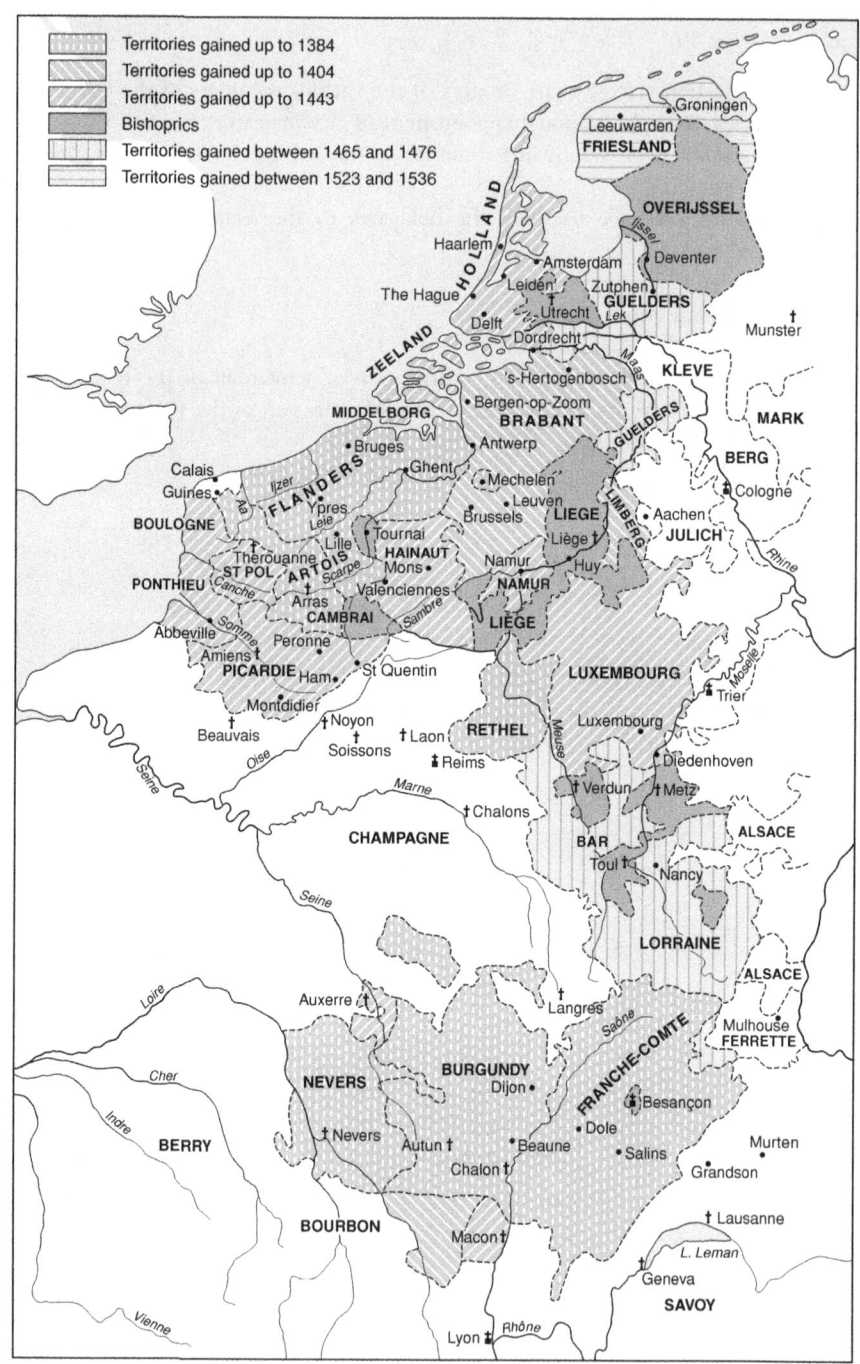

Map 1 The Burgundian Netherlands

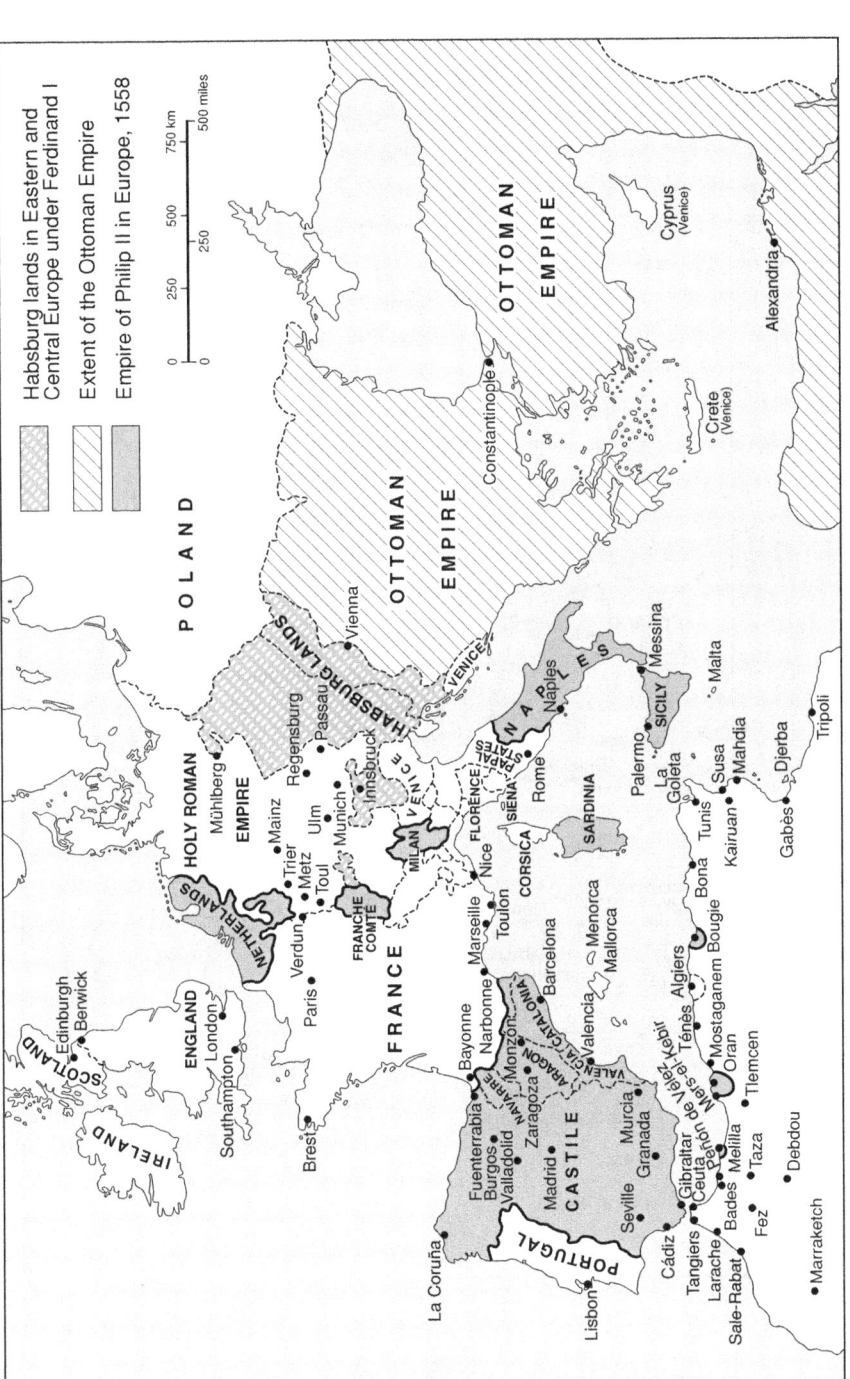

Map 2 Europe and the Mediterranean

Map 3 The Habsburg Netherlands, mid-sixteenth century

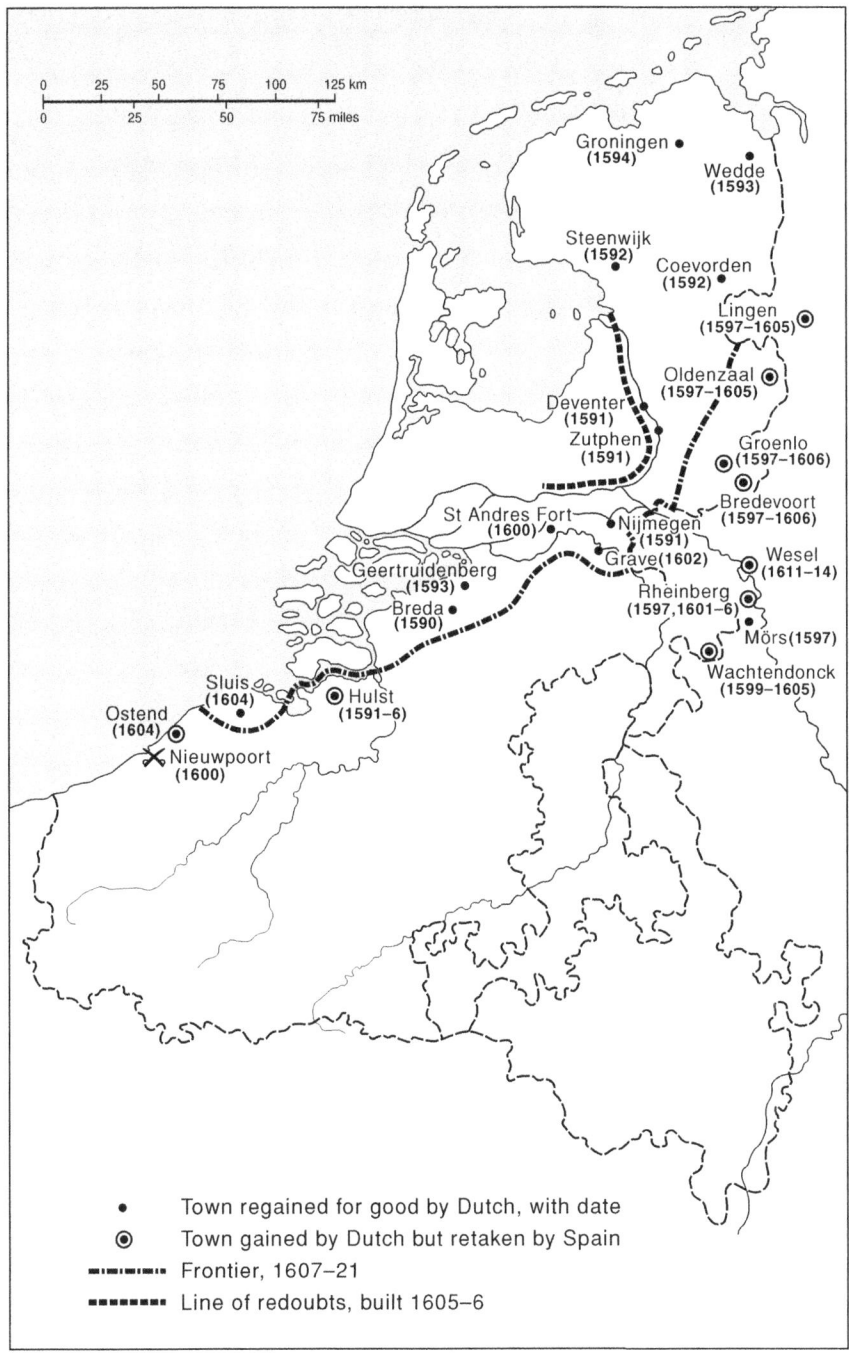

Map 4 The division of the Netherlands at the beginning of the seventeenth century (from Parker, *The Dutch Revolt*)

I

Prologue

'The state comes into existence, originating in the bare needs of life, and continuing in existence for the good life.'

(Aristotle, *Politics*, bk. I, ch. 2)[1]

ELEUTHERIA

Aristotle's epigram was the most revolutionary definition of the state in the history of political thought. Most states and, even more, most empires have been founded and run for the sake of their rulers or for the sake of the tribe. Both the tribe and the rulers have tended to justify their rule by the will of the gods or of God. The will of the gods was, of course, also held to be good for the ruled. But that was at best an afterthought and more often simply propaganda.

Not that Aristotle's thinking was original. For at least 250 years before he wrote, the good life had come to be equated with *eleutheria*, freedom or liberty, defined both as freedom of the polity from outside rule and as freedom of its citizens from tyranny, the lawless rule of a single ruler or, sometimes, group of rulers.[2] What the Greeks invented was citizenship in their polity, the polis or city-state, i.e. the participation of citizens in civic life, in the making and enforcing of laws, in agreeing to taxes and expenditure, in the taking of decisions about relations with the city's neighbours and, if necessary, in serving in the armies of the state. All this was done through dialogue, the dual activity of speaking and listening and the rational conclusions which emerged from this dual activity. It was a dynamic relationship, open-ended, uncertain in its conclusions, and always in danger of being overwhelmed by its opposite: rule and servitude, command and obedience, certainty and acceptance.[3]

To the Greeks, only life in this participatory citizenship constituted genuine political freedom. In practice they found this freedom – what Machiavelli in the

---

[1] Aristotle, *The Politics and Constitution of Athens*, ed. S. Everson, transl. B. Jowett (Cambridge, 1996), 13.
[2] M. Ostwald, 'Freedom and the Greeks', in R. W. Davis, ed., *The Origins of Modern Freedom in the West* (Stanford, 1995), 35–63.
[3] Cf. Manfred Riedel, 'Auf der Suche nach dem Bürgerbund', in P. M. Schmidhuber, ed., *Orientierungen für die Politik* (Munich, 1984), 83–99. Of course, Greek practice did not always live up to this idealised description.

sixteenth century was to call *un vivere politico* – difficult to achieve, and when they succeeded it was only within the narrow circle of the polis and of its full citizens. Women, foreigners and slaves were excluded, although women were regarded as free when married to a citizen. Aristotle was interested only in the polis. When he sent his students to study constitutions outside Athens – one of the most extensive research programmes ever undertaken in political science – he sent them only to other city states in the Mediterranean. What was revolutionary was his definition of the principle of the purpose of the state: the good life.

Since the rediscovery by Latin Christendom of his *Politics*, in the twelfth century, it has had the most profound influence on the practice of and the thinking about politics in Europe and, lately, in those civilisations outside Europe influenced by European thought, even when such influence has not been openly acknowledged. Sometimes the principle has been deliberately ignored, even in our own age, and usually with disastrous consequences for the inhabitants of the state itself and for its neighbours.

In the middle ages the reception of Aristotle's principle fell on fertile ground. The principles of *eleutheria* had never been entirely lost in the Roman Empire. In its successor states they were reinforced by the practice of Germanic kings to summon their free warriors to general meetings, there to discuss the policies pursued by their kings and the counsel (*consilium*) and help (*auxilium*) which his vassals could give him.[4]

REPRESENTATION

This was all very well for relatively small units and the practice survived in some fringe parts of Europe, several of the Alpine valleys and some less accessible coastal areas of Friesland, Norway or Iceland. The problem was to devise some form of participatory relationship in larger political units. The solution of this problem had eluded the Greeks of classical times. Or rather they had not seen it as a problem. Concentrating their political discussions on the polis, they had written off big states, such as the Persian Empire or the Macedonian kingdom, as being in any case devoid of the principle of *eleutheria*.

In medieval Europe the principles of the feudal relationships between lords and vassals were not in themselves the basis for *eleutheria*. Characteristically, the principal medieval virtue, the ideal towards which all young men were educated, was loyalty. It was not a questioning ideal. The lord or the king would ask for advice and help from his vassals; but for discussion and debate only from those he chose for this purpose. Something else was needed which would systematically associate

---

[4] Cf. G. C. Mor, 'Modificazioni strutturali dell'assemblea nazionale longobardo nel secolo VIII', in *Album Helen Maud Cam*, vol. II (Louvain, 1961), 1–12. T. N. Bisson, 'The Military Origins of Medieval Representation', *American Historical Review*, 71 (1966) 1199–218.

much wider sections of the community with the king's policies. From this need arose the principle of representation.

Representation was originally an unpolitical practice derived from Roman law when an attorney represented his client or clients in civil cases. Not surprisingly we find it first among churchmen, overwhelmingly that section of medieval society which could read Latin. The great international orders found representation convenient for increasing the mutual cohesion of their separate houses. Thus, in the thirteenth century the Dominicans developed a complex system of a hierarchy of elected councils, representing individual houses, provincial meetings and, eventually, the whole order.

Even before the Dominicans had fully developed their system of representation, the popes of the twelfth century summoned prelates from the Papal States for consultation. In 1213 Innocent III went a step further. In convening the Fourth Lateran Council he summoned not only the Christian clergy, as represented by their prelates, the bishops and the abbots of the great monasteries, but also the ambassadors of kings and of some of the Italian city-states.[5]

Somewhat more tentatively, secular rulers also began to summon their great vassals in person and, sometimes, representatives of the clergy and of the cities. Failure to do so could have unforeseen and unfortunate consequences. In 1158 the emperor Frederick I, Barbarossa, summoned a great feudal assembly, a diet, at Roncaglia in Italy to obtain taxes on a certain type of trade, on minting and on mining rights. These were traditionally regarded as the king's or emperor's prerogative, the regalia. Frederick's magnates, mostly German, made no difficulty over having these taxes imposed on the emperor's Italian cities. But these cities had not been consulted. They formed leagues against the emperor and fought him successfully until they obtained virtual independence from his rule.

More successfully, some princes summoned assemblies in which prelates, nobles and cities were all represented. Such was the first Spanish Cortes of the king of León in 1188. Such meetings were as yet sporadic and not institutionalised. It was the theologians and especially the canon lawyers who, from the twelfth to the fourteenth centuries, developed systematic theories of representation and related them to the Aristotelian precept of the state existing for the good of its citizens. For now the feudal vassals had become citizens (even if the magnates and the prelates would hardly have relished this description) and they were engaged in a latter-day Greek-style dialogue with their prince and among themselves.

There were good reasons for the concentration on this subject in late medieval clerical political thought. Basically, there was Jesus' saying about rendering unto Caesar the things which were Caesar's and unto God the things which were God's. But this precept alone was not sufficient to explain the development of elaborate political theories. Nothing like it occurred in Byzantine theology, nor in its offshoot,

---

[5] B. Tierney, 'Freedom and the Medieval Church', in Davis, *Origins*, 83.

the Russian Orthodox Church. In the Byzantine Empire and in Russia (and, *a fortiori*, in the Islamic successor states to the Roman Empire) any real opposition between the emperor and the church (or the khalifs and the laws of Islam) was unthinkable. But in the West the collapse of the Roman Empire in the fifth century had left the head of the church, the pope, virtually independent of the emperor. Although for a long time they did not think in terms of opposition, it was impossible that in the long run their interests, whether political or theological, should always coincide.

It took several centuries for the full intellectual consequences of this contingent and, in terms of world history, anomalous situation to be fully appreciated. It became unavoidable, however, when from the eleventh to the fourteenth centuries both the popes and the Holy Roman Emperors, and later also the kings of the separate European states, began to claim supremacy. At times there was open war and throughout these centuries there was a vigorous propaganda campaign on both sides. All protagonists wrote in Latin and all accepted the Bible as the ultimate source of authority. This situation forced men into rational argument. Unavoidably, especially after the rediscovery of Aristotle's *Politics* which became a basic text in the university training of civil and canon lawyers, these rational arguments had to concern themselves with the nature of the state and of political authority. Men had to argue quite fundamentally about both the locus and the limits of authority and about what remedies there were if authority were misused by a tyrant. For while Jesus had also taught that all power came from God, there remained the practical question of how kings had obtained their power: whether directly from God or indirectly, by grant of the people. And if power came from the people, what right did the people have to take it back from a tyrannical king or, at least, what right to limit his powers? Who had the authority to make laws and was the prince subject to the laws he or his ancestors had made? Indeed, what laws could he legitimately make, such as imposing a certain tax, which did not conflict with God-given natural law? And natural law, significantly, included rights of property.[6]

Such arguments were not necessarily pursued in every assembly that princes now summoned. But all these arguments were the fundamental issues which determined the scope and the claims of representative assemblies. They were reinforced by a principle derived from the Justinian Codex: *quod omnes tangit ab omnibus approbetur*: what concerns all has to be approved by all. Again, this had been a purely technical point of procedure in Roman law. It applied in civil cases, such as the guardianship of a minor by several persons. But in the course of the thirteenth and fourteenth centuries, this technical point, sometimes with a slightly

---

[6] *Ibid., passim*. In my discussion of the medieval canonists I have largely followed Professor Tierney's arguments. Cf. also H. G. Koenigsberger, 'Parliaments and Estates', in *ibid.*, 135–40. H. G. Koenigsberger, *Medieval Europe* (Harlow, 1987), 167–8, 174–5, 234–43.

different wording, became a political principle. It proved to be a principle with enormous resonance and power. It was used by those who summoned assemblies in order to get the support of their kingdom; this was the case of Edward I of England when he summoned the 'Model Parliament' in 1295. It was also regularly used by those who felt they ought to be summoned. For giving advice had a dual aspect: it was the duty of the vassal towards his lord or prince and it also came to be seen as his right. Thus the principle of *quod omnes tangit*, coupled with the principle of representation, came in a sense to reproduce the Greek principle of participation, of policy decisions arrived at through rational dialogue and 'approved by all'.

REPRESENTATIVE ASSEMBLIES

In the later middle ages the principle of representation spread throughout Catholic Christian Europe. It fitted in with both the needs of princes and with the traditions of local self-government. These traditions varied greatly, from the attendance of landowners at English hundred and county courts to the virtual self-government of village communities in different parts of Europe[7] and, above all, to the town corporations, with their royal or episcopal charters which set out the nature and details of their rights.

The princes, for their part, needed all the help they could get from their subjects in the fierce military competition which had become the European norm after the great empires of the Franks and Danes had disappeared into an unrepeatable past. Princes received both information and help from their assemblies. In the course of the thirteenth century it became convenient to summon not only the magnates but also the cities; for it was the cities which could most readily provide the money for their princes' warfare.

For the towns it was a nuisance and it was expensive to send representatives to the assemblies; but it was also a good opportunity to have their charters confirmed, to discuss matters of common interest, such as trade relations with foreign powers or the local coinage, and above all to keep taxation within reasonable bounds. The towns might form leagues, such as the *hermandades* of Castile which met regularly from 1282 onwards and which came to develop regular institutions to guide their league. In areas where towns predominated and where the conditions of travel allowed, we find an almost continuous series of assemblies. In Flanders, representatives of the four Members, the principal towns of Bruges, Ghent, Ypres and the area of small towns and castelries between Bruges and the sea, called the Franc de Bruges (het Vrije van Brugge) had more than 4,000 meetings between 1384 and

---

[7] For southern Germany and the Alpine regions *see* T. A. Brady Jr., *Turning Swiss: Cities and Empire, 1450–1550* (Cambridge, 1985), *passim*; P. Blickle, ed., *Verborgene republikanische Traditionen in Oberschwaben* (Tübingen, 1998), *passim*.

1506, often in several different places at one time. In Holland between 1401 and 1433 there were over 700 meetings.[8] Their main purpose was the discussion of commercial matters. In more extended principalities and in largely rural areas meetings tended to be dominated by the lay and ecclesiastical magnates, even when some towns participated. Such meetings were much less frequent, sometimes with intervals of several years but, in contrast to the largely urban assemblies, much more elaborate and formal. Often the prince himself was present.

The immediate surprise is that the Italian city-states, as they developed their independence in the long struggle with the German emperors, did not take part in the movement towards setting up representative assemblies. Their leagues, such as the Lombard League which fought Frederick Barbarossa, were little more than alliances of independent units, just as were somewhat later the members of the Hanseatic League in northern Europe. The Hanseatic League had its occasional diets: meetings of the representatives of some, but rarely all, of the Hanseatic cities. These assemblies never developed into formal institutions with a fixed membership.

The Italian city-states developed a very strong tradition of political liberty. Just like the Greek *eleutheria*, this liberty was seen as both freedom from outside domination and from internal tyranny. The Italian humanist political theorists, including Machiavelli, never doubted that true liberty had to be republican. Their arguments were over the nature of the republican regime: whether it should be aristocratic, democratic or mixed. Representation was something which happened in monarchies and was therefore not considered a *vivere politico*, even though Machiavelli thought that when it was lost it might have to be re-established by a man of *virtù*.[9]

At the same time there were practical reasons for the rejection of representation by the Italian city-states. They behaved towards their surrounding areas and subject towns, their *contado*, rather like princes. They subjugated them, taxed them and used them as recruiting grounds for the soldiers who fought their internecine wars for them. The towns of the *contado* and the rural nobility were not consulted about these wars and the nobles were summoned only when they were needed as individuals in the army. As for the subject cities, a city with a relatively large number of these, such as Florence, would never want to summon the representatives of the Tuscan cities together and thus provide them with an opportunity for combining their forces against the 'imperial' city. This anti-estates tradition was so strong that it prevented the development of representative assemblies even where a city-republic had become a principality, as happened in Milan, Verona and other cities.

---

[8] W. P. Blockmans, 'The Parliamentary History of the Netherlands and Belgium compared to that of Sweden', in N. Stjernquist, ed., *The Swedish Riksdag in an International Perspective* (Stockholm, 1989), 36. Cf. ch. 2, p. 22.
[9] Q. Skinner, *The Foundations of Modern Political Thought*, vol. I, (Cambridge, 1978), 158–62.

Prologue

Thus, neither a prevalence of cities, nor of feudal relationships, nor even an abundance of ecclesiastical corporations and the presence of canon lawyers were alone enough to account for the appearance of representative institutions. One further condition was absolutely necessary, an element that was inherent in the very idea of representatives of localities, corporations and estates coming together in an assembly. This was a feeling of community in a given political structure. Outside the cities, which certainly developed community feelings but in which, as we have seen, representation did not develop, such feelings could originally be tribal. But much more frequently, during the central and later middle ages, tribal origins were overridden by traditions of political and military cooperation with, and obedience to, a local prince.

Thus, in 1128 during a succession crisis in Flanders, members of the nobility and several of the great cities formed leagues to deal with the crisis and to elect a new count of Flanders. As yet these leagues were not representative assemblies (although some historians have characterised them as pre-parliaments) and there is no evidence that the 'what-concerns-all' maxim was used. But these events did show cooperation between nobility and towns and prevented Flanders from splitting up into independent city-states like northern Italy. This was the more remarkable as the principal cities, Bruges, Ghent and Ypres, behaved in many ways as if they were city-states, dominating and exploiting their surrounding countryside and smaller towns like an Italian *contado*. From the end of the twelfth and during the thirteenth century the counts were driven to cooperate regularly with assemblies of their estates to defend themselves against the kings of France who tried to re-establish their ancient lordship over the county.

In this case, as indeed happened very frequently in the relations between princes and their representative assemblies, the course of events and the eventual balance of power was not determined solely by the internal history of the country in question but also by foreign intervention. The history of princes and parliaments hardly ever took place in a closed system.

This was so even in the case of island parliaments. The history of Magna Carta might well have been different if the baronial movement against King John, in 1215, had not been supported by help from France. At the same time, and crucially showing the development of a spirit of community in the country, the rights and privileges which the barons extorted from the king, notably trial by one's peers according to law, were meant to apply to all free men. After John's death the regency government for his minor son re-issued the charter three times. Although some details differed, these copies were sent to the county courts, thus deliberately involving the community of the whole realm. This was certainly the way in which Magna Carta came to be interpreted. Successive parliaments insisted on its re-issue. The reputation of parliaments and of Magna Carta as safeguards of the basic rights of Englishmen reinforced each other and grew together to form the characteristic symbiosis of the idea of government under the law, the rights and privileges of the ruler's subjects and the representation of the whole community.

It took time for regular meetings of Parliament to be established in England and the same was true of representative assemblies on the continent. Inevitably, their development took place over different time scales, from the thirteenth to the fifteenth centuries. Inevitably too the assemblies took different forms in different countries. There were the classic three estates – clergy, nobility and commons; or again there was a principality such as Holland, where the assemblies were usually confined to the nobility and six major cities (although, on occasion, many more small towns were also summoned), with no estate of the clergy at all. In Poland only the nobility was regarded as the community. The towns were left altogether out of the Sejm, the diet of the whole kingdom, although they dominated the provincial assembly of Royal Prussia. In Sweden, by contrast, not only the prelates but the local clergy were represented in the estate of the clergy and there was even an estate of the peasants. Much depended on the development of estates as self-conscious groups or groupings within an estate, such as the division between magnates (*ricos hombres*) and lower nobility (*hijos-dalgo*) in the Cortes of Aragon.

There were representative assemblies everywhere outside the city-states apart from a few peasant communities in some Alpine valleys and in the tidal marshes of the Frisian North Sea coast, which had preserved ancient traditions of meetings of all free men.

What representative assemblies never were was democratic. Only in England was there anything like elections of the actual members of Parliament and no one imagined that such elections were democratic. Democracy was admired by some of the humanists. But outside some of the Italian and Swiss city-states and the few independent peasant communities, democracy was despised and shunned. Representation appeared in ecclesiastical orders and in monarchies. It was certainly meant to involve the community in political life but it was never meant to change the social structure of the community. It was revolutionary in the Aristotelian sense of providing for the good life by defending the liberties, the specific privileges of corporations and groups, within the community. It was meant to preserve the community from arbitrary rule by its prince. But representation was not meant to produce equality or equal rights. The exact form of the assemblies and their relations with their prince depended on the social structure of the communities they represented. These relations, in turn, were often influenced by alliances with, and interventions of, neighbours. Once established, the assemblies tended to take on an institutional form. As such, they began to develop a life of their own with certain traditional and sometimes rigid forms, and they did this even when the socio-political conditions of their origins had changed. While the appearance of representative assemblies depended on the existence of a certain degree of community feeling, the assemblies themselves helped to further this feeling.

Prologue

The princes had an ambivalent attitude towards their assemblies. They saw them as useful for assuring the support of the community, the observance of royal laws and increasingly for the grant of money in the form of taxes. In 1282 the Sicilians overthrew their king of the French House of Anjou (the 'Sicilian Vespers') and called upon the king of Aragon to take the crown and help them to maintain their independence. Peter III of Aragon, while claiming the crown of Sicily by hereditary right, summoned a succession of parliaments in Sicily to have himself confirmed as king. These parliaments prevented the kingdom from breaking up into a number of separate city-states, as in northern Italy, and they obtained from King Peter a number of privileges, in return for money grants for the war with the House of Anjou which was still established in Naples. It comes as no surprise that King Peter also summoned an assembly in his home principality of Catalonia, to obtain financial support for his Sicilian policy.

Yet princes were well aware of the danger of raising up the assemblies as potential rivals to their authority. They and their lawyers were always very touchy on this subject. While the Roman law maxim *quod omnes tangit* had been generally taken on board, so, almost as generally, had the Roman law maxim of the prince as *legibus solutus*, being above the law. For some royal lawyers this principle was reinforced by the dictum from Justinian's Codex, *quod principi placuit leges habet vigorem*: that what the prince wishes has the force of law. What exactly was meant by these Roman law maxims was a matter for debate and of learned and subtle arguments by the civil and canon lawyers. Most commonly it was held that the prince alone had the right to formulate laws which it was then the job of the representative assembly to confirm.

But what of royal laws which resulted from the presentation of grievances? Such presentation was one of the recognised functions of the assemblies. At the very least, princes were anxious to preserve their right to accept or reject suggestions by their assemblies. On occasion, especially when there was a disputed succession, the assemblies met on their own initiative. But princes always disliked such independent actions and insisted that they alone had the right to summon, prorogue or dissolve parliaments.

Yet parliaments and representative assemblies were not identical to an extended royal council. In the absence of an extensive civil service, parliaments were useful to the polity precisely because they represented interests, information and authority independent of those of the prince and the council he appointed. They could provide a political dialogue for the community.[10]

---

[10] The foregoing section is based on my 'Parliaments and Estates', in Davis, *Origins*, 135–77. See also Tierney, 'Freedom and the Medieval Church', in *ibid.*, 64–100; W. P. Blockmans, 'Representation since the Thirteenth Century', in *New Cambridge Medieval History*, vol. VII (Cambridge, 1998), ch. 2, 29–64.

CONCILIARISM

The basic ambiguity of this late medieval balance of forces became apparent in the first half of the fifteenth century in the history of the great church councils and their confrontation with the papal monarchy. It was not meant to be a confrontation. The leaders of Christian Europe, both clerical and lay, set out to end the scandal of the papal schism (since 1378). A council at Pisa (1408-9), convoked by a group of cardinals, was denounced by both popes and ended up by adding a third pope to the two feuding ones. The next council, at Constance (1414-18) was summoned at the instance of the Holy Roman Emperor and was attended by a number of European kings and princes or their representatives, as well as by an impressive array of prelates and theologians. This time it successfully deposed all three warring popes and elected a new one, Martin V, who was generally accepted. All this was very similar to the actions of a local representative assembly, such as that of the estates of Flanders which had deposed an unworthy prince and elected a new one – but now, with the Council of Constance, on a disproportionately larger stage. Being attended, or at least avidly followed, by the cream of European intellectuals, the council naturally produced an intellectual justification for its actions. It did this in the famous decree *Haec Sancta* (6 April 1415) which claimed that the universal council derived its authority directly from Christ and that this authority was superior to that of the pope, the successor of St Peter and vicar of Christ. The fathers were careful to claim such authority only in matters of faith; but how were such matters to be distinguished from organisational and political matters? For the council then proceeded to the reorganisation of the church and the election of a new head. Here were the basic problems of the nature of authority which the theologians had been debating in the abstract over centuries. And, again, they were basically analogous to the problems of the authority of princes and of their representative assemblies. The confrontation became an open one in the course of the next council, at Basle (1431-49). Characteristically, the clashes now developed over Pope Eugenius IV's attempt to dissolve the council, over the council's counter-claim that only it could prorogue or dissolve itself and by the formulation of an even more far-reaching decree than *Haec Sancta*, namely that the council had simply superior authority to that of the pope.

The conciliar position was argued especially by the universities, with the theology faculty of Paris in the forefront. In the end the theologians could not resist the pope's advantage of playing the different secular powers against each other. Morever, he had the advantage in spiritual propaganda from having concluded an apparently successful union with the Greek Orthodox Church (1437). By the middle of the fifteenth century the papacy had emerged successfully as an autocratic monarchy from its confrontation with the principles of representation of the conciliarists. No one foresaw that the papacy would now become vulnerable not only to the church reformers – everyone saw the need for reform – but to the quest

Prologue

for ecclesiastical independence and control over their own churches by the secular princes.

Looking back on the confrontations of the fifteenth century, the surprising aspect is not that the conciliar movement eventually failed. Its protagonists' interests were too diverse. The sheer scale of the conciliar operation and the huge area over which it had to be coordinated defeated even its most committed defenders. Thus, Nicolas of Cusa, one of the outstanding minds of the age, gave up on the conciliarists and changed to the papalist side. The real surprise is how far the conciliarists managed to get. This was a function of the still remarkable vitality of the idea of the unity of Christendom, the analogue to the sense of community which was so essential for the success of the idea of representation in the individual European states.[11]

Was the idea of representation then defeated with the defeat of conciliarism? History is not as logical or as symmetrical as that. The notion of a council survived as an idea, an aspiration, a means of healing the ills of the times. It was still strong in the first generation of the Reformation and it was so on both sides of the Reformation divide. But the connection of councils with representation dropped more and more into the background, yielding to the growing certainties of dogma on both sides. In the Council of Trent (1545–64) few were still interested in representation except for the crude notion that the Protestants thought their voices ought to be heard and the Catholics thought they should be denied.

COMPOSITE STATES AND STATES GENERALS

The church councils of the fifteenth century were a grandiose but doomed attempt to create a composite representative institution. The idea itself, however, was by no means dead, nor were the councils of Constance and Basle its only examples. Composite representative assemblies were the logical consequence of the appearance of composite or multiple monarchies. For in the later middle ages such monarchies had become the overwhelmingly most important form of polity in Europe. The more powerful a monarchy was – and power was the international object of most monarchies – the less likely it was to be uniform. The constituent parts of a multiple monarchy came together in most cases by common consent, as in the case of Sicily and Aragon, or even more commonly by marriage or dynastic inheritance, as did most of the dominions of the House of Austria, or England and Scotland by the succession of James VI and I in 1603.

In all such cases the prince swore to observe the existing laws and privileges of his newly acquired state. By the fifteenth century these laws and privileges usually included a representative assembly which would see it as its duty to defend its own

---

[11] For a summary account of the vast literature on the conciliar movement, see A. Black, 'Popes and Councils', in *ibid.*, ch. 3, 65–86.

and its constituents' rights. In the relatively few cases when a monarchy had acquired a state or a province by pure conquest, it was held to have the right to dispense with its existing laws and privileges. In practice, however, the monarchy's powers were limited by its need to reconcile at least an important part of the elite of the newly conquered territory. Machiavelli counselled his prince either to destroy a new province, reside in it himself (and dispense generous patronage to the natives) or let it live with its own laws.[12] Even when the inhabitants of a province which changed hands were not consulted over the change, it was expected that these rules would be observed. In 1482 Mary of Burgundy was forced by her States General to conclude the Treaty of Arras and to hand over Artois and Franche-Comté to France, as dowry for her infant daughter who was to marry the dauphin. The prospective bridegroom (who, in the event, never did marry the princess Margaret) was asked 'to hold in special commendation the counties of Artois and Burgundy and their poor inhabitants whom you will find to be good and loyal subjects'.[13]

Powerful, skilful or just lucky princes could thus add province after province, state after state, to their realm, each with its already developed laws and institutions. To achieve greater unity of his different dominions the prince often found it convenient to summon their representative assemblies together. He could not take it for granted that all his provinces would support a particular policy, especially war, which he regarded as essential. Thus in 1485 the estates of Royal Prussia, a German-speaking province which, since 1466, lived quite contentedly under the king of Poland, refused to support his war with the Ottoman Turks. They even claimed that, according to their privileges, the king of Poland was obliged to protect them from aggression, but not the other way round.[14]

The French monarchy had already had rather similar experiences in the fourteenth century. Some of the French provinces were not interested in the war with England and preferred to keep their resources for themselves. The French kings therefore summoned multiple assemblies for the whole kingdom, the *états généraux*, only rarely and then not always with great success. There was, moreover, the danger that a states general, a composite assembly for a large and articulated realm, might become very powerful and begin to usurp royal authority. This also happened in France when King John II was taken prisoner by the English at the battle of Poitiers (1356). The Estates General voted taxes for the continuation of the war and for the payment of the huge ransom for the captured king. At the same time

[12] N. Machiavelli, *Il Principe*, chs. V, XX. I have based this section of this chapter on my article 'Composite States, Representative Institutions and the American Revolution', *Historical Research*, 62, 148 (1989), 137–53. For composite monarchies, see also J. H. Elliott, 'A Europe of Composite Monarchies', *Past and Present*, 137 (1992), 48–71.
[13] L. P. Gachard, ed., *Lettres inédites de Maximilien . . . sur les affaires des Pays-Bas*, pt. 1, in *BCRH*, ser. 2, vol. II.C (Brussels, 1851), 38. See also ch. 3.
[14] M. Biskup, 'Die Stände in Preussen Königlichen Anteils 1466–1526', in H. Boockmann, ed., *Die Anfänge der ständischen Vertretung in Preussen und seinen Nachbarländern* (Munich, 1992), 83–99.

they attempted to reform the central government whose incompetence had led to the military disaster. But an Estates General for a country as big and varied as France proved too unwieldy, and the new, energetic king, Charles V, preferred to rule without it. The French monarchy was the only one, apart from some Italian principalities, which had managed to build up its tax-collecting administration for at least a large part of the country. From the time of Charles V it acquired the reputation of being a *dominium regale*, a regime which could impose important taxes at will. This was in contrast to the more common *dominium politicum et regale* where the monarchy had no such rights.[15] The line between the two types of regime was not always sharp, but contemporaries were quite clear that this line existed and which side France was on. Perhaps the situation was best summed up, as a Venetian ambassador reports it, by a joke supposedly told by Francis I. Francis claimed that the emperor Maximilian had said to him that he, the emperor, was a king of kings because no one did his bidding; Ferdinand the Catholic was a king of men, because men did his bidding but only when they thought fit to do so; but Francis, the king of France, was a king of beasts because everyone always did his bidding.

This joke was, of course, an exaggeration. The historian, though, may well wonder why King Francis appears to have dined out on it. Chief Justice Fortescue, to whom we owe the particular formulation of the nature of the two regimes, did not, however, in the fifteenth century, snatch his terms out of thin air. The adjective 'political' was derived from Aristotle's *Politics* and was frequently used on the continent to indicate a limited or mixed regime.[16]

If the rulers of multiple monarchies had ambivalent feelings about multiple representative assemblies, so had the estates of the individual provinces. Those of the Austrian Habsburgs in central Europe were often unwilling to send their deputies outside their own provincial boundaries. The Bohemians, for instance, refused to go to Austria. The privileges which the rulers had sworn to observe were always the local privileges of the particular province. One did not set such privileges aside lightly, for fear of losing them altogether. If one still found it necessary to do so, one would insist all the more strongly on one's other privileges. While in meetings of states generals the smaller provinces would often follow the lead of the bigger ones, for instance in granting taxes, all would resist stubbornly any notion of majority voting, especially in financial matters.

Here was also one of the reasons why, with very few exceptions, states generals functioned only in contiguous territories. A stretch of sea between dominions

---

[15] The exact expressions were coined by the fifteenth-century English Chief Justice, Sir John Fortescue, in *In Praise of the Laws of England*, ed. S. Lockwood, (Cambridge, 1997).
[16] See Skinner, *The Foundations of Modern Political Thought*, 54; P. Blickle, 'Kommunalismus und Republikanismus in Oberdeutschland', in H. G. Koenigsberger and E. Müller-Luckner, eds., *Republiken und Republikanismus im Europa der frühen Neuzeit* (Munich, 1988), 57–75; H. G. Koenigsberger, 'Dominium regale or dominium politicum et regale', in Koenigsberger, *Politicians and Virtuosi* (London, 1986), 1–25.

under one crown was a particularly serious obstacle. But even in such cases, the histories of England and Ireland, of Sweden and Finland, and of Aragon and Sardinia showed that the sea was not an absolute barrier.

These instances, however, were relatively rare and the main reason was that constituents of states generals, even more than those of single dominions, insisted on restricting the powers of their deputies and required them in important matters to refer back to those who had sent them. There were good reasons for this practice. The burgomasters, aldermen and town secretaries found it naturally much easier to be brave among their colleagues inside their familiar town halls than when travelling as deputies and facing the great lords of the king's council or even the king or his regent himself. Refusing government demands was much easier when one could claim that one had no power personally to decide the matter. Conversely, it was easier for the government to bully single deputies than the whole council of a big city. Nevertheless, it was not always clear whom the deputies represented. Was it the provincial assemblies or the parliamentary cities and ecclesiastical corporations? Nor was it always clear what role the magnates played in the assemblies, especially if they were also members of the king's council. The history of the states generals cannot therefore be neatly separated from the history of the assemblies of the constituent provinces of a multiple monarchy. Men do not willingly give up power which they have exercised or which they feel they ought to exercise. If the ideal of *dominium politicum et regale* was cooperation for the good of the community, there could be very different views as to who and what the community was.

There could also be passionately held views as to what was good, Aristotelian or otherwise. And if such differences led to overt conflicts, as they often did, it was inevitable that neighbours should be drawn into such conflicts. The historian can therefore observe certain tendencies or even regularities in these histories. But contingencies were always likely to affect their outcome. What the historian cannot do is to predict or retrodict the outcome of these histories, either for the whole of Europe or for single states.

A comprehensive comparative history of states generals would therefore approximate to a comprehensive comparative political history of early modern Europe. Even if it were possible to write this – and there has been no such thing up to now – it would not give us a general law of the historical relations between monarchies and parliaments. I have therefore chosen a different format: that of presenting in some depth the relations between the monarchy and the States General of the Netherlands over a period of two hundred years. The reason for this choice is the almost infinitely varied story of this relationship. Here was a composite polity within a multiple state, open both to ideas and to intervention from outside. The lion at one time managed to alienate nearly all the leopards from his command. Half of them chose to return to it, for a variety of reasons and, not least, for fear of

Prologue

the sheep with dogs' teeth. The other half of the leopards chose not to return to the lion's command because they chose not to change their spots. Everyone chose to keep the sheep, toothed or not, simply blind. Shakespeare's Richard II summed up this attitude, too, when he characterised the unnaturalness of Bolingbroke's rebellion:

> Ourselves and Bushy . . .
> Observed his courtship of the common people,
> How he did seem to dive into their hearts,
> With humble and familiar courtesy,
> What reverence he did throw away on slaves,
> Wooing poor craftsmen with the craft of smiles.
>   (*Richard II* 1.4. 23–8)

2

The beginnings of the States General

'Hence, to continue my argument, is there a king or other lord who has power, outside his domain, to levy even a penny on his subjects without the grant and consent of those who have to pay it, unless it were by tyranny or violence?'

Philippe de Commynes, *Mémoires*, 7, 18

On 5 January 1477 Duke Charles the Bold was killed at the battle of Nancy. Within three months the States General had taken effective control of the government of the Netherlands. They got rid of the late duke's councillors, abolished an important part of his centralised administration, negotiated with foreign powers, ceded several provinces to France which Louis IX's armies had occupied, and finally forced the young duchess, Mary, to grant a charter with unprecedented privileges for the provinces. It was a most startling revolution. Quite soon, however, ducal power was re-established and many of the recently granted privileges were lost again. But the States General itself remained a definitely established institution whose existence was not to be called into question for almost a hundred years.

THE PROVINCES OF THE NETHERLANDS

There was nothing inevitable about this history, or even about the existence of the States General. The state which the States General represented or, more accurately, the loose confederation of duchies, counties and lordships in north-western Europe, had been brought together under one rule only in the previous fifty years. In 1384 the House of Burgundy, a younger branch of the French royal House of Valois, had inherited the counties of Flanders and Artois, together with the lordship over the cities of Lille, Douai and Orchies and some others. All these were fiefs of the French crown. Only in the late 1420s did Philip the Good, the third of the Burgundian dukes, successively take over control of Holland, Zeeland and Hainaut from their last independent countess, Jacqueline of Bavaria, one-time wife of Humphrey, duke of Gloucester. Not until 1433 did Jacqueline finally transfer all her rights to Philip. Three years earlier, in 1430, the estates of the duchy of Brabant had chosen the Burgundian as their duke, from a list of claimants which included the emperor Sigismund. In 1429 Philip had inherited the small county of Namur and, in 1443, he conquered the duchy of Luxembourg, to which he had

Plate 1 Rogier van der Weyden (attrib.), *Philip the Good*. Groeningemuseum, Bruges

hereditary claims, as he also had to Brabant. The two duchies and the four counties were all part of the Holy Roman Empire.

The economic and political centre of gravity of the Burgundian dominions had therefore shifted outside the French frontiers. Gradually, the political interests of the dukes also shifted. From playing the role of leaders of one of the French parties trying to control the French crown, they tended more and more to become the external opponents and rivals of a re-unified kingdom of France. In this role they sought to strengthen and unify their newly acquired provinces; and the provinces, in their turn, found in their need to defend themselves against France a unifying force, a motive for cooperation.

Except for Luxembourg, separated from Brabant by the prince-bishopric of Liège, the provinces were contiguous; but they differed in economic and social structure and in their political institutions more than most other areas of similar size in Europe. The south-western provinces adjoining France, Hainaut and Artois, were largely rural and their towns were relatively small. They were dominated by a landowning nobility, by a large number of wealthy monasteries and by the cathedral chapters of Arras and Tournai. The richest of the nobles formed interrelated clans, owning estates, castles, villages and sometimes small towns in many of the Netherlands provinces and even in France. As yet their loyalties were far from firmly fixed on the Burgundian dukes. The Croy, the greatest of these clans, were notorious for their French interests and the francophile policies they tried to impose on the dukes. Their greatest rival in the mid-fifteenth century, Louis de Luxembourg, count of St Pol, was made constable of France by Louis XI as part of the peace settlement after the War of the Public Weal, a civil war among the French high nobility.[1] This did not mean that St Pol actually changed his allegiance.

It was precisely to strengthen the allegiance to the House of Burgundy of his French-speaking nobility that Philip the Good founded the new chivalric Order of the Golden Fleece in 1430.[2] But for most of the rest of the fifteenth century, at least, the pull of France remained strong. Philippe de Commynes, the memoirist, son of a knight of the Golden Fleece and godson of the duke himself, was the most famous though not the most important of those who actually exchanged Burgundian for French service as late as the 1470s. The shift of allegiance could also go in the opposite direction, as it did in the case of the Chalon family, princes of the small Rhone principality of Orange[3] – a shift which was to have the most profound, but at the time quite unforeseeable, consequences a hundred years later when their descendant, William of Orange, led the revolt against Spain.

Since the fourteenth century both Hainaut and Artois had representative assemblies, organised in the classic form of the three estates, clergy, nobility and towns.

---

[1] G. Chastellain, *Chronique des ducs de Bourgogne*, ed. A. C. Buchon (Paris, 1883), 248f; R. Vaughan, *Philip the Good* (London, 1970), 391.
[2] Vaughan, *Philip the Good*, 57.
[3] R. Vaughan, *Charles the Bold* (London, 1973), 231ff.

The beginnings of the States General

By the mid-fifteenth century the estates of Hainaut had become a regular institution with a permanent administrative office and its own seals, responsible mainly for the collection of the *aides*, the money grants which the states made to the duke. The *receveur*, the official supervising the collection of the *aides*, was appointed by the duke but on the proposal of the estates and reponsible both to the highest ducal official, the *bailli* (always a nobleman), and to the states.[4] It was the *bailli* (sometimes called *grand bailli*) who issued the summons for the estates at the instance of the duke.[5] There were twelve peerages and twenty-two baronies in Hainaut, together with a great number of minor nobility. Rarely more than half a dozen of the richest nobles attended the meetings of the estates. Much the same was true of the abbots and of the twenty-two towns that were summoned. Most left it to Mons, Valenciennes and two or three others to represent the interests of the towns.[6]

In Artois the preponderance of the first two estates was almost as great as in Hainaut. Both were summoned in their capacity of holders of fiefs from the count. The clergy comprised the bishops of Arras and Thérouanne, twenty abbots and other ecclesiastics. Over sixty nobles had the right to attend, although usually far fewer did so and some sent proxies. Ten cities were summoned and sometimes even more, but usually only Arras, St Omer, Béthune and Aire sent their deputies.[7]

Bordering Hainaut and Artois to the north was the large county of Flanders, the most populous, the most industrialised and the richest territory in Europe north of the Alps and, notoriously, the most difficult to govern. Its three large towns, Bruges, Ghent and Ypres, had grown prosperous in the middle ages by international trade and by textile manufacturing. They had reached their apogee in the early fourteenth century. In the fifteenth century Ypres had fallen on hard times, its woollen manufactures starved of English wool and unable to compete with English and other Flemish cloth makers, its population shrunk from over 20,000 to little more than half that figure.[8] Bruges was having trouble with the silting of its river access to the sea and, more seriously, with growing competition from Antwerp in its international trade. Even Ghent, with more varied manufacturing than Ypres, had declined from its former peak and the 64,000 population which it had in 1356, even after the appalling death-toll of the Black Death.[9] We have only

---

[4] C. Piérard, 'Les Etats de Hainaut', *APAE*, 33 (1965), 65ff.
[5] L. Devillers, 'Participation des états de Hainaut aux assemblées des états généraux des Pays Bas (1438–1790)', in *BCRH*, vol. LXXIV (1905), 32.
[6] L. Devillers, *Inventaire analytique des archives des états de Hainaut*, vol. I (Mons, 1884).
[7] C. Hirschauer, *Les états d'Artois de leurs origines à l'occupation française, 1340–1640*, vol. I (Paris, 1923), 36ff.
[8] R. Mols, *Introduction à la démographie historique des villes d'Europe*, vol. II (Louvain, 1952), 520.
[9] H. van Werweke, 'Het bevolkingscijfer van de stad Gent in de viertiende eeuw', in *Miscellanea L. Van der Essen*, vol. I (Brussels and Paris, 1947), 345. Cf. also W. Prevenier, 'La démographie des villes ... de Flandres aux XIVe et XVe siècles', *Revue du Nord* 65 (1983).

partial population figures for the fifteenth century, but Ghent was evidently still a big town, with well over 40,000 inhabitants.[10]

Bruges and Ghent, though not Ypres, were still immensely rich. They dominated and exploited their surrounding countryside almost as effectively as the Italian city-states dominated their *contado*. As early as the twelfth century, the counts of Flanders had summoned them or indeed they had assembled on their own initiative, to discuss important political and financial matters. Together with Lille and Douai, Arras and St Omer, they formed the 'Members' of Flanders and claimed to represent the whole county. They certainly did represent its most powerful, organised entities. By the fifteenth century, Lille and Douai had been lost to Flanders and, with the little town of Orchies, formed a province of their own. But Bruges, Ghent and Ypres still called themselves the Members of Flanders and maintained their earlier claims. The counts tried to balance this alarming concentration of urban power by organising the Franc de Bruges (Het Vrije van Brugge), a wealthy area of small towns, castles and lordships between Bruges and the sea coast, as a fourth Member. This Member was dominated by the local nobility and was likely to side with the count against the three cities. At times the Burgundian dukes also summoned the full three estates of Flanders, when the prelates, the nobility and representatives of the smaller towns all appeared in the assemblies. But the four Members were too firmly established and too powerful to allow themselves to be displaced by the three estates.[11]

Bruges and Ghent had a long history of defiance of their prince. The town patriciates, the *poorters*, were rich merchants and manufacturers who owned much urban property and intermarried with the local landed nobility. They filled most of the city offices and effectively controlled the city councils. Through centuries of struggling with the counts or of giving them financial help, the patricians had acquired charters and privileges which gave them not only economic monopolies and trading benefits but also control over the administration of their cities and substantial freedom from interference by the count in their internal affairs. These privileges and rights they were willing to defend with great tenacity. But at least from the first half of the fourteenth century onwards they had had to share some of their power in their town councils with the guilds. Class struggle had become endemic in the Flemish towns, for it was rooted in the enormous property differences of the various sections of the urban population and the economic exploitation of the mass of the working people.[12]

---

[10] W. P. Blockmans, 'Peilingen naar de sociale strukturen te Gent tijdens de late 15e eeuw', *APAE*, 54 (1971), 254.

[11] For the whole preceding paragraph see W. Prevenier, 'Les états de Flandre depuis les origines jusqu'en 1790', *APAE*, 33 (1965), 15–59. J. Dondt, 'Les origines des états de Flandre', *APAE*, 35 (1966), 1–52. J. Dondt, 'Les assemblées d'états en Belgique avant 1795', *ibid.*, 325–400.

[12] There is a vast literature on the late medieval Flemish cities. Cf. for instance Blockmans, 'Peilingen', and W. P. Blockmans, 'Nieuwe gegevens over de gegoede burgerij van Brugge en de 13e en vooral 14e eeuw', *APEA*, 54 (1971), especially table III, 148–50.

The beginnings of the States General

In the three-cornered struggles between the Burgundian dukes, as counts of Flanders, the Flemish patricians and the common people, alliances shifted and were further complicated by the commercial rivalries of the cities with each other. In 1432 the weavers of Ghent rose against their council while proclaiming their loyalty to the duke.[13] In 1437, however, duke and patricians found themselves in alliance against the lower classes. The Brugeois, after months of rising tension, killed one of their burgomasters because 'he worked with the prince to keep down the common people of Bruges'.[14] After an affray with the duke's troops in Bruges, Philip the Good had to wage a regular campaign for several months to subdue the city.[15]

But it was in Ghent that opposition to the duke went furthest. The trouble started when the city refused to impose a salt tax proposed by Philip in 1447. The duke tried to interfere in the annual council elections in order to exclude the most determined opponents of the tax. Factional strife in Ghent continued to grow and, towards the end of 1451, the common people took to the streets, overthrew the regular magistrate and set up a revolutionary government which carried out a policy of executions of those patrician councillors and supporters of the duke who had not managed to escape from the city. This time it took Philip more than a year to crush the Ghenters. They had appealed to the other cities of Flanders and even to Charles VII of France for help. But everyone feared to support a popular revolution and, in the end, the Ghenters were left to their fate. When the city had submitted, the duke changed its constitution to reduce the great power of the deans of the major guilds from the council and restrict Ghent's control over the surrounding countryside.[16]

But the weavers and the other guildsmen were not finally subdued. In the following 130 years they rose four times more and set up popular dictatorships. Rebellions were a constant possibility in Flemish and Netherlands politics, and no one was likely to forget it. In 1461 the Milanese ambassador wrote to his duke, voicing no doubt a common opinion at the court of Burgundy:

The king of France . . . also has the people of Ghent bound to him, who are close upon the back of the duke of Burgundy, and it is the most powerful city in all this country . . . Sometimes they have set on his back and chest 4,000 combatants, whom he could not shake without sweat, and they are a troublesome people to the duke of Burgundy.[17]

Adjoining Flanders on the north side of the Scheldt estuary and stretching along the coast were the two counties of Zeeland and Holland. Here life was dominated by water – the sea and the great tidal estuaries, lakes and meres. Between these, narrow stretches of land had to be constantly defended by dykes against the recurring

---

[13] Vaughan, *Philip the Good*, 85f.
[14] Quoted from Jan van Dixmude's *Kronyck van Vlaenderen*, in *ibid.*, 87.
[15] *Ibid.*, pp. 88ff.
[16] For the rebellion of Ghent, see *ibid.*, 304–33.
[17] Prospero di Camulio to Francesco Sforza, Bruges, 18 June 1461. *Calendar of State Papers. Milan.* vol. I, 99.

threats of spring tides and gales. It was a lifestyle that made for cooperation and, at the same time, for self-reliance by closely knit communities. Fishing, ship-building, navigation and trade were their principal occupations. From the fifteenth century, and even more in the sixteenth, farmers bred cattle and made butter and cheese, rather than grow cereals, as people did in most other parts of Europe. Or, when they did grow cereals, it was mostly barley for beer. The nobility were landowners, as they were everywhere, and often they functioned as dyke wardens (*dijk-graven*) and local judges (*baljuwen*, *drosten*),[18] but they never established full-blown feudal relationships: fishermen and merchants are not easily made into serfs.

No other part of Europe outside Italy, not even Flanders, was as highly urbanised as Holland. Almost half its population of perhaps 300,000 lived in towns.[19] None of these were as populous as the great Flemish towns; but Dordrecht, Amsterdam, Leiden, Haarlem, Delft and Gouda all had more than 10,000 inhabitants[20] – more than any English town except London. It is therefore no wonder that these six towns dominated the Estates of Holland. They each had one vote, while all the nobles together had only one. The other, smaller towns were summoned only rarely and the prelates, relatively poorer here than in other provinces, were not summoned at all.[21]

Zeeland, even more of a water province than Holland, was different again. Only the abbot of Middelburg represented the clergy. A varying but diminishing number of noblemen and towns usually appeared at the assemblies.[22]

These constitutional arrangements of Holland and Zeeland suited the dukes well enough. The party of the Cods (*Kabeljauwen*), the majority party in the cities, had supported Philip the Good against the party of the Hooks which had favoured Jacqueline of Bavaria. Philip could thus repay his political debts while being able to control the Estates of Holland better than most other provincial estates; for the towns, often at odds with each other over commercial privileges, could be more easily handled than powerful nobles and prelates with their sometimes awkward *esprit de corps*.[23]

---

[18] H. A. Enno van Gelder, 'De Hollands Adel in de Tijd van den Opstand', *TG*, 45 (1930), 114f.

[19] A. M. van der Woude, section on Holland in 'Population Changes and Economic Development in the Netherlands: a Historical Survey', *AAGB*, 12 (1965), 50–3, gives the population as about 275,000 in 1514, calculated from the number of communicants, with 46 per cent living in towns. He argues, however, that there was a marked demographic decline in the last quarter of the fifteenth century. A population figure of about 300,000 for the earlier fifteenth century would therefore seem to be a reasonable guess.

[20] Mols, *Démographie historique*, vol. II, 520.

[21] R. Fruin and T. H. Colenbrander, *Geschiedenis der Staatsinstellingen in Nederland tot den val der Republiek*, 2nd edn (The Hague, 1922), 79f. P. A. Meilink, 'Archieven van de Staten van Holland en de hen opgevolgde gewestelijke Besturen', pt. 1, in Meilink, *Archieven van de Staten van Holland voor 1572* (The Hague, 1929), 1ff.

[22] F. H. J. Lemmink, *Het Ontstaan van de Staten van Zeeland en hun Geschiedenis tot het Jaar 1555* (Roosendaal, 1951), 146ff.

[23] T. S. Jansma, 'Raad en Rekenkammer in Holland en Zeeland tijdens Hertog Philips van Bourgondië', *Bijdragen van het Instituut voor middeleeuwsche Geschiedenis . . . te Utrecht*, 18 (1932), 194f.

The beginnings of the States General

The large inland duchy of Brabant was economically and socially more varied than Holland. Its countryside, with soils of varying quality, was dominated by the large estates of nobles and of Cistercian and Premonstratensian monasteries. Rural overpopulation and stagnating markets, flooding from the great rivers and the depradations of the soldiery produced much rural poverty.[24] About one-third of the population lived in towns – not as great a proportion as in Holland and Flanders, but still considerable for fifteenth-century Europe. The small towns, once thriving centres of a woollen industry based on imported English wool, had been hit by the decline and increasing price of English wool exports and by the competition of more recently developed textile centres, such as Leiden in Holland. The bigger towns, however, were doing well. They expanded their economic base by building up specialised luxury industries in metal working, leather, tapestries, furs and the fulling, dyeing and finishing of semi-finished English cloth and, most visibly, in the building industry. Brussels came to function more and more as the seat of government for the dukes of Burgundy, and its citizens benefited greatly from the presence of an extravagant court. Louvain had the benefit of a recently founded university (1425), and 's-Hertogenbosch could take advantage of its strategic commercial position on the trade routes between Brabant, Holland and western Germany.

The most successful of the Brabant cities was Antwerp. Slowly but steadily its almost year-round cycle of fairs, together with those of its satellite town of Bergen-op-Zoom, built up its international trade, not so much in competition than as a complement to Bruges. In 1440 the population of Antwerp was about 20,000, perhaps a third less than Brussels. By 1500 it had overtaken Brussels and reached 50,000 and in the next half century it would double again.[25]

The Estates of Brabant on the whole reflected this economic and social reality. The prelates, i.e. the abbots of the great monasteries, represented the clergy and blocked all attempts by the secular clergy to send their own representatives.[26] The great landowning nobility (*baenrodsen*) and the knights together formed the second estate. But the great number of towns had, by the fifteenth century, come to be represented by the four 'capitals': Brussels, Antwerp, Louvain and 's-Hertogenbosch.[27]

The towns, like most other towns of the Netherlands, were effectively controlled by small groups of patrician families, but the guilds had a voice in the town councils.

---

[24] H. J. van Xanten, section on Bois-le-Duc ('s-Hertogenbosch) in Woude, 'Population Changes', 102f.
[25] Mols, *Démographie historique*, vol. II, 520. For the economic history of Brabant in the fifteenth century, see H. van der Wee, *The Growth of the Antwerp Market and the European Economy*, vol. II (The Hague, 1963), ch. III.
[26] 'Des charges publicques'. Eighteenth-century copy of sixteenth-century document, in BBR, MS 16248, 22–6.
[27] E. Lousse, 'Les états du pays et duché de Brabant', *APAE*, 33 (1965), 6–13. The names of all prelates, nobles and towns are listed in a document of the fifteenth or early sixteenth century. AGRB, Fonds Mercy Argeneau, no. 32, fos. 128r–129v. I wish to thank the archivist, Dr P. Gorissen, for kindly allowing me to see a typescript of this document.

In the flourishing craft trades wages were relatively high, and the small masters formed a modest but fairly numerous bourgeoisie. Here perhaps was the basis of the common view of the great prosperity of Flanders and Brabant, 'the promised land, more than any other principality on earth', as Commynes wrote.[28] Commynes attributed this happy state of affairs to long years of peace and to the goodness of the prince (Philip the Good) who taxed his subjects lightly and whom he contrasted with his son, Charles the Bold, the prince whose service Commynes had left for that of his great opponent, Louis XI, and whom in consequence he always denigrated.[29]

The northern provinces of the house of Burgundy were therefore highly varied in their social structures, economic interests and political traditions. To these variations was added a cultural one which even at present – or indeed perhaps more than ever before – is still causing great tensions: the division of languages. French was spoken in Hainaut, Artois and Walloon Flanders, from a line that ran further south and west than it does at present. North and east of this line people spoke Flemish-Dutch (*dietsch, thiois*) and in Luxembourg a high German dialect and also French. In the sixteenth century a fourth language, Frisian, was added with the acquisition of Friesland and Groningen. Since the dukes, their courts and most high government officials spoke French, the Estates of the provinces insisted that official business be done and official documents be drafted in their own languages.

These rights to their own languages were usually incorporated in the *joyeuses entrées* (*blijde inkomsten*), the charters of privileges which the dukes had to swear to observe on first entering each province after their accession. The most far-reaching of these charters was the *joyeuse entrée* of Brabant which went back to 1356. Its clauses included the duke's obligation to observe all earlier charters, notably those granted to the towns (clause 2), the reservation of all public offices to legitimately born natives of the province (clauses 4 and 14), the need for the dukes to obtain consent for all taxes and impositions (clause 5), for the striking or devaluation of the coinage (clause 7) and for the waging of war (clause 10). No part of Brabant was to be alienated (clause 7) and this was interpreted to include the selling of the duke's domain without the consent of the Estates, and no Brabanter was to be judged by a court outside the duchy (clause 12).[30]

REPRESENTATIVE ASSEMBLIES IN THE NETHERLANDS AND FRANCE

These privileges, and the somewhat less extensive but basically similar ones of the other provinces, were not intended to make for unity or cooperation among the

---

[28] P. de Commynes, *Les Mémoires* (The Hague, 1682), livre I, ch. 2. Also quoted by Van der Wee, *The Growth of the Antwerp Market*, vol. II, 72f.
[29] Commynes, *Les Mémoires*.
[30] Text published by R. van Bragt, 'De blijde Inkomst van de Hertogen van Brabant Johanna en Wenceslas (3 Januari 1356)', *APAE*, 13 (1956), 95–107.

provinces. They had been won and were defended in order to ensure the balance of power between the prince and his most powerful subjects in each individual dukedom or county. This was the type of regime which the fifteenth-century English Chief Justice, Sir John Fortescue, called *dominium politicum et regale* and whose virtues, especially in keeping down taxation and hence assuring the prosperity of the subjects and their ability to bear arms in their prince's service, he contrasted with *dominium regale*. This was the regime in France where, according to Fortescue, the king could tax his subjects without their consent.[31] For the later Whig tradition of both England and the Netherlands, this distinction gave a comforting sense of order and destiny to European history. For Fortescue's contemporaries, the distinction was based on experience and made perfectly good sense, although we now know that the position in France was a great deal more complex than the English Chief Justice realised or was willing to admit. While it is true that Charles VII's experiments with an Estates General for the whole of France were failures and while the king could and did impose the *taille* and certain other taxes without consent, his ability to raise taxes on his own authority remained in practice limited. The provincial assemblies continued to flourish and this in many of the *pays d'élection* as well as in the *pays d'états*. They defended local rights, privileges and customs very much like the provincial Estates of the Burgundian dominions. However, they remained unwilling to cooperate with each other, as they showed only too clearly in the Estates General of Tours in 1484. But their greatest weakness was the unintended and unforeseen result of the way in which the king's financial administration worked in practice. Ever since the fourteenth century royal officials collected taxes not only from the royal domains but also from the vassals and tenants of the nobility. To make this practice more acceptable to the nobles the crown came to share the proceeds with many of the magnates, sometimes to the tune of a third of the taxes which its officials collected. It was a very convenient arrangement by which the crown and the nobility together exploited the peasants; but, naturally, it blunted the nobility's keenness to resist royal tax demands.[32]

In the Netherlands the Valois dukes of Burgundy pursued the same policy,[33] and in Hainaut and Artois it seems to have worked as satisfactorily for them as it did for the Valois kings of France. But in those parts of the Netherlands where the towns paid a great part of the taxes and where, in consequence, they played a larger

---

[31] J. Fortescue, *The Governance of England*, ed. C. Plummer (Oxford, 1885), 114ff. For a discussion of the history of the phrase see G. Stourzh, 'Staatsformenlehre und Fundamentalgesetze... im 17. und 18. Jahrhundert', in R. Vierhaus, ed., *Herrschaftsverträge, Wahlkapitulationen, Fundamentalgesetze* (Göttingen, 1977), 294–327.

[32] J. Russell Major, *Representative Government in Early Modern France* (New Haven and London, 1980), 28–9 and *passim*.

[33] C. A. J. Armstrong, 'Had the Burgundian Government a Policy for the Nobility?' in J. S. Bromley and E. H. Kossmann, eds., *Britain and the Netherlands*, vol. II (Groningen, 1962), 11.

role in the assemblies of the estates, the system did not work nearly as satisfactorily for the monarchy. The towns could not be bought off like individual magnates, at the expense of the peasants, if for no other reason than that the peasants were an important market for the produce of the towns. In Flanders the countryside was not allowed to pay any taxes without the consent of the Member, i.e. Bruges, Ghent, Ypres or the Franc, to which they belonged. When the Burgundian dukes assembled the different Netherlands provinces under their rule they were therefore necessarily in a weaker position in relation to their Estates than their cousins, the kings of France. Not that this was immediately obvious. The conditions of this relationship had still to be worked out. As yet, the provinces did not even have a collective name. Their dukes referred to them as *ces* (or *les* or *nos*) *pays de pardeça*, as against *les pays de pardelà*, the duchy and county of Burgundy; and sometimes, when the dukes happened to reside in Burgundy, they logically but confusingly reversed these appellations. Towards the end of the fifteenth century there was a gradual change to *ces pays d'embas* meaning, either or both, 'these countries down here' or 'these low countries'. Only about the middle of the sixteenth century did the name Les Pays Bas, the Low Countries, used as a proper name, become common.

What changed right away, from about 1430, was the power relationship between the duke and the provinces. The Estates of the individual provinces had been able to build up their privileges because they were a match for their own, unaided rulers. Philip the Good, however, had the resources of all his provinces at his disposal to deal with opposition in any one of them. In the rebellions of Bruges, 1436–8, and of Ghent, 1447–53, this superior ducal power became immediately apparent.[34]

THE BEGINNINGS OF COMPOSITE ASSEMBLIES

It seems that the Estates of the different provinces were slow to draw the logical conclusion from this changed relationship by cooperating systematically in order to balance the duke's greatly increased power. Cooperate they did, but not in the first place for power-political reasons. The towns were used to dealing with everything that touched their international trade, including the sending of embassies abroad to negotiate with foreign powers. Their rulers were, on the whole, quite willing to leave such mundane and expensive matters to them. Between 1384, when the first Burgundian duke inherited Flanders, and 1506, the four Members

---

[34] W. P. Blockmans, 'De volksvertegenwoordiging in Vlaanderen in de beginperiode van de nieuwe tijden (1384–1505)', *Wetenschappelijke Tijdingen*, 33, 2 (Ghent, 1974), 124. For a general discussion of the importance of composite states in the history of early modern representative institutions, see H. G. Koenigsberger, 'Dominium regale or dominium politicum et regale: Monarchies and Parliaments in Early Modern Europe' (inaugural lecture, London 1975), in *Politicians and Virtuosi*.

of Flanders met 4,054 times, on average for three to nine days. Up to 1435 at least half the topics they discussed were economic. Much the same happened in the Estates of Brabant and Holland, although their meetings were not quite as frequent as those of the Four Members of Flanders.[35] Sometimes the towns of neighbouring provinces also found it convenient to have joint meetings, and this happened especially in the case of Holland, Zeeland and Hainaut who had the same ruler from the fourteenth century on.[36]

The dukes, for their part, were equally willing to take the initiative in combining assemblies from different provinces. Thus in 1427 Philip the Good summoned the Four Members of Flanders and the Estates of Artois and Picardie to Valenciennes, where they asked the Estates of Hainaut to recognise the duke as governor of the county to which he had not yet legally succeeded as count.[37] Whether this assembly is to be regarded as a States General, a matter on which there has been some debate among historians, is a question of definition and not in itself very important.

The next combined meeting, in 1431, was due to the initiative of the towns. This time the Four Members of Flanders met with the deputies of the towns of Brabant, Hainaut, Holland and Zeeland in Malines (Mechlin or Mechelen), i.e. all the major provinces which were by then ruled by the duke in the Netherlands. The purpose was to concert action to force the English to lower the price of wool in Calais where they had recently raised it. No sooner were the deputies assembled than the duke intervened and ordered them to continue their meetings in his presence, in Brussels. There is no indication that Philip summoned deputies from the clergy or the nobles of any of the provinces to join the deputies of the towns.[38]

The English wool and cloth trade was a matter touching all the provinces, and another combined meeting of the towns of Flanders, Brabant, Holland and Zeeland, together with Malines, held in Ghent in March 1434, induced the duke to issue an embargo on English cloth imports (9 June 1434).[39] The initiative for this embargo came from Bruges which was trying to protect the Flemish cloth industry. The Brabanters, with no similar industry to protect, were apparently willing to go along with Bruges but then simply ignored the embargo and continued happily to import English cloth, both for their textile finishing industries and for resale at the international fairs at Antwerp.[40]

---

[35] Blockmans, 'De volks vertegenwoordiging', 122. W. P. Blockmans 'A Typology of Representative Institutions in Late Medieval Europe', *Journal of Medieval History*, 4 (1978), 200–1.
[36] R. Wellens, *Les Etats Généraux des Pays-Bas des origines à la fin du règne de Philippe le Beau (1464–1506)*, vol. I, *APAE*, 64 (1974), 96ff.
[37] *Ibid.*, 98. J. Cuvelier, ed., *Actes des Etats Généraux des anciens Pays-Bas*, vol. I: *Actes de 1427 à 1477* (Brussels, 1948), 1–7.
[38] *Ibid.*, 8–11.
[39] *Ibid.*, 12–14 and 13 n.4.
[40] W. Brulez, 'Brugge en Antwerpen in de 15e en 16e eeuw: een tegenstelling?', *TG*, 83, 1 (1970), 16–17.

The most important common economic concern of the provinces, however, was their coinage. In the middle ages, control of the coinage, the right of minting, had been held to be an attribute of sovereignty and hence a prerogative right of princes. From the fourteenth century, however, scholastic writers had taught that control of the coinage was a public service. This theory naturally appealed to the Estates and especially to the towns. They were anxious to have a stable currency for the benefit of commerce and, at the same time, to prevent the prince from using his right of minting as a form of taxation over which they had no control. Even before the *joyeuse entrée* of 1356 the Estates of Brabant and of other provinces had insisted on consultation in monetary matters. In 1434 Philip the Good, having finally established his legitimate rule over the Netherlands provinces, decided to unify its coinage. It was a sensible and forward-looking move but it also offended local traditions and vested interests. In accordance with the privileges of the provinces, the duke had in the first place to get the consent of their Estates.

From that moment it became a matter in which all the provinces were vitally interested. *Quod omnes tangit ab omnibus approbari.* Nowhere was this venerable medieval formula of representation more obviously appropriate than in the case of the coinage. Our sources, mainly the mint ordinances, are too sparse to allow us to know whether anyone actually said this on these occasions. But actions speak clearly enough. An assembly of all the states, not only the towns, was summoned to Antwerp for 3 December 1437 specifically to discuss coinage questions.[41]

As it turned out, this assembly was a kind of prototype for the regular meetings of the States General, although nobody of course thought of it in quite this way. The meeting at Antwerp was preceded by meetings of the provincial Estates. In Flanders the duke had summoned ten small towns and castellanies, as well as the Four Members, and the clergy and the nobility. The Estates then decided that, because of the excessive expense, the deputies of the small towns and castellanies should go home again and entrust the decision-making to the rest of the Estates. These, in their turn, then briefed the deputies for the Antwerp meeting.[42] The States General was therefore an assembly of deputies with strictly limited instructions, briefed either by the provincial Estates or, sometimes, directly by the towns – more like a conference of ambassadors than a session of the English Parliament whose members enjoyed full powers to take binding decisions. Nevertheless, these were not deputations which the duke summoned together simply for the convenience of informing them all of his proposed decisions or negotiating with each deputation in the same place. The accounts of the different cities, which are our principal source for the States General, make it quite clear that the deputies were to confer with those of the other provinces. It is indeed hardly conceivable that

---

[41] The argument about the importance of the coinage in the development of the States General is based on P. Spufford, 'Coinage, Taxation and the States General of the Burgundian Netherlands', *APAE*, 40 (1966), 61–88.

[42] Cuvelier, *Actes des Etats Généraux*, 17ff.

The beginnings of the States General

such an assembly should not have led to mutual discussions among the deputies of the different provinces, even when there was no formal debate.[43]

The States General was summoned twelve times between 1437 and 1461, and nine of its meetings were concerned mainly with coinage and monetary matters.[44] Here then was one of the main reasons for the summoning of the States General. It was a severely practical, indeed virtually inescapable, reason, once the duke had decided on a unified monetary policy; and in this policy too he had little choice, given the economic circumstances of his dominions. Yet, quite early on he seems to have had ambivalent feelings about his dependence on the Estates in monetary questions. In 1440 Philip the Good told the Estates of Brabant that matters of coinage lay exclusively within his prerogative and that he consulted the Estates only as a matter of grace. The Estates, as they were frequently to do in the future, preferred not to contradict their prince outright, but to deny his claim more obliquely. All would be well, they replied, if only the formally agreed values of the coins were universally accepted.[45]

They had given nothing away and later they even demanded to send a committee to supervise the assaying of coins by the mint masters.[46] Duke Philip evidently did not think it worthwhile to return to the charge. Characteristically, however, his son, Charles the Bold, did. After 1470 this duke did not bring coinage matters before the States General any more and in 1474, over the protests of Flanders, he issued a monetary ordinance without reference to the Estates.[47] Important as the question of the control of the common coinage clearly was, Charles the Bold's action would suggest that a strong and determined duke could manage the coinage without the States General or even the provincial Estates. It is a different matter whether the duke's policy contributed to his unpopularity and the strong antimonarchical reaction in the country after his death.

The subjects discussed by the States General in its first thirty-odd years were strictly limited to matters of common economic or monetary interest. The duke made no financial demands or requests for *aides* or taxation. Such demands were still being presented, as they had been traditionally, to the separate provinces. Even when the duke attempted to introduce a salt tax in all his dominions, he presented it to the provinces individually. In Ghent he put the proposal to the city

---

[43] E.g. Louvain, Compte communal, in *ibid.*, 20, no. 3. 'Item, op een vaert gheseint t'Antwerpen, 3 in December, 2 heeren, 1 clerc en 2 cnapen . . . omme te gadere te spreken van der munte en van den gelde.' Compte de la ville d'Ypres, in *ibid.*, 21, no. 7. 'Meester Florenis Wielant . . . t'Antwerpen, daer seekere heeren van den rade ons geduchta heeren waren, metgaders den ghedeputerden van de staten van den landen van Brabant, Henegauwe, Hollant ende Zeelant, ende ghehandelt up tonderhouden vander munte.'
[44] Spufford, 'Coinage', 78. P. A. Meilink, in a review article of Cuvelier, *Actes*, did not accept the other three assemblies as proper States Generals. 'Dagvaarten van de Staten-Generaal 1427–1477', *BGN*, 5 (1950), 198–212.
[45] Spufford, 'Coinage', 78.
[46] *Ibid.*, 68.
[47] *Ibid.*, 80.

council (*collatie*), that he would 'seek the agreement of all my lands here to this law, but I shall not impose it in Flanders alone if it is accepted there but refused elsewhere; for I have no wish to tax my good land of Flanders more than any other'.[48] Flanders, led by Ghent, refused. It was this refusal which set in motion the events leading to the great rebellion of Ghent in 1452–3. Philip managed to cope with this rebellion; but for almost a hundred years the dukes preferred not to burn their fingers again with a similar proposal.

Political matters had been brought up by the duke mainly, it seems, for information or for formal approval. This had happened in 1427 over the governorship of Hainaut and again in March 1438 when the duke publicly pronounced sentence against the rebellious city of Bruges, although at that time the three deputies of the Estates of Hainaut 'conferred several times together and tendered monseigneur their advice in writing'.[49] We may assume that the advice was what the duke wanted to hear; otherwise we would have expected our sources to mention the duke's reaction. Philip, in spite of the sobriquet 'the Good' which his subjects bestowed on him after his death, did not take kindly to criticism.

THE STATES GENERAL OF 1464

What really established the States General as a regular institution was a quite specific political event or, rather, series of events. The great Hainaut family of the Croy, for decades favoured by Duke Philip, had become so powerful that, in the words of the chronicler Chastellain, 'none who was not in their service or their ally could obtain anything . . . and even the duke's own officials, whether nobles or clerics, trying to obtain office or benefices of marriages or anything else, remained behind them'.[50] Naturally, the Croy had enemies and, inevitably, their most determined opponents were, firstly, the great Flemish cities, whom they despised but over whom they had no control and, secondly, the duke's son Charles, count of Charolais. Charles was particularly incensed over the Croys' support of Louis XI's policy of redeeming a number of towns in Picardie, the so-called Somme towns. Duke Philip had acquired them in 1435 in the Treaty of Arras, against a loan of 400,000 gold crowns to the king of France.[51] There followed a breach between Philip and Charles which, characteristically, came to a head in a quarrel over the appointment of a chamberlain to the count's household. Philip wanted this key position to go to a Croy. Charles wanted it for one of his own clients.

---

[48] V. Fris, ed., *Dagboek van Gent*, vol. I (Ghent, 1901), 68, translated and quoted in Vaughan, *Philip the Good*, 310. My thanks to Prof W. P. Blockmans for drawing my attention to the significance of this quotation.
[49] Chastellain, *Chronique*, 248.
[50] *Ibid.*, 249.
[51] Vaughan, *Philip the Good*, 355.

The beginnings of the States General

All this was no more than an entirely conventional neo-feudal and dynastic quarrel. The next move, however, turned the quarrel first into a farce and then gave it a political significance which it had not previously possessed. Early in December 1463 it became known that Duke Philip intended to go on a crusade. Immediately, rumours began to fly that he intended to divide the guardianship of his dominions, leaving Holland and Zeeland to Edward IV of England and the other provinces to Jean de Croy.[52] Charolais was at this time in Holland where he had for some time been building up a personal clientele. His relations with the Estates of Holland had been entirely amicable. In 1462 he had obtained from them the handsome grant of 50,000 lions per annum for ten years, their recognition of his position as heir and, rather less to the old duke's liking, for it was a matter in which he wanted to keep the initiative, a request that the other Burgundian Estates also recognise Charles.[53] What more natural than that Charolais should now protest to the friendly Estates of Holland about his father's evil councillors and their pernicious advice? Thereupon the Estates took matters into their own hands and, apparently without further prompting from Charolais,[54] the towns of Holland and Zeeland wrote to the Four Members of Flanders to propose a joint meeting of all Netherlands towns to discuss the crisis. The Flemish and Brabant towns immediately agreed.

This action forced the hands of the two princes. Fearing to lose the initiative, both Philip and Charles sent out their own summons for meetings of the States General. There followed two weeks of confusion, with delegates hurrying to different meeting places, until on 9 January 1464 all finally coincided in Bruges.[55] Philip was furious. He wrote to the towns:

We are greatly marvelling how the inhabitants of our towns of Holland dare to be so presumptuous as to assemble on their own authority and to desire our subjects to assemble, seeing that it is by no means up to them to do this in our province of Holland, nor in Flanders, nor anywhere else; but that this right belongs to us, as your prince and lord and to no one else . . . It seems to us, moreover, that you must think us very simple or ignorant to imagine that we would leave this country without providing [for its government].[56]

Here was a pattern that was to repeat itself: the Estates did what they thought necessary and practical in a specific situation. The monarchy took a longer, constitutional view of the matter and showed itself touchy about its prerogatives and about the precedents which the action of the Estates might set. In the event, the Estates could well afford to ask Philip's pardon for their 'presumption'. It took

---

[52] Wellens, *Etats Généraux*, 103.
[53] P. A. Meilink, 'Holland in het conflict tusschen Philips de Goede en zijn zoon van 1463/64', *BVGO*, 7th ser. (1935), pt. 5, 132–52.
[54] *Ibid.*, pt. 6, 57.
[55] Cuvelier, *Actes des Etats Généraux*, 53ff. Wellens, *Etats Généraux*, 105ff.
[56] Philip to the towns, 31 Dec. 1463. Cuvelier, *Actes*, 72. H. G. Koenigsberger, *Estates and Revolutions* (Ithaca, 1971), 131f.

31

another five weeks after the first meeting of the States General, on 9 January, for Philip and Charles to be formally reconciled, on 12 February. During this time they issued repeated apologias for their previous actions. In the circumstances, these apologias were inevitably addressed to the States General. Equally inevitably, the States General found themselves in a position to have to do rather more than a Greek chorus. They continued with their initiative by appointing committees to negotiate with both sides.[57] Both princes thanked the deputies for their efforts in effecting the reconciliation, and Philip summoned the States General to meet again almost immediately, in March 1464, to discuss the proposed crusade.[58]

There is therefore some substance in the modern historiographical tradition of seeing the assembly of January–February 1464 as the first States General of the Netherlands. It was not really that; but it was the first assembly which concerned itself not just with technical problems of trade and coinage but with the arcana of politics, the location of ultimate power.

Nevertheless this was not a subject which was discussed again in any of the seven meetings of the States General during the remaining three years of Philip the Good's reign.[59] The assembly still did not even have this name. In the formal session of 27 April 1465, which recognised the count of Charolais as Duke Philip's heir, there was reference in Latin only to 'the reverend fathers, lords, prelates and illustrious counts, barons and other nobles . . . together with the cities and communes of the towns, the three estates of his [Philip's] dukedoms, counties and lordships'.[60] Most sessions were still summoned to discuss the coinage. The April 1465 session, however, stands out not only for the recognition of the duke's heir but also as the first session of the States General from which the duke demanded the grant of money.

This was probably a matter of convenience; for the dukes had regularly demanded and been granted *aides* from the separate provincial Estates. But the duke and his advisers realised that such a request to the States General needed some preparation. The chancellor, Pierre de Goux, therefore gave an account of the political situation and blatantly flattered the deputies: the duke, 'following his good and laudable custom, which was to inform his subjects of his and the country's great affairs, had summoned the deputies of the said Estates to assemble before him' to expound to them what was happening in France and the reasons for the need of Burgundian intervention.[61] The actual financial request had not been thought out quite so carefully. The town council of Mons, in Hainaut, complained to their deputies that they could not really answer the duke's request as no definite sum had been mentioned. In the meantime the deputies were to plead the poverty

---

[57] Wellens, *Etats Généraux*, 111–17.
[58] Cuvelier, *Actes*, 91f.
[59] *Ibid.*, 96–145. Wellens, *Etats Généraux*, allows the name of States General to only four of these meetings.
[60] Cuvelier, *Actes*, 113.
[61] *Ibid.*, 121. Wellens, *Etats Généraux*, 120.

of Hainaut compared with the duke's other provinces.[62] Only gradually did the governments of the dukes realise that they had to include specific sums or rates of tax in the original letters of summons sent out to the provinces.

CHARLES THE BOLD: THE FIRST CLASHES BETWEEN STATES GENERAL AND PRINCE

The succession of Charles the Bold, in 1467, did not immediatly change the duke's relations with his Estates. A meeting of the States General in March 1470 was again preoccupied with the unfortunate fact that inferior foreign coins drove the good Netherlands coins out of circulation. On this highly technical level there was no difficulty in generally maintaining amicable relations, even when the experts of the different provinces disagreed on what exactly should be done.[63] But Charles's excellent former relations with Flanders had already gone sour in 1467. During his 'joyous entry' into Ghent there had been a popular commotion directed against a local tax and the patrician council. The duke himself and his daughter had only managed to leave the city unharmed by promising hateful concessions. After his conquest of Liège, in 1468, he was able to take his revenge. Ghent had to submit publicly. Its charter was publicly destroyed and, specifically, the city's right to the free elections of its magistrates was taken away.[64]

From 1470, as the duke's foreign policy became more and more adventurous, his financial demands on his subjects increased and his relations with the Estates steadily deteriorated. The first clash was again with Flanders, even though the council of Ghent was now filled with the duke's own creatures. In May 1470 the duke requested from the Four Members an *aide* of 120,000 crowns per year for three years, to be levied on all his countries. It seems that the duke's government was still not yet quite clear when to make requests to the individual provinces in the traditional way or when to make requests to the States General for a global sum. In this case they had mixed up the two methods and produced confusion. The Four Members of Flanders replied with a memorandum of three points:

1. The chancellor had spoken of all the duke's lands being asked for the 120,000 crowns, but the duke himself had spoken only of the *pays de pardeça*, 'which was a great difference'.
2. The quota to be paid by Flanders was not specified.
3. Equally, nothing was said about how fiefs and mesne fiefs (which the duke had previously wanted to tax) would be affected. When these points had been cleared up 'they would loyally do their duty'.[65]

[62] Cuvelier, *Actes*, 124f.
[63] *Ibid.*, 151–5.
[64] Vaughan, *Charles the Bold*, 6–9.
[65] L. P. Gachard, *Collection de documents inédits concernant l'histoire de la Belgique*, 3 vols. (Brussels, 1833–5), vol. I, 216–19.

Plate 2 Rogier van der Weyden (attrib.), *Charles the Bold*. Staatliche Museen zu Berlin, Preussischer Kulturbesitz, Gemäldegalerie (Photo: Jörg P. Anders)

The beginnings of the States General

The duke chose to be offended and, in reply, harangued the deputies of the Four Members. On point 1 there was no difference between what the chancellor and he himself had said, 'for I understand [by this] that my *pays de pardeça* are Holland, Zeeland, Flanders, Brabant, Luxembourg, Hainaut, Picardie, the castellanie of Lille, the Boulonnais and the county of Guynes, which are those which habitually help me with *aides* and subventions'. The Burgundian lands, he continued, had no money but they produced the best soldiers in all his lands, a third of the whole army.[66] Though Luxembourg and Limbourg would not often send deputies to the States General and though Picardie and the Boulonnais were to be lost again to France, the duke's implication was surely correct, that at this time the definition of the *pays de pardeça* was already fully accepted and that the Flemings were making a pure debating point.

In fact, however, it was over point 2 that Charles accused them of 'subtlety and malice' and of never having granted anything liberally, either to his father or to himself. 'Your Flemish heads,' he stormed at them, 'are so thick and hard and you always want to persist in your evil opinions, but you might bear in mind that others, too, are as clever as you and that they also have heads. I am half French and half Portuguese and I'll have you know what I can do with your heads [and what I will do].' Then, with a sudden characteristic shift back into rational argument, he added that 120,000 crowns was very little. It would cover only a third of the cost of the standing army of 1,000 lances (5,000 combatants) and these were needed because of the mutability of the king of France against whom he had to be constantly on his guard.[67]

The duke's most interesting points, however, were made on the matter of his ordinance on fiefs and mesne fiefs for which he had proposed a tariff according to which vassals could commute the military service that was due from them. Not only had all the other provinces agreed to his proposals, he said, but 'you want to take what is mine by your privileges; but you have none . . . and if you say and maintain that I have sworn to uphold them, it is true; but you, too, have sworn to serve me and to be good and obedient subjects'.[68] The two-sided nature of the medieval view of privilege and prerogative could not have been stated more clearly.

For all the duke's thunder, it took until August of the following year, 1471, before the States General, at Abbeville, got down to fixing the provincial quotas of the 120,000 crowns, and until November before Charles published his ordinance setting up his new standing army. Naturally, every province, and especially those forming the frontier with France, had been anxious to plead poverty and destruction of the countryside by the soldiery.[69]

---

[66] *Ibid.*, 220.
[67] *Ibid.*, 220–2.
[68] *Ibid.*, 214f, 223.
[69] Wellens, *Etats Généraux*, 129–31. Cuvelier, *Actes*, 164–73. My thanks to M. A. Louant, conservateur des Archives de l'Etat de Mons, for pointing out to me that the quota for Hainaut was 6,500 écus and not 65,000 as printed in Cuvelier, *Actes*, 170.

By the end of 1472 the duke needed more money and he summoned the States General to assemble in Bruges, in January 1473. His new chancellor, Guillaume Hugonet, like most of the duke's high officials a Burgundian, addressed the deputies. He started with a discussion of human society, both as natural to man and as part of the divine hierarchy of the universe. Of the three forms of government, monarchy, aristocracy and democracy, monarchy was the most fruitful and natural, like the human body in which the head controlled the members. All this was the common coinage of Aristotelian ideas, modified towards the preference for monarchy, as they were expounded by chancellors to representative assemblies at the time. Nobody ever argued about them, least of all on such formal occasions. On this morning Hugonet continued with a eulogium of the Belgian part of Gaul, as described by Julius Caesar and as it had developed its free institutions especially under the House of Burgundy. He contrasted this with France whose inhabitants had to live under the heavy exactions which their king imposed on them. From this point Hugonet found an easy transition to the duke's efforts and expenses in defending his country against France, how his wars were his subjects' business, just as theirs were his, and how without the former English alliance the costs of this war were now greater than ever.[70]

All this was a propaganda exercise and not an objective description of the relations between the prince and his Estates, whether in the Netherlands or in France. Hugonet had been careful not to mention the duke's ambitions in the Empire and his projected conquests of Guelders and Alsace.[71] The duke himself followed his chancellor's speech by asking for money to pay for 10,000 soldiers. The deputies, after conferring among themselves, got down to the practicalities of the demand: how much would it cost? The answer was not more than 600,000 and not less than 500,000 écus per year, and the duke wanted this sum for ten years, both in war and in peace time; but in return he would give up all previous *aides*.

The deputies had no powers to grant this sum and were therefore sent back to their provinces. On 15 February they assembled again, in Brussels, and continued to negotiate with the government until 1 April. From the Artois account we know that the deputies wanted to discuss the matter with the deputies of all the other provinces, but the duke would not allow it. Unofficial contacts, however, made it clear that everyone would grant the lower sum of 500,000 écus. The period for which this was offered varied from three to six years. Finally, and after several deputations had to go home again for further instructions, the duke got his way with a grant for six years. In return, however, he had to make considerable concessions including their right to raise taxes as they pleased. In the case of Flanders this also meant the right to raise capital sums by selling annuities funded on the revenues of the cities (*rentes*).[72]

---

[70] J. Bartier, 'Un discours du chancellier Hugonet aux Etats Généraux de 1473', in *BCRH* (1942), 127–56. Cuvelier, *Actes*, 178–89.
[71] Wellens, *Etats Généraux*, 136.
[72] *Ibid.*, 138–42. Cuvelier, *Actes*, 199–220.

The beginnings of the States General

The year 1473 was the high water mark of Charles the Bold's fortunes. From then on his difficulties multiplied and he was forced to call on further help from his subjects. On 12 July 1475 the duke had an exchange with the Estates of Flanders at Bruges which showed how strained relations had become. In a speech which again showed his gift for mixing political argument with startling invective, the duke accused the Flemings of treason. They had failed to supply the pioneers, wagons and other support for the military which he had demanded. All their fine promises had been no more than the 'smoke of alchemy'; since evidently they did not wish to be governed by him as children by a father, he would disinherit them and take away their property; for God had given him this power, as they could read in the Books of Kings in the Bible.[73]

The Four Members replied with a remonstrance, answering the detailed charges, and then argued that they 'knew and recognised as good and loyal subjects that they had to obey your noble commandments according to their ability and power, as long as these are reasonable'. They had sworn this at his accession; but he, too, had sworn to observe the privileges, franchises and liberties of Flanders which his predecessors had granted, and this included freedom from the payment of any sum of money or any other charge to which the Four Members had not consented in the name of all the inhabitants of the country.[74] Once more the duke answered with abuse. They would not content him 'with good words and a baked apple' like children. He knew well that they wanted to be lords and princes themselves but, if such was their intention, they were very much mistaken.[75]

Were these simply the outbursts of a short-tempered man? Were they calculated threats with which a clever politician interspersed his cajoling of recalcitrant Estates? Or were they the reasoned statements of a political philosophy of the divinely ordained absolutism of princes? All these interpretations of Charles the Bold's behaviour were not necessarily mutually contradictory. In the event he avoided the threatened breach with the Four Members of Flanders; partly, because they did accord him a grant, but mainly, it seems, because his personal attention was just then diverted south towards Alsace, Lorraine and Savoy. The sequel was to show that he had thoroughly frightened the Flemings and that they would not forgive him. Just how much the duke was willing to upset the traditional balance between prince and Estates, *dominium politicum et regale*, was shown in his treatment of Guelders.

In the independent imperial duchy of Guelders, Duke Adolf of the House of Egmont had deposed and imprisoned his father, Duke Arnold, in 1465. The four principal cities of the duchy, Arnhem, Nijmegen, Roermond and Zutphen, supported Adolf as more likely to preserve their liberties and the duchy's independence

---

[73] Gachard, *Documents inédits*, vol. I, 249–59.
[74] *Ibid.*, 259–66.
[75] *Ibid.*, 267–70.

from its powerful and voracious neighbour, Burgundy. Charles the Bold moved slowly and tortuously from early support of Adolf to mediation between father and son, then to support of Arnold and finally, having kidnapped and imprisoned Adolf, to the conquest and annexation of Guelders in 1473. His opponents were, very clearly, the Estates of the duchy, led by the four principal cities. It was they, and especially Nijmegen, which organised the military resistance against Burgundy, while the knights (*ridderschap*) remained divided.[76] Charles the Bold, having conquered the duchy and, as he said, 'reduced it completely to my obedience',[77] won over a great part of the knights by offering them service in his armies. But he imposed reparations of 250,000 Rhenish florins on the Estates and treated them as no more than an audience for his pronouncements. He placed his own officials into the town councils, he subordinated the finances of the duchy to his treasury at Lille (*chambre des comptes, Rekenkammer*) and its judicial system to the newly established *parlement* of Malines.[78] With his power thus firmly established and awkward privileges simply set aside, the duke saw no problem in completing the integration of Guelders into the *pays de pardeça* by summoning the Estates of Guelders to the next meeting of the States General. *Dominium regale*, or absolutism as understood in the fifteenth century, could see uses in assemblies of Estates – provided they were tame and did what they were told. The question in the fifteenth century was, however, how to keep them tame.

This was the central problem in Charles the Bold's last States General, in April and May 1476. There is no indication that he foresaw it. His defeat at Grandson, on 2 March 1476, had left him with the need for further military resources but also with every expectation that he could rapidly recoup his fortunes.[79] Otherwise he would hardly have asked for his only daughter and heiress, Mary, to be sent from the Netherlands to visit him in Burgundy. The duchess Margaret of York (Charles's third wife and Mary's stepmother) and Chancellor Hugonet presented the request for a suitably safe and magnificent escort for Mary's journey to the deputies assembled in the Augustinian monastery in Ghent, on 26 April. They also demanded that all holders of fiefs, mesne fiefs and non-feudal property in the cities should serve the duke according to the value of their property. Alternatively, they should provide substitutes and/or money payments. The forces raised in this way were partly to serve as frontier garrisons and partly to join the duke's field army fighting against the Swiss.

The assembly was the most complete States General yet, including Brabant, Flanders, Limbourg, Outremeuse, Artois, Lille-Douai-Orchies, the Somme towns, the towns of Picardie, Ponthieu, Hainaut, Holland, Friesland, Namur, Luxembourg

---

[76] Vaughan, *Charles the Bold*, 112–20. W. Jappe Alberts, *De Staten van Gelre en Zutphen (1459–1492)*, pt. II (Groningen and Jakarta, 1956), 89–106.
[77] Vaughan, *Charles the Bold*, 120.
[78] *Ibid.*, 120–2. Alberts, *Gelre en Zutphen*, 89–106.
[79] Vaughan, *Charles the Bold*, 378.

and the newly conquered Guelders. Flanders was represented not only by the Four Members but by its three estates, including a large number of the smaller towns. We are very well informed about this assembly by a report, written most probably by the pensionary (secretary and legal officer) of Brussels, Gort Roelandts, who acted as spokesman for the States General.[80]

The first proposition, the princess's proposed journey, was received with some sympathy, but the deputies would have to refer the decision to their respective provincial Estates. This point the government was willing to concede. The second proposition, the defence ordinances, the deputies turned down flat. It contravened the promises given to them in 1473 when they had granted 500,000 écus for six years on condition that nothing further would be asked. They said that, as it was, the duke had expected all sorts of supplementary military services (such as those over which he had quarrelled with Flanders in the previous year) and the country was now exhausted.[81] This claim was more than a debating point. In the last ten years of Philip the Good's reign annual expenditure had varied from about 300,000 to 480,000 livres, with an average of about 360,000. Under Charles the Bold the average had nearly doubled, to almost 700,000 livres.[82] Flanders alone had contributed the following approximate annual *aides*:[83]

1471	340,000 livres
1472	390,000 livres
1473	315,000 livres
1474	350,000 livres
1475	910,000 livres
1476	412,000 livres

Hugonet was not to be put off so easily by these arguments. He claimed that the duchess had no powers to countermand the orders which the duke had already issued on military service. Evidently not only the deputies, but the duke's government too, could use the lack of full powers to score tactical points. The chancellor now suggested that the States General appoint a committee to negotiate with the government on its proposals. He argued that it was easier to discuss matters in this way than 'with a great multitude' which might well include persons not really belonging to the States General who would not keep the negotiations secret. In any case, he argued, the views of the committee would not bind the States General.[84]

The duke's council were no doubt as obsessed with secrecy and the danger of leaks as most governments. But it seems likely that they also hoped, by persuasion,

---

[80] L. P. Gachard, 'Les états de Gand en 1476', in *Trésor national*, vol. III (Brussels, 1842), 258–73. Cuvelier, *Actes*, 225–49. Wellens, *Etats Généraux*, 143–52.
[81] Cuvelier, *Actes*, 333–4.
[82] J. Bartier, 'Karel de Stoute', in J. A. van Houtte, ed., *AGN*, vol. III (Utrecht, 1951), 293.
[83] W. P. Blockmans, 'Autocratie ou polyarchie? La lutte pour le pouvoir politique en Flandre de 1482 à 1492', in *BCRH*, vol. CXL (1974), 259 n. 2.
[84] Cuvelier, *Actes*, 335.

bribery and bullying, to get a more favourable response from a committee than from the full assembly. Such committees were quite common in other countries. They were usually known as 'deputations' (*deputazione* in Sicily and Friuli, *diputació* in Catalonia) and, mostly, their behaviour confirmed Hugonet's hopes. This was certainly how the Netherlands deputies took the proposal. They did not even comment on the point of secrecy but said firmly that 'those who are deputed do not have power to depute others'. They only offered to report the duke's proposals to their provincial assemblies. The chancellor had to accept the reference back and, in the meantime, reluctantly agree to suspend the duke's ordinances (30 April).[85]

The States General reassembled on 24 May. The Flemish-speaking provinces remained adamant in their refusal. In the French-speaking provinces opinion was divided. In Artois the nobles and the clergy agreed to meet the duke halfway. The towns, however, refused. The lieutenant general of the province summoned a new assembly but got the same results. He therefore declared that a majority of the Estates had agreed to the *aide* and that it was therefore legally valid. The towns countered 'that if all estates are not agreed in a common accord, nothing could come out of it'. The lieutenant general had to assemble the towns once again and, eventually, they also agreed to a modest offer. But on the constitutional issue both sides stuck to their own interpretation. In practice, the government did not in future normally dare to break the principle of unanimity, except in extraordinary circumstances; and it did so in 1477.[86]

In the States General relations between the chancellor and the deputies became more and more acrimonious. So as not to dishonour the duke in public, the chancellor demanded on 27 May that the deputies give their conclusions in the form of an opinion (*avis*) rather than as a formal reply (*non point par forme de response*). No, said the deputies; they had no authority to give anything but a formal reply. Hugonet lost his temper. Was their authority also limited to the number of times they were allowed to drink on their journey, he asked sarcastically. 'This remark was not well taken by the estates', Roelandts reports, 'and they said to the chancellor: go on, go on, you can say what you like; but we will make the reply we have to make'.[87]

After five hours of fruitless discussion Hugonet finally tried threats: 'Be careful what you do', he said to the spokesman of the States General (Roelandts?); 'Don't dare to say a word which might displease my redoubtable sovereign prince. Your heads are at stake.' But the spokesman, according to Roelandts, though much afraid, 'took courage' and replied: 'I trust in God that I will not say a word that is not full of reverence and obedience to my redoubtable sovereign lord.' Then, falling on his knees, he made response 'without leaving out anything' according to the charge he had been given.[88]

[85] *Ibid.*, 236–7.
[86] Hirchauer, *Les états d'Artois*, 66–7.
[87] Cuvelier, *Actes*, 256.
[88] *Ibid.*

The beginnings of the States General

The next day's discussions, after the drama of the previous evening, were desultory and inconclusive. The States General refused to convert the military service demanded by the duke into a global money payment. Hugonet and the duchess could not even get an unequivocal agreement on the princess's proposed journey. They saw no alternative but to prorogue the assembly until July. The news of Charles the Bold's defeat at Morat, on 22 June, caused further postponements of the States General. It did not meet again before his death.

In the spring of 1476 no one could have foreseen the full significance of Charles the Bold's last States General. Apparently they had, while protesting their loyalty, simply refused some specific, although certainly important, requests by the government. There was a good chance that the next meeting would arrive at least at a compromise, just as the States General of 1473 had done. On that occasion Hugonet had pointedly asked the nobles whether they actually denied their obligation of military service and they had most emphatically rejected this suggestion: 'Nenni!'[89] A Burgundian victory over the Swiss would have further enhanced the duke's prestige. But this was precisely what did not happen. In the meantime the government had exhausted its credits on the international money markets of Bruges and Antwerp.[90] The deputies had voiced the whole country's revulsion for Charles the Bold's spiralling financial and military demands. Against the government's rationalising and centralising policies and the duke's and his chancellor's bullying style, they had set a pedantic and legalistic, but also brave and dignified insistence on their provinces' privileges and liberties. When revolution broke out in the following year, men with totally different motivations would look to the States General as the instrument to achieve their aims and as the one fixed and acceptable institution in a suddenly fluid and frightening situation. The myth of the States General had begun.

[89] *Ibid.*, 238.
[90] Van der Wee, *The Antwerp Market*, vol. II, 87.

3

The first crisis (1477–1494)

'The States of our said lands, for the profit of our common country, and also the Estates of each particular province for particular matters concerning such province should be able to assemble together in a place of their choice . . . as they see fit, without having to obtain leave from us or our heirs, without incurring any indignation or displeasure.'

Article 14 of the Great Privilege of Mary of Burgundy[1]

When the definite news of Charles the Bold's death arived in the Netherlands, more than two weeks after the battle of Nancy (5 January 1477), his government acted with commendable speed and decision. In the name of the duchess Mary and her step-mother, the dowager duchess Margaret of York, they summoned the States General to Ghent for 3 February.[2] At the same time they announced the suspension of the current *aides* which had caused so much ill feeling in the last year of Duke Charles's reign. All such matters, they promised, would from now be treated with the Estates with 'great sweetness, good justice and discretion'.[3] The delegates of Hainaut were even asked to go to Ghent a week early.

THE GREAT PRIVILEGE OF MARY OF BURGUNDY

There was indeed no time to lose. Louis XI, on hearing of the death of his great adversary, had immediately invaded Burgundy and Artois. His armies were threatening Hainaut. Many of the Burgundian nobility in these border provinces defected to France. The Gueldrians renounced their forced allegiance to the House of Burgundy and the Burgundian officials fled from the duchy.[4] In the big cities of Flanders and Brabant there were rumblings of popular revolt and actual outbreaks within the following weeks. It seems likely that it was to ward off these two immediate and deadly dangers, French invasion and social revolution, while at the same time assuring the acceptance of Mary's succession, that the government, the high nobility and the patrician Estates agreed on an immediate programme of

---

[1] 'Algemeen Privilegie', in W. P. Blockmans, ed., *Le privilège général et les privilèges régionaux de Marie de Bourgogne: 1477*, APAE, 80 (Kortrijk-Heule, 1985), 93.
[2] Cuvelier, *Actes des Etats Généraux*, 288. P. A. Meilink, 'Dagvaarten van de Staten-Generaal 1427–1477', *BGN*, 5, 3–4 (1951), 205f.
[3] Wellens, *Etats Généraux*, 153ff. Cuvelier, *Actes des Etats Généraux*, 288.
[4] Wellens, *Etats Généraux*, 151. Commynes, *Mémoires*, bk. 5, chs. 10–12.

The first crisis (1477–1494)

constitutional reforms. These reforms were enshrined in a charter which modern historians have called the Great Privilege of Mary of Burgundy. It was signed on 11 February, only eight days after the opening of the States General. The charter, composed in the traditional medieval form without any clear order of its separate articles, dealt with two sets of problems. The first was the remedy for specific recent grievances. These included the provision of payment for military service outside their home province by holders of fiefs and mesne fiefs (an issue that had given rise to the most acrimonious debates in the States General of the previous year),[5] restrictions of ducal appointments to ecclesiastical dignities and benefices, and the reaffirmation of the rights of merchants to travel freely throughout the duke's dominions and to be charged tolls only where these were both legal and reasonable. These articles were evidently meant to ensure the support of all three estates, clergy, nobility and towns.

The second set of articles dealt with the relations between the dukes and the Estates. The States General was given the formal right to assemble without a ducal summons and, from now on, the duchess and her heirs would need the consent of the States General in order to wage either an offensive or a defensive war. If the duchess failed to observe this privilege, her subjects were absolved from their duty of obedience to her.[6]

In consenting to such important legislation the deputies of the States General of 1477 had undoubtedly far exceeded their powers. Understandably, the provinces and cities which had sent them to Ghent were not displeased. They ratified the Great Privilege and then made sure of their advantage by demanding and obtaining special charters which reaffirmed privileges often claimed to have been enjoyed in the good old days before Duke Philip, i.e. before the provinces had been united under one ruler. These charters laid special stress on commercial privileges and on legal safeguards for individuals against unlawful arrest and the search of private houses. All provinces insisted on the right of their inhabitants to have their lawsuits tried within their province.

Partly to accommodate these last demands but, more immediately and more importantly, in order to placate Louis XI, Mary's government abolished the *parlement* of Malines. This was the supreme court which Charles the Bold had set up in 1473 to give more institutional unity to his Netherlands provinces and to stress their independence from the French crown and from the jurisdiction of the *parlement* of Paris. But, from the beginning, the *parlement* of Malines had been unpopular because it had tended to trespass on the rights of the provincial courts by calling up cases pending before them. The *parlement* of Paris had objected because it claimed jurisdiction over Flanders and Artois as French crown fiefs. Since, however,

---

[5] Alberts, *Gelre en Zutphen*, pt. II, 107.
[6] Blockmans, *Le privilège général, passim*. E. Lousse, 'The Great Privilege of Mary of Burgundy for the Netherlands', *Schweizer Beiträge zur Allgemeinen Geschichte*, 14 (1965), 37–46. P. van Ussel, *De Regering van Maria van Bourgondië over de Nederlanden* (Louvain, 1943), 30ff.

a supreme court for the Netherlands was still desirable, the judicial functions of the *parlement* of Malines were returned to the duchess's council, from which they were held to have emanated. This council, now reconstituted as a Great Council, was to consist half of noble councillors, drawn from the different provinces, and half of lawyers, in effect mainly the former judges of the *parlement* of Malines. As happened almost invariably in Western Europe in this period, the two functions of the Great Council, the political and the judicial, were rapidly separated again. The lawyers appropriated for themselves the name of Great Council and moved back to Malines. The politicians remained in attendance on the ruler in the Privy Council.[7]

None of this suggests that the provinces wanted to reverse the union which the Valois dukes of Burgundy had imposed on them in the previous half century. The point of having councillors from all the provinces in the Great Council was simply a logical extension to all provinces of the traditional demand of medieval states that their prince's councillors should be natives. Here it seemed particularly appropriate because of the strong feeling of the Netherlanders against the many Burgundians in the duke's councils. Few of the individual provisions of the Great Privilege were unprecedented or unusual. Most of them, even the right to assemble on their own initiative, had been claimed in the *joyeuses entrées* of Brabant since the middle of the fourteenth century. These rights were now extended to all the provinces, i.e. to the States General. Even for the States General the claim of autonomous assembly was not really new. In 1464 they had at least started to assemble on their own initiative and the delegates never admitted that they had at any time acted illegally.[8] As to war and peace, even in France, Fortescue's example, *par excellence*, of a *dominium regale*, the notoriously autocratic Louis XI agreed in 1482, i.e. only five years after the Burgundian Great Privilege, that his Treaty of Arras with Burgundy should be ratified by the Estates of France. The Estates were to

> undertake to support the treaty and all the points and articles contained therein; and if it should happen that the King, the Dauphin, or their successors... break the agreement... they [the French Estates] will not aid, assist or favour them, but on the contrary will give all aid, favour and assistance to my said lord, the Duke [i.e. Archduke Maximilian of Austria, widower of Mary of Burgundy], to his son [Philip of Burgundy] and to his country in order to support the said treaty.[9]

Now it is true that this clause did not imply a power of veto by the French Estates General over decisions of war and peace in the way the Great Privilege was undoubtedly intended to do for the Netherlands States General. But it did provide for a similar penalty of non-obedience in case the ruler should break the treaty to

---

[7] A. Walther, *Die burgundischen Zentralbehörden unter Maximilian I und Karl V* (Leipzig, 1909), 17ff. J. Stengers, 'Composition, procédure et activité judiciaire du grand conseil de Marie de Bourgogne (février 1477 – février 1480)', in *BCRH*, vol. CIX (1944), 2–33.

[8] Van Ussel, *Maria van Bourgondië*, 49ff. Cf. also above, ch. 2, pp. 31–2.

[9] Quoted in J. Russell Major, *Representative Institutions in Renaissance France 1421–1559* (Madison, 1960), 58.

The first crisis (1477–1494)

which the Estates had become partners. It is, of course, most unlikely that Louis XI took this clause of the Treaty of Arras very seriously or that he thought he had given away anything of the reality of royal power. Two years later, in 1484, when his daughter, Anne de Beaujeu, headed an inevitably precarious regency for her boy brother, Charles VIII, the Estates General of Tours demonstrated only too clearly that in France the Estates lacked the will seriously to challenge the royal prerogative.

In the Netherlands, in 1477, the Estates had shown this will and had translated it into constitutional action and constitutional documents. Taken together, the provisions of the Great Privilege and the setting up of the Great Council represented not perhaps a revolution but a marked shift in the balance of power within the traditional system of *dominium politicum et regale*. This shift had not been planned. It had happened as the result of an almost instinctive reaction by the traditional Netherlands ruling strata to the aggressively monarchical policies of Charles the Bold.[10] It had happened, moreover, at the very moment when such reaction usually occurred in European history, the moment of a doubtful or weak succession – in this case the succession of an inexperienced young girl, Mary of Burgundy.[11] Very soon it became apparent that no one had begun to think out the problems involved in the practical running of such a changed regime. The Netherlands establishment found, to their evident dismay, that it was the king of France and the guilds and common people of the big cities who continued to hold the political initiative, just as if the constitutional changes had never taken place.

Between January and April 1477 popular revolts broke out in Ghent and Bruges, in Antwerp, Brussels, Louvain, 's-Hertogenbosch and Lier, and in the Holland towns of Dordrecht and Gouda, as well as in Utrecht and some smaller towns. The revolts all followed a roughly similar pattern. Crowds of workmen – weavers in Ghent, seamen in Antwerp – would arm themselves and run to their guild houses and town halls and demand the restoration of their old privileges and the punishment of traitors. Traitors they called those who had signed the constitutions imposed by the dukes on the cities after earlier rebellions or, worse still, those who had actively supported the dukes on these occasions. Equally unpopular were city councillors who had been responsible for imposing new taxes or who were accused of having embezzled public funds or sold city offices to foreigners, i.e. Netherlanders

---

[10] P. van Ussel (here quoted as P. Daems-Van Ussel), 'Het charter zonder naam', in *Miscellanea L. van der Essen*, vol. I (Brussels and Paris, 1947), 439–57, for a discussion of different interpretations of the Great Privilege by modern historians. Cf. also Blockmans, *Le privilège*, 473–516.

[11] Dondt, 'Les assemblées d'états en Belgique avant 1795', 337–8, for a discussion of the question of disputed successions and the likelihood of the occurrence of such successions in the history of the origins of the Estates of Flanders in the twelfth century. For a general discussion of the likelihood of the occurrence of problematic successions, cf. H. G. Koenigsberger, G. L. Mosse and G. Q. Bowler, *Europe in the Sixteenth Century*, 2nd edn (London, 1989), 303–4. Cf. also J. Kunisch and H. Neuhaus, eds., *Der dynastische Fürstenstaat: Zur Bedeutung von Sukzessionsordnungen für die Entstehung des frühmodernen Staates* (Berlin, 1982), *passim*.

Plate 3 'The tree of class struggle' – nobility, clergy and commons fight to reach the top. MS 9079 f. 10v (H. Bovet, *L'arbre des batailles*, c. 1461). Bibliothèque Royale de Belgique, Brussels

from outside the city. These men were arrested, often tortured to obtain confessions or denunciations, and then tried with mostly rather doubtful legality. Some, but certainly not all, of the accused were condemned and executed.[12] There is no evidence that these popular movements were sparked off by economic distress except the very real hardship cause by Charles the Bold's taxes and the disruption of trade and consequent unemployment caused by his wars. Prices of grain had remained fairly steady and reasonably low for some years.[13] The crowds did not, as happened so frequently in this period, threaten grain merchants and storm bakeries; they demanded the abolition of urban taxes and excise duties. The *rentmeester* of Antwerp, the official charged with the administration of the rents, i.e. the annuities which the city sold to private investors, recorded with horror that the guildsmen, both in his and in other cities, remained under arms for six or seven weeks, drinking beer without paying excise duties.[14] He did not say that they did not pay for the beer. In some Flemish towns there were quite deliberate moves to break the virtual monopolies of the big brewers.[15]

These political and constitutional moves had the support of sections of the urban patriciates. In Holland the disturbances merged into the old party quarrels of the Hoeks and Kabeljauws. In Ghent some 700 persons whom Charles the Bold had banished in 1468 were allowed to return and these certainly included patricians. Ghent had all its privileges of the period before its rebellions against Philip the Good and Charles the Bold restored. In the renewal of the law, in February, i.e. the annual elections of the city magistrates, several of the leaders of these rebellions or members of their families were elected or re-elected to the city council.[16] The citizens of Bruges did even better. Not only did they obtain the restoration of all their old privileges but also the exemption of their merchants from tolls throughout Flanders. Foreign merchants were to be allowed to sell foreign goods only, which meant that the sale of the famous Flemish cloth and of other local manufactures was now reserved for merchants from Bruges. In the villages cloth manufacture was restricted to where it had previously been practised. This was the traditional policy of the urban guilds, designed to maintain their

---

[12] 'Journal du tumulte arrivé à Gand, 1476 (o.s.)', *BARSBL*, 6, pt. 2 (1839), 233–6. Nicholaes Despars, *Cronijk . . . van Vlaenderen*, ed. J. de Jonghe, pt. 4 (Bruges, 1840), 120–58. Geerard Bertrijn, 'Rolle of Memorie van "De quay Werelt"', in P. Génar, ed., *De Gebroeders van der Voort en de Volksopstand van 1477–78*, Maatschappij der Antwerpsche Bibliophilen (Antwerp, 1879), 4–8. *Chronicle* of Lodewijk van Caukercken in *ibid.*, 19–21. For Holland, cf. H. Kokken, *Steden en Staten. Dagvaarten van steden en staten van Holland en het eerste regentschap van Maximiliaen van Oostenrijk (1477–1494)* (The Hague, 1991), 51.
[13] E. Scholliers, *De Levensstandaard in de XVe en XVIe Eeuw te Antwerpen* (Antwerp, 1960), 124. C. Verlinden and J. Craeybeckx, *Documents pour l'histoire des prix et des salaires en Brabant (XVe–XVIIIe siècles)* (Bruges, 1959), 35–51. Van der Wee, *The Antwerp Market*, vol. II, 93.
[14] Lodewijk van Caukercken, *Chronicle*, 19–20.
[15] Despars, *Cronijk*, 158.
[16] V. Fris, *Histoire de Gand* (Brussels, 1913), 145–6. V. Fris, 'Rym, Guillaume', *BN*, vol. XIX, 986–8. Van Ussel, *Maria van Bourgondië*, 67–85.

Plate 4 'Not all is strife' – urban May celebrations. MS II 158 f. 5v (*Book of Hours of Notre Dame*). Bibliothèque Royale de Belgique, Brussels

The first crisis (1477–1494)

manufacturing monopoly against the spread of capitalist-organised manufactures in the countryside, outside guild control. Most significant of all was the abolition of the Franc de Bruges as a separate political unit and as one of the four Members of Flanders.[17] The small towns and lordships of the Franc were divided up between Ghent and Bruges. Bruges even obtained the right to garrison some of the castles, notably the strategic port of Sluys.[18]

Ghent and Bruges and, to a lesser extent, Ypres were clearly trying to re-establish their virtual autonomy as city-states. Just as with the Italian city-states, the Swiss cantons and the imperial cities of Germany this meant the economic exploitation and the political control of the surrounding countryside.[19] There was, however, this difference: that the Flemish cities were economically more integrated with the rest of the Netherlands and that they had a more powerful ruler at hand than the Italian, Swiss and German city-states. For these reasons they continued to be vitally interested in the central government of the Netherlands and especially in its defence policy; and the obvious way of exerting leverage on the duchess and her council was through the Estates of Flanders and, in so far as they could obtain the support of other provinces, through the States General. Since the towns had won their immediate objectives over their own government and over the economic control of their *contado*, their surrounding countryside, the next confrontation was likely to come precisely over the conduct of the central government.

In January and February 1477 neither the duchess's advisers nor the States General thought that the Netherlands could resist the French armies. There seemed to be no alternative but to buy off Louis XI. Hugonet therefore led a high-powered embassy, which included some representatives of the Flemish cities, to the French king and offered Mary's hand to the six-year-old dauphin, Charles (VIII). Louis, evidently well informed of the mood in Flanders, treated the Flemish representatives with special cordiality, but he barely modified his extreme demands: restitution to the French crown of the duchy of Burgundy and of all French territories won by Philip the Good and Charles the Bold. Boulogne and the Somme towns were to be ceded immediately. In the meantime the king would not even grant a truce beyond March. Such terms the embassy was not prepared to accept and left France.

At home, the States General, clearly led by Flanders and perhaps persuaded by the king's favourable reception of the Flemish representatives in Hugonet's embassy, decided to have one more try. They therefore despatched an embassy of their own with the express purpose of assuring the king that the Estates had not been responsible for the late duke's wars.[20] This embassy included aristocratic clerics and burgomasters or pensioners (secretaries) of the cities, most of whom

---

[17] See above, ch. 2.
[18] Kervyn de Lettenhove, *Histoire de Flandre*, vol. V (Brussels, 1850), 220–2.
[19] Blockmans, 'Autocracie ou polyarchie', 306–8.
[20] Cuvelier, *Actes des Etats Généraux*, 289ff.

actually had titles of nobility.²¹ Commynes was contemptuous, both of their social status and of their political experience.²² On the point of their inexperience he was certainly right. Louis outmanoeuvred them with ease. He enquired of the envoys whether they had authority to negotiate in the name of the duchess. They assured him that she would do nothing without the counsel and consent of the States General.²³ Thereupon Louis showed them a letter, signed by Mary, her stepmother Margaret of York, and by the seigneur of Ravenstein, brother of the duke of Cleves and Mary's uncle, assuring the king that Mary took all important decisions only with their advice and with that of Chancellor Hugonet and of the councillor Guy de Brimeu, seigneur of Humbercourt.

The embassy left the French court in confusion. On 13 March they presented their report to the States General. The ambassadors said that at the French court they had been told of 'letters sent by some great personages during the legation, tending to destroy and undermine our credibility'.²⁴ This much is certain. Commynes is more specific. He speaks of uproar in the assembly. Mary, who was present, denied having written such a letter, but the ambassadors actually produced it. Characteristically, Commynes did not blame the duchess for having deceived the States General and then lying about her deception, but the States General for its unchivalrous behaviour in having shown up the young duchess publicly.²⁵ But was he right in assuming that Mary was lying and that Louis XI was speaking the truth? Commynes was not himself present when the king produced his conjuror's trick of showing the Flemish ambassadors Mary's letter. It seems altogether too neat and too convenient to be completely believable and one may wonder whether the king had not forged the letter. Such an interpretation would certainly not be out of character.²⁶

Whatever the truth of the matter, Louis XI's *diabolus ex machina* certainly did its trick, as he undoubtedly hoped it would. The proposed marriage of Mary and

---

[21] Van Ussel, *Maria van Bourgondië*, 95–6.
[22] Commynes, *Mémoires*, bk. 5. ch. 16.
[23] *Ibid*. 'Ladite Damoiselle ... en toutes choses estoit deliberée de soy conduire par le vouloir et conseil des trois Estats de son pays'. On 21 September 1476 the Milanese ambassador to Piedmont-Savoy had quoted to the duke of Milan the opinion of the Piedmontese politician, Luigi Talliandi, about his own duke: 'that although they [the Piedmontese] have a prince, nevertheless, in every important case it is the three estates which deliberate, make decisions and govern the country; and by himself the prince is incapable of pursuing a course of action unless the three estates take a part'. A. Tallone, *Parlamento Sabaudo, Patria Cismontana*, vol. V (Bologna, 1935), 180. Just possibly the rather striking similarity of the two statements is more than a functional coincidence: Talliandi had been in Burgundian service and Commynes may have known him personally. See H. G. Koenigsberger, 'The Parliament of Piedmont during the Renaissance, 1460–1560,' in *Estates and Revolutions*, Koenigsberger, 22.
[24] 'Rapport en brief du besoigné devers le roi par les ambassadeurs de Mademoiselle la duchesse de Bourgogne et de ses Estats', in Cuvelier, *Actes des Etats Généraux*, 299.
[25] Commynes, *Mémoires*, bk. 5, chs. 16, 17.
[26] W. Paravicini, *Guy de Brimeu: Der burgundische Staat und seine adlige Führungsschicht unter Karl dem Kühnen* (Bonn, 1975), 456 n.33. Paravicini accepts the authenticity of the letter but voices some doubts.

The first crisis (1477–1494)

the dauphin would remain unconsummated for many years and, given the diplomatic habits of the time, had therefore only a very shaky prospect of ever becoming effective. In the meantime, the king might well find a more suitable bride for his son. He had his eye on Edward IV's daughter, Elizabeth of York. In any case, French troops were advancing very satisfactorily. They had taken Arras and there was as yet little sign of serious resistance from the Netherlands. On the contrary, many of the Netherlands high nobility with estates in the border provinces were rapidly changing their allegiance from Burgundy to France. What better course than to throw the maximum of distrust between Mary and the States General?[27]

But Louis' luck did not last. In March 1477 the Franche-Comté rose successfully against the French, followed in April by Arras, in May by Charolais and in June by Dijon. The lower classes in the towns did not hold with the aristocratic renegades and spearheaded these revolts.[28]

On 14 March, only a day after the dramatic session with the letter, the States General ordered the arrest of Hugonet and Humbercourt, together with several other government servants. Outside, in the streets of Ghent, the mood of the crowds had turned ugly. In the following days the city authorities executed several officials appointed by Charles the Bold. The States General set up a special tribunal to try Hugonet and Humbercourt for treason, and Mary had to agree. The Ghenters managed to pack the tribunal. We do not know exactly how this was done; but it certainly meant that the chancellor and the other accused had no chance of acquittal.[29] The Ghenters had too many old scores to settle. Just as Strafford, in 1641, so Hugonet in 1477 had come to be seen as the instigator of a hated policy of princely tyranny. Mary pleaded personally for Hugonet's and Humbercourt's lives, but they were executed on 3 April.[30] Not until Charles I was forced to sign the act of attainder against Strafford was a ruling prince again personally so humiliated by a representative assembly.

Although the States General was anxious for an agreement with Louis XI, it had as early as February 1477 begun to make plans for the military defence of the Netherlands. By 1 March it had agreed to raise an army of 34,000 and it had assigned the quotas for the individual provinces. This was a substantial force for the period, and the States General agreed to increase it to 100,000 in case of need. They voted a remarkably high and detailed scale of pay and they exempted the soldiers' horses and weapons from confiscation by unpaid creditors. There should not be any excuse, so the deputies argued, for soldiers having to live off the country. They enacted a strict code of military discipline but they also promised to

---

[27] Wellens, *Etats Généraux*, 168ff.
[28] W. Paravicini, *Karl der Kühne* (Göttingen, 1976), 116.
[29] C. Paillard, 'Le procès du chancelier Hugonet et du Seigneur d'Humbercourt', in *Académie royale. Mémoires coronnés*, vol. XXXI (Brussels, 1881), no. 8.
[30] Wellens, *Etats Généraux*, 168ff. Cuvelier, *Actes des Etats Généraux*, 303–4.

provide funds for ransoming prisoners of war and to provide wheat for war widows and orphans.[31]

It was a remarkably advanced conception of an army, although it is not clear how far these plans were put into practice or whether, indeed, the whole army remained on paper. The disillusionment with the French marriage alliance, however, was very real. Mary and her advisers therefore acted with commendable speed in resurrecting Charles the Bold's plan of a marriage alliance with the son of the emperor, the archduke Maximilian of Austria. On 29 March Mary wrote to him, urging him to come to the Netherlands and on 21 April Mary and Maximilian were married by proxy. On the same day a new session of the States General began in Louvain. It had been summoned by the Estates of Brabant on the initiative of the three Members of Flanders and with an express reference to the States General's right of autonomous assembly, obtained in the Great Privilege during the previous session.[32]

Only Brabant, Flanders, Hainaut and Malines sent representatives. Perhaps in order to reaffirm her princely rights, as her grandfather had done in 1464, Mary now issued her own summons for a States General for 7 May, still to assemble at Louvain. This time Holland, Zeeland and Namur also sent representatives. In Ghent Mary had promised not to marry without the consent of the States General and she now formally asked for this consent. The deputies gave it unanimously, without apparently referring back to their principals, demanding, however, that before consummating the marriage, Maximilian should confirm all the privileges which Mary had granted the Estates. Mary promised he would do this, provided the Estates also fulfilled their promise to defend the Netherlands against the French.[33]

MAXIMILIAN OF AUSTRIA IN THE NETHERLANDS

At first everything went well. Maximilian and Mary were married in person in Ghent on 19 August 1477 and were evidently pleased with each other, both personally and politically. An energetic young man of eighteen, intelligent and with some experience in political and military matters, Maximilian also shared all the attitudes and preconceptions of his class and rank. The charisma which German publicists were later to endow him with[34] was not very evident to the Netherlanders at this time. Later, too, Maximilian himself saw to it that such regrettable lack of perception should be remedied, at least among the Germans, if not perhaps among the Netherlanders. In the heroic poem *Theuerdank* and in the chivalric novel *Weisskunig*, Maximilian and his ghost-writer, Marx Treitzsauerwein, combined the

---

[31] L. P. Gachard, *Analectes historiques*, in *BCRH*, ser. 3, vol. X (Brussels, 1858), 5. Cuvelier, *Actes*, 342ff.
[32] Wellens, *Etats Généraux*, 175 n.2.
[33] *Ibid.*, 176ff. Cuvelier, *Actes*, 346–7.
[34] H. Lutz, 'Die deutsche Nation zu Beginn der Neuzeit', *HZ*, 234, 3 (1982), 544–5.

The first crisis (1477–1494)

Plate 5 Coin commemorating the marriage of Maximilian of Austria and Mary of Burgundy. Bibliothèque Royale de Belgique, Brussels

style and manner of Arthurian legend with romanticised autobiography.[35] In these works Maximilian represented himself as a kind of young superman whose unbelievable physical prowess, although hardly his foresight, defeated one after another of the wicked machinations of his envious enemies. Published with a wealth of superb woodcuts and engravings, these writings achieved immense popularity in Germany in the early sixteenth century, at any rate among those who could afford to buy such expensive books.

The young archduke was impressed by the wealth of the Netherlands and of Ghent in particular; but it is doubtful whether he ever fully understood how such wealth was created or on what conditions its continuance depended. There were no big trading or manufacturing cities in Austria, where he came from. In the *Weisskunig* Maximilian characteristically sneered at the Estates, 'most of whom were won over [to his marriage] by money. From which one might well think that many would have taken the money, no matter whether the queen [i.e. the duchess Mary] had married well or ill.'[36] What Maximilian understood very well were the prerogatives of a prince and the habitual competition of princes with each other. Immediately, on 27 August, he demanded from Louis XI the restoration of the lands the king had recently occupied. For the moment, Louis XI appeared as the aggressor and Maximilian as the chivalrous defender of his young wife's inheritance. He enjoyed the role and made the most of it and, later, in the *Weisskunig*, added a quip about the dauphin being 'small and hunchbacked, with a big head and short legs'.[37] What Maximilian did not then mention was that in 1491 the ugly dauphin, by then Charles VIII, had beaten Maximilian in the second round of

[35] G. S. Williams, 'The Arthurian Model in Emperor Maximilian's Writings. Weisskunig and Theuerdank', *Sixteenth Century Journal*, 11, 4 (1980), 2–22.
[36] Maximilian I, *Weisskunig*, ed. H. Th. Musper *et al.* (Stuttgart, 1956), 242.
[37] *Ibid.* For Maximilian's early history and arrival in the Netherlands see. H. Wiesflecker, *Maximilian I* (Munich, 1974).

Monarchies, States Generals and Parliaments

their competitions for the same lady, this time Anne of Brittany. Only gradually did the Netherlanders realise that Maximilian intended to make good all of Charles the Bold's territorial conquests and claims.

They realised rather sooner that he intended to exercise ducal power as his father-in-law had exercised it and that he would take no notice of the concessions to the Estates which Mary had been forced to make in the early months of 1477. The history of the sixteen years of Maximilian's government of the Netherlands, from his marriage to the duchess in 1477 to the declaration of the majority of his son in 1493, was therefore a history of conflict: intermittent but unresolvable military conflict with France and intermittent and gradually escalating political, and eventually also military, conflict with the Estates and especially with the centres of earlier opposition to the Burgundian dukes, the province of Flanders and above all the city of Ghent. It could hardly have been otherwise.

The Estates of Flanders were in session during the wedding and immediately, on 22 August, Maximilian demanded the sum of 500,000 ridders from them for defence, 'in the same way as his predecessor, Duke Charles, had had them'.[38] By 7 December the Estates granted this demand.[39] In February 1478 Maximilian followed up this success by asking Flanders to pay for 5,000 Swiss soldiers. The Estates again accepted this demand.[40] So far, the Estates were willing to stand by the bargain they had made with their duchess that they would defend the Netherlands against France.

More ominous for the prospects of future harmony was the government's treatment of Ypres. There had been a riot in the city on St Mark's day, 25 April 1477. As other cities had done in similar circumstances, Ypres had obtained a formal pardon from Mary.[41] Nevertheless, in the autumn the government appointed a commission of inquiry, consisting of members of the high nobility and ducal officials, to investigate the riot and punish those involved. The city councillors (*échevins*) protested both to Maximilian and to the Great Council against this breach of the city's privileges; but because of the expense of fighting its case before the Great Council they accepted a compromise with the government by which the commission proceeded with its inquiries but the city received letters of non-prejudice over the issue of privilege.[42] It is not clear whether this deal saved any of the rioters from punishment.

---

[38] W. P. Blockmans, *Handelingen van de Leden en van de Staten van Vlaanderen . . . (5 januari 1577–16 september 1506)* pt. 1 (Brussels, 1973), 36. For Maximilian's attempts to squeeze money out of Holland and to subvert the Great Privilege in that province, see M. Boone and H. Brand, 'De ondermijning van het Groot Privilege van Holland', *Holland Regionaal-Historisch Tijdschrift*, 24, 1 (1992), 2–21.

[39] Blockmans, *Handelingen*, 42 (editorial note).

[40] *Ibid.*, 51–6.

[41] I. L. A. Diegerick, *Inventaire analytique et chronologique des chartes et documents appartenant aux archives de la ville d'Ypres*, 7 vols. (Bruges, 1853–68), vol. IV, 34–5.

[42] *Ibid.*, 37ff.

The first crisis (1477–1494)

In September 1478, following a French spring and summer offensive, Maximilian summoned his first States General.[43] His council had carefully prepared the ground for his financial demands by presenting the deputies with a memorandum comparing ducal revenues and expenses of the time of Duke Charles with those the archduke could now expect.[44] According to this document, Charles the Bold had had revenues of just under 350,000 livres from his domains, plus 600,000 from the Estates of the Netherlands, 100,000 from those of Burgundy and odds and ends of more than 100,000, making a total of about 1,150,000 livres per annum. By contrast, the current domain revenue had shrunk to 38,800 livres. The reasons given for this catastrophic decline ranged from actual loss of domain lands in territories occupied by the French to the sale of rents (i.e. annuities) funded on domain revenue, especially in Brabant, and the introduction of new privileges, especially in Flanders.

It is quite likely that the councillors exaggerated the decline of domain revenue. Maximilian and his German companions were, after all, astonished by the lavishness of the duchess's court and court festivities. But there is no reason why the councillors should have exaggerated the figures for non-military expenditure. These came to about 240,000 livres. Of this sum 2 per cent was spent on the ducal chapel and just over 7 per cent, or 17,800 livres, on actual administration, i.e. the chancellor, eight *maîtres des requêtes*, six secretaries and various minor officials, together with the cost of embassies, messengers and stationery. As against these very modest sums the court establishment of the archduke and the duchess came to more than 150,000, or 62 per cent. Of the rest, 5 per cent went on small pensions and gifts, but 56,800 livres, or more than 23 per cent, on extraordinary pensions to just fourteen members of the high nobility.

This last figure is highly revealing of Maximilian's and his advisers' assessment of the political realities of the situation in the Netherlands. When so many of the Burgundian nobility had transferred their allegiance to the king of France, it was evidently essential to assure the loyalty of the rest by maintaining a large court establishment and by the distribution of generous pensions. Such pensions were seen not so much as bribes to the richest and most powerful persons in the country than as a public recognition of the prince's appreciation of the services they had rendered and were still expected to render.[45] Whether this assessment was correct is another matter. The huge sum of 31,000 livres, or well over half the total sum for pensions, went to members of the Cleves–Ravenstein family, the duchess's

---

[43] Wellens, *Etats Généraux*, 178ff.
[44] 'afin qu'ils [Maximilian and Mary] cognoissent et entendent la petite Revenue de leur demaine pour leur entretenement et conduite de leur estat, au Regard de la Revenue que avoit en son temps par communes années feu Monsieur le Duc Charles', *BBR*, MS 14511, fos. 530r–539r.
[45] Cf. H. G. Koenigsberger, 'Patronage and Bribery during the Reign of Charles V', in *Estates and Revolutions*, 166–75. Armstrong, 'Had the Burgundian Government a Policy for the Nobility?', especially 20–1. Since the time of Philip the Good there was the policy of half-yearly service of nobles in the ducal household.

uncles and cousins. From Maximilian's point of view, they turned out to be highly unreliable after Mary's death and one of them, Philip of Cleves, seigneur of Ravenstein, became his most determined and dangerous personal enemy.[46]

Perhaps not surprisingly, the States General, and especially the great cities of Flanders and Brabant, remained unimpressed by the government's financial revelations and argued that Maximilian himself should pay for most of the troops he claimed he needed. Only in the early months of 1479, when the French had resumed their military incursions, did the States General eventually agree to pay for a substantial army. Maximilian promptly used it to win the spectacular victory of Guinegate, on 17 August 1479.[47] But disillusionment followed rapidly. The French continued the war and egged on the Gueldrians who had not forgiven Charles the Bold's conquest of their country nor Maximilian's adoption of the title of duke of Guelders. In Holland the old feud between Hoeks and Kabeljauws broke out again. Successive meetings of the States General discussed defence but took no decisions on Maximilian's demands for further *aides*. The deputies pressed for negotiations with France[48] and the Estates of Flanders spent more and more time complaining of breaches of their privileges.[49] If we can believe the chronicler Nicholas Despars, they even thought of prescribing a budget for Maximilian according to which he would have to organise his court and pay his servants.[50] From September 1481 they began to add complaints about high grain prices and these became major worries in the following years.[51]

Since Ghent had now clearly become the moving force behind the opposition, Maximilian attempted to outflank the city by playing on the hostility of the smaller towns in Ghent's *contado*. He summoned their representatives to Bruges to obtain an *aide* from them. Ghent protested that towns and lordships in its quarter of Flanders were subject to its jurisdiction and had no right to grant money without the consent of the Ghent city council.[52] At this, the small towns and lordships, as the accounts of the small town of Oudenaarde tell us, 'very shamefacedly' acknowledged the validity of Ghent's privileges.[53]

On 27 March 1482 the duchess died after a riding accident, a victim of the aristocratic and princely mania for hunting in unsafe conditions, made more dangerous still in Mary's case by her probable pregnancy. Her death turned the growing tensions in the country into a full-scale crisis. Once again an early modern regime proved to be weakest at the point of succession. In the Netherlands the

---

[46] See below, pp. 65–8.
[47] Wellens, *Etats Généraux*, 180ff.
[48] *Ibid.*, 206.
[49] Blockmans, *Handelingen*, 147ff.
[50] Despars, *Cronijk*, 204.
[51] Blockmans, *Handelingen*, 186ff and *passim*. Van der Wee, *The Antwerp Market*, vol. II, also speaks of unemployment and famine.
[52] Blockmans, *Handelingen*, 206.
[53] *Ibid.*

laws and precedents governing successions and regencies differed from province to province and the problems were further complicated by the fact that Artois and Flanders were fiefs of the French crown, while the other provinces were fiefs of the Holy Roman Empire. Mary left a son and a daughter, Philip and Margaret, aged four and two. Everyone agreed that Philip was the rightful heir. But who was to govern during his minority?

THE REGENCY OF MAXIMILIAN

Maximilian summoned the States General to Ghent. For the first time for several years we have a good eyewitness account of the assembly, this time by Jean or Jeannet de la Ruyelle, a deputy from Namur.[54] It was a full and splendid assembly of prelates, great lords and bourgeois deputies who, on 27 April in the monastery of the Augustinians, listened to Gort Roelandts welcome the deputies in Flemish and then proposed Maximilian's *remonstrances* in French. No doubt Maximilian had deliberately chosen as his spokesman the man who had so bravely spoken for the Estates in Duke Charles's last States General. The archduke, Roelandts said, although expecting an imminent inheritance of his own in Austria and Hungary, had decided to stay in the Netherlands to maintain his children's rights and to defend their countries and subjects. For this purpose the States General should recognise him as his children's guardian and regent and help him to defend the frontiers.

The States General received this speech coolly. On 28 April Brabant complained bitterly of Maximilian's wilful conduct of foreign policy, contrary to his promises of 1477. At this moment they did not know whether there was peace or a truce with France, nor which way the archduke intended to move. In any case, the deputies argued, their province was so impoverished by its previous military efforts that a truce or a good peace was now essential. 's-Hertogenbosch alone had spent 380,000 Rhenish florins on defence against the Gueldrians. The Brabanters ended on a pious note. If only the provinces acted as brothers, united in a true union, neither the king of France nor anyone else could harm them. On the following day the Flemish delegation supported these arguments and went even further in criticising Maximilian. His rights, they said, had lapsed. They themselves had sent an embassy to Louis XI and they invited the other provinces to join in their negotiations. Only Hainaut and Holland were prepared to accept Maximilian's claims.

On 1 May news arrived that a large French army had invaded Flanders and sacked nine or ten villages. The French demanded that the cities of Aire and St Omer, in Artois, be handed over to them as the price of the betrothal of the young princess Margaret to the dauphin. This French action changed the mood of the

---

[54] '*Relation de Jeannet de la Ruyelle*', ed. L. P. Gachard, in *BCRH*, ser. 3, vol. I, 311–41.

assembly. Brabant now joined with most of the other provinces in recognising Maximilian as guardian and regent, and even the Flemings accepted him as 'head of the country'. However, they added the proviso that Flanders itself was to be governed by a council of regency in the name of the young archduke Philip. The deputies of Aire and St Omer added, almost despairingly, that they hoped the proposed French marriage would not 'place them in even greater servitude than they were in already' and that they should be consulted before they were handed over.

For Louis XI this had been almost a replay of the events of the winter and spring of 1477, except that the dauphin was this time to be engaged not to a grown woman and reigning princess but to her two-year-old daughter. But the king once again spoilt a promising political position by excessive territorial demands and by too hastily initiating military action that was provocative without being very effective.

Nevertheless, the closing of ranks which Louis' ill-considered actions had achieved in the Netherlands was at best a truce. On 12 July the three Members of Flanders concluded an 'act of eternal union' in which they pledged themselves to joint consultation and to help each other and the smaller Flemish towns in the defence of their privileges, their commerce and their industry.[55] It was a union clearly modelled on the late medieval urban leagues of South Germany and Switzerland. Bruges and Ypres now agreed to receive Maximilian as regent, but Ghent still refused. Immediately after Mary's death the Ghenters had induced the three Members of Flanders to dismiss several ducal officials and to appoint new ones. They had made the *chambre des comptes*, the ducal treasury, hand over their accounts.[56] Now, in July, they went a step further and started issuing their own coins in the name of the young duke Philip. Since the unification of the coinage had been one of the major achievements of the Burgundian dukes, and since the economic prosperity of all the provinces depended on this unified coinage, Ghent's action came perilously near to a unilateral declaration of independence. Maximilian protested that the Ghenters' actions harmed all provinces and that they offended against his honour as a prince and his credibility as the defender of the provinces. But the Flemings had actual physical possession of his children and there was nothing he could do. He even offered to dismiss from his court those to whom the Flemings objected.[57] On 23 December 1482 he reluctantly signed the Peace of Arras with France: the princess Margaret was to be married to the dauphin and to be sent immediately to France to be brought up there. Artois, Franche-Comté and several smaller Burgundian territories in eastern France were to be handed over, evidently without being consulted as to their wishes. The judicial superiority of

---

[55] Blockmans, 'Autocratie ou polyarchie', 213–20.
[56] *Ibid.*, 268–9.
[57] 'Instruction pour les ambassadeurs de Maximilien auprès des Trois Membres de Flandre au sujet de sa réception comme régent', in *ibid.*, 321–31.

the *parlement* of Paris over Flanders was to be acknowledged. In return, Louis was to give back French conquests in Luxembourg and to give up supporting his candidates for the bishoprics of Liège and Utrecht.[58]

The treaty was a defeat for Maximilian and was regarded as such by him. But did the policy of Ghent amount to treason, as modern historians have traditionally held?[59] Willem Rym, Jan van Coppenhole and the other hard-nosed patricians who had dominated the city council of Ghent since the revolution of 1477 were pursuing a deliberate policy of dominating and exploiting their 'quarter' of Flanders and of safeguarding the political privileges and commercial interests of the three Members of Flanders. This was not fundamentally different from the policies pursued by the patricians of Berne and the other Swiss cantons which still legally belonged to the Holy Roman Empire and the kingdom of Germany. However, it brought the Ghenters into inevitable conflict with Maximilian who had adopted the traditional policy of the Burgundian dukes of trying to restrict the autonomy of the great cities, of seeking to divide them from the small towns of the countryside and of pursuing dynastic territorial claims against the king of France. Quite naturally, therefore, the Ghenters sought allies in the States General and preferred accommodation with the king of France to fighting ruinous and seemingly endless and senseless wars with him. They felt the more justified in adopting this line as Flanders was a fief of the French crown and as the king gave legal backing to their claim freely to elect their own town councils. In fifteenth-century terms these attitudes and policies were no more nor less treasonable than the switch of allegiance from Burgundy to France of Philippe de Commynes, Philippe Crèvecoeur, the 'Grand Bâtard' Antoine de Bourgogne and other great lords with estates and prospects in France. As to those provinces which were to be handed over to France – well, one could put in a good word for them. The abbot of St Bertin, speaker for the Netherlands embassy which negotiated the Treaty of Arras, asked the dauphin 'to hold in special commendation the counties of Artois and Burgundy and their poor inhabitants, whom you will find to be good and loyal subjects to yourself and to Mademoiselle [i.e. the princess Margaret]'.[60]

This does not sound as if there was a strong feeling for either Netherlands or French nationality. But neither did political choice follow unequivocally either the undoubtedly strong class attitudes of the period or a purely Machiavellian calculation of reason of state. Time and again the Ghent patricians and guildsmen misinterpreted the attitude of Louis XI and, time and again the French let them down. Rationally, the kings of France should have consistently supported the Ghenters and the Flemings against their arch-enemy, Maximilian. Alternatively, for reasons of princely solidarity, they might have been expected to come to terms with Maximilian and support him against his rebellious subjects. In practice, French

---

[58] Wellens, *Etats Généraux* 194 n.96.
[59] *Ibid.*, 193-4.
[60] Gachard, *Lettres inédites de Maximilien*, 38.

policy was opportunistic, vacillating and, in the end, ineffective. The French court despised the bourgeois Flemings and seems to have felt uncomfortable in having them as allies. Commynes tells a bizarre story of how, at a critical moment in the winter of 1477, Louis XI sent his barber-favourite, Olivier le Daim, as his envoy to Ghent, of how Olivier committed various social *faux pas* in the presence of the duchess Mary and the great lords of her council and of how the Ghenters, themselves patricians and as snobbish in their own way as any courtier, resented Olivier for his low state. Commynes was puzzled by the king's action and thought that 'it seemed that God had disturbed his understanding'.[61] Perhaps so. More likely, the king may have thought that this Figaro figure would go down well in Flanders. If so, he underestimated the snobbishness of the patricians and the good burghers of Ghent. This particular misjudgement, at least, he did not repeat; but the ambivalence in Franco-Flemish relations remained.

A similar ambivalence in class attitudes affected the Netherlands high nobility. The council of regency for Flanders consisted of four members of the high nobility: Adolf of Cleves, seigneur of Ravenstein; Philippe de Bourgogne, seigneur of Beveren and son of the Grand Bâtard Antoine; Louis de Bruges, seigneur of Gruuthuse and earl of Winchester; and the Ghenter Adrien Vilain, seigneur of Rasseghem. To these were added, on equal terms, representatives of the three Members of Flanders.[62] Naturally, Maximilian was never happy with this council, for it blocked his own rights as regent and guardian of his children. At the first favourable opportunity he tried to get rid of it.

Louis XI died on 30 August 1483. In the autumn Maximilian's supporters in Holland, the Kabeljauws, won out over the Hoeks. Maximilian now felt strong enough to abolish the council of regency. The council, however, had other ideas. The four great lords seem to have been quite happy to cooperate with the townspeople. They spurned an attempted mediation by the Grand Bâtard (characteristically veering again in his loyalties towards Burgundy when the French monarchy seemed to be in trouble with the succession of a child and a prospective regency). They also rejected a compromise resolution by a majority of the council of the Order of the Golden Fleece.[63] Each side blamed the other for the breakdown of negotiations. The chroniclers certainly noticed the class hatred on both sides. The Ghenter Despars reported Maximilian as saying 'that he would have no dealings with the boors and clowns of Ghent but that he would be regent and guardian of his children, whether they liked it or not'.[64] A court chronicler makes the popular leaders of Ghent, Willem Rym and Daniel Onredene, responsible for blocking an agreement which the lords had almost achieved.[65]

---

[61] Commynes, *Mémoires*, bk. 5 chs. 13, 14.
[62] Blockmans, 'Autocratie ou polyarchie', 280–1.
[63] *Ibid.*, 281–7, 344–55. Lettenhove, *Histoire de Flandre*, vol. V, 536–58.
[64] Despars, *Cronijk*, pt. 5, 241–2. Also quoted in Blockmans, 'Autocratie', 284, n.2.
[65] *Ibid.*, 287 n.1.

The first crisis (1477–1494)

While the great Flemish towns continued to attract the support of members of the high nobility, they were rapidly losing the sympathy of the other Netherlands provinces. The Flemings' unwillingness to consider any interest but their own was becoming more and more evident. They failed to hand over the young archduke Philip to Brabant, as they had earlier agreed to do. Ypres insisted again on its old but almost defunct privilege of prohibiting the weaving of woollen cloth in the surrounding countryside. Bruges sought to prohibit merchants trading in the city from going to the Antwerp fairs and even began to build a blockhouse on the lower Scheldt to prevent ships from sailing up to Antwerp.[66] In November 1484 Maximilian summoned the States General. Flanders did not participate and the other provinces came out in full support of the archduke.[67] Maximilian now started military operations against Flanders. The French, who had promised help for Flanders, withdrew almost immediately, but not before their troops had made themselves very unpopular with their plundering. There followed coups in favour of Maximilian, first in Bruges and then also in Ghent where the boatmen's guild, in contrast to the weavers, favoured peace. The leaders of the popular party were arrested. On 13 June 1485 Rym and Onredene were publicly executed without protests from the crowd – which led the court memoirist, Olivier de la Marche, to write a characteristic disquisition on the fickleness of crowd favour.[68]

Maximilian made a conciliatory treaty with Ghent; but within a month he took the occasion of a minor disturbance as sufficient grounds to revoke the privilege which Mary and he himself had granted to the city and to restore the Franc of Bruges as the fourth Member of Flanders. The constitutional position was therefore back to where it had been before the revolution of 1477.[69] Maximilian's own position was now absolutely clear: he was going to pursue exactly the same policies as Charles the Bold had done, on the home as well as the foreign front.

Only rapid success could justify such ambitions; for Maximilian had won his victory over Ghent more because of the unpopularity of the radical party of Ghent than because of any great enthusiasm for his regency. But the campaigns against France went badly. The pillaging by the troops caused misery in the frontier districts, and the interruption of commerce caused hardship in the trading towns. At the same time taxes increased steeply. In 1485 Flanders granted 825,000 livres in *aides*; in 1486, 610,000; and in 1487, 840,000. This compared with an average of just over 400,000 during the five years of Maximilian and Mary's joint reign.[70] Just as he had attempted in 1481 and 1482, Maximilian was again by-passing the Members of Flanders, demanding money from the small towns and the open

---

[66] Blockmans, *Handelingen*, 337.
[67] Wellens, *Etats Généraux*, 196. H. Pirenne, *Histoire de Belgique*, vol. III (Brussels, 1907), 38.
[68] Quoted in Lettenhove, *Histoire de Flandre*, vol. V, 375.
[69] Blockmans, 'Autocratie', 291–2.
[70] *Ibid.*, 259 n.2; 293 n.1.

country and sending his officials to collect it.[71] Worse still was his tampering with the coinage. Under Philip the Good the mints had charged only the nominal sum of two or three groats in seignorage per mark of silver. Maximilian increased this profit on coining to 120 groats. This represented a cool 12 per cent tax on all silver coins, a tax which the states had not granted but which it was easy to collect even during a civil war. We know from the mint accounts that in 1488 the government made a profit of well over 100,000 livres from this source.[72] Philip of Cleves was to characterise this mint policy as 'the key to the coffers of the people' and to claim that it oppressed poor people more than all the *aides*.[73] It certainly helped to cause inflation. Grain and vegetable prices had fallen from high points in 1481–3; but in 1487–8 they rose again by 50 to 100 per cent and they stayed high for several years.[74] Epidemics decimated the workforce and compelled the municipal authorities to raise wages by 10 to 15 per cent. But these rises were insufficient to balance the higher food prices.[75]

By the autumn of 1487 the general discontent was becoming vocal and loud. Coppenhole and Rasseghem returned to Ghent and, on 4 November, they engineered a renewal of the magistrates which brought their followers, and notably the weavers' guild, back into power.[76] They then invited the cities of Brabant and Mons in Hainaut to send deputies to Ghent to discuss their common grievances against Maximilian: his agressive wars against France, the cessation of commerce, the depredations of the soldiers and the regent's general disregard for the privileges of the provinces.[77] This assembly did not actually take place. Maximilian reacted as Philip the Good had done in 1463 and Mary in 1477. He summoned the States General himself, to meet at Bruges in February 1488. Maximilian had been elected king of the Romans in 1486; but his new title did little to increase his prestige in the Netherlands. It seems that, by late 1487, the loyalty of at least some members of the high nobility had again become doubtful. At any rate, Maximilian felt it necessary not only to associate them with his government but effectively to hand over to them the control of his finances. By an ordinance of 26 December 1487 he set up a Council of Finance consisting of six members of the high nobility and presided over by Philip of Cleves, lord of Ravenstein. They were to spend two hours a day on council business, which meant that they controlled policy but not the details of financial administration. The king and the chancellor were expressly forbidden to sign any letters or orders about gifts, debts or wages without going through the new council. Even the full-time finance officials would be appointed

---

[71] Blockmans, *Handelingen*, 431–2.
[72] Spufford, 'Coinage', 82–3.
[73] Philip of Cleves to the towns of Brabant. Brussels, 28 Oct. 1488. Gachard, *Lettres de Maximilien*, 170.
[74] Verlinden and Craeybeckx, *Documents*, 35–45.
[75] Scholliers, *De Levensstandaard*, 124–5.
[76] V. Fris, 'Jan van Coppenhole', *Bulletin de la Société d'Histoire et d'Archéologie de Gand*, 14 (1906), 101–2.
[77] Gachard, *Lettres de Maximilien*, 68–72.

only on the advice of the six lords – an extraordinary limitation of the ruler's traditional prerogative of appointing whom he wished.[78]

All this was a very significant concession to those who wanted to see the regency government controlled by the 'lords of the blood', Archduke Philip's maternal relatives. Maximilian probably intended the new council to shield him in future from the persistent and widespread allegations that he and his German and Franche-Comtois ministers were enriching themselves at the expense of the Netherlands in general and of Archduke Philip's domain lands and personal jewels in particular. It was typical of Maximilian that he was prepared to make concessions to the high nobility but not, if he could help it, to towns and commoners. They would not have known that, a few years earlier, he had written to a boyhood friend: 'I'm afraid that one day I will have to kill off ten thousand Flemings before they give me peace.'[79] The remark was no doubt meant as a black joke; but Maximilian had only recently had leaders of riots in Flemish and Brabant towns executed.

The burghers of Bruges were certainly afraid of violence when the king arrived in their city a few days before the States General was due to meet; for his mercenary troops had been making themselves thoroughly unpopular in the small towns and villages of Flanders. With the mood in Bruges becoming tenser by the day, the king, too, became afraid and tried to introduce several hundred troops into the city. The guilds reacted immediately by shutting the gates in their faces and they blockaded the king himself in the Craenenburgh, a pottery or grocery shop on the market place (2 February 1488). Pirenne, with his unfailing historical sense, compared the scene to that of medieval popes being blockaded in the castle of St Angelo by the Roman mobs.[80]

The Brugeois had not planned this action and they were not at all sure what to do next. The Ghenters, however, were. Immediately they took the lead in setting out the terms under which the king of the Romans might be released. Both Ghent and Bruges were now effectively ruled by revolutionary regimes. In Ghent the city council was again dominated by the weavers' guild with its century-old revolutionary traditions, and led by Coppenhole and Rasseghem. Once again Ghent started to mint its own coins, this time with the revolutionary legend *equa libertas deo grata*. The people called the coins coppenolles.[81] Once again the revolutionaries took revenge on those patricians and officials who had supported the unpopular central government. Andries Paelding and Jacob Steeland, the deputies of Ypres who had been sent to support the union of the three Members were made by their

---

[78] 'Ordonnance faict sur le fait des finances', Bruges, 26 Dec. 1488, in Walther, *Die burgundischen Zentralbehörden*, 193–5. Walther's discussion of this document, 53–8. See also F. Rachfahl, 'Die niederländische Verwaltung', *HZ*, 110 (1912), 114–22.
[79] V. von Kraus, ed., *Maximilians vertraulicher Briefwechsel mit Sigmund Prüschenk* (Innsbruck, 1875), 56.
[80] Pirenne, *Histoire de Belgique*, vol. III, 46.
[81] I. L. A. Diegerick, *Correspondance des magistrats d'Ypres députés à Gand pendant les troubles de Flandre sous Maximilien* (Bruges, 1853), 63–5.

hosts to witness the public tortures and executions in order, they were told, to show the solidarity of the Flemish cities. They tried to refuse and even hid in churches. For the sake of God, Steeland wrote to the Ypres council, would they recall them or at least send them an order forbidding them to watch such horrors? But the council of Ypres was afraid of offending its mighty neighbours and refused to recall its deputies. Steeland and Paelding should cooperate with the authorities in Ghent and Bruges, they wrote.[82]

In the rest of the Netherlands the reaction to the kidnapping of the king of the Romans was little more decisive than it was in Ypres. The States General could obviously not now be celebrated in Bruges and Archduke Philip therefore summoned it to Malines for 24 February. The chancellor of Brabant read the opening speech, predictably condemning the Ghenters and the Brugeois for their action and accusing them of working hand in glove with France. This was not actually true. Not until March did Charles VIII openly promise help and legal justification for the Flemings, and it seems most unlikely that, before that, there had been any secret understanding between them. The kidnapping of Maximilian, while undoubtedly the result of growing tensions, had been entirely unpremeditated. The deputies in Malines were inclined to make peace between the parties. Their attempts to mediate were, however, sidetracked by the Ghenters' refusal to send a full delegation to Brabant and by their insistence that the States General meet in their own city.

For two months the arguments flew back and forth. The assembly moved first to Brussels and then, giving in to the Flemings, to Ghent. The Ghenters claimed they were not rebels since Maximilian had never been their prince. They justified their actions by appeals to biblical precedents, to Aristotle, to medieval theories of resistance and to Mary's Great Privilege: 'all our provinces [*de landen van herewaerts overe*] are privileged by express privileges to assemble at any time they wish and to make confederations and alliances for their advantage so as to prevent any infraction of their rights, privileges and liberties without having to ask the consent of the prince'.[83] Maximilian, having watched some of the executions, was understandably in fear of his life and willing to meet the Ghenters' demands. But how far could he be trusted? How far, indeed, would he be legally or morally bound by any undertaking given while he was a prisoner? Not surprisingly, the deputies of the States General failed to agree to a generally acceptable answer to these questions. The troops Maximilian had unsuccessfully tried to bring into Bruges were not strong enough to attack the big cities, but they took revenge by plundering small towns and villages in Flanders and by preventing the free movement of the deputies, so as to sabotage the meetings of the assembly. Philip of Cleves and other great lords were raising troops, but it was far from clear whose side they were on. For two

---

[82] *Ibid.*, 72ff.
[83] Declaration de Willem Zoëte, pensionary of Ghent, 24 April 1488, *ibid.*, appendix G.

The first crisis (1477–1494)

months the situation remained thoroughly confused. Like many others who have taken hostages, the Flemings found that the act of kidnapping was easier than the collection of the ransom.[84]

Outside the Netherlands decision-making was easier. The German princes were outraged by the indignity inflicted by the despised townsmen on the king of the Romans. For once, Maximilian's father, the usually ineffective emperor Frederick III, had no difficulty in raising a large army of some 20,000 men. By April 1488 the German army was advancing through Brabant into Flanders, preceded by the blast of a papal excommunication of the rebels, issued through the archbishop of Cologne. There is considerable doubt about whether the document was forged, but there was no doubt that the Ghenters were daily losing support. No one was keen to tangle with the emperor's army for their sake. It was time to come to terms.

On 12 May Brabant, Flanders, Hainaut and Zeeland concluded an act of union. Flanders was to be governed as in 1482 by the three Members and by a council of the lords of the blood. Maximilian was to renounce the title of count of Flanders which he had unilaterally assumed and he was to confirm all Flemish rights and privileges. In return he was to receive an annual money payment. In the other provinces he was to continue as regent during the minority of his son, but the States General was to meet at least once a year, in turn in Brabant, Flanders and Hainaut, whether summoned by the regent or not.[85]

The agreement of 12 May 1488 was a substantial victory for Ghent and, less dramatically but as it turned out more permanently, for the States General. Once again this institution emerged as the forum where in a crisis all parties wanted to present their arguments and whose support or mediation all were anxious to obtain. In the long run, this confirmation of the States General's political prestige was more important than the confirmation of its claim of autonomous assembly.

On 16 May Maximilian solemnly swore to observe the agreement and left Philip of Cleves and two German princes as hostages for the fulfilment of the treaty. But no sooner had he joined his father in Louvain than he renounced his oath. We do not know whether he meant to do so from the moment he took it. The emperor had been no part of the agreement. He and the German princes, at the head of a big army, were certainly not going to let slip such a splendid opportunity to put down the insolent Flemings. Maximilian claimed that his oath to the emperor as his feudal superior overrode an oath given to his subjects.[86] Philip of Cleves, however, when he agreed to act as hostage, had promised to join the Flemings in their defence against Maximilian if the king should break his oath. This, 'with great regret and sorrowing heart', he now declared he had to do.[87]

---

[84] *Ibid.*, appendices, pp. XXCI–XVL. Wellens, *Etats Généraux*, 204–10.
[85] *Ibid.*, 212–13. Blockmans, 'Autocratie', 298–9.
[86] J. Coene, pensionary, to the city council of Ypres; Ghent, 30 May 1488 in Diegerick, *Correspondance*, 238. Maximilian to the Estates of Hainaut, 16 June 1488, in Gachard, *Lettres de Maximilien*, 100–1.
[87] Philip of Cleves to Maximilian, 9 June 1488; Blockmans, 'Autocratie', 355–7.

65

CIVIL WAR

One may doubt whether the civil war which now broke out again followed these opposing interpretations of the finer points of feudal honour. In the *Weisskunig* Maximilian and Treitzsauerwein do not even mention them. In their version the *plab kunig*, the blue king, i.e. the king of France, simply bought the white king's (i.e. Maximilian's) best captain with money and the promise that he would rule the country. This captain (i.e. Philip of Cleves) 'drew to himself a great number of evil people, among whom there were many big mouths, and he gave these people a lot of money and promised to make them lords for all time'. But the majority prevented the minority from killing the white king and helped him to get free after a long captivity.[88] The early modern romantic hero had evidently no more need to justify his own side and his own actions than the hero of a modern spy thriller.

The Cleves family, just like that of the Grand Bâtard, Antoine de Bourgogne, and other noble families had for years hovered in their loyalties and marriage alliances between Burgundy and France. Philip of Cleves, seigneur of Ravenstein, had married Françoise de Luxembourg, the daughter of the count of St Pol who had changed his allegiance from Charles the Bold to Louis XI. Françoise's sister had married the count of Romont, a prince of the reigning House of Piedmont-Savoy which, in its turn, had close ties with the French royal family. Philip of Cleves' action cannot therefore have come as a complete surprise to his contemporaries. In Holland the Brederodes, the leaders of the Hoek faction, tried once again to raise the county against the pro-Burgundian Kabeljauws. By contrast the Hainaut families of the Croy and the Lannoy, after their quarrel with Charles the Bold, had been reinstated in their estates and, in spite of their traditional French sympathies, remained loyal to Maximilian. Such loyalty was even more pronounced with the Nassaus and Berghes who had only relatively recently acquired large estates in Brabant through the favour of the Burgundian dukes.

The cities were similarly inclined to follow their own particular interests. Brussels and Louvain, nursing old grudges against Maximilian for the taxes he had imposed, the devastations which his wars had caused in their hinterland and the harshness with which he had put down occasional riots, opened their gates to Philip of Cleves and the Flemings. By contrast, 's-Hertogenbosch, menaced by the Gueldrians, and Antwerp with its relatively free trade expanding with ducal favour at the expense of protectionist and monopolist Bruges, remained firmly on Maximilian's side.

No wonder therefore that the States General were disinclined to take sides and once again tried to mediate. Maximilian summoned them to Antwerp for 24 August, after his father's army had failed to capture Ghent. By September the Germans felt that they had done their duty and were going home. Campaigning far

---

[88] Maximilian I, *Weisskunig*, ch. 130, 279.

The first crisis (1477–1494)

from home and in the autumn and winter was not nearly as much fun as it had been in summer. Maximilian had no choice but to ask the States General to make peace for him with Flanders and France.[89] In October the States General negotiated with the Estates of Flanders and Brabant, assembled in Brussels. These latter offered Maximilian 100,000 Rhenish florins if he would leave the Netherlands and give up the guardianship of his children. The king of the Romans indignantly refused to be bought off.[90] But the Flemings had not completely misjudged their man. Later, after peace had been restored, Maximilian made a great point about his modesty in 1488 and suggested they should now let him have at least some of the money which he had so generously refused before.[91]

In December, the small Walloon province of Lille, Douai and Orchies, tired of being the constant battleground between France and the Netherlands, made a separate peace with the French.[92] But Maximilian, too, was tired of the struggle. Since 1485 Matthias Corvinus, the king of Hungary, had occupied Vienna and large parts of Austria, Styria and Carinthia. It was time for Maximilian to turn his attention to his own hereditary dominions. In February 1489 he left the Netherlands and appointed his nephew, Albert of Saxony, as his regent. Albert was an experienced soldier – he had been fighting the Hungarians for years – and a more flexible and emotionally less committed politician than Maximilian. He proved to be an excellent choice.

In the spring and summer of 1489 French policy also changed. Duke Francis II of Brittany had died and was succeeded by his young daughter, Anne. Henry VII of England, Ferdinand of Aragon and Maximilian were all anxious to prevent a French annexation of Brittany. Charles VIII, in face of this formidable, if not very cooperative, coalition decided to come to terms with Maximilian. By the Truce of Frankfort, 22 July 1489, Maximilian gave up interference in Brittany in return for an end of French help to Flanders. The truce was followed by the treaty of Montils-les-Tours, on 30 October 1489, by which Charles VIII recognised Maximilian as regent for Flanders. Most of Flanders now came to terms with Albert of Saxony. He defeated the Hoeks in a decisive naval battle, and that was the virtual end of the great Hoek–Kabeljauw feud in Holland. In November 1490 Bruges gave up the struggle. Only Ghent and Philip of Cleves, entrenched in the port of Sluys, continued to fight.

Then, once again, French policy changed. In December 1490 Maximilian married Anne of Brittany by proxy. It was a typically fantastical and unrealistic scheme, for Brittany could not by itself resist France, even for a short time, as the Netherlands

---

[89] The deputies of Brussels to the burgomaster and council of Brussels, Antwerp, 20 Sept. 1488; Gachard, *Lettres de Maximilien*, 155. Maximilian to the Estates of Hainaut, Bergen-op-Zoom, 26 Dec. 1488; *ibid.*, 180–1.
[90] Wellens, *Etats Généraux*, 216–17.
[91] Maximilian to States General, 26 Jan. 1499; Gachard, *Lettres de Maximilien*, pt. 2, 281ff. Same to same, 14 February 1503, *ibid.*, 298–300.
[92] Maximilian to the Estates of Hainaut, 31 Dec. 1488; *ibid.*, pt. 1, 186–8.

had been able to do in the parallel dynastic situation of 1477, and Maximilian was in no position to bring effective help. He could not even get there to consummate his marriage to Anne, as he had gone to consummate his marriage with Mary of Burgundy, thirteen years earlier. Old Frederick III himself characterised his son's plans as disgraceful. Charles VIII marched into Brittany and married Anne himself (9 December 1491). His unfortunate fiancée, Maximilian's daughter Margaret, was sent ignominiously back to the Netherlands. She was never to forgive the French for this indignity and later, when she was herself regent of the Netherlands for her nephew Charles V, her anti-French attitude remained one of the constants of her political inclinations. From the French point of view, and indeed from that of Western European politics in general, Charles VIII's policy was entirely rational. If it rode roughshod over the young duchess of Brittany's feelings, it made her queen of France and owner of the marvellous series of unicorn tapestries, now in the Musée Cluny in Paris and in the Metropolitan Museum of Art (The Cloisters) in New York City.

The inevitably renewed hostility between Maximilian and France allowed Ghent and Philip of Cleves to continue the struggle for some time longer. But support for their cause was steadily shrinking. Philip had had the seigneur of Rasseghem assassinated because, so he claimed, Rasseghem had been bought by the Netherlands government. The deed did nothing to improve Philip's reputation. In June 1492 the peace party in Ghent overthrew Coppenhole and executed him. On 19 July Ghent signed the Peace of Cadzand with Albert. The city finally recognised Maximilian as guardian of his children. It lost some rights of financial jurisdiction outside its quarter of Flanders and, most importantly, its guilds lost the right of freely electing their own deans, and with it the ability to control the city council. This control now passed to the duke whose commissioners organised the annual renewal of the magistrates. The city militia, the greatly feared White Hoods, was suppressed.[93] There were no reprisals against individuals by the ducal government; but once again, as in 1453, it had gained an apparently decisive influence over the administration of the city. As it turned out, this influence was not as decisive as it looked and in the sixteenth century Ghent was still able to challenge ducal authority on two famous occasions, in 1539 and in 1578. But in the second and most serious of all Ghent's challenges to its rulers, a new force, that of religion, was added to the well-remembered revolutionary traditions of the guilds.

In October 1492 Philip of Cleves finally made his peace with Albert of Saxony on generous personal terms. His annual pension was restored and was continued even when he spent some time at the French court, and he was paid compensation for having financed the repairs of the castle of Sluys during the time he had made it the centre of his rebellion against his prince. Only when, much later, Philip was

---

[93] Blockmans, 'Autocratie', 305–6. F. W. N. Hugenholtz, 'Crisis en herstel van het Bourgondisch gezag, 1477–1493', in *AGN*, vol. IV (1952), 24–5.

The first crisis (1477–1494)

proposed for membership of the Order of the Golden Fleece did Maximilian block him by threatening to send back his own collar.[94]

On 23 May 1493 Charles VIII, anxious to safeguard his rear during his proposed campaign to Naples, concluded the Peace of Senlis with Maximilian, giving up French claims to Artois, Charolais and Franche-Comté. In August of the same year Frederick III died and Maximilian effectively became emperor. It was a good opportunity for the States General of the Netherlands to request him to agree to the reception of his son Philip, now fifteen, as ruling prince. Maximilian agreed, and in the autumn of 1494 Philip the Handsome made his successive *joyeuses entrées* in the provinces of the Netherlands.[95]

The Netherlands and the Burgundian monarchy had survived fifteen years of crisis, following the death of Charles the Bold and the fearsome legacy of foreign war and internal disaffection which that ruler had left. The cost of the crisis was not borne primarily by the principal actors, only a few of whom lost their lives on the battlefield or the scaffold. Compared with the executions, burnings and mass slaughters of the sixteenth century, the politicians of the fifteenth, on both sides, showed a remarkable sense of economy – Maximilian's wilder pronouncements notwithstanding. The real sufferers were the common people, especially those of the small towns and villages. Not only did they have to bear the crushing burden of taxation which paid for the princes' political ambitions but they had to bear the robberies and brutalities of the all too often unpaid and half-starving soldiery. In Hainaut a census of 1501 revealed the loss of over 6,100 houses, well over 20 per cent of the total. We have no figures for the Flemish countryside; but the complaints of contemporaries were only too similar to those where we can check the reality of the devastation from the censuses.[96]

The inhabitants of the larger towns were safer. But they suffered from high food prices during the 1480s and from the interruption of trade and consequent unemployment due to the fighting. In Brussels, for instance, one in eight houses had become derelict by 1496.[97] But usually the situation in the towns improved when the fighting stopped. Some towns suffered from long-term shifts in trade or in industrial production. Ypres complained in a memorandum of 1486 that in 1408 it had 80,000 to 100,000 inhabitants and 3,000 to 4,000 looms. They had now dwindled to 5–6,000 inhabitants of whom a third were beggars, and only 25 or 30 looms were left.[98] These are frightening figures, even if those for the population of 1408 are two or three times too large.

---

[94] A. de Fouw, *Philips van Kleef* (Groningen, 1937), 271–4, 276–84, 330ff.
[95] Wellens, *Etats Généraux*, 233–4.
[96] J. Cuvelier, *Dénombrements des foyers en Brabant (XIVe–XVIe siècle)*, (Brussels, 1912), CLXI and CCXXXIII. H. G. Koenigsberger, 'Property and the Price Revolution (Hainaut, 1474–1573)', in *Estates and Revolutions*, 152–6.
[97] Cuvelier, *Dénombrements*, CCXXXIX.
[98] Diegerick, *Inventaire . . . d'Ypres*, vol. III, 301–4.

But the loss of one city could also be the gain of others. Much of the Ypres textile industry was taken over by industrial villages like Hondschoote in western Flanders where they made cheaper 'new draperies'; much of the trade of Ypres, like that of Bruges, shifted to Antwerp which, between 1480 and 1496, increased its housing by over 20 per cent.[99]

The credit for the survival of the Burgundian monarchy can hardly go to Maximilian's erratic leadership. He was brave and energetic; but he never really understood the economy of the Netherlands nor the mentality of the Netherlanders. In so far as he had a consistent policy at all, it was the same centralising and expansionist policy which had failed with Charles the Bold. Fortunately, it was the Estates of the provinces which, for all their preoccupation with their local interests and privileges, wanted the Netherlands, the *pays de pardeça*, to survive as a political entity. Members of the high nobility might waver in their allegiance between the duke of Burgundy and the king of France. But none of them, except possibly the leaders of the Hoeks in Holland, set provincial loyalty above loyalty to their sovereign prince – or at any rate the sovereign prince they had chosen for the moment. For, the greater their prince, the higher a nobleman would rise – a conviction which they were very happy to demonstrate by their eager support of Philip the Handsome when he claimed the succession to the kingdom of Castile. By contrast, in the only recently conquered duchy of Guelders the local nobility took the first opportunity to welcome back their native duke and to support him through interminable wars against the House of Burgundy.

The attitude of the cities was more complex. Like the German and Italian cities, they strove for autonomy and for economic, judicial and even political domination of their *contado*, including if possible also the smaller towns within their geographic and economic ambit. In Ghent and Bruges there were even some who wished to emulate the republicanism of the Swiss cantons. But none of the cities of the Netherlands had ever enjoyed full independence from their prince. Their economies, for all the notorious inter-city rivalry, had grown with the close political cooperation and eventual union of the provinces. In the end, none of the cities, not even Ghent, were economically able or psychologically prepared to go it alone and declare complete independence. The Ghenters were always trying to keep the three Members of Flanders together and to persuade Brabant and the other provinces to stand together with them in defence against Maximilian's policies. But the Ghenters' ruthless city-imperialism within Flanders alienated the rest of the provinces. Their alliance with France and with the aristocratic Hoeks was politically logical and, in the case of France, also economically sensible. But socially and psychologically it could never be anything but a misalliance, and time and again the French withdrew their support at a critical moment.

---

[99] Van der Wee, *The Antwerp Market*, vol. I, appendix, 49. Cuvelier, *Dénombrements*, CCXXXV.

The first crisis (1477–1494)

It was the States General which came out best. They did not manage, it is true, to maintain their claim, so boldly put forward in Mary's Great Privilege and repeated in 1488, to their right of assembling without summons by their prince. But this claim had been advanced not so much as a point of principle, an attempt to share sovereignty with the duke, than as a practical safeguard against the duke's arbitary policies. There were many conservatives in the Estates who did not believe in such a newfangled idea.[100] In their view, it did not help the States General that the revolutionaries of Flanders had pressed for such an autonomous assembly. In any case, from 1488 onwards the States General was summoned nearly every year and sometimes several times a year.[101] Albert of Saxony used the meetings with great skill. As soon as he had taken over the government he wrote to the *grand bailli* of Hainaut to send three or four deputies to him 'in order to provide daily with us for everything that might happen . . . for as long as our lord, the king, is absent and to take notice of, aid and conduct the affairs of the province together with the deputies of the other provinces'. He was sending them copies of his overtures to Philip of Cleves and to Brussels, Louvain and Flanders (i.e. all those who were still in rebellion against Maximilian), 'so that the Estates will know and understand that we wish them to be informed of everything'.[102]

A committee of deputies acting as a daily advisory council was something quite new. Albert claimed that the king had ordered it before he left the Netherlands. This is certainly possible since the government desperately needed the support of the loyal Estates; but it seems out of character and sounds more like Albert's own idea than Maximilian's. It is not clear whether this advisory council ever functioned. Perhaps the smaller and poorer provinces regarded it as too expensive a way of running the country – just as all over Europe smaller and poorer towns were often reluctant to incur the expense of sending deputies to assemblies. At any rate, in May of the same year of 1489 Albert was chiding the Estates of Holland for failing to carry out the king's order. They should send at least two deputies, for, 'as you can well imagine, and seeing that we do not know the nature of these provinces, we cannot conduct by ourselves . . . and we have never desired, nor do so now, to conduct the said affairs other than by your advice and judgement.'[103]

Apart from the negotiations with Flanders and with France, the most urgent business facing Albert of Saxony and the States General was the confusions of the currency caused by Maximilian's illegal devaluations and by the Flemish minting of coppenolles. Albert himself admitted that the 'great disorder in the matter of money causes the lord king, our cousin, and his country and subjects greater damage than the war'.[104]

---

[100] J. Molinet, *Chroniques*, ed. G. Doutrepont and O. Jodogne (Brussels, 1935), 618.
[101] See the chronological list of assemblies in Wellens, *Etats Généraux*, 458–525.
[102] 20 Jan. 1489. Gachard, *Lettres de Maximilien*, pt. 2, 211–13.
[103] 12 May 1489. *Ibid.*, 224–5.
[104] Albert to *grand bailli* of Hainaut, 15 Aug. 1489. *Ibid.*, 237. For the devaluations, especially of 1488–9, see Van der Wee, *The Antwerp Market*, vol. I, table XV.

In nearly every meeting of the States General deputies chosen especially for their expertise in monetary matters grappled with this problem; but they failed to find a satisfactory solution. In 1492 the Saint Andrew's guilder was fixed at 14 patards; but the coinage continued to be placed on the agenda of the States General well beyond the turn of the century.[105]

The States General was associated with all the negotiations and settlements of the early 1490s.[106] According to Olivier de la Marche, Maximilian himself summed up his experiences of the Flemish revolt in advice he gave to his son Philip: 'And to let you know the truth, I write this as a precept to you, never to give authority to those who should live under your command and authority. But I should advise you well that you should ask their counsel and aid to conduct your great affairs.'[107] *Dominium politicum et regale* had been preserved and, for the time being, was accepted by all parties.

---

[105] L. P. Gachard, 'Relation des Etats Généraux tenus à Malines au mois de février et mars 1492', in *BCRH*, ser. 3, vol. IV, 338. Spufford, 'Coinage', 83.
[106] See, for instance, Gachard, 'Relation', 344.
[107] Olivier de la Marche, *Mémoires*, ed. H. Beaune and J. d'Arbaumont, vol. I (Paris, 1883), 163.

4

The Netherlands becomes part of a composite monarchy (1506–1531): Philip the Handsome (1494–1506)

'This poor king finds himself torn by paternal love and by the credit and trust he gives his councillors, and I truly think that His Majesty finds himself at times in a great labyrinth.'
The Venetian ambassador, Dr Quirino, to the Doge. Brussels, 31 August 1505[1]

ECONOMIC GROWTH AND ECONOMIC PROBLEMS

The Netherlands recovered quickly from the civil wars of the regency of Maximilian of Austria, just as England, France and Spain recovered quickly from the civil wars which had plagued them in the second half of the fifteenth century. Much of the countryside had been devastated but had not lost its fertility. Peasant houses could be rebuilt quickly, slaughtered or stolen horses and cattle, pigs and sheep could be bought from parts of the country which had escaped the burning and plundering of the soldiery. In the thirty years from 1496 to 1526 the number of houses in Brabant rose from 75,000 to 97,000, a rise of about 30 per cent. In some areas which had suffered most cruelly during the wars, such as the Walloon part of the Louvain quarter of Brabant, the increase was nearly 100 per cent in the countryside and even more in the small towns.[2]

In Holland and Zeeland and near the great cities of Flanders and Brabant farmers began to grow specialised crops: fruit and vegetables for the tables of the well-to-do, flax and dye-stuffs for the linen and woollen industry. In the north they reared cattle for butter, cheese and meat, and they cut peat for shipping to the great cities as domestic and industrial fuel. With this growing specialisation and division of labour agricultural productivity gradually increased and with it the prosperity of the country people, as we can see in Bruegel's paintings of peasant festivities. These peasants now provided growing markets for manufactures and released capital and labour for dyking, road and canal building, for carting and barge services and for the increasing interchange of goods between the towns

---

[1] C. R. Höfler, *Depeschen des venezianischen Botschafters bei Erzherzog Philip, Dr Vincenzo Quirino, 1505–1506*. AÖG, 66 (Vienna, 1885), 148.
[2] Cuvelier, *Dénombrements des foyers en Brabant*, CCLXIX–CCLXX.

Plate 6 Albrecht Dürer, *Harbour Front at Antwerp*, 1520. Graphische Sammlung Albertina, Vienna

and the countryside.[3] In Holland leases on the land of the nobility rose by an average of 28 per cent for every ten-year period between 1500 and 1570.[4] It was a measure of population pressure, itself a sign of growing prosperity in this period, but even more of the increasing value of agricultural land. Even in a relatively underdeveloped province, such as Hainaut, a province which was also the inescapable battleground in the Habsburg–Valois wars, small farming properties managed to hold their own in the sixteenth century, while medium-sized farms did well out of rising farm prices.[5]

Most spectacular of all was the well-known expansion of international trade and the meteoric rise of Antwerp, a result both of the specific economic developments of the Netherlands and of the general economic expansion of Europe and its overseas trade in the sixteenth century.[6]

[3] For the Netherlands generally see van der Wee, *Growth of the Antwerp Market*, especially vol. II, 166ff. For the northern Netherlands see J. de Vries, *The Dutch Rural Economy in the Golden Age, 1500–1700* (New Haven and London, 1974), especially 119ff.

[4] H. F. K. van Nierop, *Van Ridders tot Regenten: De Hollandse add in de zestiende en de eerste helft van de zeventiende eeuw* (Hollandse Historische Reeks, 1984) 116–17. English version, *The Nobility of Holland: From Knights to Regents, 1500–1650*, transl. M. Ultee (Cambridge, 1993), 102.

[5] Koenigsberger, 'Property and the Price Revolution', especially 157.

[6] Van der Wee, 'The Antwerp Market', *passim*, in *NAGN*, 15 vols. (Haarlem, 1980), vol. 5, *passim*. J. de Vries, *European Urbanization 1500–1800*, (London, 1984), *passim*.

Philip the Handsome (1494-1506)

These underlying trends of economic growth were the necessary conditions for the re-establishment and extension of royal power, after the disasters which the monarchies had suffered in Western Europe in the fifteenth century. They were also the necessary conditions for the construction of the great multiple monarchies of the first half of the sixteenth century and for the financing of the wars which these composite monarchies fought with each other over specific disputed territories and, eventually, for the domination of Europe.

But the secular economic expansion of Western Europe in general, and of the Netherlands in particular, also brought with it problems, economic and social, as well as political. Real wages did not keep pace with rising prices, except in some areas such as the province of Holland. There the economic diversification seems to have caused an increasing demand for labour. But the general economic expansion was also subject to cyclical fluctuations. They were caused, like their modern counterparts, by harvest cycles, monetary fluctuations and changes in investment and in the market; but most often, and most spectacularly, they were caused by warfare which brought trade to a standstill and caused unemployment in manufacturing and shipping. In the Netherlands, which, as the deputies of the Estates never tired of telling their princes, were more dependent on trade than any other part of transalpine Europe, wars would have this baleful effect, even when they were fought as far afield as Italy or the Baltic. These fluctuations, together with epidemics and inundations of large stretches of land, which were a particular curse of the Netherlands, all contributed to give the common people a sense of the insecurity of life. This sense of insecurity explains much of the peoples' passion for the absolutely correct form of religious beliefs, the only apparent security in a life full of menace. These immediate fears and prospects were more important than the promise of secular economic trends. The political motivations and actions of both rulers and ruled cannot be understood apart from their fears.

THE GOVERNMENT OF THE NETHERLANDS IN A MULTIPLE MONARCHY

Ferdinand and Isabella, Louis XI and Louis XII, Henry VII and Henry VIII all took advantage of the economic upturn at the end of the fifteenth century and of their subjects' weariness of civil war to confirm and extend the authority of their monarchies. Building on late medieval practices they systematised and expanded the work of the royal councils and law courts. In the process they created dazzling careers and opportunities for social climbing for university-trained secular elites: a professional class recruited from the lower nobility and from commoners. These elites became the monarchies' firmest supporters and the most enthusiastic exponents of centralised and effective government.

The social origins, behaviour and attitudes of these elites in the Netherlands were no different from those of their counterparts in Spain, France and England. In 1530, for instance, the Estates of Holland were pleading their case before the regent's Privy Council against an export tax on grain (*congie*) which the government had imposed and which, so the Hollanders and especially the city of Amsterdam argued, contravened their privilege of freely exporting grain. The government had for some time disputed the validity of this privilege because, like all sixteenth-century governments, it wanted to keep control over the grain trade for fear that, in times of scarcity, free exports might raise prices to famine level. Besides, export taxes were a convenient source of revenue. Unsurprisingly, therefore, the Holland deputies got no sympathy from the council and they complained to their provincial governor, Antoine de Lalaing, count of Hoochstraten, who was himself a leading member of the regent's council. Should they take their case to the supreme court of the Netherlands, the Great Council of Malines, they asked. The governor advised against it. Never in a month of Sundays ('*numquam in aeternum*'), he said, would the Great Council hear a case touching the emperor's finances without the presence of members of the Privy Council and of the treasury. Otherwise the prince would win hardly one out of eleven cases. In fact, he won ten out of eleven.[7] Holland then appealed to the emperor himself who, in 1531, ruled in the province's favour. Characteristically for early modern government, this ruling did not settle the matter definitely. The lawyers of the Privy Council and of the treasury saw to that.[8]

In 1531 Charles V systematised the conciliar structure of his government in the Netherlands, very much on the lines that his grand-chancellor, Mercurino di Gattinara, had done for him in Castile in the 1520s.[9] A Council of Finance was to supervise all government finances, and a new Privy Council, or Secret Council, was to take charge of all administrative and judicial matters, prepare government legislation and supervise appointments under all forms of government patronage. Both these councils contained members of the high nobility, but they were staffed primarily by men of the long robe, i.e. professional lawyers and administrators. Officially, the Privy Council was not meant to interfere in actual court cases. In practice, as the example of Holland and the *congie* demonstrated, it did so as a matter of course when it judged that a case touched public interest, and sometimes the Privy Council even produced judgements in specific cases.[10]

The third central or 'collateral' council was the Council of State which superseded the old Great Council and Privy Council. Just like its Spanish prototype, it was to advise on matters of general policy and especially on defence and all military

---

[7] A. Jacopszoon, *Prothocolle van alle de Reysen . . . gedaen zedert ick de Stede van Aemstelredamme gedient heb gehadt . . . 2–15 May 1530*. MS in the Amsterdam Gemeente Archief, Archief Burgemeesters no. 5029; inventory nos. 721, 722. Microfilm no. 6656, vol. II, 166.

[8] H. G. Koenigsberger, 'Patronage and Bribery during the Reign of Charles V', in *Estates and Revolutions*, 169–72.

[9] F. Walser, *Die spanischen Zentralbehörden und der Staatsrat Karls V*, ed. and completed by R. Wohlfeil (Göttingen, 1959), pt. 4.

[10] H. de Schepper, 'De grote raad van Mechelen, hoogste rechtscollege in de Nederlanden?', *BMGN*, 93, 3a (1978), 390–1.

Philip the Handsome (1494–1506)

matters; and again, just like the *consejo de estado*, it did not have a fixed membership. Charles V appointed twelve councillors, mostly from the high nobility and, at least in theory, all knights of the Order of the Golden Fleece had the right to be summoned to the meetings of the Council of State. In practice, the regent worked with a much smaller group of intimate advisers, both from the nobility and from the 'long robe'. Thus the first president of the Council of State was Jean de Carondelet, a lawyer from Franche-Comté, who acted at the same time as president of the Privy Council. The emperor had arranged his election as archbishop of Palermo, so that his rank, if not his social status, was superior to that of the great seigneurs. One of the original members of the Netherlands Council of State was also a member of the Spanish *consejo de estado*. This was again a minor nobleman, a Walloon, Jean Hannart. He had risen to become sieur de Liedekerke and vicomte de Lombeke, having made his career in the imperial service as a protégé of Gattinara. The ordinance setting up the council specifically provided for the right of the members of the emperor's own council to attend the regent's Council of State when they happened to be in the Netherlands.[11]

With this reorganisation of the councils Charles V did not change the basic nature of the central government of the Netherlands as it had been under the dukes of Burgundy. The main difference was that the high nobility had now shed its ambivalent loyalties. Since the end of the fifteenth century none of them had switched allegiance, as Commynes, Crèvecoeur and members of the Croy family had done at the time of Charles the Bold,[12] or as Antoine de Bourgogne, the Grand Bâtard, and Philip of Cleves had done at the time of Maximilian's first regency.[13] Almost everywhere in Western Europe the great feudal magnates were giving up their quest for independent princely status, a quest which the German magnates had earlier pursued with spectacular success. By the sixteenth century the great lords could do much better by hitching their fortune to the star of their king. In the composite monarchies of the period some could aspire to the position of viceroy or governor general of a whole kingdom. Such a one was Charles

---

[11] M. Baelde, *De Collaterale Raden onder Karel V en Filips II (1531–1578)*, Verhandelingen van de Koninklijke Vlaamse Academie voor Wetenschappen, Letteren en Schone Kunsten, Klasse der Letteren XXVII, 60 (Brussels, 1965), ch. 3. M. Baelde, 'Monarchie in Opbouw: de eerste Instructie voor de Raad van State (1531)', in *Miscellanea Roger Petit*. Archives et Bibliothèques de Belgique, LXI, nos. 3–4 (Brussels, 1990), 314, 327.

[12] Even at that time switching allegiance could be a tricky business. The count of St Pol, of the Luxembourg family, was a principal minister of Charles the Bold but went over to Louis XI who made him *connétable*. His niece, Elizabeth Woodville, married Edward IV of England and the count's career seemed to be flourishing. But he continued to manoeuvre between France, Burgundy and England. Charles and Louis combined against him. He was captured and beheaded in Paris in 1475. Commynes added to this story both a judgement of St Pol's ineptitude – Commynes had changed sides himself without coming to grief – and a moralistic disquisition on the nature of fortune which was really God's will. Commynes, *Mémoires*, bk. 4, ch. 12.

[13] For a discussion of the switching of loyalties as a historical phenomenon, see A. Walther, *Die Anfänge Karls V* (Leipzig, 1911), 9–15.

de Lannoy, a relative of the Croy, whom Charles V appointed as his viceroy of Naples. Many more in the Netherlands, just as in France, were appointed as provincial governors. In this position they were held to represent both the person of the prince in the province and the interests of the community of the province at the prince's court. Such a dual and, inevitably, contradictory role of representation was common in similar offices all over Europe. We find it not only in the Netherlands and France but in the provinces of the crowns of Aragon and Castile, and as far afield as Royal Prussia, an autonomous province under the crown of Poland.[14]

In the Netherlands the provincial governors organised the public security and defence of the province and they commanded the aristocratic provincial militias, the *bandes d'ordonnance*. These were the Netherlands equivalent of the French *gens d'armes*. In the absence of standing armies these *bandes* were often the only troops readily available to the central government in the provinces. The governors would enforce ordinances of the central government and they could often do this without being hampered by all the legal precedents, traditions and *esprit de corps* of the lawyers in the provincial courts. Since the governors were appointed for life they were most favourably placed to advance their own and their families' interests and influence in the province. They appointed young noblemen to commissions in the *bandes d'ordonnance* and they channelled royal patronage in the church and in the royal administration to their own clients. They themselves were linked by marriage or cousinage to the other great families of neighbouring kingdoms. The Egmonts were a junior branch of the dukes of Guelders and the famous Lamoral, count of Egmont who was executed for his role in the early opposition to Philip II, was married to a princess from the Palatine Wittelsbachs. The Burgundian family of Chalon, which had inherited the principality of Orange, married into the House of Nassau, a German princely family with vast properties in the Netherlands. The Montmorency, counts of Hoorn, were cousins of the French Montmorency whose head was the redoubtable *connétable* of Francis I, Henry II and Charles IX.

The younger sons of the provincial governors would often marry into the local noble families just below their own exalted rank, and these latter, in their turn, linked with other local noble and gentlemanly families. Such webs of family alliances and patronage–clientage relationships similarly existed in all other Western European countries. Everywhere they gave stability and coherence to the ruling elites. There were of course differences. In England the powers of the lord lieutenants of the counties were not nearly as great as those of the provincial governors of France and the Netherlands. The Spanish viceroys and governors general, while they had even more extensive powers, were not appointed for life and therefore had less success in placing their families at the head of the local nobility. It was not

---

[14] Biskup, 'Die Stände in Preussen königlichen Anteils', 87.

Philip the Handsome (1494–1506)

for want of trying.[15] But the counterpart of this social cohesion and local power of the nobility was the need of the monarchies to govern with the broad consent of the nobility.

In the first half of the sixteenth century the alliance of the monarchies and their nobilities worked well. Charles V, Francis and Henry II enjoyed loyal and effective service from their provincial governors. Even splits in the allegiance of noble families during the wars between their princes were acceptable in the ethos of the time. One was expected to follow one's own prince without affecting the family honour. Such prominent families as the Egmont and the Montmorency experienced such divided allegiances. When wars were dynastic power struggles a nobleman's honour was fully preserved by loyal service to his own prince. When, however, the *connétable* Bourbon changed sides from Francis I to Charles V, his huge clientele and even his own family were not prepared to follow him.

For the provinces and their Estates the dual role of their governors and of other royal officials held both advantages and dangers; for divided loyalties in public officials were a perennial problem. Thus in February and March 1523 the Estates of Holland debated the position of the advocate of Holland, Albert de Loo. He was the legal representative of the Estates but he was also an imperial councillor. He was often required 'to speak for the province against the emperor and he does so with fear'.[16] A century later a member of the English Parliament put the same point even more succinctly: 'king's livery hindereth sight'.[17] In de Loo's case some rather obvious enmities complicated the matter. But no one liked dismissing an official, and one deputy's query as to who might be the advocate's successor was regarded as being in thoroughly bad tast (*honteux*). Some deputies, however, argued that there was the danger that the emperor would make the advocate of the province into his own official 'against the will and profit of the province, and that thus the advocate would be against the province when he should be for it'. In the end they all agreed to sack de Loo after all.[18]

The governor himself could not of course be sacked by the Estates. All they could do when they disapproved of his action or inaction was to tell him they felt 'he had not shown himself a true stadtholder'. The Estates of Holland did this rather pointedly to Hoochstraten in 1529 when he had argued that the emperor had the right to levy the export tax on corn by his own authority. Even so, they had second thoughts about a proposal to signify their displeasure by not bidding

---

[15] For patronage and clientage in general, see A. Mączak, ed., *Klientelsysteme im Europa der Frühen Neuzeit* (Munich, 1988). For the Netherlands, see in the same volume W. P. Blockmans, 'Patronage, Brokerage and Corruption as Symptoms of Incipient State Formation in the Burgundian–Habsburg Netherlands', 117–26; for the provincial governors see P. Rosenfeld, 'The Provincial Governors from the Minority of Charles V to the Revolt', *APAE*, 17 (Louvain and Paris, 1959), *passim*.

[16] Jacopszoon, *Prothocolle*, 22 Jan. 1523, vol. I, 6.

[17] *Journal of the House of Commons*, vol. I, 456. My thanks to Dr P. H. Williams for drawing my attention to this aphorism.

[18] Jacopszoon, *Prothocolle*, vol. II, 6–10.

him a formal goodbye when he had to travel to Brussels.[19] The governor, after all, had his uses – provided one treated him right. The matter of the export tax on grain (*congie* or *verlofgeld*) came up again in the autumn of 1535 when the government once more published a general prohibition of grain exports. Hoochstraten was a member of the regent's Council of State and he kept the Estates of Holland informed. He had done the same in the long-running *congie* dispute: in 1528, for instance, he had told the Estates that 'the court [i.e. the government in Brussels] is like an eel. You think you have it firmly in your hand but it will escape one way or another.'[20] Now, in 1535, he advised the Estates to win over two important councillors, the counts of Nassau and Bueren. Nothing much could be done about the Estates' most determined opponent, the treasurer general Ruffault, because he had been promised the receivership of the tax. The Estates took their governor's advice and resolved 'that the great lords should be rewarded by bribes and corruption if they supported us'. These tactics worked. Early in 1536 the government dropped the proposed export tax and the Estates of Holland paid their part of the bargain: 400 pieces of wainscotting to the counts of Hoochstraten and Nassau, 200 each to Berghes and Molembaix. Wainscotting or panelling was a form of high-class tip, perhaps because the panelling of rooms was just becoming fashionable and the Dutch merchants imported high-quality timber from the Baltic. Other members of the regent's council received money payments. Treasurer Ruffault did not get anything, and the secretaries Philip Nigri and Louis Schoere, who had voted to retain the tax, declined the gratuities which the Hollanders offered them, for, they said, they had not performed a service to the province.[21] In the next century Chancellor Bacon was to argue the opposite: he had accepted gifts but had not acted corruptly because he had not allowed these gifts to influence his decisions.[22]

It is typical of this incident in the long saga of the *congie* and, generally, of the relations of the provincial Estates with their governors and with the central government that the lawyers in the regent's council started by arguing the case for the tax on theoretical grounds. Carondelet, the president of the Council of State, demanded of the Holland deputies to know whether they were arguing that the emperor did not have the power to do as he liked. The deputies would not allow themselves to be led on to the thin ice of political theory. They did not want to argue 'about the power of princes', they said; but they knew very well that the emperor would not want to do anything which would harm the country, and the proposed tax would do just that. The ministers then shifted their ground and argued that the other provinces had complained about the free export of grain, both because it raised prices in the Netherlands and because it gave the Hollanders

---

[19] *Ibid.*, vol. II, 143–4.
[20] *Ibid.*, vol. II, 41.
[21] Koenigsberger, 'Patronage and Bribery', 170–2. For the use of wainscotting as tips see J. Wagenaar, *Vaderlandsche Historie*, vol. V (Amsterdam, 1751), 104.
[22] J. Hurstfield, *The Queen's Wards* (London, 1958), 182–4.

Philip the Handsome (1494–1506)

an unfair advantage over the merchants from Zeeland. All this was probably quite true, but the decision was eventually taken from much more mundane considerations and certainly not because of the 'scholastic talk', as the secretary of Amsterdam scornfully characterised the lawyers' arguments.[23]

A similar pattern recurred when, a year later in March 1537, the government proposed the imposition of a chimney tax to pay for the renewed war with France. The Estates of Holland demanded the redress of grievances before voting for this tax. The most important of these grievances concerned the fisheries. The admiral, the seigneur de Beveren, had made an agreement with the admiral of France for the mutual issue of safe conducts. Beveren sold them at the rate of 15 stuivers per cod fisherman and 25 per herring fisherman. This, he claimed, was his right as admiral which he and his forebears had enjoyed for fifty years. His claim seemed justified to a court which thought highly of hereditary aristocratic property rights. They did not equally impress the Dutch fishermen nor the patrician town councils. The deputies of the Holland cities accused Beveren of having made a private deal with the French admiral at the expense of the Dutch fishing industry. What did they have to do with the admiral of the Netherlands, anyway? They would be commanded by their stadtholder, their governor, in the name of the emperor. This last argument was a recurring point of friction in a composite state. The Estates of Holland had made it before on other occasions. This time, the advocate stated his case before the Council of State so violently that Secretary Nigri said his words came close to rebellion. But the government desperately needed the agreement of the Estates of Holland and proposed a compromise. Hoochstraten, in his capacity as a member of the regent's council, promised the Estates that Beveren would grant 600 free safe conducts.

On this occasion, however, the Estates behaved tactlessly and failed to give Hoochstraten a present for his efforts on their behalf. This turned out to be a mistake. When the deputies tried to make the advocate's peace with the governor for his ill-considered speech in the council, Hoochstraten rounded on them. They were constantly asking him to plead their interests but they did not consult him and said things without asking his advice. They had given Beveren 'a fat gratuity', but not him. 'I am not as stupid as you take me for', Andries Jacopszoon, the secretary of Amsterdam, quotes him as saying. 'If someone gives me so much pleasure (pointing to his hand) I will give him that much pleasure (pointing to his forearm). But equally, if someone gives me so much displeasure, I will do the same to him or I will set him back as much (pointing as before). And do you think I keep pigs while others keep lambs?'[24] One of the deputies asked the governor whether he wanted a gratuity; Jacopszoon does not tell us whether disingenuously or ironically. Perhaps Hoochstraten did not know either; for all he answered was:

---

[23] Koenigsberger, *Estates and Revolutions*, 170.
[24] *Ibid.*, 174.

'You know what you have to do.' We have no indication that they gave him anything on this occasion. On other occasions the Estates of Holland had been quite generous and they had defended their governor against accusations of corruption.[25] Not surprisingly, however, Holland's quarrel with the admiral and the government over the safe conducts for the fishermen dragged on. In 1540 the emperor finally gave the solomonic judgement that each side should retain its rights.[26]

Everyone knew the language of *dominium regale* and *dominium politicum et regale*, even if they did not use Fortescue's terms. This language defined the basic attitudes of politicians and lawyers in government service and of the patricians of the city councils and their deputies in the Estates. The practice of government, however, was more down to earth. Strategically, effective government in Western Europe was based on the monarchy's alliance with the nobility, on increasing the efficiency of conciliar government by bringing in more professionals and on the extension of government authority in the country by the extension of the competence of royal courts at the expense of independent seigneurial, municipal and provincial jurisdiction. Tactically, effective government depended on patronage and clientage to make its wheels go round. Patronage and clientage were the civilian form of an earlier feudal–military relationship. The church had become part of this system; for the clergy were looking more and more to their own princes, rather than to Rome, for benefices and advancement in their careers. In return they provided the monarchies with the moral backing of their religious teaching.

The use of patronage was pervasive throughout society. Only very gradually did an ethos of public service gain ground among public officials. Francesco Taverna, Charles V's chancellor of Milan, refused to contribute to a government loan from his salary on the grounds that his salary was not a matter of grace, a *grazie*, which he might be expected to pledge in the hope of a future, better *grazie*. Rather, he argued, his salary was his due for the public services he performed. If he did not perform them satisfactorily he would expect to be dismissed. But such an attitude was still rare, especially outside Italy. Italy was the only part of Europe where the term 'state' was beginning to be used in its modern sense, before the second half of the sixteenth century.[27]

The necessary obverse of patronage was the judicious handing out of gifts to political patrons. Great lords, such as Hoochstraten, looked upon such gifts as their due. Here again we have a kind of civilian development of an earlier

---

[25] Jacopszoon, *Prothocolle*, vol. II, 217. Cf. Wagenaar, *Vaderlandsche Historie*, vol. V, 23ff.

[26] A. van der Goes, *Register van alle die Dachvaerden by deselve Staten gehouden*, vol. I, (The Hague, 1772), 379, marginal note.

[27] F. Chabod, *Lo stato di Milano nell'impero di Carlo V* (Rome, 1934), 172ff. The dukedom of Milan was often called *lo stato*, a term which did not imply anything about the nature of this political entity. Cf. M. Stolleis, 'Grundzüge der Beamtenethik (1550–1650)', in R. Schnur, ed., *Die Rolle der Juristen bei der Entstehung des modernen Staates* (Berlin, 1986), 273–302.

Philip the Handsome (1494–1506)

feudal–military relationship – although even this military relationship was far from dead, as the second half of the sixteenth century was to show, especially in France during the Wars of Religion. Where there was no clear patron–client relationship, as there was not in the case of Admiral Beveren and the Dutch fishermen, then the nobleman could expect a fee for his service. All officials in royal service, noble or commoner, would expect a fee, and this regardless of the salary they drew from the public purse. To the client, or to those dependent on a public service, gifts and fees appeared in a cruder light: they were simply bribes.

If this was a source of friction, a division between bourgeois and aristocratic mentality, it did not in itself prevent this society from functioning. The professional armies which the monarchies built up during this period were not primarily intended to uphold the power of the monarchies in their own states, although everyone knew that, on occasion, this might and did happen. The patrician city councils, having only very inadequate police forces and a not always reliable citizen militia to call upon, relied in the last resort on the prince's soldiers to contain riots and popular movements or to protect the city's and the citizens' property outside the city walls.[28] The main purpose of the princes' professional armies was rather to fight other monarchies. The principal relation of armies to society was twofold: firstly and most directly, people had to endure the impositions and robberies of their own prince's soldiers; secondly, they had to pay for the armies and navies and for their equipment, and for the enormously expensive new style of city fortifications which were coming into vogue. Here was the most immediate and most frequent point of friction between the prince and his subjects. In a *dominium politicum et regale* it dominated the relations between the prince and his provincial Estates and the States General.

Friction did not necessarily mean conflict. Clergy, nobles and townsmen, and their representatives in the assemblies of Estates, would generally be willing to support wars which appeared to be defensive. The right of princes to ask for aid in defensive wars had been generally accepted since the beginning of parliaments and even before that. Arguments between monarchy and Estates maintained a considerable degree of rationality, and agreement was helped precisely by what some were beginning to call corruption: the smooth functioning of the patronage–clientage and payment-for-favours relationships, of which Andries Jacopszoon, the secretary and deputy of Amsterdam, gives such splendid examples.[29] A century later, during the enormously difficult negotiations of the peace congress of Westphalia, they invented a special term for such practices: *Realdankbarkeit*, practical gratitude.

This system of monarchical government in the sixteenth century was resilient and adaptable; but it was not stable. When professional and centralising government

---

[28] For a discussion of this point see G. E. Wells, 'Antwerp and the Government of Philip II 1555–1567' (Cornell University Ph.D. thesis, 1982), ch. 1.
[29] Koenigsberger, *Estates and Revolutions*, 170–5.

came into conflict with the interests, traditions and preconceptions of persons, groups and institutions, and with their ancient and deeply cherished privileges; when the Reformation undermined the traditional alliance of monarchy and church and injected irreconcilable passions and mortal fear into politics; then previously manageable clashes of interest became unresolvable. When the expansionist aims of military establishments, i.e. the militaristically and dynastically thinking monarchies and their equally militaristic allies, the nobles, were balked by similar aims of rival monarchies; when the fuel of economic expansion ran out, as it did in Western Europe around 1550; then the engine of state power would come to a stop and parts of it would go into reverse, fracturing the whole political system.

What then made such a crisis particularly difficult to resolve was the fact that it did not take place in a closed political system. Almost no European monarchies were national and unitary but composite, made up of pre-existing and often ethnically and linguistically divergent political units. Thus the French crown had only recently acquired the duchy of Brittany and, at times, it held the kingdom of Naples and the duchy of Milan. The king of England, or his eldest son, was also prince of Wales and Henry VIII elevated Ireland into a separate kingdom. The crowns of Aragon and Castile, each composed of several kingdoms and principalities, including in the case of Aragon the overseas crowns of Naples, Sicily and Sardinia, had recently been joined by the marriage of Ferdinand and Isabella.[30] By contrast, they acquired the kingdom of Granada, thus adding a large heterodox component to the already multi-religious population of the Spanish union. The Swiss cantons had voluntarily come together in a complex system of loose federations. The three Scandinavian crowns of Denmark, Norway and Sweden, the latter incorporating the duchy of Finland, had been joined since the end of the fourteenth century under the Danish crown which itself incorporated several duchies of the Holy Roman Empire. Poland was joined with Lithuania, and the crowns of Bohemia and Hungary each incorporated politically, ethnically and sometimes religiously diverse counties, duchies and even kingdoms.

The condition of *dominium politicum et regale* was admirably adapted to the needs of composite monarchies and goes a long way towards explaining their prevalence in early modern Europe. A prince could add province after province, kingdom after kingdom to his realm and rule each under different laws and with different powers, and the prince would swear to maintain these laws at his accession or when he acquired a new dominion. In practice there were, of course, points of friction. Princes liked to rely on advisers from their original or native dominions. They would favour their closest friends and compatriots when they dispensed

---

[30] As was often the case in early modern Europe, the legal position of both the crowns and of the rulers was ambiguous. The infanta Isabella ('the Catholic') had to defend her dubious claims to the throne of Castile against her niece. She married the infante Ferdinand of Aragon in 1469 and succeeded to the throne of Castile in 1474. Ferdinand succeeded to that of Aragon in 1479.

patronage; or, even if they did not actually do so, it would be thought that they did. The provinces defended themselves with the *ius indigenatus*, by which only natives of each particular dominion were allowed to be appointed to public offices or given ecclesiastical benefices. The provinces of the Netherlands defended this right tenaciously, both against their prince and against each other, and they also defended their right to have their laws published in their own language. Both in the Netherlands and in other composite monarchies, quarrels over appointments contrary to the *ius indigenatus* were common enough. By themselves they did not usually lead to major political crises, but they could certainly aggravate those which had arisen for other reasons.

There was therefore nothing unusual in the composite monarchy which the dukes of Burgundy had put together in the Netherlands. Moreover, in the crisis of 1477 the provinces had shown that they wanted to preserve their union, however much they might dislike the late duke's invasion of their autonomy. Nevertheless, the duchess Mary's marriage to Maximilian of Austria had introduced a complication. The main concern of the ruler of the Netherlands was now no longer the Netherlands themselves but had shifted outside to this ruler's dominions which were not contiguous with the Netherlands and which, of necessity, had different interests, concerns and priorities. A similar complication would apply to Ireland, or Naples or Milan when under French rule, but not to their metropolitan countries. For the Netherlands, this problem became first apparent in Maximilian's relations with France. It became even more evident when he left the Netherlands in the middle of a civil war to devote himself to the problems of his Austrian duchies.

Two results followed immediately. The first was that, to the menace from its neighbours which all countries had to face in more or less acute form, there was now added the much more complicated and threatening involvement with their prince's foreign policy in distant parts of Europe. In other words, the metropolitan country, or union of countries, was no longer master of its international relations – a condition of which the Italian dominions of the crown of Aragon already had long experience. So, for that matter, had the duchy of Burgundy and Franche-Comté. During the reigns of the first three Burgundian dukes of the Netherlands, Philip the Bold, John the Fearless and Philip the Good, they had been the junior partners of the dukes' composite monarchy. Charles the Bold's expansionist policies in Lorraine reversed this relationship to the disadvantage of the *pays de pardeça*, the Netherlands, and the revolution of 1477 was to some extent directed precisely against this reversal. With the Habsburgs, the interests of the Netherlands came to be subordinated to even more grandiose imperial plans than those of Charles the Bold. Maximilian dreamt of reconquering Constantinople for Christendom. To this end he sought to create a system of dynastic alliances, ranging from the Yorkists in England to the Jagiellon kings of Hungary, and including the Sforza dukes of Milan and, depending on the current political circumstances, either France or Spain.[31] Charles V picked up his paternal grandfather's ideas, and he had the added advantage of being king of Spain, a country with its own Christian–imperialist traditions. Its king, Charles V's other grandfather, Ferdinand of Aragon, had not only conquered Granada from the Moors but had obtained for himself and his heirs the claims of the Palaeologi to the imperial throne of Byzantium.[32] In such ecumenical visions the immediate interests of the Netherlands were bound to take second place in the political thinking of their rulers.

The second immediate result of the new position was the personal absence of the prince from the Netherlands. The effects of this absence were visible at once and they were continuous. When previous dukes had left the Netherlands, usually to campaign abroad, this had always occurred with the definite understanding that they would return at the end of the campaign. But when Maximilian left the Netherlands, in 1489, and appointed Albert of Saxony as governor, it was by no means clear when, or indeed whether, he would return or return for more than short periods at a time.[33]

THE REIGN OF PHILIP THE HANDSOME

Albert of Saxony was a very successful governor and there is little evidence that the Netherlanders had resented him in the way they had resented Maximilian. Even so, they took the first opportunity to declare their young duke, Philip, the son of Maximilian of Austria and Mary of Burgundy, to be of age (1494). The Netherlands now had their own resident prince again.

Philip the Handsome's reign started auspiciously. He had been brought up among the great lords of the southern Netherlands and he now appointed these lords as his councillors, with the Croy clan in a dominant role. Their policy was what it had been since the days of the duke's great grandfather, Philip the Good: peace with France, accommodation with Guelders and cooperation with the Estates.

Between 1495 and August 1506 the States General were summoned twenty-four times. Not all provinces sent delegates to all sessions; but with growing frequency of meeting, there developed also growing regularity and mutual knowledge. Artois, Flanders, Brabant, Hainaut, Holland, Lille-Douai-Orchies, Namur and Zeeland nearly always sent their delegates. Malines did so sometimes and Luxembourg and the Pays d'Outremeuse only rarely. With peace now reigning at home and abroad, the main object of the sessions was again what it had been in the time of Philip the Good: the problems of currency and the circulation of money. These were difficult and highly technical problems; but, judging from the rather sparse reports we have

---

[31] H. Angermeier, 'Der Wormser Reichstag 1495 in der politischen Konzeption König Maximilians I', in H. Lutz, ed., *Das römisch-deutsche Reich im politischen System Karls V* (Munich, 1982), 1–13.

[32] J. M. Headley, 'Germany, the Empire and *Monarchia* in the Thought and Policy of Gattinara', in *ibid.*, 15–33.

[33] See above, ch. 3.

Philip the Handsome (1494–1506)

of the meetings, the duke's government was quite willing to accept the advice of the States General.[34] For their part, the States General did not object to granting the relatively modest sums needed for the journey of the archduchess Margaret, first to Spain, to marry the infante Don Juan and, after his early death, to Savoy, to marry Duke Philibert II.[35]

The real difficulties arose from two interconnected problems: that of Maximilian and that of Charles of Egmont, duke of Guelders. It soon became apparent that Maximilian still regarded the Netherlands as part of his family domain and as an integral part of his proposed grand alliance against the Turks. To emphasise the unity of this composite monarchy he proposed to set up an Austrian chapter of the Order of the Golden Fleece. Not surprisingly, the Burgundian and Netherlands knights showed little enthusiasm for this plan.[36] But in 1496 Philip felt obliged to travel to Innsbruck to listen to his father's views. Philip and his advisers were quite willing to accept Maximilian's plans for a double Spanish marriage, of Philip to Juana and of Margaret to Don Juan. It was intended, in the first place, to ensure the alliance of Spain against the ever-threatening policies of France. The Netherlanders, however, resisted the emperor's proposals to incorporate the duchy of Guelders in the Netherlands and to revive the Burgundian claims against France. In August 1498 Philip concluded the Treaty of Paris with Louis XII which effectively reaffirmed the Treaty of Senlis. Philip gave up the pursuit of Netherlands claims to the duchies of Burgundy and of Guelders. He explained to the States General, in December of that year, that it would require a great deal of money and the cooperation of the Estates if he were to restart the war as his father wished, and he would not do this without the States General's advice.[37]

It was a clear declaration of the virtues of government with the consent of the governed. But was Philip really declaring his own political principles? And did he really have any choice in the matter? Some outside observers, at any rate, took a rather cynical view of the situation. Fuensalida, the Spanish envoy at Philip's court, thought that he was being manipulated by France and that his francophile councillors 'dragged him from banquet to banquet and from lady to lady'.[38] The Venetian ambassador thought he could detect the influence of Maximilian and saw Philip in a 'labyrinth' between his father and his councillors.[39] In other words, the

---

[34] E.g. in the States General of 4–12 Sept. 1501. AGRB, Copies du régistre aux mémoriaux de Béthune (i.e. copies from the Archives communales de Béthune), B.B.3, fos. 190v, 200v.
[35] Wellens, Etats Généraux, 242–3, 255–7. The city of Gouda, however, would have liked to deny the requests. See L. M. Rollin Couquerque and A. Meerkamp van Embden, eds., 'Goudsche Vroedschapsresoluties betreffende dagvaarten der staten van Holland en der Staten-Generaal, 1501–1524', BMHG, 37 (1916), 65.
[36] Gachard, Lettres inédites de Maximilien, pt. 2, 270–80.
[37] Wellens, Etats Généraux, 238–46.
[38] Duke of Berwick and Alba, Correspondencia de Gutierrez Gomez de Fuensalida (Madrid, 1907), XXVI.
[39] See note 1.

interests of a part of a composite monarchy could not always be made to coincide with the interests of the monarchy as a whole; and *dominium politicum et regale*, government with the consent of the governed, could not resolve this ultimate opposition.

A settlement with Guelders proved more difficult than the settlement with France. Charles the Bold had annexed the duchy with only the thinnest of legal justifications. The emperor Frederick III had then invested Maximilian and Mary with this imperial fief and, in 1504, Maximilian in his turn invested Philip with the duchy. Charles of Egmont, the son of the last independent duke, returned to a welcoming duchy in 1492 and, naturally, would not recognise the imperial investitures of the Habsburgs. Half-hearted attempts to settle the legal issue failed. Duke Charles naturally looked to France for support but had to experience the unreliability of an ally willing to support him only if such support fitted in with its own great-power politics. The result was forty years of local warfare, punctuated by armistices and treaties which failed to resolve the fundamental problem of the diametrically opposed claims of Egmont and Habsburg.[40]

For many years the States General were unwilling to pay for any action against Guelders. It was the private business of the ruling family, they argued. Maximilian was outraged. 'You are not the judge in this matter', he proclaimed to the States General, in February 1503; 'rather you are obliged to follow the true judge, that is the sovereign lord of the said land of Guelders, which we are'.[41] Not until 1505 did the States General vote substantial sums for the Guelders war, and then only as part of the 400,000 florins which Philip demanded primarily for his journey to Spain.[42]

But Maximilian had more ambitious plans than the reconquest of Guelders and more far-reaching claims on support from the States General. Already in 1499 he had written a long letter to them pointing to his great restraint in turning down the offer of 100,000 florins a year.[43] Instead, he asked for some compensation for his efforts, as well as money for a campaign to force France to agree to a more favourable treaty than the treaty of Paris of the previous year and for an eventual crusade against the Turks. The delegates of the States General discussed this matter among themselves and evidently thought little of it. But, to cover themselves, they referred Maximilian's demands back to their principals who turned them down flat.[44]

During Philip's first visit to Spain, in 1502–3, Maximilian spent some time in the Netherlands and returned to the attack. In February 1503 he demanded an *aide* of 100,000 florins, again for his crusade agains the Turks. Again the States General refused, arguing that they had to keep the country's resources intact in case any

---

[40] W. J. Formsma, 'De onderwerping van Friesland, het Sticht en Gelre', *AGN*, vol. IV, ch. 4.
[41] Quoted in Wellens, *Etats Généraux*, 261.
[42] *Ibid.*, 265–9.
[43] See above, ch. 3.
[44] Wellens, *Etats Généraux*, 249.

Philip the Handsome (1494-1506)

mishap befell their natural prince during his journey. Maximilian replied in his most grandiloquent style: if anything happened to his son, would he not immediately throw all his resources into the fight, which was more than they could do? Then he spoiled even the rhetorical effect: if they would not grant him the 100,000 florins, would they at least lend him 200 livres?[45]

Philip's second journey to Spain was a much more serious matter than his first. After Isabella the Catholic's death, on 26 November 1504, Philip claimed the crown of Castile for his wife Juana and himself, against the counter-claims of Ferdinand of Aragon. It would cost a lot more money to make good this claim and the government of the Netherlands therefore sold off or alienated a huge amount of domain property and domain rights. Many of the buyers were members of the high nobility or courtiers. To get quick results, for speed seemed to be of the essence, it was sometimes necessary to force buyers to bid for rights of jurisdiction or river tolls, 'on pain of incurring the sovereign's displeasure'.[46]

In January 1505 Philip asked the States General for an *aide* of 400,000 florins, payable over four years. Nobles and clergy were willing to support this venture. The towns showed less enthusiasm and the delegates of Flanders wanted to put off a decision. Eventually, in March, the States General followed Brabant in a reluctant approval.[47] Philip and Juana set sail in January 1506. Their disastrous journey started with the dubious reception they received from Henry VII, when bad weather drove their ships into English ports in March; it ended with Philip's sudden death in Burgos on 26 September 1506.

Philip had left Guillaume de Croy, seigneur de Chièvres, as his lieutenant general of the Netherlands, with a council of five of whom three were also Croys. Charles of Egmont who, only a year earlier, had been forced to conclude a humiliating truce, started hostilities again as soon as Philip had left the country. Since he was evidently receiving encouragement and help from France, even the francophile Croy government had to take action. Chièvres summoned the States General for the 22 August 1506 and asked for money for a levy of 8,000 infantry and 1,500 cavalry. The States General were lukewarm, and Chièvres reduced his proposal to 4,000 infantry and 1,000 cavalry. The deputies went home to consult their principals who showed little enthusiasm even for the reduced demand.

News of Philip's death arrived on 3 October and the council summoned the States General to reassemble on the 15th, 'to aid and advise as may be necessary, and without reference back, on all matters needful for the good and welfare of our said lord and his lands', i.e. for the young archduke Charles, later Charles V. Here was a typical succession crisis, the evident succession of a minor. But no one, except perhaps Chièvres and the council, seems to have thought of it with the

---

[45] Maximilian to Bruges, Antwerp, 18 March 1503. Gachard, *Lettres inédites*, pt. 2, 301-3.
[46] A. Henne, *Histoire du règne de Charles Quint en Belgique*, 10 vols. (Brussels, 1858-60), vol. I, 63 n.1, 64 n.1. BBR, MS 13352-69, fo. 192r.
[47] Wellens, *Etats Généraux*, 265-7.

urgency which was so evident in the crisis following the death of Charles the Bold in 1477. We know about the session of the States General mainly from the reports of Jehan Clauwin, secretary of the town of Béthune in Artois.[48] When the chancellor addressed the assembly in Malines, on 18 October, he admitted immediately that he did not actually speak as chancellor because his own and every other official's office had legally terminated with the duke's death. By implication, the States General were therefore the only body which could function on their own authority. But no one actually spelt this out or discussed the constitutional implications of this position. Everyone, however, expected the States General to take the necessary decisions. They did immediately confirm the council and the courts in their offices, although they argued about whether this should be done for two or four months, and the Brabanters wanted the treasury officials first to present their accounts. The government therefore functioned by the grace and authority of the States General. There were precedents for such a situation, at least in Brabant, from as early as the fourteenth century.[49]

On other issues proceedings continued in slow motion. All agreed that they had to remain united and they hardly needed a schoolmasterish letter from Henry VII to tell them so. This letter came, after all, from the king who had only recently taken advantage of their prince's forced visit to England to impose on him the *Malus Intercursus*, a trade treaty very unfavourable to the Netherlands. Now Henry was manoeuvring to marry Margaret of Austria, although nothing came of it.

THE SECOND REGENCY OF MAXIMILIAN I

The States General faced two rather more urgent problems. The first was the regency and tutorship for the young archduke and the second was the defence of the country against France and Guelders. Maximilian claimed the tutorship and the regency for his grandson as of right. The majority of the provinces were willing to accept his claim. But Flanders and Artois were fiefs of the French crown, and Louis XII had forty days in which legally to claim the regency for himself. The Flemings had their own unhappy memories of a regency of Maximilian. Artois had every reason to be scared of the French. During the years of French occupation after 1477, Louis XI had treated Artois as a conquered province and had forced the citizens of Arras to leave their city and their property – a type of wholesale punishment for the rebellion of a few which was happily less common in the fifteenth century than in the twentieth. In the event, Louis XII was more concerned with Milan than with Flanders and he allowed the forty days to pass without action.

---

[48] AGRB, Mémoriaux de Béthune, fos. 93–101.
[49] W. P. Blockmans, 'Alternatives to Monarchical Centralisation: The Great Tradition of Revolt in Flanders and Brabant', in Koenigsberger and Müller-Luckner, *Republiken und Republikanismus*, 145–54.

Philip the Handsome (1494–1506)

The deputies of the States General talked and negotiated with each other for nearly a month and, at times, returned to their provinces for further advice and instructions. The Flemings were accused by the Brabanters of doing this deliberately in order to spin out the matter of the regency. In the end they all agreed on Maximilian, if only because there was no one else with even a remotely legal claim. Some delegates mentioned Queen Juana, Prince Charles's mother; but perhaps they did not know of her mental condition and, in any case, she was in Spain. On defence there was a general consensus that something had to be done and that it had to be paid for, but must nevertheless be kept as cheap as possible. For this purpose, everything possible was to be done to keep peace with France and Guelders. It took the Estates a long time to realise that they could not square the circle of making Charles of Egmont keep agreements while their prince denied him the legal right to keep his duchy. As yet, the Hollanders complained only of a Gueldrian cattle raid during the armistice. In the following years the Gueldrian raids escalated and were to become a deadly danger to the Hollanders and Brabanters.

On 16 November a delegation of the States General left Malines to offer Maximilian the regency. To the delegates' surprise, Maximilian deliberately evaded them, always retreating eastwards. Not until January 1507 did he finally receive them in Innsbruck. He had convinced himself that French agents had poisoned Philip. Now he claimed the regency of Castile for himself and was planning to make good this claim under cover of a crusade in North Africa. Unhappily, the Venetians would not allow him to march his army over the Alpine passes. As a second best he therefore offered Ferdinand of Aragon the rule over Italy and perhaps even the imperial title (which of course was not Maximilian's to give) if Ferdinand would accept their common grandson, Charles of Burgundy, as heir in Spain.[50] Ferdinand was not fooled by these offers, but he did accept Charles as his heir, although later he had second thoughts about this.

Maximilian's Spanish plans preoccupied him more than the regency of the Netherlands about which he seems to have had little anxiety. Once it had been formally offered to him, he appointed his daughter Margaret to act in his name. In April 1507 the States General made no difficulty about accepting the sister of their late ruler and a native of the Netherlands as their new regent.[51]

In the succession crisis of 1506–7 everyone had behaved true to character. Maximilian veered from deepest depression to the most grandiose visions for himself and his house, but then settled for the attainable. The king of England remained on the sidelines, giving moral advice. The king of France made threatening noises but failed to move decisively because his immediate interests lay in Italy rather than in Flanders. The duke of Guelders took the opportunity to recapture

---

[50] Wiesflecker, *Maximilian*, vol. I, 152–5. Wiesflecker's evaluation of these plans is more positive than mine.

[51] R. Wellens, 'Les Etats Généraux et la succession de Philippe le Beau dans les Pays-Bas', *APAE*, 56 (1972), 153–9. I have substantially followed Wellens' account.

several of his towns but, in the absence of effective support from France, made only a few discreet raids outside his own frontiers. The Netherlands council, dominated by the Croy family, was diffident about its own authority but tried to preserve the smooth working of the government. The Estates were anxious to preserve the union, just as they had been in 1477, and to prevent chaos. Their delegates negotiated with each other in the States General, often even without reference back to their principals, to allow the unpopular Maximilian his legal rights as regent and tutor of his grandchildren. In contrast to 1477, neither the States General nor the Estates of any individual province tried to control the government. All parties were willing to cooperate, even though each player, including the individual provinces, was also playing his own game. The constitutional problems which arose were recognised as such, but none of the parties were anxious to pursue them. In contrast to the aftermath of Charles the Bold's autocratic regime, there was now sufficient trust between the parties for *dominium politicum et regale* to function, if not smoothly, at least effectively, and the States General had become an indispensable part of this functioning.

5

Dominium politicum et regale in a composite monarchy: the regencies of Margaret of Austria (1507–1530)

'One has to make a virtue of necessity and accept gracefully what one can, just as it is done here and in other of His Majesty's realms and lands.'
Marginal comment by Charles V, Toledo, 31 Oct. 1525, to the Mémoire au Seigneur de Praet ... de la part de Madame (Margaret of Austria)[1]

MARGARET OF AUSTRIA'S FIRST REGENCY, 1507–1515

The conditions of a *dominium politicum et regale* regime within the composite monarchy of the Habsburgs, established in the reign of Philip the Handsome, set the tone for his sister's first regency. It started effectively with Margaret's commission from her father and its acceptance by the States General, although her formal appointment did not take place until 1509. Once the constitutional questions of the succession and the regency had been settled, politics came to revolve around two problems. The first was who would take the ultimate decisions in foreign policy and with what ends in view. Were these ends simply the defence of the Netherlands against aggression from outside or were they the interests of an international monarchy? The second problem was who controlled government patronage, i.e. appointments to ministerial, military and judicial posts, to provincial governorships, to all types of profitable minor administrative positions and to ecclesiastical benefices. This second problem, of patronage, was often a matter of personalities and local interests; but in any case the two problems of foreign policy and patronage were closely linked. It was the States General which had to pay for defence, and relations between the government and the States General depended, in their turn, on the control of patronage.

Margaret's first major act was to break the ascendency of the Croy in the council and to balance the francophile policies of these Walloon seigneurs by the appointment of Jean de Berghes and other lords whose estates and centres of interest were situated in Brabant. Unlike the great cities of Flanders, for whom the English

---

[1] BBR, MS 16068–72, fo. 158.

Plate 7 Bernard-Barend van Orley, *Margaret of Austria*. Musées royaux des beaux-arts de Belgique © IRPA/KIK, Brussels

The regencies of Margaret of Austria (1507–1530)

merchants were commercial rivals and who therefore preferred friendship with France whenever French policy allowed this, Antwerp and the other Brabant cities saw the English as trading partners whose semi-finished cloths they imported and worked up for a European market. The Brabant nobility derived much of their income from lordship over small manufacturing towns or from ownership or leaseholds of local river and canal tolls. They were able to cream off some of the profits of the Brabant trade with the English and they were therefore naturally inclined to be anglophile.

Margaret's personal preferences, at least at this stage of her career, were decidedly anti-French. Having spent much of her childhood in France as the fiancée of the dauphin, she could not easily forgive being jilted in favour of the heiress of Brittany. She now presided over a council in which her noble councillors were divided in their foreign policy preferences. She therefore came to rely much more than previous rulers of the Netherlands on the professional lawyers in her council. Most of these came from Franche-Comté. After Philip the Handsome's death, Maximilian had given her Franch-Comté as a personal possession for life. It was a fief of the Holy Roman Empire and not subject to the French crown. French-speaking, but not French – and certainly not German – this was a part of Europe where the traditions of the Carolingian Empire and of the Holy Roman Empire were still alive; and this especially at the university of Dôle and its school of Roman law. Highly qualified intellectuals from a small and poor country tend to look for careers beyond its boundaries. The Valois dukes of Burgundy had brought some of the graduates from Dôle to the Netherlands in the fifteenth century. Now, with the widening of the Netherlands' political horizons, with its prince expecting to acquire the crowns of Spain and even that of the Holy Roman Empire, and with the regent's personal connections with this central part of Europe, the Franche-Comtois lawyers found their natural home in the councils of the Netherlands.[2]

Yet Margaret could not govern with the professionals alone. She needed the great lords as military commanders and as provincial governors; for neither the soldiers in wartime, nor the local nobility in peacetime would obey anyone else. She also needed them to manage the States General and the provincial Estates; for, as she wrote to Maximilian, the nobles must 'each in his region work on and persuade the common people to renew the *aides*', because in the assemblies the common people generally followed the lead to the gentlemen of the province.[3] This was of course the usual pattern in most of Europe.[4] Among the seigneurs francophilia or anglophilia were preferences based on their family and property interests. These were ways of thinking, rather than the basis of organised parties. Personal and family ambitions tended to determine tactical positions, and rivalries

---

[2] Walther, *Anfänge*, 15–26.
[3] *Ibid.*, 103–4.
[4] Cf. H. G. Koenigsberger, 'The Parliament of Piedmont during the Renaissance, 1460–1560', in *Estates and Revolutions*, 52–3.

arising from these could, at times, make the lords uncooperative. But they no longer fought each other or the regency government in the way Philip of Cleves had done in the 1480s and 1490s, and even this doughty champion of the medieval *ius resistendi*, old and disillusioned now, was content to rest on his dubious laurels.

But Margaret's government was no more in full control of Netherlands foreign policy than her brother's had been. Maximilian continued to interfere and to interfere unpredictably, except in the consistency of his claims to Guelders. Duke Charles, for his part, was equally consistent in being unwilling to give in. Political divisions in the bishopric of Utrecht and in Groningen and Friesland allowed him to extend his influence along the north-eastern flank of the Netherlands, and his mercenary bands raided deep into Holland and Brabant.

To get the support of the States General, Maximilian now changed his tune. In 1503 he had argued that his claim to Guelders was entirely his business and that the only business of the prince's subjects was to support him. Now he admitted that it was a matter of cooperation. 'What touches the king or prince of the country', he wrote to the Estates in August 1508, 'touches all his subjects and, conversely, everything that touches the subjects touches the king or prince of the country; for there have never been principalities without community, nor community without principality or government.' They should all now go to the assistance of Holland, for they were allied together as countries belonging to him and as confrères they were obliged to prevent all injuries to one of them and give him all aid, comfort and assistance. Moreover, at the last States General, at Ghent in February 1508, they had specifically promised to help and assist one another whenever one was attacked.[5]

Here was a clear statement of the purposes of a composite monarchy and particularly of the union of the Netherlands provinces. Yet neither the prince nor the provinces, represented by the States General, supported such purposes consistently. Maximilian, as the Netherlanders knew very well, had his own, private aims; although even the most cynical could hardly have predicted that in 1511 Maximilian would plan to bribe the cardinals to elect him pope or anti-pope. At that time he wrote teasingly to his daughter that then he would become a saint and she would have to adore him, which would give him great satisfaction. Characteristically, his main reasons for this plan seem to have been financial: he wanted to separate the German church from Rome and get his hands on the considerable sums which the German church regularly paid to the papacy.[6] That was, after all, more or less what Henry VIII was to do with the English church, some twenty years later, although Henry was to be content with being a kind of pope in England.

---

[5] Gachard, *Lettres inédites de Maximilien*, pt. 2, 310–11.
[6] H. Wiesflecker, 'Neue Beiträge zur Frage des Kaiser-Papstplans Maximilians I', *MIÖG*, 71 (1963), 311–29.

The regencies of Margaret of Austria (1507–1530)

In the Netherlands the provinces continued to argue that the Guelders war concerned only Holland and Brabant. Thus, in 1512, the deputies of Artois were instructed to say in the States General that their own province was the frontier and bulwark against France, that France was a more powerful and dangerous enemy than Guelders, that their contributions to defence had gone on for much longer than those of Brabant and Holland, and that Artois had spent much more money than those provinces.[7]

The uncertainty about the true centre of decision-making between Margaret's government and the constantly journeying Maximilian also made Netherlands defence policy and the resources which needed to be devoted to it uncertain. As a result the government was nearly always on the defensive in its relations with the States General. At Malines, in July 1507, Margaret proposed a hearth tax of one philipus gulden, to be paid by every household. This type of tax was not new and, of course, it bore more heavily on the poor than on the rich. But at least this time, and for the first time, it was to be paid by everyone, without the usual exemptions for the clergy, the nobility and government officials. Since it was an open-ended tax, without an agreed global sum, Artois claimed that Louis XII would see it as a deliberate provocation, a specific help to Maximilian, and that he had already threatened reprisals.[8] Brabant objected that the new tax would mean it had to compile a new census.[9] In the end, the Estates rejected the tax proposal and offered a modest conventional *aide* instead.

Things went better for the government after Margaret won her first great diplomatic success, the conclusion of the League of Cambrai (10 Dec. 1508). A unique constellation of forces in Italy brought together Maximilian, Pope Julius II, Ferdinand of Aragon, Louis XII and several small Italian states in a disreputable offensive alliance against the republic of Venice. The Netherlands government played a key role in the negotiations which brought about a temporary reconciliation between the emperor and France, with the consequent diplomatic isolation of Charles of Guelders. Louis XII saw to it that Duke Charles was included in the treaty, but he was required to give up all his conquests of the last three years.[10] Margaret's government took this opportunity to make its biggest demand yet on the States General. In March 1509, after arduous negotiations, the States General made the remarkable grant of 500,000 écus, payable over three years, for demobilising the troops of the Guelders wars. There were also handsome grants to Margaret personally and smaller ones to various imperial ministers.[11]

---

[7] AGRB, Régistre aux mémoriaux de Béthune, BBR, MS 5, fos. 26r–31r.
[8] *Ibid.*, fos. 112r–121r.
[9] Cuvelier, *Dénombrements des foyers*, CCCVIII.
[10] W. J. Formsma, 'De onderwerping van Gelre', in *AGN*, vol. IV, 77.
[11] L. P. Gachard, 'Actes de l'archiduchesse Marguerite', in *BCRH*. ser. 3. vol. I, 3348–51. L. Ph. C. van den Bergh, *Gedenkstukken*, vol. II, 156–60.

But the war with Guelders broke out again and went badly, and now the Estates were much less forthcoming. By February 1512 Margaret was reduced to asking the States General whether the war should be continued in the spring – it would need at least 6,000 foot and 1,200 horse – or whether she should negotiate a peace. Even if she did that she would need 200,000 florins to pay the garrisons and there were still 120,000 owing to the troops. The government claimed that the *aides* previously granted had never produced as much revenue as they had been intended to produce because of the many rebates (*gracien*, graces) which the towns always negotiated. The States General replied that they wanted peace. Brabant would not even pay for its frontier guards, and the deputies of 's-Hertogenbosch suggested to the other towns that they should treat directly with Guelders. Only when Gueldrian troops actually threatened Brabant did the province agree to an *aide* of 150,000 florins and then persuaded a reluctant Flanders to agree.[12]

Through the autumn of 1512 and throughout 1513 Margaret's letters to her father became more and more desperate. 'The provinces are so obstinate now [*en si mauvaise voulenté*] and the people are so full of malicious talk that I am very much afraid that, unless we can find some remedy, evil will come of it,' she wrote in November 1512.

> Therefore, Monseigneur, I beg you yet again to have pity on me for I do not know which way to turn. Trying to do my best, I have contributed personally all I possess and I have lent so much that I have not got a penny left and all is lost. I assure you, Monseigneur, that I feel so bad about all this that I am in danger of falling ill and many times I have wished I were still in my mother's belly.

Not surprisingly, her secretary, Marnix, like the good civil servant he was, would not let her send these passages. But we have got the drafts.[13]

From March 1513 we have got another letter to Maximilian, in similar mood. The States General were so evilly disposed that they could not be managed in any way without his coming. One wonders whether Margaret really wanted Maximilian to come or just to take responsibility for the situation in which her government found itself largely on his account; for she continued that because people had always found her following his wishes, both in the Guelders business and in everything else, they were now murmuring against her, 'no doubt egged on by some evil spirits'. They were saying that she only wanted to continue this war in order to destroy them. There might well be a popular uprising and there had already been scurrilous placards posted on church doors in Malines (her preferred residence). She finished again on a theatrical note: 'If all was to be lost for the sake of a thousand florins, the Treasurer tells me he would not be able to find them.'[14]

---

[12] Henne, *Histoire de Charles Quint*, vol. I, 287–94. AGRB, Régistre aux mémoriaux de Béthune, BBR, MS 5, fos. 26r–31r.
[13] Walther, 'Hubert Kreiten, Briefwechsel', *Göttingische Gelehrte Anzeigen*, 170 (1908), 166.
[14] Ibid., 380. A. Le Glay, *Correspondance de l'empereur Maximilien 1er et de Marguerite d'Autriche*, 2 vols. (Paris, 1839), vol. I, 504–7.

Maximilian proved no help and only made the lame suggestion that Margaret should tell the States General that it was all Charles of Egmont's fault and that the provinces must defend each other. This was, of course, what she had been saying to the States General all along. Now even Maximilian was persuaded that negotiations with Duke Charles could no longer be avoided. In a treaty, signed on 31 July 1513, Charles of Egmont achieved considerable gains and perhaps the most important was that, for the first time, the Netherlands government referred to him officially as duke of Guelders and count of Zutphen. Less than a year later he marched into Arnhem, in clear breach of the treaty.[15]

There was one innovation which Margaret's government proposed to the States General, apparently simply as a tactic to get agreement on a request for money, but which turned out to have far-reaching political and constitutional implications. In the States General of Malines, in February 1512, some deputies complained that money, which they had voted on previous occasions, had been used very inefficiently. The number of men-at-arms was not what it should have been, and too much was paid out to non-existent soldiers. This was a common complaint everywhere in Europe during this period, and it was the natural result of the universal system of employing military entrepreneurs. No one could see an alternative; but that did not make it any sweeter for those who had to provide the funds. The immediate reaction of Margaret's ministers to the grumbles of the deputies seems to have been irritation. Those who wanted to know how the money had been spent in the past, they said, should go to the war treasurer; and anyway, if anything had gone wrong it was because there had not been enough money in time. This was what the deputies of Artois reported about this session. But then the ministers went much further. Madame had agreed, they told the States General, that in future the council and representatives of the Estates should jointly appoint the officers of the *gendarmerie* and also reform and supervise it. Or, if they knew of any better way, Madame would listen to them, for Monseigneur (the archduke Charles), at his age (he was twelve), had no one to turn to but his loyal subjects.[16]

When Margaret wrote about this meeting of the States General to Maximilian she stressed that she had taken them into her confidence on the advice of the 'greater and saner part of the council'. This was the usual medieval formula for rulers who kept to the rules. Margaret did not mention the actual proposals but complained that the deputies had wasted time by not discussing her proposals together.[17]

In March, the Estates of Artois, meeting in Arras, discussed the government's demands for money but not, it seems, the proposals of the Estates' participation in the appointment of army officers or of the administration of army pay.[18] We do not

---

[15] Forsma, 'De onderwerping van Gelre', 78.
[16] AGRB, Régistre ... Béthune, BBR, MS 5, fos. 26r–31r.
[17] M. Bruchet and E. Lancien, *L'itinéraire de Marguerite d'Autriche* (Lille, 1934), 351.
[18] AGRB, Régistre ... Béthune, BBR, MS 5, fos. 26r–31r.

know whether any of the other provincial Estates took up the government's proposals; but it seems unlikely.

At the end of the year the government repeated its proposals of the Estates' supervision of defence spending, but found again that the Estates were more interested in peace than in advancing their control over the administration.[19] After their unhappy experience of 1477 and of Maximilian's first regency, the Estates did not show themselves anxious to take over executive functions from the government. In August 1506, in the last States General of Philip the Handsome's reign, it was proposed that the four 'capital cities' of Brabant, Brussels, Louvain, Antwerp and 's-Hertogenbosch, should administer the collection of *aides*. It was not a new idea. In 1473 Charles the Bold himself had made a similar proposal, although it is not quite clear whether it was ever implemented. Certainly, in 1506, the four cities refused to have anything to do with such a plan.[20] But in the summer of 1513 the Estates of Flanders voted 120,000 écus for strengthening the garrisons against France, and this time they insisted that the troops should be under the orders of their governor, the seigneur de Fiennes, and of commissioners appointed by the four Members of Flanders.[21]

It is possible that the Flemings remembered a similar arrangement they had insisted on when Maximilian was their prisoner in Bruges,[22] and perhaps this same memory was the reason why Margaret preferred not to mention the details of her proposal to her father. During her second regency, in the 1520s, Estates' control over financial administration was to become a serious issue, at least in the larger provinces. By 1559, together with the question of the joint discussions of the deputies in the States General, the question of who should control the financial administration had moved to the very centre, at least of the formal problems of the relations between the monarchy and the States General.

Nothing of this was foreseen or was foreseeable in 1513. A weak and divided government, in military and financial straits, had quite naturally turned for help to the States General. The provinces represented in this body had responded in an entirely traditional manner, granting some financial help although much less than the government had asked for, emphasising their willingness to cooperate but also recounting all the previous help they had given and insisting on their inability to do more. As always nearly all of them urged peace with Guelders and France. No one sought to exploit the situation to change the political relationship between States General and monarchy. It was also clear that the States General did more than defend local and sectional privileges. It was the body to whom the prince turned, and was expected to turn, in times of crisis and danger.

---

[19] Henne, *Histoire de Charles Quint*, vol. I, 311–12.
[20] BBR, Root Boeck, MS 16955-7, fos. 39–40.
[21] Henne, *Histoire de Charles Quint*, vol. II, 10. Cf. J. D. Tracy, *Holland under Habsburg Rule 1505–1566: The Formation of a Body Politic* (Berkeley, 1990), 74.
[22] Diegerick, *Correspondance des magistrats d'Ypres*, 44 and appendix, p. 7.

The regencies of Margaret of Austria (1507–1530)

Margaret achieved one more triumph, in the field in which she was most expert: international diplomacy. Just as she had done with the League of Cambrai, she now played a key role in bringing together the Holy League of the pope, the Swiss, Ferdinand of Aragon, Maximilian and Henry VIII. This time the league was directed against France. A special bonus was that Margaret managed, at the same time, to insist on the neutrality of the Netherlands. This was the best of all possible worlds. The more adventurous Netherlands seigneurs could indulge their love of fighting by taking service with the king of England and helping him capture Tournai (21 Sept. 1513). The rest of the country 'made a million in gold' from supplying the armies, as Margaret gleefully told her father.[23]

Nevertheless, Margaret's position in the Netherlands was getting weaker. At no time had she been in full control of her government. In a composite monarchy without elaborate imperial machinery, the prince could only obtain effective authority in his scattered dominions by personal control of government patronage in each of them. Less than a year after her appointment Margaret complained to her father about her own powerlessness in matters of appointment. At that point, in April 1508, Maximilian answered soothingly that she should make appointments under his seal, 'for it seems to me, as grandfather and guardian of our children, I should retain some authority to rule you, both for the sake of my own reputation and for yours which derives from it'.[24]

In practice this arrangement did not work as smoothly as Maximilian suggested. Those who disagreed with the regent's policies intrigued against her at the emperor's court. By 1510 Margaret complained that she could find hardly any help in her council when she had to negotiate with the States General.[25] Against her wishes – she would have preferred Bergues for this role – Maximilian had made Chièvres responsible for the upbringing of the young archduke Charles. Perhaps to weaken Chièvres' influence, but certainly also to please a large number of the nobility and especially those who had accompanied Philip the Handsome to Spain, Margaret now organised a separate household for Charles (October 1513). This had the unintended effect of adding a third centre of loyalty and intrigue to the already confusing polarity between herself and Maximilian. The government was paralysed in the manoeuvring of the parties. Abroad, the anti-French league dissolved. Maximilian, now effectively without allies, agreed to break Charles's betrothal to Mary Tudor, so that she might be free to marry Louis XII (March 1514). It was the greatest blow to Habsburg family pride since Margaret's rejection by Charles VIII.

---

[23] F. W. N. Hugenholtz, 'Filips de Schone en Maximiliaans tweede regentschap, 1493–1515', in *AGN*, vol. IV, 47–8.
[24] Le Glay, *Correspondance de l'empereur Maximilien*, vol. I, 122. Walther, 102. H. Kreiten, 'Der Briefwechsel Kaiser Maximilians I mit seiner Tochter Margareta', *AÖG*, 996, pt. 2 (1907). Critique and corrections by A. Walther in *Göttingische Gelehrte Anzeigen*, 179 (1908).
[25] Le Glay, *Correspondance*, vol. I, 308–9. Kreiten, 'Briefwechsel', 226.

Plate 8 Hans Bolsterer, medallion of Charles V with the pillars of Hercules on the reverse, 1548. Kunsthistorischesmuseum, Vienna

By December 1514 the States General had had enough of this unhappy situation and offered the emperor 100,000 florins if he agreed that Charles should be declared of age. It looks as if this offer was decided by the deputies without reference back to their principals. Just as in 1493, when Philip was declared of age, Maximilian was happy to be bought off. On 5 January 1515 Charles appeared before the States General as ruler in his own right and Margaret's first regency came to an end.[26]

CHIÈVRES' SECOND GOVERNMENT

Like many political leaders before and after her, Margaret blamed her fall on a conspiracy. The States General had been led astray by some evil spirits, she wrote to Maximilian. She was probably correct in ascribing the initiative of the coup to Chièvres and his francophile friends. But the Estates were not simply puppets on the strings of aristocratic puppeteers. In Hainaut, that most loyal of the provinces, the home of the Croy family[27] and the province in which Chièvres himself held the quasi-hereditary office of *grand bailli*, an office which allowed him to supervise the law courts of the province and virtually to control the annual appointment of the magistrates of Hainaut's chief city, Mons – itself no more than a medium-sized town in which the guilds had never managed to attain much influence; in Hainaut then, the city of Mons refused to pay its part of the 100,000 florins' bribe for

---

[26] Hugenholtz, 'Filips de Schone', 50.
[27] 'Inventaire des actes se rapportant aux biens de Guillaume de Croy-Chièvres', in G. Dansaert, *Guillaumes de Croy-Chièvres* (Paris, 1943), 303–7.

Maximilian. Its deputies for the States General wrote home, on 16 December 1514, that Chièvres had been adamant that no delay would be allowed and that the city would be forced to pay up. On 30 December, the city council, 'on the advice of several eminent persons', decided to stick to its refusal. It gave as its reasons the failure of the government to allow reference back by the deputies of the States General and also the exhaustion of the city's resources because of its commitment to build its own defences. On 1 January 1515 the deputies reported home that they had been promised relief from some excise duties but that they had been told that 'the city was not conducting its case with sweetness but with stubbornness and arrogance', and that Monseigneur (i.e. Charles), the nobles and the council would not suffer it. The government did not insist on the *a priori* binding force of the vote of the deputies in the States General. Evidently, this was not the time to raise such an explosive issue; but the government did argue that Mons, as a loyal city, should accept the vote since everyone else had accepted it.

This argument did not convince the city, and its council prepared to refer the case to the Great Court of Malines. No doubt it would have taken months or years to resolve the case. The government was not prepared to wait. It sent its bailiff (*huissier d'armes*) to the town hall. He ordered the councillors to remain in the hall until the city had paid 2,000 florins in gold. The city council protested strenuously against such unheard-of treatment; but Mons remained isolated. The rest of the States General had agreed to the *aide*. But both sides had now made their point, and on 23 January 1515 Chièvres arranged a compromise by which the city would pay 1,000 florins imediately as a gift to Monseigneur and that the remainder would be paid as an *aide* when he came to Hainaut for his *joyeuse entrée*.[28]

Harmony had been restored by the *dominium politicum et regale* recipe of 'sweetness' and 'rigour', as people said at the time. The role of the great lords had been crucial in this outcome. The question was to arise, however, whether the incident had not left them with an exaggerated view of their ability to manage the Estates.

Chièvres' second government was highly successful. In the spring of 1515 the young archduke made the rounds of the provinces and was everywhere enthusiastically acclaimed as ruling sovereign. Chièvres had him accept some modifications of the *joyeuses entrées*, but generally these charters remained within the Netherlands traditions. No new taxes were to be demanded during the three years in which the recently voted 450,000 florins ran. Roads were to be kept safe and the circulation of goods was to be unhindered. The famous traditional liberties of individuals in Brabant were confirmed: no arrest of persons nor entry into houses except according to the laws and privileges of the land. Only in the case of the church was there an important innovation. No ecclesiastical institution outside Brabant would any longer be allowed to acquire land, rents or other immovable property in the duchy without a specific grant from the duke and from the

---

[28] AGRB, Transcripts from the Archives of Mons, 5th Registry, fos. 141r–152r.

magistrates of the principal town of the quarter of Brabant in which such property was situated.[29]

In Flanders and Holland the government ordered a new census of all property which had fallen into mortmain, the 'dead hand' of the church, without a special grant from the sovereign.[30] It was a victory of the third estate over the first and a sign of how much the church was under pressure from the laity on the eve of the Reformation. It also contributed to the alienation of the prelates, and especially of the abbots of the great Brabantine monasteries, from the process of government – an alienation which was to become an increasingly serious problem right up to the outbreak of the Revolt.

The Estates of most of the provinces granted Charles handsome *aides*. Apart from Brabant's 450,000 florins payable over three years, Hainaut gave 28,500 over four years, Valenciennes 14,000, also over four years, but at a slightly lower rate per florin, while the small county of Namur agreed to 1,212 gold florins. When Charles came to Ghent many of its citizens hoped, romantically and without any evidence, that he would restore all the privileges of his birthplace which it had lost in the Treaty of Cadzand, after its long rebellion against Maximilian. He did not. All the same, Flanders voted the considerable sum of 200,000 écus.[31]

In spite of these successes, the financial position remained precarious as usual. Chièvres' government inherited debts from the Guelders war of some 600,000 florins and as much again in older obligations. In March 1515 the government annulled all pensions payments, in spite of solemn promises not to do so. But in return for the *aides* from Brabant and Holland, the government had to allow their demand for new censuses for the levying of parliamentary grants (*transports*) which would take into account changed economic circumstances; for the previous *transports* of these provinces had been compiled in the early fifteenth century.[32]

In October 1515 Chièvres summoned a States General to Brussels to report on the activities of his government during its first year and, more specifically, on the marriage of Charles's sister, the archduchess Mary, to King Louis II of Hungary. The deputies were also asked to discuss monetary problems.[33]

In February 1516, again at a session in Brussels, Chièvres reported on the recent treaty with Aragon and he proposed a levy of 400 men-at-arms, the aristocratic cavalry. At this point news arrived of the death of Charles's maternal grandfather, Ferdinand of Aragon. Without hesitation Chièvres plunged again into the same Spanish adventure as he had for Charles's father, Philip. This time, however, the Habsburg claim was not only for the crown of Castile but also for that of Aragon.

---

[29] Henne, *Histoire de Charles Quint*, vol. II, 91–2.
[30] *Ibid.*, 128. R. Fruin and H. T. Colenbrander, *Geschiedenis der Staatsinstellingen in Nederland tot den val der Republiek* 2nd edn (The Hague, 1922; 1st edn, 1901), 52–3.
[31] Henne, *Histoire de Charles Quint*, vol. II, 123–5.
[32] *Ibid.*, 126.
[33] *Ibid.*, 156.

The regencies of Margaret of Austria (1507–1530)

This meant not only eastern Spain but also Sicily, Naples and Sardinia, and therefore it meant inheriting Aragon's rivalry with France over the control of Italy and, with the Ottoman Turks, over the control of the whole of the Mediterranean.

On 19 February Chièvres asked the States General for 400,000 florins in gold, the same sum they had granted Philip for his expedition to Spain in 1505. Just as on that occasion, the Estates were not as enthusiastic about the venture as the great nobles and the courtiers; but in the end they agreed to the sum demanded, making it payable, however, over four years. In return the government had to promise to keep the country at peace but, if that proved to be impossible, the grant was to be used to pay for the defence of the Netherlands.[34] Erasmus wrote to his friend Thomas More lamenting the condition of the country, overrun as it was by soldiers and in which the nobles and prelates had agreed enormous sums in taxes which had to be paid by the common people.[35]

Chièvres, a political realist where Maximilian was a fantasist, did his best to leave the country at peace while Charles set out to claim the thrones of Spain. In the treaties of Paris (1515) and Noyon (1516) Charles did homage to Francis I for Flanders and Artois and effectively left Francis free to conquer Milan from Massimiliano Sforza and the Swiss. With England the unfavourable trade treaty of 1506 was renewed for another five years (January 1516). Only in Friesland did Chièvres continue an active policy directed against Charles of Guelders' attempts to extend his influence into this northern county. Maximilian and Philip had made over Friesland to Albert of Saxony in return for writing off the large sums he had lent them while he was Maximilian's governor of the Netherlands. Friesland had then experienced a long period of complex manoeuvring between Albert and his successors, the Frisians, the city of Groningen, the county of East Friesland and Charles of Guelders. In 1516 George of Saxony had sold his rights back to the House of Habsburg–Burgundy and the north-east became part of the primary struggle between Burgundy and Guelders.[36]

By September 1517 Charles and Chièvres were ready to embark for Spain, although not before having to ask the States General for another 100,000 guilders (Oct. 1516) and haggling in the following months with the Estates of the individual provinces over this sum. In June 1517 the States General were informed about the arrangements for the government of the country in Charles's absence. There was no alternative but to call again on Margaret of Austria, although she was again not formally appointed regent for several years. It was not Chièvres' fault that the delays before leaving for Spain, unavoidable because of the need to secure the safety of the Netherlands, had the effect of making the already difficult situation in

---

[34] *Ibid.*, 156–8. AGRB, Transcripts from the Archives of Mons, 5th Registry, fos. 211–16r.
[35] Quoted in Henne, *Histoire de Charles Quint*, vol. II, 157 and in J. D. Tracy, *The Politics of Erasmus* (Toronto, 1978), 92.
[36] Formsma, 'De onderwerping', 84–5. A. F. A. Mellink, 'Territoriale afronding van de Nederlanden', in *NAGN*, vol. V, 99.

Spain virtually unmanageable.[37] Chièvres' fault was of a different order. He seems to have had no understanding that, by the very efficiency with which he organised Charles's Spanish succession, he had manoeuvred the Netherlands into the backwater of a huge and growing composite polity. And this time the gods, having granted the Netherlanders a second chance to choose their destiny, did not rescue them again from their own pride by the premature death of their prince. It was no doubt this same pride which allowed Chièvres to imagine that he could manage the Cortes of Castile as successfully as he had handled the States General of the Netherlands. It was a misconception which precipitated the revolt of the Comuneros and which nearly lost Charles his Spanish thrones.

MARGARET OF AUSTRIA'S SECOND REGENCY, 1517–1530

In the Netherlands everything seemed to be going well at first, but the problems of regency government continued with a vengeance. In place of the fitful interference of Maximilian, acting as guardian for the reigning duke, this duke himself and his immediate advisers now exercised this authority permanently and continuously, even when he was out of the country, and that was most of the time. How uncompromisingly Charles intended to exercise his authority became clear in the run-up to the imperial election. Maximilian had, as usual, pursued contradictory policies with regard to this election. As late as July 1515 he had proposed to the German electors the choice of his new grandson-in-law, Louis of Hungary, as his successor to the imperial crown or, more likely, as imperial vicar. For such a position he would create for him a 'kingdom of Austria'.[38] Soon afterwards, however, he recommended Charles to the electors.[39]

After Maximilian's death, in January 1519, electioneering became hectic. Francis I later said that this was the moment from which his enmity with Charles dated, for they were two young gentlemen in pursuit of the same lady, the imperial crown. Margaret thought that the pope and the German electors would more readily accept the candidacy of Charles's younger brother, Ferdinand, than that of the man who was already the ruler of the Netherlands, of Spain and of half of Italy. Charles, characteristically going for the the grandest prize – and here he resembled his grandfather Maximilian – reacted fiercely and categorically to the suggestion by his aunt. Having none of Francis I's sense of humour or taste for flippancy, he adopted a high moral tone, based on his conviction of the divinely ordained nature of his claims. In a letter from Barcelona he wrote to Margaret that he would not think of giving up his candidacy. The whole thing smacked of a French intrigue to divide him from his brother. Even such a virtuous and victorious prince as the

---

[37] H. G. Koenigsberger, *The Habsburgs and Europe 1516–1660* (Ithaca and London, 1971), 7–9. K. Brandi, *Kaiser Karl V* (Munich, 1937/59), 82.
[38] Wiesflecker, *Maximilian I*, 189.
[39] *Ibid.*, 196.

The regencies of Margaret of Austria (1507–1530)

emperor Maximilian had experienced constant trouble in maintaining his patrimony and his imperial prerogatives, because he could rely only on his hereditary lands, the Austrian duchies. But Charles, with the backing of all his kingdoms and dominions would, if elected, 'be able to accomplish many good and great things, and not only conserve and guard the possessions which God had given us but increase them greatly and, in this way, give peace, repose and tranquillity to Christendom, upholding and strengthening our Catholic faith which is our principal foundation'.[40]

Charles had probably not intended it in this way, but it was in fact a striking declaration of the relegation of the Netherlands to a role subordinate to Charles's all-European interests and aims. In personal terms – although again this may not have been consciously intended – it meant the displacement of Chièvres by Mercurino di Gattinara as Charles's chief adviser on international affairs. Charles's success in the imperial election, even though it was achieved by massive bribes and by unashamed military blackmail, confirmed him in the belief of his God-given destiny. And Gattinara assiduously confirmed him in this belief.

In the Netherlands it soon became apparent that the honeymoon period of Chièvresque consensus politics was coming to an end. Not that in the Netherlands anyone openly objected to their prince obtaining the imperial crown in Germany, as many in Spain had done, where it was said openly that the title of king of Castile was much better than that of emperor of Germany. Brabant voted 100,000 livres towards the cost of the imperial election and Flanders, although not even part of the Holy Roman Empire, sent an embassy to Barcelona to congratulate Charles.[41] But already in April 1519 Charles, perhaps with his bruising experiences of the Cortes of the kingdoms of Castile and Aragon in mind, had commended Margaret for refusing a request by the Estates of Brabant for summoning the States General, for fear, he wrote, that they might form 'a league or confederation which would result in the diminution of our prerogatives and the misprision of our ministers'.[42] Back in the Netherlands, on his way to Aachen for his coronation, he did summon the States General, in June 1520, but found considerable difficulty in getting *aides* in a situation made bleak by an outbreak of the plague.[43]

The session of the States General in Brussels was, nevertheless, a grand affair. Charles sat between his aunt Margaret and his brother Ferdinand while Gattinara, now with the title of grand-chancellor, held forth in his long-winded lawyer's style. He compared Charles, the new emperor, to Alexander, Caesar and Hadrian, great conquerors known for their clemency. Charles desired to preserve the Netherlands in peace and tranquillity, and if he was corporeally absent, his heart would be with them. He was working for the union of all Christian princes and for this

---

[40] Koenigsberger, *The Habsburgs and Europe*, 10. Brandi, *Kaiser Karl V*, 88–9.
[41] Henne, *Histoire de Charles Quint*, vol. II, 292.
[42] Charles to Margaret, 9 April 1519. Van den Bergh, *Gedenkstukken*, vol. III, 219.
[43] Henne, *Histoire de Charles Quint*, vol. II, 318–20.

reason he had spared no effort to arrive at the imperial dignity. This charge he had accepted, not from worldly ambition, nor to live in luxury and voluptuousness, but to serve his countries, the Christian faith and the whole Christian commonwealth. For this purpose he had raised troops to fight the Turks and sent ships to the Indian Isles, 'which is called the world of gold', to lead them to the knowledge of God and good government and to draw from thence spices which grow there in excellent quality and great abundance, and from which great profit will ensue for His Majesty, his subjects and for the whole of Christendom. But the emperor had spent more than a million in gold in Germany (on his election), Gattinara continued, not counting pensions and more than 800,000 on naval expenses, as well as payments for the ordinary garrisons on the frontiers. The Frisian war had been expensive, and now he needed money to travel to Germany to the diet of Nuremberg. 'All these matters His Majesty has willingly imparted to you because of the entire confidence he has in your loyalty, so that you should know the complete state and disposition of all his affairs', and so that you should aid him with your persons and goods:

'for you are those who reap greater fruits than anyone else from the grandeur of your prince and from the conservation and exaltation of his imperial dignity. And in the future he will help and support you better and trouble you less with *aides* and impositions; and thus his countries will be preserved from commotions and live in peace and tranquillity, by which you will gain great wealth by trade and husbandry. And by participating in the great good and grandeur which will ensue for the service of God and for the whole of Christendom you will recognise that clearly the hand of God is with His Majesty.'[44]

Gattinara's speech was the most comprehensive justification of the spiritual and material benefits and of divine providence in the creation of composite monarchies and empires. No doubt his listeners were impressed and, in any case, one does not usually voice doubts on a grand ceremonial occasion. No one mentioned that, only two months earlier, similar harangues had left the deputies of the Castilian Cortes at Coruña quite unmoved and that, at this very moment, Castile was rapidly sliding into open rebellion and civil war. But the Netherlands deputies were also left in no doubt that there were limits to the emperor's 'entire confidence' in their loyalty; for the grand-chancellor ended his speech by saying that His Majesty would now declare his will, i.e. his demand for *aides*, to each province separately and that he expected good answers.

Perhaps the emperor's tax demands to the separate provinces, rather than to the assembled States General, was no more than an administrative convenience. But the custom had been for a long time to ask the States General for a global sum which was then divided between the provinces in a fixed ratio. The problem for the government was that a refusal or a serious watering down of the proposal by

[44] AGRB, Papiers d'Etat et de l'Audrence (P. d'E. A.), 1232. 'Recueil de propositions faites aux Etats Généraux des Pays-Bas', vol. I, 1473–1544, fos. 9–14.

one of the big provinces, say Brabant or Flanders, would then be followed by the whole States General. The paring down of the States General to a ceremonial opening and a 'state of the nation' address by the government, followed by separate discussions with the Estates of the individual provinces, may have seemed a convenient compromise with previous tradition. There is little evidence that, at this time, either the monarchy or the Estates regarded the new procedure as having grave constitutional significance. They were certainly not prepared to quarrel over it. Both sides had ambivalent feelings about the matter. If the provinces tended to play follow-my-leader, such a leader might also set a good example. Thus in 1522 Flanders agreed to pay for five companies of the *bandes d'ordonnance*, and Margaret asked the provinces to follow the Flemish lead. She thought of summoning the States General but was then dissuaded by her council.[45] A year later and again in 1524 she specifically summoned the States General for joint discussions on the coinage and monetary matters, and her successor, Mary of Hungary, did the same when it was a question of persuading Flanders, and especially Ghent, of the favourable attitude of all the other provinces.[46]

The Estates, for their part, were anxious to preserve their autonomy and rejected majority voting in the States General, especially in financial matters. In any case, these had to be referred back to the provincial Estates and, indeed, to the individual cities. The short distances and the relatively comfortable travel by barge on rivers and canals allowed the towns to keep much closer control over their deputies than the cities of the big Western European kingdoms could manage. Everywhere in Europe governments and representative assemblies were wrestling with the question of the powers of deputies and of the degree of control exercised over them by their principals; and the question was still a burning issue in the federalist and anti-federalist debates of the young United States of America in the 1780s. In the sixteenth century all the parties to this problem found themselves in equivocal positions. Apart from the purely physical problems of travel and communication in early modern Europe, both governments and assemblies had ambiguous and even contradictory aims. Governments wanted deputies who could take rapid and binding decisions, but were fearful that deputies with full powers might conspire together or, at least, cooperate in rejecting the government proposals. The principals of the third estate, cities or commons, wanted to limit the freedom of their deputies or even impose on them an imperative mandate, i.e. oblige them to stick to strict and detailed instructions. But too strict a mandate could easily leave a city or borough or even a whole province in isolation when it had either given in too easily to government demands or had resisted too rashly and found itself facing the government wrath alone – exactly what had happened

---

[45] Henne, *Histoire de Charles Quint*, vol. III, 268.
[46] AGRB, Transcripts from the Archives of Mons, 6th Registry, fo. 89. N. Maddens, 'De Beden in het Graafschap Vlaanderen tijdens de Regering van Keizer Karel V (1515–1550)', *APAE*, 72 (1978), 4.

to Mons in 1514-15. The ambiguities inherent in early modern *dominium politicum et regale* regimes were particularly evident in composite monarchies with composite assemblies, states generals. While therefore the actual practice of granting powers to deputies might tilt a long way towards either full powers or an imperative mandate, these patterns were never absolute nor completely consistent, no matter what the lawyers of the monarchies or the Estates claimed for them.

In Castile the monarchy had, since the early fifteenth century, tried to induce the cities represented in the Cortes to give their delegates full powers. From 1422 it even paid the deputies' salaries. The towns, however, tried to impose binding instructions on their deputies. In this aim they were successful, especially after Queen Isabella's death when the crown was weakened by the disputes over the succession between Ferdinand of Aragon and Philip the Handsome. When Charles V summoned the Cortes in February 1520 to ask for a new grant for his journey to Germany he demanded that the cities give their deputies full powers to take decisions for the service of God and the king. Several cities refused outright, and with good reason. During the session of the Cortes, Charles's government bribed the deputies with the promise of money from the grant they were being asked to vote for. This was the immediate cause for the outbreak of the revolt of the Comuneros. In several towns mobs burned down the houses of the deputies who had accepted these bribes and in Segovia the mob even lynched one deputy.[47]

The Comuneros lost the civil war which followed, and from then on the monarchy insisted that the deputies to the Cortes have full powers. In practice this policy proved to be difficult to enforce. The cities had not been completely tamed and one of the reasons for this was undoubtedly the fact that, just like the Netherlands, Castile had now become part of a composite monarchy whose king was more often absent than present and which therefore had to be governed by regencies. But in fact, given the long distances and the arduous travelling conditions of the Castilian *meseta*, the deputies simply could not report home as often as the deputies of the Netherlands cities. The Castilian city councils therefore imposed oaths on their deputies to limit their powers. It was characteristic of sixteenth-century Spain that it was left not to the law courts but to the theologians to determine how far such oaths were binding.[48]

In France there were similar problems of distance and travel, but there were far too many deputies at the Estates General for French governments to think they could get a favourable vote by bribing individual deputies. The deputies' constituents, a bewildering variety of local and provincial authorities and assemblies who chose them in an even more bewildering variety of electoral procedures, by-passed the problem of the deputies' powers by the simple expedient of not holding

---

[47] H. G. Koenigsberger, 'The Power of Deputies in Sixteenth-Century Assemblies', in *Estates and Revolutions*, 181-7.

[48] C. D. Hendricks, '*Charles V and the Cortes of Castile: Politics in Renaissance Spain*' (Cornell University Ph.D. thesis, 1976), *passim*.

themselves bound by the decisions of the Estates General. A favourable vote on a tax proposal carried some moral authority and was good for public relations. But the government still had to negotiate with the deputies of the individual provincial Estates about such taxes which it could not impose by royal prerogative. In the provincial Estates the government could and did bribe the nobility and some of the big town corporations with exemptions or even with a share of up to a third of the taxes which the monarchy and the local Estates thus imposed in happy cooperation. Thus developed the notorious phenomenon that in France, even more than in the rest of Europe, the burden of taxation fell mainly on the country population and the small towns.[49] It is therefore not surprising that the French monarchy did not bother to summon the Estates General between 1484 and 1560 and that the rest of Europe came to think of the French monarchy as being able to tax and legislate at will: that, in short, it was a *dominium regale*.

England was somewhere in between France and the Netherlands in geographical size and in the ease of travel. Since the end of the thirteenth century members of Parliament were held to represent the community of the shire or borough and also the community of the whole realm. And this realm, unlike the Netherlands and France, had long since become a unitary kingdom without provincial assemblies. Since most English boroughs were much smaller than the big towns of the Netherlands or the eighteen cities represented in the Castilian Cortes they tended to be represented by the leading gentry families of the counties. Between the interests of the landowning gentry and the great county families in England there was no such chasm as there was between the urban nobility and the grandees of Castile or between the urban patriciates and the great seigneurs of the Netherlands. Geographic, economic and social reasons therefore made the development of full powers for members of the English Parliament acceptable to their constituents, while the English monarchy, not having to face the same degree of institutionalised regionalism that most of the continental monarchies had to take into account, found it convenient to deal with a Parliament which could take immediate decisions that would bind the whole realm. The dangers inherent in this tradition did not become apparent until the seventeenth century.

In some countries a further complication in the powers of the deputies was introduced by the practice of some parliaments to depute small committees to look after their interests between sessions or to discuss details of legislation and taxes after the end of a full session and to make certain that the resolutions passed by the full assembly were carried out. Such committees were called deputations (*diputació* in Catalonia, *deputazione* in Sicily and Friuli, *Ausschuss* or *Deputation* in the German principalities). In Catalonia and in the later sixteenth and in the seventeenth centuries in Bavaria and in the Holy Roman Empire, these institutions came to

---

[49] J. Russell Major, *The Deputies to the States General in Renaissance France* (Madison, 1960), 5ff. Major, *Representative Government in Early Modern France*, 28–9, 45–6 and *passim*.

displace the full sessions of the parliaments or Reichstage. The monarchies usually thought that such deputations were more easily managed than the full assemblies. That was certainly so in Sicily; but the Habsburgs in particular were to find that this was not always the case. The Austrian provincial Estates had built up their own financial and administrative machinery during Maximilian's reign and they had consolidated their position in the two years between his death in 1519 and the installing of Charles V's brother Ferdinand as their effective ruler. Ferdinand summoned an assembly of deputations (*Ausschusslandtag*) of all the Austrian duchies in Graz, in September/October 1521, only to find that it used common discussions in a relatively small assembly as a very effective way of imposing its will. Ferdinand found the experience so disconcerting that he did not summon another *Ausschusslandtag* for a considerable time.[50] These differences in the powers of deputies in the different European countries did not by themselves determine the history of these countries, especially in composite monarchies. But they did a great deal to set the tone and the terms of political discourse between monarchy and Estates, king and parliament. This is shown clearly in the different practices of bribery in Castile and in the Netherlands. In Castile the monarchy bribed individual deputies but did not usually attempt to bribe city councils, and this pattern of political relationship continued with varying degrees of success throughout the reigns of Charles V and Philip II. In the Netherlands members of the first two estates, prelates and nobles, could be made pliant by judicious use of patronage or by outright bribery. Margaret's memoranda and her correspondence leave no doubt about this practice, and the deputies of the cities were under no illusions about it. 'God knows, they [the nobles] are always the first to consent [to taxes] which others have to pay', Jacopszoon wrote bitterly. But simple bribery did not work with the deputies of the towns, precisely because their decisions were imposed on them by an imperative mandate. The government therefore had recourse to the practice of giving *gracien*. The practice of *gracien* was originally designed, in the fifteenth century, to relieve towns which had suffered severe economic decline, such as happenend to the great medieval cloth centre of Ypres, or to towns which had been devastated by war or a great fire, or by that most frequent Low Countries calamity, floods. Later, and especially after about 1520, the government used *gracien* to induce individual towns to accept its proposals for *aides*. Dordrecht and Haarlem negotiated as much as 66 per cent *gracien* on their *aides*, and when the other towns in Holland tumbled to this ploy they naturally demanded similar cuts.[51] Amsterdam disapproved of *gracien*, perhaps because it was looking for more substantial favours still, such as the lifting of the export tax on grain. But in 1531 the city's deputies told the government commissioners that

---

[50] G. R. Burkert, *Landesfürst und Stände: Karl V, Ferdinand I und die österreichischen Erbländer im Ringen um den Gesamtstaat and Landesinteressen* (Graz, 1987), 132–6, 297.

[51] Tracy, *Holland under Habsburg Rule*, 53–4.

The regencies of Margaret of Austria (1507–1530)

gracien were 'ungodly' and cheated the small towns and the open country which received no similar rebates. They were heartily sorry that anyone should get them, the deputies said; but if other towns continued to receive them, Amsterdam would be ruined if it did not claim *gracien* too. They were offered a rebate of 1,060 gulden but were not impressed. Jacopszoon characterised the separate negotiations of the deputies of the cities with the government commissioners as 'auricular confession' which would lead to the destruction of the country: 'Each town looks after itself without thought for the welfare of the land.' The Amsterdamers were only saying what the deputies of the smaller towns had said for years. Peter Karre of Rotterdam, for instance, told the nobles and the big towns that 'they should go to a thousand devils' for having cheated them.[52]

Bribery, however, was not a one-way process. Towns and provinces needed favours from the government and for this purpose gave gratuities to their governors or to individual members of the regent's council. Hoochstraten's outburst to the deputies of Holland about the mutuality of favours[53] simply spelled out a characteristic practice of the system. From at least the late fifteenth century onwards the accounts of the Estates are full of references to pots of wine, understood both literally and metaphorically for all types of gratuities.[54]

For the deputies personally, as well as for the cities, there were definite advantages in having an imperative mandate. The English country gentleman who represented a borough in the House of Commons and who frequently had family ties with members of the House of Lords was, for all the deference he usually showed to the king and his councillors, in a much better position to exercise his *plena potestas* than the burgomaster or secretary of a Dutch town would have been, for the burgomaster was not a gentleman. 'The emperor is not a merchant' who would haggle with the towns over the exact sum of an *aide*; he would rather accept nothing at all, Hoochstraten remarked contemptuously to the deputies of Amsterdam.[55] Such haggling was, of course, precisely what the emperor's regent and ministers had to do; but that did not change their attitude. Hoochstraten was quite capable of growling that he knew how to harm Amsterdam; but on a personal level it was more alarming when he stormed at the deputies, the burgomasters Albert Boelenszoon and Cornelis Banninck, that they apparently imagined that they alone

---

[52] Jacopszoon, *Prothocolle*, vol. II, fo. 106 for 17 April 1531; vol. I, fo. 47 for 17 Jan. 1524.
[53] See above.
[54] AGRB, Transcripts from the Archives of Mons, 5th Registry, fo. 48v. Hirschauer, *Les états d'Artois*, vol. I, 63. A. Derville, 'Les pots-de-vin dans le dernier tiers du XVe siècle (d'après les comptes de Lille et de Saint-Omer)', in W. P. Blockmans, ed., *Le privilège général*, APAE, 80 (1985), 449–70. H. G. Koenigsberger, 'Patronage and Bribery during the Reign of Charles V', in *Estates and Revolutions*, 166–75.
[55] Jacopszoon, *Prothocolle*, 18 April 1531. Cf. Shakespeare, *Antony and Cleopatra*, 5. 2. 182–3: *Caesar*: 'Caesar's no merchant, to make price with you Of things that merchants sold.' Since, obviously, Shakespeare knew nothing of Hoochstraten, the phrase of the emperor not being a merchant seems to have been a sixteenth-century trope.

were governors of the city, that he could easily find others and 'that he would flatten them like dogs'. Boelenszoon replied that they did not want to govern, 'they had enough to do with their merchandising'.[56] The governor's relations with Banninck were particularly bad. 'I shall be governor when you are no longer Banninck', Jacopszoon reports him spluttering when what he evidently meant to say was 'when you are no longer burgomaster'. Jacopszoon who had a mordant sense of humour clearly thought that Hoochstraten's outburst was funny. But for Banninck it was ominous; for Jacopszoon also reports that the counts of Nassau and Bueren and the lord of Brederode were heard to remark that they would not have suffered a man like Banninck in their own towns. Master Vincent, one of the councillors, had to intercede for the burgomaster and make his peace with the lords.[57]

Banninck and the other bourgeois deputies would have been in an intolerable position if they had enjoyed *plena potestas* and had had to speak only for themselves. In England members of Parliament whom the monarch regarded as too outspoken could and did find themselves in the Tower. Nothing like this happened in the Netherlands. The deputies could always plead their instructions, and the government would not lightly offend a rich city, whatever a count of Hoochstraten might say and however much aristocratic ministers might despise bourgeois deputies. The burgomasters and aldermen, for their part, found it easier to be brave in their town councils among friends and within the familiar walls of their town halls, with their quasi-republican symbolic decorations, than in the daunting presence of the regent and the great lords of her council.[58]

But, imperative mandate or not, it was in practice never really possible to do without discussion and cooperation between the deputies, even if such discussion took place in private rather than in the full assembly. Especially when it was not a question of money, the town councils were quite happy to let their deputies exercise a great deal of discretion.[59] Even when money was involved, agreement could not be reached without some discussion. On occasion the Estates sent special deputies to other provinces to find out their reaction to government proposals.[60] Frequently the smaller provinces or towns instructed their deputies to follow the lead of the larger ones; for, as the small towns of Holland said, when the others ran they could not stand still.[61]

---

[56] Jacopszoon, *Prothocolle*, 11 Feb. 1530.
[57] *Ibid.*, 5–7 June 1535.
[58] Koenigsberger, 'The Powers of Deputies', in *Estates and Revolutions*, 195–6. On republican symbolism in Netherlands town halls, see G. Wells, 'Emergence and Evanescence: Republicanism and the *Res Publica* at Antwerp before the Revolt of the Netherlands', in Koenigsberger and Müller-Luckner, *Republiken und Republikanismus*, 155–68. T. Froeschl, 'Selbstdarstellung und Staatssymbolik in den europäischen Republiken der frühen Neuzeit', in *ibid.*, 239–71.
[59] L. Wils, 'De Werking van de Staten van Barbant, omstreks 1550–1650', *APAE*, 5 (1935), 11ff.
[60] Van der Goes, *Register van alle de Dachvaerden by deseslve Staten*, 350.
[61] Jacopszoon, *Prothocolle*, 31 May 1524. Kokken, *Steden en Staten*, 191–6.

The regencies of Margaret of Austria (1507-1530)

The government itself was not consistent in its opposition to common discussions. At a States General in Brussels in April 1522, Gattinara sketched a favourable political situation: the emperor's conquests of Milan and Tournai and his alliance with the king of England who would protect the Netherlands in the emperor's absence. But he exhorted the provinces to maintain their accustomed loyalty to Charles and 'to aid, succour and assist each other . . . and to preserve good union and intelligence between you'. The grand-chancellor ended his speech with the classical example of the bundle of arrows which when bound together could not be broken.[62] Some forty years later, Cardinal Granvelle, evidently not as good a classical scholar as Gattinara, was puzzled to find this symbol of the arrows used by the league of seigneurs directed against him. In the 1520s, however, it clearly meant that the government, for all its misgivings about cooperation in the States General, realised that the provinces had to cooperate in order to support their ruler's international policy — a point which Granvelle also failed to appreciate in the 1560s.

By excluding, wherever possible, the guilds from the town councils, by bribing the city corporations with *gracien* and the great lords with positions and honours in an expanding empire, the monarchy was able to get at least a part of the financial help it needed for its imperial policies by consensus in the States General and in the provincial Estates. Since the government had, for the time being, given up demanding global sums from the States General, it is not possible to follow the history of parliamentary taxation for the whole Netherlands as accurately for the 1520s as it has been for the period before. But from the provinces for which we have figures the trends are clear enough. For Flanders the ordinary grants remained at 140,000 gulden per annum, and it was from these 'ordinary' grants that the government granted *gracien*. But the 'extraordinary', i.e. additional grants, which had run at about 50,000 florins a year between 1515 and 1520, shot up to 275,000 and 350,000 in the next two years, in order to pay for the war with France. The year 1523 was easier, but in 1524 extraordinary grants rose again to 150,000, in 1528 to over 200,000 and in 1529 they were still at 120,000 florins.[63]

In Brabant the pattern was similar. The ordinary *aide* of 150,000 gulden for each of three years, granted in 1520, was followed in 1521 by an extraordinary grant of 150,000 crowns and in 1522 by another 140,000 gulden for two years.[64] Then, as in Flanders, the demands eased up, only to rise again both in 1528 and 1529 with extraordinary *aides* of about 250,000 gulden.

In Holland the *aides* rose from about 100,000 pounds to 210,000 in 1521, 305,000 in 1522 and 270,000 in 1523. The *gracien* were about 15 per cent in 1521

---

[62] Henne, *Histoire de Charles Quint*, vol. II, 248–50.
[63] Maddens, *De Beden in Vlaanderen*, 426–7, and *passim*.
[64] BBR, MS 17047, 'Sommier van de Beden . . . 1500 tot . . . 1575', fos. 55v–56v. E. van Bruyssel, 'Note sur les aides et les subsides levées en Brabant de 1500 à 1577', from MS 685 of the Bibliothèque de Bourgogne, but substantially similar to BBR, MS 17047, in *BCRH*, ser. 3, vol. VII (Brussels, 1865), 224–5.

and 1522, but only 8.5 per cent in 1523. In 1528 there was an even bigger vote, of 460,000 pounds, but with *gracien* running at 20 per cent. The figures remained high up to 1530.[65] Erasmus had lamented the tax burden on the ordinary people in the 1510s. By the 1520s that period must have seemed like a golden age of low taxes.

The pattern of government demands and of the *gracien* depended, firstly, on the demands of the war with France and Guelders, and then on the detailed and laborious negotiations and compromises between government and Estates. Most of the time the Estates were quite willing to pay for defence. But whose defence was it? Artois, Hainaut and Walloon Flanders were clearly in the greatest danger from French attack. Their big neighbour, Flanders, was usually willing to support them, and the government did its best to persuade the other provinces to support their endangered confederates. But Holland and Brabant also had to defend themselves against the destructive Gueldrian raids and were required to help counter the menacing Gueldrian advance into Friesland. During the autumn sessions of the Estates of Holland in 1523 the deputies blamed the government for reneging on its earlier promises that Holland would be defended by the commonality if the province helped in the defence of Artois and Hainaut. Now they were being told that these provinces had been burnt down by the enemy but that, loyal as they always were, they were still granting *aides*, and that it was up to Holland, too, to defend itself. The Holland deputies reacted bitterly. Where was the cow money now, and the beer and wine excises which they had previously granted, the burghers were asking. The ministers, pushed on the defensive, were embarrassed. Andries Jacopszoon tells us that the president of the Council of Holland produced a 'long and impertinent harangue'. The deputies of Leiden remarked that those who brought reports of government promises were liars, 'which amounts to saying', the inimitable Jacopszoon commented, 'that princes are liars, promising much but doing nothing'.[66] Machiavelli was not more explicit.

Our reports of the government's negotiations with the other provinces are much more sober than those of the happily indiscreet and outspoken secretary of Amsterdam. But there is little doubt that the Hollanders were not alone in voicing their disgust at government policy. Certainly, the regent was under no illusion about this. Already in June 1522 she warned the emperor of the desperate financial situation. Government credit on the Antwerp money market was exhausted. If all were to be lost for the lack of 10,000 florins, that small sum could not be found. With the prince absent and not likely to come back soon, with property diminished and a bad harvest in prospect, there could easily arise a conspiracy and a rebellion in the Netherlands. This was the more dangerous because of the war and the difficulty of doing anything about it. She and her council would always do their

[65] Tracy, *Holland under Habsburg Rule*, 75.
[66] Jacopszoon, *Prothocolle*, Oct.–Dec. 1523, vol. I, fos. 19–43.

best to prevent catastrophes; but they wanted His Majesty to know how things really stood and they feared that any evil which might ensue would be imputed to them. 'To leave great debts behind and few revenues in a country such as this is not conducive to keeping it in such security, obedience and peace as one would wish.'[67] This was a very different view of a composite monarchy from the one whose advantages Gattinara had so eloquently proclaimed. But Margaret's irony, more caustic than anything she had used to her father, had no more effect on Charles V's policies than the grumbling of the Estates had on her own.

While neither the provincial Estates and the States General nor the regency government could control the emperor's foreign policy, nor very much influence his strategy, there was one field in which they could develop policy without reference to him. This was the administration of government finances, at least in so far as these depended on grants by the Estates. The precedent of 1512, when the Estates obtained the right of insight into the treasurer's accounts and the right to send their own commissioners to supervise the pay parades of the troops, was never forgotten. In 1532 the Estates of Holland instructed three of their deputies to supervise the accounts of the *rentmeester*, the finance officials dealing with the sale of annuities (*renten, rentes*). These deputies soon discovered that they were shown only general receipts by the government officials, without clear indications what the sums involved were spent on. This was not surprising because government finance officials regularly used revenues not for what they had been appropriated for but to pay off the most pressing older debts. Nobody had any clear idea what such debts really amounted to. The emperor Maximilian, for instance, had left a jungle of debts. Such government debts often involved only relatively small sums, loaned by private persons on specific government revenues. The reason was that the government often granted relatively small sums to individuals, not so much for their financial value than as an act of patronage, a public or semi-public sign that the recipient enjoyed the prince's favour. The government would then obtain *contre-lettres*, secret undertakings by the recipient of the act of patronage that he would not actually claim the pension or other monies which the government had promised him. But in practice *contre-lettres* got lost. Specific revenues would be assigned to cover several different obligations, in the hope that no claims would arise.[68] They often did of course; and, when the Estates' deputies probed further, more old public debts also quickly came to light. The deputies of Holland and Hoochstraten had one of their periodic slanging matches and these led to characteristically devious manoeuvring. The Estates won over other members of the regent's council and managed to get Hoochstraten's unpopular deputy governor dismissed.

[67] Instructions to the secretary Jehan de la Sauch for Charles V, 11 June 1522, quoted in Henne, *Histoire de Charles Quint*, vol. III, 266–7.
[68] Memorandum of the Council of Finance for Charles V, May 1523. Quoted in K. Lanz, *Staatspapiere zur Geschichte des Kaisers Karls V* (Stuttgart, 1845), 10–14.

Monarchies, States Generals and Parliaments

More important than this tactical success of the Estates was their permanent involvement in the administration of the *aides* they granted and the disbursement of government money for military purposes; for not only did this give the Estates a measure of control over government finance, but it gave their deputies and officials experience and self-confidence in the business of government.[69]

By the end of the 1520s not only Holland but also Brabant and Flanders and probably other provinces too, successfully insisted on the strict appropriation of grants and they introduced their own officials into the financial administration of the *aides*. Margaret wrote to the emperor that she could no longer use these *aides* 'to help your other countries which are not strong enough to defend themselves'.[70] The Estates of the Netherlands province were thus effectively coming into line with the Estates of the Habsburg Austrian duchies which had built up quite an elaborate machinery for the control of their own grants and the financing of the defence against the Turks.[71] The government of the Netherlands had undoubtedly been obliged to give up an important area of its competence and it was aware of both the practical and the constitutional implications of this development, especially, as Margaret's comments to Charles V show, in the matter of financing the imperial policies of a composite monarchy. But for the Estates it was as yet mainly a matter of practical politics with, at least overtly, no thought of going beyond the broad band of *dominium politicum et regale*.

The most explosive of the issues which were eventually to wreck consensus politics in the Netherlands was as yet only a small cloud on the horizon: only rarely, and then not very urgently, did the Estates concern themselves with matters of religion. In September 1523 the Estates of Holland complained that the deputy from Dordrecht had revealed to the government discussions in the assembly which had then led to the arrest of the pensionary (secretary) of Delft for what he was alleged to have said about the Lutherans. The Estates also asked the regent to recall the inquisitor, Frans van der Hulst, for not acting in accordance with the laws of Holland. The Estates were especially anxious to establish that there should be no Inquisition proceedings against anyone who had read Luther's books before his excommunication and condemnation by the emperor at the diet of Worms.[72] In the following years the Estates of Holland discussed heresy on several occasions. Their attitude was unequivocal. They were good Catholics and they resented any imputation of heresy. Its spread was the fault of the popular preachers. But while the Estates called for the re-issue of the emperor's placards against heretics, they also insisted that the execution of the placards should not infringe the privileges of

---

[69] Tracy, *Holland under Habsburg Rule*, 82–9. I have here followed Professor Tracy's account.
[70] Margaret to Charles V, 23 April 1528. AGRB, P. d'E. A., 36, fo. 209; BBR, Root Boeck, MS 16955–57, fo. 46v.
[71] Burkert, *Landesfürst und Stände*, 166–70.
[72] Rollin Couquerque and Meerkamp van Embden, *Goudsche Vroedschapsresolutiën*, 133–4. Jacopszoon, *Prothocolle*, 10 Sept. 1523.

The regencies of Margaret of Austria (1507–1530)

the province and of the cities, and that there should be flexibility in the imposition of penalties.[73] No one in the 1520s foresaw that, thirty years later, during an economic crisis and through government ineptitude, religion and privileges would make an explosive mix.

Immediately much more worrisome for the government than the insistence of Holland on the observance of its privileges was the attitude of the prelates of Brabant. This had nothing to do with relgious beliefs or doctrine. The abbots of the rich Benedictine and Premonstratensian monasteries of Brabant, to a man scions of noble families, formed the first estate of the assemblies of Brabant and they frequently set the tone for the discussions of the government tax proposals. As early as 1522 Charles V declared himself amazed by the tactics of these prelates who were stonewalling an agreement for the sale of 50,000 livres of *rentes*.[74] This obstructive attitude of the prelates arose out of a dispute over the percentage of all *aides* which they were required to pay. Originally, this had been 12 per cent; but during Philip the Handsome's reign, i.e. at the time of Chièvres' government and the ascendancy of the Croy clan, they had managed to reduce their quota to 4 per cent. As late as 1520, when Chièvres' influence was again strong, Charels V and the pope had appointed Charles de Croy, a minor, to be abbot of Affligem, the richest of all the abbacies. But the other estates never accepted the legality of the reduction of the prelates' quota. The regent resolved the impasse by making up the full quota of 12 per cent from government funds. This was a common practice, called *vervangen* (substitute), and it was quite often used when the government obtained a majority vote for an *aide* but found that one town or one province was not prepared to pay its full quota. It was virtually the only way in which the government could by-pass the need for unanimity on financial votes in the States General and in the provincial Estates.

The 1520s were filled with quarrels between the government and the prelates of Brabant over three further issues. The first was the unwillingness of the monasteries to give up the right to elect their own abbots, a right which, they claimed, was enshrined in the *joyeuse entrée*. Charles V maintained that he had obtained the right of appointment from the pope in the deal he had made with Leo X in 1515. The second quarrel, closely related to the first, was over the emperor's practice of giving church benefices *in commendam*, i.e. temporarily to an appointee of his until a permanent appointment should have been made. This practice was specifically prohibited by the *joyeuse entrée*. The third point at issue was the emperor's prohibition, in 1520, of any increase in tithes on cultivated land above the rate at which they had been charged forty years before.

By 1527 relations between the regent and the prelates of Brabant had reached crisis point. Margaret set up a commission to inquire into the state of the property

[73] *Ibid.*, May 1525 and April 1527.
[74] Charles V to Margaret, Valladolid, 31 Oct. 1522, in K. Lanz, *Correspondenz des Kaisers Karl V* (Leipzig, 1844), 70.

of the monasteries. The prelates did their best to undermine the commission, and the regent began to urge the emperor to revise the *joyeuse entrée* in order to take away the prelates' right to refuse the *aides* requested of the Estates of Brabant and thereby sabotage the whole grant.[75] In an assembly of the Estates at Malines, in June 1528, the regent proposed a union between the Brabant nobles and the cities of Antwerp and 's-Hertogenbosch with the Estates of Holland in order to raise money for defence against the Gueldrian raids. The matter was urgent, for only three months previously Egmont's marshal, Maarten van Rossem, had plundered The Hague. The prelates again refused to pay more than 4 per cent of the proposed *aide*, and the city of Louvain and other Brabant towns declared that, in that case, they would not agree to the *aide* at all.[76] Margaret answered by threatening that government officials would collect the full quota of 12 per cent from the prelates and clergy. The chancellor of Brabant, however, refused to seal the act. It was contrary to the *joyeuse entrée*, he declared, which forbade sealing an act without the consent of all three estates. Thereupon Margaret took the seal from him and sealed the act herself in the presence of the whole assembly of the Estates of Brabant.[77] It was a deliberately dramatic gesture, rather like James I tearing a page out of the House of Commons journal, a hundred years later. Neither action had any immediate constitutional consequences, but neither was forgotten. Margaret was sufficiently anxious about it to ask the emperor insistently not to reverse her action.

The regent had good cause to fear that this might happen. The pattern of her relationship with her nephew had come to resemble the earlier pattern of her relationship with her father. Just as before, Margaret's opponents, or those who had not received the rewards they felt they deserved, took their grudges to the emperor; and Charles, just like Maximilian, was willing to listen. In March 1527 he wrote to Margaret that certain noblemen had complained to him that she had shown them no confidence and that she had not appreciated their faithful service. They had accused her of preferring low-class persons – no doubt they meant the lawyers – and that these enjoyed her exclusive favour. Would she therefore, the emperor continued, 'with her great prudence and experience', look at these complaints and deal with them?[78]

Margaret was not deceived by the flattery, the less so as the attack came not in a personal letter but in a memorandum delivered by a third person. She too now used the semi-public method of the memorandum to reply. She had been misrepresented,

---

[75] P. Gorissen, *De Prelaten van Brabant onder Karel V (1515–1544)*, *APAE*, 6 (1953), 9–35. E. de Moreau, 'Les familiers des ducs de Bourgogne dans les canonicats des anciens Pays-Bas', in *Mélanges d'histoire offerts à L. van der Essen*, vol. I (Brussels, 1947), 429–35.

[76] BBR, Root Boeck, MS 16955–57, fo. 47v.

[77] Margaret to Charles V, Malines, 7 July 1528. AGRB, P. d'E. A., 36, fo. 217. L. P. Gachard, *Analectes historiques*, ser. 7, in *BCRH*, ser. 2, vol. X (Brussels, 1859), 399–403.

[78] 'Instructions à . . . le Seigneur de Praet . . . devers Madame', Valladolid, 6 March 1527. '*Recueil concernant le gouvernement de Marguerite d'Autriche, 1515–1530*', BBR, MS 16068–72, fos. 189v–190r.

The regencies of Margaret of Austria (1507–1530)

she wrote, and in consequence had fallen into great disrespect and loss of reputation with the Netherlanders; for they had observed that the emperor for trivial reasons had revoked appointments she had made, according to the powers he had given her. A governor or a regent of a country, who did not have authority to punish the bad and reward the good would not be highly regarded by the prince's subjects. The prince himself would then lose authority. The regent would not be able to get money from the Estates or their support in other matters if she could not sometimes bestow some office or benefice, nor would the great lords be willing to negotiate with the Estates for her. As it was, several were reproaching her that she could do them harm or disfavour but that she had no power to do them any good. His Majesty should therefore allow her to make urgent appointments with the advice of the council. If anyone approached him directly, he should not lightly give them anything without first informing her.[79]

What Margaret was suggesting was a reversal of the traditional role of prince and regent in the bestowal of patronage. Charles was certainly not willing to contemplate such a reversal; nor could he accept any limitation, even if only by implication, of his subjects' right to petition him. In 1526 he had reaffirmed this right and also the subjects' right to petition the regent and her ministers. But he did not include the States General as a proper venue for petitions. Anyone who had his request denied and then proceeded to petition the States General would be guilty of sedition.[80] This ruling had the double purpose of sanitising whistle-blowers by forcing them to use official channels and, at the same time, of limiting the competence of the Estates.

The immediate problem for the regent in the handling of the States General, however, was not so much petitions as the obstructiveness of the first estate. Her relations with the prelates continued to deteriorate. The quarrel now centred mainly on ecclesiastical appointments.[81] Since the regent had openly flouted the *joyeuse entrée*, the prelates could now, for the first time, count on some degree of sympathy from the other estates. In January 1530 Charles V began negotiations with the pope for a dispensation from his oath to certain articles of the *joyeuse entrée*.[82] In April Margaret wrote that the Estates planned to send an embassy to him, officially to congratulate him on his coronation as emperor (February 1530), but in fact to lobby him on ecclesiastical appointments and on the *joyeuse entrée*. The embassy they had chosen was to consist of two noblemen and the abbots of Villers and Parcq, 'and these are certainly the most rebellious and who most

---

[79] 'Instructions . . . de par madame . . . donné à Messire de Rozimboz, en ce présent voyage d'Espagne', in *ibid.*, fos. 24r–27r. 'Articles proposez à l'Empereur . . . de par Madame', in *ibid.*, fos. 140r–141r.
[80] 'Extrait de la minute des apostilles sur la declaration des affaires de Flandre apportée par Mre Guillaume des Barres', BBR, MS II 358, vol. I, file 'Correspondance de l'Empereur avec Madame Marguerite de l'an 1526', fo. 385.
[81] AGRB, P. d'E. A., 36, fos. 228–331.
[82] Gorissen, *De Prelaten*, 36–44.

oppose our policies'. She told them they could travel privately, but not as representatives of the Estates.[83] Charles approved of his aunt's action. She was to tell them that he would attend to their affairs when he came to the Netherlands and that in the meantime they should employ themselves in his service. She should thank them for their good will 'in such a manner that it does not seem to them that I am rebuffing their good intentions for wanting to come and see me', and that she was dissuading them only to save on expenses.[84]

But the regent had reached the point where she wanted more decisive action. In July she proposed that the Estates be no longer allowed to make requests before agreeing to an *aide*, i.e. no more redress of grievances before supply. This aim, she suggested, could best be achieved when the emperor was in the country, either by government edict or by separate negotiations and deals with the individual provinces.[85] But the emperor, deeply involved in an attempt to achieve an accommodation with the German Protestant princes at the diet of Augsburg, put off a decision on the regent's proposals. In the autumn he travelled to the Netherlands. Just before arriving he received the news of Margaret's sudden death, on 1 December, at the relatively young age of fifty. It was time to rethink the whole position of the government of the Netherlands.

---

[83] Margaret to Charles V, 16 April 1530. BBR, MS II 358, vol. I, fos. 386–7 (seventeenth-century copy).
[84] Charles to Margaret, 11 May 1530. *Ibid.*, fo. 387.
[85] 'Articles proposez à l'Empereur . . . de par Madame', BBR, MS 16068–72, fo. 136. (Copy. The original contains the emperor's apostille. Vienna, Haus- Hof- und Staatsbibliothek, Belgien, PA 21/2, fos. 109v–110r.) My thanks to Professors Horst Rabe and Heide Stratenweit for sending me photocopies of the Vienna MS.

6

Dominium politicum et regale in a composite monarchy: the regency of Mary of Hungary, I (1531–1550)

> I am only one and I can't be everywhere; and I must be where I ought to be and where I can, and often enough only where I can be and not where I would like to be; for one can't do more than one can do.[1]
>
> Charles V to Mary of Hungary, Monzon, 6 October 1537. AGRB,
> Papiers d'Etat et de l'Audience, 30, fo. 25

MARY OF HUNGARY AS REGENT OF THE NETHERLANDS

For Charles V and his advisers the rethinking of the structure of the Netherlands government and of its position within the multiple monarchy meant the restructuring of the councils on the Spanish model. A plan had been carefully prepared and was readily accepted in the Netherlands during the emperor's sojourn, in 1531. This was not a matter for the States General. Only once before, after the death of Charles the Bold in 1477, had the States General attempted to prescribe the structure of the central government and its organs.[2] It had not been a satisfactory experience for anyone, and in 1531 no one thought of repeating it. The actual reorganisation (described in chapter 4) undoubtedly increased the effectiveness of the central government in the Netherlands. It did not, however, give the emperor more control when he was outside the country. Only a year later he was complaining that he was not being kept informed about a riot in Brussels.[3] Nor did his efforts to control patronage work any more smoothly than they had done in the past.

In January 1531 Charles appointed his sister Mary as the new regent, in succession to their aunt Margaret. Mary, at twenty-six, was the widow of the unfortunate Louis II of Hungary who had perished in the battle of Mohács against the Turks, in 1526. She had no children. Neither her portraits, with their long,

---

[1] 'Je ne suis que ung et ne puis estre à tous costés et faut que je soye où je doys et puis, et bien souvent où je puis seullement, et non où je voudroys pour ce que l'on ne peut plus que l'on peut.'
[2] See above, pp. 43ff.
[3] Baelde, *De Collaterale Raden*, 58.

Plate 9 Leone Leoni, *Mary of Hungary* (bronze). Kunsthistorischesmuseum, Vienna

chin-dominated Habsburg face, nor her letters nor indeed the comments of her contemporaries allow her the easy Burgundian charm of her grandmother Mary or of her aunt Margaret, at whose court in Malines Mary had spent much of her childhood. But very soon she showed herself just as enthusiastic a patron of literature, of music and of the hunt and, at the same time, a perhaps even more intelligent and determined politician.[4] Before her appointment she had had a much-exaggerated reputation of sympathy for religious reform. The Lutherans were always anxious to claim royalty among their supporters. Charles assured her that he had no doubts about her orthodoxy;[5] even so, when he took his leave of the States General in October 1531, thanked them for the *aides* they had granted him and assured them of his continuing love, he also proclaimed that if his father, brother, mother, sister, wife or children were infected by the Lutheran sect he would hold them to be his greatest enemies. Andries Jacopszoon was so impressed that, in his Dutch journal, he quoted the emperor verbatim and in French.[6] But was Charles simply proclaiming his faith and, in 1531, one of his major preoccupations – as he had done at the diet of Worms in 1521 in answer to Luther himself – or was he, here in Brussels, giving the new regent, his sister, a concealed personal warning?

By this time Charles had learned, if he had not known before, that his younger sister could not easily be bullied, least of all in matters which affected her personally. She had not sought the appointment; in May 1531 she described it to her brother Ferdinand as having a rope put around her neck.[7] When Charles had offered her the regency he had written that he hoped she would have in her house and about her person Netherlanders who knew the customs of the country and who would serve her more loyally and at lesser cost than courtiers who came from other nations.[8] Mary replied immediately that, of course, she would have servants from the Netherlands but that she would also take several of her gentlemen with her who had served her for a long time through good and ill.[9] As early as March 1531 her determination caused a clash of wills with her brother. Mary insisted on appointing her childhood friend, the countess of Salm, as one of her ladies of honour. Ferdinand's wife, sister of the late King Louis, would also have liked to

---

[4] J. Kerkhoff, 'Het Hof van Maria van Hongarije' and C. Lemaire, 'De Librije van Maria van Hongarije', in B. van Boogert and J. Kerkhoff, eds., *Maria van Hongarije: Konigin tussen keizers en kunsenaars 1505–1558* (Zwolle, 1993), 162–207.

[5] B. J. Spruyt, 'Verdacht van Lutherse Sympatieen: Maria van Hongarije en de religieuse controversen van haar tijd', in *ibid.*, 87–117.

B. J. Spruyt, ' "En bruit d'estre bonne luterienne". Mary of Hungary and Religious Reform', *English Historical Review*, 109, 431 (April 1994), 275–307.

[6] Jacopszoon, *Prothocolle*, vol. II, fo. 220, 7 Oct. 1531.

[7] H. Wolfram and C. Thomas, eds., *Die Korrespondenz Ferdinands I*, vol. III, pt. 1 (Vienna, 1973), 121.

[8] Draft of the instructions to the sieur de Bossu sent to Mary of Hungary, Cologne, 3 Jan. 1531. AGRB, P. d'E. A., 47, fos. 8–10.

[9] Jan. 1531. *Ibid.*, fo. 18.

have the countess,[10] while Charles would have preferred Mary to take 'a good and honest old lady from the Netherlands'. But his preferred ladies, Mme de Chièvres for instance, had refused because of age or bad health. Reluctantly the emperor gave way. The countess was German, 'but at least not a Lutheran', he wrote to Ferdinand.[11]

In most matters of patronage, however, Charles got his way and as a result his relations in this area were no better with Mary than they had been with Margaret, and for much the same reasons. When in 1538 Mary complained that he had reversed some of her appointments he wrote, in his own hand but patronisingly, that she should look again at her instructions and that his authority was more important than hers. He had to keep appointments in his own hands, he argued, for otherwise those who served him in his court would lose all hope of reward.[12]

THE DEFENCE OF THE NETHERLANDS

After the reorganisation of the councils the emperor's next move was to try to rationalise the defence of the Netherlands. For the next few years at any rate this issue overshadowed his fear of heresy in the Netherlands and also the quarrel of the regency government with the prelates of Brabant. Only when an Anabaptist mob stormed the town hall of Amsterdam and murdered Burgomaster Pieter Colijn, in May 1535, did heresy move again to the centre of his concerns.

The problem of the prelates in the Estates of Brabant, which had loomed so large in the last years of Margaret's regency, now faded into the background. Partly, at least, this was a matter of personalities. Mary managed to handle the touchy abbots much more successfully than her aunt had done and they, for their part, did not repeat their earlier *faux pas* of refusing to speak French with the regent. Not that the prelates had given up their claims to free elections. In September 1534 they formed a confederation or league to defend their privileges.[13] Compared with other religious leagues of the century, from the recently formed Schmalkaldic League of Lutheran German princes to the openly revolutionary Calvinist and Catholic French leagues during the second half of the sixteenth century, the confederation of the prelates of Brabant was a tame affair,[14] so tame that apparently the regent never even heard about it until 1544.[15] Not until the

---

[10] Ferdinand to Mary, Budweis, 10 March 1531. Wolfram and Thomas, *Die Korrespondenz Ferdinands I*, vol. III, pt. 1, 60.
[11] Charles to Ferdinand, Brussels, 29 July 1531. *Ibid.*, pt. 2, 228–9.
[12] Charles to Mary, Toledo, 22 Dec. 1538. AGRB, P. d'E. A., 50, fos. 1124v–125v.
[13] 'Statuten van de Confederatie der Prelaten van Brabant', in Gorissen, *De Prelaten*, 89–94.
[14] For a short discussion of sixteenth-century leagues see H. G. Koenigsberger, 'Liga, Ligadiszipliniund Treue zum Fürsten im Westeuropa der frühen Neuzeit', in P. Prodi and E. Müller-Luckner, eds., *Glaube und Eid: Treueformeln, Glaubensbekenntnisse und Sozialdisziplinierung zwischen Mittelalter und Neuzeit* (Munich, 1993), 173–8.
[15] Gorissen, *De Prelaten*, 56–120.

The regency of Mary of Hungary, I (1531–1550)

regency of Mary's niece Margaret of Parma in the 1560s did the action of the Brabantine prelates move again to the centre of parliamentary politics.

Defence, however, remained a perennial and much more formidable problem or, rather, a number of parallel problems. It had always been the key issue in the relations between the monarchy and the States General. At the same time, it was the key issue in the relations between the different parts of Charles V's composite monarchy and between the members of the Habsburg family who had been set to govern these different parts. Inevitably, they and their immediate advisers represented the interests of the countries they governed. In their regular correspondence with the emperor, the empress Isabella (regent of Castile), Ferdinand and Mary usually discussed only the problems of their own countries. Only occasionally did they discuss them in relation to each other and hardly ever in relation to the whole European situation, and this even though the regents and their advisers were certainly aware of this situation and sometimes had strong views about it. Since this overall situation was Charles V's main concern and since he always regarded his own authority as more important than that of any of his regents there was bound to be, for all the family loyalty of the Habsburgs, a good deal of friction between the siblings. As the emperor saw it, the most serious threat to his monarchy always came from France. In the early 1530s there was nominal peace with France and England. But Francis I and Henry VIII were known to be in touch with each other and there was no knowing what they might be plotting against the seemingly so powerful House of Austria. Italy was also at peace. But the pope and the Italian princes were unreliable from the emperor's point of view, especially as Clement VII was adamantly opposed to the summoning of a general council of the church, a council which Charles and Ferdinand wanted for the solution of the religious divisions of Germany. But the most immediate threat came from the Turks. Sulaiman the Magnificent – in their correspondence with each other the Habsburgs never allowed him a title but called him 'the Turk' – was backing Jan Zápolyai, the *woiwode* of Transylvania, who was disputing the throne of Hungary with Ferdinand. Sulaiman was organising huge armies to march through Hungary. Already in 1529 he had besieged Vienna. The Turkish threat largely determined Ferdinand's attitude towards the German princes and their religious convictions, for he needed their help in his defence against the Turks. Charles was never entirely happy about his brother's accommodating attitude; but he was also worried about the equally deadly threat which the huge Turkish fleet posed in the Mediterranean.

The obvious way to counter the double threat was to ask the Netherlands for help. The States General had been reasonably generous when Charles himself summoned them in the spring of 1531. Brabant had granted 1,200,000 gulden, spread over a period of six years,[16] Flanders the same amount,[17] and Holland

---
[16] *Ibid.*, 68–9.
[17] AGRB, transcript from the Archives de la ville d'Ypres, MS 40431, fo. 28v.

480,000, also over six years,[18] and the smaller provinces pro rata. But even with the emperor in the country the negotiations had not been easy. When, early in 1532, financial help against the Turks became urgent, Charles knew perfectly well that another request, so soon after the previous one and while it had still another five years to run, would meet with much more resistance. Mary wrote to Ferdinand that the Netherlanders were more afraid of their own neighbours than of the Turks and, she concluded dryly, she would not do these neighbours an injustice if she called them Turks.[19] The Netherlanders would only help the emperor if he came again to the Netherlands and personally asked for help.[20] But this was precisely what Charles was not willing to do for fear that they might refuse him and that such a refusal would be a great blow to his authority. Nothing seems to have come of an earlier suggestion to obtain the pope's consent for a special tax on the temporal possessions of the clergy.[21]

Whatever the military situation on the ground and on the waves and whatever the evaluations of the strategic and, hence, financial priorities of these wars, the basic patterns and the perceived moral justifications of the Habsburg–Ottoman and the Habsburg–Valois conflicts were clear enough. There was no such clarity in the emperor's and the Netherlands' attitude towards the Baltic powers. Not only were Baltic politics themselves confused and contradictory, they also showed up the contradictions in Charles V's monarchy as a whole and also of the composite polity of the Netherlands. For Holland, and most especially for Amsterdam and some of the smaller ports, it was essential to keep open the passage of the Sound. Their ships took salt, fish and manufactures to the Baltic and returned with grain and timber. In this trade the Hansards, and especially the Lübeckers, were their bitter rivals and when opportunity offered they tried to close the Sound to Dutch shipping. Such closures caused not only heavy losses to the Amsterdam merchants but immediate unemployment among sailors and shipwrights and a shortage of grain all over the Netherlands. When this happened the States General reacted in the traditional manner of early modern public authorities when faced with high bread prices and the consequent danger of public unrest: they proposed a prohibition of all export of grain from the Netherlands. The deputies of Amsterdam had to fight repeated battles to prevent, or at least to soften, such a further blow to the trade of their city.

The Lübeckers played on these differences of interest and tried to isolate the Hollanders further by offering concessions to Zeeland, Flemish and Brabant merchants, so that Holland would find no support in the States General. Charles V

---

[18] Jacopszoon, *Prothocolle*, vol. II, March–April 1531.
[19] Mary to Ferdinand, Ghent, 22 June 1532. Wolfram and Thomas, *Die Korrespondenz Ferdinands I*, vol. III, pt. 3, 586.
[20] Mary to Ferdinand, Ghent, 2 July 1532. *Ibid.*, 591–2.
[21] Ferdinand to Mary, Regensburg, 15 July 1532. *Ibid.*, 596. Charles to Mary, Regensburg, 27 March 1532. AGRB, P. d'E. A., 52, fos. 47–8.

The regency of Mary of Hungary, I (1531–1550)

came into this tangle in three ways: as ruler of the Netherlands, as brother-in-law of Christian II of Denmark and as Holy Roman Emperor, trying to extend imperial and Habsburg influence in northern Germany where, in contrast to southern Germany, such influence was virtually non-existent.

In 1523 Christian II was driven from his throne. The Hollanders were perfectly willing to recognise the successive usurper kings, Frederick I and Christian III, of the House of Holstein. Of course, the Holsteiners, as was usual in such cases, also had hereditary claims. For the Hollanders it was essential to prevent an alliance between the kings of Denmark and Lübeck and the consequent closing of the Sound. In 1531 Christian II raised troops in Germany and marched them into Holland in order to blackmail the Netherlands government into paying him the outstanding part from the dowry for Charles's sister, Isabel, and also to blackmail the Netherlands into supporting his proposed return to Denmark. The Estates of Holland had little choice but to grant him at least some support. Eventually Christian II sailed for Norway, then in a personal union with Denmark, but promptly bungled his campaign to regain his throne.

Even after Christian II was out of the way, the Danish civil war continued and Lübeck intervened against the Holstein kings and again closed the Sound. Holland fitted out a fleet but did not manage to induce the emperor to acknowledge Holland's war as his own and to give it his full support. The Habsburg family detested the heretical and adulterous Christian II almost as much as they came to detest Henry VIII; but Charles still hoped to establish his niece Dorothea and her husband, Frederick of the Palatinate, on the Danish throne.

Inevitably, other powers became involved. The Holstein king, Christian III of Denmark, was allied to Charles of Guelders, the great enemy of the Habsburg Netherlands. French and English merchants profited from the discomfiture of the Hollanders and were not at all unhappy to see the confusions of imperial policy-making. Thus when Charles V's ambassador in England demanded the restitution of some Spanish merchandise pirated by Lübecker ships in English waters, the English council preferred not to go into this rather embarrassing breach of English sovereignty but remarked to the ambassador that, since the Lübeckers were the emperor's subjects, it seemed strange that he did not punish them for making war on the Dutch and that the Spaniards should address themselves to him for justice, rather than to the king of England. Was it an instance of the inveterate English ignorance of the complications of continental politics? Chapuys, the ambassador, seems to have thought so, or diplomatically to have chosen to think so, rather than accept a snub; for he answered by treating the council to a pedantic lecture on the nature of Charles V's authority in his different realms. Or was the council's attitude a put-down by the very aristocratic councillors of the much less aristocratic ambassador? There was probably a dash of *Schadenfreude* in the council's attitude since the English Baltic merchants could only profit from the Hollanders' troubles. The duke of Norfolk then compounded the discourtesy by remarking that the world would never be at peace while one prince held so many kingdoms, but that the 'number of children your Majesty will have will bring remedy'. Later, at dinner, the duke of Suffolk tried some damage limitation by declaring that the emperor had done more than his duty against the Turks and that God would punish the French and the English for their failures in this respect.[22] But, in truth, the English were even less worried by the Turks than were the Netherlanders.

On most occasions Amsterdam and the small ports were able to get the support of the Estates of the whole county of Holland in their naval actions against Lübeck. Hoochstraten supported them in the regent's council and even gave his personal bond to Antwerp bankers who were advancing the money voted by the Estates for fitting out the warships. But Holland could not get the support of the States General and, in spite of Hoochstraten's efforts, little more than sympathy from Mary's government. At most, Brussels was on occasion prepared to bluff with the engagement of all the emperor's forces. In fact, no such engagement ever took place. The Baltic remained a side issue in the emperor's strategic thinking, and his position was further compromised by his moral support for the claims of Dorothea and her husband to the Danish throne. Not until 1544 were the relations between the Netherlands and Denmark settled, in the Peace of Speyer, and it was the Danes, and not the emperor himself, who insisted that he sign for all his dominions.[23]

Whatever else was clear in the otherwise murky relations between the Netherlands and the Baltic powers, it was difficult to get the provinces to support a coherent defence policy – a difficulty which had long been apparent in the French and Guelders wars. At the States General of Malines, in July 1534, Mary therefore proposed a defensive union of all the provinces. She had carefully prepared this proposal in her councils and by discussions with the great lords of the Order of the Golden Fleece. The provinces should treat an attack on any one of them as an attack on all. This was not a new point. At his leave-taking in 1531, Mary said, the emperor had requested the provinces to aid and assist each other 'like members of one indivisible and inseparable country'. They enjoyed more liberties and privileges than any neighbouring country, Mary continued, and His Majesty wanted to maintain and extend these liberties. Neither Charles in 1531, nor Mary now in 1534, made any mention of a Netherlandish state nor of a Netherlandish nationality which had to be defended. However, it was now suggested that the provinces make regular contributions to a standing army, according to the quota system of the tax contributions of the provinces which had been established by Charles the

---

[22] Chapuys to Charles V, 15 Sept. 1533. *Letters and Papers of the Reign of Henry VIII*, vol. VI (London, 1882), no. 1125.

[23] For Holland's relations with Lübeck and Denmark see Jacopszoon, *Prothocolle, passim*. R. Häpke, *Die Regierung Karls V und der europäische Norden* (Lübeck, 1914), 92–228. Tracy, *Holland under Habsburg Rule*, 105–14.

The regency of Mary of Hungary, I (1531–1550)

Bold. The regent assured the States General that her proposal would not interfere with the privileges of the individual provinces.[24]

The proposals had a mixed reception. In the separate meeting of the deputies of the different provinces everyone protested their amity towards the other provinces; but the deputies took the opportunity to air their particular grievances and old grudges and they whinged about having been let down in their own need after having contributed to the defence of the others. Most of the smaller provinces were in favour of the union, hoping for military and financial aid from the bigger ones. The Estates of Malines, the seat of the supreme court of the Netherlands and evidently reflecting the views of the legal establishment, were the most enthusiastic and suggested the transformation of the provinces into a kingdom with a common and sovereign justice system for all.[25] The bigger provinces, Brabant, Flanders and Holland, opposed the union.

For a year the parties negotiated. The government tried to meet the Estates' objections over quotas and over the role of the recently acquired provinces of Friesland, Utrecht and Groningen, as well as older but more distant ones, such as Luxembourg, the Pays d'Outremeuse and Overijssel. None of these usually sent deputies to the States General. Were they now to be forced to contribute to the common defence? By one calculation at least these smaller and newer provinces would have to make up a shortfall of 158,000 florins in the payment of 12,000 infantry and 4,000 cavalry for six months.[26] The legality of such a course of action remained unclear. The government argued that, if there was opposition because the emperor had promised not to impose further taxes while the present one was still running, the Estates should appreciate his expenses in fighting the Turks: more than two million in gold, and not only for the defence of Austria and Germany and the Catholic faith in general but also for the defence of the Netherlands; for if Germany, divided as it was by heresy, fell to the Turks, the Netherlands would be in immediate danger.[27]

This particular version of the domino theory did not impress the Estates any more than their own, equally hollow, argument impressed the government, namely that having a standing army would allow the French to know exactly what resistance they would meet when they attacked next time.

In the end the negotiations broke down over the role of the States General in the proposed union. As so often happened, both the emperor and the provinces had ambivalent feelings about this role. Even though in this case the government was anxious to have the provinces answer together, both Flanders and Brabant insisted

---

[24] L. van der Essen, 'Les Etats Généraux de 1534–1535 et le projet de confédération défensive des provinces des Pays-Bas', *Mélanges d'histoire offerts à Charles Moeller*, vol. II (Louvain and Paris, 1914), 122–39. AGRB, P. d'E. A., 1232, fos. 32–6.
[25] *Ibid.*, 1228, fo. 15.
[26] Van der Essen, 'Les Etats Généraux de 1534–1535', 138–9.
[27] AGRB, P. d'E. A., 1228, fos. 33–6.

on giving separate answers.[28] Rather unwillingly, the government accepted this demand. What it would not accept was the demand of the deputies of Holland that the States General should have the power to decide whether a war was just or not. The regent's council replied curtly that, firstly, the proposed union was meant to be defensive anyway, and that, secondly, the emperor recognised no earthly superior and that his subjects had no right to examine such matters as the justification of his wars. This was an issue which had recurred in nearly every crisis between monarchies and their parliaments in Western Europe since the fourteenth century. In July 1535 the States General flatly rejected a standing army. 'If we accept this project', they said, 'we would undoubtedly be more united – and we would be treated *à la mode de France*'.[29] Charles decided to drop the proposal. It was certainly not the time to have a lengthy dispute with the States General over a controversial plan.

CHARLES V AND THE CITIES

The smooth working of the government in the *dominium politicum et regale* regime of the Netherlands depended on obtaining the consent of the Estates to the financial demands of the prince, or at least to a high proportion of these demands. Such consent depended in its turn on decisions taken in the town councils; for usually, although not always, it was relatively easier to get the consent of the first two estates. The composition of the town councils and their political traditions were therefore of crucial importance to the political functioning of this highly urbanised country.

In often bitter social and political struggles, mainly in the fourteenth century, the guilds had won membership of many town councils. The structure of these councils and the exact weight and political influence of the guild masters varied from city to city, just as they did in much of the rest of Western Europe. Naturally the patricians, i.e. the rich merchants, the bankers, the urban nobility and everywhere the wealthier urban property owners and their agents, the lawyers and professional town officials, did their best to push out against the petty bourgeois craftsmen of the guilds. In the fifteenth century the guilds had mostly been able to maintain the positions they had won earlier but they rarely managed to make further political advances. Where, as in Holland, urban development had occurred late, later than in Flanders and Brabant, the patricians had managed to keep the guildsmen out of the town councils altogether. Apparently paradoxically, but in fact quite logically, the patrician homogeneity of the northern cities became a point of strength in the revolutionary politics of the Estates of Holland in the second half of the sixteenth century, for it prevented the growth of divisive populist–religious movements such as occurred in the politics of Ghent, Brussels and

---

[28] *Ibid.*, fo. 38.
[29] Van der Essen, 'Les Etats Généraux de 1534–1535', 138–9.

The regency of Mary of Hungary, I (1531–1550)

Amiens.[30] The class hostility underlying much of urban politics in the sixteenth century was an all-European phenomenon. 'If you shall suffer the commons to rule and follow their appetite and desire, farewell all good order', was the English court reaction to incidents of such hostility in Nottingham in 1512; and in 1584 the magistrates of Gloucester opined: 'Experience has taught us what a difficult thing it has always been to deal in any matter where the multitude of burgesses have a voice.'[31]

The 'commons' and the 'multitude of burgesses' in the large cities of the Netherlands could be a much more formidable force than in the small and relatively harmonious English country towns. The patrician elites were happy enough to support the respectable guild masters against the unorganised day workers who could at a moment's notice turn into rioting and plundering mobs. From about 1530, moreover, such workers tended to become enthusiastic followers of Anabaptist preachers. Even where the guilds were not directly represented in the town councils, the patrician councillors could never forget them nor the menace of popular movements, and more especially when they discussed the government's tax proposals.

But it was the princes who were the most consistent enemies of popular voices in city governments. Emotionally, the princes shared the common aristocratic disdain for the common people. Politically they were seeking to extend government control over the administration of the cities. They were well aware of the connection between popular representation in the city councils, even if such representation was only indirect, and the difficulties of obtaining consent for their tax proposals in the States General; for taxes fell mainly on the common people. A frontal attack on urban privileges, on the self-government of all the cities of the Netherlands, was out of the question. Even the duke of Alba, with all his soldiers, his special court and his contempt for the privileges of the Netherlanders, could not attempt such an attack. But Charles V used any hint of rebellion or riot to curtail the self-government of individual cities and especially to exclude the guilds from the town halls. Thus he acted in Malines in 1519, and it is not even clear whether there had been a significant commotion in the town. But the city was the seat of the supreme court and the regent Margaret used it as her capital; therefore, no doubt, even the smallest vestiges of medieval democracy were particularly abhorrent to the Habsburgs. The guilds lost the right to choose their own aldermen and thus also all direct influence over the city's finances.[32]

In Tournai Charles got his opportunity when he reconquered it from the French, in 1521. In the middle ages Tournai had been virtually autonomous under the French crown.[33] In the sixteenth century it changed masters several times. From 1513 to 1518 it was English and then, for three years, French again. To gain

---

[30] 'Les villes aux Pays-Bas septentrionaux', *Société Jean Bodin. Recueils*, 6 (Brussels, 1954).
[31] Both quotations from P. Clark and P. Slack, *Towns in Transition 1500–1700* (Oxford, 1976), 128.
[32] Henne, *Histoire de Charles Quint*, vol. II, 241.
[33] L. P. Gachard, *Extraits des régistres des consaux de Tournai, 1472–1490, 1559–1572, 1580–1581* (Brussels, 1846), 8–13.

support among a lukewarm patriciate the French brought the guilds into the government. Charles V at first promised to confirm all the city's privileges but provided himself with a convenient escape clause: that the privileges would have to be 'properly used'. The Netherlands government interpreted this clause so as to bar the elected representatives of the parishes and of the guilds from the commission which elected the city council. The rest of the commission was appointed by the government. In a further move against the guilds the government deprived the doyens of all rights of jurisdiction except for matters pertaining directly to their crafts. The government justified these measures by claiming that simple and sometime illiterate craftsmen had been elected to judicial offices and that, moreover, the exercise of public duties took the craftsmen away from their regular work and prevented them from earning a living for themselves and their families.

This was a common patrician sentiment in the sixteenth century.[34] Quite possibly it was the patricians of Tournai who petitioned the emperor to alter the city's privileges in order to confirm their rule. It comes as no surprise that in 1526–7 the lower classes of Tournai rose in revolt because, so the patricians claimed, of their continued attachment to France.[35]

The case of 's-Hertogenbosch confirmed the government in its view of the connection between guild participation in a town council and that town's vote in the Estates and both with the maintenance of law and order. In 1525 the magistrates and the urban nobility of 's-Hertogenbosch agreed to an *aide* but the 'commune', i.e. representatives of the guilds, refused. Soon there were riots. Crowds broke into several monasteries and helped themselves to the foodstuffs they found there. They forced the magistrates to abolish the imposts on milling and other taxes, said to amount to 12,000 livres per year – a substantial part of the city's revenue. Margaret tried to settle the incident by negotiation and several guild officials were indeed willing to treat; but, apparently because of popular pressure, no agreement was reached. Margaret and her council then imposed draconian measures on the city. Property of 's-Hertogenbosch citizens outside the city limits was seized. Favourable arrangements for paying the city's debts were cancelled. Six guild officials were summoned to appear before the *procureur général*, the government prosecutor. To show that it meant business, the government then

---

[34] Shakespeare, *Julius Caesar*, 1.1. The tribune Flavius berates two craftsmen:

> hence! home, you idle creatures, get you home.
> Is this a holiday?

His fellow tribune Marullus adds:

> But wherefore art not in thy shop today?
> Why doest thou lead these men about the streets?

As usual, Shakespeare is not one-sided and he knew his Londoners and therefore had 'mechanics' poke fun at the officious tribunes.

[35] A. Hocquet, *Tournai et le Tournaisis au XVIe siècle au point de vue politique et sociale*, ARSLBA, ser. 2, 1 (Brussels, 1906), 49–64.

stationed troops outside the city, although with strict instructions not to do any damage. We do not know whether they obeyed these instructions, but the government had no further trouble from 's-Hertogenbosch.[36]

This was all very well with a relatively small city; but a really big one, such as Ghent, was not so easily intimidated and the Habsburgs were well aware of Ghent's revolutionary history in the previous centuries. When in the same year as 's-Hertogenbosch, 1525, Ghent would not agree to an *aide* granted by the rest of Flanders, Charles proceeded much more cautiously. He advised Margaret to dissemble. She should treat the city's delegation with 'douceur'. When in this way Ghent had been persuaded to come into line with the other Members of Flanders, she was to inform herself secretly of the ringleaders of the opposition and then summon them to a place where she could arrest and punish them. Such punishment, the emperor wrote, 'would be an example to the others and in this way one could manage the people and bring them to reason and even get some good compensation [i.e. money] out of the affair'.[37]

Machiavelli himself could not have given clearer advice. In fact, Charles had learned such tactics in the dark days of the revolt of the Comuneros, in 1520, when Iñigo Velasco, his governor of Castile, had told him: 'Your Majesty should not be afraid of paper and ink, nor of oaths and pledges . . . for however much you do or break, they [the rebels] have broken much more.'[38] The advice was a sixteenth-century political commonplace.[39] The surprise with Charles is not that he followed it but that, at perhaps the most important moment of his career, he did not follow Velasco's advice: in 1521 he kept his word to Luther and honoured the safe conduct he had granted him to attend the diet of Worms.

The 1525–6 dispute with Ghent was settled reasonably amicably and, apparently, without the revenge Charles had called for.[40] By 1532, however, his reaction

---

[36] 'Mémoire au Seigneur de Praet . . . de la part de Madame', BBR, MS 16068–72, fos. 155–7.
[37] Charles V's answer to the 'Mémoire au Seigneur de Praet', Toledo, 12 Oct. 1525. *Ibid.*, fo. 155.
[38] Velasco to Charles V, 10 Oct. 1520. Quoted in H. L. Seaver, *The Great Revolt in Castile* (London, 1929), 177.
[39] Again, Shakespeare compressed sixteenth-century commonplaces into dramatic dialogue. In *Henry IV Part 2*, Prince John of Lancaster made a deal with the rebel lords and then, when their army had dissolved, arrested them for treason:

> *Mowbray*: Is this proceeding just and honourable?
> *Westmoreland*: Is your assembly so?
> *Archbishop*: Will you thus break your faith?
> *Prince John*: I pawned thee none.
> I promised you redress of these same grievances
> Whereof you did complain, which by mine honour
> I will perform with a most Christian care.
> But, for you, rebels, look to taste the due
> Meet for rebellion . . .
> God, and not we, hath safely fought today.

[40] N. Maddens, 'De opstandige houding van Gent tijdens de regering van Keizer Karel V', *Appeltjes van het Meetjesland*, 28 (1977), 214–17.

to popular opposition and riots had become ferocious. In August of that year there was a bread riot in the market place of Brussels, directed against the bakers and grain merchants. There was nothing very remarkable about this event and it was no different from hundreds of bread riots all over Europe during this period. The rioters' aims were usually practical and local.[41] But in Brussels the matter became more serious when the regent's men arrested several of the rioters. The crowd – the government claimed it was led by the guilds – broke into the town hall to free the prisoners and then forced the regent to accept certain guild proposals for the government of the city and to forward them to the emperor. Having apparently achieved their aims, the crowd dispersed. This gave the authorities the chance to arrest some forty 'evildoers' and to have them summarily executed.

Such was the report of the events (5–9 August 1532) which the regent sent to her brother. His immediate response was to claim that the Bruxellois had for a long time shown ill will and that the city authorities had not done enough to deal with the riots when they started. The regent should one fine night introduce two or three companies of infantry into the city and leave them there for some time at the city's expense. She should revoke not only what she had been forced to grant 'but also other bad privileges, if they have got any'. Mary also saw the emperor's letter, probably quite rightly, as a veiled attack on herself and on her government. At any rate, she now tried to justify herself. It had not been so much the high price of corn which had caused the riots, for it was only half of what it had been in the previous year, but the slump in trade because of the wars in Italy and the Baltic and the consequent unemployment. Her letter crossed with another one from Charles in which he wrote that it had always been his intention that due punishment should be imposed by severity of justice and by revoking privileges rather than by obtaining a financial profit (from fines). But he would leave it all to her to do as she saw fit.

In December a delegation from Brussels knelt before the regent. They did not mention any more the misery caused by high prices and unemployment, but abjectly declared that there had been no cause for the riots. The city not only agreed to give up the extorted privileges but agreed that all others, too, were forfeit. These latter, however, were restored by agreement, except for some concerning judicial procedure: an accused could now be convicted on the evidence of three witnesses and not, as formerly, only when he had confessed; the crown alone had the right of pardon and no privilege was valid in cases of high treason.

Clearly, the government was not trying to effect a wholesale abolition of privileges, such as the duke of Alba was to do thirty-five years later. Even so, in one of

---

[41] See for instance W. Reinhard, 'Theorie und Empirie bei der Erforschung frühneuzeitlicher Volksaufstände', in H. Fenske, ed., *Historia Integra* (Berlin, 1977), 173–200. M. Bercé, *Révoltes et révolutions dans l'Europe modern, XVIe–XVIIe siècles* (Paris, 1980). R. Pillorget, *Les mouvements insurrectionnels de Provence entre 1596–1715* (Paris, 1975). Pillorget counts 108 popular movements for the period 1596–1635. In the succeeding period of war and civil strife in France there were even more.

The regency of Mary of Hungary, I (1531–1550)

his letters to Mary, Charles spoke at least hypothetically of such a course. The points about judicial procedure were neither unreasonable nor unusual at the time. It was necessary to maintain consensus with the city patriciates.[42] In January 1533 the emperor once more spelled out his principles to his young and still relatively inexperienced regent: 'The preservation of my authority and of yours; fear of and obedience to justice and its administration'.[43]

But the preservation of the emperor's and the regent's authority was becoming more and more problematical. Already in February 1534 Mary was worried about it and advised the emperor that the budget could not be balanced even in peacetime – the deficit in 1534 turned out to be 330,000 livres and it rose to 500,000 in 1535 – and that people were murmuring against the emperor. At this point Charles was not unduly worried. He wrote reassuringly to his sister that he did not care about people's words. He had done his duty in trying to win their hearts and if, because of all his other obligations, he had not succeeded then that was not really surprising. When Mary had gained as much experience as he had, she would no longer despair over difficulties. He recognised that she was doing her best.[44]

But when the plan for the defensive union of the provinces had to be given up, when in 1536 a new war with France was looming and the financial situation was becoming more and more calamitous, Mary's letters to Charles, with warnings of imminent disaster in the Netherlands, began to read more and more like the theatrical outbursts of her aunt Margaret. On 4 January 1536 Mary wrote that she feared problems, especially in Brabant. She hoped other provinces would not follow the example of that province for there were always those 'who will spread it about that promises made to them in the past have not been kept'. All who were not actual members of the Council of Finance hated its very existence. Of course, there were good and bad people in it, but in general they had served loyally; and she herself was not so disloyal to the emperor as to cover up their faults, nor so stupid as not to know when they were dishonest. Worse still, some people suspected that money had been sent out of the country for the emperor's other needs and if this became generally known there would be real trouble. Mary thought, although she could not prove it, that there were some who would like to see the government living in such extreme poverty that it would have to do what they wanted. For 'through their privileges they [the Netherlanders, or perhaps the Estates] wanted to be the master and not the servant'. She would rather be a thousand leagues away than be responsible for a catastrophe. The emperor should come himself and, preferably, with money, although she doubted whether he could get it from his other dominions.

---

[42] Charles to Mary, Neukirch, 7 Oct. 1532. AGRB, P. d'E. A., 47, fos. 156–9.
[43] My account of the Brussels riots of 1532 is based on L. P. Gachard, 'Relation de l'émeute arrivée à Bruxelles de la reine Marie de Hongrie', in *BCRH*, ser. 3. vol. III (1862), 358–73.
[44] M. Baelde, 'Financiele politiek en domaniale evolutie in de Nederlanden onder Karel V en Filips II (1530–1560)' *TG*, 76 (1963), 25. Memorandum by Mary, 14 Feb. 1534, with Charles's apostilles. AGRB, P. d'E. A., 48, fos. 55–64.

At least, he should tell her exactly how she should conduct herself. She ended this letter by saying that she was not writing anything she would not say openly; nevertheless she advised him that this letter should be for his eyes only.[45]

Mary had not exaggerated the problems and dangers facing the Netherlands government. The year 1536 was the last for the taxes granted to Charles when he had been in the Netherlands in 1531. Charles now advised his sister to spin out negotiations with the States General for the renewal of these taxes until he had sent her special instructions. She was to raise 250,000 livres on her personal obligation and that of the great lords, and she was to sell domain land, even though the finance officials, like the good servants they were, always insisted that land mortgaged was better than land lost. As to the suggestion she had made that the Netherlands should remain neutral in the forthcoming war, the French would observe such neutrality only as long as it suited them.[46]

Throughout the spring and summer of 1536 Mary and her government negotiated with the States General and with the individual provinces for the continuation of the six-year *aide* of 1531; but the Estates were becoming more and more difficult. They wanted to grant money only for the defence of the frontier against France and they wanted the redress of their grievances before supply and especially the confirmation of their own interpretations of the *joyeuses entrées*. With Holland there was the vexed question of the export tax on Baltic grain which, typically, involved the private interests of several of Mary's councillors.[47] In France it was being said, Mary informed Charles, that he had money for only another three months of war. She therefore advised him to make peace.[48]

But the emperor continued his war and his campaign in France went badly. In October the regent informed the States General of the political and military situation. The cost of the garrisons and of the continuing war with Guelders had been more that 1,100,000 florins. The current *aides* had been anticipated up to 1538. The domain had been engaged for more than 140,000 florins. But the government had defended the frontiers of Artois and Hainaut and had prevented the soldiers from 'eating up the country'. After mature debates in the councils and with the knights of the Golden Fleece, the government had decided to propose an excise tax on beer, wine, silk and other high-quality textiles. There were to be none of the usual exemptions. 'No sweeter or more gracious means could be found',[49] and if it was objected that this was a 'novelty', they should consider that they habitually imposed excise taxes for their own local purposes.[50] But if they could think of a better method of raising taxes they were welcome to use it.

[45] Mary to Charles, Brussels, 4 Jan. 1536. *Ibid.*, fos. 1–7.
[46] Charles to Mary, Naples, 2 March 1536. *Ibid.*, fos. 20–8.
[47] See above, ch. 4.
[48] Report of the city council of Ghent, 12 June 1536. GAE, Varia, 265, fos. 16–21. AGRB, P. d'E. A., 1229, fo. 86. Maddens, 'De opstandige houding', 217 n.45.
[49] AGRB, P. d'E. A., 1229, fo. 86.
[50] *Ibid.*, 1232, fos. 69–71.

The regency of Mary of Hungary, I (1531–1550)

Soon it became clear that neither the States General nor most of the individual provinces were willing to accept the government's proposals. The government had to give them up, with the regent remarking bitterly that the Estates would have to take the blame before God and the emperor if any harm came to the Netherlands.[51] It was also becoming clear that the greatest difficulties were now coming not from Brabant but from Flanders and especially from the city of Ghent. The delegates from Flanders did not turn up at all at the meetings of the States General in November 1536. The magistrates of Ghent were so afraid of a commotion of the common people that they had not even dared to present the government's tax proposals to the city council (*collatie*) where the guilds and especially the weavers were strongly represented. What made the situation worse was that the deputies of Artois, Hainaut and Namur had instructions to follow the lead of Flanders; and these were the provinces which were always easiest to deal with and which, as frontier provinces, had been expected to set a good example.[52]

Since the proposed excise tax had not been accepted, the regent asked Flanders, in January 1537, for an *aide* of 52,000 livres per month. In order to get a quick agreement at least in principle she offered Ghent a *gracie*, a rebate, of six-sevenths of the city's quota. But the city rejected even this very generous offer.[53] Since negotiations with the Estates of Brabant were also bogged down, the government saw no alternative but to make one last appeal to the whole States General (24 March 1537). By now the king of France himself had entered the country with his troops. The regent argued that the Netherlanders were required to aid their own ruler for three reasons: Christian charity, loyalty and their own interest. They should do so without the usual delays.[54] On 27 March the government proposed a new type of tax: one carolus gulden per chimney or smoke hole (which was all that many poor people's hovels could boast). The idea seems to have been first discussed by the prelates and nobles of Brabant. Apart from being universal, with no exemptions for the normally privileged classes, the proposed chimney tax had a progressive element or, as the regent argued, 'the strong carrying the weak', because the houses of the rich had of course more chimneys than the houses of the poor. This tax was estimated to raise 200,000 florins a month, a sum which would pay for an army of 300,000 men. The Estates were invited to send their own commissioners to supervise the government's tax receivers and the pay parades of the troops.[55]

The States General were not impressed. The privileged elites, and they were the ones mainly represented, preferred the traditional methods of raising taxes and

---

[51] N. Maddens, 'De Invoering van de "nieuwe middelen" in het graafschap Vlaanderen, tijdens de Regering van Keizer Karel V', *RBPH*, 57 (1979), 346–7. Maddens, 'De Beden in het graafschap Vlaanderen', 398–9.
[52] Mary to Charles, Brussels, 12 Nov. 1536. AGRB, P. d'E. A., 49, fos. 100–1.
[53] Maddens, 'De opstandige houding', 220–1.
[54] GAE, Varia, 265, fos. 35–6.
[55] *Ibid.*, fos. 33–4. AGRB, P. d'E. A., 49, fo. 163. L. P. Gachard, *Relation des Troubles de Gand sous Charles Quint* (Brussels, 1846), 179–84. Maddens, 'Nieuwe middelen', 348–9.

it seems that the poor found the one gulden chimney tax an exceptionally heavy burden. In those places where the tax was actually levied it brought in very little. The government therefore changed tack again and allowed everyone to raise the money in any way they chose. All the provinces except Flanders now agreed to an *aide* of 1,200,000 gulden. Flanders was expected to pay its usual quota of one-third: 400,000 gulden.

THE REVOLT OF GHENT

From this point on the issue narrowed down to a confrontation between the government and Ghent. The city offered to raise troops in lieu of contributing its part of the Flemish *aide* in money. In itself this was neither an outrageous suggestion nor an unheard-of arrangement. It had been made on earlier occasions.[56] Ghent, in the middle of a long-term structural economic change, from a mainly cloth manufacturing economy to a much more diversified one, had long suffered from a high level of unemployment. Providing a militia for the government was a good way of getting the young men off the streets. The government, however, rejected the proposal. The military value of a quickly raised urban militia had always been minimal when it had to face professional troops – an experience which Machiavelli had had a generation earlier. Moreover, while the government was prepared to allow Ghent massive *gracien*,[57] it could not afford to allow the bad example which would be set by Ghent opting out altogether from paying money taxes which the States General and the rest of Flanders had agreed to pay. From the regent's point of view the dispute had shifted from haggling over taxes to a question of ultimate authority.

The key for this struggle over authority was Ghent's traditional control over its quarter, the smaller towns, villages and lordships in its surrounding countryside, the equivalent of the *contado* of the Italian city-republics. Just as Maximilian had in his conflict with Ghent in the 1480s, so his grand-daughter now tried to by-pass the city by demanding the *aide* directly from the smaller towns of Ghent's quarter. As early as the previous summer these towns had agreed to such a procedure while, at the same time, stipulating that they did not intend to separate themselves from Ghent.[58] By now, in the spring of 1537, Ghent complained that taxing its quarter was 'charging the loyal subjects against their will'.[59] It was certainly against the will of the Ghenters and, in the matter of their *contado*, the magistrates were at one with the mass of the poorer citizens. But was it also against the will of the smaller towns? Many of them were willing to pay the taxes but were afraid of reprisals from Ghent.

[56] Instructions for the deputies of Ghent, 16 April 1537. Gachard, *Relation*, 549–50.
[57] Ghent council minutes, 16 July 1537. GAE, Varia, 265, fos. 44–5.
[58] AGRB, P. d'E. A., 1228, fo. 48.
[59] GAE, Varia, 265, fos. 35–6.

The regency of Mary of Hungary, I (1531–1550)

Over the summer government agents began to arrest people from the *contado* for non-payment of the taxes. When Ghent protested, the regent offered to refer the legality of these arrests to the Great Council of Malines. Ghent, basing itself on its privileges, argued that there was no need for such a course. Interestingly enough, they did not argue that the Great Council could not be trusted to find against the government – the argument which Hoochstraten, a member of this government, had earlier put to the Estates of Holland. To the regent's amazement, the Ghenters now claimed the continued validity of Mary of Burgundy's Great Privilege of 1477. She wrote to her brother that this claim showed the Ghenters' bad will; for that privilege had been forced on their grandmother and had been revoked by their grandfather, Maximilian, in 1480.[60] She submitted the case to the Great Council herself and that court duly found in favour of the government.[61]

For the next two years the government and the Ghenters argued, negotiated and manoeuvred with increasing exasperation on both sides. The emperor wrote to Ghent that he could not accept their arguments about their poverty and about the payment of earlier *aides*, for these arguments applied to everyone else too, and everyone else had agreed to pay. Moreover, he was astonished that Ghent should claim it could prevent the inhabitants of the small towns and lordships from paying, or defend their non-payment, 'as if they were your subjects and not ours'. And he urged them again to take the matter of the arrests to the Great Council of Malines which, he insisted, had been set up to give justice without favour.[62] Mary wrote again that it was a matter of being master or servant, 'mestre ou varlet', and that she feared that Ghent's bad example would lead to complete loss of the emperor's authority in the other provinces.[63]

Evidently, the contrast between master and servants had become one of the regent's stock arguments; and the domino theory, the argument without proof of the escalation of potential disasters, was as popular in the sixteenth century as in the twentieth. All the same, her alarm and that of her court were genuine enough. The anonymous author of the *Relation des troubles de Gand sous Charles-Quint* who reflected the court's opinion spoke of wicked persons in Ghent who wanted to turn the city into an independent commune like the German and Italian city-states[64] – the same accusation which court circles in Castile had used against the cities of the Comunero revolt against Charles V, in 1520–1.[65]

To the magistrates of Ghent the dispute looked quite different. They felt themselves under real pressure from the common people to resist further taxation; and over the taxation of their 'quarter' they were certain that they were only upholding

---

[60] Mary to Charles, Brussels, Sept. 1537, Gachard, *Relation*, 194–6.
[61] 16 Jan. 1538. *Ibid.*, 202–3.
[62] Charles to city of Ghent. Barcelona, 31 Jan. 1538. GAE, Varia, 265, fos. 89–93.
[63] Mary to Charles, Brussels, 9 June 1538, Minute. AGRB, P. d'E. A., 50, fo. 78.
[64] Gachard, *Relation*, 25–6.
[65] J. A. Maravall, *Las comunidades de Castilla: una revolución moderna* (Madrid, 1963), 166–202.

the city's traditional political and economic domination. They were oblivious to the contradictions both in their position and in their arguments over taxation without consent. They did not recognise Maximilian's abrogation of Mary of Burgundy's Great Privilege and they were reluctant to accept the restrictions placed on them by the Treaty of Cadzand.[66] In 1515, when Charles had been declared of age and had made his *joyeuse entrée* into Ghent, there had been romantic hopes that he would renounce the Treaty of Cadzand and restore to his native city its lost privileges; and even when he showed no sign of doing this, loyalty to his person and trust in his favour remained strong. The Ghenters simply would not believe the regent when she warned them of the emperor's indignation. They stuck to their beliefs even when the emperor sent them a special envoy, the comte de Roeulx, to explain that the emperor would never accept their interpretation of their privileges. As late as the summer of 1539 the Ghenters organised an elaborate and expensive festival of the chambers of rhetoric. These were the cultural associations of the respectable burghers. They existed in many of the Netherlands cities, and the large city of Ghent had no fewer than five. In this festival another fourteen guest chambers from other cities took part. It was all meant to demonstrate how entirely loyal and pacific the Ghenter elites considered themselves to be.[67]

But it was already much too late. Suspicions were rife everywhere and tempers had risen too much. The chancellor of Brabant gave it as his opinion that the religious plays presented at the festival were full of wrong doctrines and tended towards Lutheranism. He advised the regent to prohibit the sale of the book of the plays. The censors of the theology faculty of the university of Louvain promptly placed the book on the index.[68]

More immediately damaging, however, was the fact that the magistrates and patricians of Ghent had lost the confidence of the common people. During the late summer of 1539 they staged a popular revolution. As often happened in early modern revolts its leaders were not guildsmen but propertied burghers and professional men. In time-honoured Ghenter revolutionary tradition they deposed the magistrates and appointed their own nominees. They arrested several of the old magistrates. One of them, the septuagenarian Lievin Pien, was tortured and then executed for allegedly having betrayed the city's privileges and his own instructions. They destroyed the *calfvel*, the official document, on calves' leather, of the Treaty of Cadzand which had restricted the powers of the guilds.

The chroniclers of the time were appalled by the brutal treatment of an old man but not surprised by the belief of the common people of Ghent that the magistrates were deliberately keeping charters favourable to the common man from the people. The belief in such conspiracies surfaced regularly in European

---

[66] See above, ch. 3.
[67] J. Decavele, 'Rederijkers', in J. Decavele, ed., *Keizer tussen stropdragers: Karel V 1500–1558* (Louvain, 1990), 89–96.
[68] *Ibid.*, 94.

The regency of Mary of Hungary, I (1531–1550)

cities during popular riots. In the decades following Luther's breach with Rome such beliefs tended to take on a religious colouring. The great majority of the revolutionaries in Ghent were good Catholics. But, psychologically, their fear that the authorities had conspired to keep their true privileges from them was similar to the belief of the German peasants that the authorities had conspired to keep the true word of God from the common man. Nor was such a belief without foundation in peoples' experience even if, on specific occasions, it was mistaken. In an age when kings spoke of the mysteries of state as transcendent matters beyond the understanding of ordinary mortals, when the Catholic Church and its priests taught that only they held the keys to the kingdom of heaven and reserved the cup of the eucharist to themselves, when writers delighted in filling their texts with hidden meanings accessible only to initiates, and when even composers, especially Flemish composers, constructed a method of musical notation by which they could secretly assimilate the chromaticism of the highly emotional contemporary Italian secular music into their own staid religious compositions, and when even, right down the social scale, guild masters jealously guarded the 'mysteries' of their crafts – in such an age a conspiracy to keep hidden truths from the common man made eminent sense. Where in the eighteenth century people talked of natural rights, in the sixteenth they talked of privileges which were being unjustly withheld from them. Conversely, to the authorities the demand for the disclosure of privileges, no matter whether they existed or not, looked subversive. The fear of the Netherlands government that social revolution and heresy went together was deeply anchored in the early modern psyche.

The *grand bailli* of Ghent, the chief law officer, fled from the city, fearing both for his life and that he would be forced to disclose his correspondence with the regent. Regular law enforcement therefore ceased in Ghent.[69] Even then, the new regime in Ghent seems to have still thought that the emperor would approve of their actions when they explained the situation to him on his return. They could not have misjudged the emperor more completely. When he left Spain for the Netherlands, in November 1539, he wrote in his instructions to Prince Philip that the Netherlands had missed a 'natural prince' for so long that they were showing themselves 'hard and difficult', with divisions, party conflicts, bad blood and mutinies, and with contempt towards whoever governed them. In some places there were so many sects that a great catastrophe was to be feared.[70] Philip was taught to distrust the Netherlanders at an early age – he was twelve at the time – and he never forgot this lesson. The Ghenters had burnt all bridges to the government. In Brussels there were rumours of a link between the revolutionaries of Ghent and the Anabaptists, and fears that they were seeking contacts with France. At this moment, however, Francis I was more interested in improving his relations

---

[69] Mary to Charles, Brussels, 21 Oct. 1539. AGRB, P. d'E. A., 50, fo. 158r.
[70] Ch. Weiss, ed., *Papiers d'Etat du Cardinal de Granvelle*, 9 vols (Paris, 1841–52), vol. II, 554.

with the emperor than in making trouble for him. Mary agreed with the emperor that until his arrival all necessary concessions should be made by her, and not by him, so that his authority should not be compromised.[71] For the rest, they planned his march through France with sufficient troops to restore the situation.

Charles entered Ghent on 14 February 1540 with 4,000 *landsknechts* and other troops. In contrast to Maximilian's experience in the 1480s Charles did not encounter any resistance at all. He was free to do as he liked. He rejected the duke of Alba's recommendation to treat Ghent as the Romans had treated Carthage, i.e. raze it to the ground and scatter the inhabitants. But he made the city pay its part of the *aide* of 1537 plus a fine of 150,000 gulden and an annuity of 6,000. On 29 April the city was convicted of rebellion and forfeited all its privileges. The leaders of the revolt were executed and other prominent citizens had to appear before the emperor with hangmen's ropes around their necks. In the new constitution imposed by the emperor the last vestiges of the medieval guild representation were now excluded from the city council. A government commission was to appoint all the magistrates. And finally a whole quarter of the city was razed to the ground to make way for an imperial fortress.[72]

The revolt of Ghent had demonstrated the weakness of regency government in a composite monarchy. In the face of Ghent's refusal to contribute to taxes which all the other provinces and even the rest of Flanders had agreed to in the States General, the government was virtually helpless. A relatively small town, such as 's-Hertogenbosch, could be coerced by quartering a couple of companies of soldiers in the surrounding countryside. With a bigger city like Brussels, the emperor thought of introducing soldiers but left the decision to the regent who thought better of it. But in the case of Ghent, a city of some 40,000 inhabitants and with a long tradition of defiance of its prince, the regent and her council did not think that they had the military means or, perhaps even more crucial, the will to use force. As early as August 1537 Mary had written to her brother that the country was no longer governable,[73] and on this and many other occasions she declared that the only remedy was his return to the Netherlands, preferably with a sum of ready money. Such a view was to be echoed many times and by many different people during the reign of Philip II.

In fact, Mary handled the crisis with great skill. By keeping cool in public (although not in her private letters to her brother); by sticking to the point of principle that the States General and even three of the four 'Members' of Flanders were supporting the government's tax demands for the reasonable cause of the defence of the Netherlands while only Ghent stood out, Mary and her council were able to keep the city isolated – very much in contrast to the 1480s when

---

[71] Charles to Mary, Madrid, 3 Oct. 1539. AGRB, P. d'E. A., 50, fo. 256r.
[72] For the revolt of Ghent see Decavele, *Keizer tussen stropdragers*. Much of, but not all, the documentation is published in Gachard, *Relation*.
[73] 'Ces pays ne sont plus gouvernables.' Mary to Charles, 27 Aug. 1537. AGRB, P. d'E. A., 50, fo. 19.

The regency of Mary of Hungary, I (1531–1550)

Ghent had been able to mobilise the rest of Flanders and a considerable section of the States General against the regent Maximilian. When in October 1539 she was discussing with the emperor the troops he would need when he came, she wrote that 2,000 Spaniards would be very effective. This was quite a small force; but even so, she feared that 'they would trouble the poor peasants a great deal'.[74] A myth was growing up already in Charles V's lifetime that he, the native Netherlander, could be trusted to look after his people in a way that his grandfather Maximilian had never been trusted and that his son, Philip II, would not be. The native Netherlander, Mary of Hungary, although never especially popular herself, did much to help the growth of this myth.

PEACE PROPOSALS WITH FRANCE: THE *ALTERNATIVA*

The emperor's entente with Francis I which had enabled him to march through France did not last. In 1542 war broke out again. Ambitious plans for an Anglo–imperial march on Paris failed, just as they had failed in 1523. The French retaliated by funding the new duke of Guelders, William of Cleves, and the terrible raids of his mercenary marshal Maarten van Rossem, 'Black Martin', the bogeyman of Dutch children. But, as so often before, French help proved to be too unreliable for the duke of Guelders. The old Egmont duke, Charles, had already lost many of his earlier gains. Friesland, Groningen, Drenthe, Overijssel and Utrecht had surrendered more or less willingly to the emperor for the prospect of a more peaceful life. Now Charles V used his considerable imperial clout in Germany to isolate William of Cleves. After that, it needed only a short campaign to make Duke William surrender and give up the Egmont claim to Guelders and Zutphen (1543).

The eastern frontier of the Netherlands was now secure and the provinces were finally rid of warfare on their own soil, apart from incursions from France. The Guelders wars had been both destructive and expensive. The Estates of Holland calculated that they had spent 485,000 guilders in the two years from April 1542 to April 1544.[75] They had of course haggled over the size of each separate grant of the taxes.[76] But in the end they had agreed to pay, on the principle that 'it is better to give up one cow when you have two than be burnt out, suffer brandschatting or be taken prisoner'.[77] Brandschatting was blackmail or a protection racket by which armies extracted huge sums from undefended towns in return for not burning them down. The government made the most of its success over Guelders when it argued with the Estates. But it was clear that it was now also necessary to make peace with France.

---

[74] Mary to Charles, 21 Oct. 1539. *Ibid.*, fos. 160–2.
[75] Adrien van der Goes, *Register van de Saecken van den Lande van Hollant (1544–49)*, vol. II (n.p., n.d.), 53–4.
[76] The debates on the nature of the government's tax proposals will be discussed below, ch. 7.
[77] Aert van der Goes, *Register van all die Dachvaerden*, 341.

This was the Netherlands background to the Peace of Crépy (18 Sept. 1544) between Charles V and Francis I. Charles had other and, to his mind, more pressing reasons for making peace than the situation in the Netherlands. Notably, he needed to have his hands free for fighting the Protestants and the Turks. Unusually, this aim seemed at least temporarily more important than the more usual priority of fighting France. It was less than three years since the emperor's disastrous and shaming failure to take Algiers, while in Germany the attempts to solve the religious problem had reached an impasse. As was usual with international treaties, the Estates of the Netherlands were asked to ratify Crépy. Since there was no loss of Netherlands territory, there was no immediate problem about such a course of action.

But this applied only to the official version of the treaty. The Estates do not seem to have been asked to ratify its secret clauses.[78] This is not surprising, for these clauses contained the famous *alternativa*, the emperor's promise to give the whole of the Netherlands and Franche-Comté as a dowry to his daughter on her marriage with Francis I's second son, the duke of Orléans. During the emperor's lifetime they would act as his regents but after his death they would reign in full sovereignty, although Orléans would have to give up any hereditary claims to the throne of France. Alternatively, Orléans would marry the emperor's niece, King Ferdinand I's daughter, with the duchy of Milan as her dowry.

The plan was meant to provide a permanent solution to the Habsburg–Valois rivalry. Such a plan, with some variations of personalities and details of the dowries, had been discussed for years: for instance towards the end of 1539 when Charles prepared to march from Spain through France to punish rebellious Ghent.[79] At that time there had also been talk of reviving a scheme of Charles the Bold of erecting the Netherlands into a kingdom.[80] In October 1540, after the defeat of Ghent, Charles talked about the alternatives of succession to the knights of the Golden Fleece.[81] In 1544 secret clauses of the Treaty of Crépy made a decision on the *alternativa* a matter of urgency. Charles first consulted members of his family, notably Mary. Then in December 1544 it was the turn of the Council of State in Spain. Philip (II) reported the discussions at length to his father. The council was split. The generals wanted to give up the Netherlands and keep Milan, the key to Spanish Italy and the central Mediterranean; for the Netherlands, as the duke of Alba forcefully argued, were strategically not defensible unless the prince himself resided there. A quarter of a century later Alba was to do his ferocious best to prove himself wrong – and he very nearly succeeded. But, basically, he was right in 1544.

---

[78] Adrien van der Goes, *Register*, vol. II, 31.
[79] Instructions to Prince Philip, Madrid, 5 Nov. 1539, in Weiss, *Papiers d'Etat*, vol. II, 554–61.
[80] Charles to François Bonvalot, his ambassador in France, Ghent, 14 March 1540. *Ibid.*, 564.
[81] AGRB, P. d'E. A., 52, fos. 252r–253r.

The regency of Mary of Hungary, I (1531–1550)

Most of the civilian ministers and theologians in the Spanish Council of State argued for giving up Milan and retaining the Netherlands under Habsburg rule. Their arguments were the economic and financial advantages to Spain and the sentimental one – they claimed it was moral – that the emperor should not give up his oldest hereditary dominion. No one argued the advantages or disadvantages to the Netherlanders or to the Milanese. Only the secretary, Francisco de los Cobos, who himself wavered between the two views, suggested that the Netherlanders would resent being handed over to the French and especially to such an unsavoury character as Orléans, and that they would resent having to pay for the defence of Milan (during Charles V's lifetime). Cobos thought the Netherlanders should at least be consulted.[82]

Not surprisingly the tone of the discussions in the Council of State in Brussels, during February 1545, was somewhat different. The generals were rather less in evidence than in the Consejo de Estado in Valladolid, but the arguments ranged more widely, to include the likely reactions of the English, the Germans and the pope. It was thought that His Holiness, backed by several German and Italian princes, would covertly try to sabotage the Franco-imperial entente. The ministers were all agreed that the welfare of the Netherlands should be the principal consideration. They argued rather whether the great lords should be consulted individually or together, and how the confidentiality of the negotiations with France could be maintained. This last point would become an even greater problem when the treaty had to be ratified by the Estates. But in spite of all the ifs and buts which individual ministers put forward, there was no fundamental division of opinion as there was in Spain: they all wanted the emperor to keep the Netherlands in the Habsburg family and give up Milan.[83] This was also Mary's opinion and, in the end, that of Charles himself.

Before this part of the Treaty of Crépy could be put into effect, however, the duke of Orléans died, on 9 September 1545, and with him the whole plan of the *alternativa*. The Estates, however, had ratified the public part of the treaty a month before this event, just as they had ratified the treaty with Cleves. Gouda instructed its deputies that they should insist on the Estates of Holland following those of Flanders and Brabant and the other provinces which had already ratified, 'to the honour of His Imperial Majesty'.[84] There is no evidence that the Estates were informed about the *alternativa* and, more surprisingly, there does not even seem to have been a leak. It was not normal during this period that representative assemblies were involved in international diplomatic negotiations, even when the

---

[82] Prince Philip to Charles V, Valladolid, 13 Dec. 1544, in F. Fernández Alvarez, ed., *Corpus documental de Carlos V*, vol. II (Salamanca, 1975), 299–311. F. Chabod, '¿Milan o los Paises Bajos?', in *Carlos V (1500–1558). Homenaje de la Universidad de Granada* (Granada, 1958), 331–72.
[83] 'Avis des ministres', Brussels, end Febr. 1545, in Weiss, *Papiers d'Etat*, vol. III, 67–90.
[84] A. Meerkamp van Embden, ed., 'Goudse Vroedschapsresoluties betreffende de Dagvaerten der Staten van Holland', *BMHG*, 38, (1917), 267, 271. Adrien van der Goes, *Register*, vol. II, 31.

future sovereignty of their country was involved. Ten years later, when Queen Mary of England married Philip of Spain, she rounded on Parliament for so much as suggesting she should marry an Englishman.[85]

For Mary of England this was not only a practical matter of preserving confidentiality during delicate negotiations but also a matter of principle: the respective prerogatives and rights of princes and parliaments. In the discussion about the *alternativa* nobody in the Netherlands talked about principle. This is curious. As early as the twelfth century representatives of the nobility and of the major cities of Flanders had deposed a count and elected a new count.[86] In Brabant a series of succession crises, from the thirteenth to the fifteenth century, brought the Estates on to the scene as principal actors. In 1477 the States General claimed the effective right to determine the duchess's marriage and the succession to all the provinces of the Netherlands. In 1494, 1506 and 1515 the States General determined not indeed the succession – there were no legitimate alternatives to Philip I and Charles V – but who was to control the government of the Netherlands. But in 1544/5 no one mentioned these precedents. Where Mary I and, later, Elizabeth I had to lecture their parliaments Charles V and his regent clearly do not seem to have thought this was necessary. They discussed the *alternativa* in diplomatic, strategic and personal terms. As recently as 1543 the regent had justified new tax proposals to the States General by reminding them of their devotion to the emperor, their 'natural prince', and 'for nothing in the world would they wish to give up their obedience to him but rather endure all hardships than fall under the domination of the French ... and that they would preserve and defend their liberties and freedoms and not allow themselves, their wives and children to be reduced to perpetual servitude'.[87]

Only a year later, in so far as Mary and Charles thought in constitutional terms at all, it seemed to them sufficient that Orléans, if indeed he were to succeed to the Netherlands, would have to take his oath on preserving their laws and privileges. The Estates never knew about this arrangement and there is no knowing whether they would have accepted it. A generation later they definitely rejected such an arrangement with another French prince, Orléans' nephew, the duke of Anjou. But by then the whole perception of constitutional power had changed in the Netherlands.[88]

---

[85] My thanks to Prof. M. J. Rodríguez-Salgado for clarifying this point for me.
[86] J. Dhondt, 'Les origines des états de Flandre', *APAE*, 1 (1950), 13–19.
[87] Quoted in T. Juste, *Les Pays-Bas sous Charles Quint. Vie de Marie de Hongrie* (Brussels and Paris, 1858), 80.
[88] See below, ch. 13. It is at least possible that in 1545 the imperial government had decided to keep the States General in reserve and to use this body to repudiate the whole deal, if they later felt so inclined. Charles V and his advisers had certainly not forgotten how, in 1526, Francis I had used the Estates of Burgundy to repudiate the clauses of the Treaty of Madrid which stipulated the surrender of the duchy of Burgundy to the emperor. But I have found no actual mention of such a ploy.

The regency of Mary of Hungary, I (1531–1550)

THE NETHERLANDS AND THE HOLY ROMAN EMPIRE

With the *alternativa* Charles V had deliberately risked a crisis in the relations between the composite monarchy of the House of Austria and the Estates of the Netherlands in order to solve the apparently more urgent problems of his relations with the Valois. In the event the crisis did not materialise, but all the underlying problems remained unresolved. Not the least of these was the relationship between the House of Austria and the Holy Roman Empire. Charles V was head of both; but this fact made the problem only the more intractable. The injection of religious passion into the situation made it explosive. The Schmalkaldic War (1545–6) and its aftermath, the abortive search for a solution to both the religious and the constitutional problems of the Holy Roman Empire, however, left the Netherlands relatively untouched.

No one doubted that the Netherlands were part of the Holy Roman Empire. Almost equally certainly, but not quite, Flanders and Artois were not, and there were also other areas of uncertainty. At the same time the Netherlanders did not think of themselves as German, though here again there were uncertainties in some of the newly joined eastern provinces, especially Guelders. The Habsburg emperors did not want to break the connection of the Netherlands with the Holy Roman Empire but they tried to keep them as separate from imperial organisation as possible, just as they tried to do, although somewhat less successfully, with their Austrian dominions. Charles V spelt out this policy in secret instructions to his brother Ferdinand in 1531: the Netherlands were not to be subject to the jurisdiction of the Empire. But Maximilian I had set up the Burgundian Circle (although it was not entirely clear which territories belonged to it) and the Netherlands contributed to the costs of the Imperial Chamber (*Reichskammergericht*). But the Germans' most important concern, the need to pay for their country's defence against the Turks, was seen as a very low priority by the Netherlanders compared with their immediate need for defence against France and their commercial and maritime rivalry with the German Hansards, the English and the Scots.

The incorporation of Utrecht, Overijssel, Guelders and Zutphen, all of them undoubtedly imperial fiefs, brought the problem of mutual relations back into focus. Through the 1540s the emperor and the government in Brussels, on the one side, and King Ferdinand and the German Reichstag, on the other, conducted highly technical negotiations in order to clear up the legal and financial grey areas in their relations. In 1548 they concluded the Treaty of Augsburg. In contrast with the negotiations for the *alternativa*, there was no reason to keep these discussions confidential or to keep the Estates of the Netherlands in the dark.[89] For the Estates, as for the Reichstag, it was largely a practical matter. They were not very interested in the apparently paradoxical legal point that the emperor had freed the

[89] AGRB, P. d'E. A., 150, fo. 3 r and v.

provinces from investment by the emperor. But would the Empire – the Estates of Holland called it Duytslandt – help the Netherlands Estates against France and the Scots, and would they receive an act of indemnity excusing them from further contributions they might have to make to the defensive alliance which resulted from the Treaty of Augsburg? When the Estates of Holland discussed ratification, in January 1549, most of the other provinces had already ratified the treaty, and the Holland deputies agreed to the ratification without even the usual reference back to their principals.[90] For Charles V the advantages of this treaty were that the Netherlands were now united in a much more clearly defined Burgundian Circle, that they were represented in the Reichstag and, by a legal assessor, in the Imperial Chamber and that, although still a part of the Holy Roman Empire, they were also in a defensive alliance with it. The Netherlands, for their part, were expected to pay a financial contribution to the Empire at double the rate of an imperial electorate, or treble during an actual war with the Turks.[91]

By the middle of the sixteenth century Charles V seemed to have firmly established his princely authority in the Netherlands and, by the treaties of Crépy and Augsburg, to have defined and safeguarded their international position. Very soon it was to become apparent that the safeguards and definitions were paper defences. The war with France would start again and become more dangerous and costly than ever. The Netherlands' contribution to the Holy Roman Empire (though not of course to the costs of Charles V's composite monarchy and his imperial policies) remained largely unpaid; but for their part the Netherlanders were to find that the Holy Roman Empire did not regard the defensive alliance as valid against France and, later, after the outbreak of the Revolt, even less so against Spain.

---

[90] Adrien van der Goes, *Register*, vol. II. States General of Brussels, Dec. 1548. Estates of Holland in The Hague, Jan. 1549. Adriaen Sandelijn, 'Register van de Resolutien van de Dagvaerd 1548–54'. Amsterdam, Gemeente Archief, MS 5029, I, S IV. 54, fos. 24–44.

[91] In my discussion of the Netherlands and the Empire I have followed Nicolette Mout, 'Die Niederlande und das Reich im sechzehnten Jahrhundert (1512–1609)', in V. Press, ed., *Alternativen zur Reichsverfassung* (forthcoming). My thanks to Prof. Mout for sending me a copy of her article before publication.

7

The Netherlands at the centre of the Habsburg composite monarchy: the regency of Mary of Hungary, II (1550–1555)

'Whoever is in charge of this country should be very sociable with everyone in order to gain the goodwill both of the nobility and the commonality; for this country does not render the obedience which is due to a monarchy, nor is there an oligarchical order nor even that of a republic. And thus a woman, especially if she is a widow, cannot do what should be done.'

Mary of Hungary to Charles V, on the occasion of his abdication. Brussels, 1555.
Weiss, *Papiers d'Etat du Cardinal de Granvelle*, vol. IV, 474[1]

CHARLES V AND THE HABSBURG MONARCHY

In 1550 Charles V and his composite monarchy were at peace in Europe and, by common estimation, at the height of their power. The Netherlands were an important part of this monarchy and, as the discussions about the *alternativa* showed, not a part the monarchy would willingly give up. But, giving them up for the sake of permanent peace with France had been at least a matter for serious discussion. And the Netherlands were not the centre of the monarchy. The monarch did not habitually reside there, nor were their interests as a polity his principal concern. Their government, in the capable hands of, first, Charles V's aunt, and then of his sister, and with the basic support of the aristocratic-landed and the urban-commercial elites was functioning satisfactorily. Of the major threats to the tranquillity of the country, the regency governments had coped quite successfully with two popular urban rebellions and with the aggressions of the duke of Guelders. (While the Netherlanders experienced these wars as aggressive, they were really the duke's defensive response to the doubtfully legal and certainly aggressive claims of the Habsburgs to his duchy.) Only once, in each case, had Charles V needed to intervene in person: against the popular rebellion in Ghent, in 1539–40,

---

[1] 'Celuy qui a la charge de cestuy d'icy ayt grande hantisse avec un chascun, pour gaigner la voluntez tant de la noblesse que des communes, pour n'estre ce pays en l'obéissance que à monarchie appartient, ny en l'ordre de oligarquie, ny aussi du tout en république, ce que la femme, principalement estant vefve, ne peult faire comm'il sera requis'.

and against Guelders, then ruled by the duke of Cleves, in 1543. In both cases his formidable military power, drawn from his international monarchy, had assured him of quick and complete success.

There was a third threat and it could not be handled so easily: that of France. Traditionally this threat had been directed against the Netherlands and it continued to be so; but the threat was also directed against Charles V's claims to be head or leader of Christendom, whether against the Ottoman Turks or the European heretics or simply the leader of Europe *qua* emperor. Charles's military might had defeated the German Protestant princes in the Schmalkaldic War (1546–7), even if not as decisively as the rebels of Ghent and the duke of Guelders. The threat of heresy seemed to be eminently containable in the emperor's hereditary lands, always provided his regency governments remained alert to this danger. In the Netherlands the regent Mary of Hungary, whatever her personal interest in Lutheran teaching might or might not have been in the 1520s, showed every sign of being thus alert in 1550.

In these circumstances it is understandable that in the Netherlands the political basis of the Habsburg monarchy, together with its nebulous but crucial self-relationship with the monarchy of the whole Habsburg composite polity, was not seriously questioned. The imperial–universal claims of the monarch were acknowledged in triumphal arches and learned nostalgic Latin mottoes whenever he made a formal entry into a city; but they hardly entered into the internal political dialogue of the country. The relations between the monarchy and the States General were therefore on the whole perfectly amicable. This was very different from what these relations had been in the reign of Charles the Bold and during the regencies of Maximilian. There were of course grumbles. Many people resented contributing to the emperor's apparently endless wars, which did not seem to be waged in the interests of the Netherlands. The Dutch burghers felt about the Turkish threat like the German burghers in Goethe's *Faust*: faraway wars and rumours of wars, good for leisurely talk on a Sunday afternoon, so long as at home everything continued in the good old way.[2] It was quite characteristic that, on the one occasion when the Netherlands had entered into a treaty with the Empire, i.e. Germany, the interpretations the two sides put on this essentially amicable agreement were diametrically opposed: each side thought that the other had obliged itself to give help with its international problems. Both were to be disappointed.

France was a different matter. The Habsburg propaganda that the king of France's subjects had none of the liberties of the emperor's subjects of the Low

---

[2] Andrer Bürger:

>Nichts Bessers weiss ich mir an Sonn- und Feiertagen,
>Als ein Gespräch von Krieg und Kriegsgeschrei,
>Wenn hinten, weit, in der Türkei
>Die Völker aufeinander schlagen.
>
>Goethe, *Faust*, pt. I

The regency of Mary of Hungary, II (1550–1555)

Countries and that the king of France could raise taxes at will was very effective.³ The Netherlands high nobility, with some of their estates and with relatives in France, knew this argument to be an exaggeration. But, with their careers hitched to the fortunes of the emperor, they saw no reason to contradict the propaganda line which, after all, had a kernel of truth: the difference between *dominium regale* and *dominium politicum et regale*. The lawyers and civil servants did not bother very much about this distinction, provided the law was always observed and no wrong was done to anyone: thus the chancellor and the Council of Brabant, as well as the president and the judges of the Great Council of Malines, insisted to the regent. When the emperor made arrangements for his own succession, the lawyers argued, he had to have the consent of his subjects and the provinces should always be kept together, 'for the law of this land resides entirely in the person of His Majesty'.⁴ Thus the Roman law principle of the *princeps* as the fountain of all law could be used to insist on a regime based on consent.

The patrician councillors of the town halls were anxiously looking through their windows, fearful of the mood of their unprivileged fellow citizens. For this, if for no other reason, peace with France was vastly preferable to war. During the regency of Maximilian of Austria the States General had actually criticised his aggressive policy. But with his grandson, Charles V, a born Netherlander and their actual prince, they were, at least as yet, willing to accept his claim that war and peace were the prince's prerogative. But of course the town councils could ask their deputies to the provincial Estates and to the States General to try to get the burden of taxes which the government proposed reduced as much as possible. During the second half of Mary's regency her finance officers made successive attempts to deal with the deepening financial crisis. These attempts will be discussed below; but as yet they were all attempts to solve the crisis by cooperation with the Estates: by consent.

This generally manageable political situation was upset by events outside the Netherlands and outside Netherlands control. In Germany the emperor failed to negotiate or to impose a stable settlement, either of the religious question or of the relations of the imperial monarchy with the German princes. Worse still, in 1552 Charles's personal authority collapsed when he had to flee from a suddenly aggressive league of German princes which included some of his former allies. In Italy the emperor was drawn into new wars over the strategically situated republic of Siena and the principalities of Parma and Piacenza; and these wars, in turn, hopelessly compromised his relations with the papacy. In any case, the papacy, unlike the emperor, was unwilling to make any compromise with the Protestants at all.

---

³ For instance in the government's address to the States General, in July 1542. AGRB, P. d'E. A., 649, fo. 107r–v.
⁴ Council of Brabant to Mary of Hungary, Brussels, 1 June 1549. *Ibid.*, fo. 2r–v.

Monarchies, States Generals and Parliaments

Given the previous history of imperial–French relations, there was no surprise that France now became involved on the side of Charles V's enemies, both in Germany and in Italy, and that Henry II would try to persuade the sultan to attack the Habsburgs again in the Mediterranean and in Hungary.[5]

In the actual fighting which now broke out, the Netherlands were bound to become one of the focal points of the conflict. As so often before, Mary of Hungary saw this earlier and more clearly than her brother. The Habsburg family knew from experience that Charles always wanted to take final decisions himself, even when he was exasperatingly slow to make up his mind. He also expected his relatives to take full responsibility for the dominions in which he had installed them as regents. Charles prescribed their foreign policy and hence the military and financial efforts he expected these dominions to make and he did this all too often without taking account of, or sometimes even listening to, his family's opinions. Mary was to describe this situation succinctly in her letter of resignation in 1555: 'He who governs under another must render account not only to God but also to the prince and to his subjects.'[6] When things were going badly it was best to have the emperor physically by one's side, both to exert his personal authority in the requests for financial aid which had to be made to the Estates and to take personal responsibility for unpopular and sometimes plainly wrong decisions. Once war had broken out, a woman governor would be at a particular disadvantage because the generals would tend to ignore her but still blame her if anything went wrong. Thus in 1552 Mary's letters, just like those of her aunt Margaret earlier, were full of pleas for Charles to return to the Netherlands. What she could not foresee was that, when Charles did return, she herself would have to take responsibility for much of her brother's imperial policy, as well as for that of the Netherlands.

At the end of 1552 Charles chose to attack Metz, a city handed over without authority by the league of German princes to the king of France. Strategically, this move was justified because Charles had to impress the four Rhenish electors, for Henry II was wooing them for a possible imperial election. More importantly, perhaps, the French occupation of Metz was part of an ambitious French plan to block the route between the Habsburg positions in Italy and the Netherlands. But Metz, especially in winter, was virtually impregnable. Mary and most of Charles's military experts vainly tried to dissuade him from his move against the fortress. The campaign turned into one of the emperor's greatest military disasters and financially a very expensive one at that.

---

[5] For the extraordinarily complicated international relations of these years, see H. Lutz, *Christianitas Afflicta: Europa, das Reich und die päpstliche Politik im Niedergang der Hegemonie Kaiser Karls V (1552–1556)*, (Göttingen, 1964), *passim*, and M. J. Rodriguez-Salgado, *The Changing Face of Empire: Charles V, Philip II and Habsburg Authority 1551–1559* (Cambridge, 1988), *passim*.

[6] This is the passage which precedes the quotation at the beginning of this chapter.

The regency of Mary of Hungary, II (1550–1555)

CHARLES V IN THE NETHERLANDS

In February 1553 the emperor entered Brussels and stayed in the Netherlands, beyond his abdication, until September 1556, when both he and Mary finally left for Spain and retirement. While Charles was resident in Brussels the Netherlands became the centre of the Habsburg monarchy and of imperial policy-making for the first time since Maximilian had returned to Austria in 1489. Naturally, this position influenced the emperor's perspective. Germany and the German Protestant princes ceased to be the prime focus of his preoccupation. Charles left them to his brother Ferdinand to cope with – perhaps not without a touch of *Schadenfreude*, after his defeat by Ferdinand over the Habsburg succession to the Holy Roman Empire and Ferdinand's somewhat dubious attitude during the Protestant League's attack on Charles in Innsbruck in 1552. While making Ferdinand responsible, Charles continued to interfere in the politics of the Empire and he did not resign his title of Holy Roman Emperor until after he had resigned all his other titles. But his principal efforts and his waning personal ability to concentrate were now directed towards the war with France.

However, the shift in perspective did not mean that now the actual interests of the Netherlands had become paramount in Habsburg policy-making. These interests, as their Estates had never ceased arguing since the days of the Burgundian dukes, had been independence from but peace with France. But the war with France continued. The lip service which both sides had given to a united front against the Turks, the dynastic status solidarity of Habsburg and Valois which had moderated the conflict between Charles V and Francis I, and which had led Charles to such a romantic gesture as to challenge Francis to a personal combat as a judgement of God (1536), as well as the less romantic but still quixotic plans of the *alternativa* – all this disappeared in a rising tide of distrust and war fever. The other side would have to show some signs of moral repentance; so it was argued in the courts of both Paris and Brussels. For how could the imperialists trust the French who had allowed a Turkish fleet to winter in Toulon (1544) and, more recently, had asked them to support a rebellion in Corsica and even the temporary conquest of that island (1553)?[7]

For their part, how could the French trust the emperor? They knew of course of his proposal to marry his son Philip to Mary Tudor as soon as she had succeeded to the throne of England, in September 1553. And, if they had known of them, the French would probably not have been surprised by the arguments which the emperor told his ambassador, Simon Renard, to use in England: it would be beneficial if God gave the pair a son, for England and the Netherlands to be ruled by one prince; for thus the French would be kept in check and moreover, with the assistance of Spain, the kings of England would recover Guyenne, unjustly seized by the kings of France.

---

[7] Rodriguez-Salgado, *The Changing Face of Empire*, 111–18.

So here it was, what the French always feared: the encirclement and eventual dismemberment of their kingdom. If important personages in the English council had to be won over, they could be bribed, Charles suggested.[8] He did not actually say so on this occasion; but everyone believed he had won the imperial crown by massive bribes – and thus fulfilled divine providence, as his grand-chancellor Gattinara put it at the time. Renard, at least, understood this point. In submitting his master's arguments to Mary Tudor he stressed the emperor's concern for religion in the proposed dynastic alliance.[9]

The marriage of Philip and Mary was a tremendous victory for the Habsburgs; but it did nothing to forward peace. The French, as much as the imperialists, believed that one should negotiate from a position of strength or, as people said at the time, after a good victory. Then, as nearly always in international relations, it was a formula for making war endless. 'Poor Christendom' sighed the rest of Europe, watching the two principal Christian powers fighting relentlessly for political and dynastic supremacy.[10]

In the Netherlands the regent, Mary, soon found that this time the emperor's presence did little to strengthen her authority. On the contrary. Just as her aunt Mary had found with her father, the emperor Maximilian I, there were now two competing centres of authority and decision-making and two sources of patronage in the country. Almost immediately, Mary made a further miscalculation. Fearing an imminent catastrophe in the Netherlands, she persuaded Charles to summon Prince Philip from Spain, so as to strengthen the family position which she now evidently judged to be centred in the Netherlands.

To the historian it is not so obvious that there was such an imminent danger of catastrophe as she conjured up for her brother. No doubt she had information which has not come down to us. But throughout her regency she had been given to melodramatic warnings of impending catastrophe; and no wonder, because by herself and without the personal intervention of the emperor and the troops he could raise, she and the Netherlands government did not have the means to deal with anything but a very minor local crisis. The immediate result of Philip's appearance in northern Europe, at a time when the emperor was periodically suffering from debilitating illnesses, was to raise a third centre of authority, decision-making and patronage. Even before leaving Spain, Philip had already shown how formidable he could be in such a capacity by installing his sister Juana as regent, much against his father's inclinations, and by choosing Juana's council for her, without even consulting the emperor.[11]

---

[8] Charles V to Simon Renard, Valenciennes, 20 Sept. 1553. Weiss, *Papiers d'Etat*, vol. IV, 113.
[9] Renard to Mary of England, London, 11 Oct. 1553. *Ibid.*, 130.
[10] 'Christianitas afflicta', or a similar phrase in Latin or a modern language was widely used at the time. See Lutz (whom it provided with the title of his book), 16 and *passim*.
[11] On this point and on the whole complex relationship between Charles, Mary, Philip and Juana I have followed the detailed account by Rodriguez-Salgado, *The Changing Face of Empire*, especially ch. 2.

The regency of Mary of Hungary, II (1550–1555)

Nevertheless, for the moment the political problems of the Netherlands remained manageable. The three members of the Habsburg family, Charles, Mary and Philip, kept at least the outward appearance of a united front. In the country there were plenty of grumbles about the level of taxes and the robberies and violence of the soldiers, both those of the enemy and their own. Among the elite there were doubts about the emperor's Italian policy and whether it did not prolong the unpopular war with France. But such grumbles were nothing new, and the high nobility, their clients among the lower nobility and all the patrician town councils remained firmly loyal. The eventual casualty of a volatile political and personal situation turned out to be the emperor himself, eighteen months later.

WAR FINANCE

In the meantime there remained the practical problem of financing the continuing war with France. We now know that, as so often in conflict situations, both sides exaggerated the enemy's resources; but that did not make the problem of war finance any easier. All the Habsburg dominions were required to contribute to the costs of the monarchy's wars. But this was not a legal obligation. Mary of Hungary had tried to make it so for the Netherlands by persuading the provinces to form a defensive union. She had failed. No one attempted to form a defensive union for the composite monarchy as a whole. The Habsburg rulers and regents themselves felt ambivalent about pooling resources. As late as 1589, the year after the whole Habsburg monarchy had contributed to the very limit to the enormous costs of the Armada campaign, Philip II voiced his regret that such common efforts were at times unavoidable: 'Except in the most urgent cases', he wrote to the Council of Italy, 'it is not the custom to transfer the burdens of one kingdom to another. [But] since God has entrusted me with so many [kingdoms], since all are in my charge, and since in the defence of one all are preserved, it is just that all should help me.'[12] Charles V had usually tried to keep movements of money from one of his dominions to another secret. By the 1550s the veil of secrecy had worn very thin and the emperor himself, at least, does not seem to have had a bad conscience about his imperial financial practices, even though this did not mean that he regarded his composite monarchy as a unified empire.[13]

In all the Habsburg dominions, but especially in those most immediately affected by the French wars, i.e. Castile and the Netherlands, normal revenues were not nearly sufficient to meet the cost of warfare and, what made the situation worse, their collection was much too slow when the soldiers were clamouring for

---

[12] Quoted in H. G. Koenigsberger, *The Practice of Empire: The Government of Sicily under Philip II of Spain* (London and Ithaca, 1969), 56.
[13] For Naples see A. Calabria, *The Cost of Empire: The Finances of the Kingdom of Naples in the Time of the Spanish Rule* (Cambridge, 1991), chs. 3 and 4.

their pay. The governments of the separate dominions therefore engaged in sophisticated methods of deficit financing by negotiating loans with willing bankers. Varying and often heavy rates of interest had to be paid on these loans and, in the end, they had to be repaid. This could only be done by raising new taxes and tapping new resources.

It was in this financial field that, for a time, the Netherlands became the administrative centre of the Habsburg multiple monarchy. As regent of Spain, Philip worked hard to provide funds for the emperor's wars in Italy and on the Netherlands borders. At the same time, because the need was so urgent, Mary interfered with Philip's efforts by taking up loans in Antwerp for which she assigned Spanish funds by persuading the emperor to issue licences to Genoese and German bankers to export gold and silver from Spain. Twice Charles ordered the confiscation of silver imported privately in the annual treasure fleets from the Indies: nearly 600,000 ducats worth in 1553 and well over 800,000 in 1555. The owners were forced to take *juros*, the Castilian government annuities, instead. The *juros* were funded on regular Castilian government income. To preserve his standing with his most important creditors, Charles exempted the Fugger and other favoured financiers from his decree of confiscation. Philip, as regent, put the interests of the Castilian treasury first and therefore had his own preferences for exemptions. When he left for the Netherlands the new regent, his sister Juana, naturally had her own preferences. The financial confusion in Castile was now beginning to look even worse than that of the Netherlands. Already by 1552 the emperor's borrowing in Castile had reached more than 3.5 million ducats; for the last quinquennium of his reign, 1551–5, it came altogether to more than 8 million.[14]

Charles and Mary raised their loans on the Antwerp money market. That was possible only because of the export licences for precious metals from Spain; for the Netherlands had no treasure-producing colonies. Yet the Spanish–American treasure which was transmitted to Antwerp was not enough. It was still necessary to raise loans funded on Netherlands revenues. The problem was to reassure the international bankers that such revenues were sufficiently large and that they would not be diverted from paying the interest on, and eventually repaying the capital of, the loans. Government domain income had long since been sold off or pledged for years in advance. The great seigneurs, as commanding officers of the restive soldiers, would sometimes stand surety with their private property. This practice demonstrated the loyalty of the high nobility; but as a method of raising loans it was unreliable and, at best, a short-term expedient.

This left the income from the grants made by the Estates. These were, by far, the government's most inportant sources of income. They suffered, however, from

---

[14] For detailed descriptions of Spanish government finances see Rodríguez-Salgado, *The Changing Face of Empire*, 60–1; and M. Steele, 'La real hacienda', in *Historia general de España y América*, vol. VI (Madrid, 1986), 143–67.

two disadvantages. The provincial Estates and the States General made their grants for a fixed number of years and this number had to be negotiated for each separate grant. The government could pledge this income to the bankers, but then there was little or nothing left for current expenses or for the crises which tended to blow up more and more frequently. Secondly, the practice of allowing *gracien* rebates or, effectively, bribes, to the most powerful and influential cities greatly reduced the disposable income from the regular *aides*. In Flanders, Brabant and Holland, *gracien* seem to have amounted to one-third of the nominal value of the *aide*, even in the 1530s[15] and in the 1550s the position was certainly no better.

The Council of Finance therefore began to work on new methods of raising revenues. The principles underlying their thinking were, firstly, to get rid as far as possible of the traditional exemptions: the *gracien* for the towns and the immunity from taxes of the clergy, the nobility and government officials. Secondly, they aimed at achieving a fairer incidence of taxation. In 1537 these principles formed the basis of the proposed chimney tax. This tax had proved to be a failure.[16] A more sophisticated method of taxation was needed, and one which would tap more effectively hitherto exempt wealth. Meester Vincent Corneliszoon van Mierop, one of the professionals in the Council of Finance, therefore proposed a 1 per cent tax on the property of every inhabitant of the Netherlands or a 25 per cent income tax. This and other similar proposals were urgently discussed by the regent's financial advisers.[17] When war broke out again with France and Guelders, the government presented a regular budget to the States General of 1 December 1542 for the total estimated military expenditure, 300,000 livres per month, and of the sums that could be raised from domain revenues and from the ordinary grants of the Estates. The deficit was estimated at 2,400,000 livres. The regent stressed the dangers of the attack by the Gueldrian marshal, Maarten van Rossem, 'who is only a simple gentleman of lowly condition' – evidently that made the Gueldrian attack much more shameful than if it had been led by a great nobleman. If our own soldiers remained unpaid, Mary continued, they would oppress the poor country people, 'and you might afterwards ask me why I did not request more money from you to prevent such a calamity'.[18] The government did not pursue the idea of a property tax on everyone because that would have been too difficult to collect. Instead, it proposed an income tax on merchants, bankers and money lenders, as well as on owners of *immobilia*, i.e. land and houses, and of annuities. Ministers insisted to the States General that such people were mostly much richer than the commonality, especially in Holland and the other provinces 'where commerce reigns' and where the incidence of taxes was notoriously unfair. There would be no

---

[15] J. D. Tracy, 'The Taxation System of the County of Holland during the Reigns of Charles V and Philip II, 1519–1566', *Economisch- en Sociaal-Historisch Jaarboek* 48 (1985), 74–85.
[16] See above, p. 139.
[17] Tracy, 'The Taxation System', 85–6.
[18] AGRB, P. d'E. A., 1232, fos. 188–91.

great difficulty in assessing the owners of immoveables and annuities, and the government stressed that for the assessment of commercial income there would be no inspection of merchants' books and accounts. The assessment would be made by respected persons: 'gens de bien'. In other words, the new income tax would be based on self-assessment and hearsay. Poorer people would be helped because all those who, by the common opinion of their neighbours and of the tax commissioners, owned property of only 1,000 gulden or less would be exempt. There were to be no other rebates.[19]

The outlines of these proposals seem to have been made to the States General as a whole and the details were made separately to the individual provinces. This tactic was part of the government's general principle of divide and rule. Earlier in the same year, 1542, it had issued an ordinance that the deputies of the Franc de Bruges (het Vrije van Brugge) who usually tended to follow the lead of Bruges, Ghent and Ypres, should report the government proposals to their constituents but on no account consult with each other and then bring back their answers. The eighteenth-century commentator Philippe Zaman remarked about this order that the Estates of Flanders would now function like the English House of Commons would if it could no longer debate government proposals but was to leave the drawing up of the bills to London, Bristol, Cambridge and Wales.[20] Zaman belonged to the anglophile Enlightenment and his satirical analogy was well taken, although one may doubt whether the Estates of Flanders really functioned like this. In any case, with greater or lesser vehemence, the provinces objected to the proposals. But they objected even more vehemently to another government proposal, the Hundredth Penny, a tax of 1 per cent on the export of all goods. In the face of this opposition in the States General the regent declared she would impose the Hundredth Penny *ex potestate absoluta imperatoris*.

Princes who claimed imperial rights according to Roman law had been arguing for a long time that regulating and taxing trade was part of their royal prerogative. It was, however, only in the seventeenth century that the full implications of such a claim were spelt out. In 1606 Thomas Bate brought a court case against James I's government in England over an import duty on currants, a duty imposed during the previous reign, by Elizabeth I. He lost his case, but in 1610 Parliament brought it up again. This time the arguments came to involve fundamental questions of the powers of the monarchy and of Parliament, of the relation of both these to the English common law and of a free Englishman's rights of property.[21] Were the

---

[19] *Ibid.*, 1228, fos. 92–3.
[20] P. de Zaman, *Exposition des trois états dy païs et comté de Flandre* (Ghent, 1711), 220–4.
[21] J. P. Kenyon, *Stuart England* (London, 1978), 65. For the constitutional arguments see J. P. Sommerville, 'Parliament, Privilege, and the Liberties of the Subject', in J. H. Hexter, ed., *Parliament and Liberty from the Reign of Elizabeth to the English Civil War* (Stanford, 1992), 56–84; D. H. Sacks, 'Parliament, Liberty and the Commonweal', in *ibid.*, 85–121; C. Holmes, 'Parliament, Liberty, Taxation and Property', in *ibid.*, 122–54. My thanks to Dr Ian Roy and to Dr Dorothy Koenigsberger for further advice on these problems.

privileges of Parliament and its right to give consent to taxation derived from the king's authority and therefore ultimately revocable? This was the argument of James I and his lawyers, as indeed it had been of Elizabeth I. Or was the authority of Parliament independent of that of the king and therefore not revocable? This was what some of the parliamentary lawyers now claimed. Further, were both the king's and Parliament's authority ultimately derived from the English common law, which the king, for all his sovereignty, could not alter?

Such questions were at the basis of the English constitutional struggles throughout the seventeenth century, even when the actual political conflicts were dominated or triggered by more mundane political aims. The difficulty of resolving these questions was to be, even in the very different circumstances of the eighteenth century, one of the main reasons for the American Revolution.[22]

By the latter part of the seventeenth century the debate about the philosophical implications of sovereignty widened to include the basic problems of God, man and the laws of the universe. The form in which the theologians and philosophers argued these problems was essentially similar to the form in which the lawyers had argued about royal sovereignty: God was omnipotent and had created the universe. Everyone agreed on this point. But could He alter the laws He had given the universe? Or, an even more alarming question, could He have created the world with any other laws, and were these laws then independent of His divine will – as the common law of England was claimed to be independent of the royal sovereign's will?

In the 1540s the Netherlanders did not as yet engage in such speculations. The deputies to the States General traditionally preferred not to argue 'de potestate principi'. Andries Jacopszoon, the secretary of Amsterdam and that city's regular representative at both the provincial Estates and the States General, contemptuously referred to such arguments as 'scholastic talk', whenever government lawyers brought them up. It was probably more than just a deprecating remark. Quite likely he had in mind the formal debating exercises, deliberately removed from practical reality, which had been commonly practised in traditional scholastic schools for centuries. Most Netherlands schools of the early sixteenth century were still of that type.

On this occasion, in 1542, the Estates of Holland told their governor that if the emperor told the governor she could impose these taxes by his absolute power then there was no need to demand them from the Estates. They suggested that what was really happening was that Gasparo Ducci, the banker from Lucca who had made a profitable career lending money to the Netherlands government and, it was whispered, also to the king of France,[23] had lent the regent 200,000 guilders and

---

[22] H. G. Koenigsberger, 'Composite States, Representative Institutions and the American Revolution', *Historical Research*, 62, 148 (June 1989), 145–53.

[23] On Ducci see J. A. Goris, *Etudes sur les colonies marchandes méridionales à Anvers de 1488 à 1567* (London, 1925), 375–81.

that he was to have the receipt of the Hundredth Penny.[24] When they could blame a foreigner, why should they start a quarrel over ultimate rights with their prince? On the whole, they had got on perfectly well with him, and he was a born Netherlander and his regent, his sister, was also a born Netherlander who had always made a point of defending the country's liberties against the king of France; for this king, she claimed, cared nothing for his subjects' rights. It took the injection of religious passions into the political situation, and the apparently deliberately arbitrary actions of a new prince who was regarded as a foreigner, before the Netherlanders were willing to raise the question of the principles underlying princely sovereignty. It is at least suggestive that there was much grumbling in England during the last years of Elizabeth I, but that most of the points of principle were not raised until the advent of a foreign king; and in both the Netherlands and England it was the monarchy which precipitated the debate. In the 1540s it is at least possible that the regent, Mary of Hungary, knew or had been told that, twenty years earlier, her brother, Charles V, had used his *potestas principi* to abrogate, rather than impose, a customs tax for the Holy Roman Empire, proposed by the Reichstag. He did this in the interests of the imperial cities and it is certainly possible that, in the 1540s, the Estates of Holland knew about this reverse precedent. There was plenty of contact between the Netherlands and Germany and, as always, the motivations of the parties to a dispute were highly complex and sometimes contradictory.[25]

Mary certainly had a better developed political sensitivity than her nephew Philip II or King James I and his clever lawyers and she understood the limits of the authority of a regent. She demonstrated this understanding during the revolt of Ghent and she was to spell it out succinctly in her letter of resignation on the occasion of her brother's abdication in 1555. In 1542–3 she stuck with the Hundredth Penny export tax. It was mainly the Hollanders who had objected to it, claiming that it would divert the Hansards to London or Hamburg or Rouen. The dangers of such a diversion were real enough and always present; but one may doubt whether the profit expectations and the accounting procedures of the Lübeck merchants were so finely tuned that a 1 per cent *ad valorem* tax on their re-exports from the Netherlands would have determined their choice of markets.

The proposed income tax was another matter. All the provinces objected to it. As early as January 1543 the government retreated from this proposal. Instead it accepted Tournai's offer of 12,000 florins, raised in the traditional way.[26] By November 1544 this pattern was repeated for all the other provinces who were given the right to raise the sums the government demanded as they pleased.

---

[24] Van der Goes, *Register van alle de Dachvaerden*, vol. I, 252–3. Entry for 7 March 1543.
[25] G. Schmidt, *Der Städtetag in der Reichsverfassung* (Stuttgart, 1984), 440–9. S. Hofmann, 'Die Städte zwischen Kaiser und Reich', in H. Rabe, ed., *Karl V. Politik und politisches System* (Constance, 1996), 163–89.
[26] AGRB, P. d'E. A., 1228, fos. 98–9.

The regency of Mary of Hungary, II (1550–1555)

They came to a total of 636,000 florins plus four unspecified *aides* from Artois. All that was left of the government quest for a fairer method of taxation was an exhortation to the States General to raise money 'with the least burden to the poor'.[27]

But the problem could clearly not be left there. From 1552 the war with France was swallowing up unheard-of sums, and the government had to make steadily increasing demands of the States General. In January 1552 Mary spelled out to them the efforts of the king of France, or at any rate what her intelligence service told her and what she chose to pass on to the States General. King Henry had doubled the *taille*, she asserted, and forced the French towns to pay for 50,000 men for six months. Further, he had levied a cavalry tax on all fiefs. By his own authority he had imposed five or six tithes on the clergy; he had imposed forced loans on private persons and 'other methods [of raising money] which he is excogitating'. The anti-*dominium regale* propaganda is very evident; but the need to counter the French war effort was real enough. After a consultation with her provincial governors, her principal military advisers, she estimated her government's military needs as a minimum of 3 million florins. If the enemy made even greater efforts than we know of, she told the States General, they would have to raise more money accordingly. To ease the tax burden the emperor would sell annuities on his domain to the capital of 600,000 florins.[28] The document with this proposal is followed by an estimate of the *aides* granted by the Estates for the present war. It came to just under 1.5 million livres.[29]

It is difficult to give exact figures for the public finances of the 1550s. Some contemporaries had a sophisticated grasp of the intricacies of public and international finance, a fact which emerges, among other sources, from Thomas Gresham's detailed reports from Antwerp and Seville. But no one drew up a budget in the modern sense. Charles V's private dealings with the German and Genoese bankers, his interference in the public finances of all his dominions, the huge sums which the bankers transferred between these dominions and especially between Seville and Antwerp – all this makes it very difficult to disentangle Netherlands finances from the finances of the rest of the Habsburg monarchy and especially from those of Castile. There was and is general agreement among the experts that the Netherlands government vastly increased the loans it took up in 1552 and that it continued to do this, if on a slightly lower scale, until Charles V's abdication in 1555. By that time the deficit in the Netherlands had reached something like 7 million livres.[30]

How was the government able to command such extraordinary credit, pay back the huge loans and, in the meantime, pay interest on them? Repayment was usually

---

[27] *Ibid.*, 1232, fos. 232–3.
[28] *Ibid.*, 1228, fos. 161–4.
[29] *Ibid.*, fos. 163–4.
[30] Rodríguez-Salgado, *The Changing Face of Empire*, 50–4. M. Steele, 'The Financial Crises in Spain and the Netherlands during the Reign of Philip II' (London University Ph.D. thesis, 1987), ch. 3. Steele, 'La real hacienda'.

scheduled for one of the periodic financial fairs in Spain or in Antwerp. Sometimes it was possible to postpone the dates of these fairs; but this was at best a palliative and, in fact, increased the interest payable on the loans whose repayment had been postponed. This interest was high, varying from 6.25 to over 20 per cent. Traditionally the government paid interest on its loans from the income of domain lands and other regalia and from the *aides* granted by the Estates. There was, however, another method of raising money: the sale of government annuities. It was not a new method. Since the later middle ages, individuals, families, religious houses and other corporations had been looking for sources of steady income which were safer than investment in trade, and more conveniently negotiable and less burdened with obligations than land was apt to be. Governments were willing to provide such income, for it was a means of raising capital. In the Netherlands such annuities were called *rentes* (as they were also in France) or *renten*, and in Spain *juros*. Quite often, corporations or wealthy individuals would be bullied to buy *rentes*, so that in fact they became forced loans. Such forced loans had the deserved reputation of being repaid much later than promised or not at all. When the ordinary government income had been spent or had been earmarked for the repayment of earlier loans, people would refuse to buy government annuities or trade them well below par.

In some of the Habsburg dominions, for instance in the kingdom of Naples, government credit held up reasonably well.[31] In the Netherlands, however, it became clear in the 1540s that the buyers of government annuities demanded better security than the Council of Finance could provide. There was only one way to supply such security and this was through the provincial Estates. People trusted them where they no longer trusted the government. The economic expansion of the first half of the sixteenth century channelled sufficient wealth into the cities to enable them to balance their budgets, and their prosperity was there for everyone to see in the splendid town halls and churches they were able to erect and, at least in some towns, in the many religious and charitable institutions which they were able to afford. In the 1540s the Estates of the major provinces effectively took over raising, collecting and administering the extraordinary taxes granted by the Estates. The regular *aides*, diminished in any case by the practice of granting *gracien*, became a progressively smaller proportion of the total taxes. These were the taxes still controlled by the government's finance officials. The greater and increasing part of provincial income now came to be controlled by officials appointed by the Estates themselves.

We know most about this process in Flanders and Holland,[32] but it was certainly very similar in Brabant and in the smaller provinces. The reasons were partly

---

[31] Calabria, *The Cost of Empire*, 106–8.
[32] Maddens, 'De Beden . . . Vlaanderen'. N. Maddens, 'Nieuwe Middelen in het Grafschap Vlaanderen', *RBPH*, 57 (1979), 343–63. M. Baelde, 'Financiële Politie en domaniale evolutie in de Nederlanden onder Karel V en Filips II (1530–1560)', *TG*, 76 (1963), 14–33. J. D. Tracy, *A Financial Revolution in the Habsburg Netherlands: Renten and Renteniers in the County of Holland 1515–1565* (Berkeley, 1985). Tracy, 'The Taxation System in the County of Holland', 71–117.

functional; but the provinces also instructed their deputies how Flanders and Brabant were reacting to government proposals and how they were coping. The regent's intention of preventing the Estates from concerting their policies was never completely successful: nor, given the nature of politics in a composite state, is this very surprising. Nevertheless, it took time to develop the new methods (*nieuwe middelen*) and to build up the new administrative machinery, and there were important differences in the traditions of the provinces which influenced these developments. One result was that the government gave up its efforts to find new and fairer methods of taxation for the whole country and left each province to devise its own methods. All the provinces either immediately gave up the idea of an income tax or greatly reduced its rate. All of them, however, abolished the exemptions formerly enjoyed by the clergy and by certain seigneuries. For new taxes they also abolished the different *gracien* enjoyed by the towns. These new taxes which would service the annuities varied in different provinces and over time; but the most important ones were excise duties, taxes on income from land (but not from commercial property) levied on leaseholders as well as freeholders, and imposts on servants and workmen. There was no rule preventing employers from recouping this tax by paying lower wages.

Unsurprisingly, the new taxes were fiercely unpopular with the clergy and with the common people. One may at least wonder whether there was any connection between this clerical disaffection and the relatively weak resistance the secular clergy put up to the teaching of the Protestant preachers.

Up to this time the Estates had tried to control government expenditure of their extraordinary *aides* by trying to vet government accounts and to appoint their own officials to be present at the pay parades of the soldiers. The purpose was not only to keep an eye on the all-too-frequently corrupt government finance officials but, even more importantly, to prevent the government from using monies granted for current defence to pay off older debts. For then the government would come back to the Estates and blackmail more money out of them by threatening that otherwise the unpaid soldiers would live off the country.

It seems doubtful whether this method of financial supervision by the Estates was ever very effective. In Flanders, at least, the Estates do not seem to have thought so; for they were willing to give it up altogether in return for gaining complete control over the collection and administration of the *nieuwe middelen*. Moreover the new system gave the four Members of Flanders, Ghent, Bruges, Ypres and the Franc, the chance to regain at least part of the fiscal authority over the province which they had enjoyed during the Burgundian period and which the Habsburgs had always been anxious to curtail. For now, once again, the Members and their officials came to control the methods and the imposition of the taxes.

By contrast, the Estates of Holland did not give up their traditional policy of supervising the government's spending. Unlike the Flemings, the Hollanders built up the machinery for the administration of the annuities as a unified system for the whole province. Traditionally, the government had administered the province through the court of Holland at The Hague, with a staff of mainly lawyers and permanent financial officials. It was relatively easy for the Estates of Holland to take over the dwindling duties of the government receivers in the Court of Holland.

Through the 1540s the new system overcame its teething troubles. By its ability to retire loans based on annuities it was building up public confidence – a confidence which the French government and the city of Paris never came to enjoy to the same degree. When the Habsburg–Valois war broke out again, in 1552, the annual expenditure of the Netherlands government was twice that of the previous war of 1542–4. At that time the *nieuwe middelen* had only just been introduced. Now, in 1552, they were so well established and so popular as a safe form of investment that it was no longer necessary to force people to buy the *rentes*.

In their propaganda both government and Estates habitually talked about the widows and orphans who lived on these annuities and whom it would be wicked to let down. There were certainly widows and orphans who bought annuities, but far and away the principal buyers were corporations, wealthy property owners and, perhaps most significant, government ministers, city officials and deputies to the provincial Estates and the States General. In other words, the system was run for and by the patrician classes and at the expense of those on whom taxes had always fallen most heavily, the peasants and the urban workers. Only the methods and details had changed since, earlier in the sixteenth century, Sir Thomas More had declared that government was a conspiracy of the rich against the poor.

Yet the details were important. The system of the *nieuw middelen* confirmed the stability of *dominium politicum et regale*. Even the German princes and princelings, with their aspirations to emulate the *dominium regale* of the French monarchy, found that they had to hand over their public finances – finances which often tended to be confused with their personal debts – to their local Estates. It all had very little to do with the formal political theories current at the time, and it was usually done by agreement and not by confrontation. Neither Charles V nor any of the other princes of Europe who came to base their finances on the sale of annuities had needed to rely on their proclaimed imperial authority of imposing certain types of taxes. They usually managed to raise them much more comfortably by consent, even if not usually as much as they would have liked. But what the monarchies had lost was a great part of their administrative control over their financial systems. For the moment at least they preferred not to think about this. It was enough that they had found a new, or revamped, and apparently foolproof source of revenue to underpin their deficit financing of the increasingly voracious costs of warfare.

The Estates, for their part, were also doing well. Without giving up any of their privileges they had got rid of the hated clerical exemptions and of at least some of the dubious tax privileges of the nobility. Perhaps most immediately satisfying,

The regency of Mary of Hungary, II (1550–1555)

they had virtually killed off the plan for a tax on commercial income. The cohesion of the provincial elites and their experience of practical financial administration all greatly increased. It was not this which caused the later revolt; but it was a necessary condition of the successful establishment of an alternative political regime in Holland, in opposition not only to the Spanish monarchy but to much of the rest of the Netherlands.[33]

It was the government itself which was not as complacent as the Estates over the loss of its plans for a more equitable system of taxation. The appeal of heterodoxy to the poor and deprived was a well-known phenomenon to intelligent observers since the end of the middle ages. In 1546 the regent Mary had stressed the danger again. She had also linked it with the ruin Antwerp would suffer if the emperor insisted, at the beginning of the Schmalkaldic War against the German Protestants, on an embargo of Augsburg merchants. Antwerp would suffer, Mary had argued, because the embargo would frighten off all German merchants.[34]

Yet it was not the religious situation which was uppermost in the emperor's and the Netherlands' government's minds in the first half of the 1550s.[35] In so far as Charles thought about religion at this time, it was mainly about his own conscience and about his relations with the German Protestant princes or with Pope Julius III; and that meant the Council of Trent and the imperial position in Italy. But outweighing everything else in importance there was the war with France.[36] With the spiralling costs of this war, and with the growing tensions with his son Philip and his youngest daughter Juana, his successive regents in Spain, the emperor's own position now became the most problematic aspect of the Habsburg polity. The Netherlands and Castile were its two richest dominions. From the emperor's point of view they would have to bear the heaviest burden of his struggle with France and of the need, as he saw it and with which courtly Europe agreed, of establishing the reputation of his successor Philip to be as formidable a protagonist of the Habsburg monarchy as his father was. But, inevitably, the governments and regents of Spain and of the Netherlands, themselves composite countries and fiercely jealous of their autonomy, would defend their own interests against those they thought of as being only the emperor's interests or, worse still, the interests of his other dominions. Charles, Mary on his behalf, and Philip, after his arrival in northern Europe and as husband of the queen of England, all attempted to control Habsburg finances and negotiate loans from the international bankers. At times, the terms they offered rose to over 30 per cent. They interfered with each other's

---

[33] In this argument I have followed J. D. Tracy, *Holland under Habsburg Rule 1516–1566: The Formation of a Body Politic* (Berkeley, 1990), 208 and *passim*.
[34] Mary to Charles V, Brussels, 28 Nov. 1546. R. Häpke, ed., *Niederländische Akten und Urkunden zur Geschichte der Hanse*, vol. I (Munich, 1913), 443–7.
[35] F. Postma, 'Nieuw licht op een oude zaak: de oprichting van de nieuwe bisdommen in 1559', *TG*, 103 (1990), 10–27.
[36] Lutz, *Christianitas Afflicta*, especially chs. 4–6.

negotiations and all claimed to have control over the monarchy's finances and the final say about where and for what purposes the sums borrowed should be spent.

In Spain, Juana and her government felt imposed upon from Brussels and were rightly anxious about the effects of the emperor's policies on Spanish opinion. An attempt to persuade the Cortes of Castile to raise the *encabezamiento* failed. This tax had been granted to the monarchy by the cities represented in the Cortes, and it was a lump-sum composition of the generally hated sales tax, the *alcabala*. The cities could levy the *encabezamiento* as they pleased, provided it reached a definite sum. The whole arrangement was fixed for a definite number of years. In essentials it was an arrangement similar to that which the government of the Netherlands had been forced to make with the States General, in the 1540s. The system, both in Castile and in the Netherlands, was convenient for both sides; but it was not easy for the respective governments to obtain an increase in the global sums which their assemblies had granted, and in Castile the period for which it had been granted was much longer than in the Netherlands. With authority divided between Charles, Philip and Juana, the request to the Cortes for an increase in the *encabezamiento* was badly mishandled. The Cortes would not play until Philip would give them a formal agreement for a thirty-year period. In the meantime the deputies indulged in pointed criticism of royal policy which, they argued, sacrificed the interests of Castile to those of the Netherlands. In the spring of 1555 the collection of even the old rate of the *encabezamiento* virtually ceased.[37]

THE ABDICATION OF CHARLES V

In the Netherlands taxes could still be collected; but with Philip shuttling between Brussels and London, the problem of divided authority became more and more serious. It was the weak point of all early modern composite monarchies, and in the last years of Charles V's reign the problem was becoming particularly acute. By the spring and summer of 1555 it was becoming clear that something or somebody had to give – just as had been the case in 1514–15 when the States General had dealt with a similar impasse by buying off the emperor Maximilian with a lump sum. In 1555 it was more difficult. Charles V could not be simply bought off like his grandfather. He had to act himself. He was to claim that the idea of his abdication went back a long time and that it was motivated by his failing health and by his desire to spend the remainder of his life in religious devotions in a more agreeable climate. His spokesman at the abdication ceremony before the States General on 25 October 1555 added to these what was clearly meant to be a reassuring reason: the emperor was handing over his dominions one by one, in stages, so that the whole burden would not fall on Philip all at once.[38]

---

[37] Rodriguez-Salgado, *The Changing Face of Empire*, 118–27.
[38] 'Propositions aux Etats des Pays-Bas', in Weiss, *Papiers d'Etat*, vol. IV, 482.

The regency of Mary of Hungary, II (1550–1555)

No doubt these reasons were all genuine. In practice, however, the pattern and the pace of Charles V's abdications were determined by political, legal and financial circumstances. Charles would have liked to abdicate the Holy Roman Empire before the Reichstag of Augsburg and, in the event, he did not sign the Treaty of Augsburg with its famous formula of *cuius regio eius religio*. Charles would never officially accept any compromise over the unity of Christendom. Theological compromises were, of course, possible. But these were the business of the theologians, and Charles had always encouraged them to find some inclusive formulae and had hoped that a general council of the church would bring the Protestants back into the fold. But on the unity of Christendom depended Charles's claim of political leadership of Europe and of his superior status to that of the king of France.[39] This refusal to accept the Treaty of Augsburg did not prevent Charles from continuing to interfere in the affairs of the Holy Roman Empire, and quarrels with Ferdinand over imperial rights in Italy delayed Charles's final abdication of his imperial title until 1558.

In the Netherlands, too, he interfered until the very end, i.e. his long-delayed embarcation for Spain, making ecclesiastical, military and administrative appointments right up to the key position of provincial governors. Even Maximilian, for all his autocratic inclinations, had not gone so far in 1515. Was Charles V's irresponsible, autocratic interference in the government of his successors at the end of his reign a way of paying off family scores? In the case of Ferdinand and the Holy Roman Empire for his defeat in the Habsburg succession dispute and Ferdinand's alleged failure to help him sufficiently at the moment of Charles's greatest need, after his flight from Innsbruck? And were the Netherlands appointments a tit for tat for Philip's unilateral appointments to the regency council of his sister Juana in Spain? Perhaps. But we cannot tell because in the autumn of 1555 neither Charles nor Philip could afford to voice criticism of the other, even to their most intimate advisers. The formal abdication ceremony for the Netherlands before the States General was a grand occasion and stage-managed with the usual Habsburg savoir-faire for such happenings. Nearly all the senior members of the Habsburg family were present: Charles, Philip and Mary; their sister Eleanor, dowager queen of France; Charles's nephew and son-in-law, the archduke and king of Bohemia, Maximilian and his wife, the emperor's daughter Mary; his niece Christina of Denmark, dowager duchess of Lorraine; and his cousin Emmanuel Philibert of Savoy, just appointed to the post of governor general of the Netherlands. Only Ferdinand, the king of the Romans, and Juana, the regent of Spain, could not leave their posts. They were probably not sorry because their relations with both Charles and Philip were distinctly strained at this time. The States General, unlike their predecessors of 1515 which had declared Charles of age, were

---

[39] H. Rabe, 'Karl V und die deutschen Protestanten', in Rabe, *Karl V. Politik und Politisches System*, 317–45.

Plate 10 Frans Hogenberg, engraving showing a scene of the transfer of sovereignty to Philip II. MS 196 C 30, f. 11, Koninklijke Bibliotheek, The Hague

The regency of Mary of Hungary, II (1550–1555)

little more than spectators on the stage on which the Habsburg family decided the fate of its multiple monarchy. Charles's spokesman gave them four specific exhortations in his name. They were to observe and maintain religious faith and Holy Church; they were to 'honour and revere justice, for without it the mystical body of the state [*le corps mystique de la république*] cannot be sustained'; they were to stay united and help each other, for otherwise they would present their enemies with great opportunities to do them damage; and, finally, they were to show all due reverence and obedience to their prince and sovereign.[40]

The sentiments expressed in these exhortations were entirely conventional: just what one would expect on such a formal occasion. There is no evidence that the deputies to the States General or anyone regarded them as anything else. No one expected that, in the next half century, all four of Charles V's exhortations would become focal points of conflict in the Netherlands and in the whole composite monarchy of the Habsburgs: no one except perhaps the retiring regent, Mary of Hungary. Her letters to her brother had always tended to be pessimistic, sometimes verging on hysteria. Now, in the autumn of 1555 when she wrote her letter of resignation to the emperor after fourteen years of service as his regent, she spelt out the problems of this position. To those problems quoted at the beginning of this chapter she added specifically that a prince's subjects will never give his governor as much loyalty and assistance as they would himself; and when the governor is a woman 'then the difference is as between white and black'. Moreover, she saw a young generation in the country 'with whose customs I cannot and would not wish to accommodate myself'.[41]

Was it only the melancholy of ending a life's endeavour which she felt to have been inadequate? Or was it a premonition, based on long experience and her acute political sensitivity, that the change of generations she was observing implied a change in the relationship between the prince and his subjects, a change which would have tragic consequences for the Netherlands and for the House of Habsburg?

---

[40] Weiss, *Papiers d'Etat*, vol. IV, 484–5.
[41] *Ibid.*, 469–80.

8

The Netherlands at the centre of the Habsburg composite monarchy: the governor-generalship of Emmanuel Philibert of Savoy (1555–1559)

'For my part I am doing what I can and will risk my person for them [the Netherlanders] and join the army which is to defend these states and will give them all the money I have ... and for all this they thank me here by saying or thinking that I care nothing for them and that I prefer an inch of Spanish earth to a hundred leagues here. All this I cannot but feel strongly and grieve much over it, for it is so much without cause.'

Philip II to Savoy, London, 27 May 1557[1]

THE ACCESSION OF PHILIP II AND THE FINANCIAL SITUATION

For the Netherlands and for their government the abdication of Charles V, in October 1555, had been a highly emotional event. At the same time, most people expected that politics and business would go on much as before. Their new prince, King Philip II of Spain, was still in the country, and if he left it in the foreseeable future, it would be only to go to neighbouring England of which, through his marriage with Mary Tudor, he was now also king; and he would not stay in England longer than was absolutely necessary. Fortunately, as the Netherlanders though not Philip himself thought, he did not have to bother about Germany any more; for his uncle, Ferdinand, would soon be elected Holy Roman Emperor. More immediately important, negotiations were under way with France which would soon lead to the Truce of Vaucelles (January 1556). Only in Italy was war flaring up again, fanned by the hatred of the new pope, Paul IV, for the Spaniards. The Netherlanders, understandably, did not consider this war as any concern of theirs, except in so far as they were expected to help pay for it. Perhaps the Netherlands nobility would have felt differently if even a very few of their number had been given appointments in Italy, in the way Charles V had appointed the count of Lannoy, of the great Croy clan, as viceroy of Naples, in the 1520s. In 1554 Charles V had again suggested military appointments of English and Netherlands noblemen in Italy; but Philip had refused. He said that the English and the

---

[1] AGRB, Les Archives et les Bibliothèques d'Italie, vol. I, Manuscrits divers 1172, fos. 225–7 (Gachard's copy of the original in Turin).

Emmanuel Philibert of Savoy (1555–1559)

Netherlanders would not allow him to reciprocate by appointing Spaniards and Italians in their counties.[2]

For England this was probably true; for the Netherlands not quite. They did indeed insist on the *uis indigenatus*, barring non-natives from public office, and the provinces even used this law against each other. But both the imperial army in the Netherlands and imperial finances were much too international to allow the observance of such restrictive laws. Most important of all, however, the successor of their quintessentially Netherlandish regent Mary of Hungary was an Italian, Emmanuel Philibert (Emanuele Filiberto), duke of Piedmont-Savoy. He was related to the Habsburgs but, all the same, the Netherlanders managed to block the title of regent for him and to insist on the less prestigious title of governor general. Moreover, the duke himself and everybody else knew that his position was only a stop-gap while he waited to return to his own country. Since 1536 Piedmont-Savoy had been divided between occupying French and imperial troops.

For the rest Savoy's constitutional position was similar to that of his predecessor. Mary of Hungary had characterised it succintly in her letter of resignation: 'a person who governs under a prince must be wiser than the prince himself who, governing for himself, has to render account only to God ... But he who governs under another must render account to God but also to the prince and to his subjects.'[3] In practice, as Mary knew only too well, it was not only a question of responsibility but of decision-making and of patronage. The system of regencies in the Netherlands had always led to divided centres of authority and multiple centres of patronage. Courtiers, ministers, the high nobility and clergy and the ubiquitous host of patronage brokers chose their patron in government according to their political preferences, their family connections or simply according to their own private interests. Only recently Mary had insisted on Philip coming to the Netherlands, at least partly to neutralise the tension between herself and her brother, the emperor. The result had been to increase confusion, and this confusion had not diminished when Charles and Mary retired, even though its nature had shifted somewhat. After his abdication Charles had never ceased to interfere and, inevitably, many continued to look to him for decisions and patronage. Philip, now the ultimate source of authority, was away in England for months on end. More serious still, he surrounded himself with Iberian advisers: the Portuguese Ruy Gomez de Silva, prince of Eboli, and the Spaniards, the count of Feria, Juan Manrique de Lara, Bernardino de Mendoza, the ubiquitous secretary Francisco de Eraso and finally the sinister and dominating figure of the duke of Alba, at that time in Italy as viceroy of Naples and doing his best not to win the war with Pope Paul IV, but always formidable and never far from the heart of government.

---

[2] M. J. Rodriguez-Salgado, *The Changing Face of Empire*, 202.
[3] Weiss, *Papiers d'Etat*, vol. IV, 484–5.

Savoy was to show, later in his career after he returned to Piedmont, considerable political astuteness.[4] But in 1555 political observers remarked on his youth and his inexperience and political naivety.[5] In the advice given him on his appointment he was ordered always to follow the advice of his Council of State, except in the case of 'just and urgent necessity'.[6] In itself this instruction was not unusual; nor was the fact that it was not the governor general but Charles and Philip who had appointed his Council of State. The councillors were members of the high nobility and of the Order of the Golden Fleece, plus several professional administrators, notably Antoine Perrenot, bishop of Arras, son of the emperor's late chancellor and, from 1561, Cardinal Granvelle. The dominant personality in the government was Charles de Lalaing, *grand bailli* of Hainaut. Lalaing was a traditionalist, trusted especially by Mary of Hungary, like his now dead relative Antoine de Lalaing, count of Hoochstraten, and he was of an older generation than his fellow councillors, the prince of Orange and the counts of Egmont, Hoorn (Hornes), Berghes and Megen. These were the younger generation whom Mary disliked and who were to dominate the politics of the 1560s. It was, however, Lalaing who drafted the two famous memoranda about the state of the Netherlands and its unhappy position, as he saw it, in the composite monarchy of the Habsburgs (May–July and November 1556).[7]

Writing critical memoranda was not in itself remarkable. Both Margaret and Mary, helped and prompted by their Councils of State, had over the years drafted quite a number of gloomy memoranda for Charles V, outlining the desperate state of the Netherlands, the excessive taxes, the devastations caused by the wars with France and Guelders, the depredations of their own unpaid soldiery, the ill will shown by certain towns or even whole estates – in short, the imminent danger of complete disaster, as they saw it. The emperor had always remained unmoved, except for his insistence on slapping down actual rebellion or popular riots. The Lalaing–Savoy memoranda were saying in essence much the same thing as previous warnings, but they went further on two sensitive points. 'To tell the truth, Monseigneur', we read in the May–July memorandum, 'you [i.e. King Philip] are not loved and therefore a great change is to be feared, even though this might not be through the French'.[8] By contrast, Margaret and Mary had always stressed the basic loyalty of the Netherlanders, even when they gave their most gloomy warnings.

---

[4] Koenigsberger, *Estates and Revolutions*, 72–8. P. Merlin, *Emanuele Filiberto. Un principe tra il Piemonte e l'Europa* (Turin, 1995), chs. IV–VI.
[5] *Ibid.*, 64.
[6] K. J. W. Verhofstad, *De Regering der Nederlanden in de Jaren 1555–1559* (Nijmegen, 1937), 26.
[7] L. P. Gachard, 'Remonstrances faites par le duc de Savoie à Philippe II sur la situation des Pays-Bas', in *BCRH*, ser. 2 vol. VIII (1856), 118–32. Emanuele Filiberto, 'Charles de Lalaing et les remonstrances d'Emmanuel-Philibert de Savoie (juillet et novembre 1556)', in *ibid.*, vol. XCVII (1933), 155–69.
[8] *Ibid.*, 266. 'Monseigneur, car, pour le vous dire francement, vous n'en n'estes aymé et en est de craindre ung grand changement, encores que ce ni est pas les Franchois.'

Emmanuel Philibert of Savoy (1555–1559)

But almost from the moment of the emperor's abdication the tone of the dialogue between the government and the Estates changed. What had been largely technical discussions, albeit over the invariable *basso ostinato* of the provinces' complaints about their poverty, changed into bad-tempered political arguments.

Secondly, while Savoy and Lalaing did not openly criticise the existence of the Habsburg monarchy, they claimed that the king's other dominions, notably Spain, had contributed nothing to the war in Italy and to the wars with France. At the same time these dominions had escaped all the devastations which the wars had visited on the Netherlands. The king of France, so the memorandum argued, taxed his inland provinces more heavily than those, such as Picardie, which suffered from the fighting. In His Majesty's [i.e. Philip's] monarchy it was the whole of the Netherlands which should be regarded as frontier provinces and taxed more lightly than Spain; for Spain, in this sense, was an interior province, untouched by the fighting.

Such arguments were to become the staple reasoning of the Netherlanders and they help to explain the growing hatred between the Dutch and the Spaniards which, within a few years, was to lead to the Revolt and the Eighty Years War.

It is understandable that Lalaing, the elderly aristocratic warhorse from provincial Hainaut, should have been under such xenophobic illusions. But Savoy, for all his youthful inexperience, should have known better about the Spanish and Italian contributions to the war. And if he did not understand all the complicated technical financial details, he should at least have been aware of the general position. For the members of his Council of Finance and at least the professional administrators in his Council of State knew all these things perfectly well. The secretary Francisco de Eraso, the king's financial agents in Antwerp, and Gaspar Schetz, Philip's financial agent, were all in constant touch with the governor general's Council of Finance and Council of State.

It is true that the Castilian Cortes did not raise the rate of taxation. The sales tax (*alcabala*) and other taxes in Castile had been converted into fixed payments (*encabezamiento*) by the towns as far back as 1534, and the rate of the *encabezamiento* had remained fixed for twenty years.[9] But this did not mean that Spain had failed to contribute to the Habsburg war effort. The contribution took the form of loans from international banking houses (*asientos*) and the servicing of these loans from all sources of royal income, including the quite heavy clerical taxes, and from the confiscation of privately owned silver in the treasure fleets arriving in Seville from America. In 1553 these confiscations amounted to 600,000 ducats worth, in 1555 to more than 800,000 ducats and in 1556 to the enormous sum of 1.6 million. Even before these confiscations, in the disastrous year of 1552, when Charles V had to flee from the armies of the Protestant German princes, total *asientos* amounted to 3.6 million ducats and the total for the quinquennium up to Charles V's abdication

---

[9] See above, ch. 7.

was 8.2 million. The owners of the confiscated silver were compensated by state annuities (*juros*) at between 3 and 7 per cent interest. The foreign lenders received assignations on government revenues. Between 1552 and 1560 the capital invested in *juros* rose from 13 million ducats to nearly 22 million. The amount of treasure arriving from America in Seville during these years was still greater than the total of the *asientos*. Since at least some of this money was spent in Spain, the economy of the country as a whole was not impoverished.[10] On this point, at least, the Netherlanders were correct; but the problems of the Spanish government were real enough and the financial dislocations caused by its policies affected the whole country. Already in November 1554 Thomas Gresham, at that time in Seville, wrote home: 'I am not abell with my pen to set forthe unto you the great scarsity [of money] that is now through all Spayne.'[11]

The financial problems of the Spanish government were compounded in 1555 by the outbreak of the war with Pope Paul IV who promptly cancelled the king's right to levy the *cruzada* and other clerical taxes. Most of the revenues from these taxes, estimated at the time at 1.3 million ducats a year, had also been assigned to the repayment of the *asientos*, and these sums had now to be found from other government revenues. Spanish Milan, burdened with the garrison of Spanish troops and suffering from the wars with France, raised 700,000 scudi between July 1555 and January 1557; and, even so, the Spanish government had to send a further 600,000 to Milan during the same period. In Naples, meanwhile, the duke of Alba, viceroy and commander of Philip's armies, was anxious to find more money for the war against the pope and for countering the expected French attack on Milan. He therefore proposed an *alcabala*, a 10 per cent sales tax. The Neapolitans protested strongly but eventually agreed to new taxes on bread and wine which, it was hoped, would raise one million scudi per year for three years.[12]

So much then for the claim of the governor general of the Netherlands that the Netherlands alone paid for the Habsburg wars. The Lalaing–Savoy 'remonstrances' were actually translated into Spanish and read to the king in front of the whole Netherlands Council of State in November 1556. There is an air of unreality clinging to these remonstrances, and Philip must have been aware of it. Already in October 1555 the financial experts in his Council had proposed a sophisticated plan to rationalise the finances of all the dominions of the Habsburg multiple monarchy. It was suggested that the king appoint a factor general to supervise and coordinate all financial transactions between the different dominions. Under the

---

[10] A detailed account of Spanish finances and of the *asientos* is Steele, 'The Financial Crises in Spain and the Netherlands during the Reign of Philip II', ch. 3. A shorter version is Steele, 'La real hacienda', 160–2. My thanks to Dr Steele for making the typescript of his thesis available to me.
[11] Quoted in Steele, 'La real hacienda', 10.
[12] Figures for Milan and Naples from Rodrigues-Salgado, *The Changing Face of Empire*, 153–7. For the characteristic increase of government annuities sold in Naples see Calabria, *The Cost of Empire*, 106–8.

Emmanuel Philibert of Savoy (1555–1559)

factor general there were to be factors in each of the major financial centres of the monarchy. If money was plentiful in one such centre, for instance in Seville or Medina del Campo after the arrival of a treasure fleet from Peru, the factors could transfer it to where it was needed to pay the troops, say Antwerp. The factors would settle accounts with each other and, while they remained personally fully liable for the sums they handled, they would be able to speculate with government money on the international money markets and thus make profits for the monarchy which otherwise habitually accrued to the private banking houses. It was hoped that in this way and for the first time the monarchy would have a clear view of the state of its finances in all its dominions, as well as the technical means to bring to bear the resources of the whole multiple monarchy on crisis points.

In principle, the plan was similar to the system which the French monarchy gradually developed for its internal finances and which persisted until the beginning of the French Revolution. But it was wildly optimistic to think that such a system could be constructed quickly on an international level and in the middle of a severe financial crisis. From the first the Spaniards in Philip's council objected to having a Netherlander, the Antwerp banker Gaspar Schetz, as the factor general, and they induced the king to appoint Juan López Gallo as Schetz's colleague with equal standing. In practice Gallo had more power than Schetz because he was to control the most important of all financial transactions, the transfer of treasure from Spain to the Netherlands. Worse still, Juana's regency government in Spain opposed the plan altogether and did its best to sabotage it. Even Savoy's government in the Netherlands, which had perhaps most to gain from the plan, was hostile and was, moreover, half paralysed by a personal quarrel between Lalaing and Antoine Perrenot, that most professional of professional administrators. Predictably, the Netherlands grandees in the council, notably the prince of Orange and the count of Egmont, supported Lalaing in this quarrel. In the end, the plan of the 'factoría' offended too many vested interests. It never functioned properly and, by the end of 1557, it was effectively dead.[13]

To the king's financial advisers, both in Spain and in the Netherlands, it had in any case been clear for some time that they themselves had to devise some effective methods to deal with the government's mounting debts. In the Netherlands the annual deficit had risen from 3 million pounds, in 1553, to 7 million pounds (florins), in 1555. In 1556 interest payments on government loans jumped from 425,000 to 1,360,000.[14] The main reason for these staggering rises was the cost of the war with France. Most of the huge sums transferred from Spain to the

---

[13] For the scheme of the 'factoria', as the Spaniards called it, I have followed Rodríguez-Salgado, *The Changing Face of Empire*, 234–9. For the quarrel between Lalaing and Perrenot see M. van Durme, *Antoon Perrenot, Bisschop van Atrecht, Kardinaal Granvelle* (Brussels, 1953), 158–61; and Verhofstad, *De Regering der Nederlanden*, 45–7.

[14] Rodríguez-Salgado, *The Changing Face*, 55–9. For the varying rates between ducats, scudi and Flemish pounds see *ibid.*, XV–XVI.

Netherlands – in the region of 9.5 million ducats, between 1552 and 1556 – were spent in the Netherlands, even when they did not remain in the Antwerp money market. As usually happens in wartime, there were many people who did well out of this extraordinary increase in the circulation of money, from the camp followers of both sexes, at the bottom of the pile, to the provision merchants, the money lenders, big and small, right up to the big international bankers. It was, of course, a different matter for those in the way of the soldiers, even when they were not caught up in the actual fighting.

Many tears and much ink were spilt over the dangers to the civilian population, and the Netherlands government was genuinely concerned with paying the troops to prevent at least the worst horrors. Nevertheless, its primary concern was with the war against the French and even the matter of paying the troops was more a question of preventing the men from going on strike at a critical moment in the campaign than humanitarian concerns. As early as 1552 there had been talk of repudiating the government debts or of forcibly reducing the interest paid on them. Charles V had always vetoed such a course. It was inappropriate to his imperial dignity, he said. Perhaps even more important, ever since his imperial election of 1519 he knew he was dependent on the bankers and especially on his favourite banking house, the Fugger of Augsburg. They had rescued him again in 1552 when he had fled from Innsbruck and he had made promises to them which he did not want to break. For Philip it was a different matter. He did not like breaking his word any more than his father did; but it was generally accepted that a prince was not responsible for the debts of his predecessor. His succession in 1555–6 was therefore a good opportunity to do something drastic about the monarchy's debts. The trick was to repudiate the emperor's debts without completely losing credit himself.

It was not only the military situation which made action urgent. The winter of 1556–7 was a particularly severe one, and in the spring the prices of foodstuffs rose higher than at any previous time in the century. To prevent grain shortage from turning into famine the cities bought large quantities of rye, shipped from the Baltic to Amsterdam. These imports had to be paid for in cash, and here was therefore another drain on the money market of Antwerp.

The government solved the problem, at least temporarily, by a decree, drafted in April and published in June 1557. The government of Castile followed suit with similar decrees. Historians have usually called these decrees declarations of bankruptcy. But they were not really that. Neither in the Netherlands nor in Spain did the government cease trading, as private firms have to do when they go bankrupt. The funded debts, the *juros* in Spain and the *rentes* in the Netherlands, were not affected at all, and these represented the greater part of the debts of both governments. The floating debts, the *asientos* of Castile and the Netherlands, added up to about 2.6 million ducats. There were also further loans on the Antwerp market, the *emprunts de la cour des Pays-Bas*, which were included in the decree; but we do

Emmanuel Philibert of Savoy (1555–1559)

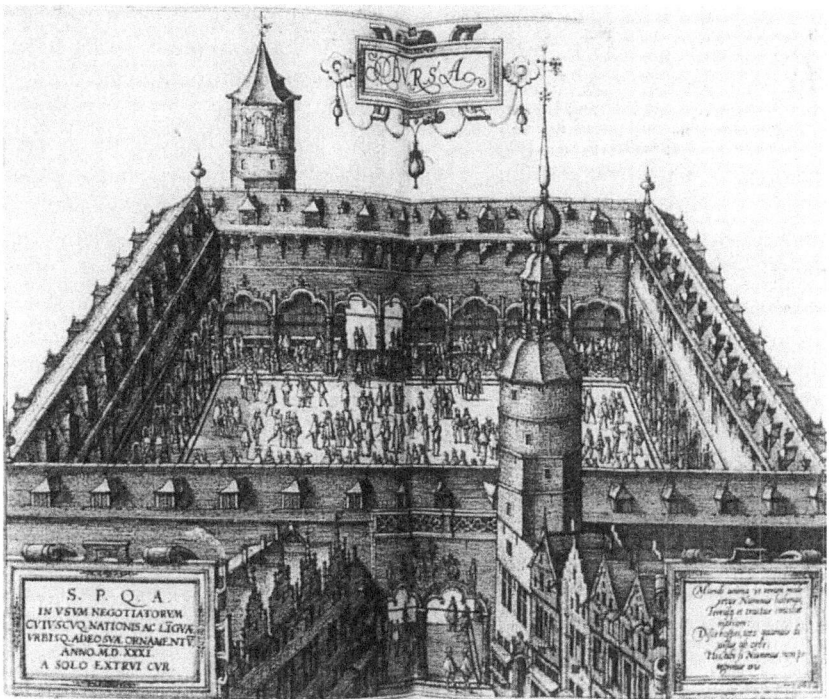

Plate 11 Petrus van der Borcht, engraving of the Antwerp stock exchange from L. Guicciardini, *Descrittione di tutti Paesi Bassi*, Antwerp, 1581

not know the exact amounts of these latter. Effectively, the holders of *asientos* and other floating debts were given *juros* and rentes as compensation.

Such were the decrees on paper. In practice Philip and Juana virtually exempted favoured bankers, although this time the Fugger, without the personal protection of the emperor, were badly hit. Since the financial practices of the sixteenth century were highly sophisticated, there were also those who did well out of speculating in *juros* and *rentes* on the open market. For a while 'bears' (i.e. those who stipulated to pay for their purchases of *juros* at a later time when, they hoped, their market value had declined) were as prominent on the money market as 'bulls' had usually been. In any case, those directly affected by the decrees were a relatively small group of financiers. Rather more were affected by the postponement of payments at the money fairs, postponements arranged to save the bankers from their own creditors. But while such postponements, at the time called prolongations, were particularly frequent in the months following the decree of June 1557, they were nothing new and had been used for years by both the government and the financiers to deal with immediate cash crises.

None of the great financial houses on the Antwerp money market actually went bankrupt, although one or two in Seville did.[15] The general public seems to have been almost unaware of the royal decree. The deputies of the provincial Estates and of the States General hardly mentioned it. In December 1557 they demanded a limitation of interest to 12 per cent – as if they had never heard of the decree of the previous June! At other times they proposed a 5 per cent limit; but a proposal from the deputies of Artois to apply such a limit also to domain rents was immediately rejected by all the other provinces. Too many burghers of the Netherlands towns held such rents.[16]

Considering how confused the Habsburg governments were about the state of their finances, it is not surprising that the general public and even the political elites should have been even more confused. Everyone hated the foreign bankers and it was convenient to blame them for financial disasters and high taxes. For, in the end, high taxes were bound to follow the excessive government borrowing, no matter how much clever finance officials and bankers played about with rescheduling government debts. The interest on all those *juros* and *rentes* which had been given to the bankers had still to be paid. That was certainly much less than the interest on the floating loans had been before the rescheduling. But the wars continued and the soldiers could not be paid with annuities. Almost immediately Philip's governments in both Spain and the Netherlands took up new loans. In Spain one could always hope for new silver shipments from Peru, and it was this expectation, more than the actual amount of treasure unloaded in Seville, which persuaded the bankers to go on lending to the Spanish government, even after their bad experience of the summer of 1557.

Much of this American silver found its way to Antwerp. But, in the end, the Netherlands government still had to find its own collateral for the loans it took up on the Antwerp money market. And this collateral could only be provided by taxes granted by the Estates. At the very moment when it seemed that the development of the system of provincial annuities had solved the financial problems of the Netherlands government, the almost limitless escalation of the costs of warfare overtook the benefits of the system. The relations between the government and the representative assemblies therefore moved again into the centre of Netherlands politics, and this at a time when the government, now in the hands of relatively inexperienced men, was in a state of confusion such as it had not been since the last days of Maximilian I.

THE STATES GENERAL OF 1556

Philip II summoned his first States General for 12 March 1556. No one thought it would give him an easy ride. The summer of 1555 had been exceptionally wet.

---

[15] For this account of the crisis I have followed Steele, 'The Financial Crisis', ch. 3.
[16] Verhofstad, *De Regering*, 125–40.

Emmanuel Philibert of Savoy (1555–1559)

Plate 12 Titian, *Philip II*, 1554. Private collection, Switzerland

Cattle normally left out in the fields until November had to be stalled much earlier and this had caused great mortality. The grain harvest had been poor and prices were rising throughout the winter to nearly double their usual level. The bakers had to make smaller loaves; the brewers brewed worse beer because the weather affected the turf which they used as fuel. The Holland fishermen reported their catches down from a normal 40 last per boat to 8 or even 6.[17] Philip asked as many of the great seigneurs as possible to attend what would undoubtedly be a difficult session, even if the gentlemen were sick and had to be carried in.

The government outlined the dire financial situation and proposed a tax of a Hundredth Penny (1 per cent) on real property and a Fiftieth Penny on commercial and industrial property. The proposed machinery for assessment was much more sophisticated than that proposed when the idea of such a tax was first mooted, in 1543. Every town or quarter was to have a commission of four, two chosen by the king and two by the locality. This commission, in turn, was to choose four notables who were to make the assessment under oath, but without requiring insight into the merchants' account books.[18]

The proposal had a universally bad reception. Just as had happened in the 1540s, the provinces offered the government substantial sums which they proposed to raise by the traditional methods. But these sums were not as much as the government had calculated it would get from its own proposals. Immediately, ministers were involved in the usual haggling. Worse still, from the government's point of view, the haggling was not only about the amounts to be raised but conditions which the provinces wanted to attach to their grants. Brabant insisted that the king come to Brussels and refused to send its deputies to him in Ghent, for fear of losing its privilege of holding the meetings of its Estates in its own province. In fact, this condition had frequently been broken before. Flanders was anxious to keep the king and his court in Ghent and was quite prepared to sabotage Brussels. Holland brought up its old grievance of the immunity from taxation enjoyed by the three great seigneurs who had extensive estates in the province, Orange, Egmont and Hoorn. Even before the meeting of the States General the Holland deputies demanded that only natives should be appointed to official positions. The government advised them against writing such a clause into their *bede* conditions because the king would regard it as blackmail and later refuse to be bound by it.[19]

During the summer and autumn of 1556 tempers frayed on all sides. The Venetian ambassador reported that the prince of Orange had publicly remarked that His Majesty should hang those who spoke against his important affairs. There is nothing here of the Orange legend which has William the Silent stand up against the king for Dutch freedom from the beginning of Philip II's reign. The marquis of Berghes, another of the 'opposition' seigneurs of the 1560s, said the king should put a Spanish garrison into Brussels, perhaps even build a fortress there. The deputies in the States General were unimpressed and replied coolly that those who defended their property did not deserve to be hanged, but that this fate should be

---

[17] *RSH*, vol. IV, Adrien van der Goes, *Register*, vol. II, 155–6, 42.
[18] Verhofstad, *De Regering*, 84–7.
[19] *RSH*, vol. IV, 89–92.

reserved for those ministers who wished to appropriate their property. If His Majesty knew how ill he was served and how well robbed, he would not think badly of the deputies.[20] At the same time they asked to see the government accounts and they insisted on the reform of the law courts before they would grant further taxes. When Philip reported to his father the insolent language of the Brabant deputies, Charles replied that he must simply bear with these obstinate thickheads (*quei ostinati cervelli di Brabant*), as the Venetian ambassador reported the incident.[21]

The ambassador was of course reporting court gossip. But the opinions he reported to the Venetian Senate and even their wording have an authentic ring to them. The great seigneurs had, at least as yet, little sympathy for the towns and their deputies, while Charles V's remark fits only too well with his well-known attitude at this time of shuffling off responsibility to his successors while still interfering and blaming them for everything that went wrong.

By the end of October 1556 Savoy had reached the point of drafting an extraordinarily strongly worded letter to the city council of Brussels. It had in fact been the representatives of the guilds and the ordinary respectable citizens in the council who had rejected the government's tax proposals. Savoy now accused the whole city council of being bad subjects and mocking their natural prince. His Majesty would show them the resentment, he wrote, of which such a prince is capable. At the very least, they must return the two acts which he, Savoy, had granted them. It is not clear which particular set of acts the governor general meant or even whether this letter was ever sent.[22]

By the end of the year 1556 most of the provinces were finally persuaded to grant considerable sums in taxes. The government had to give up its plans for uniform property and income taxes, although Philip tried to salvage at least something of the principle of greater fairness on which these plans had been based. Orange had gone to 's-Hertogenbosch to put pressure on the city council. Its third 'member', representing the ordinary citizens, demanded the abolition of the chimney tax, a tax which brought in 22,000 florins plus interest payments. The king could take over this payment himself, but it was thought that this would set a bad example. All the same, Philip wrote, if Orange could achieve a compromise, Philip would be more inclined to accept it if the payment fell on the rich rather than on the poor.[23]

Flanders offered 800,000 florins, payable by a Tenth Penny on income from immoveables and a Tenth Penny on commercial income, payable by merchants

---

[20] Badoero to Doge, Ghent, 4 Nov. 1556. Quoted in Verhofstad, *De Regering*, 97–8.
[21] Badoero to Doge, 5 Sept. 1556, *Calendar of State Papers Venetian*, vol. VI, pt. 1, 600, 612.
[22] 'Remonstrances faictes par Monseigneur le Duc de Savoye a ceulx de la loy et dixhuit choisiz par les nations de Bruxelles.' This seems to be a draft. AGRB, P. d'E. A., 1228, fo. 228.
[23] Philip to Prince of Orange, 30 Sept. 1556. Groen van Prinsterer, ed., *Archives ou correspondance inédite de la maison Orange-Nassau*, ser. 1, vol. I, 2nd edn (Leiden, 1841), 26.

reputed to have a capital of more than 300 florins. It was assumed that their income would be 6 per cent of such capital. Effectively, then, the tax amounted to 0.6 per cent on commercial capital. For Brabant the prelates and nobles offered 667,000 florins; but not all the Brabant cities could achieve the necessary unanimity in their councils and the king took over some of their quotas. In Holland the provincial Estates continued to press for a tax of 300,000 florins, instead of their usual quota of half that of Brabant, 333,333 florins. Already in July the Estates of Holland had argued that with the government's proposals of the Hundredth and Fiftieth pennies, the province would have paid less than half of Brabant's quota.[24] Negotiations between the monarchy and its parliaments tended to be full of ironic twists, and sometimes the historian has the feeling that they were quite deliberate on the part of the Estates. The deputies and their constituents were concerned much less with the extra 30,000 odd florins than with their quarrel with the government over the claims of Orange, Egmont and Hoorn for exemption from all taxes for their estates in Holland.

The States General of 1556 does not seem to have agreed a global sum for all the provinces which sent deputies, nor was any money payable before 1557. These facts did not prevent the government from negotiating loans on the Antwerp money market based on the expected extraordinary revenue. The Council of Finance extrapolated the firm offer of 800,000 florins from Flanders, for instance, to claim that they would get a total revenue of 2.5 million. Antwerp was sufficiently impressed to drop its interest rates from more than 20 per cent to the more normal 12 to 14.[25] A final twist in the irony of the situation was that the negotiations of 1556 and the *aides* granted in that year were overtaken by the financial settlements with the next States General in 1557–8.

THE NOVENNIAL *AIDE* AND THE STATES GENERAL'S CONTROL OVER NETHERLANDS FINANCE

In February 1557 the war with France started again, and not just in Italy but on the Netherlands border. The situation was critical. During the winter both sides of the Channel had been struck by a particularly virulent strain of influenza, causing a high rate of mortality.[26] Poor harvests for the second year running and warfare in the Baltic pushed up grain prices to the highest level of the century before the 1590s.[27] As we have seen, the government was working on the rescheduling of its

---

[24] *RSH*, vol. IV, 2 July 1556.
[25] Verhofstad, *De Regering*, 88–9.
[26] F. B. Fisher, 'Influenza and Inflation in Tudor England', *Economic History Review*, 2nd ser., 18 (1965).
[27] A. Friis, 'An Inquiry into the Relations between Economic and Financial Factors in the Sixteenth and Seventeenth Century, I. The Two Crises in the Netherlands in 1557', *Scandinavian Economic History Review*, I, 2 (1953), 202–3.

short-term loans, but it needed ready money for what was hoped to be the decisive campaign to force a favourable peace on King Henry II. Philip succeeded in getting England involved in this war. But there was no question of getting any money from the English for what they clearly regarded as his and not their war. Nor, as Philip wrote to Savoy, was there anyone left in Castile with money to buy royal domain.[28] In the Netherlands, or at least in Brabant, it was a breach of the *joyeuse entrée* to sell domain land without the consent of the Estates. More serious still, nobody would buy annuities unless they had been guaranteed by the Estates.[29]

There was no alternative to summoning the States General again. But everyone was thoroughly sick of the usual procedures: for the government to make its proposals to the assembled deputies, but then to negotiate separately with each province and, often enough, to have to send its own high-powered representatives, members of the Council of State or Knights of the Golden Fleece, to the meetings of provincial assemblies and even to individual town councils. This is what had happed in the previous year. So why not, people in the government began to argue, try the opposite approach? Keep the deputies together beyond the initial address and let them discuss together their traditional obligation of giving their prince advice and help in the hour of his need. An essential condition for the success of such a course would be for the deputies in the States General to have *plena potestas*, full powers to discuss all relevant issues and to take binding decisions (rather like the members of the House of Commons in England). At the very least, they should have greater powers than their provincial assemblies usually allowed them to have.

In all this, King Philip and his Spanish advisers were in known territory. Castile was the largest unified kingdom in continental Europe and in both respects, size and unification, comparable only to England. There the position was perhaps best summed up by Sir Thomas Smith in his *De Republica Anglorum* of 1583: Parliament 'representeth and hath power of the whole realm both head and bodie. For every Englishman is entended to be present, either in person or by procuration and attornies . . . And the consent of Parliament is taken to be every mans consent.'[30] In Castile the powers of the deputies to the Cortes had been a matter for controversy at least since Charles V's first visit.[31] It remained controversial throughout the sixteenth century. Constant reference back to the deputies' constituents was out of the question, by reason of sheer distance and of the difficulties of travel. These difficulties suited the monarchy which wanted the deputies to enjoy full powers. That would make negotiations easier and, if necessary, one could bribe

---

[28] Philip II to Savoy, 27 May 1557. AGRB, Manuscrits divers 1172.
[29] Englebert van der Dale, chancellor of Brabant, to Regent Mary, 11 Jan. 1552. AGRB, P. d'E. A., 647, fo. 45.
[30] H. G. Koenigsberger, 'The Powers of Deputies in Sixteenth Century Assemblies', in *Estates and Revolutions*, 177.
[31] *Ibid.*, 181–90.

individual deputies. For their part, the eighteen cities which sent deputies to the Cortes tried to keep as close control over them as possible and often made them take oaths to observe their instructions. The result was a constant tug-of-war between the government and the cities. When things got out of hand they sometimes called in the theologians to resolve their quarrels. But more commonly the deputies found themselves acting as a kind of third force, neither fully independent nor fully bound to their constituents or manipulable by the government.

In the Netherlands, by contrast, there had never been any question of full powers for the deputies. They could easily travel the relatively short distances between the meeting places of the States General and their home provinces, often quite comfortably by boat or barge. Moreover, the Netherlands was a composite polity. People did not speak of it as a state, a realm, as Sir Thomas Smith spoke of England. For a long time the provinces had considered themselves bound together only by having the same prince. Only very gradually had they come to consider themselves as a political community and they were suspicious of the word union. It was the monarchy which had given this dynastic community a legal status by negotiating the Treaty of Augsburg with the Reichstag of the Holy Roman Empire, in 1548. At the same time, no one seriously thought that this polity would be dissolved again. There were too many vested interests in keeping it alive and there always had been – which was why the monarchy and the provinces had cooperated in building the States General in the first place. And indeed, in spite of the provinces' insistence that their deputies refer back for all important decisions, there had always been a great deal of discussion behind the scenes. The smaller provinces, especially, had often instructed their deputies to follow the lead of Flanders and Barbant. The fate of Ghent in 1540 had shown only too clearly the penalties for 'going it alone'.

In 1557 it was only Antoine Perrenot, the arch-conservative Franche-Comtois, born so to speak in the red tape of government procedure – his father, we remember, had been Charles V's chancellor – who spoke in the council against the government's plans for the States General as a joint debating assembly.[32] Later he self-righteously blamed the regent Margaret of Parma's difficulties on this 'mistake' of 1557 and suggested that Lalaing and others had been deliberately trying to build up the authority of the States General, no doubt for their own aristocratic purposes, at the expense of the authority of the monarchy.

In 1557, at least, there is very little evidence for any such conspiracy. In 1536 Mary of Hungary had warned the emperor that 'there are always those who will put it into other peoples' heads that promises made to them in the past have not been kept', and that this was causing her great difficulties.[33] But at that time there

---

[32] J. I. Fortea Pérez, *Monarchia y cortes en la corona de Castilla. Las ciudades ante la politica fiscal de Felipe II* (Cortes de Castilla y Leon, 1990), especially ch. 3.
[33] Mary to Charles V, Brussels, 4 Jan 1536. AGRB, P. d'E. A., 49, fo. 4.

had been no question of formally joint discussion. In fact, the Estates had their own feelings of ambivalence. Their privileges often ante-dated the existence of the States General. They would not lightly give up such privileges as the right to take decisions on taxation after discussions in their own provincial assemblies, within the frontiers of their own provinces and with the accustomed procedures in their own language, Dutch-Flemish or Frisian, as against the French of the meetings of the States General.[34] The prince might offer letters of non-prejudice for necessary breaches of these traditions. But such letters were notoriously fragile defences against the government lawyers' arguing from both necessity and precedent.

In August 1557 the States General of all the Netherlands met at Valenciennes, near the king's headquarters in the campaign against France. In November the States General were transferred back to Brussels, their most usual meeting place. From the beginning the deputies raised procedural points. Did the States General, now that their procedures were unified, represent only the old hereditary provinces or also those acquired more recently by Charles V: Utrecht, Guelders, Overijssel, Friesland, Groningen? Utrecht did not send any deputies at first, arguing that it had nothing to do with the States General. The others at least came, including deputies from the duchies of Luxembourg and Limburg, who were not usually seen at such meetings. But now, if there was to be a general tax, as the government proposed, how was it to be apportioned? The traditional fixed proportions for the provinces went back to the 1510s. How would the new provinces fit into the old schema, even allowing for the fact that they were all relatively poor, compared with urbanised Flanders, Brabant and Holland?

The bickering about all this was bad enough; but these were practical problems which were certainly not insoluble. Much more serious for the government were two characteristics which immediately became apparent in the debates of the States General in their new format. The first was that discussions about such matters as legal procedures in the provincial courts or local privileges and exemptions, matters which had normally been discussed quietly and rationally in the relative obscurity of the provincial Estates, were now suddenly being brought into the open before the assembled representatives of the whole States General. The result was often both a waste of time for the government and a source of jealousy and friction between the provinces. Thus in April and May 1558 Holland demanded that the powers of the inquisitors should be limited according to canon law. It was the first time that this topic had surfaced in a meeting of the States General. But no one as yet took it seriously, except to show their irritation that the Hollanders had evidently not done their homework. The deputies of Brabant said that, on the basis of their *joyeuse entrée*, they did not admit any inquisitors in their province at all, canonical or otherwise. The other deputies remarked that if their provinces found any excess or unreasonableness in the actions of the inquisitors in

---

[34] E.g. discussions in the Estates of Holland, Oct. 1557. *RSH*, vol. V, 105-9.

their provinces, they would know how to deal with them.[35] It would take a great increase in both Protestant proselytising and in inquisitorial activity, together with the plan for the new bishoprics, to shift the problem of religion into the centre of the States General's relations with the monarchy. This was to happen quite soon. But as yet only the Hollanders were worried and, apparently, not very much.

The second characteristic of the new type of States General was that the deputies began as a matter of course to discuss openly matters of state and of high policy. Again, such discussions – and they were usually highly critical of the government – had previously taken place mostly in the provincial assemblies. Now they were given a public resonance which they did not have before. There was, for instance, the Treaty of Augsburg of 1548. At the time, the States General had accepted it willingly enough. Now, in December 1557, the deputies argued that the Netherlands had fulfilled their part of the treaty and faithfully paid their contributions for the defence of the Holy Roman Empire.[36] They now wanted help from the Empire in the war with France, if only, they argued, for the greater security of the Holy Roman Empire itself.[37]

Perhaps it was this bad experience with the Empire which made the States General feel ambivalent about a proposed union with England. Several of the deputies feared that the English would get more out of it than the Netherlanders.[38] But above all, and time and again, the deputies argued that the war had started in Italy for the benefit of Spain, but that it was being fought in the Netherlands and that the Netherlanders bore most of the costs.[39]

It was the unfairness of such accusations, as Philip perceived it, which led him already in the spring of 1557 to write his plaintive note to Savoy about how the Netherlanders claimed that he loved an inch of Spanish soil more than a hundred leagues in the Low Countries. By the autumn of 1557 the deputies were discussing not only matters of high policy, which on the basis of the information they had, they could do only on a very general level, but also detailed matters of military policy and organisation. There were debates on whether to use only native troops, for they would know the local roads and their pay would keep money in the country; or about who was to be appointed as commander of the *bandes d'ordonnance* and of the frontier fortresses. The general view was that, in both cases, it should be the knights of the Order of the Golden Fleece.[40] Such views were not in themselves objectionable to the government. They were, however, a clear invasion by the States General of a field which had always been regarded as strictly part of the royal prerogative.

---

[35] From a Flemish account: 'Recueil de ce que a esté faicte ès assemblées des estatz généraux ... depuis le VIIe d'avril 1557 [1558 n.s.] jusque au 4a mai, dedans la ville de Bruxelles', in *BCRH*, ser. 3, vol. VIII, 301–3.
[36] Cf. above ch. 6.
[37] Verhofstad, *De Regering*, 121–3.
[38] AGRB, Manuscrits divers, 327, fo. 40.
[39] *Ibid.*, fo. 39.
[40] *Ibid.*, fos. 40–7.

Emmanuel Philibert of Savoy (1555–1559)

We have no single personal account of the proceedings of all the sessions of the States General of 1557–9, the way we have it even for some of the sessions of the fifteenth century. What we do have are reports by individual deputies to their constituents, although these are mostly in the form of minutes with occasional comments; and we have the comments by the king, his governor general and, sometimes, by the ministers involved in the negotiations. There were no dramatic confrontations, as there had been in the States Generals of Charles the Bold. Philip II, unlike his father and his great-great-grandfather, had little taste for dramatic gestures. Both he and Savoy were mostly away, in England or at the front in the St Quentin campaign of 1557. Savoy seems to have been disapproving and bored with the whole business of negotiating with the States General. There were great passions and little good will in the Netherlands, he wrote to the king in 1557, and he advised him to keep troops ready in case of troubles, troubles which, he judged, were likely to happen.[41] Such remarks sound entirely in character for the man who later abolished the parliaments of his own duchy of Piedmont-Savoy by a military coup.[42]

Savoy was surely right about the great passions and the little good will he saw in the Netherlands, and he was also right about the danger of rebellion. But such still hypothetical rebellion would not be initiated by the States General. Its internal quarrels made it quite incapable of such action. In the 1480s it had been Flanders, and especially the city of Ghent, which had been the motor which propelled the States General into opposition and civil war against the regent, Maximilian of Austria. In the 1550s there was no such motor. Ghent, tamed in 1540 and now living under the shadow of Charles V's fortress, could not and did not dream of leading a revolt; and without the leadership of its principal city, the whole province of Flanders proved to be more amenable to government pressure than several of the other provinces. The States General's forays into the fields of foreign and defence policy might seem outrageous to conservatively minded ministers; but they were not part of a purposeful movement of opposition.

How little this was so and how undramatic were the proceedings of the States General is evident from the discussions about the main purpose for which it had been summoned: voting *aides* and providing money for paying the troops and for servicing and repaying the huge loans which the government had taken up. The deputies were, of course, well aware of the exceptionally high food prices of the winter of 1557 and the impact which further taxes would have on the common people, and they were equally aware that they themselves and their friends in the town councils would be the first targets of popular movements. Province after province was therefore claiming poverty and the burden of previous taxes

---

[41] Savoy to Philip II, 2 May 1557. Emanuele Filiberto, duke of Savoy, 'I diarii delle campagne di Fiandra', ed. E. Brunelli, *Biblioteca della società subalpina*, 113 n.s., 21 (Turin, 1928), 182–7.
[42] Koenigsberger, *Estates and Revolutions*, 74–8. Merlin, *Emanuele Filiberto*, V.

against the government proposals. To these common laments they added such well-rehearsed complaints as the arbitrary actions of customs officials, whom the deputies characteristically lumped together with 'lombards' and 'highwaymen'.[43] None of this was new. More alarming for the government were doubts raised about the wisdom of helping the government at all. The States General had not been consulted about the government's loans. If it now agreed to pay off the king's debts he would become independent of the States General; for he would simply go on making debts and presenting the deputies with *faits accomplis* and moralistic warnings of the horrendous consequences if the debts were not paid.[44]

Worse still, the Council of State itself suggested that the king had a stake in inefficiency. Holland and Zeeland demanded that the king upgrade 'bad fiefs' into 'good fiefs', immortal and heritable by any relative. Against this the council argued that such a move would deprive the king of a valuable source of patronage.[45] Similarly with monopolies. There were always merchants or financiers who argued that a salt monopoly or an alum monopoly would provide the government with a sizeable lump sum or a steady revenue while, at the same time, lowering the price to the consumer – the herring fishermen and cheesemakers of Zeeland and Holland for salt, the cloth makers of Brabant for alum, the metal workers of Namur for calamine or, in the case of proposed monopolies of French or German wine, the taverners and wine merchants everywhere. Neither governments nor deputies of representative assemblies were necessarily taken in by the sleight of hand of the supply-side arguments of prospective monopolists; but they could rarely resist the prospect of a new source of capital or of revenue, not to speak of patronage sweeteners for potential creditors.

With such problems and such clashes of interest the common discussions of the States General did not produce the speedy resolutions which the government had hoped for. The deputies still demanded on several occasions to be sent home for new instructions. They threw out a government proposal to combine the provinces into four groups, so as to speed negotiations. No one wanted to be held responsible for anyone else whose contribution fell short of their quota. But however exasperating the proceedings were for the government – and there was after all nothing new in that – there was never any real doubt that the States General would meet at least the greater part of the government's demands.[46] Indeed it was more generous than it had ever been. In May 1558 it agreed to the 'novennial *aide*', taxes worth 800,000 livres per annum for nine years. The yet uncollected taxes granted by the

---

[43] AGRB, Manuscrits divers, 327, fo. 42.
[44] Verhofstad, *De Regering*, 137–40.
[45] *Ibid.*, 140–1.
[46] The most interesting contemporary account, probably by a Flemish deputy, is printed by L. P. Gachard, 'Relation des séances des Etats Généraux à Bruxelles, 2 avril – 4 mai 1558', in *BCRH*, ser. 3, vol. VIII, 297–319. Also printed in G. Griffiths, *Representative Government in Western Europe in the Sixteenth Century* (Oxford, 1968), 356–70.

Emmanuel Philibert of Savoy (1555–1559)

Plate 13 Bartholomeus de Momper, engraving of the court of Brussels, 1558–60. Print cabinet S. II. 11445, Koninklijke Bibliotheek Albert I/Bibliothèque Royale Albert Ier, Brussels

States General of 1556, the so-called 'sexennial *aide*', were to be subsumed in the new taxes. *Dominium politicum et regale* was clearly still working and, in spite of all problems, it was still accepted by both the monarchy and by the political classes of the Netherlands.

The devil, as Perrenot and probably through him also Philip II came to see it, was in the agreements for the administration of the 'novennial *aide*' which the government had made with the States General; or, as they later came to claim, agreements which the States General had imposed on a somewhat naive and unsuspecting duke of Savoy or perhaps on an equally naive, and perhaps even malicious, Count Charles de Lalaing, whom Savoy had left in charge while he himself was with the army in France. Lalaing died in November 1558 and Savoy would soon return to his duchies in Italy. The one could not, and the other could not be bothered to, counter such innuendoes. In fact the detailed negotiations had been conducted on the government side by the president of the Council of State, Viglius van Aytta, an intelligent if unimaginative lawyer from Friesland who had made his name in the complicated legal negotiations with the Germans for the

Treaty of Augsburg, in 1548–9. Ironically, he was a protégé of Perrenot and later his most faithful ally in the Council of State.

By 1558 all the major provinces had built up their tax-gathering and tax-disbursing machinery. This development had been a functional as well as a political necessity for the great expansion of the sale of annuities. Now that the States General as a whole had granted the 'novennial *aide*', there could be no question of handing its administration back to the government's own finance officers. Nor could it be simply left to the separate provincial administrations. Even though the collection of the 'novennial *aide*' was left to the individual provinces, there now had to be some machinery for its overall administration, if only because otherwise the Antwerp money market would not take it seriously.

The head of this administration, the superintendant of finances, as he came to be called, therefore had to be appointed by the States General. But here new difficulties arose. The person to choose would need to be someone who was a good administrator and who, preferably, had contacts with the international money market. The deputies therefore chose the Antwerp banker Antoon van Straelen. The Flemish deputies, however, refused to join in this election. They were suspicious of a Brabanter because they feared he would want to increase the quota which Flanders traditionally paid in the general *aides* – a fear which was frequently voiced by several Flemish deputies – and 'because they did not want to enter into a union with the other provinces'.[47] This traditional 'unwillingnesss to enter into a union' had led to the failure of Charles V's and Mary of Hungary's attempts to rationalise the defence and foreign policy of the Netherlands in 1534. Now, nearly a quarter of a century later, it was possible to arrange a compromise. After all the deputies except those of Flanders and Holland had agreed on van Straelen, Savoy took the Flemings aside, in the same room, and persuaded them to agree to his, Savoy's, appointing van Straelen in the name of the king. An element of the ludicrous was to remain a characteristic of Netherlands politics. The Hollanders, however, held out and within three years van Straelen's administration of the 'novennial *aide*' collapsed.

[47] Gachard, 'Relation', 315–16.

9

Rule from Madrid: the regency of Margaret of Parma (1559–1567)

'Rather than suffer the least damage to religion and the service of God, I would lose all my states and a hundred lives, if I had them: for I do not propose or desire to be ruler of heretics.'

Philip II to Don Luis de Requesens, his ambassador to the pope, 12 Aug. 1566[1]

THE KING RETURNS TO SPAIN

The signing of the Treaty of Cateau-Cambrésis (2–3 April 1559) was the true end of the late emperor Charles V's grandiose imperial plans, the *plus ultra*, the dream of a universal Christian empire of the early years of his reign. The idealism, never completely negligible, had always been more a matter of self-justification and propaganda than of practical political aims. In the bitter and progressively more expensive wars on the Netherlands–French border and in Italy during the 1550s the idealism had worn very thin indeed. The peace treaty was therefore characteristically an agreement between the two dominant contending powers, Spain and France. The interests of their allies were settled according to the value the Habsburg and Valois monarchies attached to these interests in the spring of 1559 and to a good deal of horse-trading about which the unfortunate allies were never consistently consulted. It was hoped that the marriage of Philip II to Henry II's daughter, Elizabeth, would make the peace permanent. In fact, the old enmities had not been resolved and, in the opinions of the monarchs and their ministers and generals, might break out again at any moment. The old domino theory, the belief that ever greater disasters would follow even a minor setback, was still very much alive, graced (as it is also in our own time) by the argument of the need to prepare for the worst possible contingency.[2]

Such arguments have invariably had political and financial implications. One of them surfaced in the Netherlands even before Philip II had set sail for Spain, on 25

---

[1] 'que antes que sufrir la menor quiebra del mundo en lo de la religión y el servicio de Dios, perderé todos mis estados y cien vidas, que tuviesse, porque yo ni pienso ni quiero ser señor de herejes'.

[2] For the international situation in 1559 see H. G. Koenigsberger, 'Western Europe and the Power of Spain', in *New Cambridge Modern History*, vol. III, 234–7; reprinted in Koenigsberger, *The Habsburgs and Europe*, 63–8. Rodriguez-Salgado, *The Changing Face of Empire*, chs. 6–8.

August 1559. He wanted to leave a *tercio*, a regiment of 3,000 Spanish veterans, in the Netherlands. They were his most reliable troops and were meant to garrison the towns on the French border and also to act, and to be seen, as an immediately available striking force in case of any resumption of hostilities by France. Now, after Queen Mary's death, England had become a great question mark in international relations, and so the *tercio* was also meant to warn off the English from any hostile move. Finally, although this was not spelled out until later, Spanish troops might be used to intervene in the French civil wars against the Huguenots.[3]

All this made sense in terms of Philip II's overall strategy for his multiple monarchy.[4] In the king's dominions outside Spain, however, Spanish troops were never popular. In Sicily, for instance, the parliament petitioned against the garrison of 300 Spanish light cavalry and proposed the commissioning of six galleys instead to keep the coasts clear of Muslim pirates. There were even rumblings that the Sicilian parliament might refuse the grants demanded by the government if the king did not grant their petition about the cavalry. It did not come to that and the cavalry remained in Sicily until 1593. But neither parliament nor the king's government ever suggested that Philip kept these troops in the kingdom to keep the Sicilians in check.[5]

In the Netherlands the Spanish troops were as unpopular as in Italy and, moreover, their presence was not regarded as politically innocent. Three months before the decisive victory of St Quentin, in May 1557, the governor general, Savoy, advised the king that it was advisable to keep some loyal troops in the country in case of revolt.[6] In November of that year the States General discussed the whole question of what troops should be used to defend the Netherlands and who should command them and the country's fortresses.[7] These matters had been traditionally regarded as being the prince's prerogative, although the Estates of Holland had quarrelled with their provincial governor precisely over such issues in the 1530s. The discussions in the States General were meant to be secret, but the Venetian ambassador, Badoer, seems to have known about them. At any rate he wrote to the Senate about the mood of the country and of the government's intentions to keep Spanish and German troops in order to control and chastise the country. Two years later, Badoer's successor, Soriano, made the same point in his report.[8]

By the summer of 1559 this view of the Spanish troops had become widespread. The count of Egmont, next to the duke of Alba Philip's most distinguished

---

[3] Secret report [instructions?] by Philip II to Secretary Courteville for Margaret of Parma, Dec. 1561, in Weiss, *Papiers d'Etat*, vol. VI, 432–43.
[4] G. Parker, *The Grand Strategy of Philip II* (New Haven, 1998), *passim*.
[5] Koenigsberger, *The Practice of Empire*, 176–7.
[6] Savoy to Philip II, 2 May 1557. Emanuele Filiberto, 'I diarii', 182.
[7] AGRB, Manuscrits divers, 327, fos. 40–7.
[8] 'Relazione di Carlo V e di Filippo II (1557)', in E. Albèri, ed., *Relazioni degli Ambasciatori Veneti al Senato durante il secolo decimosesto*, ser. 1, vol. III, 298–358.

The regency of Margaret of Parma (1559–1567)

general, wrote cynically to his friend, the prince of Orange, that as usual things were getting worse. The king seemed determined to keep the Spanish infantry here and disband all other troops. 'I leave you to guess for what purpose.'[9] A new meeting of the States General, summoned to Brussels in June 1559, now made the removal of the Spanish *tercio* a condition for the actual disbursement of the novennial *aide*. Philip was furious and called the States General ill informed and acting with 'sinister intent'.[10] The States General remained unmoved. The deputies were bound by their instructions and, when it suited them, they could happily hide behind their limitations. They could therefore afford to remain unimpressed by royal bad temper and ministerial bluster.[11] Perrenot was convinced there was no way of keeping the Spaniards in the country and advised that the king should replace them with other loyal troops.[12]

Throughout the autumn and winter of 1559–60 the new regent, Margaret of Parma, prompted by Perrenot, pressed the king to withdraw the Spanish troops. Philip had not paid their arrears, as he had promised, and the Estates were not paying for substitute garrisons, as they had promised. Margaret's letters, even at this early stage of her regency, began to sound like those of her predecessors, warning of impending catastrophe, only that, where her great-aunt Margaret of Austria had wished to be in her mother's belly and her aunt, Mary of Hungary, had wished to be a thousand leagues away, Philip's sister, Margaret of Parma, wanted to be a hundred feet under the earth.[13] Finally Philip gave way and the Spanish troops left the Netherlands in January 1561. They were immediately sent to the Mediterranean to replace the losses of a failed coup against Tripoli which had cost the Spaniards twenty-seven galleys and 10,000 men in casualties and prisoners.

While the problem of the Spanish *tercio* in the Netherlands was now resolved, it had left a thoroughly bad taste. It was all very well for Philip to feel hurt by the Netherlanders' belief that he loved an inch of Spanish soil more than a hundred leagues in the Netherlands; he and many of his Spanish ministers had become distrustful of the Netherlanders. The king was careful not to show this distrust openly. The government he appointed for his sister, Margaret, was as traditional an aristocratic government of Netherlands seigneurs and knights of the Golden

---

[9] Egmont to Orange, 1 July 1559. N. Japikse, ed., *Correspondentie van Willem den Eerste Prins van Oranje*, vol. I (The Hague, 1934), 143.

[10] AGRB, P. d'E. A., 647, fos. 121–4.

[11] E.g. the deputies from Hainaut. Margaret to Philip, Brussels, 4 Oct. 1559. L. P. Gachard, ed., *Correspondance de Marguerite d'Autriche, duchesse de Parme, avec Philippe II*, vol. I (Brussels, 1867), 121.

[12] Perrenot to Philip II, 4 Oct. 1559. Weiss, *Papiers d'Etat*, vol. V, 653. Same to same, 9 Dec. 1559. *Ibid.*, 667.

[13] Margaret to Philip, Brussels, 17 March 1560 Most letters of this period have references to the *tercio*. Cf. also Weiss, *Papiers d'Etat*, vol. V, *passim*. For the favourite expressions of the Habsburg ladies fearing catastrophe, see H. G. Koenigsberger, 'Prince and States General: Charles V and the Netherlands (1506–1555)', *TRHS*, 6th ser. 4 (1994), 145.

Fleece as ever Chièvres had appointed for the young Charles: William of Nassau, prince of Orange and the richest nobleman in the country; Count Egmont and, later, Count Hoorn and the marquis of Berghes. There was also Count Berlaymont, a relatively poor nobleman on the make, heavily dependent on government patronage. About Orange Philip may already at this time have had to swallow hard. He was his former personal companion but he was raising doubts in the king's mind about his religious orthodoxy. He was just negotiating a very prestigious but hardly tactful marriage with the niece of the elector of Saxony. She was a Lutheran and the daughter of Charles V's arch-enemy, Maurice of Saxony, the man who had led the German princes against the emperor and, at least in imperial eyes, had betrayed Metz to the French.

Absent from this council were the members of the Croy clan. We do not know whether, at this time, this was a deliberate move to make the Croys jealous. Later on, Philip certainly tried to divide the Netherlands high nobility.[14] Again quite traditionally, Margaret's council also contained a number of professional lawyers, notably Perrenot, who from 1561 was Cardinal Granvelle, and the Frisian lawyer Viglius.

These were all Netherlanders except for Granvelle, and there were many precedents from the fourteenth and fifteenth centuries for Burgundian professionals in the council. Again according to tradition, the noble members of the council doubled as provincial governors: Orange of Holland and Zeeland, Egmont of Flanders, Berghes of Hainaut. Count Megen was appointed governor of Guelders, after Hoorn had resigned from this position with the courtesy title of admiral when he followed Philip to Spain. The king gave Margaret instructions on how to conduct herself, just as his predecessors had always done with the regents, governors general and viceroys in the Netherlands and Italy and even in Spain itself. Margaret's instructions contained the usual restrictions, notably on the appointment to all high administrative and military offices and to ecclesiastical benefices, leaving only a very small number in the regent's free gift – exactly the position about which Margaret of Austria had protested to Charles V in the 1520s. Philip, like his predecessors, was convinced that governments were controlled through patronage and, later, he was to spell out this conviction as a firm principle: 'They must depend only on me and from me only receive favours for services they have rendered me.'[15]

When Philip left for Spain, in 1559, it looked as if he intended to govern the Netherlands entirely according to tradition and this was probably what he believed himself. Look at the appointment of my sister and the ministers I have chosen for her, and stop complaining about the *tercio* and Spanish control of the government, he told the States General he attended in August 1559, just before leaving for

---

[14] E.g. Granvelle to Philip II, 10 March 1563, Weiss, *Papiers d'Etat*, vol. VII, 11–14.
[15] Koenigsberger, *Politicians and Virtuosi*, 81.

The regency of Margaret of Parma (1559-1567)

Spain.[16] It was only in the course of the next few years that the practical experience of running this government showed both Philip and an increasing number of his Netherlands subjects that the terms of this tradition no longer applied. The causes of this change were systemic, that is, in the nature and traditions of Netherlands society; they were personal, in the ambitions of the younger generation, those whom Mary of Hungary had said she no longer understood; and they were contingent on the events outside the control of the traditional government competence. These causes were interconnected and acted on each other.

For at least sixty years the Netherlands had experienced growing prosperity, even while there had been the normal economic fluctuations which always hit the poorer people hardest. But the cities, notably Antwerp and Amsterdam, had grown, the former to almost 100,000 inhabitants. The expanding middle classes had founded up to 150 secular schools which taught reading and writing, elementary arithmetic and geometry to a much greater proportion of the population than ever before. And Antwerp was only the most spectacular of many Netherlands cities whose growing prosperity and civic pride we can often still see in their sumptuous town halls. Textile industries had spread in villages and small towns in western Flanders and spawned a new proletariat of propertyless workers, a proletariat which frightened both respectable propertied burghers and the ruling elites of the cities. Some historians have seen a direct connection between these social changes, sometimes and with some exaggeration characterised as a dysfunction, a breakdown, of Netherlands society, and the social and religious troubles which started in 1566.[17]

The traditional structure of Margaret of Parma's government masked for a time the change which was occurring both in Netherlands society and in the control which the head of the multiple Habsburg monarchy would exert over decision-making. His position, too, was traditional enough; but now, for the first time, it was exercised from one country only, Spain and, as all observers gradually came to realise, by a king who preferred to take his advice from Spaniards, even about non-Spanish matters. In the Netherlands he had left Tomás de Armenteros as Margaret's secretary, and Armenteros was a cousin of his own secretary of state, Gonzalo Pérez. Other Spaniards were placed in strategic positions, in charge of finance and church affairs. Just how effective they were in providing information for Madrid and in reporting on those they suspected of unorthodox religious views was to become apparent only later. The foreign ambassadors whose job it was to keep their ears open wrote to their principals quite clearly that it was the Spaniards who controlled the king's government. This was what the Netherlanders thought.[18]

Philip's policy towards France seemed to prove their point. Governments have never found it easy to forget age-old enmities. Philip and his advisers simply did

---

[16] E.g. J. W. Smit, 'The Netherlands Revolution', in R. Forster and J. P. Greene, *Preconditions of Revolution in Early Modern Europe* (Baltimore and London, 1970).

[17] G. Parker, *The Dutch Revolt* (London, 1977), 45-6.

[18] Ibid., 46 n.20.

not trust the French. When the first French civil war broke out, in the early summer of 1562, their unease was further magnified by the danger of a victory for the Protestants, the Huguenots, or alternatively by the danger of the French monarchy using the age-old tactic of diverting attention from its internal problems by aggression abroad. The reports from Philip's ambassador in France, Granvelle's brother, the sieur de Chantonnay, became more and more alarming. As Chantonnay wrote to the duke of Alba, at least some of the French councillors were talking of the disaffection of the Netherlanders who were going to transfer their loyalty either to the emperor Ferdinand I's son, Maximilian, or even to the king of France. In a classic example of the domino theory, Spain would then lose its hold over northern Italy, its contacts with England and its transatlantic commerce.[19]

It is not clear whether such views were taken seriously in French government circles or were mischievously fed to the ambassador. But even before they reached Madrid, Philip was contemplating intervening in France to forestall a Huguenot victory and its undoubtedly baleful effects on the Netherlands. In the Netherlands itself, everyone was agreed – Margaret, Granvelle, the knights of the Golden Fleece, the Estates – that the country could not afford such an adventure. Philip felt that this attitude was both humiliating to himself and desperately dangerous to the Netherlands. These feelings coloured all his future relations with his dominion.

Such unanimity as over the proposed intervention in France, was not, however, usual in the Netherlands during Margaret of Parma's regency. The States General of 1557-8 had provided the very generous novennial *aide*; but the government had immediately anticipated at least the first years of this grant in loans from the bankers, in order to pay off the horrendous debts from the last war. Even that was not enough and some regiments remained unpaid for months or even years and began to live off the country. For those unfortunate enough to be in the path of the marauding bands of hungry and disgruntled soldiers, any peace dividend of the Treaty of Cateau-Cambrésis was conspicuous by its absence.

The problem was compounded by the need to keep effective frontier garrisons. The government argued that the Estates had promised to pay for those which were to take the place of the *tercio*. But the whole position of the Estates and their relations with the government were now thoroughly confused. Margaret asked the separate provinces for contributions. Were these separate, additional *aides*, or were they part of the deal which Savoy had worked out with the States General? The deputies had made the withdrawal of the *tercio* a condition of their grant. The king had never accepted their right to make such conditions. Nevertheless, the government had negotiated on the basis of precisely such conditions and, once the *tercio* had left, used this as an argument.

[19] For the whole episode see H. G. Koenigsberger, 'Orange, Granvelle and Philip II', *BGN*, 99. 4 (1984), 591-2.

The regency of Margaret of Parma (1559–1567)

The trouble was, however, that there were also other conditions, and there was no unambiguous agreement as to what they were. We are best informed about the negotiations with Holland. In April 1560 the province was asked for 37,500 guilders for three years, for the frontier garrisons. But we are not a frontier province, the Holland deputies replied. On the other hand, war causes indefinite interruptions of trade. Six hundred ships had been lost, and there was heavy loss of capital and high unemployment. By contrast the agricultural frontier provinces of the south could make good devastations of land warfare within a year. This was not altogether wrong about a province living mainly by commerce and fishing. But it was also a self-serving argument and wildly optimistic about recovery rates in Hainaut and Artois where houses and farm animals as well as harvests had been lost.

More serious for the government was the deputies' argument that defence was now a matter for the States General. The king himself, they said, had agreed to this argument in May 1558. In view of this fact, and because the government claimed that the other provinces had already agreed to the payment of the garrisons, were the Netherlands now in a defensive union, at least for the duration of the novennial *aide*? The ministers reacted strongly: certainly not, they argued. The regent Mary of Hungary had always resisted such a union. This was one of Granvelle's pet arguments, but he was wrong. In 1534–5, it had been Mary, prompted by Charles V, who had proposed a defensive union of the provinces and it had been these provinces, represented in the States General, which had rejected it.

But even if Granvelle's argument was accepted, it produced its own contradictions. If Holland reduced its contribution, the other provinces would reduce theirs too. But how could that be, said the Holland deputies. Either they do not know our acts, any more than we do theirs (because we are no longer supposed to have common discussions) or they misunderstand how much we have already granted. Several of the other provinces have not even granted the 1559 *aide* yet, so why should Holland? Besides, it is the king now who accepts *aides* with his own reservations, a practice formerly unheard of. Margaret now gave way so far that she promised not to insist on the last point until Brabant had consented to the 1559 *aide*.[20] The position and the arguments of the government, and the arguments and the self-perception of the provincial Estates and the States General had become thoroughly confused. Granvelle, at least according to his own claims, was and always had been consistently opposed to common discussions. His reasons were that they were very lengthy and inefficient, as well as a derogation of the king's authority. He does not seem to have known that common debates were the normal procedure of the States General before 1520. Philip II agreed with Granvelle or was persuaded by him. But what was he persuaded of? It rather looks as if he now

---

[20] Gachard, *Correspondance de Marguerite d'Autriche*, vol. I, *passim*. HSR, vols. VI and VII, *passim*.

took against all forms of the States General without even making Granvelle's distinction about the form of the debates. Yet, with the near desperate financial situation which Philip found in Spain on his return, he could not send his government in Brussels the help which he had hoped and indeed promised to send from Spain. He simply could not do without help from the Estates.

The Estates were equally confused. There was no question of denying that, together with the king's service, the safeguard of their privileges was their primary concern. Philip himself acknowledged this much, at least at this stage. For these purposes, discussions between the provinces were essential, whether they were called common discussions or not. In January 1562 the deputies of Holland explained to the regent that, since 1560, deputies from the different provinces had discussed together how they could persuade Flanders to stay in the union for the administration of the novennial *aide*. And they used the word union. But Flanders, resenting the apparent primacy of Brabant in this matter, had refused to do so. Then why, the Holland deputies argued, should not Holland also stay out of the union, especially since they were paying their part of the novennial *aide* and since the costs of van Straelen's common administration came to more than the 70,000 livres earmarked for it.[21]

In Brabant they were of course content with the Antwerp banker van Straelen's position as superintendent of finances. But they had been in the forefront of the campaign for the removal of the *tercio* and they made difficulties about the payment for the substitute garrisons and even for the current instalments of the novennial *aide*. The centre of this resistance was traditional: the guild and populist members of the town councils of Louvain and 's-Hertogenbosch. However exasperating for Margaret's government, this traditional problem could have been solved if it had been the only one. For, just as on previous occasions, the great lords in the regent's council were willing to go to the town halls and they could usually persuade the recalcitrant councils to fall into line.

THE RELIGIOUS QUESTION

But heavy taxation and war-weariness, which everyone including Granvelle and the regent herself acknowledged, were no longer the only problems. Two developments occurred over which the government in Brussels had little or no control. They came from opposite directions and, while not exactly caused by each other, they were interlinked and they first coloured and then came to dominate the perceptions of the monarchy's relations with the States General. The first was the spread of Protestant ideas in the Netherlands. This had been a relatively slow process and the States General and the provincial Estates had only occasionally taken notice of it. The great majority of the Netherlands elite, those who were

---

[21] *Ibid.*, vol. VII, 39–42.

The regency of Margaret of Parma (1559–1567)

represented in the Estates, considered themselves to be good Catholics, well able to resist the allures of the Protestant preachers. They did not greatly object to Charles V's placards, the laws against heresy which the emperor had issued since shortly after his own encounter with Luther. It was only in the 1560s, when the government appointed special inquisitors who actually hunted out heretics or alleged heretics, that the placards acquired a sinister connotation and that the Netherlands elites became seriously worried. For the inquisitors disregarded all local rights of jurisdiction, including the right of local courts to confiscate the property of convicted heretics.[22] Most alarming, however, was the inquisitors' disregard of the privilege of *de non evocando* by which an accused could be tried only in his local court. As early as 1548 the Estates of Holland had become uneasy. If the privilege *de non evocando* could be set aside, were not all privileges safeguarding life and property in danger? At that time the matter had been smoothed over. But now, in the time of Margaret of Parma, this was no longer possible.[23]

For in the meantime the king had obtained from the pope bulls for the erection of fourteen new bishoprics and for removing the Netherlands church from the authority of the metropolitan sees of Rheims and Cologne, outside Habsburg jurisdiction. The initiative for this move had originally come in the 1550s from a number of academic theologians who wished to improve the administrative, pastoral and theological effectiveness of the Netherlands church. These aims had recommended themselves to Charles V but he was too busy with the war with France to pursue them, Philip II, with the examples of the spread of heresy in France and Scotland before his eyes, took them up with enthusiasm. Apart from their normal episcopal duties, the new bishops would also function as inquisitors or, rather, they would appoint professional inquisitors to track down heretics.

It took time to organise the new bishoprics and appoint suitable incumbents. From the beginning the scheme ran into opposition from most of the cities which had been earmarked as the new sees. As especially the Antwerp magistrates argued, a bishop and his inquisitors in the city would frighten away foreign merchants, especially the Germans who were always suspect and many of whom had indeed quietly observed the Lutheran faith, without bothering anyone. And now, the political waves of this problem spread much more widely. For the first time the Estates became systematically involved.

This involvement was at least partly due to a political decision by the government. The new bishoprics had to be financed. It seemed a clever move to assign to them the income of a number of rich Brabant monasteries. Their abbots had traditionally been the leaders of the first estate of the assembly of Brabant and, since the time of Margaret of Austria in the 1520s, they had a reputation for being

---

[22] H. A. Enno van Gelder, 'Bailleul, Bronckhorst, Brederode', *De Gids*, no. 100, 219–20.
[23] In this discussion of the legal aspects of the placards I have largely followed A. Duke, 'Salvation by Coercion', in Duke, *Reformation and Revolt in the Low Countries* (London and Ronceverte, 1990).

awkward.[24] Worse still, these prelates were often the sons or younger brothers of the great lords. The move therefore seemed to be directed against the nobility.[25] Much later, Granvelle claimed that his policy was a deliberate attempt to increase government influence in the Estates of Brabant.[26] This may have been true; but at the time both he and the king accused the nobles of wanting to block the reform of the church, precisely because they did not want to lose their influence in the Estates.[27] This may also have been true. In October 1565 Egmont acquired the lordship of the huge estate of Gaesbeek for 210,050 guilders by outbidding the duke of Brunswick, the king's candidate, by 50 guilders. This acquisition made Egmont a member of the estate of nobles of Brabant. The king's advisers were divided as to whether this was good for royal policy – in the spring of that year Egmont had been persuaded in Madrid that Philip was supporting the Netherlands nobles – or whether it was a coup for the opposition. Both sides were aware that Egmont had borrowed heavily for this purchase from the towns of Flanders of which he was the governor; and it was well understood that the creditors of a noble borrower were as much his clients as those who had received favours from a patron.

Among the deputies of the Estates there circulated rumours that the king wanted to appoint Spaniards to some of the new bishoprics. Through the incorporated abbacies they would then be abbots, have seats as prelates in the meetings of the Estates and discover their secrets.[28] In February 1562 the Estates therefore sent a petition directly to the king. The abbacies of Saint Bernard and Tongerloo had now been vacant for two years, they pointed out. This was an infringement of Brabant's privileges and so was the plan to join them to bishoprics, for this would be a perpetual commendation. It would also be bad for religion; for the monastic orders, as represented by the great Premonstratensian abbacies, were especially necessary at the present time.[29] The privileges the Estates quoted were both the Great Privilege of 1477 and the *joyeuse entrée*. The Habsburgs had always rejected the Great Privilege as having been forced on Mary of Burgundy. The *joyeuse entrée* was in a different category. It had, of course, also been forced on the dukes of Brabant, but much earlier, and they and their Burgundian and Habsburg successors had always accepted it.

Philip's reply now was a denial of both the complaints and the privileges. He ended with a trump card: any privilege, however strong, had to give way to

---

[24] See above, ch. 5.
[25] M. Dierickx, *De Oprichting der Nieuwe Bisdommen in de Nederlanden onder Filips II, 1559–70* (Antwerp, 1950), 74ff. and *passim*.
[26] Parker, *The Dutch Revolt*, 48, n.24.
[27] G. Griffiths, *William of Hornes, Lord of Hèze, and the Revolt of the Netherlands* (Los Angeles, 1954), 14–15. Granvelle to Philip II, Brussels, 14 June and 12 July 1562, Weiss, *Papiers d'Etat*, vol. VI, 568 and 577. The earlier letter also quoted by Dierickx, *De Oprichting*, 165.
[28] Margaret to Philip, 17 Jan. 1562. Gachard, *Correspondance de Marguerite d'Autriche*, vol. II, 56.
[29] *Ibid.*, 131–6.

The regency of Margaret of Parma (1559–1567)

overriding necessity, as at present. In case of dispute over the interpretation of privileges, it was the prince and not the Estates who decided. And the king ended triumphantly with two well-known Latin quotations: *cum summa sit ratio quae pro religione facit* and *salus populi suprema lex sit* – religious reasons are the highest reasons and the public good must be the supreme law.[30]

The first quotation was a commonplace in medieval law; the second came from Cicero's *De Legibus*.[31] Whatever meaning Cicero may have had in mind with his phrase of *salus populi*, for Philip II the meaning was never in doubt: it was the salvation of his subjects, and God's providence had appointed him, the king, to safeguard this supreme good. Time and time again he reiterated to members of his family, to his ministers, to his generals, that the maintenance of his own service and of Holy Church must be their objects in all their public actions. Like most of his contemporaries he was convinced, and said and wrote it often, that 'a change of religion' was always followed by a 'change of state'. Philip's religious beliefs and his belief in the religious value of his own sovereignty were not precisely synonymous, but they overlapped to a high degree and he could not think of them as separate.

These were Philip II's fundamental beliefs, the bottom line, one might say, below which he would never consent to act. Thus had his father, the emperor Charles V, refused to sign the Treaty of Augsburg with the acknowledgement of the legitimacy of Lutheranism in Germany. Philip refused to contemplate in his own dominions what he regarded as the similar abominable principles underlying the successive edicts of toleration for the Calvinists in France. The categorical statement for the eyes of the pope (quoted at the head of this chapter) Philip had previously written, on other occasions, even if not always in such a lapidary form.

Uncompromising as was the king's language, it showed his beliefs, his attitude, not a plan of action; or at least not in 1562 when he, or his secretaries with his consent, wrote his answer to the petition of the Estates of Brabant. In principle, he had undercut the foundations of legitimate government of Brabant. If, for the sake of his own religious beliefs and his personal conception of what these beliefs imposed on him, he could set aside specific privileges in public law which he had sworn to uphold, then no sphere of public law was safe from his claims. Then he really was a *princeps legibus solutus*, a ruler above the law or, what amounted to the same thing, a ruler who was always able to declare what the law was.

The king was fully aware of the possible consequences of his beliefs. In his message to Pope Pius V he spelt out these consequences:

If it should be possible I will settle the religious problem of these states [i.e. the Netherlands] without taking up arms, for I know that to do so would result in their total destruction; but if everything cannot be remedied as I desire without recourse to arms, I am

---

[30] *Ibid.*, 143.
[31] Duke, *Reformation and Revolt*, 171–2.

determined to take them up ... and neither danger [to myself] nor the ruin of these states, nor all the others which are left to me, will prevent me from doing what a Christian prince, fearing God, ought to do in His service, the preservation of the Catholic faith and the honour of the Apostolic See.[32]

Here was the most fundamental reason why the conflict between the king and the Estates of the Netherlands escalated into open war and why, once this had happened, all attempts at compromise would founder. Those Netherlanders who believed in the fundamental nature of their privileges, even if they shared the king's religion, could not accept a ruler who claimed powers of omnipotence. However much he protested that, in his actions, he was representing God and His church, he could no longer be fully trusted. And a degree of mutual trust was the basis of all *dominium politicum et regale* regimes – as in the following century Charles I of England was to find. For those of a different religious persuasion the issues were even clearer. The logic of the situation drove them to the defence, and eventually the armed defence, of their country's political privileges.

But in 1562 such logic was not yet compelling for most of the actors. Traditionally, the deputies of the States General and of the provincial Estates preferred not to dispute 'the power of princes' but to concentrate on individual, concrete problems.[33] The prince, his regents and his lawyers would occasionally defend specific policies by arguments based on theoretical claims of princely or imperial prerogatives. But the general political tenor of the age was conservatism rather than rational consistency. Philip II himself, like most of his contemporary rulers, abhorred 'novelties'. He did not set out deliberately to undermine local laws and privileges simply for the sake of royal authority. The real problems arose when political power and political rights became entangled with transcendental aims. For the time being, all sides therefore continued to concentrate on the immediate issue of the bishoprics and of the specific powers needed to deal with heretics.

But it was precisely on these issues that strong emotions became involved. The Inquisition which Charles V had established in the Netherlands was the traditional medieval institution, based on the local bishoprics, not the Spanish Inquisition, founded by Ferdinand and Isabella in the late fifteenth century to deal with the perceived threat to Spanish Christianity from Jews of judaising converted Jews (Conversos) and from Islamic Moors or superficially converted Moors (Moriscos). In Spain the Inquisition was concerned only incidentally and mainly prophylactically with heretics. In the Netherlands there were no Moriscos and, as yet, very few Jews and Conversos. But the Spanish Inquisition was famous (or infamous, depending on one's point of view) for its secret trials, often involving the use of torture, of persons who had been secretly denounced. The Neapolitans, good Catholics, said, when Charles V tried to introduce the Spanish Inquisition in their

---

[32] Quoted in full in Koenigsberger, *Politicians and Virtuosi*, 87.
[33] See above p. 161.

The regency of Margaret of Parma (1559–1567)

kingdom: we simply do not trust each other enough to allow such a tribunal with such secret powers in our country. The emperor had to give way. The Milanese, led by their saintly archbishop Carlo Borromeo, and backed by Borromeo's uncle Pope Pius IV, forced a similar retreat on Philip II in 1563.

The Netherlanders thought of the new bishoprics with their inquisitorial powers and the now greatly increased activities of the travelling inquisitors in terms of the Spanish Inquisition and as another, and particularly hateful, instance of the Spanish takeover of their country. Philip II was aware of these accusations and asked his regent to assure the Netherlanders that he had no intention of introducing the Spanish Inquisition and felt rather hurt by the accusation.[34] But this was disingenuous; for in the same letter he explained that the reason for his decision was that the inquisition in the Netherlands was less merciful than in Spain, for it did not spare the life of the truly penitent heretic, whereas the Spanish Inquisition did.[35]

Most people in the Netherlands did not understand these subtle distinctions and those who did were not impressed by them. Killing people for their beliefs went against all the traditions, Erasmian and even medieval, of the Netherlands elite. Since the Estates, for their own reasons, opposed the erection of the new bishoprics, those who opposed the Inquisition also looked to the Estates to defend their resistance.[36] Voices now began to be heard calling for the States General to solve the religious problem of the Netherlands. It seemed a natural move in an age when the papacy itself was summoning councils of the whole Christian church to solve doctrinal disputes.

For Philip II, however, this was not a solution at all. He had gained the conviction, helped by Granvelle's insistent arguments to that effect, that the Estates and especially the States General were intent on reducing his own God-given authority. Even in the case of the Council of Trent, the ecumenical council summoned by the pope, he refused to publish those decrees which he regarded as infringing his royal sovereignty. By the summer of 1562 he wrote to Margaret of 'those devils of Brabant'.[37]

Devils or not, Philip and Granvelle still thought that their policy of taming the Estates of Brabant by means of the effective decapitation of the estate of the prelates would work. Granvelle himself had been appointed as archbishop of Malines and a cardinal and, hence, primate of the Netherlands church, with formal precedence over everyone after the regent. The States General could be effectively neutralised by never summoning them again in the form of 1557–8, with common

---

[34] Philip to Margaret, 17 July 1562. Gachard, *Correspondance*, vol. II, 291.
[35] Quoted from Archivo General de Simancas, MS Estado, legajo 525 in M. Dierickx, 'La politique religieuse de Philippe II dans les anciens Pays-Bas', *Hispania*, 16, 62 (Madrid, 1956), 137.
[36] E.g. objections to the placards and to the actions of the episcopal Inquisition in the Estates of Holland, 9 Jan. and 17 April 1564. *HSR*, vol. VIII.
[37] Philip to Margaret, 25 July 1562. Quoted in Dierickx, *De Oprichting*, 165.

debates. Then the expanded activities of the Inquisition would be able to root out heresy, just as it had been rooted out in Spain.

Such a scenario was not impossible, given a Netherlands government led determinedly and firmly supported by the high nobility and the town patriciates, as it had been in the time of Mary of Hungary. But these conditions no longer prevailed. Heavy taxation, the alleged takeover of the country by the Spaniards and a religious policy which ran counter to the traditions of most educated Netherlanders were eroding the government's support among the elites. At the same time firm leadership at the centre disappeared. This was the second development over which the king had little control.

WHO CONTROLS THE GOVERNMENT OF THE NETHERLANDS?

No longer did the imperative demands of war mask the growing divisions over the conduct of government. While ultimate decision-making and ultimate control over patronage had moved to Madrid, the Netherlands government was now headed by an inexperienced woman who had none of the political flair of her aunt, Mary of Hungary. Such powers as were left to her government slipped into the hands of Cardinal Granvelle. To the great Netherlands lords Granvelle was little more than an upstart civil servant from Franche-Comté. They had been the king's generals and advisers on foreign policy. Their Spanish peer, the duke of Alba, had been appointed as viceroy of Naples and was one of the king's closest advisers. Here was the basic reason why, in July 1561, Egmont and Orange wrote to the king, denouncing Granvelle's conduct of the government and complaining that they were excluded from all important decision-making in the government of the Netherlands.[38]

Over the following three years the antagonisms deepened and the dispute escalated into a struggle for power. Since all parties were agreed on the most important issues of foreign policy, that is opposition to the king's wish to interfere in France, that left the spheres of finance, religious policy and government patronage. The lords supported action against heresy, but without enthusiasm for the actions of the inquisitors. More for political than for religious reasons they were critical of the erection of the new bishoprics. The struggle therefore centred on the control of patronage. Many of the great seigneurs were governors of provinces and commanders of the aristocratic cavalry militia, the *bandes d'ordonnance*. Similar to the provincial governors in France, they represented both the king's authority, especially in organising defence and security, and the interests of the community of the province, with whose Estates they negotiated and whose arguments they might support in the regent's council.[39] Both positions, as commanders and as governors,

[38] For a fuller account with relevant sources see Koenigsberger, 'Orange, Granvelle and Philip II', 573–95.
[39] Cf. the ambivalent relations of the count of Hoochstraten with the Estates of Holland, above, ch. 5.

The regency of Margaret of Parma (1559–1567)

gave ample opportunity for the exercise of local patronage. Because the king had officially reserved all patronage decisions for himself, much of the governors' patronage was unofficial, either ignoring the king or at least putting in a good word for their clients. This power was real enough and everyone knew how the system worked.

Granvelle, in his letters to the king, was spelling out more and more insistently how Orange and his friends in the high nobility were building up their own following. He was especially alarmed by their influence on the 'renewal', the annual appointments, of city magistrates. Granvelle insisted on the lords' basic loyalty to both the king and to the Catholic religion in much the same way that Shakespeare's Mark Anthony, in his funeral speech for Julius Caesar, insisted that Brutus and Cassius were honourable men. In 1563 he even suggested to the king that he appoint Orange as viceroy of Sicily. Perhaps he wanted in this way to get rid of his most dangerous opponent. But the suggestion, which the cardinal repeated, fits in well with what we know of his conception of the Habsburg monarchy as an essentially international institution. Educated in the Franche-Comté, in the old Carolingian middle kingdom, between France and Germany, where the idea of the Roman Empire had never entirely disappeared, Granvelle had learned his politics and administration from his father, the councillor of Charles V. He continued to pursue his cosmopolitan vision when, later, he was viceroy of Naples, ambassador in Rome and, finally, the king's principal adviser in Madrid, the only non-Spaniard and non-Italian ever to reach such a position under Philip II. But, characteristically, Philip rejected Granvelle's suggestion for the prince of Orange and even his much more modest proposals of bestowing a few *encomiendas* in Spain on some Netherlands gentlemen. For every Netherlander so honoured, the cardinal argued, 25,000 would live in hope and hence complete loyalty. Philip answered that Orange was too much of a risk in such a crucial position as an Italian viceroyalty. As to the *encomiendas*, they had to be reserved for those who served near him. His father had rejected a similar suggestion about ecclesiastical benefices by the regent Margaret of Austria in just the same way.[40] Philip II undoubtedly believed in his frequent protestations that all his subjects were equally dear to him. He was deceiving himself, but he was not deceiving his subjects.

If Granvelle overdramatised the ambitions of the Netherlands lords, he was correct in the direction in which these ambitions pointed. There were fears in government circles that one of the lords would play the role of a Condé or Coligny in contemporary France and make himself head of a Netherlands Huguenot party. But no such party existed, nor did any of the lords make any move to form one. Orange's ultimate aims at this stage of his career have remained as puzzling for historians as they were for his contemporaries. If he looked to France for a model, it was to the role of the Catholic Guises during the minority of Charles IX or to the

---

[40] Cf. above pp. 120–1.

role of the *connétable* and the Montmorency clan, the relatives of Orange's friend and colleague in the Council of State, the count of Hoorn.

Neither Orange and his friends, with whom he had actually formed an anti-Granvelle league, nor the cardinal himself could afford to be entirely open about their policy of building up their respective followings among the lower nobility and the city magistrates; for this would have meant challenging the king's authority. Granvelle claimed that his actions were specifically aimed at defending this authority. The lords claimed that, if only the cardinal did not interfere and if the king would soften his religious policy, they could persuade the Estates of Brabant and hopefully those of the other provinces to pay up their quotas of the novennial *aide* and of the additional sums for the replacement of the frontier garrisons after the withdrawal of the Spanish *tercio*.

Both sides had allies at the court in Madrid: the lords among the Eboli party, Granvelle among the duke of Alba's friends. Several royal officials manoeuvred in between, for a varying mixture of religious concern and careerism. Some of these filled the king's ears with tales of the supposed softness shown to the heretics by one or other party in the Netherlands. By the end of 1563 Granvelle had lost the game in Madrid. Partly because of the temporary weakness of the Alba party and partly for the apparently good strategic reason that the king had no other military force in the Netherlands but the noble-controlled *bandes d'ordonnance*, Philip decided to cooperate with the lords and ordered Granvelle to leave the Netherlands, in March 1564.

This action was very much part of a pattern of Philip's political behaviour. Whenever a minister, governor or viceroy ran up against insuperable local opposition, it became expedient to throw him to the wolves and replace him, while leaving the king's authority intact. With the viceroys of Sicily such action became virtually institutionalised, and their tenure was never renewed beyond one or at most two three-year terms. The universal contemporary lament about the fickleness of princes had much justification; for such fickleness was built into the system of early modern government and especially of those dominions of a composite monarchy in which the king did not personally reside.

The lords, now in control of the Netherlands Council of State, did their best to deliver on the financial front. In December 1563 a States General met in Brussels, officially at least without common debates. Orange, the governor of Holland and Zeeland, would give huge dinner parties to the deputies of Flanders. Egmont, the governor of Flanders, would give similar parties to the deputies of Holland and Zeeland. But now the limitations of the quest for power by patronage became apparent. The city councils who chose and instructed the deputies were in most cases a virtually closed group of patricians. At the annual 'renewal of the law' a third of the aldermen were usually chosen either directly by the government in Brussels or by the provincial governor. In most cities this choice was limited to a list prepared by the city council, a system which severely limited the choice by

The regency of Margaret of Parma (1559-1567)

either the governor or the government. Neither Granvelle nor the lords had therefore been able to build up loyal majorities in the city councils. And these councils continued to pursue the policies they had always pursued. They depended on the monarchy for commercial and legal privileges, for the protection of their trade and, perhaps most important in the absence of effective municipal police forces, for the final guarantee of law and order and their own position and authority against popular riots and mob rule. Thus they were traditionally royalist and willing to support the regent and her government. At the same time they were touchy about the infringement of any of their privileges and, at least partly because of their fear of a popular backlash, they tried to keep down taxation. Orange and his friends in the Council of State were therefore no more successful in dealing with the recalcitrant Estates in the matter of finances than Granvelle.

Even in the matter of government patronage they found that Margaret's civil servants in the Privy Council and, most galling of all, her Spanish secretary, Armenteros, still had the decisive voice. At the same time the league of the seigneurs was beginning to show cracks. The duke of Aerschot and his powerful Croy connection had never wanted to join the league against Granvelle, accusing Egmont of not wanting to treat him as an equal. Egmont and Orange found themselves acting respectively as the somewhat reluctant champions of the Flemish cities and of Antwerp, in their perpetual competition for commercial privileges.

The king's new policy of cooperating with the Netherlands high nobility was a forlorn hope. Neither side wanted as yet to break the basic structure of the Netherlands polity nor challenge its position within the Habsburg multiple monarchy. Yet psychologically and politically the aims of the players in this game had become too contradictory to make genuine cooperation possible. The lords, both as members of the Council of State and, even more, as provincial governors, dragged their feet over the implementation of the placards, although this did not always prevent the inquisitors from doing their grisly work. Even before his fate had been decided, Granvelle wrote to the king's secretary, Gonzalo Pérez, in June 1563: 'It is laughable to send us depositions before the inquisitors in Spain so that we should look for heretics here: as if there were not thousands professing heresy to whom we dare not say anything.'[41]

THE CRISIS OF 1565-1566

In the spring of 1565 the Netherlands Council of State sent Egmont to Spain to obtain the king's approval for the post-Granvellian role the council was now playing and for a relaxation of the laws against heresy. Philip was quite certain in his mind about the need to continue the punishment of the heretics, but he was not yet clear about his tactics and was anxious not to break with the Netherlands lords.

---

[41] Weiss, *Papiers d'Etat*, vol. VII, 106.

Egmont misunderstood his attitude and the favours the king showered on him personally. It had for some time been Philip's intention to ease Egmont away from the noble opposition. Egmont returned to the Netherlands, wrongly believing that Philip had promised the relaxation of the placards. From this moment of misunderstanding, prompted by the remains of good will on both sides, events escaped from the control of both the king in Madrid and of the regency government in Brussels. Through the summer and autumn of 1565 the king reinforced his determination to uphold the Inquisition, while doing nothing to resolve the paralysis into which the government of the Netherlands had fallen.[42]

This was a systemic weakness of Philip II's political system. At much the same time, in Spain itself, in Andalucia, paralysis overtook the government, resulting from the conflicting claims and manoeuvres of the Spanish Inquisition, the *audiencia*, i.e. the supreme civil court of the province, the archbishop of Granada, his hostile cathedral chapter and the governor of the province, the only authority to protect the Moriscos of the province. Here, too, Philip did nothing to resolve the political deadlocks, but he recalled the governor and backed a repressive religious policy against the Moriscos. The result was a Morisco uprising, aided by the North African Moors, followed by two years of particularly cruel civil war.

In the Netherlands the first reaction to political paralysis and reinforced religious persecution was also an extra-constitutional action, the formation of the Compromise, although not as yet a full-scale rebellion. That would duly come a year later. The Compromise consisted of a league of some 400 members of the minor nobility and urban patricians from all the provinces of the Netherlands. It was led by the Dutch count of Brederode and by Orange's younger brother, Count Louis of Nassau. Its intention was to put pressure on the government. The lords of the council and the knights of the Golden Fleece were sympathetic but kept aloof. On 5 April 1566, some two hundred members of the Compromise marched to the regent's palace in Brussels and presented her with a petition demanding the abolition of the anti-heresy laws and the summoning of the States General to settle the religious question.

One of the regent's ministers, perhaps to reassure his mistress, seems to have referred to the procession as mere beggars. That night, at a characteristically extravagant dinner in Brussels, hosted by several of the rich lords, Brederode and his friends adopted the name of Beggars (*gueux, guizen*) with the symbols of the beggar's wooden bowl and traditional double-pouched sack as their emblem. The whole event, with its multi-faceted symbolism of carnival and of popular charivari, 'the world-turned-upside-down', was in itself profoundly conservative, a reaffirmation, through the game of inversion, of the traditional order and values of

---

[42] On the paralysis of the Netherlands government see also the instructions given to Egmont for his journey to Spain, 23 January 1565. Gachard, *Correspondance de Marguerite d'Autriche*, vol. III, 546.

The regency of Margaret of Parma (1559–1567)

society.[43] While the symbolism of the Beggars' movement and its propaganda was generally accessible to contemporaries, not all of it was to everyone. People chose from it those parts which fitted into their preconceptions or desires; and this happened with both the friends and the opponents of the movement. The result tended to be a much more radical image than most of the members of the Compromise had intended.

Both the programme of the Compromise and the petition presented to the regent had been carefully drafted to allow for the support of Catholics as well as Protestants, and this duality gave its name to the movement. The petition aimed to bring the States General once more into the centre of Netherlands public life. Yet this body was not in session and did not at that time, nor later in the year, take any active part in the movement. There was undoubtedly a great deal of support for a States General in the country. The nobility and the patricians saw themselves as defending their ancient privileges against attack. Extravagant figures of support for the Compromise circulated both in the movement itself and in government circles. As often happens with reform movements, its opponents equated the moderate majority with the small extremist wing, in this case the Calvinists.

Not unnaturally, Margaret of Parma was terrified. She rapidly agreed to a moderation of the placards and informed the provincial Estates of this move. All these Estates, often with the prelates in the van, approved of the 'Moderation'.[44] To become law, however, it needed the king's assent; and this was, equally naturally, not forthcoming.

The convinced Protestants were also unappeased. They called the 'Moderation' the murderation; but effectively the preachers now had a free rein, at least outside the cities. The authorities no longer interfered. In the Netherlands, as in France, the preachers built up their congregations into armed conventicles. By the summer they had organisations in many parts of the country and they negotiated with the Compromise about raising troops. A radical section of the movement had become, at least covertly, revolutionary.

In Madrid the confusion was almost as great as in Brussels. On the Mediterranean front Philip II and his allies had just managed to fight off the Turkish siege of Malta, in 1565, but the control of the central Mediterranean was not really secure. Sultan Sulaiman was threatening an even greater effort for 1566. Philip had little time for Netherlands affairs. At the beginning of August he wrote to Margaret approving her unwillingness to summon the States General. He would never consent to it, for he knew only too well what it would lead to, he wrote. But she should not make his resolve known and say that she was still waiting for his authorisation, so that people should not despair.[45] But what did Philip mean by

---

[43] For a detailed analysis of this symbolism, see H. van Nierop, 'A Beggars' Banquet: The Compromise of the Nobility and the Politics of Inversion', *European History Quarterly*, 21, 4 (Oct. 1991), 419–43.
[44] For a more detailed account of the events of 1566 see Parker, *The Dutch Revolt*, ch. 2.
[45] Philip to Margaret, Forest of Segovia, 2 August 1566. Gachard, *Correspondance de Marguerite d'Autriche*, vol. II, LXXVII.

States General? What Granvelle meant – common discussion – or simply the meeting together of the delegates of the provincial Estates to listen together to general propositions by the government and then discuss them separately, although of course always trying to coordinate with the other major provinces? Did Philip know himself what he meant? No one was given a chance to find out.

Margaret received the king's letter on 12 August. By that time the other actors in the drama had pushed aside the question of the States General altogether. On 10 August in the Westquartier, the Walloon part of Flanders, gangs entered monasteries and rural churches and smashed stained glass windows and images of saints. In the following two weeks this iconoclast movement spread throughout the Netherlands. Many contemporaries and later historians saw these outbreaks of violence as revolutionary movements by the proletariat of the new rural industries of west Flanders. The weavers of the 'new draperies', light and relatively cheap woollen cloths, had suffered from unemployment and high bread prices, following a failed harvest in 1565. The economic crisis was sharpened by the disruption of trade because of war in the Baltic and by one of the periodic embargoes in the endless game of commercial rivalry which punctuated the basically symbiotic economic relationship of the Netherlands and England.

Both sides of the economic divide liked to portray their opponents as motivated mainly by economic greed or the prospect of plunder.[46] They were not completely wrong. As early as May 1565 the Estates of Holland had petitioned the regent to intervene with the king of Denmark against the closing of the Sound to Dutch shipping. Grain prices, they said, had risen above the famine level of 1557 and from this would necessarily follow 'all sorts of crimes, theft, robbery and violence by the people'. In November they reiterated their fear of a popular rising 'under the cloak of high prices'. They asked for the presence of their provincial governor, the prince of Orange, but he replied that the regent needed his presence in Brussels.[47]

In Brussels there were rumours of huge popular armies of fanatical heretics swamping the whole country. In fact, the image breaking was carried out by quite small groups who, in a number of cases, were paid to do their work of destruction. They sometimes got themselves drunk in the monastic wine cellars but did not usually plunder bakeries and grain stores, nor did they steal church treaures for themselves. This was all very different from the usual sixteenth-century bread riots. In contrast with similar events in France there was little violence towards the persons of priests, monks and nuns. The aspect of ritual violence, purification by the shedding of blood,[48] was almost completely absent in the Netherlands. The

---

[46] For the most categorically economic and class-war explanation of iconoclasm see E. Kuttner, *Het Hongerjaar 1566* (Amsterdam, 1949).

[47] *HSR*, vol. VIII. Petition of 15 May 1565 and subsequent debates, notably November 1565. (There is no continuous pagination.)

[48] Cf. N. Z. Davis, 'The Rites of Violence', in Davis, *Society and Culture in Early Modern France* (Stanford, 1975), 152–87.

The regency of Margaret of Parma (1559–1567)

authorities in the towns and the countryside did not, of course, have this overall picture and, understandably, thought in terms of what was happening in France. They were terrified by the apparent prospect of a new peasant war. Above all, they were confused. Where they took firm action, as the magistrates of Amsterdam did, perhaps with memories of the Anabaptist troubles of the 1530s, they had no difficulty in stopping the image breakers. But in other cities the magistrates preferred to shut themselves up in their own houses or sometimes they even gave orders for the removal of the sacred images. They later claimed that they were safeguarding the statues and paintings from destruction – and in some cases this may have been true. The image breakers often claimed that the count of Egmont and other great noblemen or the city magistrates had commanded them to do their destructive work to safeguard the true and traditional religion. Some of the Protestant preachers also seem to have been convinced that the iconoclasm was the work of preserving the true faith, an essentially conservative action. They were not revolutionaries like the Huguenots in France, or so many of them who were not even strict Calvinists seem to have believed.[49]

The vacillations of the government in Brussels, even of the king himself, had provided the provincial authorities with some reasonable grounds for their passivity in the face of the actions of the fanatics. As late as July 1566 the Estates of Holland had again insisted that, to preserve tranquillity, the government must suspend the existing placards and the Inquisition, and the new ordinances for the whole country must be drawn up by the States General. Margaret replied that their request was just like that of the *gueux* which the king had taken very badly. Thereupon the deputies in The Hague went into a huddle and retreated, but only one step: they would leave out the clause requesting the summoning of the States General. But the regent should still make the new ordinances with the advice of this body whose summons the Estates of Holland would now graciously leave to her discretion.[50]

By the 23 August, in a reaction characteristic of authorities caught out by events, they blamed the messenger and began to argue about principles which were irrelevant to the matter in hand: how were these resolutions known in Brussels before the deputies had arrived there? The nobles then complained that the deputies had varied the petition for the summoning of the States General without referring back to their principals. In this case, they said, it was all right. But it was now essential to get the advice of their governor, the prince of Orange, and for the deputies in Brussels to find out what the other provinces were doing. From the minutes of the Estates it would seem that no one mentioned the image breaking.[51]

---

[49] In this description of the iconoclasm of 1566 I have followed Phyllis Mack Crew, *Calvinist Preaching and Iconoclasm in the Netherlands 1544–1569* (Cambridge, 1978), *passim*.
[50] *HSR*, vol. VIII. Session of 14 July 1566.
[51] *Ibid.*, session of 23 August 1566.

But of course everyone was aware of it. By October even the Holland deputies talked about it but came to the comforting populist conclusion that the riots were instigated mainly by foreigners and that these should be expelled, as had already been done in Flanders.[52] The regent, however, could not be as calm about it. In Brussels it was not possible to know exactly what was happening in different places, except that, in large parts of the country, the regent's writ did not run any more. She wrote to the king that in this country practically half the people were touched by heresy. She was consulting with the knights of the Golden Fleece, i.e. the great seigneurs. They also supported the demand for the suspension of the placards and the inquisitions and for the summoning of the States General. Margaret herself assured the king, no doubt aware of his own formulation of his most basic beliefs, that 'she would rather preserve [the Catholic religion] than the country', rather losing everything than offend God with something like the Edict of January in France.[53] This edict had allowed freedom of worship for the Calvinists, although with considerable limitations.

Half the inhabitants of the Netherlands were certainly not heretics, or touched by heretical beliefs; but certainly a large number were disaffected. Through the autumn of 1566 the provincial Estates, where they were in session, continued to demand the summoning of the States General to settle the religious question.[54] But the Estates were not the principal actors. Nor did those who were, the Calvinists, the nobles of the Compromise, the great lords, the regent and, eventually, the king himself always act consistently or logically or in symmetrical response to the actions of the others. Some of the Calvinist conventicles in alliance with Brederode and other members of the Compromise were collecting arms and trying to engage troops in Germany. No one knew whom to trust or not to trust – a frightening phenomenon which had also been observed in France on the eve of the first civil war.[55]

Government in the Netherlands had come to a standstill. But Netherlands society as a whole had not broken down or become dysfunctional.[56] The provincial Estates still spent time on their purely local business. The Estates of Holland, for instance, debated at length whether to give a substantial gratuity to their governor, the prince of Orange, just as they had usually done in the case of Orange's predecessors. There had certainly been much economic hardship for a great many people since the mid-1550s and especially in the winter of 1565–66. This hardship no doubt drove many to listen to the preachers. Yet the nobility, the leaders of the

[52] *Ibid.*, session of 5 Oct. 1566.
[53] Margaret to Philip II, Brussels, 29 Aug. 1566. II. A. Enno van Gelder, ed., *Correspondance française de Marguerite d'Autriche, Supplément*, vol. II (Utrecht, 1941), 326–32.
[54] *HSR*, vol. VIII. Meeting of 5 October, 19–20 Nov. 1566. Antwerp, Stadsarchief, H. de Moy, Tractaet van Beden, fo. 113v.
[55] E.g. Throckmorton to Cecil, Amboise, 15 March 1560. P. Forbes, *A Full View of Public Transactions in the Reign of Queen Elizabeth* (London, 1740), 375.
[56] E.g. Smit, 'The Netherlands Revolution', 19–54.

The regency of Margaret of Parma (1559–1567)

Compromise, did not suffer from a general financial crisis. In Hainaut, an essentially rural and aristocratic province, the land registers show that the peasants, whether owners or tenants, had held their own throughout the first three-quarters of the sixteenth century, far better than they had done in the period of falling prices in the fifteenth. By contrast, the nobility had not done so well and their share of income dropped from 59 to 47 per cent of all agricultural income. Yet it is doubtful whether the majority of the nobility were in a state of economic crisis. On an admittedly incomplete list of noblemen signing the Beggars' petition, we find only nineteen from Hainaut, as against twenty-one from Flanders, forty-six from Brabant, forty-nine from Holland and eighty-seven from Friesland.[57] We have not got similar land registers for the other provinces; but it is unlikely that, except for Flanders and Holland, economic developments were very different. Even in Brabant, the census compiled in 1570 for the levying of the duke of Alba's Hundredth Penny showed income from mobilia of only 20 per cent, as against 80 per cent from immoveable property, i.e. mainly land and rents. In Holland perhaps half the nobility joined the Compromise, but probably only a minority of these did so, as the royalists alleged, to enrich themselves from the property of the church and the monasteries.[58]

The sympathisers with the new doctrines included all classes and the great majority did not contemplate revolutionary action. They were often not even sympathetic to the takeover of churches by the Calvinists, let alone to the takeover of a whole city, as happened in Valenciennes.

Margaret, however, was raising troops, just as the Calvinists were doing. In the autumn of 1566 it looked as if there would be civil war, as had happened in France. It did not get beyond a few encounters. Many of the high nobility now rallied to the regent. The governor of Guelders, the count of Megen, had been sympathetic to the anti-Granvelle league. To keep on good terms with the Estates of Guelders he had made a point of recalling the situation under the independent duke, 'who tyrannised his subjects as much as any prince ever did'. He contrasted this with the excellent treatment they were receiving from the king.[59] In March 1566 Margaret sent him a strong reprimand for allowing the Estates to assemble on their own initiative.[60] By July Megen had changed sides completely and used his former reputation to introduce spies into the negotiations of the Compromise with the Calvinists.[61]

---

[57] H. G. Koenigsberger, 'Property and the Price Revolution (Hainault, 1474–1573)', in Koenigsberger, *Estates and Revolutions*, 144–65. For Holland the latest count is fifty-four. See H. F. K. van Nierop, *The Nobility of Holland: From Knights to Regents, 1500–1650*, transl. M. Ultee (Cambridge, 1993), 181.
[58] Van Nierop, *The Nobility of Holland*, 114, 184–5. In Groningen, Drenthe, Overijssel and, perhaps more surprisingly, in Zeeland, none of the nobility joined the Compromise.
[59] Megen to Margaret, Arnhem, 6 Oct. 1560. *Briefwisseling tussen Margaretha van Parma en Charles de Brimeu, Graaf van Megen ... 1560–1567*, ed. J. S. van Veen (Arnhem, 1914), 9.
[60] Margaret to Megen, Brussels, 9 March 1566. *Ibid.*, 148–9.
[61] Megen to Margaret, 24 July 1566. *Ibid.*, 151.

Monarchies, States Generals and Parliaments

Other governors of provinces, including Egmont, openly took the side of the government. The great majority of the patriciate, even those who had supported a change in the heresy laws, did nothing to help the Calvinists. By the spring of 1567 Margaret and her allies in the Netherlands establishment had triumphed all along the line. The structure of society and its ethos had remained firm. Royal authority and the safety of the Catholic religion had been re-established. Calvinist worship and preaching ceased. It was a much more comprehensive victory than the monarchy and the church were to achieve in France for forty years. The nobility and the provincial Estates had singularly failed to impose their preferred solution of all religious problems on the Netherlands government. The States General had not been summoned.

THE KING'S DECISIONS

And yet, the situation was not stable. The instability was due, in contrast to France, not to an organised Protestant party but to the fact that the Netherlands were part of a multiple monarchy and that the king had, as yet, taken very little part in the events of the 'wonderyear', as Protestant Dutch historians in the nineteenth century called 1566. Since the spring of 1566 and the news of the regent's political retreat following the petition of the Compromise, Philip and his closest advisers had debated the situation in the Netherlands with increasing urgency and increasing frequency. The Netherlands seigneurs had sent Floris de Montmorency, baron of Montigny and brother of the count of Hoorn to Madrid to urge their case against the Inquisition and for the summoning of the States General. Montigny had friends and sympathisers at court, especially among the party of Ruy Gomez, prince of Eboli. But Montigny soon found himself excluded from the king's council and throughout the summer and autumn, when the vital decisions were being taken, Philip summoned only Spaniards to discuss Netherlands policy.[62] Those who had feared that Philip II would, in a crisis, trust Spaniards more than all others, had been proved right in fearing that Charles V's multiple monarchy would be turned into a Spanish empire in Europe.

And yet, in 1566 Philip did not set out to impose Spanish rule on the Netherlands. Everyone in his council agreed that something had to be done to reaffirm the king's authority in the Netherlands and to preserve the Catholic religion. But the councillors were divided on how to achieve these aims, and the Netherlanders had at least some indirect influence through their friends. Nor were the lines of policy advocated by the different groups always consistent; for the tactics of these groups varied with their relations with each other and with the constantly changing political situation. The king had to consider not only the Netherlands but also the complex and continually changing strategic and diplomatic situation in the Mediterranean.

---

[62] Parker, *The Dutch Revolt*, 85.

The regency of Margaret of Parma (1559–1567)

The shock of the iconoclasm in August and the rapidly fading danger of a major Ottoman offensive for that year or the next, both forced and allowed the king to concentrate on the Netherlands. By November it was agreed that the duke of Alba should go to the Netherlands with an army that would be irresistible and that, within a short time, the king should follow. He would punish a few ringleaders of the disturbances but then pronounce a pardon and distribute royal favours to the faithful. Thus had his father dealt with the rebels of Ghent in 1540.

The difficulty lay in the last part of this plan. How was Spain to be governed while the king was absent? Would not the same problems arise which had arisen in the Netherlands and in France? Philip's sister Juana refused to return as regent – and no wonder, recalling her unhappy experiences in that position before 1559 and the closeness with which Spain had come to the abyss.[63] Philip's younger cousins, the sons of the emperor Maximilian II, had spent considerable time at the Spanish court and could be regarded as safe if provided with an effective council. But their father, like his cousin Philip now relieved by Sulaiman's death about anxiety about the Turks, refused to allow his sons' participation in a Netherlands policy which the German princes would have resented. The princes and the emperor were urging Philip to adopt the solution of a *Religionsfrieden* such as had been concluded in Germany in the Peace of Augsburg. But Philip would no more accept such a 'religious peace' than his father had done.

This left his son, Don Carlos. The prince wanted to be sent to the Netherlands but the king knew of his ambiguous sympathies for the Netherlands nobility and, in any case, Carlos was showing more and more signs of that mental instability which made him unfit to rule anywhere. Philip did not deliberately give up his plan of going to the Netherlands himself; but given his political preconceptions and the personal circumstances of the Habsburg family in 1566 and 1567, there was no way he could leave Spain.

In May 1567 Margaret of Parma sent a special envoy to the king to inform him of the vastly improved situation of the Netherlands government and implored him not to send an army. Once more the council debated the issue. Once more it was divided. The king himself decided that Alba's expedition was to go ahead. We do not know his precise reasons for this fateful decision. Perhaps not the least was that all the logistic and military preparations had already been made. It would not have been the only time in history that such preparations precipitated an otherwise unwanted war. But it seems most likely that Philip still believed in the romantic ideal of the just and merciful prince which he believed his father to have been.[64]

---

[63] I owe this point to Prof. Rodríguez-Salgado.
[64] For Philip II's decision to send Alba to the Netherlands see Parker, *The Dutch Revolt*, 84–90, 99–105. D. Lagomarsino, 'Court Factions and the Formulation of Spanish Policy towards the Netherlands (1559–67)' (University of Cambridge Ph.D. thesis, 1973). D. Lagomarsino, 'Philip II and the Netherlands 1559–73' (unpublished typescript). My thanks to Prof. Lagomarsino for making this typescript available to me.

Plate 14 Antonio Moro, *The duke of Alba*. Musées royaux des beaux-arts de Belgique © IRPA/KIK, Brussels

The regency of Margaret of Parma (1559–1567)

What Philip did not see was that this decision denied the fundamental basis of the politics of a multiple monarchy, and what he did not foresee was that it also undermined the basis of the regime of *dominium politicum et regale*, the trust between prince and subject on which he had taken his succession oaths.

10

The governor-generalships of the duke of Alba (1567–1573) and of Don Luis de Requesens (1573–1576)

'In newly acquired states and those which are accustomed to live according to their own laws and in liberty, there are three methods of maintaining them: the first is to destroy them; the second is to go and reside there personally; the third to let them live according to their laws.'[1]

Machiavelli, The Prince, ch. 5

DECISIONS

In Madrid in 1567 Philip II and his ministers were well aware of these alternatives, whether or not they had actually read their Machiavelli. And they were even agreed that, in a sense, the Netherlands were like a newly acquired state; for they had shown disobedience to their rightful prince and such action was held to absolve the prince from his duty to preserve their laws and privileges. The petition of the nobles of the Compromise, the Beggars, was circulating all over Western Europe[2] and in Madrid it was felt that the eyes of the world, i.e. of other Christian princes, were on the king, to see how he would react.

For the rest, there was no clarity at all. The signals arriving from the Netherlands had been plentiful and confusing[3] and there was no unanimity among the king's advisers about the possible punishment of the leaders of the rebellion. Who, indeed, was to be included in this category and what were the implications of the process of punishment for the government of the Netherlands? Few seem to have realised that there was a world of difference between punishing a relatively small

---

[1] 'Quando quelli stati che si acquistano ... sono consueti a vivere con le loro leggi, e in libertà, a volerli tenere ci sono tre modi: Il primo è rovinarli; l'altro andarvi ad abitarvi personalmente; il terzo lasciarli vivere con le sue leggi ...'

[2] Count Louis of Nassau, brother of the prince of Orange and one of the leaders of the Compromise saw to its translation and distribution among the German princes. P. A. M. Geurts, *De Nederlandse Opstand in de Pamfletten 1566–1584* (Nijmegen, 1956), 22. There is an Italian translation in Florence, Archivio di Stato, Mediceo del Principato 4254, fos. 177ff.

[3] For a discussion of the problems of evaluating information arriving at the decision-making centre of an international polity, see Parker, *The Grand Strategy of Philip II*.

number of burghers for the rebellion of Ghent, in 1540, and for punishing the rebellion of a whole country, as it was thought to have happened, in which members of all classes might or might not have been implicated. The council of Gouda, for instance, were happy to report that everything had remained quiet in their city. Bu they also thought that no one should be done to death for his beliefs, as long as he did not cause an insurrection, and at any rate until His Royal Majesty, with the advice of the States General, should have ordered otherwise.[4]

In 1540 the duke of Alba had advocated a 'Carthaginian solution': the destruction of the whole city of Ghent. The historian may speculate what would have happened at that time if Charles V had followed the duke's advice. Would there have been a general revulsion against the emperor's rule, with the almost inevitable prospect of foreign intervention? Would Alba now, in 1567, destroy the whole country in the way he and Machiavelli had suggested as a rational policy option? While we have no direct evidence, it seems likely that Alba's views of 1540 were known in the Netherlands. Somewhat later the anti-Alba pamphlets and cartoons certainly proclaimed that such was his policy. It was a policy which Philip II implemented, a few years later, against the Moriscos of Andalucia: wholesale expulsion from their homes. Were the Protestant heretics any safer from a fate which turned the stomach even of Philip's warrior brother, Don John of Austria, who had defeated the Moriscos in a long and exceptionally brutal civil war?[5]

In the autumn of 1567 when Alba arrived with his army in the Netherlands he certainly had no instructions to destroy the country or its institutions and it seems unlikely that he himself thought in such terms. The duke and most observers, except for a few cynics, thought that the king would himself come to the Netherlands, as he had promised, and would issue a general pardon. There would be no change in the traditional regime, once rebels and heretics had been punished and the military situation secured – Machiavelli's second method.

Very soon, however, it became clear that the act of punishment, as Alba envisioned it with the king's approval, would not leave the traditional regime of the Netherlands intact. The regent Margaret realised this and, somewhat guardedly, warned the king.[6] The establishment of the Council of Troubles and the arrest of Counts Egmont and Hoorn, members of the Order of the Golden Fleece, both measures fully supported by the king, could not be justified by any Netherlands public law which Philip had sworn to uphold, but only by the theory that the rebellion of 1566 had transformed the Netherlands into a country which could be treated like a conquered state. But such a transformation had not been publicly established and it is at least doubtful whether, in 1567, Philip thought consistently of the situation in such terms.

---

[4] Meerkamp van Embden, 'Goudse Vroedschap Resoluties', 322–3. 5 Nov. 1566.
[5] H. Kamen, *Philip of Spain* (New Haven and London, 1997), 131.
[6] See her letters to Philip, September to November 1567. J. S. Theissen, ed., *Correspondance de Marguerite d'Autriche, duchesse de Parme, avec Philippe II*, vol. I (Utrecht, 1925).

Monarchies, States Generals and Parliaments

A rift had opened up between the king and his Netherlands subjects about the nature of their relationship, like a geological fault which was likely to lead to an earthquake, although no one as yet could know when it would occur and how serious it would turn out to be. Margaret, who saw the rift at least dimly, quite apart from the personal offence Alba's actions caused her, resigned her regency. She warned her brother about the large number of people who, foreseeing trouble, were leaving the Netherlands. Riots and seditions, she wrote, had always been punished only in their leaders by kings and princes who wished to imitate God, and they had always pardoned the multitude. 'Otherwise, Monseigneur, if you use rigour, it is impossible that the good should not suffer with the bad and a calamity and general destruction of this state will ensue.'[7]

Philip does not seem to have seen the implications of his and Alba's actions, at least not yet, and he was not greatly worried by the mass flight. In 1566, when he heard that the prince of Orange was raising troops in Germany, he had remarked contemptuously: 'This little count apparently imagines he can wage war against me.'[8] In October 1567 he evidently thought that political life in the Netherlands would continue as before except for the punishment of the rebels and heretics. The novennial *aide* was now running out and Margaret should try to get it renewed but, as he had told her before, without summoning the States General and, preferably, without even summoning the Estates of Brabant.[9] These Estates had protested immediately against the quartering of Alba's troops in their province. It is not clear how the king visualised the extension of the novennial *aide* without the summoning of even the provincial Estates.

ALBA'S IMPOSITION OF *DOMINIUM REGALE*

To Alba, now governor general as well as commander-in-chief, it was soon becoming clear, even if he had not thought the matter out before, that he had to introduce a fundamental change of regime in the Netherlands. No doubt the culture clash between himself and his Spanish and Italian advisers and troops, on the one hand, and the Netherlanders' traditions on the other, made such clarification easier for the men on the spot than for the king, many hundred miles away. Alba found the personnel of the Netherlands public institutions both corrupt and uncooperative.

---

[7] Gachard, *Correspondance de Marguerite d'Autriche*, vol. I, XXXV–XXXVI.
[8] Quoted in K. W. Swart, 'Wat bewog Willem van Oranje de strijd tegen de Spaanse overheersing an te binden?', *BMHG*, 99, 4 (1984), 558.
[9] Philip to Margaret, Madrid, 5 Oct. 1567. The French text is ambiguous: 'Vous sçavez le respect que ay heu du passé de non laisser assembler lesdicts Estatz, ni aussi particulièrement ceulx de Brabant, seullement durant mon absence.' Was it just the Estates of Brabant which were not to be assembled in his absence or also the States General? If he meant the latter, it would mean that he contemplated summoning the States General when he himself came to the Netherlands. In other words, he did not really at this point contemplate a fundamental change in regime. On the protests by Brabant against Alba's troops see G. Janssens, 'Brabant in het Verweer', *APAE*, 89 (Kortrijk and Heule, 1989), 140–1.

There is no justice here, he wrote after five years experience of the Netherlands, 'for there is no case, civil or criminal, which is not sold like meat in a butcher's shop'.[10] To the Netherlanders Alba's regime, quite apart from the political implications of his policies, looked the exact opposite. His closest Spanish advisers were known to be making fortunes for themselves[11] and his soldiers were insolent and thieving bullies – a point of which the duke, like all sixteenth-century generals, was well aware. The policy of encouraging people to spy on their neighbours and report their alleged heretical or treasonous views to the Council of Troubles or the inquisitors was deeply resented. In this respect the Netherlanders were very different from the Spaniards. In Spain such a policy was directed mainly against those who were in any case considered outsiders: those who were supposedly judaising converted Jews and, later, sexual 'deviants'. The Milanese regarded the Spanish Inquisition as an insult to their Catholicism and the Neapolitans had said that they could not trust each other sufficiently to accept a regime of denunciations. Pedro de Toledo, the Spanish viceroy of Naples at that time was wiser than his younger kinsman, the duke of Alba, and advised the emperor to withdraw the Spanish Inquisition from Naples. In Sicily people were not worried about the inquisitorial pursuit of heretics because they did not believe that there were any in the country but, after an initial revolt against it, they allowed the Spanish Inquisition to become an effective protector of such noblemen who opposed the viceroy's policies and who protected the proto-mafia of the countryside.

In the Netherlands, however, the government's encouragement of denunciations tended to lead to a breakdown of social cohesion and established order – a development feared by those of the elite who had no synpathy for the heretics and rebels. Alba had set up his Council of Troubles, a court specifically not bound by provincial privileges, on 5 September 1567, only five days after his arrival in Brussels. It has been calculated that the Council of Troubles, which the Netherlanders dubbed the Council of Blood, altogether tried some 12,000 persons, condemned a majority of these to confiscation of their property and some 1,000 to be executed.[12] A great many had fled abroad, and the figures are not as great as was suggested by Protestant propaganda. But compared with condemnations of earlier rebellions they were still frightening, as in truth they were meant to be, even to those who were not actually tried.

Once it became clear that the king would go on postponing his coming to the Netherlands, Alba's effective authority would have to rest on his army.[13] The

---

[10] Alba to Philip II, Nijmegen, 16 April 1573. Duque de Alba, ed., *Epistolario del III Duque de Alba, don Fernando Alvarez de Toledo*, vol. III (Madrid, 1952), 334.
[11] G. Parker, *Spain and the Netherlands* (Glasgow, 1979), 152–64.
[12] A. L. E. Verheyden, *Le conseil des troubles* (Florence, 1981), *passim*.
[13] There are many modern accounts in English of Alba's governor-generalship. E.g. Parker, *The Dutch Revolt*, chs. 2 and 3; Parker, *the Grand Strategy of Philip II*; W. S. Maltby, *Alba: A Biography of Fernando Alvarez de Toledo, Third Duke of Alba, 1507–1582* (Berkeley, 1983), chs. V–XII. Koenigsberger, *The Habsburgs and Europe*, 130–8.

exiled *gueux*'s connection with the French Huguenots and other neighbours hostile to Spain, and the prince of Orange's invasion of the Netherlands in 1568, only confirmed Alba and Philip in their belief in the need for a strong military presence. The king had paid for Alba's army in the first place, but Spain, beset by its own obligations, could not go on doing so.[14] Alba therefore had no choice but to raise the money to pay for his army in the Netherlands. It was his attempt to do so which set him on a collision course with much wider circles of the elites that had opposed him before, and especially with its representative institutions.

At first Alba was optimistic about obtaining the necessary funds by bullying the Estates. Quite early in his term of office he wrote to the king: 'Although your Majesty has commanded me that to treat of this matter [the payment of the troops] or of any other, it is not appropriate to summon the States General, nevertheless if they are assembled Your Majesty may rest assured that times have changed and that they can be assembled just like the procurators of the cities [of Castile] in Valladolid.'[15] This view of the deputies of the Castilian cities did not seem unreasonable. Philip II had raised the *alcabala* unilaterally in the 1560s. Nevertheless, as it turned out, Alba underestimated their independence and their willingness to dig in against the king's demands.[16]

THE TENTH PENNY[17]

The usual grants of the Estates would be quite insufficient for the payment of Alba's troops. After all, even the exceptionally generous novennial *aide* of 1558 had left the Netherlands government with huge debts. The duke and his financial advisers therefore went back to Mary of Hungary's ideas of general taxes to be levied equally throughout the Netherlands such as income taxes and sales taxes, similar to the Spanish *alcabala*. In the 1540s the Estates had firmly rejected general taxes and Mary had been content to accept fairly generous conventional grants. Now Alba proposed a Hundredth Penny, a once and for all tax of 1 per cent. Next there was to be a Twentieth Penny, a 5 per cent tax on all sales of landed property, and finally a Tenth Penny, a 10 per cent sales tax on all commercial transactions.

Alba and his financial advisers variously estimated that these taxes would raise a huge annual revenue. Estimates up to the astronomical figure of 13,600,000 florins

---

[14] For the costs of Alba's army see G. Parker, *The Army of Flanders and the Spanish Road 1567–1659* (Cambridge, 1972), 141, 287 and *passim*.
[15] Alba to Philip II, Brussels, 19 Jan. 1568. Duque de Alba, ed., *Epistolario*, vol. II, 11.
[16] Fortea Pérez, *Monarquia y cortes en la corona de Castilla*, *passim*.
[17] There are detailed modern accounts, e.g. M.-A. Arnould, 'L'impot sur le capital en Belgique au XVIe siècle', *Le Hainaut Economique*, (Mons, 1946), 22–45. J. Craeybeckx, 'Alva's Tiende Penning, een Mythe?', *BMHG*, 76 (1962), 10–42; J. Craeybeckx, 'La portée fiscale et politique du 10e denier du duc d'Albe', in *Acta Historiae Bruxellensia*, vol. I: *Recherches sur l'histoire des finances publiques en Belgique*, ed. M.-A. Arnould *et al.* (Brussels, 1967), 343–74. F. M. H. Grapperhaus, *Alva en de Tiende Penning* (Zutphen, 1982).

Plate 15 Satirical engraving of 'Alba's throne', 1569. Atlas Van Stolk, Rotterdam

were mentioned. This was a scale of taxation of quite a different order from what Mary of Hungary had contemplated. The Council of Finance had doubts from the beginning. Schetz, the king's financial agent in the Netherlands, 'raised a hundred objections'. Alba wanted to pay back at least some of the 7 million florins sent by Spain for his army in the Netherlands. This was not the council's idea. Alba wrote to Gabriel Zayas, the king's secretary, that no one supported him and that they would like him to jump out of the window. In Madrid Alba's enemies in the Eboli clique would not support his policies either, and even his old political ally, Cardinal Granvelle, was voicing doubts about the possibility of collecting such taxes.

By the end of June 1569 Philip himself began to distance himself from his governor general's policy. 'In effect, this business is all yours', he wrote.[18] But Alba was very sure of himself or wanted to appear to be so. He had punished the heretics and rebels and he had defeated the prince of Orange's invasions of the Netherlands. 'This victory and all previous ones', he wrote to the king, 'must be attributed only to God, and I freely confess that nothing which has been done here since I have come has not been guided by His hand.'[19] Did he really believe this or was he using a conventional trope which he knew would please the king? At any rate, he did not imagine that the Almighty would advance the money he needed for his soldiers. This is probably the basic reason for his otherwise extraordinary decision to propose his new taxes to a meeting of the States General.

The king had repeatedly prohibited the summoning of the States General. Alba had never had any love or respect for a representative assembly anywhere and he had shown himself to be quite unsqueamish in using bullying tactics towards the Netherlands provincial Estates. He had also started building up his own tax-collecting bureaucracy. Why then did he not simply impose the new taxes by royal fiat? He wrote to the king that he had told the Council of Finance, who had warned him of the resistance of the Estates, that he knew how to deal with them. If he could not have a permanent tax, the king's position would be intolerable. His defence of the Netherlands would depend on the good will of the burghers of the third 'Member' of the city council of Brussels or the fourth 'Member' of the council of Louvain, the representatives of the guilds, who were concerned only with their own interests. Moreover, and this was an altogether abominable and pernicious custom, when they did make a grant they attached to it such conditions and demanded liberties such that His Majesty could not really govern nor inflict punishments in these states. It is precisely for this reason, Alba concluded, that we have suffered the catastrophes in religion and the rebellions of recent years.[20]

---

[18] L. P. Gachard, *Correspondance de Philippe II sur les affaires des Pays-Bas (1558–1577)*, 6 vols. (Brussels, 1842–72), vol. II, 104.

[19] Alba to Philip II, Cateau-Cambrésis, 22 Nov. 1568. Alba, *Epistolario*, vol. II, 113.

[20] Alba to Philip II, Brussels, December (?) 1568. *Ibid.*, 137. Twenty-five years later Philip II made the same point to the deputies of the Castilian Cortes: the deputies should not talk of reform or of the expenses of the war, 'for they can and should trust in me and in the love which I bear these kingdoms

Both the aristocratic preconceptions of the age and the rationale for *dominium regale* could not have been expressed more clearly. When Mary of Hungary had proposed general taxes, their duration was to have been strictly limited, and if they produced more revenue than the government had estimated, then the surplus was to have been returned to the Estates. By contrast, Alba wanted his taxes to be permanent and he would not dream of returning any surpluses.

This was all very well if it could be achieved. But the collection of the new taxes would take time, while the soldiers wanted to be fed and paid immediately. As always, the gap would have to be bridged by loans from the financiers in Antwerp, anticipating the revenue from the taxes. The bankers and financiers, however, were the one group in the country who could not be bullied. Just as in the case of the sale of the *rentes*, they trusted the Estates but not the government. This had been the reason why the provincial Estates had built up their own financial machinery and why the States General of 1558 had insisted on appointing their own receiver general for the novennial *aide*.

It is not clear whether this situation was fully understood in Spain. There the foreign financiers built up their own machinery for the sale of the *juros* and, above all, they could always hope to be repaid when the next silver fleet from America arrived in Seville. In the Netherlands, once Philip was no longer prepared to send huge quantities of ducats from Spain, there was no prospect of the repayment of government loans except from tax revenues. Here was one of the main reasons why most transalpine monarchies, especially the German principalities, did not, indeed could not, get rid of their representative assemblies. The more insistently an early modern prince claimed to be *legibus solutus*, i.e. to have authority to tax and legislate freely, the more shaky became his credit with the international financiers.

Alba seems to have been very well aware of this situation. He never explained it in so many words to Philip II,[21] perhaps because it could have thrown doubts on the king's and Alba's own conception of the king's sovereignty. At any rate, in September 1568 Alba wrote an agonised letter to Cardinal Espinosa, at the time the king's most influential minister, that the Genoese financier, Niccolo Grimaldi, had withdrawn a loan of 200,000 escudos, although the greater part of it had already been spent.[22]

In March 1569 Alba summoned the States General to propose his new taxes. Historians have often ascribed this extraordinary reversal of the king's policy to the absence of a sufficiently developed financial apparatus to collect the taxes and also

and the long experience I have of governing them, so that I always do what is most suitable and beneficial for them'. As he usually did, Philip stressed his personal authority and not that of the monarchy, let alone the state. Philip's reply to the Cortes, 9 May 1593. Quoted by I. A. A. Thompson, 'Oposición política y juicio del gobierno en las cortes de 1592–98'. *Studia Historica. Historia Moderna*, 17 (1997), 57 and n.80.

[21] Alba gave at least some hints of this situation in a letter to Philip, 29 Feb. 1568, Alba, *Epistolario*, vol. II, 31.

[22] Alba to Espinosa, 19 Sept. 1568. *Ibid.*, vol. II, 98.

to the duke's own precarious health which decided him not to travel in winter to the different provinces himself, as he apparently had originally planned.[23] Both points may have some validity. But the whole exercise has all the aspects of an attempt to escape the dilemma of the need for the king's untrammelled authority, which only a few weeks before he had declared magisterially to Espinosa, and the practical necessity of gaining consent.

To square this circle, Alba planned a meeting of only one day and he assured the king that no one would dare speak out of turn.[24] To make his proposals more palatable, he himself addressed the session of 20 March, accompanied by the knights of the Golden Fleece, while leaving all his Spanish advisers at home. The deputies of the several provinces would not, however, be allowed to discuss the proposals with each other.[25] The duke's financial advisers had warned him of the devastation and hardship his form of the *alcabala*, the 10 per cent tax on all commercial transactions, would have in a commercial country. Alba justified his proposals to the States General by explaining that the king had sent him to the Netherlands to restore order. Now that he had effectively completed this task, it was necessary to preserve this order by force of arms, i.e. with his soldiers.[26]

To the duke this argument seemed eminently logical. To the Estates it was a contradiction in terms. Now that the evildoers had been punished, it was the business of the loyal Estates to maintain order and obedience to the king, as they had traditionally done. This had been their position in the arguments over the Spanish *tercio* in 1559. By withdrawing this force, the king had accepted their argument. If Alba now wanted to keep his foreign soldiers in the country and build a citadel in Antwerp, then the king, or anyway his governor general, had evidently no intention of returning to the regime of mutual trust which had existed before 1566. Alba's arguments were therefore not a signal of a return to normality but a cloak to mask the setting up of a permanent military regime. For the time being, at least, the propaganda of the Orangeists was now directed not against the king but against the duke of Alba and his alleged evil genius, Cardinal Granvelle.[27]

The deputies accepted the Hundredth Penny without too much difficulty. It was a once-for-all tax which the governor general promised not to repeat. It was collected by specially appointed tax collectors responsible directly to the government. By February 1571 the tax had yielded 3.3 million florins.[28] About the other two tax proposals the deputies were not so complacent. They demanded to refer back to their principals, according to customary and legal tradition. Jacob van

---

[23] On this latter point see Grapperhaus, *Alva en de Tiende Penning*, 108.
[24] Alba to Espinosa, Brussels, 30 Jan. 1569. *Epistolario*, vol. II, 155. Alba to Philip II, Brussels 10 March 1569. Griffiths, *Representative Government in Western Europe in the Sixteenth Century*, 426–7.
[25] Grapperhaus, *Alva en de Tiende Penning*, 108–12.
[26] Janssens, *Brabant in het Verweer*, 148.
[27] Geurts, *Pamfletten*, ch. 2. H. F. K. van Nierop, 'De troon van Alva. Over de interpretatie van de Nederlandse Opstand,' *BMGN*, 110, 2 (1995), 205–23.
[28] Figures from Parker, *The Revolt*, 115 and 294 n.38.

Wesembeke, Antwerp banker and friend of Orange, later claimed that, as early as the autumn of 1566, the government had tried to pack the separate provincial assemblies with compliant deputies.[29] However that may have been, by the autumn of 1569 nearly all the provinces had agreed to the new taxes.

The governor general, however, had not got a penny in revenue. As Granvelle had warned him, the practical difficulty lay in collecting the money. The provincial Estates and their own revenue officials were effectively dragging their feet.[30] Pigeon-holing unpopular government orders was an all but universal practice by sixteenth-century officialdom. The Spaniards were particularly good at it in their faraway American colonies and they called it *obedecer y no cumplir*: 'acknowledge but sit on your hands'.

Alba claimed that his new taxes were fairer than the traditional taxes and produced a lesser burden on poor people, small towns and villages. From the beginning he was willing to modify the Tenth Penny by granting exemptions such as for the trade in spices, English cloth and Baltic grain coming into Holland.[31] But once it had become clear that the government could not insist on its initial crude proposals, the provincial Estates produced a flood of detailed objections, backed by persuasive figures and calculations of the harm the 10 per cent sales tax would do.

Backed by offers of large sums to be raised in the traditional way, these arguments were effective. They were much more effective than arguments based simply on custom and earlier royal grants. Thus throughout the previous year, 1568, the Estates of Holland had fought a running but gradually losing battle with their governor, now the count of Bossu, over the appointment of the receiver of taxes and of the naval officers of the province's warships.[32] The previous receiver, Jacob van der Eynden, had been caught up in the net of the Council of Troubles. His wife found his own cities, Delft and Leiden, reluctant to intervene and had therefore suggested the Estates of Holland as a whole should do so. Some worldly-wise deputies thought that such an intervention would be unhelpful; but that they might help Mevrouw van der Eynden to petition the governor in her own name, stressing her husband's ill health.[33] Did this advice imply that the Estates had lost their traditional influence with the government in such matters or that they had become too frightened of Alba and the Council of Troubles even to try to defend their respected officer whom they themselves had appointed? Perhaps a bit of both. Van der Eynden died in prison but was acquitted in 1571.[34]

Pusillanimity, however, can go together with stubbornness. On 22 March, the day after Alba had proposed his new taxes, he summoned the deputies of Holland

---

[29] J. de Wesembeke, *Mémoires* (Brussels, 1859), 206–7.
[30] Grapperhaus, *Alva en de Tiende Penning*, 151.
[31] Report of Holland deputies in Brussels from 22 March 1569. *HSR* 1569, 20–7.
[32] *Ibid.*, 1568, *passim*.
[33] *Ibid.*, 25 May to 19 June 1568.
[34] R. C. Bakhuizen van den Brink, 'Eerste Vergadering van de Staten van Holland, 19 July 1572', *Les Archives du Royaume des Pays-Bas*, vol. I (The Hague, 1857), 10 n.1.

to an audience. The deputies assured His Excellency that 'they would prove their affection and good will as good and faithful subjects of their natural prince' by doing everything in their power to obtain the acceptance of the proposals and that they would not take the attitude of other provinces as an excuse.[35] Nevertheless, in the meeting of the Estates of Holland, in The Hague on 5 April, all the objections to the taxes were aired: Holland merchants trading in low-value goods, such as pitch, tar, iron, coal, timber, bacon and fish made no more than a bare living; which was the reason His Majesty's predecessors had relieved them of all tolls. The new tax would be levied on goods which had not yet been sold and which still ran the risk of a sea voyage and possible loss. And how did you pay a Tenth Penny on a pennyworth of goods in the shops? Everywhere the foreigners would gain, for they would not have to pay the tax. As to the Twentieth Penny on the sale of real property, such property was usually already burdened by other obligations – presumably they meant mortgages and rents payable to relatives – and it was notorious that people sold it only from necessity or when forced by their creditors. The Estates therefore offered an extra 100,000 florins per annum, to be levied in the traditional way and with the usual *gracien*, rebates.[36]

The nobles and the city of Dordrecht were willing to accept the new tax and Bossu, the governor, argued that it was not His Excellency's intention to ruin the province. Alba himself reiterated this point at another interview with the deputies, on 7 May. He thanked the nobles and Dordrecht for their support and refused to accept the Estates' substitute offer.[37]

Negotiations continued and by 17 October Alba gave Holland the choice between the Tenth and Twentieth Penny or 271,000 guilders per annum for six years, levied in any way the Estates wanted, plus a second Hundredth Penny. The Estates argued that the province could not afford this. Negotiations continued. Bossu was becoming desperate to pay the troops for which he was responsible and on 22 November asked for an advance loan of 65,000 pounds.[38]

By March 1570 Alba had been forced to modify drastically his original proposals. All raw materials and all first sales whatever were now to be exempt and in inland sales only the last sale to the consumer was to be taxed. But the Twentieth Penny and the second Hundredth Penny were to be collected. The original proposals had been agreed by all provinces on 13 August, but His Majesty had not had any of it, and this shortfall should now be made up because the soldiers had to be paid.[39]

Here therefore was a virtual admission of Alba's need to summon the States General. Moreover, in the negotiations with the individual provinces there was,

[35] *HSR*, 1569, 22 March 1669.
[36] *Ibid.*, 5 April 1569.
[37] *Ibid.*, 7 May 1569.
[38] *Ibid.*, 22 Nov. 1569.
[39] *Ibid.*, 13 March 1570.

for all the king's prohibition of common discussions, constant reference by all sides to the grants of all the other provinces. It was simply not possible to want to impose general taxes, i.e. treat the Netherlands as a unity, and at the same time pretend that there was no unity and that such taxes could be negotiated with the individual provinces. The Estates of Holland were quite clear about this and argued that if Holland agreed to the taxes without the other provinces, it would be depopulated, for people would move to the less highly taxed provinces.[40]

In June 1570 a formal agreement was finally reached. In Madrid there was less objection than in Brussels to the substitution of an agreed payment for the Tenth and Twentieth Pennies. Since the 1530s most Castilian cities had obtained such a substitution, the *encabezamiento* in place of the *alcabala*. For the years 1570 and 1571 the Netherlands treasury received over 4 million florins per annum and the king needed to send Alba only quite small sums to pay for his troops.[41]

Inevitably, the provinces fell behind in their quotas of the huge sums which had been agreed. In July 1571 Bossu informed the Estates of Holland that the king wanted to return to the levying of the Tenth and Twentieth Pennies and that Alba had tried to persuade him to let the substitution continue for another four years.[42]

Was Alba telling the truth about the king's and his own attitudes? However that may have been, progressively more acrimonious negotiations went on with the provincial Estates. They can be followed week by week, sometimes day by day, in the *Resolutions of the Estates of Holland* (published in the eighteenth century) and in the minutes of the town council of Gouda (published in the twentieth century). The Estates found themselves between Scylla and Charybdis, the wrath of the governor general and the fury of the populace. At one time at least the council of Gouda made the heroic declaration that they would agree to the 271,000 pounds per annum but that, if the governor general insisted on levying the Tenth Penny or a second instalment of the Hundredth Penny, he would have to do this on his own authority. A week later, however, they agreed to conform to the majority opinion of the Estates.[43]

For the other provinces we do not have as detailed published documentation as for Holland; but it is certainly good enough to show that their experience of Alba's policies and their reaction to these were very similar to those of Holland. In Artois, a clerically and landowning dominated province, there had been a particularly strong reaction against the image breakers and Alba was at first welcomed. But soon resistance to the proposed Tenth Penny grew. Artois, a frontier province with much transit trade to France would have been especially hard hit. Alba would not listen to their protestations that they had always been loyal Catholics. But now

---

[40] *Ibid.*, 4 April 1570.
[41] Figures and tables in Parker, *The Army of Flanders*, 141; and Parker, *The Dutch Revolt* 162. Cf. Craeybeckx, 'La portée fiscale', 370.
[42] *HSR*, 11 Aug. 1571.
[43] 12 and 18 June 1570. Meerkamp van Embden, ed., *Goudsche Vroedschaps Resoluties*, 365–6.

the clergy, fearing they would be blamed for the new taxes, refused to exhort the people to pay these taxes if they were to be unlimited in time.[44]

In Brabant the situation was complicated by the fact that the Estates had in previous years made loans to the government for the payment of the troops, or they had anticipated the monies raised for the government by the sale of *rentes* funded on the ducal domain. Alba had to agree to subtract substantial sums from the more than 500,000 florins the province was to pay as its part of the 2 million the States General offered in place of the Tenth and Twentieth Pennies.

Much time and energy was spent, moreover, on the old problem of unanimity. The nobles and clergy agreed to the taxes but the third and fourth 'Members' of the several cities refused. The government tried, without success, to get the Estates to waive their traditional insistence on unanimity. It may even have been that the nobles quietly encouraged the bourgeois 'Members' to reject taxes which they themselves had thought it wise to openly agree to. But, naturally, there is no direct evidence of such concealed sabotage.

Alba would not listen to arguments about the need for unanimity and declared he would continue to collect the taxes. Nor would he listen to the Estates' petitions against the officials of his councils who claimed exemption from taxes.[45]

In the spring of 1572 Brabant, Artois, Hainaut and the province of Lille-Douai-Orchies all sent deputations to Madrid to petition the king against the Tenth and Twentieth Pennies. The king refused to see them, but they remained in Madrid, for the general atmosphere was changing. The king needed all his spare resources for the Mediterranean campaign against the Turks. He was not prepared to send more money to the Netherlands. At court opinion against Alba was hardening. Alava, the recently retired ambassador to France who had close contacts with the Netherlands nobility, warned the king of the mass exodus of Netherlands merchants to France and of the quiet disappearance of Alba's former aristocratic supporters from Brussels.[46] The duke had had no high opinion of them. He called them the satraps. But he could not do without them. He himself, in his mid-sixties and with recurring health problems, had for a long time asked to be relieved of his post.

Not that Alba had regrets about his policies in the Netherlands and, more clearly than his opponents, he saw the basic incompatibility of his aims with the political traditions of the Netherlands. In a long letter to the king, on 4 November 1571, he spelt out the position as he saw it. The king had been 'perplexed' because, on the one hand, the Netherlands had taken so strongly against the Tenth Penny and, on the other hand, it was necessary to obtain revenue from the country. Alba detailed how he had moderated the incidence of the sales tax, exempting raw materials, so as not to burden the poor craftsmen, and restricting the Tenth Penny

---

[44] Hirschauer, *Les états d'Artois*, vol. I, 247–51.
[45] BBR, Root Boeck, MS 1655–7, fos. 55r–62v. Janssens, *Brabant in het Verweer*, 145–52.
[46] Alva to Secretary Zayas, 4 Jan. 1572. Alva to Philip II, 5 Jan. 1572. Gachard, *Correspondance de Philippe II*, vol. II, 215–19.

to the last sale of commodities. He did, however, insist that he had done this by the exercise of royal grace, reserving for the king the right to reimpose all the taxes originally agreed. For until now His Majesty had to give up royal prerogatives for every florin which could be had from the Estates. It was this point to which the Estates, once they had understood it, objected and about which they were concerned much more than about the effects of the tax on the poor craftsmen and fishermen; for they wanted to deprive His Majesty of his rights.

This was the point, although Alba did not say this, which Mary of Hungary had made about the Ghenters, some thirty years before, when she wrote that they wanted to be masters. That had been little more than an outburst of exasperation with a single city. Mary never had any intention of changing the basic power relationship within the whole Netherlands. But that was precisely what Alba was trying to do. Do not show any graciousness to the deputies who will be coming, he advised the king, and do not think you can go back to things as they used to be if you want to be lord (*señor*) of these states. He, Alba, had with God's help placed His Majesty in the position of authority in which he now was. And, oh yes (*conviene*), nobody else should see this letter, for the Netherlanders should not know that His Majesty understood them.[47] Evidently, Alba did not think that secrets were generally kept at Philip II's court and on this point he was surely right.

Alba had written at the beginning of his letter that he would treat of nothing but the *alcabala*, and indeed he did not mention religion or the restoration of order or the punishment of rebels. Yet he proposed a fundamental change in the relations between the king and the Estates, a change which he justified entirely by arguing for the maintenance, indeed the increase, of the king's authority against the traditional rights of the Estates. At the end he wrote politely, with the conventional formula, that His Majesty would of course himself decide what was best for his service, 'for he will understand it all much better than I do'. There is nothing in this letter about the state as an institution, or reason of state, and no hint of 'state building'. When, a year earlier, he had written that the Netherlands must be governed from Madrid and not from Brussels,[48] that was precisely what the States General had feared in 1559 when Philip II left the Netherlands for Spain. Alba was a soldier and a politician, not a political theorist. It may well be that when he came to the Netherlands in 1567 he had not realised what was obvious to the Netherlanders. And it may also be that at that time he did not have the clear view of the structure of the power relationship between prince and Estates which he outlined to the king in his letter of November 1571. His ability to verbalise his conclusions may have been the result of his experience of negotiating with the Estates.

In June 1572 the king suddenly conveyed to the deputations of the Netherlands provinces his good will and on 26th he formally informed them of the abolition of

---

[47] Alba, *Epistolario*, vol. II, 268–71.
[48] Parker, *The Dutch Revolt*, 107.

the Tenth and Twentieth Pennies.[49] The reason for this reversal was the dramatic transformation of the Netherlands scene. Most of Holland and Zeeland had fallen to the *gueux* and, apparently more ominous still, the French Huguenots, in alliance with the prince of Orange, had captured Mons in Hainaut. There was now a danger of full-scale intervention by France.

It was at this time that Alba's replacement, the duke of Medinaceli, arrived in the Netherlands. His appointment was due to the Eboli faction at court, as well as Medinaceli's personal friendship with Cardinal Granvelle, and it indicated a turning away from the harshness of Alba's policies. But, just as importantly, it showed up a systemic weakness of composite monarchies in general and of Philip II's composite monarchy in the 1570s in particular. The most important dominions of composite monarchies – and the Netherlands was the most important after Castile itself – were used to regencies by members of the ruling family. This was, among other subjects, what the Netherlands delegations in Madrid in the spring of 1572 were petitioning the king about. Failing such a member of the Habsburg family – and from Margaret of Austria to Margaret of Parma they had all been that, even Emmanuel Philibert of Savoy, who was a cousin – one could only think of the highest nobility. Nobody else would be obeyed. In view of Philip's prejudices, he would also have to be a Spaniard. But there was a desperate shortage of such Spanish noblemen with the right qualifications. Medinaceli had the right social qualifications and was known for his courtesy and good will. As viceroy of Sicily (1557–65) he had been popular with the Sicilian nobility but in government he was inept and ineffective. His own ministers fought law suits against each other and betrayed him at court. Worst of all, his one foray into military campaigning had resulted in one of the greatest Spanish disasters in the Mediterranean war with the Turks, at the North African island of Djerba, in 1560.[50]

In the Netherlands Medinaceli found that Alba sidelined him as effectively as five years before he had sidelined Margaret of Parma. Medinaceli did not bring with him a clear conception of the type of regime which might now be functional in the Netherlands. Philip certainly had none. He had agreed to the abolition of the Tenth Penny; but that represented no more than a relatively minor tactical retreat, a change from *alcabala* to *encabezamiento*. With such an arrangement he had lived in Castile throughout his whole reign. For the rest, he still accepted Alba's analysis of the political situation and the consequently the logical need to support Alba in his policy of crushing the new rebellion by force. Medinaceli resigned after a few frustrating months. Soon millions of florins had to be sent again from Spain to the Netherlands to pay for Alba's campaigns.[51]

---

[49] Hirschauer, *Les états d'Artois*, vol. I, 252.
[50] Koenigsberger, *The Practice of Empire*, 179–80.
[51] Figures as for n.39. For Medinaceli's contradictory instructions see. A. W. Lovett, 'A New Governor for the Netherlands', *ESR*, 1, 2 (1971), 91.

ALBA'S FAILURE

Alba defeated the invasions from the south and the east. On 23–24 August 1572 the massacre of St Bartholomew relieved him of the danger of a full-scale war with France, at least for the foreseeable future. Madrid therefore celebrated the news of the massacre for good strategic reasons. Philip II saw it also as a just punishment for heretics and rebels. Not surprisingly, this celebration and another one in the Vatican, confirmed many in the Netherlands and in the rest of Europe in their view that the king of Spain and the pope were justifying mass murder of a prince's subjects regardless of law and legal processes. It did not help the mood of the Netherlanders that while England was receiving thousands of refugees from France, its government was pussyfooting in its reaction to the French monarchy's role in the massacre and treated shamefully the author of a pamphlet objecting for these reasons to the proposed marriage of Elizabeth and the duke of Alençon. The pamphleteer had his hand chopped off.[52]

In the north Alba's campaign failed, though he came within a whisker of success.[53] The historian may wonder whether military success, if the duke had achieved it, would have lasted. It would have depended on a continuing use of military force; for Alba had destroyed the trust of the elites on which the *dominium politicum et regale* regime of the Netherlands had depended. As for the common people, they hated the Spaniards and would turn on them at the first opportunity and refuse obedience to their magistrates.[54] Where in 1566 the religious movement of the common people had been mainly peaceful, after 1572 the mood of the people became much more political, xenophobic and menacing. It had taken the French monarchy several centuries to build up a *dominium regale* regime. Philip II's and the duke of Alba's attempt to do this in a few years caused unresolvable tensions in Netherlands society. These tensions were aggravated by two conditions. The first was the religious passions which became involved with the political tensions and which made otherwise negotiable differences unbridgeable. The second was the now virtually inevitable intervention of a country's neighbours, once its internal tensions had come into the open. For the people and the rulers of a neighbouring state the victory of the opposing religious side was not just a political setback to which they could accommodate themselves. It was rather a threat to the very life of people and rulers and even to their hope of eternal salvation. At the same time it gave at least a minority on each side an extremely good conscience in the pursuit of their political aims by all and every means. Once civil wars had broken out they

---

[52] A. G. Dickens, 'The Elizabethans and St Bartholomew', in A. Soman, ed., *The Massacre of St Bartholomew* (The Hague, 1974), 52–70.

[53] G. Parker, 'Philip II, Paul Kennedy and the Revolt of the Netherlands 1572–76: A Case of Strategic Overstretch?', in J. C. V. Johansen *et al.*, eds., *Clashes of Culture* (Odense, 1995), 50–79.

[54] E.g. Jean de Croy, comte de Roeulx to Alba, Bruges, 19 July 1572. AGRB, P. d'E. A., Lettres missives, 1725/1.

now became extremely difficult to end. In both France and the Netherlands they were to last, with longer or shorter intervals, for nearly three-quarters of a century.

THE APPOINTMENT OF DON LUIS DE REQUESENS

After the failure of the Medinaceli appointment, the problem of finding a successor to the duke of Alba remained much as before. Philip's choice fell on another great Spanish nobleman, the Comendador Mayor of Castile, Don Luis de Requesens, the current governor of Milan. With good reason Requesens was reluctant, and not only because of his feeling of personal inadequacy for the post. The king frankly admitted that he had not been able to make up his mind between those who wanted to make far-reaching concessions to the Netherlanders and those who thought that only a continuation and intensification of Alba's military policy could restore his authority and defeat heresy. Temperamentally, Philip seems to have been inclined towards the hard line of the Alba faction. 'In this [line of policy] the greatest difficulty is money', was Philip's own comment to Requesens.[55]

In the event, the king did not give his new governor general definite instructions as to what general policy to pursue but was content with the platitudinous exhortations which all Spanish governors general and viceroys habitually received at the beginning of their term of office.[56] Among the few detailed points some were two-faced and others purely negative. Thus Requesens was always to appear to place great confidence in his Netherlands officials, so as to gain their support, but 'not to allow anything detrimental to our interests'.[57] Among these latter the king mentioned especially that the States General should not be summoned without his express agreement and that this would not be forthcoming, at least for the time being.[58]

When the Comendador Mayor arrived in Brussels on 17 November 1573 he was therefore thrown back on taking his predecessor's advice. Alba was anxious to give it before he himself left, a month later. The troubles were all due to religion, the duke told his successor, especially in Holland, Friesland and Guelders, because these provinces were most open to malign influences from England and Germany. Seminaries for priests and all publishing should be closely controlled; all officials should be carefully vetted for their religious beliefs; above all, the Council of Troubles must continue its work and must under no circumstances be abolished. For the rest, Requesens should continue the policy of military reconquest. And, of course, the soldiers must be paid. That could be done by levying the Hundredth Penny for a second time. Alba estimated that it would raise 31 million florins.[59]

---

[55] Philip II to Requesens, 20 Oct. 1573. Quoted in Lovett, 'A New Governor for the Netherlands', 96.
[56] Cf. e.g. the instructions to the duke of Alcalá, viceroy of Naples, 1559. Quoted in Koenigsberger, *Politicians and Virtuosi*, 79.
[57] Lovett, 'A New Governor', 97.
[58] Janssens, *Brabant in het Verweer*, 208.
[59] Lovett, 'The Governorship of Don Luis de Requesens, 1573–76: A Spanish View', ESR, 2, 3 (1972), 276–7.

The duke of Alba and Don Luis de Requesens

Was this sincere advice or a justification for Alba's own policies which he knew were under attack in Madrid? Two years earlier, in connection with the Tenth Penny, he had produced for the king a much more subtle analysis of the opposition in the Netherlands, although even at that time he had not wanted it to be generally known. In the meantime, his military policy had come near to success. But, just like the king, Alba knew it depended on money and he must have known that his estimate for the yield of the second Hundredth Penny was pure fantasy. The first time round it had raised in total little more than 3.5 million. Could even such a sum be raised again or would there not be a repetition of the fiasco of the Tenth Penny which, in the form of an *alcabala*, had yielded hardly any revenue at all?

Understandably, Requesens, an intelligent and well-meaning man, adopted a moderate version of his formidable predecessor's policies. The king had virtually given up making clear policy decisions. The Spanish governmental system's inherent tendency towards stasis now became disastrously evident. The experienced Spanish and royalist field commanders in the Netherlands could still win victories in the field. But the troops tended to mutiny over pay precisely after a victory and it proved difficult and time-consuming to capture towns with modern, Italian-style fortifications. The *gueux* remained in control of the surrounding sea and of the inland waterways. Philip himself vetoed plans to break the dykes and flood the whole of Holland and Zeeland because of the harm it would do to the loyal neighbouring provinces and because it would give him a reputation for extraordinary cruelty.[60]

On the home front Requesens negotiated for conventional *aides* with the Estates of the individual provinces. They all, and especially Brabant, demanded the summoning of the States General and they were now supported in this demand by the Netherlands ministers in the governor general's councils. In March 1574 the king finally agreed and on 4 June the States General met in Brussels to be formally told of the king's pardon.

It was meant to be a one-day ceremony like that of 1569, and again this tactic backfired. When Requesens followed the ceremony up by giving separate audiences to the provincial Estates, they immediately brought up all their old demands: a formal abolition of the Tenth and Twentieth Pennies, a Council for the Netherlands in Madrid, in analogy to the Council of Italy, the return of the king himself or of a prince of the blood to the Netherlands, special measures against marauding Spanish soldiers and a commission of the Estates which was to supervise the regular payment of the troops. Requesens asked for an *aide* of 2 million guilders, the second Hundredth Penny and from Brabant an anticipation of its part of the grant of 440,000 guilders. The Brabant deputies demanded to consult the other Estates. The governor general, following the king's known views, refused. By the end of the summer of 1574 there was complete deadlock.[61]

---

[60] Parker, *The Grand Strategy*, ch. 4.
[61] Janssens, *Brabant in het Verweer*, 219–28.

With deadlock also reigning in the military field, the government for the first time consciously faced the consequences: the need to negotiate with the rebels and heretics. To some it seemed a nightmare. Others had foreseen that it would come to this, just as had happened time and time again in France. Even before the outbreak of the actual civil war, voices in the Netherlands Council of State had warned the king that in such a war 'it is the victor who weeps... for men's consciences will not be forced by arms... We have witnessed that emperors, kings and monarchs, after engaging in long and dangerous wars against their subjects, have been forced to treat with them.'[62]

In the meantime the war in the Mediterranean was going badly. In the autumn of 1574 Tunis and La Goletta fell to the Turks. Perhaps the Turks had even been encouraged by the prince of Orange.[63] The king finally gave permission for negotiations with the rebel provinces. The representatives of the two sides met in the Brabant town of Breda, on 3 March 1575.

They were preceded by volleys of anti-Spanish pamphlets and cartoons. The royalists did little to counter these. The reason was, at least in part, that the king regarded such propaganda as beneath his dignity. On the intellectual level the arguments had changed little on either side. On the Orangeist side they were based on the specific privileges of the Netherlands Estates which the king had sworn to observe at his *joyeuses entrées*, his 'joyous entries' into each province at his accession. Not unnaturally, the propagandists of the Estates chose the most far-reaching of the privileges. Since these were most systematically contained in the *joyeuses entrées* of Brabant of the fourteenth century, the propagandists happily claimed them for all the provinces. The 'joyous entries' included specifically a right of resistance against a prince who had sworn to observe them and had broken his oath. They were well known and reprinted, for instance in 1564, 1565 and 1566.[64]

These arguments were essentially still those of the late middle ages, although they were now often mixed with arguments against religious coercion.[65] At the same time the plural word 'freedoms' – specific privileges granted to or conquered by individual provinces, cities, corporations and individuals – now shifted more and more frequently to the word 'freedom', in the singular and having therefore a universal colouring.

The arguments had a strong appeal to a people brought up in the traditions of Netherlands political life. Before the outbreak of the 'troubles' these arguments

---

[62] 'Considérations puises et débattues, d'un costé et d'autre, au Conseil d'Etat', 3 Oct. 1566. Griffiths, *Representative Government*, 421.
[63] Parker, *The Dutch Revolt*, 165.
[64] Van Nierop, 'De troon van Alva', n.26. P. A. M. Geurts, 'Het beroep op de Blijde Inkomste in de Pamfletten uit de Tachtigjarige Oorlog', *APAE*, 16 (1958), 2–15. M. van Gelderen, 'The Position of the States in the Political Thought of the Dutch Revolt 1555–1581', *Parliaments, Estates and Representation*, 7, 2 (1987), 164–5.
[65] E.g. 'A Defence and True Declaration of the Things lately done in the Low Countries', printed in M. van Gelderen, *The Dutch Revolt* (Cambridge, 1993), 1–77.

had generally been taken for granted, rather than enunciated, and, in spite of occasional growls on the part of the emperor's and the king's regents, they had been respected; and this respect had been regularly practised and embodied in the periodic meetings of the provincial Estates and the States General. But with the introduction of religious issues into political dialogue, these medieval arguments were beginning to show their limitations. The intellectual arguments of the royalists had a universalist colouring from the beginning. The king was the sovereign. All concrete and specific privileges of his subjects had been granted by him or his predecessors. In case of necessity, any or all privileges could be revoked or set aside. For the king's overriding duty before God was to defend his subjects, and this defence was particularly important in the case of religion. In no way could religion be separated from the political sovereignty of the king. Conversely, as long as you did not want to attack directly the king's religion, you had no valid defence against the political acts by which he chose to uphold his and his subjects' religious beliefs. Moreover, the *gueux* had raised arms against the king, and a rebel forfeited all privileges. All you could do was to blame his ministers and the evil advice they gave him. And this was precisely the burden of most opposition propaganda, both in its popular and in its most sophisticated forms. The duke of Alba became the favourite target of the pamphleteers and a gift to the cartoonists. He was represented with a cruel countenance, a satanic beard and a contemptuous view of the Netherlands' privileges.

One of the pamphleteers, Junius de Jonghe, Orangeist governor of Vere in Zeeland, pushed the arguments further. He compared the States General to the Reichstag in Germany and the Estates General in France and, perhaps most tellingly, to the general council of the Catholic Church. More fundamental, however, was his adoption of the French contract theory of the state. The prince owed his position to the people. His sovereignty was therefore dependent on them and he could not take their freedom away.[66]

Here was a much more powerful attack on the royalists than that of the conventional pamphleteers. It was, however, the practical politicians and actual events which left the pamphleteers behind. The conference of Breda had failed by the summer of 1574.[67] A year later, Spanish power collapsed for the immediate reason which Philip II had always feared: the lack of money. The arguments over the fundamental nature of the state now acquired an even greater urgency.

---

[66] Janssens, *Brabant in het Verweer*, 236. Some authorities claim that Junius de Jonghe was Stephanus Junius Brutus, the unidentified author of the *Vindiciae contra Tyrannos*; but this attribution is not generally accepted.

[67] The conference will be discussed further in ch. 11.

The beginnings of parliamentary government: Holland and Zeeland (1572–1576)

'It is further resolved, because of the manifold affairs which occur daily, that several suitable persons who are apt and qualified should be appointed to work with His Grace in order to deal with and expedite government business, at the expense of the country . . . and for this the deputies of Dordrecht and Delft have been committed.'

Resolution of the Estates of Holland, Rotterdam, 25 July 1572. Bakhuizen van den Brink, 'Eerste Vergadering der Staten van Holland', 46

THE REVOLT OF HOLLAND AND ZEELAND

Ever since the discussions of the *alternativa*, in the 1540s, the duke of Alba had seen the greatest danger to his master's control of the Netherlands in aggression from the country's neighbours. In the spring of 1572 these fears were realised by the Sea Beggars' conquest of a large part of the provinces of Holland and Zeeland. The Sea Beggars' initial success was due to surprise, but their success could not have lasted if Alba had not been distracted by invasions and potential invasions from Germany and France.

This was, however, only half the story. Throughout the preceding winter there had been many voices predicting trouble. Responsibility was assigned, in varying degrees and combinations, to the activities of the Calvinists and their many sympathisers, to the hatred of the Inquisition, even among good Catholics, to the unpopularity of Alba's tax policy, to the unemployment caused by the Sea Beggars' blockade and to the behaviour of the soldiers, especially the Spanish soldiers. For all these ills the duke of Alba and his government were held responsible.

It was this background of pervasive anti-Alba and anti-government feeling which made the Sea Beggars' campaign in Holland and Zeeland so successful. The pamphleteers and cartoonists, now with safe bases from which to spread their propaganda, would not let people forget their grievances, especially not the old accusation that the Netherlands had funded the Spanish conquest of Italy. With their varying targets and with the differing emphasis of their attacks the propagandists could appeal to all classes and groups of the population and to a wide range of religious, political and economic aspirations.

The beginnings of parliamentary government

There was a basic pattern to the Sea Beggars' conquest of the towns of Holland and Zeeland; for in these provinces it was the towns which mattered.[1] When the armed Beggars approached a town they could count on a minority of the patricians to give them active support and sometimes to open the gates for them. These patricians, or some of them, were often Calvinists. But even among these active supporters of the *gueux* the Calvinists were often a minority. From such fragmentary evidence as we have, it seems that these minorities were in most towns quite small, probably smaller than the 33 per cent in Lyon, in 1562, or even the 20 per cent in Rouen, on which we have reliable information.[2] But the Beggars were also supported by large sections of the common people: sailors, fishermen, bargees, handicraft workers of every kind and especially the unemployed. Opposed to them was the minority of patricians who, for religious reasons or because they would not give up their traditional loyalty to the king's government, would resist the Beggars if that was militarily possible. Much here depended on current local politics. In Amsterdam, for instance, the party of the *schout* (sheriff, chief law officer) Willem Dirckzoon Baerdes, had for decades been excluded from the city's government by the party of the burgomaster Hendrick Dirkszoon. Quite early in this dispute the Hendrick-Dirkists had accused their opponents, the *Schoutists*, of heretical sympathies. In 1572 the Catholic Hendrick-Dirkists were in firm control and kept Amsterdam loyal to the king until 1578.[3]

In between the extreme parties there was the great majority of the population, composed of all social classes, who wanted nothing so much as a quiet life and were willing to follow whoever had effective power.

There was nothing new in this general pattern. The difference from 1566, however, was that with the Sea Beggars the opposition now had a much better military organisation than the enthusiastic bands of Protestants of 1566 and Brederode's haphazardly recruited mercenaries. William of Orange, with his sharp eye for political reality, had refused to join the revolt in 1566, but in 1572 he was its generally acclaimed leader.[4]

Moreover, the mood of the opposition had changed since 1566. The iconoclast riots of that year had been almost bloodless and politically conservative. Those involved had wanted a change in religious practices, not a change in political

---

[1] Among many accounts see Parker, *The Dutch Revolt*, 126–42. J. C. Boogman, 'De overgang van Gouda, Dordrecht, Leiden en Delft in de Zomer van het jaar 1572', *TG*, 51 (1942), 81–109. J. J. Woltjer, *Tussen vrijheidsstrijd en burgeroorlog* (Amsterdam, 1994), 9–63. K. W. Swart, *Willem van Oranje en de Nederlandse Opstande* (The Hague, 1994), 37–105. Koenigsberger, *Estates and Revolutions*, 235–9.

[2] The figures for Protestants in Rouen and Lyon are from P. Benedict, 'The Dynamics of Protestant Militancy, France 1555–1563', a paper read at the conference *'Reformation, Revolution and Civil War in France and the Netherlands'*, Amsterdam, Oct. 1997. My thanks to Prof. Benedict for making his typescript available to me.

[3] J. D. Tracy, 'Habsburg Grain Policy and Amsterdam Politics: The Career of Sheriff Willem Dirckzoon Baerdes', *Sixteenth Century Journal*, 14, 3 (1983), 293–319.

[4] Swart, 'Wat bewog Willem van Oranje', 554–60.

Plate 16 Adriaen Thomas Key, William I, prince of Orange. © Rijksmuseum, Amsterdam

regime. Some of them had thought in terms of a substitution of the prince or, at least, of his regent in the Netherlands, with a revived States General acting as peace-maker. This had all been mere fantasy. All over Europe it had been endlessly repeated, in treatises, memoranda and letters of princes and their ministers that a change of religion necessarily produced a change of regime. It had always been inconceivable that Philip II would consent to such a course. The arguments were usually only about tactics: how best to achieve the principle summed up by a French chancellor as *un roi, une loi, une foi* – one king, one law, one faith. Alba's contribution to this tactical debate was not only his support for an Inquisition which punished heterodoxy by death, but also his belief that the whole, or at least the vast majority, of the population of the Netherlands was guilty of sympathy with the heretics and therefore at least passively condoned the high treason of the supporters of the prince of Orange.

It did not matter that, as modern research has shown, the numbers actually condemned by the Inquisition and the Council of Troubles were relatively small[5] or that King Philip, albeit for very ambiguous reasons, had no intention of introducing the Spanish Inquisition in the Netherlands. The inquisitors of the Netherlands Inquisition, Netherlanders and not Spaniards, perhaps disliked their grisly task, but performed it all the same as a sacred duty.[6] Italian styles of ingrained anti-clerical cynicism were neither emotionally nor intellectually possible for either Spaniards or Netherlanders. Alba's convictions about the attitude of the majority of the Netherlanders turned out to be self-fulfilling, confirmed by his own actions and the behaviour of his troops which provided fuel for the propaganda of the Calvinists and the Orangeists.

In 1572 in Holland and Zeeland the majority of all social classes were therefore supporting the Sea Beggars or, at least, they were not prepared to oppose them actively. At the same time and at least partly as a reaction to the brutalities of Alba's regime, the restraint shown by the iconoclasts of 1566 disappeared. The Netherlands had come to resemble the contemporary France of the civil wars with its religious cleansing, its mutual atrocities and wholesale massacres. Not only were the religious images destroyed or just carefully stored away, as had happened in 1566, but priests, monks and nuns were chased out of their homes, forcibly; converted or killed, often with as much brutality as the Catholics had shown.

William of Orange, who had promised the Catholics – still the great majority of Hollanders and Zeelanders – freedom of worship and maintenance of their churches, was powerless to prevent the triumphant Sea Beggars from forcibly imposing their own beliefs. Only about a year after the conquest of Brielle was he able to dismiss the brutal but successful and popular leader of the *gueux*, the Liègeois Count

---

[5] Maltby, *Alba*, 157, compares the 1,000-odd condemned to death by the Council of Troubles with the 600 executed in England for complicity in the Northern Rebellion of 1569–70.
[6] Woltjer, *Tussen vrijheidsstrijd en burgeroorlog*, 29.

Lumey. Lumey was not a Hollander and strictly not even a Netherlander and subject of King Philip. From the beginning the revolt of the Netherlands, for all its anti-Spanish xenophobia, was not a nationalist uprising but a civil war and an international event.

The *vroedschappen*, the town councils, which had been conquered by the Beggars or had allowed the Beggars to enter, now had a formidable task on their hands: they had to prevent roaming and plundering military bands, often drunk with military victory or, more literally, with the agreeable finds they made in the cellars of the monasteries they sacked, from plunging the whole country into chaos. The *vroedschappen* wanted to maintain the power of their own class, the patrician elite, and they had to act legally or construct a new, generally acceptable, legality. Whatever people's motivation for public action, whether political or personal, religious or social or economic, everyone in the sixteenth century thought in legal terms. It was perhaps the most pervasive and powerful legacy which the Roman Empire had left to Europe and the thousand chaotic and often bloodstained years since the fall of the Roman Empire in the West had only reinforced the general longing for legality.

In pre-Reformation Europe princes had been shifting provinces and whole countries around without changing the laws of these countries or the political status of the quarrelling, international princely brotherhood. Thus it happened in 1482 when Franche-Comté and Artois were handed over to France, without consulting the inhabitants and with no more than a pious request to the dauphin to treat the poor inhabitants well.[7] Thus it happened when Charles V annexed Utrecht and Guelders and thus it was at least planned as late as 1544 during the negotiations for the *alternativa*.[8]

There were no precedents for keeping intact the traditional laws and social fabric of a polity where there was an internal shift of power. The elites of the Netherlands cities had always performed a balancing act. While fiercely defending their privileges against both rivals and the encroachments of the central government, they had had to rely, in the absence of professional police forces, on the central government and its soldiers as a defence of last resort against popular movements.[9]

The military victory of the *gueux* had knocked out this defence of last resort; or rather, it had substituted for it a force which was at least partly made up of and appealed to the popular elements against which the elites wanted to defend their positions. From the elites' point of view, the *schutterijen*, the civic guards, were not fully reliable. The *schutters* were mostly petty bourgeois property owners, master

---

[7] Gachard, *Lettres inédites de Maximilien*, 38. Cf. above, ch. 3.
[8] Cf. above, ch. 6.
[9] See, for instance, the detailed description of this position in Guy E. Wells, 'Antwerp and the Government of Philip II, 1555–1567' (Cornell University Ph.D. thesis, 1982). More generally, cf. F. R. Friedrichs, *The Early Modern City 1450–1750* (Harlow, 1995), chs 11 and 12.

The beginnings of parliamentary government

craftsmen, shopkeepers, a sprinkling of school teachers and other educated citizens. Unlike similar groups in Flemish and Brabantine cities, they had in Holland been kept firmly out of town governments. But it had been these groups, as well as the common people, who had been incensed by the duke of Alba's taxation. They did not forgive those *vroedschappen* who, for fear of Alba's revenge, had accepted the Tenth Penny. The feelings of betrayal remained, even when the tax had been modified or sabotaged and not collected at all.[10]

Worse still: the Dutch elites could not even rely any more on the civilian part of the traditional government, the Court of Holland. This court, in The Hague, had been the centre of both the traditional and the administrative branches of the central government. In the course of the sixteenth century it had steadily increased its judicial powers and widened its competence in local government. While staffed entirely by Dutch noblemen and lawyers it was, inevitably, seen as an agent of the now hated central government. When the Beggars swept triumphantly through Holland, the members of the Court of Holland fled from The Hague. Civil government for the province as a whole ceased to function, in a way that had never happened when a province had respectably changed its allegiance or even when it had been conquered by one of Machiavelli's princes acquiring a 'new principality'.

There was now only one major institution left in Holland which could claim legitimacy and demand loyalty: the Estates of Holland. In July 1572 the city council of Dordrecht issued an invitation to the *vroedschappen* of all the towns which had rebelled to send their deputies to Dordrecht. For a long time there had been arguments as to whether the Estates had the right to assemble on their own initiative. Orange, when he had been governor before 1567, had denied it. But it had been generally accepted that the Court of Holland had the right to summon the Estates in a case of emergency. The *gueux* conquest was certainly an emergency, but the Court of Holland had ceased to function. There was no alternative but for the Estates to take matters into their own hands.

In this action they were encouraged by William of Orange who argued, with very little basis in accepted public tradition, that he was still (or was it again?) the king's governor of Holland, Zeeland and Utrecht, even though he had resigned this office in 1567, and the king had appointed the Walloon nobleman, Maximilien de Hennin, count of Bossu, to take his place. On the part of Orange it was an opportunistic move by a politician whose only unwavering principle was opposition to the duke of Alba and his regime of setting aside the laws and privileges of the Netherlands. For this purpose Orange made alliances and asked for help from whomever he could obtain it, and he was willing to pay a high price for it. Just a year earlier Sir Francis Walsingham, then English ambassador in Paris, had talked with Orange's brother, Count Louis of Nassau. Louis made the old, inaccurate

---

[10] C. C. Hibben, *Gouda in Revolt* (Utrecht, 1983), 55–7. For the detailed and complex history of the Gouda *vroedschap* during the first year of the revolt, see 67–93.

propaganda point to Walsingham that Philip II wanted to introduce the Spanish Inquisition into the Netherlands. Then he proposed a grand alliance, with France, England and the Protestant German princes, which would carve up the Netherlands. France would get Artois and Flanders, England would get Zeeland and several of the Holland islands, while Brabant, Guelders and Luxembourg would be reunited with the Holy Roman Empire – strictly speaking, they had never been disunited – with the duchy of Brabant going to the house of Nassau.[11] In 1573 Orange once more offered the sovereignty over Holland and Zeeland to Elizabeth I, only to be turned down again.[12] Whatever else he was, William of Orange was not the champion of an independent Dutch state.

In the summer of 1572 his claims gave at least some sort of legal cloak, however thin, to the actions of the Estates. He reinforced these claims by also insisting that he was acting as one of the foremost members of the States General who had the right to protect the Netherlands against invasion and oppression. It was an argument no more substantial than that of Orange's governorship; but it appealed to those, especially the Calvinists, who looked to the 'lower magistrates', and especially the Estates, to defend the country against a tyrannical prince. A tyrannical prince was one who tried to impose a false religion on the true believers. This was the common coinage of Calvinist literature at the time. Later, in France, it was to be turned upside down and used by the Catholics against their own king whom they regarded as sympathetic to Calvinism.

THE ESTATES OF HOLLAND AND ZEELAND

The first task of the Estates assembled in Dordrecht was to solve the practical problems of governing the province and of defending it against the duke of Alba's counter-attack. It was on the success of coping with these two formidable tasks that the legitimacy of the Estates' regime would ultimately be judged.

It was also immediately clear that the Estates would have to shed many of their traditional habits, especially that of having their deputies refer every important point back to their principals. There simply was not enough time for continuing with this venerable tradition and, moreover, the roads and waterways were often made unsafe by loyalist troops. Some of the deputies of the Estates before 1572 had fled, because they were convinced Catholic loyalists or because they felt compromised and unsafe. But those who came to Dordrecht in July 1572 and to subsequent meetings of the Estates still came from the same class of patricians in the *vroedschappen* of the towns, often indeed from the same families. Some, such as Paulus Buys, the pensionary of Leiden, had been deputies before. Buys became

---

[11] Walsingham to Burghley, Paris, 12 Aug. 1571. *Calendar of State Papers, Foreign, 1569–71* vol. XXI (London, 1929). Walsingham to Leicester, quoted in C. Read, *Mr Secretary Walsingham*, vol. I (Oxford, 1925), 154.
[12] N. M. Sutherland, *Princes, Politics and Religion 1547–1589* (London, 1984), 223.

advocate of Holland and one of Orange's most effective supporters. Common discussions and decision-taking came naturally to such men. When Granvelle and Philip II had tried to prevent common discussions by the deputies of the States General they had mistaken the temper of that body at that time. But they were not naive. They knew how politics worked and how decisions were taken. The regular common discussions of the deputies of the Estates of Holland proved to be an indispensable innovation for the success of the revolt and of the Orangeist movement.[13]

The avowed aim of the deputies was to re-establish their traditional rights and privileges of which, as William of Orange put it, 'they had been robbed and despoiled ... by the duke of Alba and his followers'. They therefore appointed a committee to get hold of and copy their charters which had been deposited in the castle of Gouda. The deputies also made no difficulty about accepting Orange to be acting governor of Holland in the king's name.

These two decisions by the Estates were essentially conservative; but from then on their actions went far beyond the re-establishment of the old *dominium politicum et regale* position. Quite early on the Estates made a pact with Orange not to treat with the king or any of his agents in matters concerning the 'generality of the Estates' without the consent of the prince of Orange. By the king's agents they meant the duke of Alba or his successor or indeed their governor appointed legitimately by the king, the count of Bossu. By all accepted precedents such a pact, directed specifically against the king, was an act of rebellion. On a practical level of administration Orange cashiered all naval commissions and, with the advice of the *watersteden*, the coastal towns, he appointed an admiral and all sea captains. In November 1572 Orange appointed new members of the Court of Holland, on the nomination and with the advice of the Estates. At the same time he deprived the court of its previous considerable administrative functions and restricted it to a purely judicial role.

These were revolutionary acts of unprecedented interference with the royal prerogative. More significant still, as early as 28 July 1572 the deputies appointed a paid committee of their own members to advise Orange on all matters of government and, in October, they added a committee to act as 'Commissioners in all matters of war'.[14] Representative assemblies had often claimed the right to appoint members of their king's council. They had never previously achieved this ambition anywhere in Europe for more than short periods of time.

---

[13] For the Estates of 1572 see *HSR*, 1572–74 which, unfortunately but understandably, have large gaps between 1572 and 1574. *Resolutiën Staten van Noord-Holland*, MS, mainly from the archives of Alkmaar. My thanks to Dr Alastair Duke for making photocopies of this source available to me. Bakhuizen van den Brink, 'Eerste Vergadering der Staten van Holland, 19 July 1572', 11–46. J. W. Koopmans, *De Staten van Holland en de Opstand: De ontwikkeling van hun functies en organisatie in de periode 1544–1588* (The Hague, 1990), 43–6, 117–23 and *passim*. H. Lademacher, *Die Stellung des Prinzen von Oranien als Statthalter in den Niederlanden von 1572–1584* (Bonn, 1958), 41–55.

[14] *HSR*, 1572–74. 5–6.

Monarchies, States Generals and Parliaments

The most immediate problem of the new government was the age-old one of raising money to pay for the country's defence. Even before Orange himself came to Holland, his representative, Marnix van St Aldegonde, asked the Estates for an immediate grant of 100,000 crowns and for the sale of *rente*s for another 500,000 guilders. The Estates accepted this proposal and abolished the whole traditional schema of raising taxes based on nominal land values (*schiltalen* and *verpondingen*) because, as they said, conditions in Holland had greatly changed and even previously there had been many complaints about the unfairness of the old system. The new *aides* were to be raised by a Twelfth Penny (8.3 per cent) on income from land, without exemptions, two-thirds payable by the owner and one-third by the leaseholder. In addition there were excises, a method of raising money which the Estates had in fact used for many years. The resolutions are quite explicit in stating that those who refused to pay were to be forced to do so.[15]

Most startling of all was the action of the Estates in confiscating from churches, brotherhoods, monasteries and convents all moveable treasures which were not directly necessary for their religious functions. No doubt this partial secularisation of church property owed much to Calvinist pressure. But there is in fact no mention of any religious motive for this action in the *Resolutions of the Estates*. What had, a generation earlier, been done in England by formal and elaborate acts of Parliament, which of course carried the king's signature, was done by the Estates of Holland by a simple resolution, moreover a resolution taken a day before the Estates recognised Orange as governor, and therefore without even the fiction of royal assent.[16] Later, on 3 March 1575, in the middle of the Breda negotiations with the king's representatives, the Estates continued the process of establishing secular control over the church by decreeing that the magistrates of the towns and the public authorities of all villages and hamlets were annually to appoint officials to administer all church property and see to the upkeep of churches and the salaries of the ministers and the schoolmasters. A week later they even ventured into the traditionally fenced-off field of ecclesiastical legislation by declaring that marriage between first cousins was not contrary to divine or imperial law. To King Philip such a treatment of the church was of course anathema and appeared to be entirely heretical and revolutionary.

---

[15] *Excursus*: Historians of political thought have frequently expressed shock at Rousseau's doctrine that people should be forced to accept the general will, i.e. forced to be free. I do not wish to discuss the philosophical justification or otherwise of this doctrine, nor deny that twentieth-century totalitarian regimes have found it a convenient doctrine to justify coercion. But it follows from the Dutch sixteenth-century example that there are certain coercive practical measures which must inevitably be taken by those who wish to defend liberty, at least against military attack. Social scientists call this phenomenon the reification of established categories. This means that the leaders of rebellious movements tend to reproduce the state against which they are rebelling, on a smaller geographical scale but with similar coercive powers. See e.g. J. Penrose, 'Reification in the Name of Change', in J. G. Beramendi *et al.*, eds., *Nationalism in Europe Past and Present*, vol. II (Santiago de Compostela, 1994), 585–608. One could also more succinctly quote Virgil: *Sunt lacrimae rerum* – these are tears in the nature of things.

[16] *HSR*, 1572–74, 37.

The beginnings of parliamentary government

Apart from Orange's Council of State and Councils of Finance and Admiralty, for all of which the Estates had a hand in appointing the members, they also set up a whole series of committees of their own, to supervise not only the collection of the taxes they had voted but a whole host of administrative matters, from the maintenance of dykes to the evacuation of populations threatened by the advance of the duke of Alba's troops. In most cases these committees consisted of deputies; but sometimes the Estates also appointed committees of outside experts, quangos in late twentieth-century terminology. The Estates had gained a great deal of know-how and self-confidence from their experience of administering their own tax collections and *rentes*. Much of the local administration and justice in the countryside had in any case been in the hands of the local nobility and the elites of the localities. Their activities had been steadily encroached on by the Court of Holland. Its role was now taken over by the Estates and their executive committees. These comittees travelled all over the country to exhort and supervise, especially in matters of finance and military defence.

These activities by the Estates left their relations with the prince of Orange to be more clearly defined. It was in this relationship that there remained a considerable amount of confusion, a confusion made all the more intractable by the traditional concepts and practices of rhetoric in which political dialogue was conducted. And this was bound to be so because both Orange and the Estates were so anxious to appear to be acting legally and traditionally. For both of them a genuinely realistic rhetoric, which would have matched their political actions, was, at least for some time, not so much unthinkable as psychologically and propagandistically unacceptable. It was their opponents, the loyalists, the supporters of King Philip, who saw more clearly and were willing to say it, that the *gueux*, the Orangeists and the Estates of Holland were in effect setting up a republic. If this was a realistic analysis, it was also and it was meant to be a cautionary propaganda ploy in an age which thought of monarchy as natural and God-given. During a rebellion it was meant to frighten people back into obedience to the traditional regime, however much that itself had been changed. Thus it had been during the revolt of the Comuneros, in 1520, and during the revolt of Ghent, in 1537–40.[17]

Impressive as was the seizing of control of the administration of Holland by the Estates, the actual initiative for most of the resolutions seems to have come from Orange, acting through Marnix as his representative.[18] The honeymoon in these relations did not last. However much improved the procedures of the Estates were over those formerly used, for Orange they were still too slow and cumbersome. He was after all fighting the now formidable counter-offensive mounted by the duke of Alba, and he needed money, and needed it immediately, to pay his soldiers and

---

[17] For the problem of republicanism in the early modern period see H. G. Koenigsberger, 'Republicanism, Monarchism and Liberty', in R. Oresko *et al.*, eds., *Royal and Republican Sovereignty in Early Modern Europe* (Cambridge, 1997), 43–74.
[18] Swart, *Willem van Oranje en de Nederlandse Opstand*, 51.

sailors. As early as October 1572 Orange threatened the Estates with his resignation. It did not come to that; but in the following spring Marnix demanded from the Estates, meeting at Delft, a resolution about the exact extent of Orange's powers.[19]

No clear result seems to have come out of this démarche, and on 20 October 1574 Orange proposed to the Estates that they should take over the government of the land of Holland and discharge him from his heavy burdens.[20] Resignation or withdrawal, for this was what he was proposing, had long been a weapon in William of Orange's political armoury. He had used it very effectively against Cardinal Granvelle and in order to put pressure on Philip II in the 1560s. In 1574 there was, however, this difference: that it would not be the king who would have to pick up the pieces but the Estates. And this difference shows how ultimate authority had shifted from the king to the Estates and that William of Orange recognised this fact. At the same time the incident shows that his position gave Orange certain advantages over a hereditary prince who was ruler over a country *dei gratia*: by the grace of God. Such a prince might resign his crown to his heir, as Charles V had done. But he could not use the threat of resignation as a form of political blackmail, as Orange was doing.

Not surprisingly, the Estates did not accept the resignation. Through the autumn and winter of 1574-5 parallel and interlocking discussions went on about the exact nature of Orange's position and the preparations for the peace negotiations of the conference of Breda.

Orange's threat of resignation had been very carefully wrapped up in conciliatory language. He would very willingly serve 'to the last drop of his blood to defend the welfare and freedom of the country'.[21] But the common people seemed to think that the money they paid was for his personal benefit. The townspeople were saying that the troops should stay outside, in the country, and that they were brought inside the town walls only to please the soldiers. Not all the contributions agreed to by the Estates were being collected, and this meant a greater burden on those willing to pay and led to disputes between towns and individuals. The Estates were mixing up money earmarked for the pay of the soldiers with payments for provisions and obligations of their own, and this left troops unpaid and a consequent burden on the inhabitants – a polite way of saying that unpaid troops became robbers.

The Estates presented their formal answer on 12 November. During their present differences (*sic*) with the king of Spain, who had been misled by the Spanish Inquisition and its henchmen, it was necessary for the preservation of order in the country and of its privileges and liberties and, most especially, of the Christian religion to have a head and authority of the province (*Hooft ende Overigheydt*). They therefore asked His Excellency to continue his government with the name of governor or regent and 'with absolute power and sovereign command' for the

---

[19] Lademacher, *Die Stellung des Prinzen von Oranien*, 46-55.
[20] *HSR*, 20 Oct. 1574.
[21] *Ibid.*, 178.

The beginnings of parliamentary government

direction of all matters concerning the common welfare, without exception. But in all political decisions he was to consult his council. This council was nominated for him by the Estates. The Estates were also to be associated with the appointment of all principal officers and provincial councillors and with the regular renewal of the magistrates of the towns. All magistrates, militias, guilds and commons of the towns were to promise to obey all orders His Excellency and his Councils would issue, and defaulters would be liable to fines and the arrest of their persons and goods.

There were further details about finance and regulations that individual towns should not divert money voted for defence for their own purposes – just as, throughout the century, the Estates had objected to the central government diverting earmarked funds in this way.

What the Estates of Holland had done was very much what Charles V and Philip II had done with their regents and viceroys. In their instructions the monarchs had similarly assured these regents and viceroys that they were given the full sovereign powers of the prince himself, but with a long list of reservations of how he might exercise them only with the advice of their councils (appointed of course by the king) and what powers the prince reserved for himself, especially in matters of appointment and patronage.[22]

Significantly, the Estates now legislated on specific matters which would formerly have been petitions to the king. Thus they made resolutions about the Dutch nobility. The nobles were to have criminal jurisdiction in the first instance but were to be helped by the Court of Holland. This was a compromise between the nobles' traditional rights of local jurisdiction and the policies pusued by the Court of Holland. The Estates said that the nobles did not perform their duties properly because they were apparently too ready to put people into prison. This was objectionable, not because it was often too harsh a punishment for minor offences, but because keeping people in prison laid an unnecessary expense on the community. The court of Holland had, for a long time, claimed the right to call up cases from seigneurial courts and to limit or supersede their fields of jurisdiction. Such a policy was pursued by royal courts all over Europe.[23]

What this compromise meant in practice was probably far from clear at the time. The Estates did recognise that the representation of the nobility was rather thin and resolved to add the count of Culemborgh and the lord of Carnis to the college of nobles.

The resolutions of the autumn of 1574 did not resolve all the problems between the Estates of Holland and their chosen governor. On matters of taxation, beyond the limited sums the Estates allowed Orange to raise on his own authority, they

---

[22] For instructions to regents and viceroys see Koenigsberger, *The Practice of Empire*, 173–4. Koenigsberger, 'Prince and States General', 127–51. Cf. also above, ch. 4.

[23] It could be argued that this was the only field of governmental activity in which the late twentieth-century concept of state-building has any important content before the end of sixteenth century.

insisted that the deputies would still have to refer back to their principals, the *vroedschappen* of the towns, and equally so in matters concerning the political structure of the province and all constitutional questions. Since, however, it was now realised that the political and military situation demanded that the Estates remain in permanent session, they resolved that during reference back at least one deputy of each town should always remain at the session.[24]

Constitutionally, this was no doubt an advance making for greater efficiency. But Orange continued to complain about the slowness of the Estates in granting him the money he needed for paying his soldiers, just as princes had traditionally complained to their representative assemblies.

Inevitably, tense relations between Orange and the Estates of Holland would continue, however much both sides saw the need to cooperate. Much depended on Orange's skill in handling the Estates. After his assassination his friend described the prince's political virtuosity to Thomas Wilkes, the earl of Leicester's representative in The Hague. Wilkes promptly relayed this account to his queen, as his informants had probably intended that he should, and thus point up the contrast between Orange's skill and Leicester's clumsy political behaviour. The prince of Orange, Wilkes wrote, 'always entertained five or six of the most credit; the needy ones with pensions, the rest with presents, and all calling them to his table and society. Through these he wrought upon the rest and there was nothing handled in their assemblies but he knew of it beforehand.' When he had anything to propose, he always consulted with these persons 'whether the matter would pass or be impugned'. He knew the arguments that would be brought against his propositions and came 'armed with the answers and counter-reasons to the wonderful admiration of all, and so prevailed'.[25]

Perhaps Wilkes's informants exaggerated the virtuosity of Orange's methods, and perhaps Wilkes underestimated, at least by implication, the skill with which Elizabeth's ministers handled her parliaments. But his description rings true; for already during the regency of Margaret of Parma both Cardinal Granvelle and the opposition lords, Orange and Egmont, had used just such tactics to win support in the States General. The Sicilian publicist, Scipio di Castro, writing during the same period, gave similar advice to the Spanish viceroys of Sicily for the handling of the parliament in Palermo.

THE FIRST PEACE NEGOTIATIONS

In the 1570s there was still the unanswered question of how permanent the constitutional arrangements in Holland and Zeeland would be, or even how permanent the different actors meant them to be. In November 1574 Orange wrote to his

---

[24] *HSR*, 208.
[25] Wilkes to Elizabeth I, 12 July 1587. *Calendar of State Papers*, vol. XXI, pt. 3, 164.

brother John, the reigning count of the small Rhenish county of Nassau, that he was really most anxious to make peace in the forthcoming negotiations. All that was necessary was the achievement of such conditions as would give the people of the Netherlands some assurance of political liberty and of the matter of conscience.[26] There was nothing in this letter about the form of political liberty, nor of his own position or future. Yet he was definitely writing about the whole Netherlands and not just the county of Holland. The people here in Holland, he added, would gladly accept one of the emperor's sons: Orange did not specify whether as their ruler or as regent. No doubt Orange knew he had to be careful not to offend the German princes or the emperor. But the tone of his letter was personal, and his brother would have known that he was more concerned with the fate of the whole Netherlands than with his position in Holland.

The position of the Estates of Holland and the arguments they put forward were similarly unfocused and ambivalent, at least during the preparations for and at the beginning of the talks. The historian would have wished for the comments of an observer with as sharp an eye for the behaviour of politicians and as caustic a pen for the absurdities of their arguments as the incomparable Andries Jacopszoon, the secretary of Amsterdam in the 1520s and 1530s. Jacopszoon's son, still in public service, as was so frequently the case with sixteenth-century civil service dynasties, had little of his father's political acumen and none of his verbal panache. Besides, in 1575, Amsterdam was conspicuous by its absence from the peace talks. Nevertheless the resolutions, in this case the minutes of the discussions of the Estates of Holland, give perhaps in their very dryness a clear picture of the confused arguments of the two sides at the conference of Breda.

The Hollanders started with the proposition that they were not rebels against the king but were fighting only his evil ministers and they therefore rejected the very notion of a general pardon which the king's representatives offered. They wanted justice and they meant justice against Alba and his supporters who had broken the country's laws. For the rest they insisted that the king should observe all the privileges which their wise ancestors had gained. There were different views as to what these privileges were, and some of the Dutch propagandists included the terms of Mary of Burgundy's Great Privilege of 1477, a document whose validity all rulers of the Netherlands had always disclaimed as having been signed by the young duchess under duress. With the *joyeuses entrées* of Brabant and with their own charters, which they were now retrieving from the castle of Gouda, the Estates' representatives were on firmer ground. It was these privileges which the king had sworn to observe at his accession and which, so a series of pamphlets and memoranda argued, it was the right and duty of the States General to uphold.[27] The king must therefore govern with the advice of the States General.

---

[26] Orange to John of Nassau. Delft, 16 Nov. 1574. Groen van Prinsterer, *Archives de la Maison d'Orange-Nassau*, 95–7.

[27] Van Gelderen, 'The Position of the States in the Political Thought of the Dutch Revolt', 167–71.

Monarchies, States Generals and Parliaments

In itself this argument was not something strange in Spain. In the very year of the conference of Breda, in 1575, the Cortes of Castile argued that it was the kingdom, i.e. the Cortes, and not the king and his financial advisers who should control the drastic financial matters which became necessary at the time; for, as Philip's own *limosnero mayor* (director of the royal charities) told him, not God but all the demons of hell presided over his Council of Finance.[28] The problem was how the claims of the Cortes or the States General could be forced on a reluctant prince. After the Comunero revolt Spanish writers do not seem to have discussed this question at all even when, like Juan de Mariana, they stressed the importance of the Cortes in preventing abuses of royal power.[29]

Not all Netherlands writers followed the contemporary French monarchomach authors in deriving the right, or even the duty, of resistance from the king's breach of the compact with his subjects. Such arguments were certainly not part of the initial instructions of the Estates' negotiators at Breda. Nor could they be because these negotiators did not represent the States General but only the Estates of Holland and Zeeland, and even these without their largest and richest city, Amsterdam. Moreover, they left the position of the prince of Orange in these provinces in the dark – just as he himself had not attempted to define his role for the Netherlands as a whole, except as a member of the States General.

It was all very well for both sides at Breda to argue for a return to the position of prince and Estates at the time of the emperor Charles V. Both sides endowed his memory and the supposedly ideal functioning of the Netherlands government of his time with a rosy glow. The differences arose over how exactly this idealised government should now function. The royalist negotiators, probably only staking out a maximum position at the beginning of the talks, allowed that the king would summon the States General when all troubles had been settled and that he would consult them, as it was claimed that he had traditionally done, on such matters as he thought fit for them to discuss. These would certainly not include religion or sovereignty. The Catholic Church and its services would have to be re-established. Those who persisted in their heresies would no longer be persecuted but would have to leave the country quietly and without being able to exercise their religion any more. The royalist negotiators did not actually say so, but Philip himself had declared often enough that he would not be a ruler over heretics. As to the Estates' demand that he withdraw the Spanish troops, why should he do that? These soldiers were his subjects, which was more than could be said of the German, Scottish, French and other soldiers the Estates had hired. They would, moreover, have to restore all fortresses to the king's control.

---

[28] British Library, MS Egerton 330, Copia de carta que escribió al Señor Rey Phelipe II Don Luis Manrique su limosnero mayor.

[29] J. de Mariana, *Del rey y de la institución de la dignidad real*, transl. E. Barriobero y Herran (Madrid, 1930), 160.

The beginnings of parliamentary government

The reaction of the Estates to these proposals was violent. As Shakespeare's Cardinal Wolsey said, such a course would 'have left me naked to mine enemies'.[30] Orange put it this way: we have made only just demands at Breda: the withdrawal of foreigners and the convocation of the States General. But they have put conditions which are 'harder and more iniquitous than we would ever receive from the greatest tyrant in the world and our condition would become worse than that of slaves or brute beasts'.[31]

The royalist negotiators were taken aback by this reaction, as established authorities in the sixteenth century always were when challenged. Dr Leoninus, the chief negotiator, a law professor from the university of Louvain, said his commission was given in good faith, but he would report the objections to the governor general. The negotiations never quite recovered from this initial clash. The royalists made a series of concessions. Prisoners on both sides would be exchanged. Those unwilling to return to the old church would be given six months to sell their property and leave the country. The States General would be allowed to discuss the execution of the placards. This would, in effect, have meant a suspension of the Netherlands Inquisition. The king would provide safeguards before requiring the handover of the fortresses. But the bottom line remained the king's sovereignty and the maintenance of the Catholic Church and its doctrines as the sole religious faith which the king would allow.

Contemporaries on both sides realised that sovereignty and religion were the rocks on which the talks eventually foundered. But were they aware of the implications of the arguments which the king's representatives had used? The royalist negotiators had made the perfectly valid debating point that the Estates themselves had, with the oath of allegiance to the king and his forebears, sworn to uphold the Catholic religion. But they also argued that it was the right of princes to determine their subjects' religious allegiance. This had, by implication, been the effective position of the hated Henry VIII. More alarming still, this had been the basis of the *cuius regio eius religio* principle of the Peace of Augsburg of 1555. And this was the principle which the revered Charles V and Philip II himself had categorically rejected.

On the side of the Estates the bottom line was less clearly drawn. Just like the royalists they had started with the assumption that one could go back to a *dominium politicum et regale* position: the regime as it had been in the time of the emperor. Once the old law and the venerable privileges had been reaffirmed, practical problems could be solved in what was assumed to be the traditional way, by consultation between the monarch and the States General. There were two major ambiguities in this position. The first was the relation of the Estates of Holland to the States General. How far could Holland and Zeeland speak for the Netherlands

---

[30] Shakespeare, *Henry VIII*, 3. 2. 458.
[31] Orange to John of Nassau. Dordrecht, 21 March 1575. Groen van Prinsterer, *Archives*, 151.

as a whole? This ambiguity was even more pronounced in the position of William of Orange. He had always wished to speak for the country as a whole and this was one of the reasons he had insisted on his membership of the States General as well as on his royal governorship of Holland and Zeeland.

The second ambiguity was the problem of religion. For King Philip this was simply not a question open to discussion, apart perhaps from some of its administrative aspects. It was a question inherent in princely sovereignty in general and, more particularly, in the providential international position of the House of Austria. The introduction of the religious dimension into politics, by the Reformation and the Catholic reaction to it, and by the need of the Habsburgs to justify their pre-eminence over France – the oldest Christian kingdom, according to the French – these conditions gave a rigidity to political and constitutional problems which were something new in European politics.

It was only in the course of the discussion at Breda that the Estates began to grasp the implications of their own and of the royalist arguments: a return to *dominium politicum et regale*, the happy balance of the days of Charles V, was no longer possible. Religion had driven both sides into incompatible positions. Toleration of both the Reformed and the Catholic faith, in the way that Orange tried to establish it in one polity, was difficult enough. For the two sides at Breda it was impossible. For King Philip toleration was not an option. For the Estates, or at least the Calvinists within the Estates party, Philip's position was not and could not be acceptable. And this meant that princely sovereignty, as it had been traditionally understood, was also no longer an option.

What then were the alternatives? Developments in France, which in Spain and in the Netherlands were watched with either horrified or approving fascination, showed some of the alternatives to be alarming, not only to the royalists but also to anti-royalist Catholics who, in Holland and Zeeland, were still the great majority of the population. In Languedoc the provincial Estates appointed an advisory council for the military governor and this council promptly resolved to banish unrepentant Catholics from the province. The Estates of Dauphiné went even further. As well as setting up a similar advisory council, they ordered all inhabitants to attend the services of the Reformed Church and all parents were to bring their new-born children to be baptised in it. Public positions, including those of schoolmasters, could be held only by members of the Reformed Church, and their orthodoxy would be examined by the Calvinist Church colloquies.[32]

Even if the Estates of Holland did not propose to go as far as those of Languedoc or Dauphiné – and there was undoubtedly a core of Calvinists among the *gueux* who would have liked to do so – most people on all sides agreed that a change of religion would inevitably lead to a change of sovereignty. The question was, who was to be sovereign?

---

[32] Benedict, 'The Dynamics of Protestant Militancy'.

The beginnings of parliamentary government

It was precisely over this point that the Estates of Holland negotiated with William of Orange during the spring and well into the summer of 1575, at the same time that the conference of Breda sank more and more deeply into the morass of stalemate and, eventually, into the abyss of total collapse.

THE PROBLEM OF SOVEREIGNTY

The Estates and the prince of Orange were now in uncharted waters. There was a great deal of good will and both sides were agreed on the overwhelming practical necessity of continuing their defence against the military efforts of the royalists. But beyond this basic conviction there was still a great deal of confusion. It was relatively easy to find a title for William of Orange. One could use a mixture of traditional and confected terminology. In April the commissions for the negotiators had been drawn up in the name of 'William, by the grace of God, prince of Orange, count of Nassau etc., and by the nobles and knights of the county of Holland, the burgomasters, aldermen, councillors ... militias and guilds'. To this undifferentiated list were added the towns of Zeeland, 'representing the whole corpus of these towns'.[33]

A month later, in draft articles for the government, Orange is called *Souverain ende Overhooft*, sovereign and head, for as long as the military emergency should last, and he was 'to order everything that was necessary and useful for the conservation and defence of the country'.[34] The word 'sovereign' here did not mean what King Philip meant by it but rather simply head of government. For the rest of the articles detailed the limitations of his position and especially required him to take the advice of a *Landts Raedt*, a Council of the Country. It was to be chosen by the Estates from persons 'of the best quality and property' and its members were to take an oath both to Orange and to the Estates, while the officials and magistrates of the towns and of the militias were to take reciprocal oaths to each other.

Orange's answer to these drafts was that he left his own position to the discretion of the Estates 'who should give him as much or as little authority as they thought advisable for the welfare of the country'.[35] In the fourteenth century the Estates of Brabant had chosen their duke and they had taken the opportunity to have him confirm their privileges. But no duke of Brabant had ever allowed, as Orange did in 1575, that the Estates should have *carte blanche* over the powers they conferred on him.

One may doubt whether Orange really meant this, in spite of the wording of his missive to the Estates – meant it any more than they had really meant to make him

---

[33] *HSR*, 1575, 240.
[34] *Ibid.*, 294–8.
[35] *Ibid.*, 312. The exact words were: 'soo remitteert syne Excellencie al't selve ter goeder beliefte van de Heeren Staten, die hun soo veel ende so weynigh authoriteyt sulllen mogen geven, als henluyden tot welvaren van de Landen goedtduncken sal.'

'sovereign'. Negotiations went on throughout the summer about who was to be associated with all these resolutions and about the details of the personnel and the functions of the *Landts Raedt*. Orange wanted the common people associated with the proposals 'so that one would have all the better obedience from them and also that they should have no cause for complaint that the constitutional ordinances have been made without their consent and knowledge'.[36]

This did not signify a conversion of this princely arch-aristocrat to a republican style of democracy. It was rather a populist card which Orange was playing against the urban oligarchies, a card which the House of Nassau was to play from time to time for the next hundred years, and often with great success. At about the same time Orange was proposing that the small towns of Buren and Zaltbommel should together have a vote in the Estates. He himself owned Buren and would represent it.[37]

The Estates immediately blocked the proposals about the common people and Orange thought it expedient not to insist on this point. He had, after all, been given the authority to 'renew' the magistrates of the towns, even ahead of the expiry of their terms of office. He certainly used this power, for instance by appointing Pieter Adriansz van der Werff, the defender of Leiden in the famous siege, even though van der Werff did not belong to a patrician family in that city. Later, in the civil war with Don John of Austria, both sides systematically deposed opposing magistrates and had their own followers elected, or they simply appointed them. Even so, in 1575 the regents of the towns were careful to keep their fingers in the pie. They stipulated that Orange's appointment of city magistrates must be made only with the consent of the majority of those 'who represented the *vroedschap* and the corpus of these towns'.[38]

By September 1575 Orange had had enough of the *Landts Raedt*. It had not dealt swiftly enough with financial, naval and police matters, and it was not recognised in the whole of Holland and not at all in the other provinces. Orange therefore proposed a Council of State with very extensive powers, including the ability to raise 50,000 guilders without asking for further consent. The Estates would still be represented by the *Landts Raedt* which would be co-opted into the Council of State.

Not surprisingly, the Estates were alarmed by these proposals. They had, after all, given His Excellency 'complete authority', and had even offered him the title of count of Holland. They referred the proposal back to their principals. On 13 October they came back with written instructions about an abjuration of loyalty to the king of Spain (*'het verlaten van den Koning van Spaigne'*). Orange was to choose a foreign lord or prince in his place, but with the advice of the Estates.[39] We do not know which of the towns first put forward this proposal nor how the towns arrived at an agreement on it.

[36] *Ibid.*, 313.
[37] Koopmans, *De Staten van Holland*, 121.
[38] *HSR*, 20 July 1575, 523.
[39] *Ibid.*, 648–92.

The beginnings of parliamentary government

The year 1575 ended without a definitive settlement. Before the French Revolution no one used the words constituent assembly; but this was the role which the Estates of Holland had been playing since 1572 and particularly vigorously in 1575. They had assumed the authority to determine how their country was to be governed. And yet, this had not been their original intention. When they assembled after the first *gueux* victories of 1572 they had done so by the authority of the man who claimed to be the royal governor and with the avowed object of reinstating their legal privileges which, they claimed, had been illegally and tyrannically set aside by the king's governor general. From the beginning much of this argument was fiction. Over the next three years circumstances had forced them to claim always greater powers and to delegate many of them, as a practical necessity, to the prince of Orange. There had been no plan underlying these actions, no blueprint for the creation of a republic or the setting up of a new type of regime which would, later, be identified as parliamentary government.

The conference of Breda sharpened the Hollanders' perceptions of their problems; but it did so in a largely negative way. It became clear that a return to *dominium politicum et regale*, the regime of the previous two hundred years, was no longer possible. And it was impossible in the conditions of the Habsburg composite monarchy because opposed religious beliefs had produced diametrically opposed and irreconcilable views of sovereignty between the Dutch Estates and the monarchy in Madrid. It was this opposition which gave to both the conference of Breda and to the political discussions between the Estates of Holland and the prince of Orange their curious air of unreality. The peace conference collapsed and the Dutch found themselves manoeuvring, both with and against Orange, for a constitutional settlement. Their very attempts at constitution-building, however, showed both sides that they were only engaged in a political process of finding a *modus vivendi*. Orange had never given up his hope of raising the whole of the Netherlands in revolt. In the last analysis, his position in Holland and Zeeland was only a temporary stepping stone in this aim, an aim which was political rather than constitutional.

The Estates of Holland were perhaps more concerned than Orange with a definition of their own regime, a regime which would safeguard as much as possible the position of the traditional urban patriciates and their closely allied rural nobility. What they achieved was, for all its confusions, a workable polity ultimately based on the authority not of a prince but of the Estates. This polity included both South and North Holland, Zeeland and those parts of Utrecht and other provinces which the Orangeists had conquered or which had thrown in their lot with them. Thus, several of the provinces of the Netherlands had now formed the sort of defensive union which they had always rejected under Habsburg rule. It was political and military events in the spring of 1576 in the provinces outside Holland and Zeeland which overtook their efforts at constitution-building and, again as in 1572, the rationalisations and arguments of most of the political theorists and propagandists.

12

Rule by the States General: myths and realities (1576–1581)

'If he [Requesens] were to die at this juncture, it would be the ruin and confusion of the country: for everyone would want to be master, and the Estates would control the government and many evil-minded people would rush in to create a mess.'
Maximilien Morillon, vicar general of the archbishopric of Mechlin,
to Cardinal Granvelle, 18 Dec. 1575[1]

THE STATES GENERAL OF SEPTEMBER 1576

On 8 September 1576 the Estates of Brabant and Hainaut invited all the provincial Estates of the Netherlands, except those of Holland and Zeeland, to send deputies to the States General in Brussels. During the next two weeks most of them responded to this invitation.

Contemporaries compared these actions to the initiative taken by the Estates of Holland in 1463.[2] It is one of the ironies of history that in 1463 the move by Holland was directed against the influence of the Croy family at court, while the move of Brabant and Hainaut in 1576 was taken with the approval, perhaps even at the instigation, of a descendant of this family, Philippe de Croy, third duke of Aerschot. Historians have taken the events of both 1463 and 1576 as landmarks in the history of the Netherlands States General. This is fair enough; but neither move was as sudden or as innovatory as has sometimes been claimed for them. In each case the summons for a general assembly was issued by provincial Estates, rather than by the monarch, to deal with quite specific and limited problems. In each case the implications of the action went far beyond the immediate intentions of its authors.

---

[1] E. Poullet and C. Piot, eds., *Correspondance du Cardinal de Granvelle*, 12 vols. (Brussels, 1878–96), vol. V, 436. 'S'il venoit à décéder en telle conjoncture ce seroit la ruyne et confusion du pays: car chacun vouldroit estre maistre, et les Estatz embrasseroient le gouvernement et beaucoup des mauvais esprits s'advanceroient à y teiller les chartes.' My translation of the second part of this sentence is not literal but, I think, captures something of the sense of dismay in Morillon's letter. He knew that Cardinal Granvelle was desperately afraid of the power of the States General. Understatement was common in sixteenth-century correspondence where 'inconvénience' (in all Latin languages) nearly always meant not inconvenience but disaster or catastrophe.

[2] See above, ch. 2.

Rule by the States General: myths and realities

In 1463 it was the quarrel of Duke Philip the Good and and his son, the count of Charolais (Charles the Bold), and a putative crisis of a regency government. The States General succeeded in their immediate aim, the reconciliation of the princes. In the long run, however, the results were the establishment of the States General as a regular part of the regime of the composite Burgundian monarchy of the Netherlands provinces.

In 1576 the crisis was much more serious. It was the actual breakdown of monarchical government in the Netherlands. In the intervening century the composite monarchy had vastly increased its size and membership, and its political centre had shifted to Spain. Problems of the relations between the different parts of this expanded composite monarchy, of its international relations and of the consequent opaqueness of its perceived priorities and of the consequent physical and intellectual difficulties of decision-making – these had all been aggravated by the religious passions of the age and the emotions which these injected into political and personal ambitions. Philip II and Alba had tried to solve these problems by crushing all political and religious opposition. The result had been military rebellion and a shift of all conflicts on to a military plane.

Given the organisational and tactical superiority of the Spanish army over all other armies of the time, Philip's and Alba's policy very nearly worked.[3] But the decisive point is that in the end it did not. Contemporaries were very much aware of the unpredictability of the final decision, once there had been a resort to arms. All sides agreed that this final decision was in the hands of God. Since both sides claimed to be fighting the Almighty's battles, they tried to make sure that he would really be fighting for them. The best way to do this was by increasing one's armies and navies to overwhelming numbers and to build the new Italian-style fortifications for one's towns and fortresses. There was therefore an inherent and inexorable tendency to overstretch one's resources. When resources were also urgently needed for other inescapable tasks, the results were likely to be catastrophic.

This was what happened to the Spanish monarchy in the 1570s. Alba's war in the Netherlands started almost immediately after the traumatic and costly revolt of the Moriscos in Spain itself and it coincided with the still enormously dangerous and expensive naval war with the Ottoman Turks in the Mediterranean. The Spanish government's financial situation deteriorated even beyond its low points of 1557 and 1566 when royal confiscation of private treasure had led to fifty-three bank failures in Seville. In 1574 nearly 8 million florins had to be sent to the army in the Netherlands, and in 1575 it was still over 5 million. The Castilian financial fairs virtually ceased to function. In September 1575 all government debts contracted since November 1560 were simply cancelled and not converted into *juros*, as they had been in 1557. Some 15 million ducats in short-term loans were involved, owed mainly to Genoese bankers. They were given only a vague promise

---

[3] Parker, *The Grand Strategy of Philip II*.

of repayment which would be negotiated with individual bankers. Not until 1577, after 2 million ducats had arrived from Peru, did the crown manage to negotiate a compromise with its creditors.[4]

Even when it became possible again for the king to earmark funds for the Netherlands, the very efficient Genoese financial organisation which had regularly transferred money from Spain to Antwerp, had been broken. It would take time to rebuild it. In the meantime, the Spanish soldiers could not be paid. They had lost nothing of their military prowess but, precisely after each victory, they went on strike and decided to take by force what they could not be given legitimately. It was a brutal and terrifying experience for all those who happened to be nearby, whether they were Protestants or Catholics, rebels or loyalists.

A strong central government with a clear sense of direction and of political possibilities was now more necessary than ever. It is doubtful whether Requesens could have provided it, hampered as he was by rigid directives from Madrid and by his own psychological inability to break completely with Alba's analysis of the Netherlands situation. In fact, he died on 5 March 1576. The king had no alternative but to empower the Netherlands Council of State to carry on the government until he could send a new governor general. Thanks to Requesens the Council of State was now dominated by the Walloon high nobility as it had not been since the regency of Mary of Hungary. Its leading member, both socially and by experience, was the duke of Aerschot, an elegant and rather rigid aristocratic figure given to portentous and long-winded pronouncements, who found it no easier to get on with his colleagues than he had with the anti-Granvelle league of his peers in the 1560s. Requesens had vainly tried to keep him out of the council, and now he quarrelled with Gerónimo Roda, the only remaining Spanish member of the Netherlands Council of State.

Effective central government was grinding to a halt. This had happened on previous occasions in the Netherlands. It was a systemic hazard in the Habsburg system of government. Only this time the stasis had even more serious consequences than before. The provincial Estates had continued to meet, quite legally. Neither Alba nor Requesens could do without them.[5] Now they moved into the power vacuum because there was no other legitimate force which could do this. Morillon was driven to his despairing prediction which was a correct appreciation of the situation. The Estates of Brabant were demanding that the foreign soldiers should be sent away. In March 1576 they asked the Council of State directly to summon the States General, quoting the precedent of 1506 and the death of Philip I.[6]

---

[4] Steele, 'La real hacienda', 162–4.
[5] E.g. the Estates of Flanders in December 1563. AGRB., P. d'E. A., 648, fos. 1–2.
[6] Antwerp Stadsarchief, H. de Moy, Tractaet van de Beden by de hertogen van Brabant gedaen aen de Staeten general, fo. 202r. Poullet and Piot, *Correspondance . . . de Granvelle*, vol. V, 656–9.

Rule by the States General: myths and realities

There had been an increasing groundswell of this demand from the other provincial Estates. At the same time the prince of Orange and the Estates of Holland were sending a stream of propaganda south, all urging the need for a States General to re-establish the liberties of the country.[7] Perhaps the most comprehensive was the anonymous pamphlet, 'Address and Opening to make good, blessed and general peace in the Netherlands', published in the spring of 1576. It argued that the States General 'assist the lord of the country in accordance with his oath in all grave and important affairs', that it was their duty 'to bring the country peace and union'. It concluded that the Netherlands had never been governed 'by way of an absolute monarch' but rather 'by way of a Republic or civil policy [sic – polity?]'.[8]

The Council of State itself had urged Requesens to summon the States General in order to announce the king's (limited) pardon. After considerable hesitation, Philip allowed it for one day, provided the deputies of the different provinces did not engage in common discussions. This condition was as unrealistic as it had been when Alba had summoned the States General to underwrite his Tenth Penny tax. The deputies immediately presented the governor general with a list of the country's grievances and demands: the pardon should be general and unlimited; Alba's taxes should be formally abolished; the Estates should supervise the regular payment of the troops, a Council of the Netherlands should be set up in Spain (presumably in imitation of the Council of Italy); the king should come himself to the Netherlands or send a prince of the blood as regent; and, generally, the political and legal situation of the time of the emperor Charles should be restored.[9]

In Madrid the junta among Philip's advisers for Netherlands affairs was divided about how to react to these demands. Joachim Hopperus, the most senior Netherlander of this group, a friend of Viglius and Granvelle, was in favour of a hard line. Gaspar de Quiroga, the inquisitor general, appeared more accommodating. There was plenty of dislike between Spaniards and Netherlanders; but this dislike did not necessarily determine individual attitudes or advice on policy.

The king refused the abolition of the Council of Troubles but allowed the peace negotiations of Breda to take place. As Requesens had already told the deputies, there was no question of the king fulfilling his earlier repeated promises of coming himself to the Netherlands.[10] The situation in the Mediterranean was too critical for him to leave Spain. In spite of Don John of Austria's dramatic victory over the Turkish fleet at Lepanto in 1572, the Sultan was still able to outbuild the galleys which Philip II could launch. In September 1574 the Turks retook Tunis which had only recently been captured, with great Christian fanfares, by Don John of

---

[7] Geurts, *De Nederlands Opstand in de Pamfletten*, 46–58.
[8] Van Gelderen, *The Dutch Revolt*, 79–122. See also M. van Gelderen, *The Political Thought of the Dutch Revolt* (Cambridge, 1992), 126–35.
[9] Janssens, *Brabant in het Verweer*, 220–2.
[10] Ibid., 223–9.

Austria. Moreover, the lack of money and troops would not allow Philip to repeat his father's triumphal march of 1540.[11] It might have been Philip II's last opportunity to settle the Netherlands problem. It was the strategic obligations imposed on the king by the very extent of his composite monarchy which accounted for his failure.

There was, however, much else. Just before his death Requesens had given the provincial governors permission to use force against the Spanish mutineers. But when the Spaniards had captured Zierickzee in Zeeland, after a long and arduous siege, and they were still not paid, they moved into Brabant. On 25 July 1576 they captured and sacked the blameless little town of Aalst (Alost), only a few miles from Brussels. The Council of State now declared the mutinous Spanish soldiers to be enemies of the country. In Brussels there was an explosion of popular anger.

Up until then, popular movements had been inspired or directed by the Calvinists. Now, for the first time, a Catholic popular movement appeared in a big Netherlands city. The phenomenon was well known in France. In Paris, Toulouse and other big cities the Catholic mob had turned on the Huguenots as disturbers of the peace and polluters of the religious beliefs and traditional values of the majority. In Brussels, however, the enemy was the foreigner who had committed similar outrages, even though he was not a heretic. On the contrary, the Brusselers demanded peace with the rebellious and heretical provinces of Holland and Zeeland. For the moment this common aim of the propertied and ruling classes, represented in the Estates of Brabant, and of the common people overrode their traditional mutual distrust.

Even a century earlier, in the rebellion of 1477, the Estates of the provinces had not contemplated breaking up the unity of the Netherlands. By 1576 this feeling of solidarity had been strengthened by long cooperation, formally by the Treaty of Augsburg of 1548 and by the oft-expressed view that if they did not hang together, they would hang separately. In the long run, this distrust was to continue to dog the anti-Spanish movement.

The Spanish soldiers demonstrated the reality of this fear by the ease with which they brushed aside the dilettante militias and the ad hoc forces raised by the individual provinces. But, perhaps most important of all, there was the myth of the States General, the only institution which, it was now widely believed, could restore peace and the golden days of Emperor Charles V.

Even before the States General could assemble, the situation in Brussels had changed dramatically. What happened now, and the roles played by different individuals has never been established with complete clarity. On 4 September a company of the citizen guard broke into the palace and arrested the Council of State. Thomas Wilson, Queen Elizabeth's envoy, reported that the action was to 'the great liking of the people who now seem to rule . . . None of the nobility

---

[11] See above, ch. 6.

allowed of this arrest . . . except it were covertly' and that it is the people alone who rule and 'nobody dares oppose their will'.[12]

Wilson had undoubtedly observed the atmosphere in Brussels correctly, but he underestimated the covert role of the nobility. Both Aerschot and Orange, who at this time were undoubtedly cooperating, were probably involved in this coup. They were supported by the Hoorn, the Egmont and the Lalaing-Montigny families, all good patriots, no doubt, but also intent on revenge for the execution of their famous relatives in 1568 and on the retrieval of their confiscated estates. It was probably through Orange's influence that Willam of Hoorn, lord of Hèze, had been appointed commander of the Brabant troops, and it was his lieutenant commander who carried out the coup. Later, in January 1577, there was talk of a double marriage between Orange's and Aerschot's children.[13] In September 1576 it was a Council of State purged of its pro-Spanish members which agreed to the summoning of the States General by the Estates of Brabant and Hainaut, and on the immediate opening of negotiations with the prince of Orange and the provinces of Holland and Zeeland.

The driving force of Estate policy in 1477 had been Flanders. Now, in 1576, it was Brabant. Formally this was recognised by the immediate appointment of Cornelius Weellemans, the secretary of the Estates of Brabant, as secretary of the States General. Politically, the Estates of Brabant set a good example by accepting Aerschot's proposal for one million florins in taxes, including even the reimposition of Alba's Hundredth Penny, to pay for the Estates' troops. This was the sum which they had resolutely refused to Requesens and the States General unless their grievances were met first.[14]

The States General immediately staked out their aim and their predominant role in the government of the country. Within a month, all the other delegates whom they had invited appeared in Brussels, all that is except those of Groningen, Friesland and Overijssel. Luxembourg and Limbourg had not normally sent delegates to the States General. The north-eastern provinces, only fairly recently incorporated into the Netherlands, had always been chary of acknowledging authority which came from Brussels.[15] The province of Groningen (Ommelanden) was in chronic dispute with the city of Groningen, so that the two nearly always tended to choose opposite paths.

Well before the deputies of most of the provinces had arrived, the States General appointed the duke of Aerschot as chief of the Council of State, 'committed by

---

[12] Quoted in Griffiths, *William of Hornes Lord of Hèze*, 28. This is the best account in English of the events in Brussels. For a general narrative of the events in the Netherlands, see Parker, *The Dutch Revolt*, ch. 4.

[13] Swart, *Willem van Oranje en de Nederlands Opstand*, 142.

[14] De Moy, Tractaet, fo. 181r. Parker, *The Dutch Revolt*, 176.

[15] J. J. Woltjer, 'Het Noorden en de Pacificatie van Gent', in N. V. Snoeck-Ducajn *et al.*, eds., *Opstand en Pacificatie in de Lage Landen*, D. (Ghent, 1976), 79–98.

His Majesty to the government of these provinces'. The count of Lalaing, governor of Hainaut, was to be Aerschot's lieutenant general, in charge of military matters. Other noblemen were appointed to assist them.[16] In other words, the Council of State was still the king's council but was now effectively appointed by the States General – much as the government of Holland and Zeeland, after 1572, was still the king's government under the prince of Orange.

The States General never questioned their own legality. In case of doubt, there were plenty of propagandists who found more or less convincing precedents for this assembly. One of the frequently used but not very convincing precedents was Mary of Burgundy's Great Privilege of 1477. More convincing was the actual history of the Estates of Brabant and the appeals to the *joyeuses entrées* which were now happily adopted by the other provinces as well. The States General's resolutions took the form of petitions to the king's Council of State; but it was not the king's council but their own. At the same time the States General were in no doubt about the revolutionary character of their actions. When, on 12 October, they sent letters to Henry II and Catherine de Medici, they instructed their envoy to speak of 'the great and sovereign change which now had occurred' in the Netherlands.[17]

The letter to the king and queen-mother of France was only one of a barrage of letters which the States General fired off to Philip II, the pope, the queen of England, the emperor and a large number of German princes. They assured every recipient of the States General's good intentions and, where appropriate, with regard to the Catholic religion, and they asked the German princes to prevent the German soldiers in the Netherlands from making common cause with the Spanish mutineers.

On 2 October the deputies requested the Council of State to see to it that, for the purpose of getting rid of the Spaniards, the deputies from all provinces should have full powers.[18] Like the Estates of Holland, the States General appointed committees to supervise the raising of troops and their payment, even though they had themselves appointed a Council of War.[19] They negotiated for immediate loans with international bankers. Perhaps unsurprisingly, they did not find the Antwerp money market as tight as the king's agents had done.

But finance remained a problem. It was the one area where the provincial assemblies still required their deputies to refer back. Soon the Estates' commanders were complaining of their inability to pay their troops. The States General found themselves on the horns of the same dilemma as the monarchies when they went to war: it was necessary to match or exceed the number of soldiers the enemy raised

---

[16] N. Japikse, *Resolutiën der Staten-Generaal van 1576–1609*, vol. I, 5.
[17] Gachard, ed., *Actes des Etats Généraux des Pays-Bas 1576–1585*, 2 vols. (Brussels, 1861), vol. I, 17, 20.
[18] *Ibid.*, 11.
[19] *Ordonnances et instructions faicts sur la levée ... des moyens généraux, 18 Déc, 1576* (Brussels, 1577). Japikse, *Resolutiën*, vol. I, 82–111.

or was thought to be able to raise. In December 1576 the States General accepted their Council of State' proposal for taxes on a long list of foodstuffs and textiles. Each province could organise these taxes as it wished, with its own receivers, but there were to be no exemptions and they suspended all ecclesiastical and other privileges except for the king's person and for the mendicant orders. The monies collected were to be paid each month to a treasurer general of the Estates who would then pay the troops. This time there were few arguments and none of the foot dragging which there had been for similar proposals after the famous novennial *aide* of 1558–9.

The States General further streamlined its procedure. It appointed a rotating presidency. The president, assisted by one or two pensionaries (i.e. secretaries) chosen from the pensionaries of the cities who were the usual delegates to the assembly, was to preside over the meetings for one week at a time. He was to submit proposals and to receive the letters from the provincial Estates. In the afternoon the pensionaries were to act as the executive committee for the resolutions taken by the assembly.[20] Aerschot was beginning to learn how to manage such an assembly. Perhaps he had learned it from the practice of Cardinal Granvelle during the regency of Margaret of Parma, for he now also invited deputies to dinner before the actual session. Judicially managed dinners remained an important part of sixteenth-century political life in the Netherlands. They were important not least because the States General, just as the Estates of the provinces, busied themselves with a host of mundane matters, from traditional inter-provincial quarrels over river and canal tolls to the restitution of property confiscated by Alba's Council of Troubles.[21] As always happens with cases of restitution where property has changed hands several times, this involved highly complex legal and moral problems.

The monarchs and the courts of Europe, regardless of whether they were pro- or anti-Spanish, did not like representative assemblies on principle, unless they kept themselves to their traditional and preferably gradually narrowing limits. In spite of all the rivalries and even open enmity between the European states, there was a basic feeling of monarchical solidarity and a gut dislike of rebellion which limited monarchical power. Elizabeth I complained about the slowness of the States General in taking decisions and blamed it on the difficulties of negotiating with a large number of people.[22] Don John of Austria asserted that the States General did not know from one hour to the next what they had decided.[23] The prince of Orange himself complained of the States General's procedure, just as he had complained, during the previous four years, about the procedure of the Estates of Holland.

[20] *Ibid.*, 10.
[21] See the acts and resolutions published for this period by Gachard and Japikse.
[22] Report by the States General's envoy. Windsor, 17 Oct. 1577. Gachard, *Actes*, vol. II, 271.
[23] Don John of Austria to Rodrigo de Mendoza. Luxembourg, 9 Dec. 1576. A. Morel-Fatio, ed., *L'Espagne au XVIe et au XVIIe siècle*, vol. II: *Lettres de don Juan d'Autriche* (Heilbronn, 1878), 111.

Monarchies, States Generals and Parliaments

But was conventional wisdom of the greater efficiency of monarchical government, or at least government by a single person and his advisers, as against government by a representative assembly, borne out by experience? The acts and resolutions of the States General during the autumn of 1576 rather suggest extraordinary activity and efficiency. Even though the persons of the deputies were constantly being changed by their principals, the Estates of the provinces and the individual cities,[24] the States General answered letters on the day they were received or the next day and showed every willingness to take rapid decisions on a wide variety of topics. The one exception, and it was certainly an extremely important one, was taxation. This was a power which the provincial Estates would not allow their deputies to exercise without reference back. But this was nothing new. Even during Alba's regime they had insisted on this point. It was the centralised government of Philip II of Spain which had declared bankruptcy for the whole monarchy. It was the *dominium regale* government of the French monarchy which, in spite of its far-reaching powers of taxation, failed to achieve a viable solution of its financial problems. Since at least the 1540s the Estates of the Netherlands provinces had shown themselves much more competent in raising funds and imposing taxes which were actually paid than any European monarchy. As the royalists sourly observed, during the autumn of 1576 the States General imposed taxes by 'general means', sold *rentes*, mostly voluntarily, raised loans in Antwerp, like the Estates of Holland, and sold church property.[25] They set up committees to handle separate problems, as the Estates of Holland had done. Unfortunately, we have no specific study of these committees. But evidently it was a much more difficult practice in a composite assembly, representing most of the provinces, than in the Estates of the single province of Holland.

Yet the real problems of the States General were not procedural or institutional but political. The most urgent need was the ending of the war with Holland and Zeeland. Speed was of the essence, for the mutinous Spanish troops were terrorising large sections of the country. Don John of Austria, the new goveror general appointed by the king arrived in Luxembourg on 3 November and nobody was quite sure what his policy was going to be.

THE APPOINTMENT OF DON JOHN OF AUSTRIA

In fact, the appointment of Don John and the problem of his instructions was a classic instance of the inefficiency of monarchical government in general and of Philip II's government in particular. Already in May 1576, when Don John's appointment was first mooted in Brussels, Aerschot had clashed violently with

---

[24] States General to Don John of Austria, Brussels, 30 July 1577. Gachard, *Actes*, vol. II, 211. *Ibid.*, vol. II, 215.

[25] Japikse, *Resolutiën*, vol. I, 111–27. Cf. also *Ordonnance et Instruction par les Estatz généraux des pays de par-deça* (Brussels, 1577).

Rule by the States General: myths and realities

Gerónimo Roda. Never would he serve under a boy, declared the duke.[26] This was less than fair to the king's half-brother. He was a prince of the blood, as the Netherlanders were always demanding of their regents. At twenty-nine he had a glittering military reputation as commander-in-chief against the Morisco rebellion, as victor over the Turkish fleet at Lepanto and as conqueror of Tunis. But he was known to be ambitious and self-willed, and it was also know that his relations with the king were ambiguous. He had fought the Lepanto campaign against Philip's orders not to venture the Spanish fleet so far east from its bases and so late in the unpredictable Mediterranean naval season. After Don John's victory in Tunis, Philip had blocked his attempts to be given a royal title.

In the spring he failed to respond to his letters of appointment and then, definitely against Philip's orders, he went to Spain to see the king, instead of proceeding straight to the Netherlands. Knowing the court of Madrid and his brother's personal unreliability towards his ministers, Don John had every reason to wish to be certain about the policies he was being asked to pursue. Even so, Philip could not support Don John's romantic ambition to conquer England and perhaps liberate and marry Mary Queen of Scots, nor could Don John have foreseen the depths of his brother's reason-of-state treachery in conniving at the murder of his own secretary, Juan de Escobedo.[27]

Philip knew well that the delay caused by Don John's coming to Spain made a bad situation in the Netherlands worse. It was made worse still when Don John finally arrived in the Netherlands without troops, without money and with contradictory instructions. In one set of instructions the king ordered Roda to destroy the troops of the States General if they did not disband. There was no chance of that, and Orange's agents intercepted the king's letters to Roda and read them out to the States General. At the same time Philip gave totally different instructions to Don John:

> If matters are in such a state that the States General demand unilateral concessions before they recognise your authority, it seems that, safeguarding religion and my authority *as much as may be*, since matters have reached these extremes, given the need to extinguish the fire and to prevent these people from [taking] more desperate action, so that everything is lost, *we shall have to concede everything in order to bring about a conclusion and save what we can*.[28]

This looks like a complete surrender. The question of the legality of the States General was not even mentioned. On the contrary, it was a question of getting Don John recognised as governor general by the States General. This was just like Maximilian I and his daughter Margaret needing to be recognised by the States

---

[26] Janssens, *Brabant in het Verweer*, 284.
[27] Historians have had different views of Philip's guilt, or otherwise, in the murder of Escobedo. I am here following Geoffrey Parker, *Philip II* (Boston and Toronto, 1978), 133–7. For a contrary view see Kamen, *Philip of Spain*, 162–8.
[28] Quoted by Parker, *The Grand Strategy of Philip II*. Emphasis added by Parker.

Monarchies, States Generals and Parliaments

General as regents, after the death of Philip I. And that was precisely one of the justifications which the propagandists of the States General had put forward in 1576. But even leaving aside the opaque question of the respective legalities of States General and governor general, were Philip II's instructions not weasel words, simply masking a tactical withdrawal? It is true that this time, and unlike 1566 when Philip agreed to Margaret of Parma's concessions to the nobles of the Compromise, he did not formally disclaim his concessions. But perhaps he thought that such a disclaimer was no longer necessary. This was, after all, the century of Machiavelli, of the reason-of-state theorists who gave Machiavellism a godly slant, of the constable of Castile, Iñigo de Velasco, who wrote to Charles V about the Comunero revolt that 'Your Majesty should not be afraid of paper and ink', and, at the other end of the social scale, and only a few years after 1576, the English tavern song:

> We are soldiers three
> Lately come out of the Low Country
> With never a penny of money ...
> Charge it again, boys,
> Charge it again,
> As long as there's any ink in your pen –
> With never a penny of money.

Above all, it was the century when, especially in the Netherlands, the Protestants threw into the teeth of the Catholics the church's teaching that it was permissible to break faith with heretics, i.e. with all Protestants.

And yet, there is no hard evidence that, in the summer and autumn of 1576, Philip II set out to deliberately deceive his subjects. It became evident only in the following years that saving the Catholic religion and the king's authority were thoroughly ambiguous and confusing concepts in the minds of all the actors in the Netherlands drama: the king, his ministers in the Netherlands, the different Netherlands parties inside and outside the States General, and even the country's neighbours.

THE PACIFICATION OF GHENT

In the autumn of 1576 this confusion was not yet evident. Virtually everyone in the Netherlands, whatever their religious convictions, hated Alba's regime and the detritus it had left behind, the unpaid and mutinous soldiers. Added to the violent dislike of foreign soldiers, even if they behaved reasonably, there was a violent culture clash. For the common Spanish soldiers, from their often desperately poor home backgrounds in the arid villages of the Castilian *meseta* and their culture of abstemious wine-drinking, the lifestyle of the beer-swilling and apparently gluttonous Netherlanders was profoundly distasteful or envy-making. The miserable

Rule by the States General: myths and realities

wet climate and the non-payment of their wages, when around them even the common people seemed to be living in a degree of affluence unknown at home – all this made them easily believe what their respected commander-in-chief, the duke of Alba, had openly proclaimed: that all Netherlanders were heretics and traitors who deserved all they got.[29]

The Netherlanders, for their part, were even more hostile. The States General complained to their Council of State about Spanish soldiers in Antwerp shouting 'fuera bellacos' – 'out you bastards'.[30] But, in truth, everyone was rightly worried about more than the insults and bad language of the soldiers.

Almost immediately, the States General resolved that its deputies should have full powers to conclude a peace and they appointed a committee to negotiate with the representative of the prince of Orange. With Brabant calling the tune, it was Aerschot who took the initiative. While himself from the Hainaut family of Croy, he had extensive estates in Brabant and was a member of the States General: in fact he was its leading member as a Brabant nobleman. But to keep the other provinces on board, it was advisable not to concentrate all action in Brabant. The prince of Orange's troops were already swarming south into Flanders. In Ghent Orange could count on strong support. The States General therefore decided to negotiate in Ghent. Their commissioners were simply to carry on from where the conference of Breda had broken down in the previous year. Even some of those who had negotiated for Requesens at Breda now reappeared as commissioners for the States General, notably Dr Elbertus Leoninus, the law professor from Louvain. Holland and Zeeland, too, sent their most experienced negotiators, among them Paulus Buys, secretary of the Estates of Holland, and Philippe Marnix, sieur de St Aldegonde, Orange's intimate adviser and his chief propagandist.[31]

It was a wise decision by both sides in the negotiations at Ghent to appoint men who knew the problems and roadblocks from previous experience. With Don John in the wings and likely to appear on the stage at any moment, the delegates knew they had to act fast, precisely because they had the great advantage over the conference of Breda that this time they did not need the governor general's agreement for every move they made. Moreover, the military situation was getting more and more ominous.

The delegates reached agreement on 30 October 1576, less than three weeks after the beginning of the negotiations. Even so, they could hardly have foreseen the fate which overtook Antwerp a few days later: the sack of the city by the mutinous Spanish troops, in which some 8,000 people were killed and vast damage

---

[29] Cf. L. van der Essen, 'Croisade contre les hérétiques ou guerre contre les rebelles', *Revue d'Histoire Ecclésiastique*, 51, 1 (1956), 43–78.
[30] Probably a sanitised version for the chaste pages of the States General's official resolutions. Soldiers rarely shout 'rogues' or 'scoundrels'. I have therefore sharpened the translation but may well have still made it too genteel.
[31] 5 Oct. 1576. Japikse, *Resolutiën*, vol. I, 18. Griffiths, *Representative Government*, 434–6.

was done to property and the credit of the city's financiers. Neither the prosperity of the foremost commercial and financial centre of northern Europe, nor the reputation of Philip II's Spain ever fully recovered from this dreadful event, at least not during the early modern period.

It was certainly not something which Philip II had planned, any more than his father had planned the sack of Rome by the mutinous imperial army in 1527. However far Philip II was prepared to go in the punishment of heretics and rebellious Moriscos, or in praising the king of France for the massacre of St Bartholomew, he did not approve of the mass murder of his vassals, for 'it would earn us a reputation for cruelty which would be better avoided'. For thus he wrote about his generals' proposals to open the dykes of Holland. Perhaps his less than convincing humanitarian attitude should be seen in the light of the fact that the Orangeists, with the prince's approval, had themselves opened some dykes, at least locally.[32]

However that may be, the sack of Antwerp undoubtedly convinced waverers that the agreement must be signed and published immediately (8 Nov. 1576). The preamble of the Pacification unequivocally held the 'hard government of the Spaniards and their adherents' responsible for the nine or ten last years of cruel war. The provinces of the Netherlands and its inhabitants were now jointly to drive out the Spaniards and their supporters, so as to restore the citizens to their rights, privileges and liberties and to their former prosperity. By article 1 all offences following from the troubles were to be pardoned. By article 3, once the Spaniards had been driven out, the States General, summoned and held as under Charles V, would return the country into the hands of the king 'our gracious lord' and decide the issue of religion and the return to the king of all fortresses, artillery and ships taken by the Hollanders. In the meantime (article 5), all placards of the duke of Alba against heresy were revoked and no one was to be punished for the sake of religion until the States General should determine the issue. Outside Holland and Zeeland no action against the Catholic religion was to be allowed (article 4). The remaining articles dealt with the right of free movement and commerce by all Netherlanders in all provinces, the freeing of all prisoners and the return of confiscated properties, notably those of the prince of Orange. The States General was to decide how to equalise the inflated currency of Holland and Zeeland with the currency of the other provinces. They were also to decide on Orange's claim to be paid the expenses of raising the armies for his abortive campaigns before 1572.[33] On 9 January 1577 the provinces signed an act of union (Union of Brussels) in support of the Pacification.

---

[32] Philip II to Requesens, 22 Oct. 1574. Quoted in Parker, *The Grand Strategy of Philip II*. Parker makes an interesting comparison of Philip's refusal to flood Holland with President Lyndon B. Johnson's refusal to flood the Mekong delta in the Vietnam War of the 1960s.

[33] The Dutch and the French versions of the Pacification are printed in parallel in Griffiths, *Representative Government*, 433-47.

Rule by the States General: myths and realities

DON JOHN OF AUSTRIA AND THE STATES GENERAL

For a short time it looked as if the Pacification of Ghent had really restored peace in the Netherlands. It was printed and circulated in all Western European languages. By many it was regarded as a constitution and it became a kind of mantra because, apparently, everybody had agreed to it. Any action which offended the vital interests of one of the parties would be condemned by this party as breaking the Pacification, with the implication of plunging the country back into civil war.

This was exactly what happened. It was not a matter of legality. One could leave the lawyers (and later historians) to argue about that; and, curiously, no one seems to have fastened on the claim that it was the States General which was to give the country back to its rightful prince, much as the Estates of Brabant had done on several occasions in the fourteenth century, or as the parliaments of Sicily had done in the thirteenth century when they offered the crown to the House of Aragon – facts which no self-respecting princely court cared to dwell on.

Bishop Laurent Metsius of 's-Hertogenbosch, himself a member of the States General, thought that driving out the Spanish soldiers would deliver Christ's lambs to be devoured by the wolves.[34] There had certainly been 'wolves' in Holland in the first flush of revolution; but the luckless victims of the Spanish soldiery in Antwerp, most of them Catholics, evidently did not count as Christ's lambs for the pious bishop.

More important than individual hardline Catholic clerics, for the moment at least, was the refusal of Orange and of the Estates of Holland and Zeeland to ratify the Pacification, and this for opposite reasons. Already at the conference of Breda they had realised that they could not simply return to the political system of Charles V. In February 1577 Marnix spelt this out in a letter to his friend Gaspar Schetz, sieur de Grobbendoncq, one of the king's principal financial agents in Antwerp but personally sympathetic to the States General. Was the persecution of 'the poor people of the religion' (i.e. the Protestants) not initiated by the late emperor?, Marnix wrote; or, leaving out the matter of religion, was it not this emperor who had built the citadels of Ghent and Utrecht? The Pacification would allow Don John to build as many citadels in the name of the king as he pleased and re-enact all the placards. 'We would be jumping from the frying pan into the fire.'[35]

The question of trust, or rather distrust, remained crucial. Both Orange and Don John intercepted some of each other's most embarrassing letters and both had clever mathematicians who could break codes. In October 1576 the States General had deliberately fudged the question of religion in Holland and Zeeland – the words they used were *glisser ce point* – so that the matter could be settled in a future

[34] M. Baelde and P. van Peteghem, 'De Pacificatie van Gent (1576)', in *Opstand en Pacificatie in de Lage Landen* (n.p., n.d.), 34.
[35] The letter is quoted in full in Griffiths, *Representative Government*, 448–50.

States General after the Spaniards had left.[36] Don John did not want to come to Brussels because he feared for his personal safety. He had good reason; for in November Orange sent a memorandum to the States General, with a covering letter to Aerschot, urging them to secure Don John's person. He had come with few followers and no safe conduct. The action would end the war, Orange argued, for the king would then accept their just demands of withdrawing the Spanish troops.[37]

In December the Council of State and some of the deputies of the States General went to Namur to pay their respects to the new governor general. Again, the question was not one of organisation; for the deputies of both sections of the States General, those who wanted to conciliate Don John and those who were hardliners against him, had full powers to negotiate with him and take majority decisions.[38]

On 12 February 1577 Don John signed the Pacification of Ghent, putting special stress, however, on the maintenance of the Catholic religion. The States General accepted him formally as governor general. There was no universal agreement as to what his legal position had been before that date, any more than what the legal position of the States General had been. In both cases, the real question was that of political acceptance. The States General now agreed to pay the arrears of the royal troops – earlier an almost unthinkable action – and, at the end of April, the Spaniards left overland for Italy, after Don John had vainly tried to get funds to send them by sea.

The formula of a return to the regime of the emperor had deliberately not foreseen the States General as being permanently in session. Holland and Zeeland immediately protested against this agreement, the 'Eternal Edict'.[39] At a conference arranged by the governor general at the small Brabant town of St Gertruidenberg, in May 1577, Orange, with deputies from Holland and Zeeland on the one side, and deputies from the States General on the other, met to discuss their differences. For once, we have a verbatim account of a sixteenth-century conference.[40] It was written by an Orangeist, but it gives the arguments of all sides fairly enough.

The Orangeists would not submit to a royalist government and a States General summoned in the traditional form by the governor general, and this on both political and religious grounds. Nor would they give up their fortresses, artillery or ships to the traditional control of the king. The other side tried vainly to reassure

---

[36] Gachard, *Actes des Etats Généraux*, vol. II, 34.
[37] Groen van Prinsterer, *Archives*, 494–7.
[38] Japikse, *Resolutiën*, vol. I, 43.
[39] Sometimes called the Perpetual Edict.
[40] 'Vraye narration de costé et d'aultre entre les députez de don Jehan et monseigneur le prince et députez d'Hollande et Zeelande, à Gheertrudenberghe, au mois mai 1577'. Griffiths, *Representative Government*, 454–62.

them. Leoninus voiced the common reasoning against government by a large assembly and pointed to France, where the assemblies of the estates had engendered more dissensions and wars than there had been before. Orange countered that this had happened in France because of the 'partisanship and partialities of the [noble] houses', whereas in the Netherlands everyone was agreed on the Pacification of Ghent. Evidently, not everyone was. The atmosphere of the debate deteriorated until Orange exclaimed that they would not submit to the States General deciding the matter of religion because 'you want to annihilate us and we do not want to be annihilated' (*extirpés*). 'Ho', said the duke of Aerschot, 'no one wants that.' After this exchange Orange calmed down, but the debate petered out and the lawyers had a field day, discussing (in Latin for the benefit of the emperor's envoy) how far anyone who had made a law could break it. Evidently, the lawyers had formulated many of the arguments of reason of state before the political philosophers got round to discussing them.

At the same time, Don John's relations with those members of the States General who accepted the conditions of preserving the Catholic religion and the king's sovereignty remained bad. The Estates of Brabant accepted Don John only by majority vote in a late-night session, when most deputies had already gone home.[41] He did not come to Brussels until 3 May. He insisted that only he had the right to summon the Estates. He complained that he could never rely on any opinion because it would be denied the next moment and he compared himself to a tennis ball, struck from one side of the net to the other.[42] It was all the fault of Orange and of England, he wrote to the king. He was correct about the confusion on the side of the States General, but he had his own reasons for exaggerating the evil influence of Queen Elizabeth. He was still dreaming of invading England and of liberating and marrying Mary Stuart. In fact, the States General sent an embassy to London which found the English court distinctly lukewarm to their cause.

The Netherlands were becoming ungovernable. Individual governors of provinces and commanders of the regiments of the States General's troops or of the still unpaid and marauding German soldiers refused to take orders from anyone. Don John was too intelligent not to realise that he himself contributed to the universal distrust. He railed against the deputies of the States General and sometimes uttered blood-curdling threats if they did not submit to the king. More reasonably, he also suggested they should ask the king for another governor general. Orange hated the king, he wrote to Philip, and would drink his blood if he could.[43]

After only a month in Brussels, Don John left again for Namur. On 24 July he entered the citadel of Namur with his own troops, ostensibly for his personal

---

[41] L. Delfos, *Die Anfänge der Utrechter Union 1577–1587* (Berlin, 1941), 39–40.
[42] Janssens, *Brabant in het Verweer*, 335–7.
[43] J. Lefèvre, *Correspondance de Philippe II sur les affaires des Pays-Bas*, pt. 2, vol. I (Brussels, 1940). Don John to Philip II, 28 July 1577.

safety, and he promptly recalled the Spanish troops from Italy. The king's reaction was as usual confused. He accepted his brother's characterisation of the situation in the Netherlands but he was fearful of the reaction of the neighbouring states, in case war broke out again. He alone had the right to take decisions on the recall of the Spanish troops, he wrote severely to Don John. But his closest advisers, Alba and even Quiroga, insisted on a hard line. There was now peace in the Mediterranean and a treasure fleet from Peru had just arrived. Before the end of Angust Philip gave permission for the Spanish troops to return.[44] Don John's negotiations with the States General came to nothing. It seems doubtful whether he had ever meant them seriously after his Namur coup. Aerschot felt betrayed and fled from Namur. After all, Elizabeth I's envoy had rightly dubbed the Pacification of Ghent 'the Peace of the duke of Aerschot', perhaps in analogy to the 'Peace of Monsieur' (i.e. the duke of Alençon) in France in 1576. Both treaties represented the high water mark of the Politiques, those Catholics who wanted to overcome the murderous hostility of Catholics and Protestants. The States General knew that Don John was in touch with the duke of Guise. On 23 September the prince of Orange made his triumphal entry into Brussels, and on 8 October the States General formally broke with Don John.[45]

THE INTERVENTION OF THE COMMON PEOPLE

Both sides realised that the renewed war would now be a real civil war and that they would need more support than that of the established political and administrative elites and of the professional mercenary troops they were able to raise and pay for – or, as usual, not pay for. Don John was pessimistic about this: the people always followed those they thought would win and were concerned only with their own interests; and this made them partisans of the Estates.[46] The States General told Don John that he was responsible for the fact that the people were arming themselves; for his intercepted letters showed that the Spaniards had for a long time been planning 'the total extermination of the inhabitants of this country'.[47]

William of Orange deliberately courted the common people, as he had already done in Holland since 1572. In November 1576 he addressed the States General as 'representing the universal body of all the people'.[48] In August 1577 he made this point again, writing of the 'obligation which they [the States General] had towards the entire body of all the people'.[49] It was about this time that the Orangeists began

---

[44] Philip II to Don John, 1 Sept. 1577. *Ibid.*, 40. Janssens, *Brabant in het Verweer*, 243. Parker, *The Grand Strategy of Philip II*, 145.
[45] Gachard, *Actes des Etats Généraux*, vol. II, 265–6.
[46] Don John to Philip II, Namur, 4 Aug. 1577. Lefèvre, *Correspondance*, vol. II, 22.
[47] States General to Don John, Brussels, 24 Oct. 1577. Japikse, *Resolutiën*, vol. I, 239.
[48] Griffiths, *Representative Government*, 432.
[49] Gachard, *Actes des Etats Généraux*, vol. II, 214.

to call themselves Patriots. All this was very different from the obligation to maintain the Catholic religion, which was what the States General had been talking about, even after Don John's coup. Marnix looked to the Swiss cantons as a model for the Netherlands, and the Swiss were at that time regarded as very democratic.[50]

While such views were populist, no one thought in terms of equal votes for all individuals. In Brussels, where Orange had the most vocal popular support, it was the guilds, led by the guild masters who formed a Committee of Eighteen. This committee dominated, and indeed sometimes organised mobs to terrorise, the municipality, the Estates of Brabant and the States General. On the 18 October they bullied these bodies to accept Orange as governor (*ruwaard*, *surintendant*) of Brabant, a position traditionally reserved for the king's governor general.

Orange had therefore succeeded in gaining a position he had attempted but failed to gain in 1562.[51] But, just as fifteen years earlier, the duke of Aerschot felt himself slighted, both as a Catholic and as a great Brabant magnate. From his position as governor of Flanders, Aerschot tried to get the nobility and clergy of that province to condemn the prince of Orange as *ruwaard* of Brabant. But Orange outmanoeuvred him by another appeal to the populace, this time of Ghent, where Aerschot had gone. More than anywhere else in the southern Netherlands the Calvinist preachers had made converts in Ghent, the city with a large discontented proletariat and a long and well-remembered revolutionary tradition. On 28 October their leaders in the city council, Jan van Hembyze and the lord of Rijhove, arrested the duke, probably at the instigation of Marnix. They organised a popular militia and a Committee of Eighteen on the Brussels model.

This was a real popular revolution, and there were similar revolutions in other large cities in Brabant, notably Antwerp and 's-Hertogenbosch. All the classic conditions for popular revolutions were present. The unpaid Spanish soldiers had not only sacked Antwerp but levied heavy contributions on countless small towns in Brabant and Flanders with the threat of sacking and burning. The practice was called 'brandschatting' or in modern mafia language, protection money. From the countryside and the villages terrified peasants and their families fled to the larger and apparently safer cities, only to fall victim to rapidly spreading epidemics. We have price series for agricultural rents in Flanders and these stop abruptly in 1578–9. Industrial production of the famous 'new draperies' in the Flemish countryside had held up well until the late 1570s. From then it took a nose-dive.[52] The result was more unemployment and more migration into the cities to swell the urban unemployed and discontented populace.

[50] Swart, *Willem van Oranje*, 122–3. Cf. Brady, *Turning Swiss*, *passim*. R. C. Head, *Early Modern Democracy in the Grisons* (Cambridge, 1995), *passim*.
[51] Koenigsberger, *Politicians and Virtuosi*, 103. Janssens, *Brabant in het Verweer*, 357–8.
[52] E. van Cauwenberghe, 'De economische Ontwikkeling in de Nederlanden', in Baelde and Peteghem, *Opstand en Pacificatie*, 173–83. Such figures as we have, however, are patchy and contradictory. Cf. C. Verlinden, 'En Flandre sous Philippe II: Durée de la crise économique', *Annales*, 7, 1 (1952), 21–30.

Monarchies, States Generals and Parliaments

In every case of urban unrest the States General exercised the sovereign power of granting the restoration of the old urban privileges which had been abrogated by Charles V or the duke of Alba.[53] Curiously enough, Ghent got back only to the position of 1539, just before its rebellion against Charles V and did not get back its much more extensive privileges from before the Peace of Cadzant. But it was enough and it had been Aerschot's mishandling of Ghent's demands – he had called Hembyze and his colleagues rioters who deserved the gallows – which had led to his arrest.[54] The duke was soon released. But the Orange–Aerschot alliance, so effective up until then, was broken.

Many political theorists since the middle ages or even since the ancient world of Greece and Rome had warned against the fickleness of popular opinion. Orange and his classically educated and mostly aristocratic and patrician entourage were well aware of their warning. Moreover, Orange could not afford to offend his principal allies, the nobles and the patricians who were represented in the States General. A purely populist policy was therefore out of the question. Thus in October 1577 he warned his followers in Brussels to leave the actual government of the country to the States General. What he needed was an organisation, a party which could span different social groups and which was completely reliable. Already a year earlier, in October 1576, Orange had proposed an indissoluble union of all provinces. All seigneurs and gentlemen were to oblige themselves to preserve the liberty of the fatherland (*patrie*) to the last drop of their blood for the expulsion of the Spaniards. They were to undertake this 'on pain of eternal infamy and to be reputed as enemies of the fatherland'. Orange demanded that the States General organise a general council, made up of gentlemen and others from each province, and with authority to administer all matters of state and government in the name of the States General.[55]

The proposal of a union or league whose members were to take an oath to pursue a certain policy and who were to be punished by infamy and death if they broke their oath went far beyond the question of the competence or efficiency of the States General. It looks rather as if it was an attempt to imitate the religious–political leagues which had sprung up in France. There they had proved to be extraordinarily effective political organisations in the hands of the leaders of the opposed parties, Catholic and Huguenot.[56] The obligations of the members of these leagues far surpassed the normal obligations of vassals or subjects to their

---

[53] For this series of events see Parker, *The Dutch Revolt*, 185–6. Koenigsberger, *The Habsburgs and Europe*, 142.

[54] See above, ch. 3. Delfos, *Die Anfänge der Utrechter Union*, 53.

[55] 'L'advis de Monseigneur le Prince d'Oranges...' probably middle of October 1576. Groen van Prinsterer, *Archives*, 436–40.

[56] Koenigsberger, 'The Organisation of Revolutionary Parties in France and the Netherlands during the Sixteenth Century', in *Estates and Revolutions*, 224–52. Cf. P. Prodi, *Glaube und Eid: Treueformeln, Glaubensbekenntnisse und Sozialdisziplinierung zwischen Mittelalter und Neuzeit* (Munich, 1993), *passim*.

prince. Princes therefore tried to use such leagues as reinforcements or even as alternatives to the traditional ways of increasing their power through control of taxation, of law courts and of the usual forms of princely patronage. Thus, after his victory over the Schmalkaldic League of German Protestant princes and cities, Charles V proposed leagues in Germany, rather like the late medieval Swabian League. The German princes, however, were quite unwilling to grant the powers they had willingly given to a union which defended their interests and which they controlled themselves to the emperor *qua* head of the confederal polity of the Holy Roman Empire. Henry III of France had a similar experience when he tried to make himself head of a Catholic League. The League dissolved in his hands, to be reconstituted later, when it was specifically directed against him.

The Union of Brussels, of January 1577, had some aspects of such leagues and in August 1577, just after Don John's coup, passed an act very much in line with Orange's proposals. The French leagues confined themselves deliberately to either Catholics or Huguenots. Such uni-religious organisations were precisely what Orange wanted to avoid in the Netherlands. Obviously, the king would not attempt to make himself head of a multi-religious league and there was therefore no danger of the monarchical dissolving effect on leagues, which was so evident in France. But even without this danger, could such an organisation work? Before this question could be fully answered or rather fully experienced, the duke of Aerschot attempted another solution to the political problems of the Netherlands.

ARCHDUKE MATTHIAS AND THE VISION OF PARLIAMENTARY GOVERNMENT

Even before the breach between Aerschot and Orange had become open, the duke and his party had started negotiating with the new emperor, Rudolph II, to invite his brother, the archduke Matthias, Philip II's nephew, to become governor general of the Netherlands in succession to Don John of Austria. Aerschot and Matthias have had a bad press, both from their contemporaries and from modern historians. It is easy to see why. In the first place, the experiment failed, and it was not a heroic failure. Neither the duke nor the archduke became martyrs to a splendid cause, like Egmont and Hoorn and, later, William of Orange. In the second place, their cause did not triumph after their deaths, or at least so it seemed. Contemporaries rejected it and for later historians it did not fit into the comfortable teleology of a Protestant and nationalist history of the United Provinces nor of a Catholic and royalist loyalism of the southern provinces, Belgium. And yet, in sixteenth-century terms, their aims were both reasonable and humane.

Aerschot was seeking to establish what Orange, Egmont and Hoorn had striven for during the regency of Margaret of Parma: the Netherlands ruled by law and its ancient traditions, with the myriad privileges of its provinces and corporations respected and upheld, with no one persecuted for his beliefs, provided he accepted at least the outward forms of the Catholic religion; a country governed by its natural governors, the high nobility, in loyal relation with their hereditary prince and with his composite monarchy in which they expected the interests of the Netherlands would count for as much as those of the king's Spanish and Italian dominions. It went without saying that in this polity the Croy would play their traditional role of principal advisers to the king and his regent, a role which the family had played for the last hundred years. What more reasonable, therefore, that, in good Netherlands tradition, the head of the House of Croy should lead the States General to choose a governor general from within the royal family, but without the odour of Spanish militarism which Don John of Austria had exuded from the moment of his arrival? Had not Don John himself suggested that the States General should ask the king to send another 'prince of the blood' in his place? And while of course nobody could foresee this, some twenty years later King Philip himself opted for a similar solution when he made over the Netherlands to his daughter Isabella and her husband, the archduke Albert, younger brother of Matthias.

The archduke Matthias is more difficult to place. He was the son of Philip's and Don John's sister Mary who had married the emperor Maximilian II and was a lady of rigidly Catholic piety. Yet, as a young man, Matthias was exposed to a court in which there was an influential party seeking peace and compromise with the Protestants. Like their spiritual father, Erasmus, they believed not so much in toleration as in the need to find an inclusive and peaceful middle way between the religious beliefs of the time.[57] The emperor Maximilian II had once famously declared that he was neither a Protestant nor a Catholic but a Christian.[58] Madrid had always regarded him with great suspicion, not only for religious reasons but because it was he, even more than his father, Ferdinand I, who had blocked Philip's succession to the Empire.[59] Moreover, in deference to opinion in the Holy Roman Empire, he had not joined the 'Holy League' of Spain, the pope and Venice against the Turks in 1572. The Vienna Habsburgs had taken no direct part in the glorious Catholic victory of Lepanto. Nevertheless, Maximilian never wholeheartedly supported the Erasmian group at his court, in spite of his undoubted sympathy for their views. At the end of his reign they were already losing influence to the Jesuits. When the negotiations between Aerschot and Matthias came to fruition, in the autumn of 1577, Maximilian II was already dead.

The new emperor, Rudolph II, brought up at Philip II's court, was much more definitely a Catholic, and he had not been informed of his brother's plans until the last moment. For the Erasmians in Vienna, the States General's invitation to Matthias seemed to be their great chance in an otherwise deteriorating situation.

---

[57] H. Louthan, *The Quest for Compromise: Peacemakers in Counter-Reformation Vienna* (Cambridge, 1997), *passim*.
[58] *Ibid.*, 3.
[59] See above.

Rule by the States General: myths and realities

For Rudolph it was a much more difficult matter. He had to consider the opinion of the German princes, and this opinion was divided. Many of the princes, in their turn, had to consider the opinion of their subjects, or at least of the most influential of them. Many of these were Protestants, mainly Lutherans. Even many of those who were Catholics had considerable sympathy for the Netherlanders' aversion to the Inquisition, which they mostly seemed to have thought of, influenced no doubt by Orangeist propaganda, as the Spanish Inquisition, and for the Netherlanders' fight for the defence of their privileges against 'Spanish tyranny'. All the same, Emperor Rudolph could hardly give his brother unqualified support; but he could try to mediate.

In the Netherlands Matthias arrived to great acclaim, much of it based simply on hope. In Vienna his backers had been a handful of gifted professionals, perhaps most strikingly characterised in Titian's famous portrait of one of them, the architect and designer Jacopo Strada, shown as the quintessential aesthete.[60] They had no constituency of their own. They were a court party, dependent on the somewhat wayward emperor Maximilian II. Matthias, having left Vienna almost surreptitiously, arrived in the Netherlands even more alone than Don John had done a year earlier, and without Don John's legal and moral backing of the king. Even Lazarus Schwendi, his most experienced political adviser and the only one of his circle with international military and diplomatic experience, did not accompany him.

Matthias, without a strong personality himself, without political experience and without any knowledge of the complexities of the Netherlands situation, was therefore bound to become the pawn of one of the strong personalities of the Brussels scene. This should have been the role of the duke of Aerschot who had invited him. In fact, almost immediately Aerschot was outmanoeuvred and sidelined, both on a personal and on a political level, by the charismatic figure of William of Orange. Very rapidly the Orangeists produced a draft for the conditions of the reception of Matthias as governor general. The draft had to be sent to the separate provincial assemblies, and it was not until 8 December 1577 that the States General accepted the 'Conditions'.[61]

Both in their form and in their content the Conditions followed the precedents established by the Estates of Holland in 1572 and in the following years, together with the obligatory bow to the Pacification of Ghent which the new governor general was specifically required to uphold. The preamble therefore repeated the fiction that the States General were acting in the name of the king and for the sake of upholding the Catholic religion. But immediately, in articles 1 and 2, the power relationship was spelt out: the governor general and the governors of the provinces and of the cities, and all colonels and captains, were to take their oaths to both the king and the States General. The governor general was to govern with a Council of

---
[60] Now in the Kunsthistorisches Museum, Vienna.
[61] Griffiths, *Representative Government*, 463–8.

State which, while formally in the king's provision, could be chosen only from the persons designated by the States General (articles 4–7). The obligation to govern only with a council appointed by the king was entirely traditional. Charles V and Philip II had always insisted on this point in their instructions to their regents. Indeed, it was part of the common currency of princely ethics that a Christian ruler took important decisions only with the advice of trusted councillors. This was always a convenient safeguard for the prince. Even at that time in the Netherlands people still blamed Granvelle and Alba rather than King Philip for the 'Spanish tyranny'. What was new in the Conditions was that now even officially the ministers were chosen by the States General. Earlier States Generals had made such demands and, as at the time of Maximilian I's regency, they had on occasion even been successful in imposing their nominees. But the Habsburg rulers had never accepted such a practice as a matter of principle. Now, by articles 18 to 22, this States-General-appointed council was to make all military and financial appointments. It was also to handle all foreign alliances (article 23) and especially relations with the Holy Roman Empire (article 28). The States General were to remain in session according to their own judgement and meet whenever they thought fit (article 13).

None of these conditions were entirely new. Every one of them had been proposed by the States General at some time or other during the previous hundred years. However, taken altogether, they amounted to a constitution which was clearly revolutionary, for it transferred effective political power from the monarch to the representative assembly. Don John, for one, said this in so many words. The one really new constitutional problem which the Conditions threw up was the relationship between the States General and the Estates of the individual provinces in this new situation of parliamentary government in a confederal polity. Article 8 confirmed that the governor general and his council must not take any decisions of importance, such as the imposition of taxes, declarations of war or foreign alliances, nor should they issue important placards or ordinances without the consent of the States General nor 'the advice and agreement of the Estates, legitimately assembled for this purpose and according to their habits and customs, in each province [forming part of] the States General when this becomes necessary'.[62]

This was a thoroughly confusing statement and this confusion may well have been deliberate because the authors of the Conditions were unwilling openly to face the almost insoluble problem of the relations between the States General and the provincial Estates. For, once the governor general and his council were acknowledged to have become completely dependent on the States General, this body could no longer be regarded as functioning simply, or even mainly, as a

---

[62] *Ibid.*, 465. 'Ledict Gouverneur et conseil ne feront chose dimportance et qui concerne la généralité... sans consentement des Estatz généraux... sans en avoir ladvis et accord des Estatz sur et legittement assemblez respectivement en chacune province selon les fachons et coustumes dicelle mesmes des Estatz generaux si besoing est.'

Rule by the States General: myths and realities

delegation of the provincial Estates. It was bound to develop a mind and policies of its own. Effectively, this had been so since the Estates of Brabant and Hainaut had summoned the States General in August 1576. Now this fact was acknowledged in the very confusion of article 8 of the Conditions agreed to with Matthias. Or was this matter imposed on him? Again, this point remained happily obscure.

The confusion surfaced immediately at the point where it was bound to do so: the religious clauses of the Pacification of Ghent. In fifteen of the seventeen provinces the Pacification had been accepted precisely because it had promised to maintain the Catholic religion. In the other two provinces, Holland and Zeeland, Catholic worship was to be at least tolerated. But toleration had simply not been observed, even though the principle of mutual toleration had been reiterated, after heated debate, by the States General in the so-called Second Union of Brussels (10 December 1577). In many cities of Holland and Zeeland Catholic worship was effectively outlawed. In Amsterdam, in May 1578, the previously exiled city councillors and the Calvinists carried out a successful coup in this city whose council had until then remained Catholic and royalist. About the same time Haarlem and other remaining royalist centres fell to the Orangeists.

Worse still, from the Catholic point of view, was the spread of Calvinism in the southern provinces. Its centre now was Ghent. In the earlier popular revolutions in Ghent religion had played very little part. It was mainly the opponents of the Ghent revolutionaries who had accused them of heterodoxy. This was a common pattern of anti-revolutionary propaganda which had been used even against such obviously orthodox Catholics as the Comuneros of Castile, in 1519–20. But in Flanders, in the spring and summer of 1578, economic misery, traditional revolutionary passion and religious ardour did combine in an explosive mixture. The Ghenters set up a Council of Eighteen, on the Brussels model, and carried their populist and Calvinist revolution through the length and breadth of Flanders and its big cities. In Brussels, however, the Council of Eighteen remained firmly Catholic, according to the age-old religious traditions of their masters, the guilds.[63] There was no simple correlation between Calvinism and popular revolution in the Netherlands, any more than there was in France.

Orange and his circle saw the problem clearly enough. Both the Catholics and the Calvinists still hoped that they could convert the other side. By conversion they meant, in practice, the imposition of their own doctrines. The only alternative which had become thinkable was a religious peace (*Religionsvrede, Religionsfrieden*). At the time this seemed to be working in Germany, following the Peace of Augsburg, with its *cuius regio eius religio* principle, i.e. religion depending on the preference of the prince. It was a corollary of this principle that individuals who did not accept the religion of their prince would emigrate to a principality more congenial to their beliefs. It was a characteristic arrangement between autonomous princes and,

[63] Griffiths, *William of Hornes*, 69.

significantly, the position of the autonomous cities remained obscure, an obscurity which contributed to the eventual breakdown of the Augsburg system in the seventeenth century.

In France similar arrangements were being tried out, and while cities were clearly included in these treaties, these were characteristically still arrangements between sections of the ruling elites. But, unlike the Holy Roman Empire, France was politically too integrated and the religious–political parties spanned too obviously different social classes for such convenient religious divisions to be viable. The *Religionsfrieden*, the peace treaties, never lasted for more than a few years, at least not until, in the late 1590s, religious divisions had concentrated themselves in relatively clearly defined geographical areas, and the fight against Spanish interference had become as overwhelmingly important to most of the nation as it was in the Netherlands in 1576.

With a German governor general and with an eye on the apparently happy experience of the Holy Roman Empire, William of Orange tried to solve the Netherlands problem by introducing the Augsburg system in the seventeen provinces. At the same time he tried to associate the widest sections of the population with his anti-Spanish policies. The second Union of Brussels was to be signed by all persons in secular or ecclesiastical authority and by propertied persons in the towns and villages.[64] Marnix was fascinated by the Swiss cantons and by what was regarded at the time as Swiss democracy[65] and the ability of Protestant and Catholic cantons to live peacefully side by side. But the Netherlands provinces were not politically or economically as independent from each other as the Swiss cantons. The populist movements of the cities, especially in Brussels, found it difficult to distinguish between the States General, representing each and all of the provinces, and the Council of State as an executive organ in which some of the provinces, notably Flanders, Holland and Zeeland, were not represented at all. The functioning of an effective parliamentary government in a composite state had not been fully thought out, because the different players all had different goals in view. Unsurprisingly, therefore, the States General rejected Orange's plans of a *Religionsfrieden*. Too many people still believed in the aims of the Pacification of Ghent, the reconciliation of religious differences, rather than their peaceful coexistence.

They did not believe in a religious peace in Madrid either. Philip II and his father Charles V had refused to sign the Peace of Augsburg and Philip had said, on many occasions, that he would never accept it for his own subjects. This did not mean that outside his own dominions he would necessarily engage in a Catholic crusade. Such a crusade was feared by some, especially in France. In the neighbouring kingdom he had indeed interfered, with a greater or lesser commitment of

---

[64] 'Het Cort verhaal ende gherechte Oorsaecken ende Redenen, die de Generale Staten der Nederlanden ghedwongen hebben, he te versiene tot haerder beschermenisse, teghen den Heere Don Iehan van Oostenrijk.' B.L. *Tracts*, T 1721, no. 6. fos. 83–4.
[65] Swart, *Willem van Oranje*, 122–3.

Rule by the States General: myths and realities

his resources, since the beginning of the French civil wars in the early 1560s. His avowed justification was always the danger of heresy spreading to his own dominions, especially the Netherlands. These fears were certainly not ungrounded and nor were their political implications. In the resulting actions, as Philip's support for the duke of Alba had shown, he felt justified in breaking his own promises and the public laws to which he had sworn adherence at his coronations, his 'joyous entries'.

Further afield, some people were willing to give him the benefit of all doubts. At one point, it seems, the Lutheran elector of Saxony even suggested Philip of Spain should be chosen as the next emperor. The laws of the Holy Roman Empire, which of course he would have to swear to observe, would force him to come to terms with the provinces of the Netherlands which were part of the Holy Roman Empire.[66] Whatever the elector may have imagined, the other German princes would have been most unlikely to accept this unrealistic argument. What many of them, including several of the Catholic ecclesiastical princes, did support was the proposal by the emperor Rudoph II to mediate between Philip and the Netherlands States General.[67]

THE CONFERENCE OF COLOGNE AND THE FAILURE OF COMPROMISE

While in Madrid the ultimate rejection of a religious peace was never questioned, there remained almost as much confusion about everything else as in the Netherlands. Through the spring and summer of 1578 a junta of Philip's Council of State discussed the whole problem of the Netherlands. There was never any question of accepting the archduke Matthias as governor general. That would have been an intolerable infringement of the king's sovereignty. When Don John of Austria was dying, in September 1578, he nominated the king's nephew, Alexander Farnese, prince and later duke of Parma, as his successor. Philip, perhaps out of relief at the demise of a brother whose ambitions he distrusted, was willing to accept Don John's nomination. At least it was his appointment and not, like Matthias, that of some lordlings who were his subjects. In the event, Parma was by far the best appointment Philip could have made. As a politician he was in the class of William of Orange; as a general he was as superior to him as the duke of Alba had been. Although, as an Italian, Parma always had enemies in Madrid, Philip did not seriously begin to distrust him until after the disaster of the Armada in 1588.

The Pacification of Ghent was a different matter. It had been accepted at least in the slightly modified form of the Perpetual Edict by the king's legally appointed governor general, Don John of Austria. Perhaps this was the reason why the

---

[66] I owe this curious point to Dr Thomas Froeschl, Vienna.
[67] Cf. T. Froeschl, 'In Frieden, Ainigkeit und Ruhe beieinander sitzen: Das heilige römische Reich und die Politik Kaiser Rudolfs II im ersten Jahrzehnt seiner Regierung, 1576–86' (Habilitationsschrift for the University of Vienna, 1997), 240–65. My thanks to Dr Froeschl for making this typescript available to me.

discussion in the Council of State hardly touched upon the detailed role of the States General in the actual government of the country. This role had been a central issue for the framers of the Pacification and, even more, for the authors of the 'Conditions' imposed on Matthias. What primarily concerned the Spanish junta was how to preserve the Catholic religion. The role of the States General would be automatically reduced again to the important but clearly subordinate position it had occupied during the reign of Charles V. After all, everyone had agreed to wanting to return to the emperor's good old days, except of course the heretics of Holland and Zeeland.

But all this was aspiration, not a political programme. The Spaniards were no clearer about what was meant in concrete terms by the privileges and political conditions of this supposed golden age than were the Netherlanders; nor did they consider the political changes which had taken place during the emperor's long reign. There were the hardliners, inevitably led by the duke of Alba, who thought that only military action, followed by a strict application of the precepts of the Council of Trent, especially in education, could restore the king's position and that of the Catholic religion. Some thought that the States General should be lured into a false sense of security by the promise of concessions which would induce them to give up their arms. Such views were not new, and no doubt Iñigo Velasco, the constable of Castile, he who during the Comunero revolt had advised Charles V not to be afraid of paper and ink, would have approved. The majority of the junta, however, advised accepting the emperor's mediation. For them too religion remained the central issue. The implications of accepting the States General as a negotiating partner were not discussed at all. In so far as politics came into the matter, it was the fear of foreign intervention, especially from France and England. From the beginning of the revolt there had been talk in the Netherlands of making their country over to another prince, perhaps one from the Vienna branch of the Habsburgs or even a Frenchman or other foreigner. In 1578 the triumphal reception of Archduke Matthias and the spasmodic interventions by the duke of Angoulême/Anjou in Hainaut, or even of complete outsiders such as the Calvinist count John Casimir of the Palatinate in Flanders – all these events made these fears of the Spaniards seem far from groundless.

By March 1579 all sides, whatever their misgivings, were at least willing to engage in negotiations with the imperial mediators. The king's delegation was led by Carlo d'Aragona, duke of Terranova. Related to a collateral branch of the royal House of Aragon he was the greatest landowner in Sicily and had twice served as viceroy of that kingdom.[68] Unlike nearly all other viceroys of Sicily he had managed to retain his reputation both in the island and among an influential party at the king's court in Madrid.[69]

[68] Strictly, his title had been president because Sicilians were not granted the title of viceroy when they served in that position in Sicily.
[69] Koenigsberger, *The Practice of Empire*, 182–3.

Rule by the States General: myths and realities

The conference which finally met in Cologne did not, however, give Terranova the chance to shine as a diplomat or negotiator. He did not, like Don John, heap abuse on the States General, but he was strictly bound by the instructions given him by the king and by Parma who was himself no great believer in the value of the conference. The delegations met in separate rooms,[70] providing probably one of the first instances of shuttle diplomacy. This was in itself a measure of the effect of religious conflict through the involvement of large sections of the general public in politics. For shuttle diplomacy allowed the parties to negotiate while claiming that they had no face-to-face dealing with the devil, i.e. with those of the opposed religion. This practice of gesture politics was to reach its apogee in the negotiations in two separate towns, Münster (Catholics) and Osnabrück (Protestants), which ended the Thirty Years War with five years of negotiations. After 1648 shuttle diplomacy seems to have been given up, only to be resumed in the second half of the twentieth century.

At the beginning of the conference the royalist side was willing to make extraordinary concessions to the archdevil. If Orange would leave the Netherlands, he was offered a large sum of money, the payment of his debts and the return of his eldest son who was being held and educated in Spain. Orange was at first willing to engage in such negotiations. As so often in his career, it is difficult to know his ultimate aims. Did he really think he could get enough from the king or was he making a demonstration of loyalty to his own side by rejecting the king's apparently very generous terms? Conversely, how sincere was Philip with his offer? At any rate, this was not what the delegations in Cologne were negotiating about.

The final break came in the autumn, after it had become clear that the two sides meant opposite and incompatible things by adherence to the Pacification of Ghent. For the king the freedom of religion given to Holland and Zeeland could never be permanent, even though he was now willing to allow the Protestants four years to sell their property and emigrate. At least in the long run he would not have to rule over heretics. For the Protestants, forced emigration, even on these more generous terms, remained unacceptable, the more so as by now Calvinism had spread widely outside the two provinces.

Just as impossible was a return to the political regime of Charles V. For this would have meant the return of the States General to virtual impotence in important political and religious issues. The States delegation had proposed the legal extension of the Brabant *joyeuse entrée*, a claim which had been voiced throughout the revolt. But the *joyeuse entrée* specifically allowed the right of resistance; and how could that be exercised if the States General were to hand back the control of the fortresses and the armed forces to the king? Even if the king agreed once more to withdraw his Spanish troops, he would still have all the levers of military control in his hands. This was precisely what was to happen in the Union of Arras.

---

[70] Louthan, *The Quest for Compromise*, 150.

In the autumn of 1579 the conference broke up. The reasons lay basically not in the personalities of the delegates, the clumsy practice of shuttle diplomacy or the awkwardness of the need to refer major points back not only to the States General but to the separate provincial Estates. It was rather that the two sides insisted on fundamentally incompatible positions, and that the Orangeists, both Protestant and Catholic on the one side, and the royalists on the other, did not trust each other. An accommodation on the basis of the Pacification of Ghent was no longer possible. The importance of the conference of Cologne was not that it resolved anything. It did not do that. What it did was to clarify the positions and aims of the principal players. Only the imperial mediators had had hopes of success. But their position, and with it that of the compromisers, the moderate Catholics in the Netherlands such as the Estates of Tournai-Tournésis, had been undermined by the emperor Rudolph II himself. Matthias certainly realised this. In April 1579 he sent a special envoy to his brother, complaining of the lack of support he had had and warning the emperor that the majority of the Estates no longer believed in the possibility of reconciliation with King Philip. The House of Austria was in danger of losing the Netherlands altogether, for they were likely to choose another prince and he, Matthias, would be sent home 'in shame and mockery'.[71]

Perhaps Matthias' memorandum was drafted by Orange. It was certainly an accurate forecast of future events and it put its finger on the central weakness of the archduke's position as governor general: without the emperor's active support he would never have a party of his own in the Netherlands. Rudolph, for his part, could not afford such support without risking a breach with King Philip and isolation in the event of a renewed Turkish offensive in Hungary.

The different parties were all going their own way. The States General gave a vote of thanks to the arch-peacemaker, the duke of Aerschot, but excused itself from rewarding him further for his good services. In June 1580 Leoninus and the other members of the Netherlands Council of State handed their resignations to the States General. In July Matthias followed their example.[72]

THE UNION OF ARRAS

In the southern Netherlands support for the States General was fragmenting. Contemporaries had for many years observed a connection between economic discontent in the cities and revolutionary movements. Such movements could be either Calvinist-led, as in Ghent, or remain staunchly Catholic, as in Brussels. The difference would depend on the traditions of the particular city, especially the traditions of its guilds and on such contingencies as the effectiveness, or otherwise, of the popular preachers.

---

[71] Froeschl, 'In Frieden', 242.
[72] Gachard, *Actes des Etats Généraux*, vol. II, 316. J. C. H. de Pater, *De Raad van State nevens Matthias (1578–1581)*, (The Hague, 1917), 136–7.

Rule by the States General: myths and realities

For the nobility, the patricians and the country population there was very little economic correlation with political movements. For Hainaut it can be shown statistically that there was no long-term economic crisis for landowners.[73] It is likely that economic developments were similar in Artois and in at least parts of southern Brabant. In spite of its big cities and the huge metropolis of Antwerp, the censuses compiled in the 1570s for the duke of Alba's Hundredth Penny show that in Brabant only 10 per cent of all income derived from mobilia, and these included *rentes*.[74] The propertied classes and especially the nobility of these provinces had for a long time resented the government's encroachments on what was left of their feudal rights of jurisdiction, rights which could be a considerable source of income. But basically these classes were conservative and royalist, and they had supported the States General and its claims because they had come to hate the duke of Alba and his Spanish troops. By 1578 it had become clear that the Pacification of Ghent did not restore the *status quo ante* and that heresy was spreading in the southern provinces. The Ghenters were spreading their Calvinist beliefs throughout Flanders and often linked them with attacks on the local nobility. In the name of 'the people', they were imposing a worse tyranny than that of the Spaniards, the seigneur de Masnuy wrote to the prince of Orange in December 1578.[75] Many of the Walloon cities followed Ghent's example, or were forced to do so by the Ghenters, in setting up revolutionary committees. Commanders of towns and local commanders of the States General's troops manoeuvred against each other. Families split in their allegiances. The duke of Anjou had established himself in Hainaut. John Casimir of the Palatinate, the Calvinist *condottiere*, was called in by the Ghenters. Both brought their own largely unpaid and marauding troops with them. Both maintained varying political and financial relations with the governors of the provinces and with Orange and the queen of England.[76]

A number of noble commanders of unpaid troops joined their soldiers, first in demanding their back pay from the States General and, when the money was not forthcoming, in breaking with the States General and making contact with the royalists or the duke of Anjou.[77] They called themselves the Malcontents and they have been compared, rather generously, with the Politiques in contemporary France. In practice, their aims were as confused as those of the other parties. At least one of their leaders, William of Hoorn, lord of Hèze, and a relative of Alba's famous victim, Count Hoorn, made one switch of sides too many when he later moved back to the States General. Parma had him arrested and executed for treason.

[73] Koenigsberger, 'Property and the Price Revolution (Hainault, 1474–1573)', in *Estates and Revolutions*, 144–65.
[74] Arnould, 'Impot sur le capital en Belgique au XVIe siècle', 44 and *passim*.
[75] L. P. Gachard, *Correspondance de Guillaume le Taciturne*, 6 vols. (Brussels, 1847–66), vol. IV, 130–1.
[76] For a detailed history of this confused period, see for instance C. H. Th. Bussemaker, *De Afscheiding der Waalsche Gewesten van de Generale Unie* (Haarlem, 1895). Griffiths, *William of Hornes*.
[77] *Exhortation faite par Monseigneur l'Archiduc... aux Etats généraux... 11 avril 1579* (Antwerp, 1579).

The leaders of the States General had no clear, or only partially effective, answers to these problems. In December 1578 Orange and his patrician allies in Ghent engineered a coup against the radicals. But it was too late to reconcile the disgruntled nobles. In April 1579 Matthias still urged the States General to establish a closer union of the provinces and to give their deputies 'sufficient authority to listen to, debate and if necessary determine and resolve all occurrences'. Dr Leoninus followed this up with the argument that it was not the insufficient forces of the provinces but their lack of cooperation which had caused all the damage and prevented the relief of Maastricht, besieged by Parma.[78] Nor was Orange's plan for a religious peace able to reconcile the warring factions. It became itself a focus of dissension and strife. This was not the fault of the States General or of the limited powers of their deputies. On the contrary, they continued to act intelligently and expeditiously. Their weakness was that they could not impose themselves on the provincial Estates and on the other local powers. Their agents, both those travelling, as in Holland and Zeeland, and those resident in the localities, could not control the situation dominated by a plethora of warlords.

The king was well pleased with this situation. He wrote to Parma that the great division among the Estates was just what one would wish for, and Parma was to see to it that this division continued.[79] This was also the governor general's view. He had been willing to negotiate from the beginning. On 6 April 1579 the deputies of the provinces of Walloon Flanders wrote to the States General about their negotiations with Parma, arguing that their purpose was the expulsion of the Spaniards.[80] But already in January 1579, and largely on the initiative of the prelates of Artois, the Estates of that province, of Hainaut and of Walloon Flanders concluded the Union of Arras. In May 1579 they recognised the authority of the king again.

The 'Articles of Peace and Reconciliation' between the king and the provinces of Artois, Hainaut and Lille-Douai-Orchies, which made up the Treaty of Arras, began with a preamble detailing the reasons which led to this act and comprised twenty-seven articles. They started with a ringing declaration that the Pacification of Ghent and the Eternal Edict remained in force (article 1), followed by an equally emphatic commitment to the Catholic religion, but with an amnesty for all previous actions or words (article 2). Everything ordered by the archduke Matthias and all appointments made by him and confirmed by the Estates were to be recognised, except the appointments to the Council of State, the Finance and the Privy Councils (article 3). Most of the other articles dealt with military matters. All foreign troops were to be sent away by both sides and could be recalled only in case

---

[78] Marc Antonio Colonna, viceroy of Sicily, to Philip II, 24 May 1582. 'I have never seen Your Majesty's affairs in danger, or lost, for lack of money, men or munitions, but because there was an abundance in one part and want in another.' Archivo General de Simancas, MS Estado, legajo 1152.

[79] Philip II to Parma, Madrid, 15 Nov. 1578. Gachard, *Correspondance d'Alexandre Farnèse... avec Philippe II* (Brussels, 1853), 41.

[80] Gachard, *Actes des Etats Généraux*, vol. II, 175.

Rule by the States General: myths and realities

of foreign war or 'necessity recognised and approved by the said estates' (article 5). All military and political appointments were to be made with the advice of the Estates and the appointees were to take an oath to uphold the Catholic religion and the Pacification of Ghent. They were not to change or admit new garrisons without the advice of the Estates, although (again) 'necessity' could override this condition.

Parma's correspondence throughout 1579 does not suggest that he thought of this last clause as a loophole for a *coup d'état*; nor did the king. That it was an effective loophole became evident only in the following years of continuing civil war.

The governor general, the treaty proclaimed, should always be a prince of the blood. His or her Council of State were all to be native Netherlanders and two-thirds of their number had to be approved by the Estates. The many appointments of town magistrates which the prince of Orange had engineered were all revoked. But all old privileges were to be confirmed and especially that of no taxation without the consent of the Estates.[81]

With this treaty the nobility and the prelates appeared to have gained the idealised position of what they had been striving for during the regency of Margaret of Parma and the myth of the golden age of the emperor Charles V. In fact they went a good deal further than the reality of those times, in the restrictions they imposed on the government and the rights of assembly and control over appointments which were allowed to the Estates. The towns were less enthusiastic, and some, especially those in which Calvinism had spread, were openly hostile. As late as April 1578 there had been an Orangeist, but still largely Catholic, revolution in Arras. The city then concluded an alliance with the cities of St Omer, Béthune and Aire, directed against both Don John and the duke of Anjou.

The Union of Arras was not meant to be confined to the Walloon provinces, nor was it a self-consciously francophone alliance directed against the Flemish-Dutch-speaking provinces. Even before the actual signing of the treaty, in February 1579, the Estates of the Walloon provinces wrote to the States General in Antwerp asking them to join in the reconciliation. The States General replied that they were only 'proposing to cover the iron and chains of a Spanish servitude with the glitter of false gold'.[82]

Parma was pleased with the treaty, although he was well aware of the problems it would throw up. The king was much less pleased, especially about the military clauses. In spite of Parma's protests, he would not speak of 'reconciliation' but of

---

[81] *Articles de la Paix et Reconciliation faictes en la ville d'Arras le XVIIIe de May XVc LXXIX avec sa majesté par les Provinces d'Arthois, Haynault, Lille, Douay et Orchies* (Mons, 13 Sept. 1579). English translation by H. H. Rowen, *The Low Countries in Early Modern Times* (New York, 1972), 361–6, based on the text published by J. Dumont, *Corps universel diplomatique du droit des gens*, vol. V, pt. 1 (Amsterdam 1728), 350–5.

[82] *Lettres des Estats d'Arthois et des Deputés de Haynaut & Douay aux Deputés des Estats generaux des païs bas ... Avec la responce sur icelles donnée par desdits Deputés des Estats generaux* (Antwerp, 1579). Cf. Archduke Matthias to city of Valenciennes, 2 Oct. 1579. Gachard, *Actes des Etats Généraux*, vol. II, 270–1.

the provinces' 'reduction to obedience'. In the classic style of the self-righteous autocrat he blamed the provinces for all the evil which had befallen their country, while he himself had shown them exemplary clemency for their malevolence.[83]

The main reason why the Estates of the Walloon provinces had been able to achieve such relatively favourable terms for their 'reconciliation' was the presence in the Netherlands of the duke of Anjou. Immediately after the coup of September 1576, the Estates of Brabant Hainaut and Flanders had written to Henry III of France and his brother the duke of Alençon (later Anjou) for assistance against the Spaniards. In July 1578 Anjou entered Hainaut and in August the States General bestowed on him the title of 'Defender of the Liberties of the Low Countries'. He, in turn, promised to bring 12,000 troops.[84]

For Parma and the king this was a very sinister development. There were voices in the Netherlands urging a change of the ruling house. The German princes were highly alarmed, and this was one of the reasons why they and the emperor urged both sides at the conference of Cologne to compromise. Elizabeth I was also alarmed. For a long time it had been, and continued to be, English policy to prevent the Netherlands falling to the French. It was England which paid for the incursion of John Casimir of the Palatinate into Brabant as an ally of the Calvinist wing of the States General (August 1578). The civil war in the Netherlands had not only come to engage mercenaries from all over Europe – the Treaty of Arras even mentioned Albanians[85] – but it had become an all-European issue which the great powers were now fighting by proxy and, a few years later, directly. Very soon, Parma's and Philip's worst fears about Anjou's intervention were to be realised.

THE UNION OF UTRECHT AND THE ACT OF ABJURATION

At the same time as the Walloon provinces were negotiating their reconciliation with the king, the States General were engaged in a similar attempt in the doomed negotiations in Cologne. Also, at the same time, the war continued. More and more the States General occupied themselves with this problem. Orange continued to urge them to give the executive more power and to ensure the financial contributions from the provinces to finance their army. Here too, as in the Walloon provinces, the ambiguous presence of the duke of Anjou served to concentrate peoples' minds.

---

[83] Philip II to Parma, San Lorenzo de Escorial, 12 Sept. 1579. Gachard, *Correspondance d'Alexandre Farnèse*, 119–20.
[84] Parker, *The Dutch Revolt*, 191.
[85] Although in *Così fan tutte* da Ponte and Mozart treated the transformation of the girls' lovers into Albanian noblemen as a great joke the appearance of such personages in Western Europe was far from unheard of. Like other bored young men wanting to escape extreme poverty at home, the Albanians, like the Irish and the Scots, served in armies all over Europe in the early modern period.

Rule by the States General: myths and realities

It was in this context, rather than as an answer to the Union of Arras, nor in opposition to the States General, that the Union of Utrecht was formed. The preamble to the Act of Union stated expressly that it was formed not in order to split from the general union made by the Pacification of Ghent, but that the provinces which signed the Union should 'remain joined together for all time . . . as if they constituted only a single province'.[86]

Orange and his circle had urged a closer union of the provinces for some time. The initiative for the Closer Union (*Nadere Unie*) which was signed in January 1579 came not from Orange but from Holland and Zeeland and from Orange's brother, John of Nassau who was governor of Guelders at the time. From the beginning this initiative gave the Union a much more pronounced Calvinist slant than the States General had exhibited since its break with Don John of Austria. The Union of Utrecht was signed by Holland, Zeeland, Utrecht, Friesland, Guelders and the Ommelanden (the province, but not the city, of Groningen).

Orange was not pleased with his brother's initiative. It undermined his policy of keeping Protestants and Catholics together in the struggle against Spain. Only after several months did he accept the Union. There was no intention by the promoters of the Union of Utrecht to confine it to the Protestant or the Dutch-Flemish-speaking provinces. The Catholic province of Tournai-Tournésis, frightened by the presence of Anjou and his French troops in neighbouring Hainaut, was happy to join the Union. But the religious peace which Orange had been advocating was now interpreted not as a *modus vivendi* until the final resolution of the religious differences, but as *carte blanche* for the dominant religion in each province to prohibit the open exercise of the opposite confession. Effectively, one had arrived at a German-style *Religionsfrieden*. A resolution of the religious differences by a future States General was now more unlikely than ever. Just as in Germany in the first half of the seventeenth century, so in the Netherlands in the late sixteenth, the religious differences could now be settled, or rather made permanent, only by civil war. And this civil war was inevitably fought not only, or not even principally, over religion but over political issues, sharpened by religious passions. Just as in the Thirty Years War, the civil war merged into a European war because the great powers could not afford to see the victory of the opposing religion; or at least not until the horrors and futilities of these wars themselves gradually caused religion to cease being the principal driving force of international politics. In the Netherlands there were sharp differences of opinion and sometimes acrimonious debates about the aims of the war against the royalists. Was it *religionis ergo* or *libertatis ergo*? For most people, however, liberty came to mean more and more political liberty and at least freedom from persecution in the belief, if not always the exercise, of one's chosen religious persuasion. Marnix put it succinctly: 'We do not abjure [*destituons*] the king because he is not of our religious persuasion

---

[86] Rowen, *The Low Countries in Early Modern Times*, 69–70.

but because he is a tyrant ... and by the destruction of those of the true religion he designs to suppress all the liberties of the country.'[87]

In the meantime, in 1579 and 1580, the Union of Utrecht established its own war council and gave teeth to the collection of taxes in the provinces and cities. Thus, for instance, Amsterdam was punished for non-payment by the confiscation of its merchants' goods outside the city. This was an almost venerable practice which had been used sporadically throughout the century to coerce hostile or recalcitrant cities. Officials appointed by the Union had to take their oath to the Union. The king was now left out of the new formula.

The Union set up its own executive and this met at least some of the objectives which Orange had been consistently proposing to the States General of the Generality (*generaliteit*), as it was called. Even so, the Closer Union was still far from creating a 'single province'. The Union's Council of State, while it had greater powers than the official council of the archduke Matthias, was still meant to represent the constituent provinces. Each of these provinces was to have a fixed number of councillors. The implications of parliamentary government in a composite state had not yet been fully thought out, or were perhaps not yet thinkable.[88]

From the beginning of the Union of Utrecht there was a good deal of cooperation between its assembly, which was permanently in session, and the States General of the Generality. This cooperation increased after the failure of the conference of Cologne. Thus in December 1579 the States General adopted the Union's monetary regulations, equalised the rate of exchange between the provinces and ordered the striking of new coins without the king's head.[89] Quite soon it became evident that, with so much overlap in functions, there was no sense in having two governmental organisations and two separate representative assemblies. In the summer of 1580 the Union and the States General merged. There was no single act to this effect, but in May 1580 the States General required an oath from all delegates to the general union and to the Union of Utrecht.[90] In October 1580 a new oath for the inhabitants of Antwerp read that they swore loyalty, to 'the High Authority of the States General of the Netherlands united in the Closer Union'.

Throughout the year 1580 and the first half of 1581 the last shreds of trust between the king and the States General disappeared. More and more the pamphleteers stressed the right of resistance to a tyrannical prince and the assumption that the king now only desired vengeance.[91] In the summer of 1580 the States General negotiated the transfer of rulership over the Netherlands to the duke of

---

[87] Marnix to Orange. Antwerp, 27 March 1580. Griffiths, *Representative Government*, 482–3.
[88] For a detailed account of the Closer Union see Delfos, *Die Anfänge der Utrechter Union, passim*.
[89] Gachard, *Actes des Etats Généraux*, vol. II, 309–10.
[90] *Ibid.*, 337–8.
[91] A particularly good example, already published in 1579, is the 'Brief Discourse on the Peace Negotiations taking place at Cologne ...' (Leiden, 1579), ed. and transl. M. van Gelderen, *The Dutch Revolt*, 123–64.

Anjou.⁹² For the king this meant that the worst scenario had come true. It was much worse than the States General's invitation of Archduke Matthias to the governor-generalship. He was at least a Habsburg and, nominally at any rate, invited to govern in the name of the king. With Anjou there was not even this fiction and there was, on the contrary, the prospect that the king of France himself might become involved. It was not immediately obvious that Henry III could no more afford full military and political support for his brother than Rudolph II had been able to afford for his.

From the point of view of Madrid, the worst of it was that the king could not mount an immediate and crushing military riposte to this new danger. He was engaged in the succession and conquest of Portugal, and for this purpose he had summoned Cardinal Granvelle to Madrid. It seems to have been Granvelle who persuaded the king to eliminate the person of the prince of Orange by accusing him publicly of treason and putting him and his adherents under a ban and a price on his head.

The king did achieve his object of the elimination of the man he regarded as his arch-enemy, but not until four years later. However, Granvelle had once again misjudged the mood of the Netherlands. In Philip II's *fatwa* – the late twentieth-century term, taken over by the West from the pronouncements of certain fanatical Muslim clerics, although Philip would no doubt have been appalled by such an analogy – the king spoke of himself as 'absolute prince and sovereign'.⁹³ Even though this term was probably not intended as a constitutional definition but as a traditional description of his position as king and as God's representative on earth to whom Orange had broken all oaths, the term did not go down well in the Netherlands. For absolute sovereignty was precisely what the Netherlanders now did not want to accept. Just about the same time, they had insisted on this very point in their negotiations with the duke of Anjou.⁹⁴ Orange's reply to the ban was a propaganda victory at the time and, in its personal attack on the integrity of the king, became one of the principal sources of the 'black legend' of Philip II and Spain.

The prince's 'Apology' was drafted, with his approval, by his court chaplain, De Villiers and by the French publicists Hubert Languet and Philippe Du Plessis-Mornay, the latter probably the author of the most famous of all resistance-theory texts of the sixteenth century, the *Vindiciae contra tyrannos*.⁹⁵ Apart from their personal attacks on Philip II they argued that the king had shown his true aims already at the beginning of his reign by forbidding the summoning of the States General. It was this body which the prince of Orange now explicitly recognised

---

⁹² The constitutional problems involved in this transfer will be discussed below, ch. 13.
⁹³ Rowen, *The Low Countries*, 78.
⁹⁴ Cf. below pp. 298–302.
⁹⁵ 'Apologie de Guillaume IX, Prince d'Orange, contre la Proscription de Philippe II, Roy d'Espagne', ed. and transl. Rowen, *The Low Countries*, 80–91.

Monarchies, States Generals and Parliaments

as his only superior. To reinforce this point he recalled that in 1578 the States General had ordered its own seal, showing a lion with seventeen arrows in his right paw.[96] The symbol of the bundle of arrows, used by the Netherlands lords who opposed Granvelle in the 1560s, had become the symbol of the seventeen provinces of the Netherlands. The lion, the universal symbol of royalty, had been transferred to the States General. As an allegory of a parliamentary regime it could not have been clearer. The problems in terms of sovereignty inherent in this symbolism, the location of ultimate political authority, had yet to be resolved.

The Rubicon had now been crossed, The veiled and not-so-veiled threats of the previous two years to choose another prince had become an urgent programme accepted by all who did not want to, or could not be bribed to, reconcile themselves with the king. At the same time there was as yet little overt republicanism. This was so, even though the admired role model, the Swiss cantons, were republics. Orange, looking for help from abroad against the might of the king of Spain was now convinced that such help could only be obtained by offering a monarchical position to a powerful prince. Since the Netherlands were a composite polity the individual provinces had to debate such a solution. There were historical precedents for such a transfer. In the thirteenth century the Sicilians had thrown out their French Angevin king and their parliament had transferred the crown to the king of Aragon. In the fourteenth and fifteenth centuries the Estates of Brabant had adjudicated disputed successions to their duchy and had written their right to do so into their *joyeuse entrée*. In 1578 John of Nassau had told the Estates of Holland and Zeeland that 'they were chosen by God Almighty from the people to choose a king or governor'.[97] These two provinces in fact did not use the king's name any more in their acts and proclamations.

On the other side there were those who, while agreeing with the need to choose another prince, were fearful of appearing to declare war on King Philip, not least because of the obvious vulnerability of Dutch merchants in Spain and Portugal. On this point it turned out that there was in the long run a kind of tacit gentlemen's agreement to allow this 'trade with the enemy' (*handel op de vijand*). Neither side could do without this trade in order to keep on fighting each other. There were only occasional interruptions to this undercover agreement when certain politicians suffered from bouts of religious puritanism or when they saw a tactical advantage in stopping the trade. During the earl of Leicester's governor-generalship both these motives determined a policy which was greatly to contribute to the earl's failure.[98]

The Act of Abjuration (*Plakkaat van Verlatinge*) of 22 July 1581 was a compromise arrived at by the States General after extensive discussions in the Estates of the individual provinces – just as the American Declaration of Independence of 1776 was to be preceded by lengthy discussions in the assemblies of the individual American

---
[96] Swart, *Willem van Oranje*, 196.
[97] Quoted in N. Mout, *Plakkaat van Verlatinge 1581* (The Hague, 1979), 39.
[98] Cf. below, ch. 13.

Rule by the States General: myths and realities

states. The Dutch text, written by Jan van Asseliers, an official of the States General, does not match Jefferson's ringing periods. Instead of the eighteenth-century Enlightenment invocation of natural human rights, the *Plakkaat* concentrated on the right of resistance to tyranny and the failure of the king to fulfil his God-given task. 'It is generally agreed that God has appointed a prince to protect and safeguard them [i.e. his subjects] from all injustice, harm and violence, as a shepherd protects his flock, and that the subjects are not created for the sake of the prince ... like slaves. On the contrary, the prince is there for the sake of the people.'[99]

The metaphor of the king as the shepherd of his flock and the arguments following from this were entirely conventional. One may wonder, though, whether van Asseliers deliberately adopted the phraseology current at Philip II's court in order to heighten the moral impact of his argument. Here, for instance, are the king's instructions to the duke of Alcalá, his viceroy of Naples:

The first thing you must realise is that the community was not made for the prince but rather that the prince was created for the community ... Your principal object and intention must be to work for the community which is in your charge so that it may live and rest in full security, peace, justice and quiet ... and to take heed that you are not accepting this office to be idle or to live at your pleasure nor for any benefit of your own.[100]

There is no direct evidence for the influence of Philip's 'secret instructions', which, like most such documents in the sixteenth century, was far from secret and circulated widely; but the similarities are at least suggestive. Philip could of course have argued that by doing everything in his power to preserve the Catholic religion he was working for the benefit of the community.

The *Plakkaat* was not, strictly, a declaration of independence. It was rather, as its title said clearly enough, the 'leaving' of a prince by his subjects because he had failed to live up to his duties as a Christian prince. It was indeed an Act of Abjuration, as it is usually and quite appropriately called in English. The bells were not rung, as they were for the signing of the Union of Utrecht, and there was little immediate reaction on either side. And yet, as it turned out, its effects were those of a declaration of independence for the polity which, since the signing of the Union of Utrecht, had come to be called 'The United Provinces of the Netherlands'. The authority by which this act had been performed was the States General. The act itself did not transfer the crown and the sovereignty of the country to another prince, as the parliament of Sicily and the Estates of Brabant had done in earlier centuries. The States General themselves had assumed sovereignty over the country. However, it took time before this fact was generally recognised and even more time before its meaning had been fully understood even by the Dutch Estates themselves.

---

[99] *Placcaert Vande Staten general ... by den men verclaert den Coninck van Spaegnien vervallen van de Overheyt end Heerschappije van dese voors. Nederlanden ...* (Leiden, 1581), in Mout, *Plakkaat*, 71.
[100] Koenigsberger, *The Practice of Empire*, 172 and 172 n.2.

13

Parliamentary government and *dominium regale* (1580–1600)

'I foresaw and predicted this disaster to messieurs [Marnix] de St Aldegonde and des Pruneaux [councillor of the duke of Anjou] when, in England, I told them that their negotiations would result in the ruin of our prince [Anjou] and of the Low Country, knowing the contrary customs and humours of the two peoples and their differences over the question of liberty which they [the Netherlands] would not give up, since they control the citadels which make them the prince's masters: for it is certain that he who is master of the armed forces is master of the state and owes obedience only where he pleases. Thus sovereignty, which can never be divided, is split between the prince and the subjects, and this would cause the ruin of the state.'

Jean Bodin to M. Trouillart, his father-in-law, Antwerp, 21 Jan. 1583[1]

ANJOU

It took the prince of Orange eight months to persuade the Netherlands to accept the duke of Anjou as their prince in place of Philip II. The matter had been discussed sporadically as early as 1578. In January 1580 it was proposed to the States General. Understandably, the delegates did not think they could decide a matter of such fundamental importance on their own authority and they insisted on referring it back to their own provincial assemblies. In these, in turn, the delegates referred back to their own principals, the town councils of the major cities. There were serious misgivings. The Hollanders and Zeelanders were set against giving authority to another Catholic prince. The north-eastern provinces,

---

[1] In Griffiths, *Constitutional Government*, 505. 'J'ai prévue et prédit malheur en Angleterre à Monsieur de Sainct-Aldegonde et des Pruneaux, lorsque je leurs dis que leurs négociations tiroit après soy la ruine de nostre prince et du Bas-Païs, cognoissant la contrariété de meurs et d'humeurs des deux peuples, et la différence de cela à la possession de liberté, laquelle jamais ils ne voudroient quicter, ayant eu les citadelles, pour estre maistres du prince: car il est bien certain que celuy est maistre de l'Estat qui est maistre de la force publicque, et ne preste obéissance que ce qu'il lui plaist, en sorte que la souveraineté, ne souffrant jamais division, se trouveroit partie entre le prince et les subjectz, qui causeroit la ruine d'un Estat.'

Also partly quoted in M. P. Holt, *The Duke of Anjou and the Politique Struggle during the Wars of Religion* (Cambridge, 1986), 180. Holt dates Bodin's letter 23 Jan. 1583. In any case, it was written after the 'French Fury' in Antwerp, 17 January, during which Bodin was taken prisoner by the Antwerpers.

Parliamentary government and dominium regale

joined to the Netherlands only in the course of the sixteenth century, always distrusted initiatives from Brussels or Antwerp. It was to Antwerp that the government and the States General had fled after Don John of Austria's victory over the States army at Gembloux, in January 1577. The Flemings and the Brabanters traditionally hated the French, and even the French-speaking Walloon provinces had bad memories of French aggression and occasional French occupation. It was not least for this reason that their nobility and higher clergy had preferred reconciliation with the king of Spain in the Treaty of Arras.

In the end Orange's arguments of the necessity of outside military assistance won the day. During the conference of Cologne it had become all too clear that no help was to be expected from Germany. It was Flanders which broke the deadlock and pledged support for Anjou. William of Orange's successful coup against the radical populist–Calvinist party in Ghent, in August 1579, had come too late to save his alliance with the Walloon nobility; but it did remove the anti-French opposition. Astute politician that Orange was, he even used the evident anti-French feeling in the country as an argument for the acceptance of Anjou: the duke would not be able to govern against the will of the country.[2]

Reluctantly, the other provinces followed Flanders' lead. By August 1580 Orange had achieved the support of the majority of the States General. Even then, this majority depended on the votes of Holland and Zeeland who had effectively distanced themselves from this policy, both by their insistence on their right to prohibit all Catholic worship and by their action, during the spring of 1580, of appointing Orange as their 'Highest authority for the government of Holland and with such a title as he might wish to have'.[3]

If the provinces of the Netherlands had mixed feelings about inviting the duke of Anjou to be their new prince, the governments in Madrid, Paris and London found themselves walking diplomatic tightropes. Madrid was clear enough that the king would never accept any right of the Estates to transfer the sovereignty of the Netherlands, least of all to the brother of the king of France. But here precisely was the danger. Would the French interfere massively, and for Spain disastrously, in the civil war in the Netherlands at the very moment when King Philip was occupied with the conquest of Portugal?

For Henry III and Catherine de Medici the situation was the mirror image of that of Philip II. In principle, they would have liked to see Anjou as the new lord of the Netherlands. But to give him full support risked, at the very least, further interference by Spain in the fraught situation in France. Even purely tactically they needed Anjou and his Politique following to help reconcile the antagonistic Catholic and Huguenot parties in Provence. In the worst case, they would find

---

[2] Swart, *Willem van Oranje*, 210–11.
[3] *Ibid.*, 213. *Resolutiën van de Heeren Staten van Hollandt* . . . 28 March 1580. Orange accepted the proposal on 5 July with the title *Hooge Overigheid en Regeringe* or *Souveraineté et Gouvernement*, 'at least for some time'. Griffiths, *Representative Government*, 506–9.

themselves at open war with Spain. Catherine at least feared, just as she had feared in the summer of 1572, when it seemed that Coligny was pushing Charles IX into just such a war, that France was militarily in no condition to take on the full power of Spain and its mighty war machine.

And again, as in 1572, the key to the situation seemed to lie in England. At that time Elizabeth had reneged on what Coligny had taken to be the promise of an anti-Spanish Anglo-French alliance. Catherine had escaped from what she regarded as a fatal trap for France by the assassination of Coligny and the massacre of St Bartholomew (24 August 1572). This time, in 1580, Catherine and Henry III would trust Elizabeth only if she bound herself by marriage to Anjou.

But this was precisely what Elizabeth would not, or indeed could not, do. Quite apart from her personal feelings, public opinion in England was dead set against such a marriage and her own council was divided, the majority being strongly against. It was in England's interest to keep Spain occupied in the Netherlands and to prevent Parma from gaining an outright victory, just as it was, again in a mirror image, in Spain's interest to keep France occupied with its civil and religious problems, however much Philip might detest the Huguenots and fear Calvinist contagion in his own dominions. This point was fully understood both in France and the Netherlands. 'I deplore our miseries and calamities [in France], but more than this I fear another drawback, that these [Dutch] provinces cannot be assisted if this continues', wrote Philippe Du Plessis-Mornay, the reputed author of the famous *Vindiciae contra tyrannos*; and the deputies of Flanders said: 'There is nothing more prejudicial to this negotiation [with Anjou] than seeing the forces of France banded together against one another.'[4]

But traditionally the English did not want to see the French firmly established in the Netherlands. Moreover, just like Catherine, Elizabeth feared being dragged into an open war with Spain without an assurance that the other great anti-Spanish power would stick to the alliance. In spite of all Anjou's promises, Henry III had not committed himself. For England it was safer to support John Casimir, the administrator of the Palatinate, in the Netherlands. For all his personal ambition, this prince was little more than a Calvinist *condottiere* who did not and could not indulge in the imperialism of a great power.[5]

Against this ambiguous and shifting background of international relations, where offers of support dissolved into moralistic talk or slid into covert betrayal, the States General sent their deputation to offer the duke of Anjou the lordship over the Netherlands – on conditions. The meeting in Anjou's château of Plessis-les-Tours, near the city of Tours on the Loire in September 1580 was a grand affair. The States General's deputation was led by Orange's right-hand man, Marnix. On Anjou's side there was the marshal de Cossé, several great noblemen and governors of French

---

[4] Both quotations from Holt, *The Duke of Anjou*, 131.
[5] For the very complex international relations of the period see *ibid.*, chs. 6 and 7.

Parliamentary government and dominium regale

provinces and a number of lawyers in the duke's service. Of these latter, the great Jean Bodin was not present; but there seems little doubt that his ideas about the indivisibility of sovereignty were already circulating among the duke's advisers.

It was over the question of sovereignty that the two delegations appeared to differ most. Even before the formal opening of the discussions the Dutch delegation had harangued Anjou 'on how it is admirable and of great renown for princes and lords to govern and command a people who have their liberty at heart and who defend it, so that on both sides there will disappear all constraints to affection and devotion'.[6] During the discussion itself the Estates' delegation rejected the appellation 'sovereign' for Anjou, claiming it smacked of absolute power and that in Dutch there was no such term but only 'gracious lord' (*genadighe heerre* or *geduchte heere*). This was both pedantic and unfounded – the word sovereign had often been used, even in Dutch – but eventually the two sides agreed on the vague phrase 'with such pre-eminences and prerogatives as our preceding lords'. This was really meaningless since they specifically excluded not only King Philip but also Emperor Charles who, in contrast to the formulation of earlier documents of the revolt such as the Pacification of Ghent, was now held responsible for all the ills that had befallen the country, because in Worms he had issued edicts against heresy without consulting the Estates of the Netherlands. The king of Spain, however, had so consistently violated their laws and his own promises that they had been constrained to take up arms against him. They had not done this lightly, knowing the ruin and desolation which would befall their country, but they could not allow any change in their ancient liberties.

The actual discussions and arguments with the duke's representatives were therefore severely practical: the States General should be summoned at least once a year and, in any case, they would have the right to assemble on their own initiative if they felt it necessary. This was a point which representative assemblies had been making in many European countries for the last two hundred years and it had never been formally conceded by any prince, or at least not for more than very short periods of crisis, and it had habitually been revoked as soon as the crisis had passed. Anjou and his advisers regarded this demand in just such a traditional way, but nevertheless they gave way on it.

They also gave way on the demand that all members of the duke's Council of State and of his finance and judicial councils had to be native Netherlanders, nominated by the Estates. Only on temporary military appointments did the States General give way. Those officers who risked their lives and property for the sake of the Netherlands would be granted access to the councils of war.[7]

The key of the agreement, however, was financial; and here the arguments were not about the nature and conduct of government but about the very practical

---

[6] Griffiths, *Representative Government*, 490.
[7] Ibid., 497–504.

problem of who was to pay and how much for the war against Parma and his loyalist and Malcontent allies. Henry III would no more give a definite promise to finance his brother than Emperor Rudolph had done for his own brother. The best that Anjou could promise was that he would do his best to gain the active support of the king of France. The States General, for their part, promised to provide Anjou with 2.4 million florins a year. On the basis of these wildly optimistic promises the two sides agreed on 25 September 1580. Anjou wrote to the States General: 'At the risk of losing my life [was he deliberately echoing King Philip's well-known pronouncements about rather losing his life than ruling over heretics?] I will undertake to restore your former and ancient liberties, to maintain your state, laws, privileges and customs, and to protect, defend and secure your lives, property and families.'[8]

From then on events moved in slow motion. First, Anjou was held up in France on Henry III's business. Then he went to England on his unsuccessful bridal quest for the twenty-years-older Elizabeth. These ventures were not, however, complete failures. Both the king of France and the queen of England promised him secret aid for the Netherlands. In August 1581 he managed to relieve Cambrai which Parma had been somewhat half-heartedly besieging. It was to be Anjou's only significant military success. In February 1582 he finally came to Antwerp. With the usual splendid festivities and the now obligatory fireworks, only recently introduced into Europe from China, Anjou was installed as duke of Brabant and marquis of the Holy Roman Empire.

To the *parlement* of Paris Anjou had justified his actions because:

the provinces of Brabant, Flanders, Holland, Zeeland, Malines, Friesland and the Ommelanden . . . after long deliberation and universal consent of their people . . . threw themselves into my arms and asked me to take them under my wing in a just and legitimate rulership . . . not for my own particular glory but . . . to the service of the king my lord and brother . . . for the conservation of his state and the augmentation of his crown.[9]

The Treaty of Plessis-les-Tours and Anjou's installation in Antwerp have sometimes been regarded as both revolutionary and constitution-building actions by the States General. This was by no means clear to contemporaries. The States General had severely restricted Anjou's powers and, as he himself boasted, had called upon him, elected him, as their prince. Was this different in principle from earlier occasions when the Estates of Brabant had elected a new duke? Anjou's title was to be hereditary and he was still to be styled 'by the grace of God'. He could claim at least a glimmer of hereditary right, in an age which viewed such rights as conferred by divine providence. The ubiquitous and obsequious learned antiquarians were not slow in recalling the glories of the fourteenth- and fifteenth-century dukes of Burgundy, like Anjou members of the royal house of Valois. Yet, however confused

[8] Quoted in Holt, *The Duke of Anjou*, 143.
[9] *Ibid.*, 151.

Parliamentary government and dominium regale

the Netherlands ruling classes were about what they had done constitutionally and what the exact constitutional role of the prince should be, they were clear enough about the limitations they had imposed on him in order to safeguard their own liberties. And the separate provinces and their Estates saw the essence of their liberties in not being dominated by a central government. They showed this attitude in the way they had always done, by dragging their feet over payments to the government or by keeping the money they collected within their province for their own defence. The campaign against Parma came to a virtual standstill, while Parma himself slowly and systematically reconquered town after town.

For Anjou this situation was intolerable from every point of view: political, financial and military. The Netherlanders had 'made a Matthias of him', he said.[10] In January 1583 he reacted as Don John had reacted in his not altogether dissimilar situation of July 1577. It turned out to be an even greater mistake than that of Don John and, moreover, it was completely bungled. Anjou's troops tried to make themselves masters of Antwerp but the States General's troops and the Antwerpers cut the French troops to pieces.

Jean Bodin, in the anguish of having been taken prisoner with the French troops in Antwerp, penned a brilliantly concise, donnish account of this disaster (quoted at the head of this chapter). But his definition of sovereignty had not yet become as popular with the courts of Western Europe as it was shortly to be. To the actors in this drama, in 1583, the situation was, in essence, even more simple and crude: Anjou had accepted the offer of the States General because he desperately wanted to be a prince in his own right. Catherine de Medici, his own mother, had insisted to him that, even as heir apparent to the French crown, he was his brother's subject.[11] Whatever his sophisticated advisers at Plessis-les-Tours had negotiated, the duke himself had been brought up in the French tradition of kingship, *dominium regale* (which was not, it is worth repeating, seen by its adherents as being inconsistent with the rule of law or the maintenance of ancient privileges). By contrast, the Netherlands ruling classes only wanted a prince whom they had installed and whose authority derived from them, but a prince with sufficient status and resources to continue the fight against the king of Spain. There was no way these two preconceptions and aims could be combined.[12]

---

[10] Quoted in Parker, *The Dutch Revolt*, 206.
[11] Holt, *The Duke of Anjou*, 143.
[12] *Excursus*: It was one of history's ironies (although Anjou could not have known of it, since he died of tuberculosis in June 1584) that from 1608 to 1611 the much-despised Matthias organised, or at least presided over, a highly successful series of coups against his brother, Rudolph II, which gave him the crowns of Hungary and Bohemia and, eventually, the imperial crown. In a further twist of historical irony, Matthias' coups were one of the immediate causes of an even more dreadful civil war than the one he had tried to appease in the Netherlands, some thirty years earlier. Perhaps it was a merciful providence which carried off this mediocre man, who was always manipulated by his entourage but who strove for compromise, peace and harmony, before the full horrors of the Thirty Years War became apparent. He died peacefully in his bed in March 1619, an end which was not given to all leading personalities of the period.

Yet, what alternative was there? The Netherlanders now hated Anjou and his entourage even more than they had always hated the French, and some of the common people and their pamphleteers claimed (wrongly) that Orange had approved of Anjou's attempted coup. But William of Orange's arguments still held good. There was no one else to help the Netherlanders and if they antagonised Anjou completely there was always the danger that, for religious reasons and for reasons of princely solidarity, he might join forces with the Spaniards. Parma immediately, although unsuccessfully, tried to persuade him to do so. Most of the money which the States General actually paid him – much less than the 2.4 million per annum which they had promised – came to him after his attempted coup. This curious fact was hardly the result of any greater trust in the duke's military prowess, but was probably the result of the byzantine complexity and slowness of the States General's practice of raising money. Between May 1581 and October 1583 Anjou got by far the most money from Henry III, nearly 950,000 livres tournois, but the French royal army which he had promised never made an appearance. He got some 630,000 livres from Elizabeth I, 450,000 livres from his own apanages in France and somewhat less than 350,000 livres from the States General.[13] Financially, the Netherlanders had not done all that badly from their connection with the duke of Anjou. Politically and militarily he had been a failure, but it is at least possible that his presence slowed down Parma's advance.

THE ASSASSINATION OF WILLIAM OF ORANGE

Anjou's attempted coup led to the collapse of the central government. The members of his Council of State all resigned. Practical authority returned to where it had been before, the States General. They were led by the prince of Orange in his capacity of *ruward* of Brabant and of all the other dignities which he had accumulated in the different provinces. In September 1583 the States General appointed Orange as governor general and head of a reconstituted Council of State.

In a sense, these were the acts of a republic, choosing not a new prince but an effective head of government. Yet this was not the way most Netherlanders were thinking. In Flanders and Brabant, Parma was capturing town after town. In many cases he won the consent of the local authorities and local military commanders by his policy of promising, and evidently observing, the maintenance of old local privileges. He confirmed this policy by the judicious distribution of royal patronage. In Ghent it was the leaders of the Calvinists and populists who had managed once more to seize power. In their hatred of the patricians and of Orange, they now started negotiations with Parma. They were overthrown once more and their leader, Hembyze, was publicly executed for treason. But the revolution in Ghent,

---

[13] Figures from Holt, *The Duke of Anjou*, table 1, 246.

Parliamentary government and dominium regale

both in its populist and in its Orangeist forms, had now effectively committed suicide. Parma found little resistance in taking the town (17 Sept. 1584).

The Hollanders drew the logical constitutional conclusion. They offered to make the prince of Orange their hereditary count, just as the Estates of Brabant had made the duke of Anjou their hereditary duke. The proposal had been discussed, on and off, for several years. Orange had always rejected it, mainly because it would have interfered with his attempts to offer the lordship of the whole Netherlands to a potentially powerful prince who would fight the king of Spain. But in the autumn and winter of 1583-4 he seems to have been inclined to accept the offer. Perhaps because the king had outlawed him and because several attempts had been made on his life, he wanted to ensure the position of his family.[14] It was not an altogether attractive offer. The Estates of Zeeland did not join in it at all, and several of the major cities of Holland, including Amsterdam, objected. Moreover, the new count's powers would be more restricted than they had been when he was the king's provincial governor.

Nothing came of these plans. After the death of the duke of Anjou, Orange wanted to offer the sovereignty of the Netherlands to Henry III of France. He could hardly do so if he was himself the hereditary count of one the country's constituent provinces.[15] In any case, he himself was doomed, as doomed as Admiral Coligny had been whose daughter he had just married. The age believed in the assassination of political opponents. On 10 July 1584 the assassination attempts sponsored by Philip II finally succeeded.

LEICESTER

On the day William of Orange was assassinated in Delft, the States General were in session there. They reacted with commendable speed. They wrote immediately to the members of the Union of Utrecht asking them to send deputies with full powers to take decisions on the government of the Union. The Estates of Holland and Zeeland invited their deputies to a separate meeting of the three provinces. The Utrechters, however, distrusted their powerful neighbours. They instructed their deputies to oppose absolute powers for deputies in the negotiations to confirm the Union of Utrecht. No one should have absolute powers to decide on the government of the country and, moreover, in Utrecht nobody could be found of sufficient intelligence to exercise such powers, they wrote. The deputies should only consult with those of the other provinces and then refer their proposals back to the Estates of Utrecht.[16] This distrust of Holland was to become a permanent feature of the politics of the United Provinces of the Netherlands.

---

[14] Swart, *Willem van Oranje*, 245-7.
[15] *Ibid.*
[16] 15 July 1584 (o.s.), 'Instructie voor den edelen . . . Meester Floris Heermade', in M. L. van Deventer, *Gedenkstukken van Johan van Oldenbarnevelt*, 3 vols. (The Hague, 1860), vol. 1, 50ff.

Monarchies, States Generals and Parliaments

Nevertheless, after heated debates, there was general agreement about continuing the Union. (*Acte van Vereeninge*, 18 August 1584). They appointed a new Council of State to be the highest executive organ. The young Maurice of Nassau, the son of William of Orange, was immediately chosen to be the First Councillor.

This arrangement still left open the question of effective leadership. Maurice was still too young to fill such a role. Most people still thought in terms of a prince, a monarch for the whole country, and such a prince was still generally known and addressed as sovereign. Such a person seemed necessary to give cohesion to the provinces and cities and their separatist interests. They might still rouse themselves to a 'patriotic' defence when attacked by the Spaniards and their Netherlands allies. But the war was usually localised and the 'patriots' were not anxious to admit that for a long time it had effectively been a civil war.[17] The problem was to find a prince who could bring substantial military help to the Union and who was yet willing to give up a great many of the powers which, in common sixteenth-century thought, pertained to a prince.

William of Orange had managed to fulfil these apparently contradictory conditions. He had reiterated them once more in his *Apologie*, his attack on the political practices of Philip II, following his own outlawry by the king; and he had

---

[17] *Excursus*: After Gembloux, in January 1568, there were few pitched battles and such as there were were not decisive. While small units of cavalry sometimes made long-distance raids and, generally, made life for the country population a misery, it was a war of sieges and counter-sieges. The soldiers dug trenches around fortified towns and those who tried to relieve sieges would dig trenches around the besiegers. At the same time the ubiquitous rivers and canals would allow quite large bodies of troops, artillery and munitions to be shifted rapidly from one theatre of war to another. In the Netherlands the waterways played a role in tactics analogous to the railways in the trench warfare of the American Civil War and World War I. One might think that Mephistopheles' characterisation also fitted this sixteenth-century civil war which was fought mainly by professionals (Goethe, *Faust II*, Act 2):

> Man streitet, heisst's, um Freiheitsrechte.
> Genau beschn sinds Knechte gegen Knechte.
> (They say they fight for freedom.
> Looked at closely, it's mercenaries against mercenaries.)

The reaction of the common soldiers was just as cynical but more earthy, as for instance in the contemporary English tavern song quoted on p. 270. The German soldiers, of whom there were many in the Netherlands, serving on both sides, had a very similar attitude:

> Der Wirt muss borgen,
> Er darf nicht rappelköppig sein,
> Sonst kehrn wir morgen
> Beim andern ein.
> (The landlord must give credit,
> He must not be pigheaded,
> Otherwise tomorrow we'll go to another inn.)
> (From the popular song *Wenn wir marschieren*)

Evidently, it was not only governments who borrowed and held the whiphand over their creditors. One may wonder, though, whether the notoriously rough *Landsknechte* did not threaten more dire penalties against a recalcitrant landlord than the withdrawal of their dubious custom.

Parliamentary government and dominium regale

especially blamed Philip for his failure to consult the States General.[18] But for the central practical problem, the survival of the Union, he had still favoured the appointment of a prince.

In European court society, the ambience of all possible invitees, a prince was still regarded and often addressed as sovereign, and this was so even at courts of countries which had an effective *dominium politicum et regale* regime. After the death of the duke of Anjou, in July 1584, and Henry III's rejection of the offer to become sovereign of the Netherlands, the States General approached Elizabeth I once more. The offer was quite impossible for her to accept. It would have involved the unappeasable enmity of the unforgiving house of Habsburg. But Elizabeth was quite willing to give the Dutch military and financial help. She hoped in this way to bring pressure on Philip II to give up his support for the party of Mary Queen of Scots and to offer the Dutch an acceptable compromise (Treaty of Nonsuch, 20 Aug. 1585, with the Dutch).

The treaty, however welcome to the States General, resolved none of the contradictions inherent in the situation. After the failure of the conference of Cologne six years before, the States General had given up hope of any acceptable compromise by the king. Nor, with Parma's continuing successes, was the king inclined to make further concessions. At the same time, the problems of the political–constitutional position of the queen's representative, the earl of Leicester, remained basically unresolved. The States General agreed to allow Leicester 'full authority and absolute power ... in matters of policy and justice, just as the governors general of the Netherlands had at all times lawfully exercised, especially at the time of Emperor Charles V'. This last phrase spelt trouble because there had been voices for years, notable Marnix of St Aldegonde, who had held Charles V's regime responsible for all the later troubles.

More confusion was to come. 'His Excellency [Leicester] would have the right to summon the States General ... whenever he thought fit.' But this phrase was followed immediately by the declaration 'that the said Estates ... shall assemble as they think fit for the welfare of the country'; and all this without prejudice to the rights and freedoms of the States General and of the individual provinces.[19] The position was further complicated because Leicester himself acknowledged a sovereign; and this sovereign, the queen of England, thought that Leicester had accepted powers and titles beyond the brief she had given him.

Leicester was no William of Orange, neither in the knowledge of the country he had come to govern, nor in general political *savoir faire*. He did not have Dutch and, surprisingly for an Elizabethan official, very little French. Soon he was at odds with the States General over finance. Following the advice of a south Netherlander, Ringault, Leicester minted large numbers of English coins on which

---

[18] Griffiths, *Representative Government*, 526–7.
[19] *Ibid.*, 529.

he imposed an artificially high rate of exchange. It was a deliberate inflation of Netherlands coins, a tax for which Leicester did not ask the consent of the States General. The Netherlanders resented Ringault, just as during Mary of Hungary's time they had resented Ducci and her other Italian financial advisers. Leicester also quarrelled with the Estates of Holland over the personnel of his council. The Estates were now led by their advocate, Jan van Oldenbarnevelt, a patrician of patricians, anxious to defend the privileges of the traditional Dutch ruling classes. Quite naturally, Leicester came to rely more and more on the congenial Calvinist preachers with their popular following and on refugees from the southern Netherlands.

Quite apart from the actual difficulty of extracting the promised sums from the States General – the same problem which had paralysed the duke of Anjou – Leicester quarrelled with Holland over the *handel op de vijand*, trade with the enemy. The Estates of Holland claimed that the profits of this trade were necessary to pay for their soldiers, and they were afraid that it might fall into the hands of the Hansards and other neutrals. Leicester, like his Calvinist preacher friends, thought the trade abominable, and he tried to prohibit it and declared it to be treason. But apart from his moral reasons, he also had practical financial arguments for his position. He could sell licences for this trade and, more dubious still, he could extract heavy conversion fees in lieu of death penalties from those who had been convicted of the illegal trade.

In February 1587 English commanders betrayed the city of Deventer and the fortifications of Zutphen to the Spaniards. The Dutch were outraged and there were popular demonstrations and even violence against English soldiers. Elizabeth blamed the Dutch Estates for not paying her troops and thus driving them to deal with the enemy or starve. She had a point; but to the Dutch it was adding insult to injury. Oldenbarnevelt took the opportunity of purging Leicester's partisans from his Council of State and having young Maurice of Nassau appointed commander-in-chief.

There was no open breach between the Union and England. Both sides needed each other, however much they now preferred to stay at arm's length. In Holland they were now discussing the possibility of becoming a republic. Leicester returned to England to retrieve his own shaken position and, if possible, to raise more money. In March 1587 Thomas Wilkes, the English representative at The Hague and a persistent critic of Leicester, tried to clarify the governor general's position in a memorandum, in French, addressed to the States General and the Estates of Holland. 'Sovereignty, in the absence of the legitimate prince', Wilkes wrote, presumably still regarding Philip II as the legitimate prince, 'belongs to the people and not to you, gentlemen, who are only servants, ministers and deputies of the said people; and all your instructions and commissions are limited not only in time but also in subject matter.' Sovereignty, he continued, was limited neither in power nor in time. The deputies of the States General did not represent this sovereignty; for the people had given the 'general and absolute government' to His Excellency (i.e. Leicester). He could exercise it and was the guardian of this

Parliamentary government and dominium regale

sovereignty until the prince or the people chose to revoke it. In the present state of the United Provinces only the people, and not the deputies of the States General or of the provicial Estates, could revoke this sovereignty or take any power away from the governor general. The deputies had not received any such commission. They had either not understood this position, Wilkes triumphantly concluded his argument, or they were guilty of the crime of disobedience.

Wilkes had no doubt read Bodin. His argumentation was hardly original. But the Estates of Holland took the memorandum seriously enough to entrust Franchois Vranck, the pensionary of Gouda, with drawing up a formal reply.[20] Vranck argued that sovereignty in Holland and Zeeland did not reside in the common people, as Wilkes had maintained, nor in the thirty or forty deputies at the meetings of the Estates. Holland and Zeeland had been ruled for 800 years by counts and countesses to whom the nobles and the towns, i.e. the Estates, had entrusted sovereignty. In cases of the minority or incapacity of the ruler, the Estates had exercised this sovereignty by appointing guardians. The origins of the present wars were due to Philip II's attempts to introduce Spanish and other foreign soldiery into the country and to force it to do what the Estates had not approved. The towns were governed by the councils constituted by the most notable persons of the community, anything from twenty-four to forty. These bodies, the *vroedschappen*, were as old as the towns themselves, and their members took their oaths to their cities, not to their prince. They served for life and filled vacancies by co-option. They elected the burgomasters and the other officers. These councils, together with the nobles, therefore represented the whole state. They sent their deputies to the meetings of the Estates with such powers as they chose to give them. For the present circumstances, Vranck reiterated, their powers were 'to discuss and resolve all matters concerning the welfare and the preservation of the state'. But they were not sovereign, for their powers were derived from their principals.

Vranck concluded his argument with a peroration which still assumed a monarchical form of government, but one in which the *dominium politicum et regale* argument was pushed to the extreme of the limitation of the powers of the prince: 'For what is the power of a prince, unless he were a tyrant', Vranck asked, without a good understanding of his subjects?

What understanding can he have, what support can he draw from them, if he lets himself be persuaded to become a partisan against the Estates who represent the community or, to speak more clearly, against his own people? And, secondly, how can the state continue to exist if it should happen that the community should be persuaded to become a partisan against the Estates, that is against the nobles, the magistrates and the councils of the towns?

---

[20] For Leicester's governor-generalship see J. den Tex, *Oldenbarnevelt*, transl. R. B. Powell, 2 vols. (Cambridge, 1973), vol. I, chs. 2 and 3. For the Wilkes–Vranck debate, see Koenigsberger, *Estates and Revolutions*, 204–8. For Bodin's famous definitions see his *Les six livres de la république*, bk I, ch. VIII (Paris, 1583), 122ff.

Monarchies, States Generals and Parliaments

The historical part of Vranck's argument was largely a fantasy. The claim that the *vroedschappen* represented the whole community was quite arbitrary. But he was right about the actual seat of power as it had developed in Holland. Vranck's 'Deduction' became a primary text for Dutch aristocratic-patrician political theory. The theory of the sovereignty of the Estates of Holland and, by logical extension, of the other provinces of the Union came to be generally accepted. The States General itself so pronounced it in 1621 and the great Hugo Grotius accepted it in his treatise on the government of Holland.[21]

Even Thomas Wilkes was impressed. By July 1587 he wrote to Queen Elizabeth that, if she refused the proffered sovereignty for herself, she would think that it should 'remain with such as now, by the laws of those countries, do retain the same, which is not the common people, as some are persuaded [i.e. as he himself had argued] but in the *Vroedschap*, who are the chiefest burgers in the cities and out of whom are drawn the magistrates and out of them the persons called the Estates'. This *Vroedschap*, Wilkes continued, were very jealous of their liberties 'and now make war against their lawful sovereign'. Evidently the question of sovereignty in the Netherlands was still causing great confusion.

This was not what Elizabeth was primarily concerned about. She wanted to have an acceptable peace with Spain, both for England and the Netherlands. To achieve this, she was willing to offer the king cities in the Netherlands which were not hers to offer, and this until the very moment the Spanish Armada appeared in the English Channel, in July 1588. Between the divergent aims of the Dutch and the English Leicester's mission came to grief and would probably have done so even if he had not been as personally inadequate for the part he was asked to play.

In July 1587 Leicester returned once more on his 'most perylous and crooked voyage' to the Netherlands, as he called it. By then Oldenbarnevelt and the States General had lost whatever desire they had had to cooperate with him on his terms. Leicester reacted as Don John of Austria and the duke of Anjou had reacted in similar situations: he tried a military coup by throwing English troops into several Dutch towns. Unsurprisingly, he failed as dismally as Anjou had done. By the end of 1587 he left the Netherlands for good.

Leicester's coup is an indication of the chasm which had opened up between the mentalities of a society in which the prince claimed to be sovereign, however much he might agree that he should observe his country's laws, and the mentalities of the patrician classes of his country. The prince as sovereign and his regents or governors general thought it entirely justified to use force against their own subjects, regardless of what happened to the innocent, if they thought that this was the way to achieve their ultimate greater good, in religion or otherwise.

---

[21] Vranck's 'Deduction' in P. Bor, *Oorspronck, begin ende vervolgh der Nederlandsche Oorlogen*, 3 vols. (Amsterdam, 1621), vol. III, bk. 22, fos. 49–54. Cf. van Gelderen, *The Dutch Revolt*, 227–38. Van Gelderen, *The Political Thought of the Dutch Revolt*, 204–7. H. Grotius, *Verantwoordingh van de Wettelijke Regieringh van Hollandt* (Paris, 1622), 8.

Parliamentary government and dominium regale

By contrast, the patricians and their representative assemblies stressed their defensive role against the aggressions of their prince. But after the Act of Abjuration the emphasis on the right of resistance gave way to the new burning question of sovereignty.[22] In the process the very concept of sovereignty shifted its location and had to be redefined. The process of working this out took time, and it is not surprising that people, including such an acute observer as Thomas Wilkes, were confused about it. As it turned out, the chasm between the two mentalities was real and proved to be unbridgeable.

REPUBLIC AND PARLIAMENTARY GOVERNMENT

Once again, the politicians were ahead of most of the political theorists. There were certainly discussions of republicanism in the luxuriant pamphlet literature of the time and it was fashionable to look to the Swiss cantons for inspiration. For not only were the cantons republics and some of them, like the Grisons, were even democracies; they also seemed to have solved that most intractable of problems of the period, the coexistence of differing and hostile religious confessions, by allowing each canton in the Helvetic Confederacy to determine its own religious denomination. But most writers still thought in terms of a limited monarchy with safeguards for the observance of the country's laws and privileges. In the universities of Leiden and Franeker the professors taught and commented on monarchies as late as the 1620s.[23]

Nevertheless, after the ignominious disappearance of Leicester, the leading minds of the Estates of Holland and of the States General concluded that it was better to do without a foreign 'sovereign'. By force of circumstances they now had to organise the Union of Utrecht as a republic, or rather as a federation of sovereign republican provinces. These provinces were as jealous of their separate rights as they had always been; and yet they had to act together if they were not to fall again separately under Spanish rule. This problem had led them into successive unions since 1576. They had used the organ of their unions, the States General, to tame their princely sovereign or his governor general. Since this pattern was no longer available, there was no alternative to having the States General itself as the ultimate source of authority and centre of the federal government. This was not an easy conclusion to accept, either politically or psychologically. The government, although not sovereignty, might be conveniently exercised by the Council of State. But even Anjou and Leicester had had to accept the States General's nominees for this body or, at least, they had been required to choose their councillors from the States General's nominees. The Council of State therefore derived

---

[22] N. Mout, 'Ideales Muster oder erfundene Eigenart', in Koenigsberger and Müller-Luckner, *Republiken und Republikanismus im Europa der frühen Neuzeit*, 170–1.
[23] *Ibid.*, 169–87.

its authority from the States General, but it was not directly responsible to that assembly. The separate provinces tried, although not always successfully, to place their own. natives in the Council. This was an impossible situation. The States General had effectively to degrade the Council of State into a largely administrative organ.[24]

The lead in these transformations and political clarifications was taken by Jan van Oldenbarnevelt, the advocate, i.e. the political secretary of the Estates of Holland. Now that most of Flanders and Brabant had been lost to the Union, Oldenbarnevelt used his position and the economic and financial predominance of Holland over the other provinces, to make the States General into an effective centre of government. Contemporary courtly observers in France and England deplored this messy form of government. It seemed to lack institutional centralisation, so beloved by the lawyers of early modern monarchies. It also seemed to lack a clearly recognisable central authority and decision-making machinery. Many modern historians have adopted the same point of view They have argued from the supposed inefficiency of large assemblies, although in fact the States General was a rather small assembly, and even the much larger ones of the 1570s had often acted with remarkable speed and efficiency. They, like their contemporaries, also pointed especially to the absence of full powers for the deputies of the States General and even for the provincial Estates, and of their need to refer financial and constitutional matters back to their principals.

In practice, the *ruggespraak*, the need for reference back, was not nearly as much of a hindrance to effective government as was generally thought in court circles outside the Netherlands. With the relatively short distances of the Union and the excellent waterways, reference back could often be achieved quite quickly. More importantly, for all non-financial and non-constitutional matters the deputies had in fact full powers and mostly proceeded by majority voting. It was not as if the financial demands of *dominium regale* regimes were usually capable of being settled quickly and easily. In Castile itself, in 1596, the Cortes refused to renew the tax of the *milliones* and did not consent to renew it until 1600, two years after Philip II's death. In *dominium politicum et regale* regimes such as England, parliaments had usually to be first summoned and then they tended to debate financial demands at considerable length, even where the deputies enjoyed *plena potestas* or full powers.

The most important reason why the Netherlands system worked was the position of Holland in the Union. The smaller provinces could be, and often were, awkward. Not only did they want to keep their money for their own defence; they also put pressure on the States General to plan the year's campaigning for their own benefit. Yet in most cases the smaller provinces were willing to follow the lead of Holland, just as, before the civil wars started, they had followed the lead of Holland, Brabant and Flanders.

---

[24] Den Tex, *Oldenbarnevelt*, vol. I, 151–2.

Parliamentary government and dominium regale

William of Orange had known how to make use of these traditions, by clever management of the Estates of Holland and of the States General. Jan van Oldenbarnevelt was Orange's equal in the virtuosity of parliamentary management. The Estates of Holland and the States General met close together. The advocate was able to go personally from one to the other and lead both. Oldenbarnevelt the patrician (although his own origins were rather in the professional bourgeoisie) saw no need, as the prince had done, to rely on populist support. In Utrecht, for instance, he managed to overthrow the populist regime led by the Calvinist preachers which Leicester had vainly hoped to play against the regents of Holland. With most provincial regimes dominated by narrow regent oligarchies, Oldenbarnevelt had a solid party to support his policies. The essence of these policies was the continued fight against Spain and the maintenance of a relatively tolerant and inclusive religious policy in the Union.

With these policies the advocate headed a remarkably effective government, at least as long as the war lasted. The majority of the non-patrician population were willing to support this government, although they were effectively excluded from direct participation in it, just as they had been during the various monarchical regimes. There had, it is true, always been exceptions to this pattern. The most recent and dramatic had been the popular revolutions and populist Calvinist dictatorship in Ghent, between 1577 and 1583. But William of Orange who had at first favoured this movement turned against it, to preserve his broad coalition against Spain.[25] Ghent became a kind of cautionary case for the regent class and this anti-democratic feeling played its part also in the coolness of contemporary intellectuals towards republicanism. For the Ghent of the populist Calvinists had loudly proclaimed its republicanism and had consciously looked towards the arch-Calvinist republic of Geneva.

Oldenbarnevelt's position was not unlike that of a modern prime minister who depends on a parliamentary majority for his authority. Most of his energies went into foreign policy. In directing the United Provinces – this name was now coming into use – he insisted on equal treatment with the other great powers, and he achieved this status in the triple alliance with France and England against Spain in 1596.

It was not easy psychologically. Even old-established sister republics could not completely shed the monarchical preconceptions of the age. In the early seventeenth century the ambassador of the allied republic of Venice claimed precedence over his Dutch colleague because the Serenissima ruled, or had ruled, over several kingdoms while the United Provinces included 'only' dukedoms and counties.[26]

In practice it was again a matter of diplomatic tightrope-walking between the divergent aims of France and England and the detritus left by the Treaty of

---

[25] H. A. Enno van Gelder, *Revolutionaire Reformatie* (Amsterdam, 1943), *passim*. J. Decavele, 'De mislukking van Oranjes "demokratische" politiek in Vlaanderen', *BMGN*, 99, 4 (1984), 626–50.

[26] Koenigsberger, 'Schlussbetrachtung', in Koenigsberger and Müller-Luckner, *Republiken und Republikanismus*, 290.

Nonsuch of English claims to political and military rights in the United Provinces. In spite of the apprehensiveness of some of his more cautious colleagues, Oldenbarnevelt on occasion blocked the policies of the redoubtable queen of England, calculating correctly that the two countries still needed each other, in spite of the many points of friction during and after Leicester's governor-generalship.

Nor were relations with France entirely smooth. In 1596 and on several later occasions Henry IV made it known that he wanted to take up the offer of sovereignty which the Dutch had made to Henry III after the assassination of William of Orange. It is not clear how seriously Henry IV meant these claims to be taken or whether they were only moves in the diplomatic game of chess. Oldenbarnevelt, at least, had to take them seriously and he made sure that they were blocked.

The growing political and diplomatic self-assurance of the republic depended to a large extent on its military successes during the 1590s. These successes were due in the first place to events over which the United Provinces had no direct control: the diversion of Spanish resources, first to the Armada campaign against England in 1588, and then to Parma's intervention in the French civil wars in 1590 and 1592. At the same time Dutch military efforts were becoming more effective than they had ever been. This was due to the financial support for the army which the States General were able to organise in spite of all the contemporary complaints about their inefficiency. Secondly, it was due to the successful cooperation between Oldenbarnevelt and his principal military commander, William of Orange's son, Maurice.

Like everything else in the republic, Maurice's position was complex and not easily understood outside the country. He was appointed stadholder of Holland and Zeeland and of several other provinces, by their Estates, but not of Friesland or Guelders. The stadholder enjoyed powers similar to the royal governors of the individual provinces, including the right of appointing the magistrates of the cities and the command of the provinces' military forces. He held no federal military command except that of admiral.[27] Yet in practice he was a kind of commander-in-chief and it was his cautious professionalism and Parma-like grasp of strategic possibilities which ensured Dutch success in the reconquest of the eastern provinces of the Netherlands and even of some towns in Brabant and Flanders. This professionalism spread the fame of Maurice as a commander and as a supreme exponent of the art of war all over Protestant Europe.

Inevitably, Maurice of Nassau, the outstanding military commander of the age and surrounded by a kind of court of young noblemen, came to be regarded, both inside and outside the republic, as the head of the state. Inevitably, there grew up frictions between himself and the Estates of Holland and the States General, just as there had been in his father's case. These frictions, however exasperating, remained manageable as long as the war with Spain lasted. All parties agreed to

---

[27] H. H. Rowen, *The Princes of Orange: The Stadtholders in the Dutch Republic* (Cambridge, 1988), 32–6.

Parliamentary government and dominium regale

give priority to the fight against the common enemy. But as soon as a truce was concluded, the old rivalries between the military and the Estates reappeared. Characteristically, the open breach came over religion: not Catholicism and Protestantism this time, but the rigid Calvinism of the preachers with their populist appeal and the tolerant Erastianism, i.e. state control over the church, of the regent class. Inevitably the House of Nassau became involved in these disputes over political power within the republic. Inevitably, too, these disputes took on a personal colouring between the head of the House of Orange-Nassau, in his capacity as stadholder and commander of the Dutch armies, Maurice and, later, William II and William III, and the advocate and leader of the regents, party, Oldenbarnevelt and, later, Jan de Witt. To the dismay, although perhaps not to the surprise, of contemporaries the republic of the United Provinces re-enacted many of the conflicts between the different provinces and their principal cities and between an executive government and a representative assembly, conflicts which had been characteristic of the princely regimes of *dominium pociticum et regale*.

THE SOUTH: TOWARDS *DOMINIUM REGALE*

The Treaty of Arras had seemed to be a victory of the conservative Estates of the Walloon provinces over both the populist Calvinism of the cities and the absolutist tendencies of Philip II. The first part of this victory was to be permanent. In some of the Walloon cities, notably in Lille, neither a Calvinist nor a Catholic popular party had ever seriously menaced the established Catholic–patrician order.[28] Other cities, such as Tournai and Arras, were relatively small urban islands in a sea of rural nobility and rich monasteries. Against these, the religious democrats could not stand up, once support from Flanders and Brabant had disappeared with Parma's conquests. In these two provinces, with their big cities, the populist regimes like Ghent or the Catholic ones like Brussels, disappeared for the same reason, Parma's reconquests.

The second part of the victory, that over the king, very rapidly proved to be illusory. In the first place, it was not really a victory over the king at all, in spite of Philip II's misgivings over the terms which Parma had negotiated. It was, on the contrary, a deliberate 'reconciliation' with the king by men who had always thought of themselves as his loyal vassals who had protested or even fought only against the excesses of some of the king's ministers and the unbearable damage inflicted on the country by the king's soldiers in the civil war.

But the civil war continued. The Walloon provinces on their own were unable to bear the costs of this war. Within two years of the Treaty of Arras, Parma recalled his Spanish and Italian troops, with the consent of the Walloon Estates. By

---

[28] Cf. R. S. Duplessis, *Lille and the Dutch Revolt: Urban Stability in an Era of Revolution* (Cambridge, 1991), ch. 8 and *passim*.

1586 the money sent from Castile to the Netherlands had reached new heights,[29] and these troops and resources enabled Parma to reconquer most of Flanders and Brabant and the provinces of the eastern fringe of the Netherlands.

The cost to the country was appalling. Antwerp and its trade were blockaded by the Dutch, after the city had surrendered to Parma in 1585. Many towns lost between a half and two-thirds of their inhabitants. Large stretches of the countryside were depopulated. Country industries, such as the famous serge cloth manufactures of the small Flemish town of Hondschoote, collapsed almost completely.[30]

The 1590s saw some very modest beginnings of an economic recovery. But the Estates of the provinces of the Union of Arras had lost the economic ability to defend themselves on their own from Maurice of Nassau's counter-offensive; and with this loss they had also lost the ability and, to a large extent even the will, to counterbalance the king's governor general politically.

For some years this situation was masked by the confusion surrounding this office. In 1591-2 Parma was mortally ill in Spa, in the archbishopric of Liège. The old count of Mansfelt was appointed as interim governor general and he and Parma governed at cross-purposes from Brussels and Spa. Parma had lost the confidence of the court of Madrid. The king sent the count of Fuentes to arrest him. Like Don John of Austria, Parma died just in time to be spared this ultimate disgrace of Philip II's habitual betrayal. It had been bad enough that in 1580 Philip had sent Margaret of Parma back to the Netherlands to take over once more the political government of the country while reducing her son to the position of captain general. Parma refused point blank this division of powers with his mother, and the king had to give in.[31] It seems very doubtful whether the double act, even with mother and son as principals, would have worked any better than the duo of Margaret and Alba in 1568.

When Parma died in the middle of his second campaign in France against Henry IV and the Huguenots, in December 1592 the States General of the Union of Arras officially took over the government. In practice it was Fuentes who controlled it, without bothering to make known his precise instructions. In Brussels he replaced Parma's Italian advisers with Spaniards. Even so, he complained that he had insufficient control over decision-making.[32] For all the fashionable complaints and wise shakings of grizzled heads in the European courts over the inefficiency of the political decision-making process in the republican United Provinces, the confusions in the monarchical regime in Brussels were worse.

The short interlude of the governor-generalship of Philip's nephew, the archduke Ernest, did nothing to improve matters. Ernest who believed in 'force' and

---

[29] Parker, *Spain and the Netherlands*, 187.
[30] *Ibid.*, 183. Verlinden, 'En Flandre sous Philippe II', 21-30.
[31] H. de Schepper, 'De "Reconquista" mislukt. De katholieke gewesten 1578-1588', in *NAGN* (Haarlem, 1980), vol. VI, 265.
[32] *Ibid.*, 281.

Parliamentary government and dominium regale

'rigour' summoned an assembly of some of the Estates and of the knights of the Golden Fleece in January 1595, and immediately found himself overwhelmed by complaints and grievances. He died shortly afterwards, and Fuentes now officially took over the government. This was too reminiscent of Alba and it was too much for the great Walloon seigneurs. Charles of Mansfelt joined the imperial army in Hungary. Most of the others withdrew from the Council of State, just as the trio of Orange, Egmont and Hoorn had done in the 1560s. The old duke of Aerschot left the country to spend his remaining days in that ultra-aristocratic and snobbish but strictly constitutional state of Venice.[33]

Aerschot, for all his class-conscious narrowness and his political mistakes had consistently stood for peace, reconciliation and the maintenance of the Netherlands privileges, for Catholicism without persecution and for constitutional government under the king's sovereignty. His flight – for it was that, although no one pursued him – marked symbolically the defeat of the Politiques party in the Netherlands and the effective end of *dominium politicum et regale* in the Union of Arras.

Not everyone immediately saw it in this way. Shortly before his death, in September 1598, Philip II proposed to make over the sovereignty of the Netherlands to Archduke Albert, brother of the recently deceased Archduke Ernest and also of the emperor Rudolph II, and marry him to his favourite daughter, Isabella. Even though the Council of State did not think it necessary, the States General, assembled in August 1598, were informed of this decision by the president of the Council of State, Jean Richardot. Richardot was a lawyer and civil servant in the conservative tradition of Viglius and of the contemporary French, Spanish and English secretaries of state, all of them civil servants who felt happy with an autocratic regime. It allowed them the exercise of great decision-making powers, with responsibility only to their prince. Richardot reassured the States General: 'This change, gentlemen, which has at first surprised us, is in fact no change, for nothing has changed except to our great advantage.'[34]

Formally, this was true enough. Isabella took an oath on the observance of the Perpetual Edict of 1577 and the Treaty of Arras of 1579. King Philip had meant to include all seventeen provinces in his bestowal of sovereignty on his daughter and son-in-law – apparently just what Aerschot and the Politiques had hoped to achieve when they summoned Archduke Matthias, Albert's elder brother, to Brussels in 1577. In 1598 the States General symbolically left benches open for the participation of deputies from the 'rebel' provinces.

In fact, the political set-up was very different. This became immediately clear even on a relatively minor point. The States General petitioned Albert not to return to Spain, as he intended. Richardot thereupon read them a lecture on the

---

[33] L. van der Essen, 'Politieke geschiedenis van het Zuiden, 1585–1609', in *AGN*, vol. V, 265–6.
[34] G. de Hautecloque, 'Le Président de Richardot et les Etats Généraux des Pays-Bas de 1598', *Mémoires de l'Académie des Sciences, Lettres et Arts d'Arras*, 2nd series, 10 (1878), 151.

authority of kings 'to which you should conform yourselves, realising that there may be a mystery which we do not understand and which God, who governs and directs the actions of princes . . . has ordered for our great good'.[35]

Here was a succinct formulation of the 'mystery' of matters of state and of the divine and absolute right of kings, such as was becoming a fashionable creed at this time in Western Europe. James I would no doubt have approved, if he had read Richardot's speech.

When 'the Archdukes', as they now came to be known, arrived in the Netherlands, there was another debate about the need to summon the States General. The fact that this was debated at all would have surprised Charles V and perhaps even Philip II. We have an anonymous memorandum — could it have been by Richardot? — which set out the arguments both for and against a States General.[36] The arguments for were conventional. It had been the practice of the ancient Belgians. The States General represented an amiable conference between the princes and their subjects and the princes could reject their subjects' humble supplications and requests as they thought fit. The assembly gave public and solemn authority to the prince's resolutions. It was the true basis of their authority, the 'honest liberty' of the people and the sign of 'a sweet and courteous dominion'. Novelties were perilous, especially for a new prince who had still to establish himself and gain the hearts of the people. Not to summon the States General would make people fear that the prince would not observe the laws and customs he and his predecessors had sworn to uphold.

But even these arguments in favour of a States General were interspersed with cautionary remarks about the 'many great difficulties which often ensue' and 'the too great authority and liberty of speech which the Estates assume', as was happening in England, Denmark and other northern countries.

The opposite view was argued much more incisively: such an assembly would be a poison rather than medicine, as could be witnessed in France. States Generals weakened the grandeur and power of the prince and strengthened those of the subjects. They confused a royal state with an aristocratic or popular one, binding the prince's hands and subjecting him to the law and thus reducing him to servitude. This was especially so for a new prince who was not yet absolute master of the state or of the hearts of his subjects (shades of Machiavelli here?). They would insist on the departure of foreigners and on peace with Holland at any price. If the *aides* were discontinued — it was the Cortes of Castile which had just discontinued the tax of the *milliones*; the States General of the Netherlands had never actually abolished an *aide*, although they had often reduced the initial demand — if, then, the *aides* were discontinued, it would lead to plundering and brandschatting of the

---

[35] *Ibid.*, 156–7.
[36] 'S'il est expédient d'assembler les Etats Généraux?' Its main points are quoted or summarised by Gachard, *Actes des Etats Généraux de 1600* (Brussels, 1849), VIII–XIV.

Parliamentary government and dominium regale

people and the evident ruin and dissolution of the prince's state. This was not easy to remedy as, once the evils and miseries which had crept in 'by the length and malice of the time', people would put the blame on the prince. In short, 'the prince is not bound by the laws of the state. He can change, uphold or abolish them, according to the good, the needs and the peace of his subjects; for he is above the law, he is himself the living and breathing law; and he does not have to give any account of his actions to anyone but God.'

Here was a clear and succinct exposition of *dominium politicum et regale* and of *dominium regale* which was now interpreted as the divine, absolute right of princes as God's viceregents.

The fact that this memorandum was anonymous suggests that it reflected opinions current at the court of Brussels. Its general thrust was clearly anti-States General. Nevertheless, the Archdukes chose the conservative and time-honoured option of summoning the States General. There was the practical consideration that the mutinous Spanish soldiers in the castles of Antwerp, Ghent and Lier could only be appeased with money from a special loan, and this loan could only be raised if it was guaranteed by the Estates of Brabant. For the Archdukes it was essential to avoid a repetition of the events of 1576 when the mutinies of the unpaid Spanish soldiers had led the States General to meet on their own initiative and to conclude peace with Holland, without regard for the king. The Archdukes took their revenge on the mutinous soldiers by encouraging, although with some misgivings, the country people to massacre stragglers or even small groups of the retreating soldiers. It was not only the Calvinists of the House of Orange who could play the populist card.

All the same, it was as well to take precautions. Just as had happened at the accession of Philip II, the governorships of the provinces were distributed to members of the high nobility. To make doubly sure of the loyalty of the States General, the Archdukes wrote confidentially to these provincial governors to make certain only persons of great authority and prudence were elected as deputies and that they should be 'easily manageable persons who will allow themselves to accept what is proposed to them'.[37] There had been earlier occasions, since the days of Charles V, when the Brussels government had tried to influence the selection of deputies. But never before had there been such a consistent attempt at 'packing'.

In spite of this packing, the States General, meeting in August 1600, attempted to repeat the actions of their predecessor of 1557–8. They had some cards to play; or, at least, they seem to have thought so. Dark rumours were circulating in Brussels that they would make their own peace with the Hollanders. They tried to appoint a treasurer for the sums they voted and they tried to have their own representatives at the pay parades of the soldiers. The government firmly rejected all these attempts. The key administrative positions were now much more firmly in

---

[37] *Ibid.*, XV.

the hands of Spaniards than they had been in 1558. There was no chance that the Spaniards would give up control of the money that was sent from Spain for the troops,[38] nor would they agree that only native Netherlanders should command the fortresses. The government demanded an *aide* of 325,000 florins a month but allowed themselves to be beaten down to 300,000 – still an enormous sum, compared to the 800,000 florins per year of 1558, even allowing for inflation. Moreover, a smaller and now much devastated area had to pay it. The government proposed to raise this money by 'general means': a chimney tax and excise taxes on foodstuffs. Flanders and Brabant agreed, but the other provinces did not. Eventually, and much against their better judgement, the Archdukes allowed every province to raise its quota as it pleased. Inevitably, there was a shortfall from the total sum.

From the government's point of view, the States General had behaved as awkwardly and as slowly as it had always done. Some of its deputies had been given full powers to negotiate and conclude; others had repeatedly to refer back to their principals. Nor did they manage to negotiate an agreement with the States General of the United Provinces. Apart from quarrelling over which of the two assemblies had the right to call itself the States General of the Netherlands, each side expected the other to join with them on its terms, and these terms were incompatible. The Brussels assembly asked the assembly at The Hague to accept the sovereignty of the Archdukes. After all, sovereignty now no longer lay with the king of Spain. The Hague assembly asked Brussels to rid the country once and for all of all the Spaniards.

By October 1600 the government of the Archdukes had lost its patience and dissolved the assembly. The leave-taking remained amicable. The Archdukes did not want to offend the Belgian elite unnecessarily. In fact, however, the States General had lost out. The government had agreed only to the most general of its demands, such as that it would try to curb the plundering and blackmailing of the country population by the soldiers. It collected the 300,000 florins a month, even though there had been no formal act of acceptance by the States General, and continued to do so, as if a permanent *aide* had been voted.[39]

Madrid was even less impressed than Brussels with the value of summoning a States General. Philip III formally forbade it, and it was not a point on which the Archdukes insisted by virtue of their sovereignty. They could manage without the States General, just as Henry IV did in France, by simply collecting taxes on their own authority. For the rest, their position was little different from that of earlier governors general. All important decision-making was done in Spain. When Archduke Albert died the former position was even formally restored.

[38] G. Parker, 'The Decision-making Process in the Government of the Catholic Netherlands under the Archdukes, 1596–1621', in Parker, *Spain and the Netherlands*, 164–75.
[39] For the detailed negotiations of the States General see Gachard, *Actes des Etats Généraux de 1600*, *passim*. Cf. also a contemporary Spanish account, 'Relacion de la que han consentido los estados generales en el eño de 1600', AGRB, P. d'E.A., 663, fos. 140r–144v.

Parliamentary government and dominium regale

Isabella, now governor general and no longer sovereign, summoned the States General one last time, in 1632, and this against the wishes of her nephew, Philip IV. Once more, the idea was to come to an agreement with 'Their High Mightinesses', as the deputies of the States General at The Hague now called themselves. The two sides were bitterly divided over what concessions would be acceptable. In the north, not only the different provinces but individual towns disagreed with each other. In the south the different views of the Brussels States General and the Spaniards became more and more evident.[40] Peace and truce negotiations ground to a halt. Isabella died in December 1633. The States General sent the duke of Aerschot to Madrid to plead their cause. There he was arrested, as Montigny had been arrested in Spain in 1567.[41] In 1634 the States General were dissolved.

Philip IV declared that 'States Generals are pernicious at all times and in all monarchical countries, without exception'.[42] Neither the Spanish nor the Austrian Habsburgs summoned the States General again before 1789. The provincial Estates survived, as they did in some provinces in France; but it was the end of *dominium politicum et regale* in the Netherlands.

[40] J. I. Israel, *The Dutch Republic and the Hispanic World* (Oxford, 1982), 227–49.
[41] P. Geyl, *The Netherlands in the Seventeenth Century*, pt. 1, 2nd edn (London, 1961), 107.
[42] Quoted in J. Gilissen, *Le régime représentatif avant 1790 en Belgique* (Brussels, 1952), 117.

14

Epilogue

'Our ancestors ... arranged many things wisely to keep kings within the bounds of modesty and balance, so that they should not abuse their power; for its excess is the cause of the destruction of all public felicity. Among those matters which they determined with much prudence was the one that nothing of importance should be decided without the consent of the nobles and the people and without electing from all classes of the state persons who should assemble in the Cortes of the kingdom.'[1]

LIBERTY AND SOVEREIGNTY

The relations between the monarchy and the States General of the Netherlands were about power and freedom. In the one and three-quarter centuries of their history they were, of course, about a lot of other things as well. But power and freedom were always the basic issues. All others were no more than variations on this theme, however distant the keys and harmonies, and however strange the dissonances they chose to explore.

In the later middle ages most European monarchies had worked out a system of balance and harmony in which monarchies and representative assemblies shared power and in which, ideally, they cooperated for a common end: the greater glory of the monarchy and the welfare of the community over which the monarchy ruled. This was the point of Juan de Mariana's encomium in Spain in 1598, and it was the point of a dialogue, at the other end of Europe, between the Swedish chancellor, Axel Oxenstierna, and Cromwell's ambassador to Sweden, Bulstrode Whitelocke, in 1654.

Both the chancellor and the ambassador were anxious to impress each other with the stability of their political regimes and, hence, their admirable status as political and trading partners.

---

[1] Mariana, *Del rey y de la institución de la dignidad real*, 60. 'nuestros mayores ... sancionaron muchas cosas sabiamente, para contener a los reyes dentro los límites de la modestia y templanza, de suerte que no abusen de su potestad, cuyo exceso es la causa de la distrucción de la felicidad pública. Entre aquellas cosas que determinaron con mucha prudencia, una de ellas fué que en ningun negocio de importancia se sancionase sin la voluntad de la nobleza y del pueblo antes de elegir de entre todas las clases del Estado, individuos para reunirse en Cortes del reino.'

Epilogue

We hold the government of England, as to the fundamentals of it, to be the same now as when we had a king; the same laws, the same supreme power, and the same magistrates. Forrein negotiations, matters of peace and warre, raysing of moneys, and making of lawes, were the proper business of parlements in the time of our kings, so admitted by the best and most successful of them; and though some of them, growing in power, would encroach more than others. Yett all acknowledged the power of parlements in those matters, and so it is still.[2]

Oxenstierna tactfully refrained from raising the point that the English Parliament had recently abolished the monarchy and the House of Lords. He concentrated rather on the Riksdag, the Swedish parliament, remarking that the only real difference was that the Riksdag discussed only what the king wanted it to discuss. This had been one of the principal points at issue between Philip II and the States General of the Netherlands. Whitelocke thought that in Sweden, too, this should have been an important issue: 'This may be a good way to preserve your quiet; but may it not be ill for the rights and liberty of the people?' The king would hardly propose a new law for liberty, he thought, which derogated from his power.

Oxenstierna had a ready answer:

This were an inconvenience if the peoples' rights and libertyes were not already settled; but by our lawes the boundaries of the king's power and the peoples' rights are sufficiently known and established; as the king can make no law, nor alter or repeale any, nor impose any taxe, nor compell men to go out of the kingdom, without the assent of the riksdag: and in that councell which is supreme in this kingdome, every man's vote and assent is included, by the deputies of the clergy, burroughs, and boores, which are respectively elected, and by the chiefs of the nobility; so that all sorts of people have their share, either in person or by deputies in the supreme councell of the kingdome by whom only those great matters are done.[3]

Here was the idealised description of *domininium politicum et regale* in which the king's prerogatives and the subjects' liberties complement each other. This was what the dukes of Brabant had sworn to uphold in their famous *joyeuses entrées*, and which most European princes had sworn for their own countries, with only relatively minor variations. This was the basis of Henry VIII's famous address to Parliament, in 1543, that 'we at no time stand so highly in our estate royal as in time of Parliament, wherein we as head and you as members are conjoined and knit together into one body politic'. Both the idea behind the declaration and, indeed, its formulation were far from original. As early as the twelfth century a canonist had said: 'The pope with a council is greater than the pope without one.'[4]

---

[2] B. Whitelocke, *A Journal of the Swedish Embassy*, ed. C. Morton, 2 vols. (London, 1772), vol. I, 320.
[3] *Ibid.*, vol. II, 224–6.
[4] G. R. Elton, ed., *The Tudor Constitution* (Cambridge, 1960), 270. The quotation from the canonist is in B. Tierney, 'Freedom and the Medieval Church', in Davis, *The Origins of Modern Freedom in the West*, 74.

Monarchies, States Generals and Parliaments

This is what countless kings and their chancellors said in countless addresses at the opening of parliamentary sessions in the fifteenth and sixteenth and sometimes the seventeenth centuries. Debates, disagreements and quarrels would come later. The engravings which we have of parliaments during this period all represent the assemblies at precisely such openings or other formal ceremonies. They all look remarkably alike: a big rectangular hall, with the prince and his ministers at one end, facing the viewer, and with the deputies, according to their estate and rank, on benches along the sides or, sometimes, facing the throne. Change the wall hangings and the coats of arms, and you could easily exchange one engraving for another. The pictures tell us about the idealised relationship, but very little about the working of the institution. A symbolic visual division between government supporters and opposition, let alone a semi-circular seating arrangement reflecting different shades of opinion, did not appear until the late eighteenth century. Before that time, when constitutional opposition was looked on as treason, such arrangements were not even thinkable.

THE INSTABILITY OF *DOMINIUM POLITICUM ET REGALE*

The harmony shown at the opening session did not often last. There was an inbuilt clash of interests in the regime of *dominium politicum et regale*. Princes were anxious to increase their powers, from personal ambition to pursue their favourite occupation, i.e. waging war; or because they could claim that they represented the whole realm as against the allegedly private interests of magnates, cities and even the church and its prelates. A clever prince could play on the divisions and balance different interest groups against each other.

The prince's lawyers and other officials reinforced his personal ambitions. They had learned from Roman law about the absolute authority of the Roman emperor, the *princeps legibus solutus*, the ruler above and beyond the law, with no earthly superior. Early and effortlessly, the lawyers made the leap from the Roman emperor, the *princeps* of the Justinian Codex, to the much more limited ruler of their own country. When Henry VIII claimed that the realm of England was an empire, and therefore not subject to the authority of the pope or the Holy Roman Emperor, Henry, or rather his lawyers, were claiming no more than the lawyers of continental kings had been claiming for generations.

Beyond the personal ambition of princes there were the impersonal pressures on heads of government and ministers. As the complexities and problems of government increased, as warfare became ever more expensive and absorbed an increasing proportion of the country's resources, and as royal justice superseded local jurisdictions, governments were driven to increase their powers. For a time, and with competent leadership at the top, much of this increase could be accommodated within the traditional political system. Henry VII, Henry VIII and Elizabeth I in England, Gustavus Adolphus in Sweden, Charles V in the Netherlands all

Plate 17 Engraving of the Polish Sejm, with Sigismund II Augustus presiding, from A. Guagninus, *Sarmatiae Europae Descriptio*, 1581. British Library, London

Plate 18 Elizabeth I in Parliament, from Sir Simonds d'Ewes, *Journals of the Parliaments of Queen Elizabeth*, 1672. British Library, London

Epilogue

Plate 19 Engraving of the French Estates General, 1614. Bibliothèque Nationale, Paris

Plate 20 Engraving of the Regensburg Reichstag, 1653. Photo courtesy of the late Professor Dr Volker Press

managed this problem without breaking the basic political consensus in their countries. But the divisions were real, and the tactical initiative lay nearly always with the monarchies.

Yet princes did not usually attempt a frontal assault on privileges. Apart from their coronation oaths and their profound dislike of all 'novelties', which they shared with most of their subjects, there were two basic conditions which made such assaults difficult. There was firstly the fact of multiple monarchies. The prince had to rule most of his dominions by deputies. The regents, viceroys or governors general never had the authority of the prince himself and found it difficult to pursue a consistent policy of increasing royal power. The exception was the duke of Alba, and he precipitated a civil war and was, in the end, disowned by his king. At least in the case of the Habsburgs, the very existence of their extended multiple monarchy made it difficult, if not impossible, for them to concentrate systematically on increasing monarchical power, even in the dominion in which they resided.

The second condition was a more technical one. It was the difficulty of financing increased government activity, especially warfare. All governments had to take up

Epilogue

loans, for even the resources of the European and overseas silver mines were insufficient to pay for the ever-swelling armies and navies and for the more and more urgent building costs for the new type of fortifications, necessitated by advances in artillery. These loans, as it turned out, could often only be raised by corporate cities and representative assemblies. For the unromantic international bankers regarded these institutions and their tax- and annuity-raising abilities as much more creditworthy than the prince and his theoretical claim of being *legibus solutus*.

One may therefore use the metaphor of geological plates, rather than that of a parallelogram or mechanical balance of forces. In a regime of *dominium politicum et regale* one may live on these plates safely for a considerable period of time, disturbed only by occasional rumbles. However, because of long-term economic changes and the long-term political policies of the monarchies, tensions gradually increase and through prolonged pressure there is an earthquake. Such an event necessitates an adjustment, a new arrangement of political forces. Such earthquakes took place in Denmark and Sweden where the monarchies, in 1660–5 and 1680 respectively, got rid of their parliaments altogether. In Spain and its dependencies this happened more slowly. In the course of the seventeenth century the Spanish monarchy deliberately ceased to summon the States General of the southern Netherlands and the Estates of Naples, Sardinia, Aragon and eventually Castile itself. In their last century of rule the Habsburgs deliberately transformed their monarchy into a *dominium regale*, just as the American and Asian colonies had been from the beginning. In the early eighteenth century the Bourbons then had little difficulty in building up the royal administrative apparatus into French-style absolutism.

Political earthquakes, due to gradual shifts in the tectonic plates, were not, however, the only hazards of the *dominium politicum et regale* regimes. There were also volcanic eruptions. Such eruptions were occasionally due to social movements. But social movements by themselves, while frequent in this period, were usually purely local and were relatively easily contained.[5] It was the Reformation and Counter-Reformation, and the reaction of the monarchies to them, which gave these movements coherence and clearly defined their purposes, widening their social appeal and spreading them nationally and internationally.

Unavoidably, parliaments became involved, either directly in the religious movements or in reaction to the monarchies' reaction to these movements. This did not inevitably mean a clash between a parliament and its prince. Very often they were on the same religious side, whether in defence of the Catholic Church, as in Spain, or in opposition to it, as in England under Henry VIII and in Sweden under Gustavus Vasa. But where the monarchy and its parliament, or an important

---

[5] For a more detailed discussion of such movements and their implications, especially in the seventeenth century, see H. G. Koenigsberger, 'The Crisis of the Seventeenth Century: a Farewell?' in Koenigsberger, *Politicians and Virtuosi*, 149–68.

section of the parliament, were on opposite sides, a clash became practically unavoidable. For the monarch's reaction to a religious challenge had political and constitutional consequences, and it also tended to involve property. This was precisely what happened in the Netherlands, even while the great majority of the people and the political classes continued to support the old church. It was the monarchy's initiative in its actions against the heretics which rode roughshod over a whole array of highly prized privileges, liberties and property rights. Here was the connection between religious dissent, even when it was not one's own dissent, and the parliament's or States General's primary obligation to defend the subjects' liberties.

Religion gave both sides coherent political arguments and appeared to justify the use of force. And since this force caught up strata in society which were not normally engaged in political discourse at all, it made the traditional compromises by which political differences used to be settled much more difficult to achieve. Unless one side gave in completely or won a complete victory, the quarrels were now likely to result in civil wars which became self-feeding and could go on for a very long time.

Three consequences followed for the political life of countries hit by such eruptions. The first was the widening of the concept of specific liberties into the general concept of liberty. This transformation was often due to the religious dimension of the new politics. The process is very clear in the history of the resistance theories of the Protestants in France and in the Netherlands. By the middle of the seventeenth century the concept of liberty had widened beyond its religious connotation and entered purely secular discourse. This is very evident in the conversations between Oxenstierna and Whitelocke.

The second consequence was the internationalisation of the conflicts. All European countries feared heterodoxy, both for itself, its threat to the accepted path of individual salvation and the threat of divine vengeance for a regime which had allowed this to happen, and because it was generally agreed that 'a change in religion produced a change in the state'. A political upheaval could threaten an individual king, as Gustavus Vasa's Lutheran revolt caused the downfall of the Danish king of Sweden and as, eventually, the Dutch Protestant revolt caused the downfall of the king of Spain in Holland. More likely still, religious heterodoxy in one's neighbour could threaten to spread to one's own state; or, alternatively, religious repression by a neighbour could threaten one's own precarious balance. In either case there was a strong incentive to intervene in the neighbour's civil war. Again unavoidably, when this happened, the religious–political decision-making became mixed up with power-political considerations.

THE QUESTION OF MUTUAL TRUST

The third consequence of a civil–religious eruption was the effective end of *dominium politicum et regale*, the *Ständestaat*, the *monarchia mixta*, the balanced monarchy.

Epilogue

Such a regime was built on trust. It was this trust which the religious division and the consequent civil strife destroyed. In the Netherlands this became clear as early as 1575 in the conference of Breda. Both sides wished to return to the balance of the reign of the emperor Charles V. Both sides found this impossible. The Dutch found that they could no longer trust the king with the powers his father had formerly exercised in a supposedly perfect balance. And since motives are never pure or unicausal, the Dutch also found themselves unwilling to give up the powers which the Estates of Holland had exercised since the beginning of the effective revolt in 1572.

The Hollanders never returned to a regime of *dominium politicum et regale*. With much trial and error they evolved a regime which may best be characterised by the modern term of 'parliamentary government'. In this regime the executive power was derived from the Estates, or the *vroedschappen*, which the Estates represented, and was so recognised as deriving. In the seventeenth century, for all the political problems between the Estates and the executive, this basic position was never seriously questioned.

For the monarchy the position represented a kind of mirror image. When the financial machinery for paying the army in the Netherlands collapsed, the king, having unsuccessfully tried to rule the country with a *dominium regale* regime, agreed to a new version of a balance of powers in the Pacification of Ghent. Very rapidly, it became clear to his new governor general, Don John of Austria, that he could not trust the States General. He attempted to solve his problems by a military coup; but this led inevitably to a continuance of the civil war and to foreign intervention.

The king and the Netherlanders made one final attempt to restore the old balance, the Treaty of Arras. But the demands of the continued civil war made the attempt unworkable. Rapidly, the relations with the king and the Estates changed to a regime of *dominium regale*. The Estates lost their powers of military appointments and of consent in political decision-making. Gradually, *dominium regale* was transformed into absolutism. The States General, summoned only twice again, became an anachronism and were treated as such by the States General of the United Provinces. The Catholic elite of the Spanish Netherlands were willing to accept this, not least because it safeguarded them from the danger of populist Calvinism. In the late 1570s and early 1580s this had been a very real danger in many of the cities of Flanders and the Walloon provinces. By contrast, this was a prospect which the *vroedschappen* of the cities of Holland had always been able at least to minimise. Fear of the populace was bad enough, even without a religious dimension. Shakespeare's Richard II voiced his disgust with the usurper Bolingbroke[6] and thus, had he been given the poet's command of words, might Philip II have apostrophised the usurper William of Orange. After

---

[6] Shakespeare, *Richard II*, I. 4. 23–36. Quoted above, p. 15.

Plate 21 The seal of the Estates of Holland, in use from 1572, with the lion of sovereignty as its emblem. Rijksarchief, The Hague

Parma's reconquest of Ghent there were no more revolutions in that revolution-prone city.

Throughout the seventeenth and eighteenth centuries Europe experienced the same collapse of the centre. In 1619 in Bohemia the rebellious Estates not only dethroned their legitimate king and chose another, Frederick of the Palatinate, to take his place; they also issued an act of confederation, the Confederation Bohemica, effectively a legislative act, a clear act of parliamentary government; for the king had no say in the legislation whatsoever. As soon as the emperor Ferdinand II had defeated the Bohemian Estates he went to the opposite extreme. In his *Landesordnung*, the new constitution he gave Bohemia, he stated specifically: 'We reserve for ourselves and our heirs... the right to make all laws and everything

Epilogue

which the *ius leges ferendae* involves.' The sole right to make laws is the most important prerogative of royal absolutism.[7]

It was precisely conflict over this problem and the consequent destruction of mutual trust which led to the breach between king and Parliament in England. In 1628, in the middle of the La Rochelle campaign against France, Charles I was trying to raise extra taxes and find billets for his soldiers. He also justified imprisonment of men suspected of subversion without the normal process of law. If cause had to be shown for such imprisonment, he wrote to the House of Lords, 'the service of the king would thereby be destroyed and defeated'. The judges could not follow any rule of law 'in cases of that transcendent nature which, happening so often, the very intermitting of the constant rule of government . . . would soon dissolve the very foundation and frame of our monarchy . . . and without overthrow of our sovereignty we cannot suffer this power to be impeached'.[8] In other words, the king claimed that for reasons of state he could set aside normal law and make his own laws. The House of Commons certainly saw it this way. 'Reason of state', said Sir Benjamin Rudyard, 'as it is used has not only eaten up law but almost all religion of Christendom.'[9]

In speech after speech, during that spring of 1628, members of the House of Commons proclaimed their trust in the king, their desire to uphold his prerogative, their willingness to grant aid for the country's defence. But the stark truth was that they did not, could not, trust a king who imposed taxes without consent and imprisoned men at will, according to laws he was making up himself. 'I fear more the violation of rights at home than a foreign army', proclaimed Sir Robert Phelps, on 22 March. He concluded his speech with a famous peroration:

Oh improvident ancestors! oh unwise forefathers! to be so curious in providing for the quiet possession of our lands and the liberties of Parliament, and to neglect our persons and bodies and to let them lie in prison . . . remediless. If this be law, what do we talk of our liberties? why do we trouble ourselves with the dispute of laws, franchises, propriety of goods . . . what may a man call his if not his liberty?[10]

But when the king accepted the Petition of Right (7 June 1628) as a declaration and not as a law, prohibiting the billeting of troops, the imposition of taxes without consent, and imprisonment without cause shown, he tacitly reserved his own prerogative right to do all these things when he, and not Parliament, judged them to be necessary.

With the king's acceptance of the Petition of Right, *dominium politicum et regale* had been re-estalished, at least formally. No one as yet foresaw that there would be

---

[7] J. Kunisch, 'Staatsraison and Konfessionalisierung als Faktoren absolutistischer Gesetzgebung: Das Beispiel Böhmen (1627)', in B. Dölemeyer and D. Klippel, *Gesetz und Gesetzgebung im Europe der Frühen Neuzeit* (Berlin, 1998), 142–8.
[8] R. C. Johnson *et al.*, eds., *Commons Debates 1628*, vol. III (New Haven and London, 1977), 372.
[9] *Ibid.*, 28 April 1628, 134.
[10] *Ibid.*, 22 March 1628, 61–3.

civil war fourteen years later. To the historian, however, with his inescapable hindsight, it is clear that the dilemma of liberty and sovereignty was bound to lead to confrontation, and this confrontation would have to be resolved. For too many of the political elite the traditional mutual trust with the monarch, so evident during the Armada campaign, had been eroded. The erosion was accelerated because of the greatly diminished common danger from abroad and because the English monarchy had become, much more evidently than in the sixteenth century, a multiple monarchy. This position was further complicated because its three main constitutents, England, Ireland and Scotland, all followed different confessions. This fact made the control of the armed forces the life-and-death issue which it was on the continent.

A wise government, following the basic principle of multiple monarchies of leaving the outlying dominions well alone, might have prevented the catastrophe. Charles I, untrustworthy as a monarch as well as personally, precipitated civil war in all three of his kingdoms and lost them, together with his head and the monarch's crown.[11]

In the Restoration both monarchy and Parliament were restored, but the balance of power between them remained problematical. A new viable balance was found, again without a previous blueprint, in the practical arrangements after the revolution of 1688–9. The monarchy, after a last and unsuccessful try to establish *dominium regale*, gave up its struggle and joined those it could not beat. It was effectively parliamentary government, although behind the veil of the curious Bodinian theory of the absolute sovereignty of the King-in-Parliament. This worked well in England and Scotland because they combined their parliaments in 1707.[12] It did not work at all in Catholic Ireland. The American colonies maintained their status of outlying dominions of a *politicum et regale* regime. When the Westminster King-in-Parliament attempted to rule the colonies according to its concept of Bodinian sovereignty, the situation did not prove manageable from any previous experience. Very rapidly trust between the two sides disappeared. The result was another civil war, usually called the American Revolution or the American War of Independence. The American constitution established a new type of *dominium politicum et regale*, with independent executive and legislature, but with the crucial difference from earlier systems that the independent executive was no longer a hereditary monarchy but an elective presidency. The once-despised common people had captured the monarchy, and sovereignty now resided in the republic as a whole, the state as such.[13]

---

[11] C. Russell, *The Causes of the English Civil War* (Oxford, 1990), *passim*. C. Russell, *The Fall of the British Monarchies 1637–1642* (Oxford, 1991), *passim*.

[12] At the time of writing, there are some doubts about the continuance of the union. The terms of the Union of 1707 are certainly being changed and there is, for the first time since 1707, a Scottish parliament again.

[13] Koenigsberger, 'Composite States, Representative Institutions and the American Revolution', 142–53.

Epilogue

An explosive situation could, however, also generate the trust which the monarchy needed to get rid of *dominium politicum et regale*, provided the really distrusted power was an outsider. This happened in Piedmont-Savoy and in Portugal. From 1536 to 1559 the western part of Piedmont-Savoy was occupied by French troops, the eastern part by Spanish-imperial troops. At the Treaty of Cateau-Cambrésis, in 1559, Emmanuel Philibert was reinstated in his duchy. As Philip II's governor general of the Netherlands he had had to deal with the States General and he was determined not to repeat this scary experience in his own duchy. He was clever enough not to let on. The parliament he summoned for its first independent session since 1536 was a kind of Kahki Parliament such as the one which Lloyd George summoned in Britain after victory in the First World War in 1919, and which was filled with enthusiastic patriots. They welcomed Emmanuel Philibert and voted him a huge tax. With the money thus legally obtained by the excessive trust of the ruling classes, the duke paid his army and from then onwards was able to raise taxes without ever having to summon parliament again. What the duke of Alba failed to achieve in the composite polity of the Netherlands, which was itself part of the huge Habsburg composite monarchy, Emmanuel Philibert accomplished easily in his compact ducal state. For a generation, distrust had been directed at the foreign rulers of the state, and the duke was now happy to share this distrust with his subjects. Moreover, he had the great advantage of having no significant religious problem in his country.

Emmanuel Philibert kept the nobility on board by judicious and generous use of patronage. It kept the native monopoly of offices and did not interfere with the nobles' exploitation of the peasants. Serfdom was not effectively abolished until the eighteenth century. But taxation rose from an average of 70-90,000 ducats p.a. before the French invasion to over 500,000 for Emmanuel Philibert's reign, a much greater increase than the rise of prices during this period. The pattern of a military autocracy with noble support which the House of Hohenzollern was to build up in Brandenburg-Prussia during the seventeenth and eighteenth centuries was very similar to that which the House of Savoy had already established in the sixteenth century.[14]

In Portugal distrust was also directed against outsiders: the Castilians who, so the Portuguese claimed, had ridden roughshod over their privileges. When they threw out the Castilians, in 1640, and proclaimed the duke of Braganza as their king, all were happily united in this action. As in Piedmont, there was no religious dimension in the conflict. Revenues from gold and other precious metals from Brazil then allowed the monarchy to neglect the Cortes and quietly establish one of Europe's most effective absolutisms.

---

[14] H. G. Koenigsberger, 'The Parliament of Piedmont during the Renaissance 1460-1560', in Koenigsberger, *Estates and Revolutions*, 19-79.

Monarchies, States Generals and Parliaments

It did not go so smoothly for the monarchy everywhere. In the sixteenth century Catalonia's rarely summoned Cortes (*corts*) had presented no more problems to the monarchy than was normal in a *dominium politicum et regale* regime. But it was the monarchy which precipitated a crisis by giving up its previous policy of benevolent neglect and attempting to force the unwilling Catalans into an active role in the Spanish war with France. Trust, which had never been great, now vanished altogether and the traditionally bitterly divided Catalans combined in a successful revolt against the king in 1640, a few months before the Portuguese did the same. Eventually, after a short interval as a republic and a rather longer one as a French province, the principality was reconquered by the Spanish monarchy. Madrid had now learnt its lesson and negotiated a kind of Treaty of Arras with the Catalans. It restored the previous regime of *dominium politicum et regale*. Without a religious problem or a continued civil war, this regime then lasted for another half century until Catalonia was caught up in the great-power struggles of the War of the Spanish Succession. In the end Catalonia was lost to the Habsburgs, together with its *dominium politicum et regale* regime and was absorbed by the absolutist Spanish regime of the Bourbons.

THE MYTH

While the question of trust was crucial in the history of early modern parliaments, there was another, equally important, psychological question: the myth, or indeed the absence of such a myth, of a parliament as an institution with its own independent authority providing remedies for the country's ills during a severe crisis. In the Netherlands the States General had built up such a myth in the fifteenth century. This myth had received a great boost because of Philip II's ill-advised policy of trying to prevent the meeting of the States General after 1559. In England something similar happened after Charles I's similarly ill-advised policy of not summoning Parliament after 1629. In Castile there were the beginnings of such a myth, also in the fifteenth century. But the myth never fully recovered after the defeat of the Comunero revolt. This failure was certainly one of the main reasons for the ease with which the weak government of Charles II easily managed to effectively abolish the Cortes in the 1660s.

By contrast, in Poland the Sejm had built up a most formidable myth as the central point of the *aurea libertas poloniae*, the golden Polish liberty. The weakness in this position was that the golden liberty was pushed to such extremes as to make efficient government almost impossible. At the same time, this liberty was also too restrictive. The towns were virtually excluded from it, the peasantry remained in serfdom and the mass of the lower nobility, the *sçlachta*, who nominally profited from this regime were economically and politically completely dependent on a handful of rich magnates. Even then, it took the three most powerful neighbouring states, in the late eighteenth century, to overthrow the *rzespospolita*, the noble

Epilogue

republic of Poland with its elected king and its new, quasi-democratic written constitution.

The most interesting case of the role of the parliamentary myth is that of France. Nearly all provinces of France boasted some sort of representative institution. The monarchy summoned the Estates General only rarely, but it maintained a living myth throughout the fifteenth century. The first turning point was in 1484 when the Estates General met for the classical reason of adjudicating different claims to the throne after the death of the king, Louis XI, and the hereditary succession of a minor, Charles VIII. Much was expected of this meeting to solve the constitutional and financial problems of the kingdom. But the different regions of France and their deputies failed to cooperate, and the reputation and the myth of the Estates General never fully recovered. It was not summoned again for seventy-five years. Few people seemed to mind, not least because few Frenchmen thought of France as a true political unit. For those who did, the monarchy was an effective symbol of unity. The rest were content with their provincial assemblies. And so France became the model of the *dominium regale* regime, not only for Sir John Fortescue but for most of his contemporaries all over Europe.

The few Estates Generals which were summoned during the Wars of Religion, between 1560 and 1593, were unable to appease the murderous religious and partisan passions, and themselves appeared to many to become vehicles of these passions. Frenchmen therefore turned to their monarchy. When, in the middle of the seventeenth century and during another regency, the authority of the government was again seriously questioned, no one thought it worthwhile to summon the Estates General.

And yet the myth had not completely died. In 1789 the monarchy, *in extremis*, summoned the Estates General once more. Almost immediately it became clear that it was a ghost from a previous era; but it was a ghost which still had enough vitality to transform itself into a living organism, a popular assembly and a constitutional convention.

ROYAL ABSOLUTISM

By the early eighteenth century *dominium regale* or absolutism had triumphed in most European countries. There were exceptions: the United Provinces of the Netherlands, Great Britain, Poland and, with some swings of the pendulum, Sweden. In Sweden Charles XI's coup of 1680 had not fully resolved the problem of the distribution of power. When, after the death of Charles XII in 1718, a dubious succession coincided with resounding military defeat, the *dominium regale* regime of the Vasas was once more overthrown. Significantly, the new regime was a fully parliamentary government, based largely on the British model. From 1772 until 1792 the monarchy managed to re-establish a kind of absolutism, but it did not survive the assassination of the king, Gustavus III.

In Hungary, *a dominium politicum et regale* regime survived until the middle of the eighteenth century when the Habsburgs managed to abolish it without much fuss. Similar regimes also survived in several minor German principalities, notably Württemberg and Mecklenburg. It did so also in Sicily. The island kingdom was shuffled around the great powers, none of whom liked its old system with what was one of Europe's oldest parliaments. But all of them – Spaniards, Piedmontese and Austrians – shied away from tampering with a regime in what was a notoriously difficult but also completely unrevolutionary country. Such an attempt was left to the Neapolitan viceroy, the marquis Domenico Caracciolo, in 1783. Caracciolo had spent ten years as ambassador in Paris, where he had made friends with d'Alembert and his circle of *philosophes*. In Caracciolo's view of the superiority of enlightened absolutism, the Sicilian parliament seemed nothing but a bastion of privilege of those who exploited the country for their own benefit. But the Sicilian elite had friends at court in Naples. Caracciolo was outmanoeuvred at the centre of political power[15] – just as other would-be reformers of Sicilian institutions had found themselves outmanoeuvred before, in the multiple monarchies of which Sicily had always formed a part, and just as they were to find themselves outmanoeuvred into the twentieth century.

Nevertheless, the victory of absolutist monarchy was very impressive. Few of its actions show more clearly the chasm which separated it from traditional monarchy than its treatment of newly acquired states or provinces. Under *dominium politicum et regale* regimes the prince swore to respect the existing laws of a newly acquired country. But when he had conquered an unwilling country he could dispense with this need. In practice this was not a good idea, as even Machiavelli realised, although such a realisation did not change the basic conditions of that early modern phenomenon, the multiple or composite monarchy. But the absolutist regime of Louis XV conquered and incorporated Corsica as a French province in 1769, and immediately abolished the democratic constitution of 1755.[16]

Much the same happened in Poland. At least one of the main reasons for the Second and Third Partitions (1792 and 1795) was precisely the desire of the neighbouring absolutist monarchies of Russia, Prussia and Austria to end the danger of a possible infection by Polish constitutionalism.

The absolutist monarchies managed to acquire a considerable degree of moral and intellectual justification which went beyond the traditional loyalty demanded by *dominium regale* kings. The abolition of judicial torture, the beginnings, at least, of the emancipation of the serfs, the rationalisation of tax and judicial procedures and of local administration, the first glimmers of religious toleration – these were real and not always easy advances and not to be written off lightly.

---

[15] D. Mack Smith, *A History of Sicily*, 2 vols. (London, 1968), vol. II, 318–19.
[16] D. Carrington, 'The Corsican Constitution of Pasquale Paoli (1755–1769)', *English Historical Review*, 88 (July 1973), *passim*. D. Carrington, 'Pasqual Paoli et sa constitution (1755–1769)', *Annales Historiques de la Révolution Française* (Oct.–Dec. 1974), *passim*.

Epilogue

CONCLUSION

But the monarchies had to pay a price. This price was the hollowing out of the personal position of the monarch. It was a slow process and it had started in the sixteenth century, or sometimes even earlier, with the growing complexity of governmental functions. For the more complex these became and the wider their scope, the more they became institutionalised and the less they were seen as functions of the person of the monarch.

At the beginning of the sixteenth century Machiavelli had concentrated his rationalistic arguments on the person of the prince. His followers, the reason-of-state theorists, reintroduced religion into their political analysis; but they were as cavalier about normal moral precepts as the master had been, provided always they could make the Almighty responsible. One does not need to doubt the theorists' personal Christian faith; but more and more the abstract state took the place of the king-by-the-grace-of-God. Charles V always and Philip II nearly always talked of the obligation of service to themselves personally, *mi servicio*, and not of service to the state. With the spread of reason-of-state arguments, reinforced by Bodinian theories of sovereignty, the person of the monarch dropped more and more into the background.

This phenomenon did not go unobserved. James I and other monarchs tried to counter it by developing the theory of divine, hereditary right. It was an essentially defensive theory and it did not outlast the seventeenth century. For this was the century of the *privado*, the all-powerful first minister, the century of Lerma and Olivares, of Richelieu and Mazarin, of Buckingham and Strafford (the last-named significantly in a dependent dominion of a composite monarchy). They worked for the state and only secondarily for the king-by-the-grace-of-God.

By the end of the eighteenth century personal position and attributes were no longer sufficient to guarantee the stability of a regime. The society of orders, often deliberately undermined by enlightened monarchs and professional civil servants, and a society where the nobility had personal powers – all these had become unacceptable, as aristocratic and popular audiences of Beaumarchais' plays and Mozart's opera demonstrated when they cheered the come-uppance which Count Almaviva suffered for trying to re-enact his mythical feudal rights; a come-uppance which he suffered at the hands of Figaro, his clever barber-valet, and of Susanna, his wife's pert and humane lady's maid.

There was no resting place, no final end to the quest for the Aristotelian good life in any of the regimes discussed in this book; nor did any of them represent the preliminary stage for the attainment of an ideal society. The tectonic plates continued to grind together. Volcanoes continued to erupt. The lions had not changed the leopards' spots, although lions might have become states and leopards international corporations. Lions and leopards still needed the sheep to legitimise their positions and, at times, the sheep would show their teeth. The striving would have to continue. As Goethe's Faust said, at the end of his long life and before his redemption by the feminine aspect of the Godhead:

> Das ist der Weisheit letzter Schluss:
> Nur der verdient sich Freiheit wie das Leben,
> Der täglich sie erobern muss.
> (Here wisdom speaks its final word and true,
> None is of freedom or of life deserving,
> Unless he daily conquers it anew.)[17]

---

[17] Goethe, *Faust II*, Act 5, transl. P. Wayne, in Goethe, *Faust Part Two* (Harmondsworth, 1975), 269.

Bibliography

MANUSCRIPTS

Archives Générales du Royaume à Bruxelles (AGRB)

Copies du régistre aux mémoriaux de Béthune
Fonds Mercy Argenau, no. 32, fos. 128r–129v
Manuscrits divers, 327
Manuscrits divers, 1172. Les Archives et les Bibliothèques d'Italie, vol. I
Papiers d'Etat et de l'Audience, 30, 36, 47–50, 52, 150, 647–9, 663, 1228, 1229, 1232, 1723, Lettres missives 1725/1
Transcripts from the Archives de la ville d'Ypres, 40431
Transcripts from the Archives of Mons, 5th Registry, 6th Registry

Alkmaar and other small cities, Archives

MS, Resoluties Staten van Noord-Holland.

Amsterdam, Gemeente Archief

Adriaen Sandelijn, Register van de Resolutien van de Dagvaerd 1548–54, MS 5029, I S IV. 54
A. Jacopszoon, *Prothocolle van alle de Reysen gaedaen zedert ick de Stede van Aemstelredamme gedient heb gehadt*, 2 vols. inventory nos. 721, 722

Antwerp Stadsarchief

H. de Moy, Tractaet van Beden

Brussels, Bibliothèque Royale (BBR)

Des charges publicques, MS 16248, 22–6
... la Revenue en temps [de] feu Monsieur le Duc Charles, MS 14511
Root Boeck, MS 16955–7
MS 5, II 358 vol. I, 13352–9, 16068–72, 17047

Florence, Archivio di Stato

Mediceo del Principato, 4254

Bibliography

Ghent, Archives de l'Etat (GAE)

Varia, 265

London, British Library

Copia de carta que escribió al Señor Rey Phelipe II Don Luis Manrique su limosnero mayor, MS Egerton 330

Simancas, Archivo General

MS Estado, legajo 525, 1152

Vienna, Haus- Hof- und Staatsbibliothek

Belgien, PA 21/2

PRINTED SOURCES

Alba, duque de, ed., *Epistolario del III Duque de Alba, don Fernando Alvarez de Toledo*, 3 vols. (Madrid, 1952).
Albèri, E., ed., *Relazioni degli Ambasciatori Veneti al Senato durante il secolo decimosesto*, ser. 1, vol. III (Florence, 1858).
Alberts, W. Jappe, *De Staten van Gelre en Zutphen (1459–1492)*, (Groningen and Jakarta, 1956).
Angermeier, H., 'Der Wormser Reichstag 1495 in der politischen Konzeption König Maximilians I', in H. Lutz, ed., *Das römisch-deutsche Reich im politischen System Karls V* (Munich, 1982), 1–13.
Aristotle, *The Politics and the Constitution of Athens*, ed. S. Everson, transl. B. Jowett (Cambridge, 1996).
Armstrong, C. A. J., 'Had the Burgundian Government a Policy for the Nobility?', in J. S. Bromley and E. H. Kossmann, eds., *Britain and the Netherlands*, vol. II (Groningen, 1962).
Arnould, M.-A., 'L'impot sur le capital en Belgique au XVIe siecle', *Le Hainaut Economique*, 1 (Mons, 1946), 22–45.
Baelde, M., *De Collaterale Raden onder Karel V en Filips II (1531–1578)*. Verhandelingen van de Koninklijke Vlaamse Academie voor Wetenschapen, Letteren en Schone Kunsten, Klasse der Letteren XXVII (Brussels, 1965).
'Financiële Politie en domaniale evolutie in de Nederlanden onder Karel V en Filips II (1530–1560)'. *TG*, 76 (1963).
'Monarchie in Opbouw: de eerste Instructie voor de Raad van State (1531)', *Miscellanea Roger Petit*. Archives et Bibliothèques de Belgique LXI, 3–4 (Brussels, 1990).
Baelde, M. and Peteghem, P. van, *Opstand en Pacificatie in de Lage Landen*, Acta Historiae Neerlandicae, vols. XI, XIII (n.p., n.d.).
Bakhuizen van den Brink, R. C., 'Eerste Vergadering van de Staten van Holland, 19 July 1572', in *Les Archives du Royaume des Pays-Bas*, vol. I (The Hague, 1857).

Bibliography

Bartier, J., 'Un discours du chancellier Hugonet aux Etats Généraux de 1473', in *BCRH* (1942), 127–56.
'Karel de Stoute', in J. A. van Houtte, ed., *Algemene Geschiedenis der Nederlanden*, vol. III (Utrecht, 1951).
Benedict, P., 'The Dynamics of Protestant Militancy. France 1555–1563'. Paper read at the conference 'Reformation, Revolution and Civil War in France and the Netherlands', Amsterdam, Oct. 1997.
Bercé, M., *Révoltes et révolutions dans l'Europe moderne, XVI–XVIIe siècles* (Paris, 1980).
Bergh, L. Ph. C van den, ed., *Gedenkstukken tot opheldering der Nederlandsche Geschiedenis*, 3 vols. (Utrecht, 1849).
Bertijn, G., 'Rolle van Memorie van "De quay Werelt"', in Génar, P., ed., *De Gebroeders van der Voort en de Volksopstand van 1477–78*, Maatschappij der Antwerpsche Bibliophilen III (Antwerp, 1879).
Berwick and Alba, duke of, *Correspondencia de Gutierrez Gomez de Fuensalida* (Madrid, 1907).
Biskup, M., 'Die Stände Preussens Königlichen Anteils 1466–1526', in H. Boockmann, ed., *Die Anfänge der ständischen Vertretung in Preussen und seinen Nachbarländern* (Munich, 1992), 83–99.
Bisson, T. N., 'The Military Origins of Medieval Representation', *American Historical Review*, 71 (1966), 1199–218.
Black, A., 'Popes and Councils', in *New Cambridge Medieval History*, vol. VII (Cambridge, 1998), ch. 3.
Blickle, P., 'Kommunalismus und Republikanismus in Oberdeutschland', in Koenigsberger and Müller-Luckner, *Republiken und Republikanismus im Europa der frühen Neuzeit*, 57–75.
ed., *Verborgene republikanische Traditionen in Oberschwaben* (Tübingen, 1998).
Blockmans, W. P., 'Algemeen Privilegie', in W. P. Blockmans, ed., *Le privilège général et les privilèges régionaux de Marie de Bourgogne: 1477*, APAE, 80 (Kortryk-Heule, 1985).
'Alternatives to Monarchical Centralisation: The Great Tradition of Revolt in Flanders and Brabant', in Koenigsberger and Müller-Luckner, *Republiken und Republikanismus in der frühen Neuzeit*, 145–54.
'Autocratie ou polyarchie? La lutte pour le pouvoir politique en Flandre de 1482 à 1492', in *BCRH*, vol. CXL (1974).
'De volksvertegenwoordiging in Vlaanderen in de beginperiode van de nieuwe tijden (1384–1505)', *Wetenschapplijke Tijdingen*, 33, 2 (Ghent, 1974).
Handelingen van de Leden en van de Staten van Vlaanderen, 2 parts (Brussels, 1973).
'Nieuwes gegevens over de gegoede burgerij van Brugge en de 13e an vooral 14e eeuw', *APAE*, 54 (1971).
'The Parliamentary History of the Netherlands and Belgium Compared to that of Sweden', in N. Stjernquist, ed., *The Swedish Riksdag in an International Perspective* (Stockholm, 1989).
'Patronage, Brokerage and Corruption as Symptoms of Incipient State Formation in the Burgundian–Habsburg Netherlands', in Mączak, *Klientelsysteme im Europa der frühen Neuzeit*.
'Peilingen naar de sociale strukturen te Gent tijdens de late 15e eeuw', *APAE*, 54 (1971).
'Representation since the Thirteenth Century', in *New Cambridge Medieval History*, vol. VII (Cambridge, 1998), ch. 2.

Bibliography

'A Typology of Representative Institutions in Late Medieval Europe', Journal of Medieval History, 4 (1978).
Bodin, J., *Les six livres de la république* (Paris, 1583).
Boogman, J. C., 'De overgang van Gouda, Dordrecht, Leiden en Delft, in de Zomer van het jaar 1572', *TG*, 51 (1942), 81-109.
Boone, M. and Brand, H., 'De ondermijning van het Groot Privileg van Holland', *Holland Regionaal-Historisch Tijdschrift*, 24, 1 (1992), 2-21.
Bor, P., *Oorspronck, begin ende vervolgh der Nederlandsche Oorlogen*, 3 vols. (Amsterdam, 1621).
Brady, T. A., *Turning Swiss: Cities and Empire 1450-1550* (Cambridge, 1985).
Bragt, R. van, 'De blijde Inkomst van den Hertogen van Brabant Johanna en Wenceslas', *APAE*, 13 (1956), 95-107.
Brandi, K., *Kaiser Karl V* (Munich, 1937/1959).
Briefvisseling tussen Margaretha van Parma en Charles de Brimeu, Graaf van Megen... 1560-1567, ed. J. S. van Veen (Arnhem, 1914).
Bruchet, M. and Lancien, E., *L'itinéraire de Marguerite d'Autriche* (Lille, 1934).
Brulez, W., 'Brugge en Antwerpen in de 15e en 16e eeuw: een tegenstelling', *TG*, 83, 1 (1970).
Bruyssel, E. van, 'Notes sur les aides et les subsides levées en Brabant de 1500 à 1577', *BCRH*, ser. 3, vol. VII (Brussels, 1865).
Burkert, G. R., *Landesfürst und Stände: Karl V, Ferdinand I und die österreichischen Erbländer im Ringen um den Gesamtstaat und Landesinteressen* (Graz, 1987).
Bussemaker, G. H. Th., *De Afscheiding der Waalsche Gewesten van de Generale Unie* (Haarlem, 1895).
Calabria, A., *The Cost of Empire: The Finances of the Kingdom of Naples in the Time of the Spanish Rule* (Cambridge, 1991).
Calendar of State Papers, Foreign, 1569-71, vol. XXI (London, 1929).
Calendar of State Papers, Milan, vol. 1.
Calendar of State Papers, Venetian, vol. VI, pt. 1.
Carrington, D., 'The Corsican Constitution of Pasquale Paoli (1755-1769)', *English Historical Review*, 88 (July 1973).
'Pasquale Paoli et sa constitution (1755-1769)', *Annales Historiques de la Révolution Française* (Oct.-Dec. 1974).
Caukercken, Lodewijk van, *Chronicle*, in P. Génar, *De Gebroeders van der Voort en de Volksopstand van 1477-78*, Maatschappij der Antwerpsche Bibliophilen III (Antwerp, 1879).
Cauwenberghe, E. van, 'De economische Ontwikkeling in de Nederlanden', in M. Baelde and P. Peteghem, Opstand en Pacificatie (n.p., n.d.).
Chabod, F., *Lo stato di Milano nell'impero di Carlo V* (Rome, 1934).
'¿Milan o los Países Bajos?', in *Carlos V (1500-1558). Homenaje de la Universidad de Granada* (Granada, 1958).
Chastellain, G., *Chronique des ducs de Bourgogne*, ed. A. C. Buchon (Paris, 1883).
Clark, P. and Slack, P., *Towns in Transition 1500-1700* (Oxford, 1976).
Commynes, P. de, *Les Mémoires* (The Hague, 1682).
Craeybeckx, J., 'Alva's Tiende Penning, een Mythe?', *BMHG*, 76 (1962), 10-42.
Craeybeckx, J., 'La portée fiscale et politique du 100e denier du duc d'Albe', in *Acta Historiae Bruxellensia*, vol. I (Brussels, 1967).

Bibliography

Crew, Phyllis Mack, *Calvinist Preaching and Iconoclasm in the Netherlands 1544–1569* (Cambridge, 1978).
Cuvelier, J., *Actes des Etats Généraux des anciens Pays-Bas, vol. I: Actes des 1427 à 1477* (Brussels, 1948).
Dénombrements des foyers en Brabant (XIVe–XVIe siècle), (Brussels, 1912).
Dansaert, G., *Guillaume de Croy-Chièvres* (Paris, 1943).
Davis, N. Z., 'The Rites of Violence', in Davis, *Society and Culture in Early Modern France* (Stanford, 1975), 152–87.
Davis, R. W., ed., *The Origins of Modern Freedom in the West* (Stanford, 1995).
Decavele, J., 'De mislukking van Oranjes "demokratische" politiek in Vlaanderen', *BMGN*, 99, 4 (1984), 626–50.
— ed., 'Rederijkers', in J. Decavele, *Keizer tussen stropdragers: Karel V 1500–1558* (Louvain, 1990).
Delfos, L., *Die Anfänge der Utrechter Union, 1577–1587* (Berlin, 1941).
Derville, A., 'Les pots-de-vin dans le dernier tiers du XVe siècle', in Blockmans, *Le privilège général*, 449–70.
Despars, Nicholaes, *Cronijk... van Vlaenderen*, ed. J. de Jonghe (Bruges, 1840).
Deventer, M. L. van, ed., *Gedenkstukken van Johan van Oldenbarnevelt*, 3 vols. (The Hague, 1860–5).
Devillers, L., *Inventaire analytique des archives des états de Hainaut*, vol. I (Mons, 1884).
— 'Participation des états de Hainaut aux assemblées des états généraux des Pays-Bas (1438–1790)', in *BCRH* (1905).
Dhondt, J., 'Les origines des états de Flandre', *APAE*, 1 (1950), 13–19.
— 'Les assemblées d'états en Belgique avant 1795', *APAE*, 35 (1965), 325–400.
Dickens, A. G., 'The Elizabethans and St Bartholomew', in A. Soman, ed., *The Massacre of St Bartholomew* (The Hague, 1974), 52–70.
Diegerick, I. L. A., *Correspondance des magistrats d'Ypres députés à Gand pendant les troubles de Flandres sous Maximilien* (Bruges, 1853).
— *Inventaire analytique et chronologique des chartes et documents appartenant aux archives de la ville d'Ypres*, 7 vols. (Bruges, 1853–68).
Dierickx, M., *De Oprichting der Nieuwe Bisdommen in de Nederlanden onder Filips II, 1559–70* (Antwerp, 1950).
— 'La politique religieuse de Philippe II dans les anciens Pays-Bas', *Hispania*, 16, 62 (1956).
Don John of Austria to Philip II, 1 Sept. 1577. British Library Tracts T 1721 b 28.
Duke, A., *Reformation and Revolt in the Low Countries* (London and Ronceverte, 1990).
Dumont, J., *Corps universel diplomatique du droit des gens*, vol. V, pt. 1 (Amsterdam, 1728).
Duplessis, R. S., *Lille and the Dutch Revolt: Urban Stability in an Era of Revolution* (Cambridge, 1991).
Durme, M. van, *Antoon Perrenot, Bisschop van Utrecht, Kardinaal Granvelle* (Brussels, 1953).
Elliott, J. H., 'A Europe of Composite Monarchies', *Past and Present*, 137 (1992), 48–71.
Elton, G. R., ed., *The Tudor Constitution* (Cambridge, 1960).
Emanuele Filiberto of Savoy, 'Charles de Lalaing et les remonstrances d'Emmanuel-Philibert de Savoie', in *BCRH*, 2nd ser, vol. XCVII (1933), 155–69.
— *I diarii delle campagne di Fiandra*, ed. E. Brunelli, Biblioteca della società subalpina, 112 n.s., 21 (Turin, 1928).

Bibliography

Enno van Gelder, H. A., 'Bailleul, Bronckhorst, Brederode', *De Gids*, no. 100.
  'De Hollandse Adel in de Tijd van den Opstand', *TG*, 45 (1930).
  Revolutionaire Reformatie (Amsterdam, 1943).
  ed., *Correspondance française de Marguerite d'Autriche. Supplément*, 2 vols. (Utrecht, 1941).
Essen, L. van der, 'Croisade contre les hérétiques ou guerre contre les rebelles', *Revue d'Histoire Ecclésiastique*, 51, 1 (1956), 43–78.
  'Les Etats Généraux de 1534–1535 et le projet de confédération défensive des provinces des Pays-Bas', in *Mélanges d'histoire offerts à Charles Moeller*, vol. II (Louvain and Paris, 1914).
  Mélanges d'histoire offerts à L. van der Essen, 2 vols. (Brussels, 1947). *Exhortation faite par Monseigneur l'Archiduc . . . aux états généraux . . . 11 avril 1579* (Antwerp, 1579).
  'Politicke geschiedenis van het Zuiden, 1585–1609', in *AGN*, vol. V (Utrecht, 1952).
Fernández Alvarez, M., ed., *Corpus documental de Carlos V*, 4 vols. (Salamanca, 1973–9).
Fisher, F. B., 'Influenza and Inflation in Tudor England', *Economic History Review*, ser. 2, 18 (1965).
Forbes, P., *A Full View of Public Transactions in the Reign of Queen Elizabeth* (London, 1740).
Formsma, W. J., 'De onderwerping van Friesland, het Sticht en Gelre', in *AGN*, vol. IV (Utrecht, 1952).
Fortea Pérez, J. I., *Monarchia y cortes en la corona de Castilla. Las ciudades ante la política fiscal de Felipe II* (Cortes de Castilla y León, 1990).
Fortescue, Sir John, *The Governance of England*, ed. C. Plummer (Oxford, 1885).
  In Praise of the Laws of England, ed. S. Lockwood (Cambridge, 1997).
Fouw, A. de, *Philips van Kleef* (Groningen, 1937).
Friedrichs, F. R., *The Early Modern City 1450–1750* (Harlow, 1995).
Friis, A., 'An Inquiry into the Relations between Economic and Financial Factors in the Sixteenth and Seventeenth Century. I. The Two Crises in the Netherlands in 1557', *Scandinavian Economic History Review*, 1, 2 (1953).
Fris, V., *Historie de Gand* (Brussels, 1913).
  'Jan van Coppenhole', *Bulletin de la Société d'Histoire et d'Archéologie de Gand*, 14 (1906).
  'Rym, Guillaume', in *BN* vol. XIX, 986–8.
  ed., *Dagboek van Gent*, vol. I (Ghent, 1901).
Froeschl, T., 'In Frieden, Ainigkeit und Ruhe beieinander sitzen: Das Heilige Römische Reich und die Politik Kaiser Rudolfs II im ersten Jahrzehnt seiner Regierung, 1576–86' (Habilitationsschrift for the University of Vienna, 1997).
  'Selbstdarstellung und Staatssymbolik in den europäischen Republiken der frühen Neuzeit', in Koenigsberger and Müller-Luckner, *Republiken und Republikanismus*, 239–71.
Fruin, R. and Colenbrander, T. H., *Geschiedenis der Staatsinstellingen in Nederland tot den val der Republiek*, 2nd edn (The Hague, 1922; 1st edn, 1901).
Gachard, L. P., *Correspondance de Philippe II sur les affaires des Pays-Bas (1558–1577)*, 6 vols. (Brussels, 1842–72).
  'Relation des Etats Généraux tenus à Malines au mois de février et mars 1492', in *BCRH*, ser. 3, vol. IV, 338.
Gachard, L. P., 'Actes de l'archiduchesse Marguerite', in *BCRH*, ser. 3, vol. I.

Bibliography

Analectes historiques, in *BCRH*, ser. 3, vol. X (Brussels, 1858).
'Les états de Gand en 1476', in *Trésor national*, vol. III (Brussels, 1842), 258-73.
'Relation de Jeannet de la Ruyelle', in *BCRH*, ser. 3, vol. I, 311-41.
'Relation de l'émeute arrivée à Bruxelles de la reine Marie de Hongrie', in *BCRH*, ser. 3, vol. III (1862).
'Relation des séances des Etats Généraux à Bruxelles, 2 avril – 4 mai 1558', in *BCRH*, ser. 3, vol. VIII.
Relation des troubles de Gand sous Charles Quint (Brussels, 1846).
'Remonstrances faictes par le duc de Savoie à Philippe II sur la situation des Pays-Bas', in *BCRH*, ser. 2, vol. VIII (1856), 118-32.
ed., *Actes des Etats Généraux des Pays-Bas 1576-1585*, 2 vols. (Brussels, 1861).
ed., *Actes des Etats Généraux de 1600* (Brussels, 1849).
ed., *Collection de documents inédits concernant l'histoire de la Belgique*, 3 vols. (Brussels, 1833-5).
ed., *Correspondance d'Alexandre Farnèse . . . avec Philippe II* (Brussels, 1853).
ed., *Correspondance de Guillaume le Taciturne*, 6 vols. (Brussels, 1847-66).
ed., *Correspondance de Marguerite d'Autriche, duchesse de Parme, avec Philippe II*, 3 vols. (Brussels, 1867).
ed., *Extraits des régistres des consaux de Tournai, 1472-1490, 1559-1572, 1580-1581* (Brussels, 1846).
ed., *Lettres inédites de Maximilien . . . sur les affaires des Pays-Bas*, pt. 1, in *BCRH*, ser. 2, vol. II. C (Brussels, 1851).
Gelderen, M. van, *The Dutch Revolt* (Cambridge, 1993).
The Political Thought of the Dutch Revolt (Cambridge, 1992).
'The Position of the States in the Political Thought of the Dutch Revolt 1555-1581', *Parliaments, Estates and Representation*, 7, 2 (1987).
Geurts, P. A. M., 'Het beroep op de Blijde Inkomste in de Pamfletten uit de Tachtigjarige Oorlog', *APAE*, 16 (1958), 2-15.
De Nederlandse Opstand in de Pamfletten 1566-1584 (Nijmegen, 1956).
Geyl, P., *The Netherlands in the Seventeenth Century*, pt. 1, 2nd edn (London, 1961).
Gilissen, J., *Le régime représentatif avant 1790 en Belgique* (Brussels, 1952).
Glay, A. Le, *Correspondance de l'empereur Maximilien 1er et de Marguerite d'Autriche*, 2 vols. (Paris, 1839).
Goes, Adrien van der, *Register van de Saeken van den Lande van Hollant (1544-49)*, vol. II (n.p., n.d.).
Goes, Aert van der, *Register van alle die Dachvaerden by deselve Staten gehouden*, vol. I (The Hague, 1772). Part of *Resolutiën van de Heeren Staten van Holland en Westfriesland, 1524–* , 269 pts. (The Hague, 1670–).
Goris, J. A., *Etudes sur les colonies marchandes méridionales à Anvers de 1488 à 1567* (London, 1925), 375-81.
Gorissen, P., 'De Prelaten van Brabant onder Karel V (1515-1544)', *APAE*, 6 (1953).
Grapperhaus, F. H. M., *Alva en de Tiende Penning* (Zutphen, 1982).
Griffiths, G., *Representative Government in Western Europe in the Sixteenth Century* (Oxford, 1968).
William of Hornes, Lord of Hèze and the Revolt of the Netherlands (Los Angeles, 1954).

Bibliography

Grotius, H., *Verantwoordingh van de Wettelijke Regieringh van Hollandt* (Paris, 1622).
Häpke, R., *Die Regierung Karls V and der europäische Norden* (Lübeck, 1914).
ed., *Niederländische Akten und Urkunden zur Geschichte der Hanse*, 2 vols. (Munich, 1913).
Hautecloque, G. de, 'Le Président de Richardot et les Etats Généraux des Pays-Bas de 1598', *Mémoires de l'Académie des Sciences, Lettres et Arts*, ser. 2, 10 (1878).
Head, R. C., *Early Modern Democracy in the Grisons* (Cambridge, 1995).
Headley, J. M., 'Germany, the Empire and Monarchia in the Thought and Policy of Gattinara', in H. Lutz, ed., *Das römisch-deutsche Reich im politischen System Karls V* (Munich, 1982).
Hendricks, C. D., 'Charles V and the Cortes of Castile: Politics in Renaissance Spain' (Cornell University Ph.D. thesis, 1976).
Henne, A., *Histoire du règne de Charles Quint en Belgique*, 10 vols. (Brussels, 1858–60). 'Het Cort verhaal..., die de Generale Staten ghedwongen hebben, he te versiene... teghen de Heere Don Jehan van Oostenrijk', *British Library Tracts*, T 1721 no. 6, fos. 83–4.
Hibben, C., *Gouda in Revolt* (Utrecht, 1983).
Hirschauer, C., *Les états d'Artois de leurs origines à l'occupation française, 1340–1640*, vol. I (Paris, 1923).
Hocquet, A., 'Tournai et le Tournaisis au XVIe siècle au point de vue politique et sociale', *ARSLBA*, ser. 2, 1 (Brussels, 1906).
Höfler, C. R., 'Depeschen des venezianischen Botschafters bei Erzherzog Philip, Dr Vincenzo Quirino, 1505–1506', *AÖG*, 66 (Vienna, 1885).
Hofmann, S., 'Die Städte zwischen Kaiser und Reich', in H. Rabe, ed., *Karl V. Politik und politisches System* (Constance, 1996), 145–53.
Holland Staten Resolutien, see *Resolutien van de Staten van Holland*.
Holmes, C., 'Parliament, Liberty, Taxation and Property', in J. H. Hexter, ed., *Parliament and Liberty from the Reign of Elizabeth to the English Civil War* (Stanford, 1992), 122–54.
Holt, M. P., *The Duke of Anjou and the Politique Struggle during the Wars of Religion* (Cambridge, 1986).
Hugenholtz, F. W. N., 'Crisis and herstel van het Bourgondisch gezag, 1477–1493', in *AGN*, vol. IV (Utrecht, 1952).
'Filips de Schone en Maximiliaans tweede regentschap, 1493–1515', in *AGN*, vol. IV (Utrecht, 1952).
Hurstfield, J., *The Queen's Wards* (London, 1958).
Israel, J. I., *The Dutch Republic: Its Rise, Greatness and Fall, 1477–1806* (Oxford, 1995).
The Dutch Republic and the Hispanic World (Oxford, 1982).
Jansma, T. S., 'Raad en Rekenkammer in Holland en Zeeland tijdens Hertog Philips van Bourgondie', *Bijdragen van het Instituut voor middeleuwsche Geschiedenis... te Utrecht*, 18 (1932).
Janssens, G., 'Brabant in het Verweer', *APAE*, 89 (Kortrijk and Heule, 1989).
Japikse, N., ed., *Correspondentie van Willem den Eerste, Prins van Oranje*, vol. I (The Hague, 1934).
Resolutiën der Staten-Generaal van 1576–1609, 10 vols. (The Hague, 1913–30).
Johnson, R. C. *et al.*, eds., *Commons Debates 1628*, vol. III (New Haven and London, 1977).
Journal of the House of Commons, vol. I.
'Journal du tumulte arrivé à Gand, 1476 (o.s.)', *BARSBL*, 6, pt. 2 (1839).

Bibliography

Juste, T., *Les Pays-Bas sous Charles Quint. Vie de Marie de Hongrie* (Brussels and Paris, 1858).
Kamen, H., *Philip of Spain* (New Haven and London, 1997).
Kenyon, J. P., *Stuart England* (London, 1978).
Kerkhoff, J., 'Het Hof van Maria van Hongarije', in B. van Boogert and J. Kerkhoff, *Maria van Hongarije: Konigin tussen keizers en kunsenaars 1505–1558* (Zwolle, 1993), 162–74.
Koenigsberger, H. G., 'Orange, Granvelle and Philip II', *BGN*, 99, 4 (1984), 591–2.
'Composite States, Representative Institutions and the American Revolution', *Historical Research*, 62, 148 (1989), 137–53.
Estates and Revolutions (Ithaca, 1971).
The Habsburgs and Europe 1516–1660 (Ithaca and London, 1971).
'Liga, Ligadisziplin und Treue zum Fürsten im Westeuropa der frühen Neuzeit', in P. Prodi and E. Müller-Luckner, eds., *Glaube und Eid: Treueformeln, Glaubensbekenntnisse und Sozialdisziplinierung zwischen Mittelalter und Neuzeit* (Munich, 1993), 173–8.
Medieval Europe (Harlow, 1987).
'Parliaments and Estates', in Davis, *The Origins of Modern Freedom in the West*.
Politicians and Virtuosi (London, 1986).
The Practice of Empire: The Government of Sicily under Philip II of Spain (London and Ithaca, 1969).
'Prince and States General: Charles V and the Netherlands (1506–1555)', *Transactions of the Royal Historical Society*, 6th ser. 4 (1994).
'Republicanism, Monarchism and Liberty', in R. Oresko et al., eds., *Royal and Republican Sovereignty in Early Modern Europe* (Cambridge, 1997), 43–74.
Koenigsberger, H. G. and Müller-Luckner, E., eds., *Republiken und Republikanismus in der frühen Neuzeit* (Munich, 1988).
Koenigsberger, H. G., Mosse, G. L. and Bowler, C. Q., *Europe in the Sixteenth Century*, 2nd edn (London, 1989).
Kokken, H., *Steden en Staten. Dagvaarten van steden en staten van Holland en het eerste regentschap van Maximiliaen van Oostenrijk (1477–1494)* (The Hague, 1991).
Koopmans, J. W., *De Staten van Holland en de Opstand: De ontwikkeling van hun functies en organisatie in de periode 1544–1588* (The Hague, 1990).
Kraus, V. von, ed., *Maximilians vertraulicher Briefwechsel mit Sigmund Prüschenk* (Innsbruck, 1875).
Kreiten, H., ed., 'Der Briefwechsel Kaiser Maximilians I mit seiner Tochter Margareta', *AÖG*, 996 (1907).
Kunisch, J., 'Staatsraison und Konfessionalisierung als Faktoren absolutistischer Gesetzgebung: Das Beispiel Böhmen (1627)', in B. Dölemeyer and D. Klippel, *Gesetz und Gesetzgebung im Europa der Frühen Neuzeit* (Berlin, 1998).
Kunisch, J. and Neuhaus, H., eds., *Der dynastische Fürstenstaat: Zur Bedeutung von Sukzessionsordnungen für die Entstehung des frühmodernen Staates* (Berlin, 1982).
Kuttner, E., *Het Hogerjaar 1566* (Amsterdam, 1949).
Lademacher, H., *Die Stellung des Prinzen von Oranien als Statthalter in den Niederlanden von 1572–1584* (Bonn, 1958).
Lagomarsino, D., 'Court Factions and Formulation of Spanish Policy towards the Netherlands (1559–67)' (Cambridge University Ph.D. thesis, 1973).
'Philip II and the Netherlands (1559–73)' (unpublished typescript).

Bibliography

Lanz, K., *Staatspapiere zur Geschichte des Kaisers Karls V* (Stuttgart, 1845).
ed., *Correspondenz des Kaisers Karl V* (Leipzig, 1844).
Lefèvre, J., ed., *Correspondance de Philippe II sur les affaires des Pays-Bas*, 2 vols. (Brussels, 1940).
Lemaire, C., 'De Librije van Maria van Hongarije', in B. van Boogert and J. Kerkhoff, eds., *Maria van Hongarije: Konigin tussen keizers en kunsenaars 1505-1558* (Zwolle, 1993), 179-207.
Lemmink, F. H. J., *Het Ontstaan van de Staten van Zeeland en hun Geschiedenis tot het Jaar 1555* (Roosendaal, 1951).
'Les villes aux Pays-Bas septentrionaux', *Société Jean Bodin. Recueils*, 6 (Brussels, 1954).
Lettenhove, Kervyn de, *Histoire de Flandre*, 5 vols. (Brussels, 1850).
Letters and Papers of the Reign of Henry VIII, vol. VI (London, 1882).
Lettres des Estats d'Arthois . . . aux Députées des Estats Generaux (Antwerp, 1579).
Lousse, E., 'Les états du pays et duché de Brabant', *APAE*, 33 (1965).
'The Great Privilege of Mary of Burgundy for the Netherlands', *Schweizer Beiträge zur Allgemeinen Geschichte*, 14 (1965).
Louthan, H., *The Quest for Compromise: Peacemakers in Counter-Reformation Vienna* (Cambridge, 1997).
Lovett, A. W., 'The Governorship of Don Luís de Requesens, 1572-1576, A Spanish View', *ESR*, 2, 3 (1972).
'A New Governor for the Netherlands', *ESR*, 1, 2 (1971).
Lutz, H., *Christianitas Afflicta: Europa, das Reich und die päpstliche Politik im Niedergang der Hegemonie Kaiser Karls V (1552-1556)* (Göttingen, 1964).
'Die deutsche Nation zu Beginn der Neuzeit', *HZ*, 234, 3 (1982).
Mack Smith, D., *A History of Sicily*, 2 vols. (London, 1968).
Mączak, A., ed., *Klientelsysteme im Europa der Frühen Neuzeit* (Munich, 1988).
Maddens, N., 'De Beden in het Graafschap Vlaanderen tijdens de Regering van Keizer Karel V (1515-1550)', *APAE*, 72 (1978).
Maddens, N., 'Nieuwe Middelen in het Grafschap Vlaanderen', *RBPH*, 57 (1979), 343-63.
'De Invoering van de "nieuwe middelen" in het graafschap Vlaanderen, tijdens de Regering van Keizer Karel V', *RBPH*, 57 (1979).
'De opstandige houding van Gent tijdens de regiering van Keizer Karel V', *Appeltjes van het Meetjesland*, 28 (1977).
Major, J. Russell, *The Deputies to the States General in Renaissance France* (Madison, 1960).
Representative Government in Early Modern France (New Haven and London, 1980).
Representative Institutions in Renaissance France 1421-1559 (Madison, 1960).
Maltby, W. S., *Alba: A Biography of Fernando Alvarez de Toledo, Third Duke of Alba, 1507-1582* (Berkeley, 1983).
Maravall, J. A., *Las comunidades de Castilla: una revolución moderna* (Madrid, 1963).
Marche, Olivier de la, *Mémoires*, ed. H. Beaune and J. d'Arbaumont (Paris, 1883).
Mariana, J. de, *Del rey y de la institución de la dignidad real*, transl. E. Barriobero y Herran (Madrid, 1930).
Maximilian I, *Weisskunig*, ed. Th. Musper *et al.* (Stuttgart, 1956).
Meerkamp van Embden, A., ed., 'Goudse Vroedschapsresoluties betreffende de Dagvaerten der Staten van Holland', *BMHG*, 38, 39 (1917).

Bibliography

Meilink, P. A., *Archieven van de Staten van Holland voor 1672* (The Hague, 1929).
 'Dagvaarten van de Staten-Generaal 1427–1477', *BGN*, 5 (1950), 198–212.
 'Holland in het conflict tusschen Philips de Goede en zijn zoon van 1463/64', *BVGO*, 7th ser. (1935), pt. 5, 132–52.
Mellink, A. F. A., 'Territoriale afronding van den Nederlanden', in *NAGN*, vol. V (Haarlem, 1980).
Merlin, P., *Emanuele Filiberto: Un principe tra il Piemonte e l'Europa* (Turin, 1995).
Molinet, J., *Chroniques*, ed. G. Doutrepont and O. Jodogne (Brussels, 1935).
Mols, R., *Introduction à la démographie historique des villes d'Europe*, 2 vols. (Louvain, 1952).
Mor, G. C., 'Modificazioni strutturali dell'assemblea nazionale longobardo nel secolo VIII', in *Album Helen Maud Cam*, vol. II (Louvain, 1961), 1–12.
Moreau, E. de, 'Les familiers des ducs de Bourgogne dans les canonicats des anciens Pays-Bas', in *Mélanges d'histoire offerts à L. van der Essen*, vol. I (Brussels, 1947).
Morel-Fatio, A., ed., *L'Espagne au XVIe et au XVIIe siècle*, vol. II: *Lettres de don Juan d'Autriche* (Heilbronn, 1878).
Mout, N., 'Ideales Muster oder erfundene Eigenart', in Koenigsberger and Müller-Luckner, eds., *Republiken und Republikanismus*.
 Plakkaat van Verlatinge 1581 (The Hague, 1979).
 'Die Niederlande und das Reich im sechzehnten Jahrhundert (1512–1609)', in V. Press, ed., *Alternativen zur Reichsverfassung* (forthcoming).
Nierop, H. F. K. van, 'A Beggars' Banquet: The Compromise of the Nobility and the Politics of Inversion', *European History Quarterly*, 21, 4 (Oct. 1991), 419–43.
 Het verrad van het Noorderkwartier. Oorlog, terreur en rechts in de Nederlandse Opstand (Amsterdam, 1999).
 The Nobility of Holland; From Knights to Regents, 1500–1650, transl. M. Ultee (Cambridge, 1993).
 'De troon van Alva. Over de Interpretatie van de Nederlandse Opstand', *BMGN*, 110, 2 (1995), 205–23.
 Van Ridders tot Regenten: De Hollandse adel in de zestiende en de eerste helft van de zeventiende eeuw (Hollandse Historische Reeks. De Bataafsche Leeuw, 1984).
Ordonnance et Instruction par les Estatz généraux des pays de par-deça (Brussels, 1577).
Ordonnances et instructions faicts sur la levée . . . des moyens généraux, 18 Déc. 1576 (Brussels, 1577).
Ostwald, M., 'Freedom and the Greeks', in Davis, ed., *The Origins of Modern Freedom in the West*, 35–63.
Paillard, C., 'Le procès du chancelier Hugonet et du Seigneur d'Humbercourt', in *Académie royal. Mémoires couronnés*, vol. XXXI (Brussels, 1881), no. 8.
Paravicini, W., *Guy de Brimeu: Der burgundische Staat und seine adlige Führungsschicht unter Karl dem Kühnen* (Bonn, 1975).
 Karl der Kühne (Göttingen, 1976).
Parker, G., *The Army of Flanders and the Spanish Road 1567–1659: The Logistics of Spanish Victory and Defeat in the Low Countries Wars* (Cambridge, 1972).
 The Dutch Revolt (London, 1977).
 The Grand Strategy of Philip II (New Haven and London, 1998).
 Philip II (Boston and Toronto, 1978).

Bibliography

'Philip II, Paul Kennedy and the Revolt of the Netherlands 1572-76', in J. C. V. Johansen *et al.*, eds., *Clashes of Culture* (Odense, 1995), 50-79.

Spain and the Netherlands (Glasgow, 1979).

Pater, J. C. H. de, *De Raad van State nevens Matthias (1578-1581)*, (The Hague, 1917).

Penrose, J., 'Reification in the Name of Change', in J. G. Beramendi *et al.*, eds., *Nationalism in Europe Past and Present*, vol. II (Santiago de Compostela, 1994).

Piérard, C., 'Les Etats de Hainaut', *APAE*, 33 (1965), 65-78.

Pillorget, R., *Les mouvements insurrectionnels de Provence entre 1596-1715* (Paris, 1975).

Pirenne, H., *Histoire de Belgique*, 3 vols. (Brussels, 1907).

Postma, F., 'Nieuw licht op een oude zaak: de oprichting van de nieuwe bisdommen in 1559', *TG*, 103 (1990).

Poullet, E. and Piot, C., eds., *Correspondance du Cardinal de Granvelle*, 12 vols. (Brussels, 1877-96).

Prevenier, W., 'La démographie des villes... de Flandre aux XIVe et XVe siècles', *Revue du Nord*, 65, 257 (1983), 155-75.

'Les états de Flandre depuis les origines jusqu'en 1790', *APAE*, 33 (1965), 15-59.

Prinsterer, Groen van., ed., *Archives ou correspondance inédite de la maison Orange-Nassau*, ser. 1, 8 vols., 2nd edn (Leiden, 1835-47).

Prodi, P., *Glaube und Eid: Treueformeln, Glaubensbekenntnisse und Sozialdisziplinierung zwischen Mittelalter und Neuzeit* (Munich, 1993).

Rabe, H., 'Karl V und die deutschen Protestanten', in H. Rabe, ed., *Karl V. Politik und Politisches System* (Constance, 1996).

Rachfahl, F., 'Die niederländische Verwaltung', *HZ*, 110 (1912), 114-22.

Read, C., *Mr Secretary Walsingham*, 2 vols. (Oxford, 1925).

'Recueil de ce que a esté faicte ès assemblées des estatz généraux... depuis le VIIe d'avril 1557 (1558 n.s.)', in *BCRH*, ser. 3, vol. VIII.

Reinhard, W., 'Theorie und Empirie bei der Erforschung frühneuzeitlicher Volksaufstände', in H. Fenske, ed., *Historia Integra* (Berlin, 1977).

Resolutiën van de Staten van Holland, vols. V, VIII (The Hague, 1772-).

Riedel, M., 'Auf der Suche nach dem Bürgerbund', in P. M. Schmidhuber, ed., *Orientierungen für die Politik* (Munich, 1984), 83-99.

Rodríguez-Salgado, M. J., *The Changing Face of Empire: Charles V, Philip II and Habsburg Authority 1551-1559* (Cambridge, 1988).

Rollin Couquerque, L. M. and Meerkamp, van Embden, A., eds., 'Goudshe Vroedschaps-resoluties betreffende dagvaarten der staten van Holland en der Staten-Generaal, 1501-1524', *BMHG*, 37 (1916).

Rosenfeld, P., 'The Provincial Governors from the Minority of Charles V to the Revolt', *APAE*, 17 (1959).

Rowen, H. H., *The Princes of Orange: The Stadtholders in the Dutch Republic* (Cambridge, 1988).

ed., *The Low Countries in Early Modern Times* (New York, 1972).

Russell, C., *The Fall of the British Monarchies 1637-1642* (Oxford, 1990).

Russell, C., *The Causes of the English Civil War* (Oxford, 1991).

Sacks, D. H., 'Parliament, Liberty and the Commonweal', in J. H. Hexter, ed., *Parliament and Liberty from the Reign of Elizabeth to the English Civil War* (Stanford, 1992), 85-121.

Bibliography

Schepper, H. de, 'De grote raad van Mechelen, hoogste rechtscollege in de Nederlanden?', *BMGN*, 93, 3a (1978).
'De "Reconquista" mislukt. De katholieke gewesten 1578-1588', in *NAGN*, vol. VI (Haarlem, 1980).
Schmidt, *Der Städtetag in der Reichsverfassung* (Stuttgart, 1984).
Scholliers, E., *De Levensstandaard in de XVe en XVIe Eeuw to Antwerpen* (Antwerp, 1960).
Seaver, H. L., *The Great Revolt in Castile* (London, 1929).
Skinner, Q., *The Foundations of Modern Political Thought*, vol. I (Cambridge, 1978).
Smit, J. W., 'The Netherlands Revolution', in R. Forster and J. P. Greene, *Preconditions of Revolution in Early Modern Europe* (Baltimore and London, 1970).
Sommerville, J. P., 'Parliament, Privilege, and the Liberties of the Subject', in J. H. Hexter, ed., *Parliament and Liberty from the Reign of Elizabeth to the English Civil War* (Stanford, 1992), 56-84.
Spruyt, B. J., '"En bruit d'estre bonne luterienne." Mary of Hungary and Religious Reform', *English Historical Review*, 109, 431 (April 1994), 275-307.
'Verdacht van Lutherse Sympatieen: Maria van Hongarije en de religieuse controversen van haar tijd', in B. van Boogert and J. Kerkhoff, eds., *Maria van Hongarije* (Zwolle, 1993).
Spufford, P., 'Coinage, Taxation and the States General of the Burgundian Netherlands', *APAE*, 40 (1966), 61-85.
Steele, M., 'The Financial Crisis in Spain and the Netherlands during the Reign of Philip II' (London University Ph.D. thesis, 1987).
'La real hacienda', in *Historia general de España y America*, vol. VI (Madrid, 1986).
Stengers, J., 'Composition, procédure et activité judiciaire de grand conseil de Maria de Bourgogne (février 1477 - février 1480)', in *BCRH*, vol. CIX (1944), 2-33.
Stolleis, M., 'Grundzüge der Beamtenethik (1550-1650)', in R. Schnur, ed., *Die Rolle der Juristen bei der Entstehung des modernen Staates* (Berlin, 1986).
Stourzh, G., 'Staatsformenlehre und Fundamentalgesetze ... im 17. und 18. Jahrhundert', in R. Vierhaus, ed., *Herrschaftsverträge, Wahlkapitulationen, Fundamentalgesetze* (Göttingen, 1977), 294-327.
Sutherland, N. M., *Princes, Politics and Religion 1547-1589* (London, 1984).
Swart, K. W., 'Wat bewog Willem van Oranje de strijd tegen Spaanse overheersing an te binden?', *BMHG*, 99, 4 (1984).
Willem van Oranje en de Nederlandse Opstand (The Hague, 1994).
Tallone, A., *Parlamento Sabaudo, Patria Cismontana*, vol. V (Bologna, 1935).
Tex, J. den, *Oldenbarnevelt*, 2 vols., transl. R. B. Powell (Cambridge, 1973).
Theissen, J. S., ed., *Correspondance de Marguerite d'Autriche, duchesse de Parme, avec Philippe II*, 3 vols. (Utrecht, 1925).
Thompson, I. A. A., 'Oposición política y juicio del gobierno en las cortes de 1592-98', *Studia Historica. History Moderna* (1997).
Tierney, B., 'Freedom and the Medieval Church', in Davis, *The Origins of Modern Freedom in the West*.
Tracy, J. D., 'Habsburg Grain Policy and Amsterdam Politics: The Career of Sheriff Willem Dirckszoon Baerdes', *Sixteenth Century Journal*, 14, 3 (1983), 293-319.
A Financial Revolution in the Habsburg Netherlands: Renten and Renteniers in the County of Holland 1515-1565 (Berkeley, 1985).

Bibliography

Holland under Habsburg Rule 1516–1566: The Formation of a Body Politic (Berkeley, 1990).
The Politics of Erasmus (Toronto, 1978).
'The Taxation System of the County of Holland during the Reigns of Charles V and Philip II, 1519–1566', *Economisch- en Sociaal-Historisch Jaarboek*, 48 (1985).
Van Ussel, P. (Daems-Van Ussel, P.), 'Het Charter zonder naam', in *Miscellanea van der Essen*, vol. I (Brussels and Paris, 1947), 439–57.
De Regering van Maria van Bourgondië over de Nederlanden (Louvain, 1943).
Vaughan, R., *Charles the Bold* (London, 1973).
Philip the Good (London, 1970).
Veen, J. S. van, *Briefwisseling tussen Margaretha van Parma en Charles de Brimeu, Graaf van Megen... 1560–1567* (Arnhem, 1914).
Verheyden, A. L. E., *Le conseil des troubles* (Florence, 1981).
Verhofstad, K. J. W., *De Regering der Nederlanden in de Jaren 1555–1559* (Nijmegen, 1937).
Verlinden, C., 'En Flandre sous Philippe II: Durée de la crise économique', *Annales*, 7, 1 (1952).
Verlinden, C. and Craeybeckx, J., *Documents pour l'histoire des prix et des salaires en Brabant, XVe–XVII siècles* (Bruges, 1959).
Vries, J. de, *The Dutch Rural Economy in the Golden Age, 1500–1700* (New Haven and London, 1974).
European Urbanization 1500–1800 (London, 1984).
Wagenaar, J., *Vaderlandsche Historie*, vol. V (Amsterdam, 1751).
Walser, F., *Die spanischen Zentralbehörden und der Staatsrat Karls V*, ed. and completed R. Wohlfeil (Göttingen, 1959).
Walther, A., *Die Anfänge Karls V* (Leipzig, 1911).
Die burgundischen Zentralbehörden unter Maximilian I und Karl V (Leipzig, 1909).
'Hubert Kreiten, Briefwechsel', *Göttingische Gelehrte Anzeigen*, 170 (1908).
Wee, H. van der, 'The Antwerp Market', in *NAGN*, vol. V (Haarlem, 1980).
The Growth of the Antwerp Market and the European Economy, 3 vols. (The Hague, 1963).
Weiss, Ch., ed., *Papiers d'Etat du Cardinal de Granvelle*, 9 vols. (Paris, 1841–52).
Wellens, R., 'Les Etats Généraux et la succession de Philippe le Beau dans les Pays-Bas', *APAE*, 56 (1972).
'Les Etats Généraux des Pays-Bas des origines à la fin du règne de Philippe le Beau (1464–1506)', I, *APAE*, 64 (1974).
Wells, G. E., 'Antwerp and the Government of Philip II 1555–1567' (Cornell University Ph.D. thesis, 1982).
'Emergence and Evanescence: Republicanism and the *Res Publica* at Antwerp before the Revolt of the Netherlands', in Koenigsberger and Müller-Luckner, eds., *Republiken und Republikanismus*, 155–68.
Werweke, H. van, 'Het bevolkingscijfer van de stad Gent in de vierteente eeuw', in *Miscellanea L. van der Essen*, vol. I (Brussels and Paris, 1947).
Wesembeke, J. de, *Mémoires* (Brussels, 1859).
Whitelock, B., *A Journal of the Swedish Embassy*, ed. C. Morton, 2 vols. (London, 1772).
Wiesflecker, H., *Maximilian I*, vol. I (Munich, 1974; abridged version: Vienna, 1991).
'Neue Beiträge zur Frage des Kaiser-Papstplans Maximilians I', *MIÖG*, 71 (1963), 311–29.

Bibliography

Williams, G. S., 'The Arthurian Model in Emperor Maximilian's Writings. Weisskunig and Theuerdank', *Sixteenth Century Journal*, 11, 4 (1980), 2-22.

Wils, L., 'De Werking van de Staten van Brabant omstreks 1550-1650', *APAE*, 5 (1935).

Wolfram, H. and Thomas, C., eds., *Die Korrespondenz Ferdinands I*, vol. III, pt. 1 (Vienna, 1973).

Woltjer, J. J., 'Het Noorden en de Pacificatie van Gent', in D. N. V. Snoeck-Ducajn *et al.*, eds., *Opstand en Pacificatie in de Lage Landen* (Ghent, 1976).

Tussen vrijheidsstrijd en burgeroorlog (Amsterdam, 1994).

Woude, A. M. van der, 'Population Changes and Economic Development in the Netherlands: a Historical Survey', *AAGB*, 12 (1965).

Xanten, H. J. van, Section on s'Hertogenbosch in Woude, *AAGB*, 12 (1965), 102-3.

Zaman, P. de, *Exposition des trois états dy païs et comté de Flandre* (Ghent, 1711).

Index

Note: Page references in *italics* indicate illustrations.

Aalst (Alost; Brabant) 264
Abbeville, and States General 35
absolutism
   and Charles the Bold 37
   and *dominium regale* 331–2, 333, 335, 337–8
   and Philip II 295, 315
Act of Abjuration (1581) 296–7, 311
Adolf of Cleves, seigneur of Ravenstein 50, 60
Adolf of Egmont, duke of Guelders 37–8
Aerschot, Philippe de Croy, third duke
   and Archduke Matthias 279–80, 281, 317
   and Council of State 262, 265–6
   flight to Venice 317
   and Granvelle 209
   and John of Austria 268–9
   and States General 260, 267, 288, 321
   and William of Orange 265, 271, 274–6, 277–9, 281
aides
   and Charles V 103, 104, 107–8, 115–19, 125, 144, 159, 164–5
   and Charles the Bold 33–4, 36, 39–40, 100
   in France 19
   and Margaret of Austria 95, 97–8, 120, 122
   and Margaret of Parma 198–200, 222
   and Mary of Burgundy 42
   and Mary of Hungary 134–5, 138–41, 163
   and Maximilian 56, 61–2, 88–9
   and Philip II 184, 189, 190–2, 195, 224, 227, 237, 267, 318
   and Philip the Good 29, 32
   and Philip the Handsome 89, 100
   and Union of Arras 318, 320–1
   and William of Orange 248
Aire 19, 57–8, 291
Alba, Fernando Alvarez de Toledo, duke of 198, 208, *218*, *225*
   and abolition of privileges 133, 136
   and *alternativa* 146, 240
   and the Compromise 215
   and Estates 233, 246, 247, 249, 262, 268, 282
   failure of 235–6, 329, 335
   as governor-general of Netherlands 217, 220–35
   and imposition of *dominium regale* 222–4, 227, 235
   and Margaret of Parma 221, 222, 316
   and religious rebellions 220–2, 234–6, 239, 243, 253, 261–2, 267, 270–2, 276, 286
   and revolt of Ghent 144, 221
   and States General 224, 226, 227–8, 230–1, 263
   and taxation 224–34, 236–7, 240, 245, 263, 265, 289
   as viceroy of Naples 173, 176, 206
Albert, archduke 280, 317–20
Albert of Saxony 67, 70, 86, 105
alcabala 168, 175, 176, 224, 228, 231, 233–4, 237
Alcalá, duke of 297

356

Index

Alençon, duke of *see* Anjou, duke of
Alsace 36, 37
alternativa 146–8, 151, 155, 240, 244
Alva (Spanish ambassador to France) 232
America
  as *dominium politicum et regale* 334
  and federalism 109
Amiens, and populist-religious movements 133
Amsterdam 22, 197
  and Anabaptists 126, 213
  and Baltic states 128, 130
  and Catholicism 283
  and *gracien* 112–13
  and iconoclasts 213
  and religious revolts 241, 253, 254, 283
  and trade 76
  and Union of Utrecht 294
  and William of Orange 305
Anabaptists 126, 133, 143
Andalucia, and Philip II 210, 221
Angoulême, duke of *see* Anjou, duke of
Anjou, duke of
  death 305, 307
  in Hainaut 286, 289, 292–3
  and rule of Netherlands 148, 294–5, 298–304, 305
  and States General 294–5, 300, 301–4, 310, 311
  and Union of Arras 291–2
Anne of Brittany 54, 67–8, 95
Anne de Beaujeu 45
annuities (*rentes*), sale of 36, 119, 163, 164–6, 176, 178–80, 185, 192, 227, 248–9, 289
Antoine de Bourgougne ('Grand Bâtard') 59, 60, 66, 77
Antwerp 28, 61, 197
  and Anjou 302–3
  and Maximilian 61, 66
  money market 41, 116, 130, 158, 178–80, *179*, 184, 192, 227, 266
  and new bishopric 201
  revolt of 1477 45–7
  revolt of 1577 277
  sack of (1576) 271–2, 273, 277
  and States General 28–9, 66–7, 299
  and taxation 100, 120, 262
  and trade 19, 23, 27, 66, 70, 74, 95, 167, 289, 316
  and Union of Arras 319
  and Union of Utrecht 294
Aragon
  and Castile 84
  and Charles V 104–5
  as composite monarchy 84
  and Cortes 8, 107
  and France 105
  and Naples 9, 105
  and Sardinia 14, 105
  and Sicily 9, 11, 85, 105, 273, 296
  'Archdukes' *see* Albert, archduke; Isabella (daughter of Philip II)
Aristotle, *Politics* 1–2, 3–4, 13, 36, 64
Armenteros, Tomás de 197, 209
army, imperial 173
  financing of 175–80
army, Netherlands
  and brandschatting 145
  effects on peasant population 69, 83, 105, 159, 198
  and Margaret of Austria 99
  and Mary of Burgundy 51–2
  and Mary of Hungary 130–1, 159
  and Maximilian 55–6, 62–4
  and society 69, 83
  and States General 99–100, 105, 131–2, 188–9, 266–7, 314
army, Spanish
  and Alba 217, 223–31, 236, 240, 261, 270–1, 289
  and England 194
  mutineers 264, 266, 268, 319
  payment of 224–7, 230–1, 236–7, 262, 264, 271, 274, 318–19
  and Requesens 237–8
  and sack of Antwerp 271–2, 273, 277
  and States General 195, 198
  withdrawal of 198, 208, 228, 254, 274, 276, 287
Arnhem 37–8, 99

Index

Arnold of Egmont, duke of Guelders 37–8
Arras 18, 51, 90, 315
  and Orangeist revolt 291
  and representative assemblies 19, 20
Arras, Treaty (1435) 30
Arras, Treaty (1482) 12, 44–5, 58–9, 290, 299, 315, 317, 331
Arras, Union of *see* Union of Arras
Artois
  and Burgundy 16
  and economy 289
  Estates 19, 99–100, 138–9, 290
  and France 12, 42, 43, 57–8, 69, 90, 97, 105, 116, 199, 231, 244
  and Holy Roman Empire 149, 246
  and language 24
  representative assemblies 18–19, 25–6
  and States General 27, 36, 38, 40, 86, 99, 180
  and taxation 25, 40, 163, 231–2
  and Union of Arras 290
asientos 175–6, 178–9
Asseliers, Jan van 297
Augsberg, diet of 122
Augsburg, Treaty (1548) 186, 188, 192, 264, 283
  and Charles V 149–50, 169, 203, 217, 255, 284
  and Philip II 203, 255, 284
  and States General 150, 188
  and William of Orange 284
Austria
  Estates 13, 112, 118
  and Holy Roman Empire 149

Bacon, Francis 80
Badoer (Venetian ambassador) 194
Baerdes, Willem Dirckzoon 241
bailli, in Hainaut 19, 71
Baltic states
  and Charles V 128–9
  and Philip II 212
  and trade 80, 128–30, 138, 162, 212, 229
bandes d'ordonnance 78, 109, 188, 206, 208

Banninck, Cornelis 113–14
Basle, Council of (1431–49) 10
Bate, Thomas 160
Beggars' movement (*gueux*) 210–11, 215, 220, 249, 256
  in exile 223–4
  successes of 213, 234, 237, 239, 240–6, 259
Bergen-op-Zoom 23
Berghes family 66, 80
Berghes, Jean de 93, 101
Berghes, marquis of 174, 184, 196
Berlaymont, Count 196
Béthune 19, 291
Beveren, seigneur de 81, 83
Boccalini, Traiano viii
Bodin, Jean 298, 301, 303, 309, 334
Boelenszoon, Albert 113–14
Bohemia
  and Estates 13, 332–3
  and Hungary 84
Bolsterer, Hans *102*
Borcht, Petrus van der *179*
Borromeo, St Carlo 205
Bossu, Maximilien de Hennin, count of 229–31, 245, 247
Boulogne 49
Boulonnais, the 34
Bovet, H. *46*
Brabant (duchy)
  and Baltic trade 128
  and Calvinism 292
  and Catholicism 103–4, 119–20, 126–7, 264
  and Charles V 103–4, 107, 109, 115, 137
  and defeat by Parma 315–16
  and defensive union 131–2
  and *dominium politicum et regale* 323
  and England 93–5
  and France 58
  and *gratien* 159
  and Guelders 91, 97–8, 116
  and Maximilian 56, 57–8, 61–2, 64–5, 66–7, 70, 91
  and new bishoprics 188, 201, 205

358

Index

and peace negotiations 271
and Philip II 182–3, 184, 232
and Philip the Good 16–18, 23–4
and prelates 103–4, 119–20, 126–7, 201–2, 205
prosperity 24, 73, 289
representative assemblies 23–4
and revolt of 1477 42
and States General 27–9, 31, 38, 86, 89–91, 187, 237, 266
and taxation 100, 115, 118, 119, 127, 139, 159, 164–5, 184, 199–200, 208, 215, 232
and textile industry 23, 27, 94
and towns 23
and Union of Arras 320
and union of provinces 200
and Union of Utrecht 312
see also joyeuse entrée
Brabant (duchy), Estates of 23–4, 257
and Committee of Eighteen 277
and duke of Anjou 292, 305
early meetings of 27
and Granvelle 202, 208
and John of Austria 275
and Margaret of Austria 107, 118, 119–20, 201–2
and Margaret of Parma 200, 201–2, 222
and Mary of Hungary 139, 148
and Philip II 182, 185, 203, 262
and Philip the Good 28–9
and religious revolt 264
and revolt of Holland and Zeeland 265
and States General 52, 107, 139, 148, 260, 262, 265, 283
and taxation 118, 165, 232, 319
brandschatting 145, 277, 318–19
Breda, conference of (1575) 238, 253–7, 259, 263, 271
and Estates of Holland 248, 250, 254–6, 273
failure of 239, 257, 331
Brederode, count of 66, 210, 214, 241
bribery 112–13
Brittany, and France 67–8, 84

Bruges
and Charles the Bold 33–4, 37
and Maximilian 56, 58, 61–4, 67, 100
money market 41
and representative assemblies 5, 7, 19–21, 26, 30, 49
revolt of 1436–8 26
revolt of 1477 45–7
and States General 31–2, 35, 37, 39, 62–4
and taxation 33–4, 35, 37, 165
and trade 19, 47, 61, 70
Brussels
and Baltic states 130
and bread riots of 1532 136
and Committee of Eighteen 277, 283
and Council of State 147, 191–2
and court 23, *191*
and Maximilian 66–7, 69, 71
and Philip II 182–3
popular revolt of 1477 45
and populist-religious movements 132–3, 288, 315
and States General 27, 36, 64, 104, 107, 115, 187, 194, 237, 318–21
and taxation 36, 100, 144
and Union of Arras 316–21
uprising of 1576 264–5
Buren (town) 258
Burgundian Circle 149–50
Burgundy
and Dutch provinces 16–20, 26–9, 42–3, 83–5
and France 16–18, 35–6, 42–4, 49–51, 55, 58, 87
and Guelders 105
Buys, Paulus 246–7, 271

Cadzand, Peace of (1492) 68, 104, 142, 278
Calvinism
and the Compromise 211, 215–16
in France 203, 214, 256, 284
in Holland and Zeeland (1572) 240–6, 248, 256, 264, 283, 287
and iconoclasm 213

and Leicester 308, 313
populist 308, 313, 315, 331
in southern provinces 277, 283, 289, 304
and Union of Arras 291
and union of provinces 293
see also Huguenots
Cambrai 302
Caracciolo, Domenico 338
Carlos (son of Philip II) 217
Carondelet (president of Council of State) 80
Castile
  and Aragon 84
  and bribery 112
  and Charles V 104–5, 106, 107, 108, 110
  as composite monarchy 84, 110
  and Cortes 68, 106, 107–8, 110, 185–6, 226–7 n.20, 254, 312, 318, 336
  and France 157
  and *hermandades* 5
  and imperial revenues 158, 163, 176, 178, 185, 234, 261, 316
  and Maximilian 91
  and Philip the Handsome 70, 89, 110
  and taxation 167–8, 175
  see also Comuneros
Castro, Scipio di 252
Catalonia, and representative assemblies 9, 40, 336
Cateau-Cambrésis, Treaty (1559) 193, 198, 335
Catherine de Medici 266, 299–300, 303
Catholic League 279
Catholicism
  and Charles V 107, 108, 125, 131, 167, 201
  and Pacification of Ghent 272, 274–5, 277, 281, 283–4
  and Philip II 216, 254–5, 270, 286, 297
  and popular movements 264
  and States General 266, 281
  and Union of Arras 290–1
  and William of Orange 243
  see also church
Chalon family 18, 78

change, social 197, 216
Chapuys (Dutch ambassador in England) 129
Charles I of England and Scotland 51, 204, 333–4, 336
Charles II of Spain 336
Charles V, Emperor 68, 89, *102*
  abdication 162, 168–71, 172–3
  and *alternativa* 146–8, 149, 151, 155, 244
  and Baltic states 128–30
  and the church 121–2, 125
  and the cities 132–40
  and Council of State 76–7, 80–1, 146–7, 282
  and defence of the Netherlands 126–32, 138–9, 144, 150, 192, 199
  and *dominium politicum et regale* 123–50, 255–6, 331
  and expansionism 86, 193, 244
  and Francis I 105, 106, 127, 143–4, 145–6, 155
  and Germany 153, 279
  and government of Chièvres 102–6
  and Habsburg monarchy 151–4
  and heresy 125, 126, 152, 201
  and imperial elections 106–8, 121, 154, 178
  and Inquisition 204
  and Italy 127, 153, 157, 158, 169, 175, 193
  joyeuses entrées 103, 121, 142
  and Mary of Hungary 125–6, 154
  in Netherlands 122, 127–8, 155–7
  and papacy 153, 167
  and Peace of Augsburg 149–50, 169, 203, 255, 284
  and Philip II 167–8, 183
  and regency 89, 90–1, 93, 101–2
  and religion 167, 169, 171
  and religious divisions 153, 201, 203, 255
  and revenues and taxation 102, 104–5, 107–9, 115, 117, 119–21, 127–8, 137–8, 163–4

360

and Spanish succession 91, 95, 104–6, 110, 112
and States General 102, 105, 107–9, 115, 127–8, 148, 152–3, 169–71, 286, 287, 301, 324
and structures of government 76–8, 79, 123, 149–50
and war with France 116, 137–9, 145–6, 150, 154, 155–7, 178
Charles V of France 13
Charles VII of France 21, 25
Charles VIII of France 45, 49–51, 337
and Maximilian 53–4, 64, 67–9, 101
and proposed marriage to Margaret of Austria 12, 57–8, 68, 95, 101
Charles IX of France 300
Charles XI of Sweden 337
Charles XII of Sweden 337
Charles the Bold of Burgundy 24, *34*, 43, 51, 54, 70
and coinage 29, 33
as count of Charolais 30–2
death 16, 42, 69, 90, 123
and *dominium politicum et regale* 37
and *dominium regale* 38
and expansionism 70, 85
and expenditure 39
and Guelders 37–8, 56, 88
and Lorraine 85
and Netherlands as kingdom 146
and States General 16, 33–41, 45, 92, 152, 261
and taxation 33–7, 39–41, 47, 55, 100
Charles de Croy 119
Charles of Egmont, duke of Guelders
and Baltic states 129
and Charles V 105, 120, 145
and Maximilian 95, 96, 97, 99
and Philip the Handsome 87, 88, 89
and succession crisis (1506–7) 91
Charles of Mansfelt 316–17
Charolais 51, 69
Chastellain, G. 30
Chièvres, Guillaume de Croy, seigneur de 89, 101, 102–6, 107, 119, 196

chimney tax 139–40, 159, 183, 220
Christian II of Denmark 129
Christian III of Denmark 129
Christina of Denmark 169
church
and creation of bishoprics 188, 201–4, 206
secularisation of 248, 268
see also Catholicism
Cicero, Marcus Tullius, *De Legibus* 203
cities
and Charles V 132–40
and early representative assemblies 5–8, 19, 22, 23–4, 26–7
and effects of civil war 69–70
and Maximilian 59–61, 63, 66, 70
and Philip the Good 31
prosperity 19–20, 24, 73–5, 164, 197, 199, 215, 289
and religious revolt 244–5
and States General 102–3, 112–13
and Union of Arras 291
see also guilds; town councils
citizenship
in Greece 1–2
and representation 3
civil wars
and Don John of Austria 258, 276–9, 299, 303
under Maximilian 66–72, 73, 85
under Philip II *see* revolt against Spain
and religion 293
see also France; revolt against Spain
class attitudes, in towns 20–1, 26, 45–7, *46*, 59–60, 133
Clauwin, Jehan 90
Clement VII, Pope 127
clergy
as estate 8, 19, 22, 23, 27, 103–4
and patronage 82, 173
prelates of Brabant 103–4, 119–20, 126–7, 201–2, 205
and taxation 159, 165, 166, 175–6
and Union of Arras 291, 299
Cleves–Ravenstein family 55–6

Closer Union (1579) 293–4
coinage, control of 28–9, 32, 58, 62, 63, 71–2, 86–7, 109, 294, 307–8
Coligny, Gaspard II de, seigneur of Châtillon 300, 305
Colijn, Pieter 126
Cologne conference (1578) 287–8, 292, 294, 299, 307
Committee of Eighteen 277, 283
community, and representation 7, 8–9, 14, 96
Commynes, Philippe de 18, 59–60, 77
  Mémoires 16, 24, 50
Compromise, the 210–11, 214–15, 216, 220, 270
Comuneros, revolt of (1520–1) 106, 110, 135, 141, 249, 254, 283, 286, 336
conciliarism 10–11
Conditions of 1577 281–3, 286
congie (export tax) 76, 79–80
consent
  to taxation 3, 24, 25, 37, 132, 133, 142, 153, 166, 282, 291, 333
  to war 85–6, 88–9, 98, 132, 153, 282
Constance, Council of (1414–18) 10, 11
Coppenhole, Jan van 59, 62, 63, 68
Corsica, and Ottoman Turks 155
Cossé, Marshal de 300
Council of Finance
  of Charles V 76, 137, 159, 164
  of Emmanuel Philibert 175, 184
  of Maximilian I 62–3
  and Philip II 226, 254
  and William of Orange 249
Council of State
  of Charles V 76–7, 80–1, 146–7, 282
  of Emmanuel Philibert 174, 175, 176
  and Granvelle 174, 186, 192, 196, 263, 282
  of Margaret of Austria 94, 101
  of Margaret of Parma 195–7, 209
  of Mary of Hungary 174, 262
  of Matthias 281–2
  of Philip II 176–7, 185, 190, 208–9, 238, 262, 264–5, 282, 285–6
  and States General 265–7, 274, 288, 311–12
  of Union of Arras 301, 304, 317
  of Union of Utrecht 294
  and William of Orange 174, 177, 196, 208–9, 249, 251, 259
Crépy, Peace of (1544) 146–7, 150
Crèvecoeur, Philippe 59, 77
Croy family 260, 280
  and Charles V 78, 172
  and Charles the Bold 77
  and France 18
  and Margaret of Austria 93, 102
  and Maximilian 66, 102
  and Philip II 196
  and Philip the Good 18, 30–1, 86
  and Philip the Handsome 86, 89, 92, 119
  see also Aerschot, Philippe de Croy, third duke
Croy, Philippe de *see* Aerschot, Philippe de Croy, third duke

De Silva, Ruy Gomez 173, 216
De Villiers, 295
debt, public 117, 178–9, 190, 198, 224, 261–2
defence policies
  of Charles V 126–32, 138–9, 150, 192, 199
  of Philip II 194, 198–200
  and provinces 95–100, 115–16, 130–2, 138, 144
Delft 22, 305
democracy, and representation 8
Denmark
  and Charles V 129–30
  as composite monarchy 84
  and House of Holstein 129
  and Norway and Sweden 84, 129, 330
  and parliament 329
deputations 111–12
Des Pruneaux, 298
Despars, Nicholas 56, 60
Deventer 308
D'Ewes, Sir Simonds *326*

Index

Dijon 51
Dirkszoon, Hendrick 241
Dôle, university of 95
Dominican Order, and concept of representation 3
dominium politicum et regale 13–14, 82, 255–6, 322–4
  in America 333
  in Brabant 323
  in composite monarchies 83–5, 88, 93–122, 123–50, 259
  in England 312, 333–4
  in Hainaut 103
  instability of 324–30
  and Maximilian 45, 72, 92
  and taxation 25, 166, 191
  and Union of Arras 317
  see also trust, mutual
dominium regale 82
  and absolutism 331, 333, 335, 337–8
  in England 333–4
  in France 13, 25, 44, 111, 163, 235, 268, 303, 337
  in Guelders 37–8
  imposition of 222–4, 227, 235, 331
  in Spain 312, 329
  and taxation 13, 166, 227, 268
  and Union of Arras 317, 319–21
Don John *see* John of Austria
Dordrecht 22
  and Estates of Holland 118, 230, 245, 246
  and *gracien* 112
  popular revolt of 1477 45
  and taxation 230
Dorothea of the Palatinate 129, 130
Douai *see* Lille-Douai-Orchies
Drenthe, and Guelders 145
Du Plessis-Mornay, Philippe 295, 300
Ducci, Gasparo 161–2, 308

Eboli, Ruy Gomez de Silva, prince of 173, 216
economy
  under Maximilian 73–4
  under Philip II 197, 212, 214–15
  and popular revolt 288–9
  see also textile industry; trade
Edward I of England 5
Edward IV of England 31, 51
Egmont, counts of *see* Adolf of Egmont; Arnold of Egmont; Charles of Egmont; Lamoral, count of Egmont
Egmont family 78, 79
Eleanor, dowager queen of France 169
eleutheria 1–2, 6
Elizabeth I of England
  and Anjou 235, 292, 302, 304
  and France 300
  and John of Austria 275–6
  and Parliament 161, 252, 324, *326*
  and States General 267, 307–8, 310
  and United Provinces 310, 314
  and William of Orange 246
Elizabeth of France, and Philip II of Spain 193
Elizabeth of York 51
Emmanuel Philibert of Piedmont-Savoy 169, 173–92, 335
  and Council of Finance 175, 184
  and Council of State 174, 175, 190, 192
  and Philip II 174–6, 194, 335
  and States General 180–92, 196, 198
encabezamiento 168, 175, 231, 234
England
  and Brabant 93–5, 149
  and Charles V 115, 127, 129–30, 155–6
  as composite monarchy 11, 14, 84, 85
  as *dominium politicum et regale* regime 312, 333–4
  and France 12, 155–6, 235, 292, 300, 302
  and John of Austria 269, 275
  and Parliament 5, 8, 111, 113–14, 160–1, 185, 323, *326*, 333–4, 336
  and Philip II 172–3, 185, 194
  proposed union with 188
  and representative assemblies 7–8
  and Spain 300, 307, 310, 314
  and trade 27, 90, 94, 105, 212, 308
  and Triple Alliance (1596) 313
  and United Provinces 313–14

Index

Erasmus, Desiderius 105, 116, 280
Eraso, Francisco de 173, 175
Erastianism 315
Ernest, archduke 316–17
Escobedo, Juan de 269
Espinosa, Cardinal 227–8
'Eternal Edict' 274, 285, 290, 317
Eugenius IV, Pope 10
Eynden, Jacob van der 229

Ferdinand I, Emperor 107, 125–6, 146, 149, 169
  and deputations 112
  and Hungary 127
  and imperial elections 106, 169, 172
  and Italy 169
  and Philip II 280
  and religious divisions of Germany 127, 155
  and Turkish threat 127–8
Ferdinand II, Emperor 332–3
Ferdinand of Aragon 13, 67, 91
  and expansionism 86
  and Holy League 101
  and Isabella of Castile 75, 84, 89, 110, 204
  succession to 104–5
  and Venice 97
feudalism 22, 289
  and *eleutheria* 2
  and representation 2–3, 7
Fiennes, seigneur de 100
Fiftieth Penny tax 181, 184
Finland, and Sweden 14, 84
Flanders
  and Anjou 292, 299
  and Burgundy 16
  and Calvinism 277, 283, 289, 304
  and Charles V 104, 105, 107, 109, 115, 139
  and Charles the Bold 29, 33–4, 37
  and Council of Eighteen 283
  defeat by Parma 315–16
  and defensive union 131–2, 200
  four members *see* Bruges; Franc de Bruges; Ghent; Ypres
  and France 7, 43, 49–51, 55–6, 57–61, 67, 70, 90, 93–5, 116
  and *gratien* 159
  and Guelders 98
  and Holy Roman Empire 149, 246
  and language 24
  and Maximilian 56, 57–65, 67–72, 90–1
  and peasants 20–1, 26, 45–7
  and Philip II 182, 183–4
  and Philip the Good 21, 27–30
  prosperity 19–20, 24
  representative assemblies 5–7, 19–21, 24, 26, 49, 71, 147
  and revolt of 1477 42
  and States General 28–9, 31, 37–9, 49, 52, 61, 86, 90–1, 139, 189
  and taxation 47, 61, 89, 100, 115, 118, 127, 139–40, 159, 164–5, 183–4, 192
  and textile industry 19, 27, 47, 61, 69–70, 140, 197, 212, 277
  and trade 19, 21, 128
  and Union of Arras 320
  and union of provinces 200
  and Union of Utrecht 312
  and William of Orange 271
  see also Bruges; Franc de Bruges; Ghent; Walloon Flanders; Ypres
Flanders, Estates 10, 20, 165, 290
  and Charles V 160
  and Charles the Bold 37
  and Margaret of Austria 100, 118
  and Mary of Burgundy 49
  and Maximilian 54, 56
  and Philip the Good 28
Florence, and representation 6
foreign policy
  in multiple monarchy 85–6, 93–4, 96, 105–8, 115–17, 127–8, 154, 206
  and representative assemblies 147–8
  see also France; Ottoman Turks
Fortescue, Sir John 13, 25, 44, 82, 337
Franc de Bruges
  and Charles the Bold 33–4, 37
  and Estates General 31, 39, 44–5

Index

and Maximilian 61, 64, 67
and representative assemblies 5–6, 20, 26–7, 49
and taxation 33–4, 37, 160, 165
France
  and *alternativa* 146–8, 151, 155
  and Aragon 105
  and Brittany 67–8, 84
  and Burgundy 16–18, 35–6, 42–4, 49–51, 55, 58, 87
  and Calvinism 203, 214, 256, 284
  and Charles V 127, 137–9, 145, 152–4, 155–7
  civil wars 194, 198, 214, 243, 285, 314, 316
  as composite monarchy 84, 85
  and *dominium regale* regime 13, 25, 44, 111, 163, 268, 303, 325, 337
  and Estates General 12–13, 25, 44–5, 110–11, 239, 275, 318, 327, 337
  and Flanders 7, 42, 43, 49–51, 55–6, 57–61, 67, 70, 90, 93–5, 100
  and Habsburgs 146, 149, 152–3, 155
  and Hainaut 42, 116, 234, 292, 293
  and Holy League 101
  and Ottoman Turks 155
  and parliamentary myth 337
  and Philip II 197–8, 206, 284–5
  and Reformed Church *see* Calvinism
  and regency of Netherlands 90, 91
  religious-political leagues 126, 278–9, 284
  and Spain 87, 193, 299–300
  and taxation 13, 25, 111, 153, 163, 175, 268
  and Triple Alliance (1596) 313
  and United Provinces 313–14
  war with
    and Alba 234, 235
    and Charles V 116, 137–9, 145–6, 150, 154, 155–7, 178
    financing of 157–68, 174, 175–80, 198–200
    and Italy 154, 157, 184, 193
    and Mary of Hungary 154, 157–8
    and peace negotiations 146–7, 150, 153, 172
    and Philip II 184–5
    and States General 187–8
  Wars of Religion 83, 194, 198, 337
  see also Artois; Charles VIII; England; Francis I; Henry II; Henry III; Henry IV; Huguenots; Louis XI; Louis XII; Valois monarchy
Franche-Comté 51, 58, 69, 85, 244
  and *alternativa* 146
  and France 12
  and Margaret of Austria 95
Francis I of France 13, 79
  and Charles V 105, 106, 143–4, 145–6, 155
Francis II, Duke of Brittany 67
Françoise de Luxembourg 66
Frankfort, truce of (1489) 67
Frederick I Barbarossa 3, 6
Frederick I of Denmark 129
Frederick III, Holy Roman Emperor 65, 66, 68, 69, 88
Frederick of the Palatinate 129, 332
freedom *see* liberty
Friesland 24, 38, 187
  and Charles V 108, 131, 145
  and Guelders 105, 116, 145
  and religious rebellions 236
  and States General 265
  and Union of Utrecht 293
Friuli, and representative assemblies 40
Fuensalida, Gutierrez Gomez de 87
Fuentes, count of 316–17
Fugger banking house 158, 178–9

Gallo, Juan López 177
Gattinara, Mercurino di 76–7, 107–8, 115, 117, 156
Gembloux, battle (1577) 299, 306 n.17
Generality, and Union of Utrecht 294
George of Saxony 105
Germany
  and conference of Cologne 292, 299
  and *dominium regale* 166

and Estates 166
and imperial cities 49
and imperial elections 106, 108, 154, 169
Lutheranism in 201, 203
and Reichstag 149–50, 169, 239, *328*
and religious divisions 127, 131, 146, 152, 153, 155, 167, 217, 281, 283–4, 293
and religious-political leagues 126, 279
and representative assemblies 227
and urban leagues 58
see also Holy Roman Empire; Schmalkaldic War

Ghent
and Calvinism 277, 283, 289, 299, 304, 313, 315
and Charles V 104, 139, 141–5
and Charles the Bold 33–4, 37–8
and France 58–60, 68, 143
and *gracien* 139, 140
and Maximilian 54, 56, 58–9, 61–6, 67–8, 70, 140, 144–5
and populist-religious movements 132–3, 288, 299, 304–5, 313, 315, 332
and representative assemblies 5, 7, 19–21, 26, 49, 68
and republicanism 313
revolt of 1452–3 21, 26, 30, 135
revolt of 1477 45–7, 51, 189, 264
revolt of 1492 67–8
revolt of 1539–40 68, 140–5, 151, 162, 186, 217, 221, 233, 249, 278
revolt of 1578 68
and States General 27, 29–30, 31, 39, 42–3, 57, 64
and taxation 33–4, 37, 109, 139, 140–2, 144, 165
and town council 135
and Union of Arras 319
and William of Orange 271, 277–8, 304–5, 313
Ghent, Pacification of *see* Pacification of Ghent
Goethe, J. W. von, *Faust* 340

Golden Fleece, Order of
and Alba 228
and Charles V 77, 138, 146
and defence of Netherlands 188
and Mary of Hungary 130
and Maximilian 60, 69, 77
and Philip II 174, 185, 195–6, 198, 210, 214, 221
and Philip the Good 18
and royalists 317
Gouda 22, 45, 87 n.35, 146, 221, 231
gracien 98, 112–13, 115–16, 139, 140, 159, 164–5, 230
Granada, kingdom of, and Ferdinand and Isabella 84, 86
grand bailli
in Flanders 143
in Hainaut 19, 71, 102, 174
Grandson, battle (1476) 38
Granvelle, Antoine Perrenot, Cardinal
and Alba 226, 228–9, 234
and control of government 206–9
and Council of State 174, 186, 192, 196, 263, 282
and defensive union of provinces 199
and Lalaing 177, 186
and Spanish troops 195
and States General 115, 186, 191, 200, 205, 212, 230, 247, 252, 260 n.1, 267
and William of Orange 206–9, 250, 295
Great Council
and Mary of Burgundy 44, 45, 54
and Mary of Hungary 141
and Philip the Handsome 76
Great Privilege (1477) 42–9, 54, 253, 266
and the church 202
and States General 43–5, 52, 71
and towns and cities 47–9, 61, 64, 141–2
Gresham, Thomas 163, 176
Grimaldi, Niccolo 227
Groningen 24, 105, 131, 145, 187, 265, 293
Grotius, Hugo 310
Guagninus, A. *325*

Index

Guelders, Charles of Egmont, duke of
  see Charles of Egmont
Guelders (duchy)
  and Burgundy 105
  and Charles the Bold 37–8, 56, 88
  Estates 38, 215
  and France 42, 56, 91–2
  and Holy Roman Empire 149, 151–2, 187, 244, 246
  and Maximilian 56, 57, 66, 70, 87, 88, 91, 96–8
  and Philip the Handsome 70, 88, 89
  and religious rebellions 236
  and States General 39, 88, 97–8, 100, 116
  and Union of Utrecht 293
  wars with provinces 104, 120, 138, 145, 151, 159, 174
Guelders, dukes of see Adolf of Egmont; Arnold of Egmont; Charles of Egmont; William of Cleves
guilds 45–9, 143, 283, 288
  and civil war 277
  and town councils 21, 23–4, 62–3, 68, 102, 115, 132–4, 136, 139, 144, 183, 200
Guinegate, battle (1479) 56
Gustavus III of Sweden 337
Gustavus Adolphus of Sweden 324
Gustavus Vasa of Sweden 329, 330
Guyenne 155

Haarlem 22, 112, 283
Habsburgs
  and defence policies 127, 150
  and financing of war 157–8
  and imperial revenues 158, 163–4, 167–8, 172–80
  and multiple monarchy 13, 127, 328–9, 335
  and Netherlands 85, 88, 93, 118, 146–8, 149–50, 152, 155–7, 171, 172–92, 307
  and Turkish threat 118, 127–8, 131–2, 146, 149, 154
  and Valois monarchy 146, 149, 152–3, 155, 166, 193, 256
  see also Charles V; Holy Roman Empire; Maximilian I
Hainaut
  and Albert of Saxony 71
  and Burgundy 16–18
  and Charles V 104, 138–9
  and duke of Anjou 292
  Estates 19, 30
  and France 42, 116, 234, 292, 293
  and language 24
  and Maximilian 57, 62, 65, 69, 102–3
  and Philip the Good 27, 30
  and prosperity 74, 199, 215, 289
  and religious wars 234
  representative assemblies 18–19, 25
  and States General 27, 33, 38, 42, 52, 86, 260, 265, 283
  and taxation 19, 25, 32–3, 232
  and Union of Arras 290
Hannart, Jean 77
Hansards 128, 149, 162, 308
Hanseatic League 6
hearth tax 97
Hembyze, Jan van 277–8, 304
Henry II of France 79, 154, 163, 185, 193, 266
Henry III of France 279, 292, 295, 299–300, 302, 304–5, 307
Henry IV of France 314, 320
Henry VII of England 67, 75, 89, 90, 324
Henry VIII of England 75, 84, 127, 255
  and Holy League 101
  and papacy 96
  and Parliament 323, 324
  and Reformation 329
heresy see Calvinism; Lutheranism; Protestantism; revolt
's-Hertogenbosch 23, 57
  and Guelders 98
  and Maximilian 57, 66
  popular revolt of 1477 45
  popular revolt of 1577 277

Index

and taxation 100, 120, 144, 183, 200
and town council 134-5
Hèze, William of Hoorn, lord of 265, 289
Hoeks 22, 47, 56, 60, 66-7, 70
Hogenberg, Frans *170*
Holland (county) 31
  and agriculture 73
  and Baltic trade 80, 128-30, 138, 229
  and Catholicism 118, 243, 254, 283, 299
  and Charles V 76, 104, 115-16, 331
  and the Compromise 215
  and Court of Holland 166, 245, 247, 249, 251
  and defensive union 131-2, 199-200, 259
  and *gracien* 159, 230
  and Guelders 91, 97, 116, 145
  and iconoclasm 213-14
  and Maximilian 56, 57, 71
  and Pacification of Ghent 273, 287
  and peace negotiations 252-6, 258-9, 263-5, 268, 271
  and Philip II 182, 184, 287
  and Philip the Good 16, 18
  and popular revolts (1477) 45-7
  and prosperity 73-5
  and religious revolt 234, 236-7, 240-6, 252, 318, 330
  representative assemblies 6, 8, 21-2, 27
  and States General 31, 38, 52, 86, 91, 187-8, 190, 260, 265, 290
  and taxation 115-16, 127-8, 159, 164, 165-6, 184, 199-200, 229-31
  and trade 22
  and Union of Arras 318-19
  and Union of Utrecht 305, 312-13
  and United Provinces 305-6
  and urbanisation 22, 132
Holland, Estates of 214, 281, 296
  and Anjou 298-9
  and Charles the Bold 31
  and Conference of Breda 248, 250, 254-6, 273
  as constituent assembly 259
  and defence policies 129, 130, 194, 198-200

  early meetings of 27
  and Gueldrian war 120, 145
  and heresy 118-19
  and Inquisition 118, 187, 201, 213
  and Leicester 251, 308-9
  and Maurice of Nassau 314-15
  and Maximilian 71
  and parliamentary government 331
  and Peace of Augsberg 150
  and peace negotiations 147, 253-5
  and provincial governor 79-82, 245
  and revolt 132, 245-52
  seal *332*
  and secularisation of the church 248
  and sovereignty 309-10, 311-12
  and States General 255-6, 263, 274, 313
  and taxation 75-6, 80-1, 116-18, 160-2, 165-6, 184, 229-31, 248, 251-2
  and towns 22
  and William of Orange 212-13, 245-6, 247-52, 257-9, 263, 266, 299, 305, 313
Holstein, House of 129
Holy League 101, 280
Holy Roman Empire
  and Charles V 149-50, 169
  and fiefdoms 57, 94, 149
  and Maximilian II 280
  and Netherlands 87-8, 146-8, 149-50, 151, 186, 188, 282, 288
  and papacy 4, 10, 96, 106, 121, 127, 147
  and Philip II 285
  and Philip the Good 18
  see also Charles V; Frederick III; Germany; Habsburgs; Maximilian I
Hondschoote, textile industry 70, 316
Hoochstraten, Antoine de Lalaing, count of 76, 79-82, 113-14, 117, 130, 141
Hooks, party of *see* Hoeks
Hoorn, counts of 78, 174, 182, 184, 196, 208, 221
Hopperus, Joachim 263

Index

Hugonet, Guillaume (chancellor) 36, 38, 39–41, 49–51
Huguenots 213, 224, 264
 and Henry III 299
 and Henry IV 316
 in Netherlands 207, 234
 and political leagues 278, 299
 and Wars of Religion 194, 198
Hulst, Frans van der 118
Humbercourt, Guy de Brimeu, seigneur 50, 51
Humphrey, duke of Gloucester 16
Hundredth Penny tax
 and Alba 215, 224, 228, 230–1, 236–7, 289
 and Charles V 160, 162
 and Estates 265
 and Philip II 182, 184
Hungary
 and Bohemia 84
 dominium politicum et regale regime 338
 and Ottoman Turks 123, 127, 288

iconoclasm 212, 213–14, 241, 243
income tax 159–60, 162, 165, 167, 183–4, 224
Innocent III, Pope 3
Inquisition 213–14, 216, 240, 255
 and Charles V 204–5
 and Estates of Holland 118, 187, 201, 213
 in Naples 204–5, 223
 and Philip II 201, 204–5, 209, 210, 243, 246, 250
 in Spain 204, 210, 223, 243, 246, 250, 281
 and States General 187–8, 213
Ireland, and England 14, 84, 85
Isabel of Denmark 129
Isabella of Castile 89
 and Ferdinand of Aragon 75, 84, 110, 204
Isabella (wife of Archduke Albert) 280, 317, 321
Isabella (regent of Castile) 127

Italy
 and Aragonese and French rivalry 105
 and Charles V 127, 153, 157, 158, 169, 172–3, 175, 193
 city-states 3, 6–8, 9, 20, 49, 140, 141
 and Maximilian 97
 and papacy 3, 172, 173, 176
 and the state 82
 and war with France 154, 157, 184, 193
ius indigenatus 85, 173

Jacopszoon, Andries de 81, 83, 112–14, 116, 125, 161, 253
Jacqueline of Bavaria 16, 22
James I and VI of England and Scotland 11, 160–1, 318, 339
Jean de Carondelet 77
Jean de Croy 31
John II of France 12
John of Austria 221, 258, 263–4, 267, 285, 291
 and civil war 259, 276–9, 299, 303
 as governor general of Netherlands 268–70, 271, 279–80, 285
 and States General 269–70, 273–6, 280, 282, 310, 331
John Casimir, count of the Palatinate 286, 289, 292, 300
John the Fearless of Burgundy 85
John of Nassau 253, 293, 296
Jonge, Junius de 239
joyeuse entrée 69, 266, 296, 323
 and the church 119–20, 121, 187, 202
 and inviolability of domain land 185
 and language rights 24
 and local privileges 138, 142, 238, 253
 and right of assembly 44
 and right of resistance 238, 287
 and taxation 103, 120
Juan, infante 87
Juana I, regent of Spain 156, 158, 167–8, 169, 177, 179, 217
Juana ('the Mad') of Castile 87, 89, 91
Julius II, Pope 97
Julius III, Pope 167

Index

juros (annuities) 176, 178–80, 227, 261
Justinian Codex 4, 9, 324

Kabeljauws 22, 47, 56, 60, 66–7
Karre, Peter 113
Key, Adriaen Thomas *242*

La Ruyelle, Jean/Jeannet de 57
Lalaing, Antoine, count of Hoochstraten
   see Hoochstraten, Antoine de
   Lalaing, count of
Lalaing, Charles de, *grand bailli* of Hainaut
   174–7, 186, 191
Lamoral, count of Egmont 78, 202
   and Council of State 174, 177, 196,
     209–10
   and Perrenot 206, 208
   and religious revolts 213, 216, 221
   and Spanish troops in Netherlands
     194–5
   and States General 252
   and taxation 182, 184
Landts Raedt (Holland) 257–8
languages 24
Languet, Hubert 295
Lannoy, Charles de 77–8
Lannoy family 66, 172
Lara, Juan Marique de 173
League of Cambrai 97, 101
Leicester, Robert Dudley earl of 251, 296,
   307–10, 313–14
Leiden 22, 23, 116, 258
Leo X, Pope 119
Léon, Cortes 3
Leone, Leoni *124*
Leoninus, Elbertus 255, 271, 275, 288,
   290
Lepanto, battle (1572) 263, 269, 280
Les Pays Bas 26
liberty 1–2, 6, 103, 152–3, 252, 301–3,
   318
   and religion 238–9, 255, 293–4, 330
   and sovereignty 322–4, 333–4
Liège, prince-bishopric 18, 33, 59
Lier 45, 319

Lille, and Catholic oligarchy 315
Lille-Douai-Orchies
   and Burgundy 16
   and France 67
   representative assemblies 20
   and States General 38, 86
   and taxation 232
   and Union of Arras 290
Limbourg (duchy) 34, 38, 187, 265
Lithuania, and Poland 84
Lombard League 6
Loo, Albert de 79
Lorraine, and Charles the Bold 37, 85
Los Cobos, Francisco de 147
Louis II of Hungary 104, 106, 123, 125
Louis IX of France 16
Louis XI of France 18, 24, 30, 42–3, 75
   and Artois 42, 43, 57, 90
   death 60, 337
   and Estates 44–5
   and Flanders 49–50, 57, 59–60
   and Maximilian 53, 58
Louis XII of France 75, 90
   and Guelders 87, 97
   and Mary Tudor 101
Louis XV of France 338
Louis, count of Nassau 210, 220 n.2,
   245–6
Louis de Bruges, seigneur of Gruuthuse
   60
Louis de Luxembourg, count of St Pol 18,
   66, 77 n.12
Louvain 23, 52, 66, 71
   popular revolt of 1477 45
   and taxation 100, 120, 200
   university 142
Low Countries 26
Lübeck, and Baltic trade 128–30, 162
Lumey, count 243–4
Luther, Martin 118, 135, 143, 201
Lutheranism 118, 125, 142, 152, 201, 203
Luxembourg (duchy) 18, 59, 131
   and language 24
   and Philip the Good 16–18
   and States General 34, 38, 86, 187, 265

Index

Maastricht, siege of 290
Machiavelli, Niccolo viii, 1–2, 6, 12, 140,
   220–1, 270, 318, 338, 339
Madrid, Treaty (1526) 148 n.88
Magna Carta 7–8
Malcontents 289, 302
Malines (Mechlin; Mechelen) 52, 64, 98
  and Estates 120
  and Great Court 76, 103, 133, 141, 153
  parlement 38, 43–4
  royal court 125
  and States General 27, 38, 86, 90–1, 97,
    99, 130–1
  and town council 133
Malta, Turkish siege (1565) 211
Mansfelt, Charles, count of 316–17
Margaret of Austria 94, 125
  and the church 119–20, 121–2, 201
  death 122
  and first regency 91, 93–102
  and France 68, 95
  marriages 87, 90
  proposed marriage to Charles VIII 12,
    57–8, 68, 95, 101
  revenues and taxation 97–100, 109,
    116–18, 120–1
  and second regency 100, 105, 106–22,
    196
  and States General 91, 93, 97–9, 101–2,
    107–9, 121
Margaret of Parma
  and the Compromise 210–11, 216, 270
  and control of government 206–9, 267
  and Council of State 195–7, 209
  and duke of Alba 221, 222, 234, 316
  and heresy 209–16, 221
  and Protestantism 200–1, 211, 213–14,
    215–16
  regency 127, 186, 195–219, 220–2, 279,
    316
  and social change 197, 216
  and States General 198, 211, 213, 252
Margaret of York, duchess of Burgundy
  38, 42, 50
Mariana, Juan de 254, 322

Marnix (Secretary of Margaret of Austria)
  98
Marnix Van St Aldegonde, Philippe
  and Charles V 307
  and duke of Anjou 298, 300–1
  and Pacification of Ghent 273
  and Philip II 293–4
  and Swiss cantons 277, 284
  and William of Orange 248, 249–50
Martin V, Pope 10
Mary of Burgundy 38–9, 41, 42, 60, 124
  death 56–7
  and Great Council 44, 45
  and Maximilian 52, 54–6, 68, 85, 88
  proposed marriage to Charles VIII 50–2
  and States General 16, 42–5, 49–52,
    71
  and Treaty of Arras 12, 44–5
  see also Great Privilege
Mary of Hungary 109, *124*, 192, 197, 199
  and *alternativa* 146–7
  and the church 126
  and Council of State 174, 262
  and defensive union 157
  first regency (1531–50) 123–50, 186
  marriage 104
  and religious reform 125, 126, 152, 167
  second regency (1550–5) 151–71, 173
  and States General 130–1, 138–9, 144,
    148, 159–60, 163, 206, 308
  and taxation 127–8, 134–9, 163–5,
    224–7, 233
  and war with France 154, 157–8
Mary Queen of Scots 269, 275, 307
Mary (sister of Philip II) 280
Mary Tudor of England 101, 194
  marriage to Philip II 147, 155–6, 167, 172,
    194
Masnuy, seigneur de 289
Matthias, archduke 279, 286, 290, 303
  n.12, 317
  and Philip II 285, 288
  and States General 280–3, 290, 294,
    295
Matthias Corvinas of Hungary 67

Index

Maurice of Nassau 306, 308, 314
  as stadholder 314–15
  and Union of Arras 316
Maurice of Saxony 196
Maximilian I, Holy Roman Emperor 13, 44, 52
  and Anne of Brittany 67–8
  and Austria 112
  and Burgundian Circle 149
  and civil wars 66–72, 73, 85
  and coinage 62, 63
  and council of regency 60
  and crusade against Turks 87, 88–9, 91
  death 106
  as Emperor 69, 106
  and Estates 53–4
  and expansionism 54, 70, 85
  first regency 57–65, 86, 100, 152, 189, 282
  and Great Privilege 141–2
  and Guelders 56, 57, 66, 70, 87, 88, 91, 96–7
  and Holy League 101
  and Italy 97
  and Mary of Burgundy 52, 54–6, 85
  in Netherlands 52–7, 88–9
  and regency of Margaret of Austria 91, 95–9, 101–2
  revenues and taxation 55–6, 61–2, 66, 88–9, 117
  second regency 90–2, 152
  and States General 55–6, 57, 61–2, 64–5, 66–7, 69, 88–9, 90–2, 152–3, 168, 269–70
  Theuerdank 52
  Weisskunig 52–3, 66
Maximilian II
  as Emperor 217, 280, 281
  as king of Bohemia 169, 198
Medinaceli, duke of (governor general of Netherlands) 234, 236
Megen, count of 174, 196, 215
Mendoza, Bernardino de 173
Metsius, Laurent, bishop of 's-Hertogenbosch 273

Metz 154, 196
Middelburg 22
Mierop, Vincent Corneliszoon van 159
Milan (duchy) of
  and Charles V 115, 146–7
  and France 84, 85, 90, 105, 146
  and representation 6
  and Spain 176, 205, 223
Mohács, battle (1526) 123
Molembaix, counts of 80
Momper, Bartholomaeus de *191*
monarchy, composite 11, 74, 329, 334–5, 338, 339
  and administration of finances 174–80
  balanced 330–6
  and defensive union 157
  and division of authority 167, 168, 173, 216
  and foreign policy 85–6, 93–4, 96, 105–8, 115–17, 127–8, 154, 206
  and government of Netherlands 75–86, 149–50, 151–71, 218–19, 261–4, 280
  and maintenance of unity 87–8, 157–8, 171
  and parliament 324–30
  and personal position of monarch 339–40
  and regency government 93–122, 144, 234
  and States General 253–6, 260–1, 322–4
  see also dominium politicum et regale; *dominium regale*; sovereignty
Mons 19, 32, 62, 102–3, 110
Montigny, Floris de Montmorency, baron of 216, 321
Montils-les-Tours, treaty (1489) 37
Montmorency family (counts of Hoorn) 66, 78, 79
Morat, battle (1477) 41
More, Thomas 105, 166
Morillon, Maximilien 260, 262
Moriscos, uprising 210, 221, 261, 269, 272
Moro, Antonio *218*

Index

Namur 38
  and Charles V 104, 139
  and John of Austria 275–6
  and Philip the Good 16
  and States General 38, 52, 86
Nancy, battle (1477) 16, 42
Naples, kingdom of
  and Aragon 9, 105
  and France 69, 84, 85
  and imperial revenues 164, 176
  and Inquisition 204–5, 223
Nassau, House of 66, 78, 80, 258
Netherlands
  and absence of ruler 85
  and composite assemblies 26–30
  and Holy Roman Empire 87–8, 146–8, 149–50, 151, 186, 188, 282, 288
  and parliamentary government 279–85, 286, 295, 298–331
  representative assemblies 24–6
  see also States General; provinces
Nicolas of Cusa 11
Nigri, Philip 80–1
Nijmegen, and Charles the Bold 37–8
nobility
  and Charles V 76–82, 103, 153, 157
  as estate 7–8, 19–20, 22, 23, 27
  and Margaret of Austria 95–6, 101
  and Maximilian 59–61, 62–3
  and patronage 78, 82–3, 112, 173, 206–9, 335
  and pensions 55–6
  and Philip II 195–6, 202, 206, 209, 214–16
  and provincial loyalties 62–3, 70, 77, 79, 95–6
  and revolt of Holland 251, 264–5
  and States General 289
  and taxation 159, 165, 166
  and Union of Arras 291, 299, 319
  see also princes
Nonesuch, Treaty (1585) 307, 314
Norway, and Denmark 84, 129
Noyon, Treaty (1516) 105

Oldenbarnevelt, Jan van 308, 310, 312–15
Olivier de la Marche 61, 72
Olivier le Daim 60
Ommelanden, and Union of Utrecht 293
Onredene, Daniel 60–1
Orange (principality) 18, 78
Orange, William 'the Silent' of Nassau, prince of 182–3, 195, *242*
  and Aerschot 265, 271, 274–6, 277–9, 281
  and Anjou 298–9, 304
  'Apology' 295–6, 306
  and Archduke Matthias 281, 288
  assassination 305, 314
  and common people 276–7
  and Council of State 174, 177, 196, 208–9, 249, 251, 259
  and Estates of Holland 212–13, 245–6, 247–52, 257–9, 263, 266, 299, 313
  and Flanders 271
  as governor of Brabant 277, 304
  and Granvelle 206–9, 250, 295
  invasion of 1568 224, 226
  and John of Austria 274, 276
  and negotiations with England 245–6
  and Ottoman Turks 238
  and Pacification of Ghent 273, 275
  and peace negotiations 252–5, 274–5, 283–4, 287
  and Philip II 182, 250, 287, 295–6, 305, 306–7, 331
  and religion 212–13, 222, 293
  and religious wars 18, 234, 241–3, 249–50, 283–4, 290
  and sovereignty 257–9
  and States General 252, 255–6, 263, 267, 269, 274–5, 276–7, 278, 284, 292, 294–5, 298–9, 313
  and taxation 182, 184, 259
  and union of provinces 278, 293, 306–7
  and uprising of Brussels 265
Orangeists
  and Archduke Matthias 281
  and conference of Cologne 287–8

Index

and Pacification of Ghent 274–5, 283, 288
as Patriots 276–7
and religious revolt 238–9, 243, 247, 259, 272, 291
Orchies *see* Lille-Douai-Orchies
Orléans, duke of, and *alternativa* 146–8
Orley, Bernard-Barend van *94*
Ottoman Turks 87, 88, 149
  and Charles V 108, 127–8, 130–1, 146, 152
  and control of Mediterranean 105, 154, 232, 234, 237, 261, 263–4
  and France 154, 155
  and Hungary 123, 288
  and Philip II 211, 217, 232, 261
  and Poland 12
  and siege of Malta (1565) 211
Oudenaarde 56
Outremeuse, pays d' 38, 86, 132
Overijssel, incorporation into Holy Roman Empire 49, 131, 145, 187, 265
Oxenstiena, Axel 322–3, 330

Pacification of Ghent 270–2, 331
  and Archduke Matthias 281, 283
  and Catholicism 272, 274–5, 277, 281, 283–4
  and conference of Cologne 287–8
  and Holland and Zeeland 273, 287
  and John of Austria 274–6, 285
  and States General 272, 273, 286
  and Union of Arras 290–1
  and Union of Brussels 272, 279
  and Union of Utrecht 293
Paelding, Andries 63–4
papacy
  and Charles V 153, 167
  and concept of representation 3, 4
  and conciliarism 10–11
  and Holy Roman Empire 4, 10, 96, 106, 121, 127, 147
Paris, *parlement* 43, 59, 302
  University 10
Paris Treaty (1498) 87, 88

Paris Treaty (1515) 105
parliament
  and monarchy 324–30
  myth of 336–7
  see also England; representation; States General
Parma, Alexander Farnese, duke of 289–90, 302–5
  and conference of Cologne 287
  conquests 303, 305, 307, 315–16, 332
  and England 300
  and France 314, 316
  and Philip II 285, 315, 316
  and Treaty of Arras 291–2, 315–16
Parma, principality 153
participation, principle of 1–2, 5
Patriots 276–7
patronage
  under Charles V 126, 156, 173
  under Emmanuel Philibert 335
  under Margaret of Austria 93, 101, 112, 117, 121
  under Mary of Hungary 123, 126, 156, 173
  under Philip II 156, 173, 190, 196, 206–9, 304
  under Philip the Handsome 78, 82–5
Paul IV, Pope 172, 173, 176
Pérez, Gonzalo de 197, 209
Perpetual Edict 274, 285, 290, 317
Perrenot, Antoine *see* Granvelle, Antoine Perrenot, Cardinal
Peter III of Aragon 9
Petition of Right (England; 1628) 333
Phelps, Sir Robert 333
Philibert II, duke of Savoy 87
Philip II 112, 143, 144, 146, *181*
  and abdication of Charles V 167–8, *170*
  and Act of Abjuration 297
  and Alba 221, 223–4, 226, 234, 236, 261
  and Anjou 299, 301
  and Archduke Albert 317
  and Archduke Matthias 285, 288
  and civil war in Netherlands *see* revolt against Spain

Index

and the Compromise 220, 270
and control of government 206–9
and Council of State 190, 208–9, 238, 282, 285–6
and France 185, 197–8, 206, 284–5
and Holy Roman Empire 280, 285
and Inquisition 204–5, 243, 246, 250
and John of Austria 268–9
and marriage to Elizabeth of France 193
and marriage to Mary Tudor 147, 155–6, 167, 172, 194
mistrust of 145, 195–6, 204, 219, 228, 294
in Netherlands 156–7, 168, 172–3, 237, 263
and new bishoprics 188, 201–4, 206
and Parma 285, 315, 316
and Peace of Augsburg 203, 217, 255, 284
as regent of Spain 112, 143, 144, 146, 157–8, 167–8
and religion 193, 196, 197, 201–6, 256, 270
and religious revolt 209–11, 216–19, 220–2, 235
and religious wars 243, 254–5, 263–4, 290–6
and revenues and taxation 172–80, 181–3, 198–200, 226–7, 233–4, 239, 261–2, 268
and revolt of Holland and Zeeland 248
and sack of Antwerp 272
in Spain 193–200, 217, 233, 254
and Spanish troops in Netherlands 194–5, 315
and States General 205–6, 211–12, 222–4, 226, 236–7, 247, 253–4, 286, 295, 307, 323, 336
of 1556 180–4, 188, 191
of 1557–9 195, 199–200
of 1576 260–8, 270
and Union of Arras 291–2
and Union of Utrecht 293–5
and William of Orange 182, 250, 287, 295–6, 305, 306–7, 331
see also Spanish Armada

Philip III of Spain 320
Philip IV of Spain 321
Philip the Bold of Burgundy 85
Philip of Cleves, seigneur of Ravenstein 56, 62, 64–5, 66–9, 72, 77, 96
Philip the Good of Burgundy *17*, 26–30, 47, 85
and Brabant 16–18, 23–4, 29
and Charles the Bold 30–2
and coinage 28–9, 32, 62
expenditure and taxation 21, 29–30, 32–3, 39
and Flanders 21, 27, 30
and Holland and Zeeland 16, 22
and States General 27–9, 31–2, 43, 86, 261
Philip the Handsome of Burgundy 44, 86–92
and Castile 70, 89, 110
death 89, 91, 95
and regency 57–65
and revenues and taxation 89, 105, 119
and States General 86–9, 100
and succession crisis 90–2
Philippe de Bourgogne, seigneur of Beveren 60
Piacenza, principality 153
Picardie
and Burgundy 34
and France 30, 175
and States General 27, 38
Piedmont-Savoy, and *dominium politicum et regale* 335
Pien, Lievin 142
Pierre de Goux (chancellor) 32
Pirenne, H. 63
Pisa, Council of (1408–9) 10, 11
Pius IV, Pope 205
Pius V, Pope 203–4
placards 118, 201, 209, 210–11, 213–14, 255, 272, 282
Plakkaat van Verlatinge see Act of Abjuration
Plessis-les-Tours, Treaty (1582) 302–3
Poitiers, battle (1356) 12

375

Index

Poland
  and absolutism 338
  and Lithuania 84
  and Royal Prussia 9, 12, 78
  and Sejm 8, *325*, 336–7
politics
  and economy 288–9
  and religion 203, 242–3, 256, 261, 293, 315, 329–30
Politiques 276, 289, 299, 317
Pontieu 38
Portugal
  and House of Braganza 335–6
  Spanish conquest of 295, 299, 335
preachers, Protestant 211, 213–14, 216, 277, 288, 308
princes
  and city government 133
  and representative assemblies 5–9, 110, 267–8
  see also monarchy; nobility
Privy Council
  of Charles V 76, 77
  and Margaret of Parma 209
property tax 159, 181, 224, 230
Protestant League 155
Protestantism
  and Charles V 125, 126, 152, 167, 169, 201
  and the Compromise 211
  and Margaret of Parma 209–16, 221
  and Philip II 220–1
  and revolt 143, 167, 212–19, 220–2, 234, 235–8
  spread of 200–6
  see also Calvinism; Huguenots; Lutheranism
provinces 16–24, 25, 43–4
  and defence policies 95–100, 115–16, 130–2, 138, 144
  defensive union 130–2, 199, 259
  divisions between 289–90
  and financial administration 100, 117–18, 165–7, 191–2
  and *ius indigenatus* 85, 173
  and local loyalties 62–3, 70, 77, 79, 115
  Orange's proposed union of 278, 293, 306–7
  provincial governors 77–82, 93, 113–14, 163, 196, 206–7, 215–16, 264, 275, 319
  as sovereign republics 311
  and States General 52, 107, 108–15, 117–18, 139, 148, 185–7, 228–9, 255–6, 260–3, 265, 274, 282–3, 290, 298
  and taxation 158–60, 164–7, 182–4, 189–92, 228–33, 237
  see also individual provinces

Quirino, Vincenzo 73, 87
Quiroga, Gaspar de 263, 276

Rasseghem, Adrien Vilain, seigneur 60, 62, 63, 68
Reformation
  political effects of 203, 256, 329–30
  social effects of 84, 216
  see also Calvinism
regency *see* Margaret of Austria; Margaret of Parma; Mary of Burgundy; Mary of Hungary; Maximilian I
Regensburg, Reichstag *328*
Relation des troubles de Gand sous Charles-Quimt (anon.) 141
religion
  and monarchy 239, 329–30
  and politics 203, 242–3, 256, 261, 293, 315, 329–30
  and revolt 78, 209–11, 216–19, 220–2, 234, 235–8, 240–6, 309
  and toleration 256, 280, 283, 313
  see also Anabaptists; Calvinism; Catholicism; Lutheranism
Religionsfrieden 283–4, 293
Renard, Simon 155–6
rentes 36, 119, 164–6, 176, 178–80, 185, 192, 227, 232, 248–9, 289

representation 2–4
  and coinage 28–9
  and composite assemblies 26–30, 110
  and conciliarism 10–11
  and estates 8, 18–19
  and representative assemblies 4, 5–9, 11–15, 24–6, 267–8
  see also parliament; States General
republicanism 70, 263, 296, 304, 311, 313
  and liberty 6
  and revolt of Holland and Zeeland 249, 258
Requesens, Luis de 236–9, 262–4, 265, 271
resistance, right of 238, 254, 287, 294, 297, 311
revolt
  of 1566 212–19, 241–3
  and heresy 143, 167, 212–19, 220–2, 234, 235–8, 243, 254, 272
  of Holland and Zeeland (1572) 234, 236–7, 240–6, 252, 318, 330
  and peace negotiations 234, 252–6, 258–9, 263–5, 268, 271
revolt against Spain 276–9
  and peace negotiations 287–8, 292–3, 320–1
  and reconciliation with Philip II 315–16
  and rule by States General 260–97
  and transfer of sovereignty 294–5, 298–304, 305, 317
  see also Union of Arras; Union of Utrecht
Richardot, Jean 317–18
Ringault, 307–8
Roda, Gerónimo 262, 268–9
Roelandts, Gort 39, 40, 57
Roermond, and Charles the Bold 37–8
Roeulx, comte de 142
Rossem, Maarten van ('Black Martin') 120, 145, 159
Royal Prussia 9, 12, 78
Rudolph II, Emperor
  and Archduke Albert 317
  and Archduke Matthias 279–81, 288, 302, 303 n.12
  and Philip II 280, 285, 295

Rudyard, Sir Benjamin 333
Ruffault (treasurer general) 80
Rym, Willem 59, 60–1

St Bartholomew's Day massacre 235, 272, 300
St Omer 57–8, 291
  and representative assemblies 19, 20
St Pol, Louis de Luxembourg, count of 18, 66, 77 n.12
St Quentin, battle (1557) 194
Sardinia, and Aragon 14
Savoy, duke of *see* Emmanuel Philibert of Piedmont-Savoy
Schetz, Gaspar 175, 177, 226, 273
Schmalkaldic League 126, 279
Schmalkaldic War (1545–6) 149, 152, 167
Schoere, Louis 80
Schwendi, Lazarus 281
Scotland, and England 11
Sea Beggars 240–5
self-government, local 5, 132–6, 144
Senlis, Peace of (1493) 69, 87
Sforza, Massimiliano 105
Shakespeare, William
  Henry VIII 255
  Richard II viii, 15, 331
Sicily
  and Aragon 9, 11, 105, 234, 273, 296
  and Denmark 330
  and deputations 111–12
  and Inquisition 223
  and representative assemblies 9, 40, 252
  and Spanish troops 194
Siena, republic of 153
Sigismund II Augustus of Poland *325*
Sigismund, Emperor 16
Sluys, port 49, 67, 68
Smith, Sir Thomas, *De Republica Anglorum* 185–6
Somme towns 30, 38, 49
Soriano (Venetian ambassador) 194
sovereignty
  and contract theory 239
  divine right 339

Index

and division of authority 167, 168, 173
and liberty 322–4, 333–4
and Pacification of Ghent 275
and parliamentary government 311–15, 334
popular 308–9
and religion 161, 162, 239, 254–6, 257–9
and States General 278, 297, 309–10
transfer of 294–5, 298–304, 305, 317
see also absolutism
Spain
  and bullion exports 158, 175–7, 180, 227, 261
  and Charles V 104–6, 110, 146–7
  as composite monarchy 84, 167
  Cortes *see* Aragon; Castile; Léon
  and Council of the Netherlands 263
  as *dominium regale* 312, 329
  and England 198, 300, 307, 310, 314
  and France 87, 193, 299–300
  and imperial revenues 158, 163, 167–8, 174–80, 261–2
  and Inquisition 204, 210, 223, 243, 246, 250, 281
  and Italy 198, 240
  Morisco uprising 210
  and Philip II 174–7, 193–200, 217
  and taxation 175
  and Triple Alliance (1596) 313
  see also alcabala; Aragon; Castile; *encabeziamento*; Philip II; revolt against Spain
Spanish Armada 157, 285, 310, 314, 334
Speyer, Peace of (1544) 130
state, composite 11–14
  contract theory 239
States General
  of 1464 30–3
  of 1476 38–41
  of 1556 180–4
  of 1576 262–8
  and administration of army 99–100, 188
  and Alba 224, 226, 227–8, 230–1, 263

and Albert of Saxony 71–2
and Anjou 294–5, 300–4, 310, 311
and Charles V 102, 105, 107–9, 115, 127–8, 148, 152–3, 169–71, 286, 287, 301, 324
and Charles the Bold 16, 33–41, 45, 92, 152, 261
and coinage 28–9, 32, 71–2, 86–7, 109, 294, 308
and consent to war 85–6, 88–9, 98, 132, 153, 282
and defence policies 95–100, 115–16, 127–32, 138–9, 189, 194, 199–200
early history of 16–41
and Emmanuel Philibert 180–92, 196, 198
and financial administration 100, 117, 192
and foreign policy 93, 189, 206
and France 49–51
and Granvelle 115, 186, 191, 195, 200, 205, 212, 230, 247, 252, 260 n.1, 267
and John of Austria 269–70, 273–6, 280, 282, 310, 331
and Margaret of Austria 91, 93, 97–9, 101–2, 107–9, 121
and Margaret of Parma 198, 211, 213, 252
and Mary of Burgundy 16, 42–5, 49–52, 71
and Mary of Hungary 130–1, 138–9, 144, 148, 159–60, 163, 206, 308
and Matthias 280–3, 290, 294, 295
and Maximilian I 55–6, 57, 61–2, 64–5, 66–7, 69, 88–9, 90–2, 152–3, 168, 269–70
and monarchy 253–6, 322–4
and myth of independent parliament 264, 336–7
and parliamentary government 279–85, 286, 295, 298–331
and payment of armies 51–2, 54, 56, 99, 105, 117, 165, 224, 266–7, 289, 314

petitions to 121
and Philip II 205–6, 211–12, 222–4, 226, 236–7, 247, 253–4, 286, 295, 307, 323, 336
and Philip III of Spain 320
and Philip the Good 27–9, 30–3, 43, 86, 261
and Philip the Handsome 86–9, 100
president 267
and provincial Estates 52, 107, 109–15, 117–18, 139, 148, 185–7, 228–9, 255–6, 260–3, 265, 274, 282–3, 290, 298
and religion 188, 205, 210–11, 214
and Spanish troops 195
and succession 148
and Union of Arras 316, 317–21
and Union of Utrecht 294, 305, 312
and United Provinces 297, 320, 331
and William of Orange 252, 255–6, 263, 267, 269, 274–5, 276–7, 278, 284, 292, 294–5, 298–9, 313
see also taxation
states generals
and royal power 12–14, 123
see also France; States General
Steeland, Jacob 63–4
Strada, Jacopo 281
Straelen, Antoon van 192, 200
Sulaiman the Magnificent 127, 211, 217
Sweden
and Denmark 84, 330
and *dominium regale* regime 337
and Finland 14, 84
and representative assemblies 8, 322–3, 324, 329
Switzerland
city-states 8
federations of cantons 49, 70, 84, 277, 284, 296, 311
and Holy League 101

taille 25, 163
Talliandi, Luigi 50 n.23
Taverna, Francesco 82

taxation
and consent 3, 24, 25, 37, 132, 133, 142, 153, 166, 282, 291, 333
and costs of war 81, 83, 88–9, 97–8, 104–5
and *dominium politicum et regale* 25, 166
and *dominium regale* 13, 166, 227
on exports 76, 79–80, 112, 138, 160, 162
and representative assemblies 5, 9
salt tax 21, 29
and States General 29–30, 32, 33–6, 39–41, 108–9, 115, 133, 138–9, 144, 159–60, 163, 181–2, 187, 189–91, 267–8, 291
see also aides; alcabala; encabezamiento; chimney tax; Hundredth Penny; income tax; Tenth Penny; Twentieth Penny
Tenth Penny tax 183–4, 224, 228–34, 237, 245, 263
Terranova, Carlo d'Aragona, duke of 286–7
textile industry
and English wool 27, 94
of Flanders 19, 27, 47, 61, 69–70, 140, 197, 212, 277
of Holland 23
The Hague
and Court of Holland 166, 245
and Gueldrian raids 120
Thérouanne 19
Titian (Tiziano Vecellio) *181*, 281
Toledo, Padro de 223
toleration, and religion 256, 280, 283, 313
Tournai (city) 18, 101, 115, 133–4, 315
Tournai-Tournésis (province) 162, 288, 293
Tours, Estates General 25, 45
town councils 114–15, 132–5, 153, 157, 208–9, 309–10
and guilds 21, 23–4, 62–3, 68, 102, 115, 132–4, 136, 139, 144, 183, 200

379

and Sea Beggars 244
and taxation 184, 189
and transfer of sovereignty 298–9
towns
and corporations 5, 166
see also cities
trade
Baltic 80, 128–30, 138, 162, 212, 229
with England 27, 90, 94, 105, 212, 308
see also Antwerp
Treitzsauerwein, Marx 52–3, 66
Trent, Council of (1545–64) 11, 167, 205, 286
Triple Alliance (1596) 313
Troubles, Council of 221, 223, 229, 236, 243, 263, 267
trust, mutual 92, 132–40, 143–5, 235, 330–6
and Philip II 145, 195–6, 204, 219, 228, 294
Twelfth Penny tax 248
Twentieth Penny tax 224, 230, 231–2, 234, 237

Union of Arras 287, 288–92, 315–17
as *dominium politicum et regale* 317, 319–21
and States General 316, 317–21
and taxation 319–20
and United Provinces 320–1
Union of Brussels
Jan. 1577 272, 279
'Second' of Dec. 1577 283–4
Union of Utrecht 292–7
and Leicester 305–9
as republic 311, 314–15
and sovereignty 310
and States General 294, 305, 312
see also United Provinces
United Provinces 297, 313–15
and States General 297, 320, 331
and Union of Arras 320–1
Utrecht
bishopric 59
and Calvinism 313

incorporation into Holy Roman Empire 131, 145, 187, 244
popular revolt of 1477 45
and union of provinces 293
and William of Orange 259
Utrecht, Union of see Union of Utrecht

Valenciennes 19, 27, 104, 186, 215
Valois monarchy
and duke of Anjou 302
and Habsburgs 146, 149, 152–3, 155, 166, 193, 256
Vaucelles, Truce of (1556) 172
Velasco, Iñigo de 135, 270, 286
Venice 97
Verona, and representation 6
Viglius van Aytta 191–2, 196, 263, 317
Vranck, Franchois 309–10

Walloon Flanders
Estates 290–2, 315–17
and France 116, 299
and iconoclasm 212, 213–14
and language 24
and nobility 262, 289, 299
and Union of Arras 290–2, 313
see also Lille-Douai-Orchies
Walsingham, Sir Francis 245–6
Weellemans, Cornelius 265
Werff, Pieter Adriansz van der 258
Wesembeke, Jacob von 228–9
Weyden, Rogier van der 17, 34
Whitelocke, Bulstrode 322–3, 330
Wilkes, Thomas 252, 308–11
William II of Orange-Nassau 315
William III of Orange-Nassau 315
William of Cleves, duke of Guelders 145, 152
William 'the Silent' of Nassau see Orange, William 'the Silent' of Nassau
Wilson, Thomas 264–5
Wit, Jan de 315
Woodville, Elizabeth 77 n.12
Worms, diet of (1521) 118, 125, 135, 301
Woude, A. M. van der 22 n.19

Index

Ypres
  and Charles the Bold 33–4, 37
  and *gracien* 112
  and Maximilian 54, 58, 61, 69–70
  and popular rising 54
  and representative assemblies 5, 19–20, 26, 49
  and States General 27, 31, 39, 63–4
  and taxation 33–4, 37, 165

Zaltbommel (town) 258
Zaman, Philippe 160
Zápolyai, Jan, *woiwode* of Transylvania 127
Zayas, Gabriel 226
Zeeland (county) 31
  and agriculture 73
  and Baltic trade 128
  and Catholicism 243, 283, 299
  Estates 31, 296, 298–9, 309
  and Maximilian 65
  and Pacification of Ghent 273, 287
  and peace negotiations 252–6, 258–9, 263–5, 268, 271
  and Philip II 287
  and Philip the Good 16, 22
  and religious revolt 234, 237, 240–6, 252, 264
  representative assemblies 21–2, 27
  and States General 52, 86, 190, 260, 265, 274, 290
  and union of provinces 293
  and William of Orange 257, 266, 299, 305
Zierickzee (Zeeland) 264
Zutphen 37–8, 308
  incorporation into Holy Roman Empire 145, 149

CAMBRIDGE STUDIES IN EARLY MODERN HISTORY

The Old World and the New*
J. H. ELLIOTT

The Army of Flanders and the Spanish Road, 1567–1659: The Logistics of Spanish Victory and Defeat in the Low Countries Wars*
GEOFFREY PARKER

Richelieu and Olivares*
J. H. ELLIOTT

Absolutism and Society in Seventeenth-Century France: State Power and Provincial Aristocracy in Languedoc*
WILLIAM BEIK

The Princes of Orange: The Stadholders in the Dutch Republic*
HERBERT H. ROWEN

Lille and the Dutch Revolt: Urban Stability in an Era of Revolution
ROBERT S. DUPLESSIS

The Continuity of Feudal Power: The Caracciolo di Brienza in Spanish Naples
TOMMASO ASTARITA

The Nobility of Holland: From Knights to Regents, 1500–1650
H. F. K. VAN NIEROP

Early Modern Democracy in the Grisons: Social Order and Political Language in a Swiss Mountain Canton, 1470–1620
RANDOLPH C. HEAD

War, State and Society in Württemberg, 1677–1793*
PETER H. WILSON

From Madrid to Purgatory: The Art and Craft of Dying in Sixteenth-Century Spain
CARLOS M. N. EIRE

The Reformation and Rural Society: The Parishes of Brandenburg-Ansbach-Kulmbach, 1528–1603
C. SCOTT DIXON

Labour, Science and Technology in France, 1500–1620
HENRY HELLER

The King's Army: Warfare, Soldiers, and Society during the Wars of Religion in France, 1562–1576
JAMES B. WOOD

Spanish Naval Power, 1589–1665: Reconstruction and Defeat
DAVID GOODMAN

State and Nobility in Early Modern Germany: The Knightly Feud in Franconia 1440–1567
HILLAY ZMORA

The Quest for Compromise: Peace-Makers in Counter-Reformation Vienna
HOWARD LOUTHAN

Charles XI and Swedish Absolutism, 1660–1697
A. F. UPTON

Noble Power during the French Wars of Religion: The Guise Affinity and the Catholic Cause in Normandy
STUART CARROLL

The Reformation of Community: Social Welfare and Calvinist Charity in Holland, 1572–1620
  CHARLES H. PARKER
Henry IV and the Towns: The Pursuit of Legitimacy in French Urban Society, 1589–1610
  S. ANNETTE FINLEY-CROSWHITE
The Limits of Royal Authority: Resistance and Obedience in Seventeenth-Century Castile
  RUTH MACKAY
Defiled Trades and Social Outcasts: Honor and Ritual Pollution in Early Modern Germany
  KATHY STUART
Kingship and Favoritism in the Spain of Philip III, 1598–1621
  ANTONIO FEROS
Richelieu's Army: War, Government and Society in France, 1624–1642
  DAVID PARROTT
The Emergence of the Eastern Powers, 1756–1775
  H. M. SCOTT
Monarchies, States Generals and Parliaments: The Netherlands in the Fifteenth and Sixteenth Centuries
  H. G. KOENIGSBERGER

Titles available in paperback marked with an asterisk*

The following titles are now out of print:

French Finances, 1770–1795: From Business to Bureaucracy
  J. F. BOSHER
Chronicle into History: An Essay in the Interpretation of History in Florentine Fourteenth-Century Chronicles
  LOUIS GREEN
France and the Estates General of 1614
  J. MICHAEL HAYDEN
Reform and Revolution in Mainz, 1743–1803
  T. C. W. BLANNING
Altopascio: A Study in Tuscan Society 1587–1784
  FRANK MCARDLE
Gunpowder and Galleys: Changing Technology and Mediterranean Warfare at Sea in the Sixteenth Century
  JOHN FRANCIS GUILMARTIN JR
The State, War and Peace: Spanish Political Thought in the Renaissance 1516–1559
  J. A. FERNÁNDEZ-SANTAMARIA
Calvinist Preaching and Iconoclasm in the Netherlands, 1544–1569
  PHYLLIS MACK CREW
The Kingdom of Valencia in the Seventeenth Century
  JAMES CASEY
Filippo Strozzi and the Medici: Favor and Finance in Sixteenth-Century Florence and Rome
  MELISSA MERIAM BULLARD
Rouen during the Wars of Religion
  PHILIP BENEDICT

The Emperor and His Chancellor: A Study of the Imperial Chancellery under Gattinara
  JOHN M. HEADLEY
The Military Organisation of a Renaissance State: Venice c. 1400–1617
  M. E. MALLETT AND J. R. HALE
Neostoicism and the Early Modern State
  GERHARD OESTREICH
Prussian Society and the German Order: An Aristocratic Corporation in Crisis c. 1410–1466
  MICHAEL BURLEIGH
The Changing Face of Empire: Charles V, Philip II and Habsburg Authority, 1552–1559
  M. J. RODRÍGUEZ-SALGADO
Turning Swiss: Cities and Empire 1450–1550
  THOMAS A. BRADY JR
Neighbourhood and Community in Paris
  DAVID GARRIOCH
The Duke of Anjou and the Politique Struggle during the Wars of Religion
  MACK P. HOLT
Society and Religious Toleration in Hamburg 1529–1819
  JOACHIM WHALEY
Frontiers of Heresy: The Spanish Inquisition from the Basque Lands to Sicily
  WILLIAM MONTER
Rome in the Age of Enlightenment: The Post-Tridentine Syndrome and the Ancien Régime
  HANS GROSS
Renaissance and Revolt: Essays in the Intellectual and Social History of Modern France
  J. H. M. SALMON
Louis XIV and the Origins of the Dutch War
  PAUL SONNINO
The Cost of Empire: The Finances of the Kingdom of Naples during the Period of Spanish Rule
  ANTONIO CALABRIA
The Armada of Flanders: Spanish Maritime Policy and European War, 1568–1668
  R. A. STRADLING
After the Deluge: Poland and the Second Northern War 1655–1660
  ROBERT FROST
Classes, Estates and Order in Early Modern Brittany
  JAMES B. COLLINS

Made in the USA
Monee, IL
24 April 2022